C Language Reference

Microsoft®
Visual C++®
Language Reference

PUBLISHED BY
Microsoft Press
A Division of Microsoft Corporation
One Microsoft Way
Redmond, Washington 98052-6399

Library of Congress Cataloging-in-Publication Data
Microsoft Visual C++ Language Reference / Microsoft Corporation.
     p.   cm.
   Includes index.
   ISBN 1-57231-521-0
   1. C++ (Computer program language)   2. Microsoft Visual C++.
 I. Microsoft Corporation.
 QA76.73.C153M533   1997
 005.26'8--dc21   97-2404
                                        CIP

Printed and bound in the United States of America.

1 2 3 4 5 6 7 8 9   MLML   2 1 0 9 8 7

Distributed to the book trade in Canada by Macmillan of Canada, a division of Canada Publishing Corporation.

A CIP catalogue record for this book is available from the British Library.

Microsoft Press books are available through booksellers and distributors worldwide. For further information about international editions, contact your local Microsoft Corporation office. Or contact Microsoft Press International directly at fax (206) 936-7329.

Acquisitions Editor: Eric Stroo
Project Editor: Maureen Williams Zimmerman

Contents

Contents

Chapter 4 Expressions and Assignments 93

Chapter 5 Statements 135

Appendixes

Appendix B   Implementation-Defined Behavior   189

Contents

Tables

Introduction

Organization of the C Language Reference

- Elements of C
- Program Structure
- Declarations and Types
- Expressions and Assignments
- Statements
- Functions
- C Language Syntax Summary
- Implementation-Defined Behavior

Scope of this Manual

C is a flexible language that leaves many programming decisions up to you. In keeping with this philosophy, C imposes few restrictions in matters such as type conversion. Although this characteristic of the language can make your programming job easier, you must know the language well to understand how programs will behave. This book provides information on the C language components and the features of the Microsoft implementation. The syntax for the C language is from ANSI X3.159-1989, *American National Standard for Information Systems – Programming Language – C* (hereinafter called the ANSI C standard), although it is not part of the ANSI C standard. Appendix A, C Language Syntax Summary, provides the syntax and a description of how to read and use the syntax definitions.

This book does not discuss programming with C++. See *C++ Language Reference* for information about the C++ language.

Note For information on Microsoft product support, see the PSS.HLP file.

ANSI Conformance

Microsoft® C conforms to the standard for the C language as set forth in the ANSI C standard. Microsoft extensions to the ANSI C standard are noted in the text and syntax of this book as well as in the online reference. Because the extensions are not a part of the ANSI C standard, their use may restrict portability of programs between systems. By default, the Microsoft extensions are enabled. To disable the extensions, specify the /Za compiler option. With /Za, all non-ANSI code generates errors or warnings.

Elements of C

This chapter describes the elements of the C programming language, including the names, numbers, and characters used to construct a C program. The ANSI C syntax labels these components "tokens." This chapter explains how to define tokens and how the compiler evaluates them.

The following topics are discussed:

- Tokens
- Comments
- Keywords
- Identifiers
- Constants
- String literals
- Punctuation and special characters

The chapter also includes reference tables for trigraphs, floating-point constants, integer constants, and escape sequences.

"Operators" are symbols (both single characters and character combinations) that specify how values are to be manipulated. Each symbol is interpreted as a single unit, called a token. For more information, see "Operators" on page 99 in Chapter 4.

Tokens

In a C source program, the basic element recognized by the compiler is the "token." A token is source-program text that the compiler does not break down into component elements.

Syntax

token :

    keyword

    identifier

    constant

    string-literal

    operator

    punctuator

Note See the introduction to Appendix A, "C Language Syntax Summary," for an explanation of the ANSI syntax conventions.

The keywords, identifiers, constants, string literals, and operators described in this chapter are examples of tokens. Punctuation characters such as brackets ([ ]), braces ({ }), parentheses (( )), and commas (,) are also tokens.

White-Space Characters

Space, tab, linefeed, carriage-return, formfeed, vertical-tab, and newline characters are called "white-space characters" because they serve the same purpose as the spaces between words and lines on a printed page—they make reading easier. Tokens are delimited (bounded) by white-space characters and by other tokens, such as operators and punctuation. When parsing code, the C compiler ignores white-space characters unless you use them as separators or as components of character constants or string literals. Use white-space characters to make a program more readable. Note that the compiler also treats comments as white space.

Comments

A "comment" is a sequence of characters beginning with a forward slash/asterisk combination (/*) that is treated as a single white-space character by the compiler and is otherwise ignored. A comment can include any combination of characters from the representable character set, including newline characters, but excluding the "end comment" delimiter (*/). Comments can occupy more than one line but cannot be nested.

Comments can appear anywhere a white-space character is allowed. Since the compiler treats a comment as a single white-space character, you cannot include comments within tokens. The compiler ignores the characters in the comment.

Use comments to document your code. This example is a comment accepted by the compiler:

```
/* Comments can contain keywords such as
   for and while without generating errors. */
```

Comments can appear on the same line as a code statement:

```
printf( "Hello\n" );  /* Comments can go here */
```

You can choose to precede functions or program modules with a descriptive comment block:

```
/* MATHERR.C illustrates writing an error routine
 * for math functions.
 */
```

Since comments cannot contain nested comments, this example causes an error:

```
/* Comment out this routine for testing

    /* Open file */
    fh = _open( "myfile.c", _O_RDONLY );
    .
    .
    .
 */
```

The error occurs because the compiler recognizes the first */, after the words Open file, as the end of the comment. It tries to process the remaining text and produces an error when it finds the */ outside a comment.

While you can use comments to render certain lines of code inactive for test purposes, the preprocessor directives **#if** and **#endif** and conditional compilation are a useful alternative for this task. For more information, see "Preprocessor Directives" in the *Preprocessor Reference*.

Microsoft Specific →

The Microsoft compiler also supports single-line comments preceded by two forward slashes (//). If you compile with /Za (ANSI standard), these comments generate errors. These comments cannot extend to a second line.

```
// This is a valid comment
```

Comments beginning with two forward slashes (//) are terminated by the next newline character that is not preceded by an escape character. In the next example, the newline character is preceded by a backslash (\), creating an "escape sequence." This escape sequence causes the compiler to treat the next line as part of the previous line. (For more information, see "Escape Sequences" on page 16.)

```
// my comment \
   i++;
```

Therefore, the i++; statement is commented out.

The default for Microsoft C is that the Microsoft extensions are enabled. Use /Za to disable these extensions.

END Microsoft Specific

Evaluation of Tokens

When the compiler interprets tokens, it includes as many characters as possible in a single token before moving on to the next token. Because of this behavior, the compiler may not interpret tokens as you intended if they are not properly separated by white space. Consider the following expression:

```
i+++j
```

In this example, the compiler first makes the longest possible operator (++) from the three plus signs, then processes the remaining plus sign as an addition operator (+). Thus, the expression is interpreted as (i++) + (j), not (i) + (++j). In this and similar cases, use white space and parentheses to avoid ambiguity and ensure proper expression evaluation.

Microsoft Specific →

The C compiler treats a CTRL+Z character as an end-of-file indicator. It ignores any text after CTRL+Z.

END Microsoft Specific

Keywords

"Keywords" are words that have special meaning to the C compiler. In translation phases 7 and 8, an identifier cannot have the same spelling and case as a C keyword. (See a description of "translation phases" in the *Preprocessor Reference*; for information on identifiers, see "Identifiers" on page 5.) The C language uses the following keywords:

auto	**double**	**int**	**struct**
break	**else**	**long**	**switch**
case	**enum**	**register**	**typedef**
char	**extern**	**return**	**union**
const	**float**	**short**	**unsigned**
continue	**for**	**signed**	**void**
default	**goto**	**sizeof**	**volatile**
do	**if**	**static**	**while**

You cannot redefine keywords. However, you can specify text to be substituted for keywords before compilation by using C preprocessor directives.

Microsoft Specific →

The ANSI C standard allows identifiers with two leading underscores to be reserved for compiler implementations. Therefore, the Microsoft convention is to precede Microsoft-specific keyword names with double underscores. These words cannot be used as identifier names. For a description of the ANSI rules for naming identifiers, including the use of double underscores, see "Identifiers" on page 5.

The following keywords and special identifiers are recognized by the Microsoft C compiler:

__asm	**dllimport**[2]	**__int8**	**naked**[2]
__based[1]	**__except**	**__int16**	**__stdcall**
__cdecl	**__fastcall**	**__int32**	**thread**[2]
__declspec	**__finally**	**__int64**	**__try**
dllexport[2]	**__inline**	**__leave**	

[1] The **__based** keyword has limited uses for 32-bit target compilations.

[2] These are special identifiers when used with **__declspec**; their use in other contexts is not restricted.

Microsoft extensions are enabled by default. To ensure that your programs are fully portable, you can disable Microsoft extensions by specifying the /Za option (compile for ANSI compatibility) during compilation. When you do this, Microsoft-specific keywords are disabled.

When Microsoft extensions are enabled, you can use the keywords listed above in your programs. For ANSI compliance, most of these keywords are prefaced by a double underscore. The four exceptions, **dllexport**, **dllimport**, **naked**, and **thread**, are used only with **__declspec** and therefore do not require a leading double underscore. For backward compatibility, single-underscore versions of the rest of the keywords are supported.

END Microsoft Specific

Identifiers

"Identifiers" or "symbols" are the names you supply for variables, types, functions, and labels in your program. Identifier names must differ in spelling and case from any keywords. You cannot use keywords (either C or Microsoft) as identifiers; they are reserved for special use. You create an identifier by specifying it in the declaration of a variable, type, or function. In this example, `result` is an identifier for an integer variable, and `main` and `printf` are identifier names for functions.

```
void main()
{
    int result;

    if ( result != 0 )
        printf( "Bad file handle\n" );
}
```

Once declared, you can use the identifier in later program statements to refer to the associated value.

A special kind of identifier, called a statement label, can be used in **goto** statements. (Declarations are described in Chapter 3, "Declarations and Types." Statement labels are described in "The goto and Labeled Statements" on page 141 in Chapter 5.)

Syntax

identifier :

> *nondigit*
> *identifier nondigit*
> *identifier digit*

nondigit : one of

> _ a b c d e f g h i j k l m n o p q r s t u v w x y z
> A B C D E F G H I J K L M N O P Q R S T U V W X Y Z

digit : one of

> 0 1 2 3 4 5 6 7 8 9

The first character of an identifier name must be a *nondigit* (that is, the first character must be an underscore or an uppercase or lowercase letter). ANSI allows six significant characters in an external identifier's name and 31 for names of internal (within a function) identifiers. External identifiers (ones declared at global scope or declared with storage class **extern**) may be subject to additional naming restrictions because these identifiers have to be processed by other software such as linkers.

Microsoft Specific →

Although ANSI allows 6 significant characters in external identifier names and 31 for names of internal (within a function) identifiers, the Microsoft C compiler allows 247 characters in an internal or external identifier name. If you aren't concerned with ANSI compatibility, you can modify this default to a smaller or larger number using the /H (restrict length of external names) option.

END Microsoft Specific

The C compiler considers uppercase and lowercase letters to be distinct characters. This feature, called "case sensitivity," enables you to create distinct identifiers that have the same spelling but different cases for one or more of the letters. For example, each of the following identifiers is unique:

```
add
ADD
Add
aDD
```

Microsoft Specific →

Do not select names for identifiers that begin with two underscores or with an underscore followed by an uppercase letter. The ANSI C standard allows identifier names that begin with these character combinations to be reserved for compiler use. Identifiers with file-level scope should also not be named with an underscore and a lowercase letter as the first two letters. Identifier names that begin with these characters are also reserved. By convention, Microsoft uses an underscore and an uppercase letter to begin macro names and double underscores for Microsoft-specific keyword names. To avoid any naming conflicts, always select identifier names that do not begin with one or two underscores, or names that begin with an underscore followed by an uppercase letter.

END Microsoft Specific

The following are examples of valid identifiers that conform to either ANSI or Microsoft naming restrictions:

```
j
count
temp1
top_of_page
skip12
LastNum
```

Microsoft Specific →

Although identifiers in source files are case sensitive by default, symbols in object files are not. Microsoft C treats identifiers within a compilation unit as case sensitive.

The Microsoft linker is case sensitive. You must specify all identifiers consistently according to case.

The "source character set" is the set of legal characters that can appear in source files. For Microsoft C, the source set is the standard ASCII character set. The source character set and execution character set include the ASCII characters used as escape sequences. See "Character Constants" on page 15 for information about the execution character set.

END Microsoft Specific

An identifier has "scope," which is the region of the program in which it is known, and "linkage," which determines whether the same name in another scope refers to the same identifier. These topics are explained in "Lifetime, Scope, Visibility, and Linkage" on page 32 in Chapter 2.

Multibyte and Wide Characters

A multibyte character is a character composed of sequences of one or more bytes. Each byte sequence represents a single character in the extended character set. Multibyte characters are used in character sets such as Kanji.

Wide characters are multilingual character codes that are always 16 bits wide. The type for character constants is **char**; for wide characters, the type is **wchar_t**. Since wide characters are always a fixed size, using wide characters simplifies programming with international character sets.

The wide-character-string literal L**"hello"** becomes an array of six integers of type **wchar_t**.

```
{L'h', L'e', L'l', L'l', L'o', 0}
```

The Unicode specification is the specification for wide characters. The run-time library routines for translating between multibyte and wide characters include **mbstowcs**, **mbtowc**, **wcstombs**, and **wctomb**.

Trigraphs

The source character set of C source programs is contained within the 7-bit ASCII character set but is a superset of the ISO 646-1983 Invariant Code Set. Trigraph sequences allow C programs to be written using only the ISO (International Standards Organization) Invariant Code Set. Trigraphs are sequences of three characters (introduced by two consecutive question marks) that the compiler replaces with their corresponding punctuation characters. You can use trigraphs in C source files with a character set that does not contain convenient graphic representations for some punctuation characters.

Table 1.1 shows the nine trigraph sequences. All occurrences in a source file of the punctuation characters in the first column are replaced with the corresponding character in the second column.

Table 1.1 Trigraph Sequences

Trigraph	Punctuation Character	Trigraph	Punctuation Character
??=	#	??<	{
??(	[	??!	|
??/	\	??>	}
??)	]	??-	~
??'	^		

A trigraph is always treated as a single source character. The translation of trigraphs takes place in the first translation phase, before the recognition of escape characters in string literals and character constants. Only the nine trigraphs shown in Table 1.1 are recognized. All other character sequences are left untranslated.

The character escape sequence, \?, prevents the misinterpretation of trigraph-like character sequences. (For information about escape sequences, see "Escape Sequences" on page 16.) For example, if you attempt to print the string What??! with this **printf** statement

```
printf( "What??!\n" );
```

the string printed is What| because ??! is a trigraph sequence that is replaced with the | character. Write the statement as follows to correctly print the string:

```
printf( "What?\?!\n" );
```

In this **printf** statement, a backslash escape character in front of the second question mark prevents the misinterpretation of ??! as a trigraph.

Constants

A "constant" is a number, character, or character string that can be used as a value in a program. Use constants to represent floating-point, integer, enumeration, or character values that cannot be modified.

Syntax

constant :

>*floating-point-constant*
>*integer-constant*
>*enumeration-constant*
>*character-constant*

Constants are characterized by having a value and a type. Floating-point, integer, and character constants are discussed in the next three sections. Enumeration constants are described in "Enumeration Declarations" on page 55 in Chapter 3.

Floating-Point Constants

A "floating-point constant" is a decimal number that represents a signed real number. The representation of a signed real number includes an integer portion, a fractional portion, and an exponent. Use floating-point constants to represent floating-point values that cannot be changed.

Syntax

floating-point-constant :

>*fractional-constant exponent-part* ~opt~ *floating-suffix* ~opt~
>*digit-sequence exponent-part floating-suffix* ~opt~

fractional-constant :

>*digit-sequence* ~opt~ **.** *digit-sequence*
>*digit-sequence* **.**

exponent-part :

>**e** *sign* ~opt~ *digit-sequence*
>**E** *sign* ~opt~ *digit-sequence*

sign :   one of

>**+ –**

digit-sequence :

>*digit*
>*digit-sequence digit*

floating-suffix :   one of

>**f l F L**

You can omit either the digits before the decimal point (the integer portion of the value) or the digits after the decimal point (the fractional portion), but not both. You can leave out the decimal point only if you include an exponent. No white-space characters can separate the digits or characters of the constant.

The following examples illustrate some forms of floating-point constants and expressions:

```
15.75
1.575E1     /* = 15.75  */
1575e-2     /* = 15.75  */
-2.5e-3     /* = -0.0025 */
25E-4       /* =  0.0025 */
```

Floating-point constants are positive unless they are preceded by a minus sign (–). In this case, the minus sign is treated as a unary arithmetic negation operator. Floating-point constants have type **float**, **double**, **long**, or **long double**.

A floating-point constant without an **f**, **F**, **l**, or **L** suffix has type **double**. If the letter **f** or **F** is the suffix, the constant has type **float**. If suffixed by the letter **l** or **L**, it has type **long double**. For example:

```
100L  /* Has type long double  */
100F  /* Has type float        */
100D  /* Has type double       */
```

Note that the Microsoft C compiler maps **long double** to type **double**. See "Storage of Basic Types" on page 81 in Chapter 3 for information about type **double**, **float**, and **long**.

You can omit the integer portion of the floating-point constant, as shown in the following examples. The number .75 can be expressed in many ways, including the following:

```
.0075e2
0.075e1
.075e1
75e-2
```

Limits on Floating-Point Constants

Microsoft Specific →

Limits on the values of floating-point constants are given in Table 1.2. The header file FLOAT.H contains this information. *

Table 1.2 Limits on Floating-Point Constants

Constant	Meaning	Value
FLT_DIG	Number of digits, q, such that a	6
DBL_DIG	floating-point number with q	15
LDBL_DIG	decimal digits can be rounded into	15
	a floating-point representation and	
	back without loss of precision.	

Table 1.2   Limits on Floating-Point Constants   *(continued)*

Constant	Meaning	Value
FLT_EPSILON DBL_EPSILON LDBL_EPSILON	Smallest positive number x, such that $x + 1.0$ is not equal to 1.0	1.192092896e–07F 2.2204460492503131e–016 2.2204460492503131e–016
FLT_GUARD		0
FLT_MANT_DIG DBL_MANT_DIG LDBL_MANT_DIG	Number of digits in the radix specified by **FLT_RADIX** in the floating-point significand. The radix is 2; hence these values specify bits.	24 53 53
FLT_MAX DBL_MAX LDBL_MAX	Maximum representable floating-point number.	3.402823466e+38F 1.7976931348623158e+308 1.7976931348623158e+308
FLT_MAX_10_EXP DBL_MAX_10_EXP LDBL_MAX_10_EXP	Maximum integer such that 10 raised to that number is a representable floating-point number.	38 308 308
FLT_MAX_EXP DBL_MAX_EXP LDBL_MAX_EXP	Maximum integer such that **FLT_RADIX** raised to that number is a representable floating-point number.	128 1024 1024
FLT_MIN DBL_MIN LDBL_MIN	Minimum positive value.	1.175494351e–38F 2.2250738585072014e–308 2.2250738585072014e–308
FLT_MIN_10_EXP DBL_MIN_10_EXP LDBL_MIN_10_EXP	Minimum negative integer such that 10 raised to that number is a representable floating-point number.	–37 –307 –307
FLT_MIN_EXP DBL_MIN_EXP LDBL_MIN_EXP	Minimum negative integer such that **FLT_RADIX** raised to that number is a representable floating-point number.	–125 –1021 –1021
FLT_NORMALIZE		0
FLT_RADIX _DBL_RADIX _LDBL_RADIX	Radix of exponent representation.	2 2 2
FLT_ROUNDS _DBL_ROUNDS _LDBL_ROUNDS	Rounding mode for floating-point addition.	1 (near) 1 (near) 1 (near)

Note that the information in Table 1.2 may differ in future implementations.

END Microsoft Specific

Integer Constants

An "integer constant" is a decimal (base 10), octal (base 8), or hexadecimal (base 16) number that represents an integral value. Use integer constants to represent integer values that cannot be changed.

Syntax

integer-constant :
>> *decimal-constant integer-suffix* opt
>> *octal-constant integer-suffix* opt
>> *hexadecimal-constant integer-suffix* opt

decimal-constant :
>> *nonzero-digit*
>> *decimal-constant digit*

octal-constant :
>> **0**
>> *octal-constant octal-digit*

hexadecimal-constant :
>> **0x** *hexadecimal-digit*
>> **0X** *hexadecimal-digit*
>> *hexadecimal-constant hexadecimal-digit*

nonzero-digit : one of
>> **1 2 3 4 5 6 7 8 9**

octal-digit : one of
>> **0 1 2 3 4 5 6 7**

hexadecimal-digit : one of
>> **0 1 2 3 4 5 6 7 8 9**
>> **a b c d e f**
>> **A B C D E F**

integer-suffix :
>> *unsigned-suffix long-suffix* opt
>> *long-suffix unsigned-suffix* opt

unsigned-suffix : one of
>> **u U**

long-suffix : one of
>> **l L**

64-bit integer-suffix:
>> **i64**

Integer constants are positive unless they are preceded by a minus sign (–). The minus sign is interpreted as the unary arithmetic negation operator. (See "Unary Arithmetic Operators" on page 110 in Chapter 4 for information about this operator.)

If an integer constant begins with the letters **0x** or **0X**, it is hexadecimal. If it begins with the digit **0**, it is octal. Otherwise, it is assumed to be decimal.

The following lines are equivalent:

```
0x1C    /* = Hexadecimal representation for decimal 28 */
034     /* = Octal representation for decimal 28 */
```

No white-space characters can separate the digits of an integer constant. These examples show valid decimal, octal, and hexadecimal constants.

```
/* Decimal Constants */
10
132
32179

/* Octal Constants */
012
0204
076663

/* Hexadecimal Constants */
0xa or 0xA
0x84
0x7dB3 or 0X7DB3
```

Integer Types

Every integer constant is given a type based on its value and the way it is expressed. You can force any integer constant to type **long** by appending the letter **l** or **L** to the end of the constant; you can force it to be type **unsigned** by appending **u** or **U** to the value. The lowercase letter **l** can be confused with the digit 1 and should be avoided. Some forms of **long** integer constants follow:

```
/* Long decimal constants */
10L
79L

/* Long octal constants */
012L
0115L

/* Long hexadecimal constants */
0xaL or 0xAL
0X4fL or 0x4FL

/* Unsigned long decimal constant */
776745UL
778866LU
```

The type you assign to a constant depends on the value the constant represents. A constant's value must be in the range of representable values for its type. A constant's type determines which conversions are performed when the constant is used in an expression or when the minus sign (–) is applied. This list summarizes the conversion rules for integer constants.

- The type for a decimal constant without a suffix is either **int**, **long int**, or **unsigned long int**. The first of these three types in which the constant's value can be represented is the type assigned to the constant.

- The type assigned to octal and hexadecimal constants without suffixes is **int**, **unsigned int**, **long int**, or **unsigned long int** depending on the size of the constant.

- The type assigned to constants with a **u** or **U** suffix is **unsigned int** or **unsigned long int** depending on their size.

- The type assigned to constants with an **l** or **L** suffix is **long int** or **unsigned long int** depending on their size.

- The type assigned to constants with a **u** or **U** and an **l** or **L** suffix is **unsigned long int**.

Integer Limits

Microsoft Specific →

The limits for integer types are listed in Table 1.3. These limits are defined in the standard header file LIMITS.H. Microsoft C also permits the declaration of sized integer variables, which are integral types of size 8-, 16-, or 32-bits. For more information on sized integers, see "Sized Integer Types" on page 82 in Chapter 3.

Table 1.3 Limits on Integer Constants

Constant	Meaning	Value
CHAR_BIT	Number of bits in the smallest variable that is not a bit field.	8
SCHAR_MIN	Minimum value for a variable of type **signed char**.	–128
SCHAR_MAX	Maximum value for a variable of type **signed char**.	127
UCHAR_MAX	Maximum value for a variable of type **unsigned char**.	255 (0xff)
CHAR_MIN	Minimum value for a variable of type **char**.	–128; 0 if /J option used
CHAR_MAX	Maximum value for a variable of type **char**.	127; 255 if /J option used
MB_LEN_MAX	Maximum number of bytes in a multicharacter constant.	2
SHRT_MIN	Minimum value for a variable of type **short**.	–32768
SHRT_MAX	Maximum value for a variable of type **short**.	32767

Table 1.3   Limits on Integer Constants *(continued)*

Constant	Meaning	Value
USHRT_MAX	Maximum value for a variable of type **unsigned short**.	65535 (0xffff)
INT_MIN	Minimum value for a variable of type **int**.	−2147483647−1
INT_MAX	Maximum value for a variable of type **int**.	2147483647
UINT_MAX	Maximum value for a variable of type **unsigned int**.	4294967295 (0xffffffff)
LONG_MIN	Minimum value for a variable of type **long**.	−2147483647−1
LONG_MAX	Maximum value for a variable of type **long**.	2147483647
ULONG_MAX	Maximum value for a variable of type **unsigned long**.	4294967295 (0xffffffff)

If a value exceeds the largest integer representation, the Microsoft compiler generates an error.

END Microsoft Specific

Character Constants

A "character constant" is formed by enclosing a single character from the representable character set within single quotation marks (' '). Character constants are used to represent characters in the execution character set.

Syntax

character-constant :
    '*c-char-sequence*'
    L'*c-char-sequence*'

c-char-sequence :
    c-char
    c-char-sequence c-char

c-char :
    Any member of the source character set except the single quotation mark ('),
    backslash (\), or newline character
    escape-sequence

escape-sequence :
    simple-escape-sequence
    octal-escape-sequence
    hexadecimal-escape-sequence

simple-escape-sequence : one of
    \a \b \f \n \r \t \v
    \' \" \\ \?

octal-escape-sequence :
   \ *octal-digit*
   \ *octal-digit octal-digit*
   \ *octal-digit octal-digit octal-digit*

hexadecimal-escape-sequence :
   \x *hexadecimal-digit*
   hexadecimal-escape-sequence hexadecimal-digit

Character Types

An integer character constant not preceded by the letter **L** has type **int**. The value of an integer character constant containing a single character is the numerical value of the character interpreted as an integer. For example, the numerical value of the character a is 97 in decimal and 61 in hexadecimal.

Syntactically, a "wide-character constant" is a character constant prefixed by the letter **L**. A wide-character constant has type **wchar_t**, an integer type defined in the STDDEF.H header file. For example:

```
char    schar = 'x';   /* A character constant            */
wchar_t wchar = L'x';   /* A wide-character constant for
                           the same character              */
```

Wide-character constants are 16 bits wide and specify members of the extended execution character set. They allow you to express characters in alphabets that are too large to be represented by type **char**. See "Multibyte and Wide Characters" on page 7 for more information about wide characters.

Execution Character Set

This book often refers to the "execution character set." The execution character set is not necessarily the same as the source character set used for writing C programs. The execution character set includes all characters in the source character set as well as the null character, newline character, backspace, horizontal tab, vertical tab, carriage return, and escape sequences. The source and execution character sets may differ in other implementations.

Escape Sequences

Character combinations consisting of a backslash (\) followed by a letter or by a combination of digits are called "escape sequences." To represent a newline character, single quotation mark, or certain other characters in a character constant, you must use escape sequences. An escape sequence is regarded as a single character and is therefore valid as a character constant.

Escape sequences are typically used to specify actions such as carriage returns and tab movements on terminals and printers. They are also used to provide literal representations of nonprinting characters and characters that usually have special meanings, such as the double quotation mark ("). Table 1.4 lists the ANSI escape sequences and what they represent.

Note that the question mark preceded by a backslash (\?) specifies a literal question mark in cases where the character sequence would be misinterpreted as a trigraph. See "Trigraphs" for more information.

Table 1.4   Escape Sequences

Escape Sequence	Represents
\a	Bell (alert)
\b	Backspace
\f	Formfeed
\n	New line
\r	Carriage return
\t	Horizontal tab
\v	Vertical tab
\'	Single quotation mark
\"	Double quotation mark
\\	Backslash
\?	Literal question mark
\ooo	ASCII character in octal notation
\xhhh	ASCII character in hexadecimal notation

Microsoft Specific →

If a backslash precedes a character that does not appear in Table 1.4, the compiler handles the undefined character as the character itself. For example, \x is treated as an x.

END Microsoft Specific

Escape sequences allow you to send nongraphic control characters to a display device. For example, the ESC character (\033) is often used as the first character of a control command for a terminal or printer. Some escape sequences are device-specific. For instance, the vertical-tab and formfeed escape sequences (\v and \f) do not affect screen output, but they do perform appropriate printer operations.

You can also use the backslash (\) as a continuation character. When a newline character (equivalent to pressing the RETURN key) immediately follows the backslash, the compiler ignores the backslash and the newline character and treats the next line as part of the previous line. This is useful primarily for preprocessor definitions longer than a single line. For example:

```
#define assert(exp) \
( (exp) ? (void) 0:_assert( #exp, __FILE__, __LINE__ ) )
```

Octal and Hexadecimal Character Specifications

The sequence *ooo* means you can specify any character in the ASCII character set as a three-digit octal character code. The numerical value of the octal integer specifies the value of the desired character or wide character.

Similarly, the sequence \x*hhh* allows you to specify any ASCII character as a hexadecimal character code. For example, you can give the ASCII backspace character as the normal C escape sequence (**\b**), or you can code it as **\010** (octal) or **\x008** (hexadecimal).

You can use only the digits 0 through 7 in an octal escape sequence. Octal escape sequences can never be longer than three digits and are terminated by the first character that is not an octal digit. Although you do not need to use all three digits, you must use at least one. For example, the octal representation is **\10** for the ASCII backspace character and **\101** for the letter A, as given in an ASCII chart.

Similarly, you must use at least one digit for a hexadecimal escape sequence, but you can omit the second and third digits. Therefore you could specify the hexadecimal escape sequence for the backspace character as either **\x8**, **\x08**, or **\x008**.

The value of the octal or hexadecimal escape sequence must be in the range of representable values for type **unsigned char** for a character constant and type **wchar_t** for a wide-character constant. See "Multibyte and Wide Characters" on page 7 for information on wide-character constants.

Unlike octal escape constants, the number of hexadecimal digits in an escape sequence is unlimited. A hexadecimal escape sequence terminates at the first character that is not a hexadecimal digit. Because hexadecimal digits include the letters **a** through **f**, care must be exercised to make sure the escape sequence terminates at the intended digit. To avoid confusion, you can place octal or hexadecimal character definitions in a macro definition:

```
#define Bell '\x07'
```

For hexadecimal values, you can break the string to show the correct value clearly:

```
"\xabc"    /* one character  */
"\xab" "c" /* two characters */
```

String Literals

A "string literal" is a sequence of characters from the source character set enclosed in double quotation marks (" "). String literals are used to represent a sequence of characters which, taken together, form a null-terminated string. You must always prefix wide-string literals with the letter **L**.

Syntax

string-literal :
 "*s-char-sequence* _{opt}"
 L"*s-char-sequence* _{opt}"

s-char-sequence :
 s-char
 s-char-sequence s-char

s-char :
 any member of the source character set except the double quotation mark ("),
 backslash (\), or newline character
 escape-sequence

The example below is a simple string literal:

```
char amessage = "This is a string literal.";
```

All escape codes listed in Table 1.4 are valid in string literals. To represent a double quotation mark in a string literal, use the escape sequence \". The single quotation mark (') can be represented without an escape sequence. The backslash (\) must be followed with a second backslash (\\) when it appears within a string. When a backslash appears at the end of a line, it is always interpreted as a line-continuation character.

Type for String Literals

String literals have type array of **char** (that is, **char[ ]**). (Wide-character strings have type array of **wchar_t** (that is, **wchar_t[ ]**).) This means that a string is an array with elements of type **char**. The number of elements in the array is equal to the number of characters in the string plus one for the terminating null character.

Storage of String Literals

The characters of a literal string are stored in order at contiguous memory locations. An escape sequence (such as \\ or \") within a string literal counts as a single character. A null character (represented by the \0 escape sequence) is automatically appended to, and marks the end of, each string literal. (This occurs during translation phase 7. Note that the compiler may not store two identical strings at two different addresses. The /Gf (Eliminate Duplicate Strings) compiler option forces the compiler to place a single copy of identical strings into the executable file.

Microsoft Specific →

Strings have static storage duration. See "Storage Classes" on page 42 in Chapter 3 for information about storage duration.

END Microsoft Specific

String Literal Concatenation

To form string literals that take up more than one line, you can concatenate the two strings. To do this, type a backslash, then press the RETURN key. The backslash causes the compiler to ignore the following newline character. For example, the string literal

```
"Long strings can be bro\
ken into two or more pieces."
```

is identical to the string

```
"Long strings can be broken into two or more pieces."
```

String concatenation can be used anywhere you might previously have used a backslash followed by a newline character to enter strings longer than one line.

To force a new line within a string literal, enter the newline escape sequence (**\n**) at the point in the string where you want the line broken, as follows:

```
"Enter a number between 1 and 100\nOr press Return"
```

Because strings can start in any column of the source code and long strings can be continued in any column of a succeeding line, you can position strings to enhance source-code readability. In either case, their on-screen representation when output is unaffected. For example:

```
printf ( "This is the first half of the string, "
         "this is the second half ") ;
```

As long as each part of the string is enclosed in double quotation marks, the parts are concatenated and output as a single string. This concatenation occurs according to the sequence of events during compilation specified by translation phases.

```
"This is the first half of the string, this is the second half"
```

A string pointer, initialized as two distinct string literals separated only by white space, is stored as a single string (pointers are discussed in "Pointer Declarations" on page 68 in Chapter 3). When properly referenced, as in the following example, the result is identical to the previous example:

```
char *string = "This is the first half of the string, "
         "this is the second half";

printf( "%s" , string ) ;
```

In translation phase 6, the multibyte-character sequences specified by any sequence of adjacent string literals or adjacent wide-string literals are concatenated into a single multibyte-character sequence. Therefore, do not design programs to allow modification of string literals during execution. The ANSI C standard specifies that the result of modifying a string is undefined.

Maximum String Length

Microsoft Specific →

ANSI compatibility requires a compiler to accept up to 509 characters in a string literal after concatenation. The maximum length of a string literal allowed in Microsoft C is approximately 2,048 bytes. However, if the string literal consists of parts enclosed in double quotation marks, the preprocessor concatenates the parts into a single string, and for each line concatenated, it adds an extra byte to the total number of bytes.

For example, suppose a string consists of 40 lines with 50 characters per line (2,000 characters), and one line with 7 characters, and each line is surrounded by double quotation marks. This adds up to 2,007 bytes plus one byte for the terminating null character, for a total of 2,008 bytes. On concatenation, an extra character is added for each of the first 40 lines. This makes a total of 2,048 bytes. Note, however, that if line continuations (\) are used instead of double quotation marks, the preprocessor does not add an extra character for each line.

END Microsoft Specific

Punctuation and Special Characters

The punctuation and special characters in the C character set have various uses, from organizing program text to defining the tasks that the compiler or the compiled program carries out. They do not specify an operation to be performed. Some punctuation symbols are also operators (see "Operators" on page 99 in Chapter 4). The compiler determines their use from context.

Syntax

punctuator : one of
    [ ] ( ) { } * , : = ; ... #

These characters have special meanings in C. Their uses are described throughout this book. The pound sign (#) can occur only in "preprocessing directives."

CHAPTER 2

Program Structure

This chapter gives an overview of C programs and program execution. Terms and features important to understanding C programs and components are also introduced. Topics discussed include:

- Source files and source programs
- The main function and program execution
- Parsing command-line arguments
- Lifetime, scope, visibility, and linkage
- Name spaces

Because this chapter is an overview, the topics discussed contain introductory material only. See the cross-referenced information for more detailed explanations.

Source Files and Source Programs

A source program can be divided into one or more "source files," or "translation units." The input to the compiler is called a "translation unit."

Syntax

translation-unit :
          external-declaration
          translation-unit external-declaration

external-declaration :
          function-definition
          declaration

"Overview of Declarations" on page 39 in Chapter 3 gives the syntax for the *declaration* nonterminal, and the *Preprocessor Reference* explains how the translation unit is processed.

Note   See the introduction to Appendix A, "C Language Syntax Summary," for an explanation of the ANSI syntax conventions.

The components of a translation unit are external declarations that include function definitions and identifier declarations. These declarations and definitions can be in source files, header files, libraries, and other files the program needs. You must compile each translation unit and link the resulting object files to make a program.

A C "source program" is a collection of directives, pragmas, declarations, definitions, statement blocks, and functions. To be valid components of a Microsoft C program, each must have the syntax described in this book, although they can appear in any order in the program (subject to the rules outlined throughout this book). However, the location of these components in a program does affect how variables and functions can be used in a program. (See "Lifetime, Scope, Visibility, and Linkage" on page 32 for more information.)

Source files need not contain executable statements. For example, you may find it useful to place definitions of variables in one source file and then declare references to these variables in other source files that use them. This technique makes the definitions easy to find and update when necessary. For the same reason, constants and macros are often organized into separate files called "include files" or "header files" that can be referenced in source files as required. See the *Preprocessor Reference* for information about macros and include files.

Directives to the Preprocessor

A "directive" instructs the C preprocessor to perform a specific action on the text of the program before compilation. Preprocessor directives are fully described in the *Preprocessor Reference*. This example uses the preprocessor directive **#define**:

```
#define MAX 100
```

This statement tells the compiler to replace each occurrence of MAX by 100 before compilation. The C compiler preprocessor directives are:

#define	**#endif**	**#ifdef**	**#line**
#elif	**#error**	**#ifndef**	**#pragma**
#else	**#if**	**#include**	**#undef**

Pragmas

Microsoft Specific →

A "pragma" instructs the compiler to perform a particular action at compile time. Pragmas vary from compiler to compiler. For example, you can use the **optimize** pragma to set the optimizations to be performed on your program. The Microsoft C pragmas are:

alloc_text	data_seg	inline_recursion	setlocale
auto_inline	function	intrinsic	warning
check_stack	hdrstop	message	
code_seg	include_alias	optimize	
comment	inline_depth	pack	

See Chapter 2, "Pragma Directives," in the *Preprocessor Reference* for a description of the Microsoft C compiler pragmas.

END Microsoft Specific

Declarations and Definitions

A "declaration" establishes an association between a particular variable, function, or type and its attributes. "Overview of Declarations" on page 39 in Chapter 3 gives the ANSI syntax for the *declaration* nonterminal. A declaration also specifies where and when an identifier can be accessed (the "linkage" of an identifier). See "Lifetime, Scope, Visibility, and Linkage" on page 32 for information about linkage.

A "definition" of a variable establishes the same associations as a declaration but also causes storage to be allocated for the variable.

For example, the main, find, and count functions and the var and val variables are defined in one source file, in this order:

```
void main()
{
}

int var = 0;
double val[MAXVAL];

char find( fileptr )
{
}

int count( double f )
{
}
```

The variables var and val can be used in the find and count functions; no further declarations are needed. But these names are not visible (cannot be accessed) in main.

Function Declarations and Definitions

Function prototypes establish the name of the function, its return type, and the type and number of its formal parameters. A function definition includes the function body.

Both function and variable declarations can appear inside or outside a function definition. Any declaration within a function definition is said to appear at the "internal" or "local" level. A declaration outside all function definitions is said to appear at the "external," "global," or "file scope" level. Variable definitions, like declarations, can appear at the internal level (within a function definition) or at the external level (outside all function definitions). Function definitions always occur at the external level. Function definitions are discussed further in "Function Definitions" on page 155 in Chapter 6. Function prototypes are covered in "Function Prototypes" on page 169 in Chapter 6.

Blocks

A sequence of declarations, definitions, and statements enclosed within curly braces ({ }) is called a "block." There are two types of blocks in C. The "compound statement," a statement composed of one or more statements (see "The Compound Statement" on page 137 in Chapter 5), is one type of block. The other, the "function definition," consists of a compound statement (the body of the function) plus the function's associated "header" (the function name, return type, and formal parameters). A block within other blocks is said to be "nested."

Note that while all compound statements are enclosed within curly braces, not everything enclosed within curly braces constitutes a compound statement. For example, although the specifications of array, structure, or enumeration elements can appear within curly braces, they are not compound statements.

Example Program

The following C source program consists of two source files. It gives an overview of some of the various declarations and definitions possible in a C program. Later sections in this book describe how to write these declarations, definitions, and initializations, and how to use C keywords such as **static** and **extern**. The **printf** function is declared in the C header file STDIO.H.

The main and max functions are assumed to be in separate files, and execution of the program begins with the main function. No explicit user functions are executed before main.

```
/****************************************************************
                  FILE1.C - main function
 ****************************************************************/

#define ONE      1
#define TWO      2
#define THREE    3
#include <stdio.h>

int a = 1;                    /* Defining declarations    */
int b = 2;                    /*  of external variables   */

extern int max( int a, int b );  /* Function prototype      */

int main()                    /* Function definition      */
{                             /*  for main function       */
    int c;                    /* Definitions for          */
    int d;                    /*  two uninitialized       */
                              /*  local variables         */

    extern int u;             /* Referencing declaration  */
                              /*  of external variable    */
                              /*  defined elsewhere       */
    static int v;             /* Definition of variable   */
                              /*  with continuous lifetime */
```

```
int w = ONE, x = TWO, y = THREE;
int z = 0;
z = max( x, y );                        /* Executable statements    */
w = max( z, w );
printf( "%d %d\n", z, w );
return 0;
}


/******************************************************************
        FILE2.C - definition of max function
******************************************************************/

int max( int a, int b )               /* Note formal parameters are  */
                                      /* included in function header */
{
   if( a > b )
      return( a );
   else
      return( b );
}
```

FILE1.C contains the prototype for the max function. This kind of declaration is sometimes called a "forward declaration" because the function is declared before it is used. The definition for the main function includes calls to max.

The lines beginning with #define are preprocessor directives. These directives tell the preprocessor to replace the identifiers ONE, TWO, and THREE with the numbers 1, 2, and 3, respectively, throughout FILE1.C. However, the directives do not apply to FILE2.C, which is compiled separately and then linked with FILE1.C. The line beginning with #include tells the compiler to include the file STDIO.H, which contains the prototype for the **printf** function. Preprocessor directives are explained in the *Preprocessor Reference*.

FILE1.C uses defining declarations to initialize the global variables a and b. The local variables c and d are declared but not initialized. Storage is allocated for all these variables. The static and external variables, u and v, are automatically initialized to 0. Therefore only a, b, u, and v contain meaningful values when declared because they are initialized, either explicitly or implicitly. FILE2.C contains the function definition for max. This definition satisfies the calls to max in FILE1.C.

The lifetime and visibility of identifiers are discussed in "Lifetime, Scope, Visibility, and Linkage" on page 32. For more information on functions, see Chapter 6, "Functions."

The main Function and Program Execution

Every C program has a primary (main) function that must be named **main**. If your code adheres to the Unicode programming model, you can use the wide-character version of **main**, **wmain**. The **main** function serves as the starting point for program execution. It usually controls program execution by directing the calls to other functions in the program. A program usually stops executing at the end of **main**, although it can terminate at other points in the program for a variety of reasons. At times, perhaps when a certain error is detected, you may want to force the termination of a program. To do so, use the **exit** function. See the *Run-Time Library Reference* for information on and an example using the **exit** function.

Functions within the source program perform one or more specific tasks. The **main** function can call these functions to perform their respective tasks. When **main** calls another function, it passes execution control to the function, so that execution begins at the first statement in the function. A function returns control to **main** when a **return** statement is executed or when the end of the function is reached.

You can declare any function, including **main**, to have parameters. The term "parameter" or "formal parameter" refers to the identifier that receives a value passed to a function. See "Parameters" on page 167 in Chapter 6 for information on passing arguments to parameters. When one function calls another, the called function receives values for its parameters from the calling function. These values are called "arguments." You can declare formal parameters to **main** so that it can receive arguments from the command line using this format:

main(int *argc*, **char** **argv*[ ], **char** **envp*[ ])

When you want to pass information to the **main** function, the parameters are traditionally named *argc* and *argv*, although the C compiler does not require these names. The types for *argc* and *argv* are defined by the C language. Traditionally, if a third parameter is passed to **main**, that parameter is named *envp*. The type for the *envp* parameter is mandated by ANSI, but the name is not. Examples later in this chapter show how to use these three parameters to access command-line arguments. The following sections explain these parameters.

See "Using **wmain**" for a description of the wide-character version of **main**.

Using wmain

Microsoft Specific →

In the Unicode programming model, you can define a wide-character version of the **main** function. Use **wmain** instead of **main** if you want to write portable code that adheres to the Unicode programming model.

You declare formal parameters to **wmain** using a similar format to **main**. You can then pass wide-character arguments and, optionally, a wide-character environment pointer to the program. The *argv* and *envp* parameters to **wmain** are of type **wchar_t***. For example:

wmain(int *argc*, **wchar_t** **argv*[ ], **wchar_t** **envp*[ ])

If your program uses a **main** function, the multibyte-character environment is created by the run-time library at program startup. A wide-character copy of the environment is created only when needed (for example, by a call to the **_wgetenv** or **_wputenv** functions). On the first call to **_wputenv**, or on the first call to **_wgetenv** if an MBCS environment already exists, a corresponding wide-character string environment is created and is then pointed to by the **_wenviron** global variable, which is a wide-character version of the **_environ** global variable. At this point, two copies of the environment (MBCS and Unicode) exist simultaneously and are maintained by the operating system throughout the life of the program.

Similarly, if your program uses a **wmain** function, a wide-character environment is created at program startup and is pointed to by the **_wenviron** global variable. An MBCS (ASCII) environment is created on the first call to **_putenv** or **getenv**, and is pointed to by the **_environ** global variable.

For more information on the MBCS environment, see "Internationalization" in the *Run-Time Library Reference.*

END Microsoft Specific

Argument Description

The *argc* parameter in the **main** and **wmain** functions is an integer specifying how many arguments are passed to the program from the command line. Since the program name is considered an argument, the value of *argc* is at least one.

The *argv* parameter is an array of pointers to null-terminated strings representing the program arguments. Each element of the array points to a string representation of an argument passed to **main** (or **wmain**). (For information about arrays, see "Array Declarations" on page 66 in Chapter 3.) The *argv* parameter can be declared either as an array of pointers to type **char** (char *argv[]) or as a pointer to pointers to type **char** (char **argv). For **wmain**, the *argv* parameter can be declared either as an array of pointers to type **wchar_t** (wchar_t *argv[]) or as a pointer to pointers to type **wchar_t** (wchar_t **argv). The first string (argv[0]) is the program name. The last pointer (argv[argc]) is **NULL**. (See **getenv** in the *Run-Time Library Reference* for an alternative method for getting environment variable information.)

The *envp* parameter is a pointer to an array of null-terminated strings that represent the values set in the user's environment variables. The *envp* parameter can be declared as an array of pointers to **char** (char *envp[]) or as a pointer to pointers to **char** (char **envp). In a **wmain** function, the *envp* parameter can be declared as an array of pointers to **wchar_t** (wchar_t *envp[]) or as a pointer to pointers to **wchar_t** (wchar_t **envp). The end of the array is indicated by a **NULL** *pointer. Note that the environment block passed to **main** or **wmain** is a "frozen" copy of the current environment. If you subsequently change the environment via a call to **_putenv** or **_wputenv**, the current environment (as returned by **getenv**/**_wgetenv** and the **_environ** or **_wenviron** variables) will change, but the block pointed to by *envp* will not change.

Expanding Wildcard Arguments

Microsoft Specific →

When running a C program, you can use either of the two wildcards—the question mark (?) and the asterisk (*)—to specify filename and path arguments on the command line.

Command-line arguments are handled by a routine called **_setargv** (or **_wsetargv** in the wide-character environment), which by default does not expand wildcards into separate strings in the *argv* string array. You can replace the normal **_setargv** routine with a more powerful version of **_setargv** that does handle wildcards by linking with the SETARGV.OBJ file. If your program uses a **wmain** function, link with WSETARGV.OBJ.

To link with SETARGV.OBJ or WSETARGV.OBJ, use the /link option. For example:

```
cl typeit.c /link setargv.obj
```

The wildcards are expanded in the same manner as operating system commands. (See your operating system user's guide if you are unfamiliar with wildcards.) Enclosing an argument in double quotation marks (" ") suppresses the wildcard expansion. Within quoted arguments, you can represent quotation marks literally by preceding the double-quotation-mark character with a backslash (\). If no matches are found for the wildcard argument, the argument is passed literally.

END Microsoft Specific

Parsing Command-Line Arguments

Microsoft Specific →

Microsoft C startup code uses the following rules when interpreting arguments given on the operating system command line:

- Arguments are delimited by white space, which is either a space or a tab.

- A string surrounded by double quotation marks is interpreted as a single argument, regardless of white space contained within. A quoted string can be embedded in an argument. Note that the caret (^) is not recognized as an escape character or delimiter.

- A double quotation mark preceded by a backslash, \", is interpreted as a literal double quotation mark (").

- Backslashes are interpreted literally, unless they immediately precede a double quotation mark.

- If an even number of backslashes is followed by a double quotation mark, then one backslash (\) is placed in the *argv* array for every pair of backslashes (\\), and the double quotation mark (") is interpreted as a string delimiter.

- If an odd number of backslashes is followed by a double quotation mark, then one backslash (\) is placed in the *argv* array for every pair of backslashes (\\) and the double quotation mark is interpreted as an escape sequence by the remaining backslash, causing a literal double quotation mark (") to be placed in *argv*.

This list illustrates the rules above by showing the interpreted result passed to argv for several examples of command-line arguments. The output listed in the second, third, and fourth columns is from the ARGS.C program that follows the list.

Command-Line Input	argv[1]	argv[2]	argv[3]
"a b c" d e	a b c	d	e
"ab\"c" "\\" d	ab"c	\	d
a\\\b d"e f"g h	a\\\b	de fg	h
a\\\"b c d	a\"b	c	d
a\\\\"b c" d e	a\\b c	d	e

```c
/* ARGS.C illustrates the following variables used for accessing
 * command-line arguments and environment variables:
 * argc  argv  envp
 */

#include <stdio.h>

void main( int argc,    /* Number of strings in array argv */
 char *argv[],          /* Array of command-line argument strings */
 char **envp )          /* Array of environment variable strings */
{
    int count;

    /* Display each command-line argument. */
    printf( "\nCommand-line arguments:\n" );
    for( count = 0; count < argc; count++ )
        printf( "  argv[%d]   %s\n", count, argv[count] );

    /* Display each environment variable. */
    printf( "\nEnvironment variables:\n" );
    while( *envp != NULL )
        printf( "  %s\n", *(envp++) );

    return;
}
```

One example of output from this program is:

```
Command-line arguments:
  argv[0]   C:\MSC\TEST.EXE

Environment variables:
  COMSPEC=C:\NT\SYSTEM32\CMD.EXE

  PATH=c:\nt;c:\binb;c:\binr;c:\nt\system32;c:\word;c:\help;c:\msc;c:\;
  PROMPT=[$p]
  TEMP=c:\tmp
  TMP=c:\tmp
  EDITORS=c:\binr
  WINDIR=c:\nt
```

END Microsoft Specific

Customizing Command-Line Processing

If your program does not take command-line arguments, you can save a small amount of space by suppressing use of the library routine that performs command-line processing. This routine is called **_setargv** (or **_wsetargv** in the wide-character environment), as described in "Expanding Wildcard Arguments" on page 30. To suppress its use, define a routine that does nothing in the file containing the **main** function and name it **setargv** (or **_wsetargv** in the wide-character environment). The call to **_setargv** or **wsetargv** is then satisfied by your definition of **_setargv** or **_wsetargv** , and the library version is not loaded.

Similarly, if you never access the environment table through the *envp* argument, you can provide your own empty routine to be used in place of **_setenvp** (or **_wsetenvp**), the environment-processing routine.

If your program makes calls to the **_spawn** or **_exec** family of routines in the C run-time library, you should not suppress the environment-processing routine, since this routine is used to pass an environment from the spawning process to the new process.

Lifetime, Scope, Visibility, and Linkage

To understand how a C program works, you must understand the rules that determine how variables and functions can be used in the program. Several concepts are crucial to understanding these rules:

- Lifetime
- Scope and visibility
- Linkage

Lifetime

"Lifetime" is the period during execution of a program in which a variable or function exists. The storage duration of the identifier determines its lifetime.

An identifier declared with the *storage-class-specifier* **static** has static storage duration. Identifiers with static storage duration (also called "global") have storage and a defined value for the duration of a program. Storage is reserved and the identifier's stored value is initialized only once, before program startup. An identifier declared with external or internal linkage also has static storage duration (see "Linkage" on page 36).

An identifier declared without the **static** storage-class specifier has automatic storage duration if it is declared inside a function. An identifier with automatic storage duration (a "local identifier") has storage and a defined value only within the block where the identifier is defined or declared. An automatic identifier is allocated new storage each time the program enters that block, and it loses its storage (and its value) when the program exits the block. Identifiers declared in a function with no linkage also have automatic storage duration.

The following rules specify whether an identifier has global (static) or local (automatic) lifetime:

- All functions have static lifetime. Therefore they exist at all times during program execution. Identifiers declared at the external level (that is, outside all blocks in the program at the same level of function definitions) always have global (static) lifetimes.

- If a local variable has an initializer, the variable is initialized each time it is created (unless it is declared as **static**). Function parameters also have local lifetime. You can specify global lifetime for an identifier within a block by including the **static** storage-class specifier in its declaration. Once declared **static**, the variable retains its value from one entry of the block to the next.

Although an identifier with a global lifetime exists throughout the execution of the source program (for example, an externally declared variable or a local variable declared with the **static** keyword), it may not be visible in all parts of the program. See "Scope and Visibility" on page 34 for information about visibility, and see "Storage Classes" on page 42 in Chapter 3 for a discussion of the *storage-class-specifier* nonterminal.

Memory can be allocated as needed (dynamic) if created through the use of special library routines such as **malloc**. Since dynamic memory allocation uses library routines, it is not considered part of the language. See the **malloc** function in the *Run-Time Library Reference*.

Scope and Visibility

An identifier's "visibility" determines the portions of the program in which it can be referenced—its "scope." An identifier is visible (i.e., can be used) only in portions of a program encompassed by its "scope," which may be limited (in order of increasing restrictiveness) to the file, function, block, or function prototype in which it appears. The scope of an identifier is the part of the program in which the name can be used. This is sometimes called "lexical scope." There are four kinds of scope: function, file, block, and function prototype.

All identifiers except labels have their scope determined by the level at which the declaration occurs. The following rules for each kind of scope govern the visibility of identifiers within a program:

File scope   The declarator or type specifier for an identifier with file scope appears outside any block or list of parameters and is accessible from any place in the translation unit after its declaration. Identifier names with file scope are often called "global" or "external." The scope of a global identifier begins at the point of its definition or declaration and terminates at the end of the translation unit.

Function scope   A label is the only kind of identifier that has function scope. A label is declared implicitly by its use in a statement. Label names must be unique within a function. (For more information about labels and label names, see "The goto and Labeled Statements" on page 141 in Chapter 5.)

Block scope   The declarator or type specifier for an identifier with block scope appears inside a block or within the list of formal parameter declarations in a function definition. It is visible only from the point of its declaration or definition to the end of the block containing its declaration or definition. Its scope is limited to that block and to any blocks nested in that block and ends at the curly brace that closes the associated block. Such identifiers are sometimes called "local variables."

Function-prototype scope   The declarator or type specifier for an identifier with function-prototype scope appears within the list of parameter declarations in a function prototype (not part of the function declaration). Its scope terminates at the end of the function declarator.

The appropriate declarations for making variables visible in other source files are described in "Storage Classes" on page 42 Chapter 3. However, variables and functions declared at the external level with the **static** storage-class specifier are visible only within the source file in which they are defined. All other functions are globally visible.

Summary of Lifetime and Visibility

Table 2.1 is a summary of lifetime and visibility characteristics for most identifiers. The first three columns give the attributes that define lifetime and visibility. An identifier with the attributes given by the first three columns has the lifetime and visibility shown in the fourth and fifth columns. However, the table does not cover all possible cases. Refer to "Storage Classes" on page 42 in Chapter 3 for more information.

Table 2.1   Summary of Lifetime and Visibility

Attributes:			Result:	
Level	**Item**	**Storage-Class Specifier**	**Lifetime**	**Visibility**
File scope	Variable definition	**static**	Global	Remainder of source file in which it occurs
	Variable declaration	**extern**	Global	Remainder of source file in which it occurs
	Function prototype or definition	**static**	Global	Single source file
	Function prototype	**extern**	Global	Remainder of source file
Block scope	Variable declaration	**extern**	Global	Block
	Variable definition	**static**	Global	Block
	Variable definition	**auto** or **register**	Local	Block

The following example illustrates blocks, nesting, and visibility of variables:

```
#include <stdio.h>

int i = 1;                /* i defined at external level           */

int main()                /* main function defined at external level */
{
    printf( "%d\n", i );  /* Prints 1 (value of external level i)  */
    {                              /* Begin first nested block       */
        int i = 2, j = 3;         /* i and j defined at internal level */
        printf( "%d %d\n", i, j );    /* Prints 2, 3                */
        {                          /* Begin second nested block      */
            int i = 0;            /* i is redefined                 */
            printf( "%d %d\n", i, j ); /* Prints 0, 3               */
        }                          /* End of second nested block     */
        printf( "%d\n", i );      /* Prints 2 (outer definition      */
                                  /*   restored)                     */
    }                              /* End of first nested block       */
    printf( "%d\n", i );          /* Prints 1 (external level        */
                                  /* definition restored)            */
    return 0;
}
```

In this example, there are four levels of visibility: the external level and three block levels. The values are printed to the screen as noted in the comments following each statement.

Linkage

Identifier names can refer to different identifiers in different scopes. An identifier declared in different scopes or in the same scope more than once can be made to refer to the same identifier or function by a process called "linkage." Linkage determines the portions of the program in which an identifier can be referenced (its "visibility"). There are three kinds of linkage: internal, external, and no linkage.

Internal Linkage

If the declaration of a file-scope identifier for an object or a function contains the *storage-class-specifier* **static**, the identifier has internal linkage. Otherwise, the identifier has external linkage. See "Storage Classes" on page 42 in Chapter 3 for a discussion of the *storage-class-specifier* nonterminal.

Within one translation unit, each instance of an identifier with internal linkage denotes the same identifier or function. Internally linked identifiers are unique to a translation unit.

External Linkage

If the first declaration at file-scope level for an identifier does not use the **static** storage-class specifier, the object has external linkage.

If the declaration of an identifier for a function has no *storage-class-specifier*, its linkage is determined exactly as if it were declared with the *storage-class-specifier* **extern**. If the declaration of an identifier for an object has file scope and no *storage-class-specifier*, its linkage is external.

An identifier's name with external linkage designates the same function or data object as does any other declaration for the same name with external linkage. The two declarations can be in the same translation unit or in different translation units. If the object or function also has global lifetime, the object or function is shared by the entire program.

No Linkage

If a declaration for an identifier within a block does not include the **extern** storage-class specifier, the identifier has no linkage and is unique to the function.

The following identifiers have no linkage:

- An identifier declared to be anything other than an object or a function
- An identifier declared to be a function parameter
- A block-scope identifier for an object declared without the **extern** storage-class specifier

If an identifier has no linkage, declaring the same name again (in a declarator or type specifier) in the same scope level generates a symbol redefinition error.

Name Spaces

The compiler sets up "name spaces" to distinguish between the identifiers used for different kinds of items. The names within each name space must be unique to avoid conflict, but an identical name can appear in more than one name space. This means that you can use the same identifier for two or more different items, provided that the items are in different name spaces. The compiler can resolve references based on the syntactic context of the identifier in the program.

Note   Do not confuse the limited C notion of a name space with the C++ "namespace" feature. See "Namespaces" in the C++ *Language Reference* for more information.

This list describes the name spaces used in C.

Statement labels   Named statement labels are part of statements. Definitions of statement labels are always followed by a colon but are not part of **case** labels. Uses of statement labels always immediately follow the keyword **goto**. Statement labels do not have to be distinct from other names or from label names in other functions.

Structure, union, and enumeration tags   These tags are part of structure, union, and enumeration type specifiers and, if present, always immediately follow the reserved words **struct**, **union**, or **enum**. The tag names must be distinct from all other structure, enumeration, or union tags with the same visibility.

Members of structures or unions   Member names are allocated in name spaces associated with each structure and union type. That is, the same identifier can be a component name in any number of structures or unions at the same time. Definitions of component names always occur within structure or union type specifiers. Uses of component names always immediately follow the member-selection operators (−> and .). The name of a member must be unique within the structure or union, but it does not have to be distinct from other names in the program, including the names of members of different structures and unions, or the name of the structure itself.

Ordinary identifiers   All other names fall into a name space that includes variables, functions (including formal parameters and local variables), and enumeration constants. Identifier names have nested visibility, so you can redefine them within blocks.

Typedef names   Typedef names cannot be used as identifiers in the same scope.

For example, since structure tags, structure members, and variable names are in three different name spaces, the three items named student in this example do not conflict. The context of each item allows correct interpretation of each occurrence of student in the program. (For information about structures, see "Structure Declarations" on page 58 in Chapter 3.)

```
struct student {
    char student[20];
    int class;
    int id;
    } student;
```

When student appears after the **struct** keyword, the compiler recognizes it as a structure tag. When student appears after a member-selection operator (–> or .), the name refers to the structure member. In other contexts, student refers to the structure variable. However, overloading the tag name space is not recommended since it obscures meaning.

Declarations and Types

This chapter describes the declaration and initialization of variables, functions, and types. The C language includes a standard set of basic data types. You can also add your own data types, called "derived types," by declaring new ones based on types already defined. The following topics are discussed:

- Overview of declarations
- Storage classes
- Type specifiers
- Type qualifiers
- Declarators and variable declarations
- Interpreting more complex declarators
- Initialization
- Storage of basic types
- Incomplete types
- Typedef declarations
- Extended storage-class attributes

Overview of Declarations

A "declaration" specifies the interpretation and attributes of a set of identifiers. A declaration that also causes storage to be reserved for the object or function named by the identifier is called a "definition." C declarations for variables, functions, and types have this syntax:

Syntax

declaration :

        declaration-specifiers init-declarator-list _{opt} **;**

declaration-specifiers :
  storage-class-specifier attribute-seq opt *declaration-specifiers* opt
            /* *attribute-seq* opt is Microsoft specific */
  type-specifier declaration-specifiers opt
  type-qualifier declaration-specifiers opt

init-declarator-list :
  init-declarator
  init-declarator-list , *init-declarator*

init-declarator :
  declarator
  declarator = *initializer*

Note This syntax for *declaration* is not repeated in the following sections. Syntax in the following sections usually begin with the *declarator* nonterminal.

The declarations in the *init-declarator-list* contain the identifiers being named; *init* is an abbreviation for initializer. The *init-declarator-list* is a comma-separated sequence of declarators, each of which can have additional type information, or an initializer, or both. The *declarator* contains the identifiers, if any, being declared. The *declaration-specifiers* nonterminal consists of a sequence of type and storage-class specifiers that indicate the linkage, storage duration, and at least part of the type of the entities that the declarators denote. Therefore, declarations are made up of some combination of storage-class specifiers, type specifiers, type qualifiers, declarators, and initializers.

Declarations can contain one or more of the optional attributes listed in *attribute-seq*; *seq* is an abbreviation for sequence. These Microsoft-specific attributes perform a variety of functions, which are discussed in detail throughout this book. For a list of these attributes, see Appendix A, "C Language Syntax Summary."

In the general form of a variable declaration, *type-specifier* gives the data type of the variable. The *type-specifier* can be a compound, as when the type is modified by **const** or **volatile**. The *declarator* gives the name of the variable, possibly modified to declare an array or a pointer type. For example,

```
int const *fp;
```

declares a variable named fp as a pointer to a nonmodifiable (**const**) **int** value. You can define more than one variable in a declaration by using multiple declarators, separated by commas.

A declaration must have at least one declarator, or its type specifier must declare a structure tag, union tag, or members of an enumeration. Declarators provide any remaining information about an identifier. A declarator is an identifier that can be modified with brackets ([ ]), asterisks (*), or parentheses (( )) to declare an array, pointer, or function type, respectively. When you declare simple variables (such as character, integer, and floating-point items), or structures and unions of simple variables, the *declarator* is just an identifier. For more information on declarators, see "Declarators and Variable Declarations" on page 52.

All definitions are implicitly declarations, but not all declarations are definitions. For example, variable declarations that begin with the **extern** storage-class specifier are "referencing," rather than "defining" declarations. If an external variable is to be referred to before it is defined, or if it is defined in another source file from the one where it is used, an **extern** declaration is necessary. Storage is not allocated by "referencing" declarations, nor can variables be initialized in declarations.

A storage class or a type (or both) is required in variable declarations. Except for **__declspec**, only one storage-class specifier is allowed in a declaration and not all storage-class specifiers are permitted in every context. The **__declspec** storage class is allowed with other storage-class specifiers, and it is allowed more than once. The storage-class specifier of a declaration affects how the declared item is stored and initialized, and which parts of a program can reference the item.

The *storage-class-specifier* terminals defined in C include **auto**, **extern**, **register**, **static**, and **typedef**. In addition, Microsoft C includes the *storage-class-specifier* terminal **__declspec**. All *storage-class-specifier* terminals except **typedef** and **__declspec** are discussed in "Storage Classes" on page 42. See "Typedef Declarations" on page 86 for information about **typedef**. See "Extended Storage-Class Attributes" on page 88 for information about **__declspec**.

The location of the declaration within the source program and the presence or absence of other declarations of the variable are important factors in determining the lifetime of variables. There can be multiple redeclarations but only one definition. However, a definition can appear in more than one translation unit. For objects with internal linkage, this rule applies separately to each translation unit, because internally linked objects are unique to a translation unit. For objects with external linkage, this rule applies to the entire program. See "Lifetime, Scope, Visibility, and Linkage" on page 32 in Chapter 2 for more information about visibility.

Type specifiers provide some information about the data types of identifiers. The default type specifier is **int**. For more information, see "Type Specifiers" on page 49. Type specifiers can also define type tags, structure and union component names, and enumeration constants. For more information see "Enumeration Declarations" on page 55, "Structure Declarations" on page 58, and "Union Declarations" on page 63.

There are two *type-qualifier* terminals: **const** and **volatile**. These qualifiers specify additional properties of types that are relevant only when accessing objects of that type through l-values. For more information on **const** and **volatile**, see "Type Qualifiers" on page 51. For a definition of l-values, see "L-Value and R-Value Expressions" on page 95 in Chapter 4.

Storage Classes

The "storage class" of a variable determines whether the item has a "global" or "local" lifetime. C calls these two lifetimes "static" and "automatic." An item with a global lifetime exists and has a value throughout the execution of the program. All functions have global lifetimes.

Automatic variables, or variables with local lifetimes, are allocated new storage each time execution control passes to the block in which they are defined. When execution returns, the variables no longer have meaningful values.

C provides the following storage-class specifiers:

Syntax

storage-class-specifier :
> **auto**
> **register**
> **static**
> **extern**
> **typedef**
> **__declspec** (*extended-decl-modifier-seq*) /* Microsoft Specific */

Except for **__declspec**, you can use only one *storage-class-specifier* in the *declaration-specifier* in a declaration. If no storage-class specification is made, declarations within a block create automatic objects.

Items declared with the **auto** or **register** specifier have local lifetimes. Items declared with the **static** or **extern** specifier have global lifetimes.

Since **typedef** and **__declspec** are semantically different from the other four *storage-class-specifier* terminals, they are discussed separately. For specific information on **typedef**, see "Typedef Declarations" on page 86. For specific information on **__declspec**, see "Extended Storage-Class Attributes" on page 88.

The placement of variable and function declarations within source files also affects storage class and visibility. Declarations outside all function definitions are said to appear at the "external level." Declarations within function definitions appear at the "internal level."

The exact meaning of each storage-class specifier depends on two factors:

- Whether the declaration appears at the external or internal level
- Whether the item being declared is a variable or a function

"Storage-Class Specifiers for External-Level Declarations" on page 43 and "Storage-Class Specifiers for Internal-Level Declarations" on page 45 describe the *storage-class-specifier* terminals in each kind of declaration and explain the default behavior when the *storage-class-specifier* is omitted from a variable. "Storage-Class Specifiers with Function Declarations" on page 48 discusses storage-class specifiers used with functions.

Storage-Class Specifiers for External-Level Declarations

External variables are variables at file scope. They are defined outside any function, and they are potentially available to many functions. Functions can only be defined at the external level and, therefore, cannot be nested. By default, all references to external variables and functions of the same name are references to the same object, which means they have "external linkage." (You can use the **static** keyword to override this. See information later in this section for more details on **static**.)

Variable declarations at the external level are either definitions of variables ("defining declarations"), or references to variables defined elsewhere ("referencing declarations").

An external variable declaration that also initializes the variable (implicitly or explicitly) is a defining declaration of the variable. A definition at the external level can take several forms:

- A variable that you declare with the **static** storage-class specifier. You can explicitly initialize the **static** variable with a constant expression, as described in "Initialization." If you omit the initializer, the variable is initialized to 0 by default. For example, these two statements are both considered definitions of the variable k.

```
static int k = 16;
static int k;
```

- A variable that you explicitly initialize at the external level. For example, int j = 3; is a definition of the variable j.

In variable declarations at the external level (that is, outside all functions), you can use the **static** or **extern** storage-class specifier or omit the storage-class specifier entirely. You cannot use the **auto** and **register** *storage-class-specifier* terminals at the external level.

Once a variable is defined at the external level, it is visible throughout the rest of the translation unit. The variable is not visible prior to its declaration in the same source file. Also, it is not visible in other source files of the program, unless a referencing declaration makes it visible, as described below.

The rules relating to **static** include:

- Variables declared outside all blocks without the **static** keyword always retain their values throughout the program. To restrict their access to a particular translation unit, you must use the **static** keyword. This gives them "internal linkage." To make them global to an entire program, omit the explicit storage class or use the keyword **extern** (see the rules in the next list). This gives them "external linkage." Internal and external linkage are also discussed in "Linkage" on page 36 in Chapter 2.

- You can define a variable at the external level only once within a program. You can define another variable with the same name and the **static** storage-class specifier in a different translation unit. Since each **static** definition is visible only within its own translation unit, no conflict occurs. This provides a useful way to hide identifier names that must be shared among functions of a single translation unit, but not visible to other translation units.

- The **static** storage-class specifier can apply to functions as well. If you declare a function **static**, its name is invisible outside of the file in which it is declared.

The rules for using **extern** are:

- The **extern** storage-class specifier declares a reference to a variable defined elsewhere. You can use an **extern** declaration to make a definition in another source file visible, or to make a variable visible prior to its definition in the same source file. Once you have declared a reference to the variable at the external level, the variable is visible throughout the remainder of the translation unit in which the declared reference occurs.

- For an **extern** reference to be valid, the variable it refers to must be defined once, and only once, at the external level. This definition (without the **extern** storage class) can be in any of the translation units that make up the program.

Example

The example below illustrates external declarations:

```
/***********************************************************
                  SOURCE FILE ONE
***********************************************************/

extern int i;               /* Reference to i, defined below */
void next( void );          /* Function prototype            */

void main()
{
    i++;
    printf( "%d\n", i );    /* i equals 4 */
    next();
}

int i = 3;                  /* Definition of i */

void next( void )
{
    i++;
    printf( "%d\n", i );    /* i equals 5 */
    other();
}
```

```
/*****************************************************************
                     SOURCE FILE TWO
*****************************************************************/

extern int i;                /* Reference to i in  */
                             /* first source file  */
void other( void )
{
   i++;
   printf( "%d\n", i );      /* i equals 6 */
}
```

The two source files in this example contain a total of three external declarations of i. Only one declaration is a "defining declaration." That declaration,

```
int i = 3;
```

defines the global variable i and initializes it with initial value 3. The "referencing" declaration of i at the top of the first source file using **extern** makes the global variable visible prior to its defining declaration in the file. The referencing declaration of i in the second source file also makes the variable visible in that source file. If a defining instance for a variable is not provided in the translation unit, the compiler assumes there is an

```
extern int x;
```

referencing declaration and that a defining reference

```
int x = 0;
```

appears in another translation unit of the program.

All three functions, main, next, and other, perform the same task: they increase i and print it. The values 4, 5, and 6 are printed.

If the variable i had not been initialized, it would have been set to 0 automatically. In this case, the values 1, 2, and 3 would have been printed. See "Initialization" on page 74 for information about variable initialization.

Storage-Class Specifiers for Internal-Level Declarations

You can use any of four *storage-class-specifier* terminals for variable declarations at the internal level. When you omit the *storage-class-specifier* from such a declaration, the default storage class is **auto**. Therefore, the keyword **auto** is rarely seen in a C program.

The auto Storage-Class Specifier

The **auto** storage-class specifier declares an automatic variable, a variable with a local lifetime. An **auto** variable is visible only in the block in which it is declared. Declarations of **auto** variables can include initializers, as discussed in "Initialization" on page 74.

Since variables with **auto** storage class are not initialized automatically, you should either explicitly initialize them when you declare them, or assign them initial values in statements within the block. The values of uninitialized **auto** variables are undefined. (A local variable of **auto** or **register** storage class is initialized each time it comes in scope if an initializer is given.)

An internal **static** variable (a static variable with local or block scope) can be initialized with the address of any external or **static** item, but not with the address of another **auto** item, because the address of an **auto** item is not a constant.

The register Storage-Class Specifier

Microsoft Specific →

The Microsoft C/C++ compiler does not honor user requests for register variables. However, for portability all other semantics associated with the **register** keyword are honored by the compiler. For example, you cannot apply the unary address-of operator (**&**) to a register object nor can the **register** keyword be used on arrays.

END Microsoft Specific

The static Storage-Class Specifier

A variable declared at the internal level with the **static** storage-class specifier has a global lifetime but is visible only within the block in which it is declared. For constant strings, using **static** is useful because it alleviates the overhead of frequent initialization in often-called functions.

If you do not explicitly initialize a **static** variable, it is initialized to 0 by default. Inside a function, **static** causes storage to be allocated and serves as a definition. Internal static variables provide private, permanent storage visible to only a single function.

The extern Storage-Class Specifier

A variable declared with the **extern** storage-class specifier is a reference to a variable with the same name defined at the external level in any of the source files of the program. The internal **extern** declaration is used to make the external-level variable definition visible within the block. Unless otherwise declared at the external level, a variable declared with the **extern** keyword is visible only in the block in which it is declared.

Example

This example illustrates internal- and external-level declarations:

```
#include <stdio.h>
int i = 1;
void other( void );

void main()
{
    /* Reference to i, defined above: */
    extern int i;

    /* Initial value is zero; a is visible only within main: */
    static int a;

    /* b is stored in a register, if possible: */
    register int b = 0;

    /* Default storage class is auto: */
    int c = 0;

    /* Values printed are 1, 0, 0, 0: */
    printf( "%d\n%d\n%d\n%d\n", i, a, b, c );
    other();
    return;
}

void other( void )
{
    /* Address of global i assigned to pointer variable: */
    static int *external_i = &i;

    /* i is redefined; global i no longer visible: */
    int i = 16;

    /* This a is visible only within the other function: */
    static int a = 2;

    a += 2;
    /* Values printed are 16, 4, and 1: */
    printf( "%d\n%d\n%d\n", i, a, *external_i );
}
```

In this example, the variable i is defined at the external level with initial value 1. An **extern** declaration in the main function is used to declare a reference to the external-level i. The **static** variable a is initialized to 0 by default, since the initializer is omitted. The call to printf prints the values 1, 0, 0, and 0.

In the other function, the address of the global variable i is used to initialize the **static** pointer variable external_i. This works because the global variable has **static** lifetime, meaning its address does not change during program execution. Next, the variable i is redefined as a local variable with initial value 16. This redefinition does not affect the value of the external-level i, which is hidden by the use of its name for the local variable. The value of the global i is now accessible only indirectly within this block, through the pointer external_i. Attempting to assign the address of the **auto** variable i to a pointer does not work, since it may be different each time the block is entered. The variable a is declared as a **static** variable and initialized to 2. This a does not conflict with the a in main, since **static** variables at the internal level are visible only within the block in which they are declared.

The variable a is increased by 2, giving 4 as the result. If the other function were called again in the same program, the initial value of a would be 4. Internal **static** variables keep their values when the program exits and then reenters the block in which they are declared.

Storage-Class Specifiers with Function Declarations

You can use either the **static** or the **extern** storage-class specifier in function declarations. Functions always have global lifetimes.

Microsoft Specific →

Function declarations at the internal level have the same meaning as function declarations at the external level. This means that a function is visible from its point of declaration throughout the rest of the translation unit even if it is declared at local scope.

END Microsoft Specific

The visibility rules for functions vary slightly from the rules for variables, as follows:

- A function declared to be **static** is visible only within the source file in which it is defined. Functions in the same source file can call the **static** function, but functions in other source files cannot access it directly by name. You can declare another **static** function with the same name in a different source file without conflict.

- Functions declared as **extern** are visible throughout all source files in the program (unless you later redeclare such a function as **static**). Any function can call an **extern** function.

- Function declarations that omit the storage-class specifier are **extern** by default.

Microsoft Specific →

Microsoft allows redefinition of an **extern** identifier as **static**.

END Microsoft Specific

Type Specifiers

Type specifiers in declarations define the type of a variable or function declaration.

Syntax

type-specifier :

   void
   char
   short
   int
   long
   float
   double
   signed
   unsigned
   struct-or-union-specifier
   enum-specifier
   typedef-name

The **signed char**, **signed int**, **signed short int**, and **signed long int** types, together with their **unsigned** counterparts and **enum**, are called "integral" types. The **float, double,** and **long double** type specifiers are referred to as "floating" or "floating-point" types. You can use any integral or floating-point type specifier in a variable or function declaration. If a *type-specifier* is not provided in a declaration, it is taken to be **int**.

The optional keywords **signed** and **unsigned** can precede or follow any of the integral types, except **enum**, and can also be used alone as type specifiers, in which case they are understood as **signed int** and **unsigned int**, respectively. When used alone, the keyword **int** is assumed to be **signed**. When used alone, the keywords **long** and **short** are understood as **long int** and **short int**.

Enumeration types are considered basic types. Type specifiers for enumeration types are discussed in "Enumeration Declarations" on page 55.

The keyword **void** has three uses: to specify a function return type, to specify an argument-type list for a function that takes no arguments, and to specify a pointer to an unspecified type. You can use the **void** type to declare functions that return no value or to declare a pointer to an unspecified type. See "Arguments" on page 173 in Chapter 6 for information on **void** when it appears alone within the parentheses following a function name.

Microsoft Specific →

Type checking is now ANSI-compliant, which means that type **short** and type **int** are distinct types. For example, this is a redefinition in the Microsoft C compiler that was accepted by previous versions of the compiler.

```
int   myfunc();
short myfunc();
```

This next example also generates a warning about indirection to different types:

```
int *pi;
short *ps;

ps = pi;  /* Now generates warning */
```

The Microsoft C compiler also generates warnings for differences in sign. For example:

```
signed int *pi;
unsigned int *pu

pi = pu;  /* Now generates warning */
```

Type **void** expressions are evaluated for side effects. You cannot use the (nonexistent) value of an expression that has type **void** in any way, nor can you convert a **void** expression (by implicit or explicit conversion) to any type except **void**. If you do use an expression of any other type in a context where a **void** expression is required, its value is discarded.

To conform to the ANSI specification, **void**** cannot be used as **int****. Only **void*** can be used as a pointer to an unspecified type.

END Microsoft Specific

You can create additional type specifiers with **typedef** declarations, as described in "Typedef Declarations" on page 86. See "Storage of Basic Types" on page 81 for information on the size of each type.

Data Type Specifiers and Equivalents

This book generally uses the forms of the type specifiers listed in Table 3.1 rather than the long forms, and it assumes that the **char** type is signed by default. Therefore, throughout this book, **char** is equivalent to **signed char**.

Table 3.1 Type Specifiers and Equivalents

Type Specifier	Equivalent(s)
signed char[1]	**char**
signed int	**signed, int**
signed short int	**short, signed short**
signed long int	**long, signed long**
unsigned char	—
unsigned int	**unsigned**
unsigned short int	**unsigned short**
unsigned long int	**unsigned long**
float	—
long double[2]	—

[1] When you make the **char** type unsigned by default (by specifying the /J compiler option), you cannot abbreviate **signed char** as **char**.

[2] In 32-bit operating systems, the Microsoft C compiler maps **long double** to type **double**.

Microsoft Specific →

You can specify the /J compiler option to change the default **char** type from signed to unsigned. When this option is in effect, **char** means the same as **unsigned char**, and you must use the **signed** keyword to declare a signed character value. If a **char** value is explicitly declared signed, the /J option does not affect it, and the value is sign-extended when widened to an **int** type. The **char** type is zero-extended when widened to **int** type.

END Microsoft Specific

Type Qualifiers

Type qualifiers give one of two properties to an identifier. The **const** type qualifier declares an object to be nonmodifiable. The **volatile** type qualifier declares an item whose value can legitimately be changed by something beyond the control of the program in which it appears, such as a concurrently executing thread.

The two type qualifiers, **const** and **volatile**, can appear only once in a declaration. Type qualifiers can appear with any type specifier; however, they cannot appear after the first comma in a multiple item declaration. For example, the following declarations are legal:

```
typedef volatile int VI;
const int ci;
```

These declarations are not legal:

```
typedef int *i, volatile *vi;
float f, const cf;
```

Type qualifiers are relevant only when accessing identifiers as l-values in expressions. See "L-Value and R-Value Expressions" on page 95 in Chapter 4 for information about l-values and expressions.

Syntax

type-qualifier :
    const
    volatile

The following are legal **const** and **volatile** declarations:

```
int const *p_ci;        /* Pointer to constant int */
int const (*p_ci);      /* Pointer to constant int */
int *const cp_i;        /* Constant pointer to int */
int (*const cp_i);      /* Constant pointer to int */
int volatile vint;      /* Volatile integer        */
```

If the specification of an array type includes type qualifiers, the element is qualified, not the array type. If the specification of the function type includes qualifiers, the behavior is undefined. Neither **volatile** nor **const** affects the range of values or arithmetic properties of the object.

This list describes how to use **const** and **volatile**.

- The **const** keyword can be used to modify any fundamental or aggregate type, or a pointer to an object of any type, or a **typedef**. If an item is declared with only the **const** type qualifier, its type is taken to be **const int**. A **const** variable can be initialized or can be placed in a read-only region of storage. The **const** keyword is useful for declaring pointers to **const** since this requires the function not to change the pointer in any way.

- The compiler assumes that, at any point in the program, a **volatile** variable can be accessed by an unknown process that uses or modifies its value. Therefore, regardless of the optimizations specified on the command line, the code for each assignment to or reference of a **volatile** variable must be generated even if it appears to have no effect.

  If **volatile** is used alone, **int** is assumed. The **volatile** type specifier can be used to provide reliable access to special memory locations. Use **volatile** with data objects that may be accessed or altered by signal handlers, by concurrently executing programs, or by special hardware such as memory-mapped I/O control registers. You can declare a variable as **volatile** for its lifetime, or you can cast a single reference to be **volatile**.

- An item can be both **const** and **volatile**, in which case the item could not be legitimately modified by its own program, but could be modified by some asynchronous process.

Declarators and Variable Declarations

The rest of this chapter describes the form and meaning of declarations for variable types summarized in this list. In particular, the remaining sections explain how to declare the following:

Type of Variable	Description
Simple variables	Single-value variables with integral or floating-point type
Arrays	Variables composed of a collection of elements with the same type
Pointers	Variables that point to other variables and contain variable locations (in the form of addresses) instead of values
Enumeration variables	Simple variables with integral type that hold one value from a set of named integer constants
Structures	Variables composed of a collection of values that can have different types
Unions	Variables composed of several values of different types that occupy the same storage space

A declarator is the part of a declaration that specifies the name that is to be introduced into the program. It can include modifiers such as * (pointer-to) and any of the Microsoft calling-convention keywords.

Microsoft Specific →

In the declarator

```
__declspec(thread) char *var;
```

char is the type specifier, __declspec(thread) and * are the modifiers, and var is the identifier's name.

END Microsoft Specific

You use declarators to declare arrays of values, pointers to values, and functions returning values of a specified type. Declarators appear in the array and pointer declarations described later in this chapter.

Syntax

declarator :

> *pointer* opt *direct-declarator*

direct-declarator :

> *identifier*
> (*declarator*)
> *direct-declarator* [*constant-expression* opt]
> *direct-declarator* (*parameter-type-list*)
> *direct-declarator* (*identifier-list* opt)

type-qualifier-list :pointer :

> * *type-qualifier-list* opt
> * *type-qualifier-list* opt *pointer*

type-qualifier

> *type-qualifier-list type-qualifier*

Note   See the syntax for *declaration* in "Overview of Declarations" on page 39, or see Appendix A, "C Language Syntax Summary," for the syntax that references a *declarator*.

When a declarator consists of an unmodified identifier, the item being declared has a base type. If an asterisk (*) appears to the left of an identifier, the type is modified to a pointer type. If the identifier is followed by brackets ([ ]), the type is modified to an array type. If the identifier is followed by parentheses, the type is modified to a function type. For more information about interpreting precedence within declarations, see "Interpreting More Complex Declarators" on page 72.

Each declarator declares at least one identifier. A declarator must include a type specifier to be a complete declaration. The type specifier gives the type of the elements of an array type, the type of object addressed by a pointer type, or the return type of a function.

Array and pointer declarations are discussed in more detail later in this chapter. The following examples illustrate a few simple forms of declarators:

```
int list[20]; /* Declares an array of 20 int values named list */
char *cp;     /* Declares a pointer to a char value */
double func( void ); /* Declares a function named func, with no
                        arguments, that returns a double value */
int *aptr[10]        /* Declares an array of 10 pointers */
```

Microsoft Specific →

The Microsoft C compiler does not limit the number of declarators that can modify an arithmetic, structure, or union type. The number is limited only by available memory.

END Microsoft Specific

Simple Variable Declarations

The declaration of a simple variable, the simplest form of a direct declarator, specifies the variable's name and type. It also specifies the variable's storage class and data type.

Storage classes or types (or both) are required on variable declarations. Untyped variables (such as var;) generate warnings.

Syntax

declarator :
          pointer ₒₚₜ *direct-declarator*

direct-declarator :
          identifier

identifier :
          nondigit
          identifier nondigit
          identifier digit

For arithmetic, structure, union, enumerations, and void types, and for types represented by **typedef** names, simple declarators can be used in a declaration since the type specifier supplies all the typing information. Pointer, array, and function types require more complicated declarators.

You can use a list of identifiers separated by commas (,) to specify several variables in the same declaration. All variables defined in the declaration have the same base type. For example:

```
int x, y;        /* Declares two simple variables of type int */
int const z = 1; /* Declares a constant value of type int */
```

The variables x and y can hold any value in the set defined by the **int** type for a particular implementation. The simple object z is initialized to the value 1 and is not modifiable.

If the declaration of z was for an uninitialized static variable or was at file scope, it would receive an initial value of 0, and that value would be unmodifiable.

```
unsigned long reply, flag; /* Declares two variables
                              named reply and flag     */
```

In this example, both the variables, reply and flag, have **unsigned long** type and hold unsigned integral values.

Enumeration Declarations

An enumeration consists of a set of named integer constants. An enumeration type declaration gives the name of the (optional) enumeration tag and defines the set of named integer identifiers (called the "enumeration set," "enumerator constants," "enumerators," or "members"). A variable with enumeration type stores one of the values of the enumeration set defined by that type.

Variables of **enum** type can be used in indexing expressions and as operands of all arithmetic and relational operators. Enumerations provide an alternative to the **#define** preprocessor directive with the advantages that the values can be generated for you and obey normal scoping rules.

In ANSI C, the expressions that define the value of an enumerator constant always have **int** type; thus, the storage associated with an enumeration variable is the storage required for a single **int** value. An enumeration constant or a value of enumerated type can be used anywhere the C language permits an integer expression.

Syntax

enum-specifier :

      enum *identifier* $_{opt}$ { *enumerator-list* }

      enum *identifier*

The optional *identifier* names the enumeration type defined by *enumerator-list*. This identifier is often called the "tag" of the enumeration specified by the list. A type specifier of the form

enum *identifier* { *enumerator-list* }

declares *identifier* to be the tag of the enumeration specified by the *enumerator-list* nonterminal. The *enumerator-list* defines the "enumerator content." The *enumerator-list* is described in detail below.

If the declaration of a tag is visible, subsequent declarations that use the tag but omit *enumerator-list* specify the previously declared enumerated type. The tag must refer to a defined enumeration type, and that enumeration type must be in current scope. Since the enumeration type is defined elsewhere, the *enumerator-list* does not appear in this declaration. Declarations of types derived from enumerations and **typedef** declarations for enumeration types can use the enumeration tag before the enumeration type is defined.

Syntax

enumerator-list :
    enumerator
    enumerator-list , *enumerator*

enumerator :
    enumeration-constant
    enumeration-constant = *constant-expression*

enumeration-constant :
    identifier

Each *enumeration-constant* in an *enumeration-list* names a value of the enumeration set. By default, the first *enumeration-constant* is associated with the value 0. The next *enumeration-constant* in the list is associated with the value of (*constant-expression* + 1), unless you explicitly associate it with another value. The name of an *enumeration-constant* is equivalent to its value.

You can use *enumeration-constant* = *constant-expression* to override the default sequence of values. Thus, if *enumeration-constant* = *constant-expression* appears in the *enumerator-list*, the *enumeration-constant* is associated with the value given by *constant-expression*. The *constant-expression* must have **int** type and can be negative.

The following rules apply to the members of an enumeration set:

- An enumeration set can contain duplicate constant values. For example, you could associate the value 0 with two different identifiers, perhaps named null and zero, in the same set.

- The identifiers in the enumeration list must be distinct from other identifiers in the same scope with the same visibility, including ordinary variable names and identifiers in other enumeration lists.

- Enumeration tags obey the normal scoping rules. They must be distinct from other enumeration, structure, and union tags with the same visibility.

Examples

These examples illustrate enumeration declarations:

```
enum DAY             /* Defines an enumeration type    */
{
    saturday,        /* Names day and declares a       */
    sunday = 0,      /* variable named workday with    */
    monday,          /* that type                      */
    tuesday,
    wednesday,       /* wednesday is associated with 3 */
    thursday,
    friday
} workday;
```

The value 0 is associated with `saturday` by default. The identifier `sunday` is explicitly set to 0. The remaining identifiers are given the values 1 through 5 by default.

In this example, a value from the set DAY is assigned to the variable `today`.

```
enum DAY today = wednesday;
```

Note that the name of the enumeration constant is used to assign the value. Since the DAY enumeration type was previously declared, only the enumeration tag DAY is necessary.

To explicitly assign an integer value to a variable of an enumerated data type, use a type cast:

```
workday = ( enum DAY ) ( day_value - 1 );
```

This cast is recommended in C but is not required.

```
enum BOOLEAN  /* Declares an enumeration data type called BOOLEAN */
{
    false,       /* false = 0, true = 1 */
    true
};
```

```
enum BOOLEAN end_flag, match_flag; /* Two variables of type BOOLEAN */
```

This declaration can also be specified as

```
enum BOOLEAN { false, true } end_flag, match_flag;\
```

or as

```
enum BOOLEAN { false, true } end_flag;
enum BOOLEAN match_flag;
```

An example that uses these variables might look like this:

```
if ( match_flag == false )
    {
      .
      .    /* statement */
      .
    }
    end_flag = true;
```

Unnamed enumerator data types can also be declared. The name of the data type is omitted, but variables can be declared. The variable `response` is a variable of the type defined:

```
enum { yes, no } response;
```

Structure Declarations

A "structure declaration" names a type and specifies a sequence of variable values (called "members" or "fields" of the structure) that can have different types. An optional identifier, called a "tag," gives the name of the structure type and can be used in subsequent references to the structure type. A variable of that structure type holds the entire sequence defined by that type. Structures in C are similar to the types known as "records" in other languages.

Syntax

struct-or-union-specifier :
        struct-or-union identifier _{opt} { *struct-declaration-list* }
        struct-or-union identifier

struct-or-union :
        struct
        union

struct-declaration-list :
        struct-declaration
        struct-declaration-list struct-declaration

The structure content is defined to be

struct-declaration :
        specifier-qualifier-list struct-declarator-list ;

specifier-qualifier-list :
        type-specifier specifier-qualifier-list _{opt}
        type-qualifier specifier-qualifier-list _{opt}

struct-declarator-list :
        struct-declarator
        struct-declarator-list , *struct-declarator*

struct-declarator :
        declarator

The declaration of a structure type does not set aside space for a structure. It is only a template for later declarations of structure variables.

A previously defined *identifier* (tag) can be used to refer to a structure type defined elsewhere. In this case, *struct-declaration-list* cannot be repeated as long as the definition is visible. Declarations of pointers to structures and typedefs for structure types can use the structure tag before the structure type is defined. However, the structure definition must be encountered prior to any actual use of the size of the fields. This is an incomplete definition of the type and the type tag. For this definition to be completed, a type definition must appear later in the same scope.

The *struct-declaration-list* specifies the types and names of the structure members. A *struct-declaration-list* argument contains one or more variable or bit-field declarations.

Each variable declared in *struct-declaration-list* is defined as a member of the structure type. Variable declarations within *struct-declaration-list* have the same form as other variable declarations discussed in this chapter, except that the declarations cannot contain storage-class specifiers or initializers. The structure members can have any variable types except type **void**, an incomplete type, or a function type.

A member cannot be declared to have the type of the structure in which it appears. However, a member can be declared as a pointer to the structure type in which it appears as long as the structure type has a tag. This allows you to create linked lists of structures.

Structures follow the same scoping as other identifiers. Structure identifiers must be distinct from other structure, union, and enumeration tags with the same visibility.

Each *struct-declaration* in a *struct-declaration-list* must be unique within the list. However, identifier names in a *struct-declaration-list* do not have to be distinct from ordinary variable names or from identifiers in other structure declaration lists.

Nested structures can also be accessed as though they were declared at the file-scope level. For example, given this declaration:

```
struct a
{
    int x;
    struct b
    {
        int y;
    } var2;
} var1;
```

these declarations are both legal:

```
struct a var3;
struct b var4;
```

Examples

These examples illustrate structure declarations:

```
struct employee    /* Defines a structure variable named temp */
{
    char name[20];
    int id;
    long class;
} temp;
```

The `employee` structure has three members: `name`, `id`, and `class`. The `name` member is a 20-element array, and `id` and `class` are simple members with **int** and **long** type, respectively. The identifier `employee` is the structure identifier.

```
struct employee student, faculty, staff;
```

This example defines three structure variables: student, faculty, and staff. Each structure has the same list of three members. The members are declared to have the structure type employee, defined in the previous example.

```
struct                /* Defines an anonymous struct and a */
{                     /* structure variable named complex  */
    float x, y;
} complex;
```

The complex structure has two members with **float** type, x and y. The structure type has no tag and is therefore unnamed or anonymous.

```
struct sample   /* Defines a structure named x */
{
    char c;
    float *pf;
    struct sample *next;
} x;
```

The first two members of the structure are a **char** variable and a pointer to a **float** value. The third member, next, is declared as a pointer to the structure type being defined (sample).

Anonymous structures can be useful when the tag named is not needed. This is the case when one declaration defines all structure instances. For example:

```
struct
{
    int x;
    int y;
} mystruct;
```

Embedded structures are often anonymous.

```
struct somestruct
{
    struct      /* Anonymous structure */
    {
        int x, y;
    } point;
    int type;
} w;
```

Microsoft Specific →

The compiler allows an unsized or zero-sized array as the last member of a structure. This can be useful if the size of a constant array differs when used in various situations. The declaration of such a structure looks like this:

struct *identifier*
  {
    set-of-declarations
    type array-name[ ];
  };

Unsized arrays can appear only as the last member of a structure. Structures containing unsized array declarations can be nested within other structures as long as no further members are declared in any enclosing structures. Arrays of such structures are not allowed. The **sizeof** operator, when applied to a variable of this type or to the type itself, assumes 0 for the size of the array.

Structure declarations can also be specified without a declarator when they are members of another structure or union. The field names are promoted into the enclosing structure. For example, a nameless structure looks like this:

```
struct s
{
    float y;
    struct
    {
        int a, b, c;
    };
    char str[10];
} *p_s;
.
.
.
p_s->b = 100;   /* A reference to a field in the s structure */
```

See "Structure and Union Members" on page 106 in Chapter 4 for information about structure references.

END Microsoft Specific

Bit Fields

In addition to declarators for members of a structure or union, a structure declarator can also be a specified number of bits, called a "bit field." Its length is set off from the declarator for the field name by a colon. A bit field is interpreted as an integral type.

Syntax

struct-declarator :
　　declarator
　　type-specifier declarator _{opt} **:** *constant-expression*

The *constant-expression* specifies the width of the field in bits. The *type-specifier* for the *declarator* must be **unsigned int**, **signed int**, or **int**, and the *constant-expression* must be a nonnegative integer value. If the value is zero, the declaration has no *declarator*. Arrays of bit fields, pointers to bit fields, and functions returning bit fields are not allowed. The optional *declarator* names the bit field. Bit fields can only be declared as part of a structure. The address-of operator (**&**) cannot be applied to bit-field components.

Unnamed bit fields cannot be referenced, and their contents at run time are unpredictable. They can be used as "dummy" fields, for alignment purposes. An unnamed bit field whose width is specified as 0 guarantees that storage for the member following it in the *struct-declaration-list* begins on an **int** boundary.

Bit fields must also be long enough to contain the bit pattern. For example, these two statements are not legal:

```
short a:17;        /* Illegal! */
int long y:33;     /* Illegal! */
```

This example defines a two-dimensional array of structures named screen.

```
struct
{
   unsigned short icon : 8;
   unsigned short color : 4;
   unsigned short underline : 1;
   unsigned short blink : 1;
} screen[25][80];
```

The array contains 2,000 elements. Each element is an individual structure containing four bit-field members: icon, color, underline, and blink. The size of each structure is two bytes.

Bit fields have the same semantics as the integer type. This means a bit field is used in expressions in exactly the same way as a variable of the same base type would be used, regardless of how many bits are in the bit field.

Microsoft Specific →

Bit fields defined as **int** are treated as signed. A Microsoft extension to the ANSI C standard allows **char** and **long** types (both **signed** and **unsigned**) for bit fields. Unnamed bit fields with base type **long**, **short**, or **char** (**signed** or **unsigned**) force alignment to a boundary appropriate to the base type.

Bit fields are allocated within an integer from least-significant to most-significant bit. In the following code

```
struct mybitfields
{
   unsigned short a : 4;
   unsigned short b : 5;
   unsigned short c : 7;
} test;

void main( void );
{
   test.a = 2;
   test.b = 31;
   test.c = 0;
}
```

the bits would be arranged as follows:

```
00000001 11110010
ccccccccb bbbbaaaa
```

Since the 8086 family of processors stores the low byte of integer values before the high byte, the integer 0x01F2 above would be stored in physical memory as 0xF2 followed by 0x01.

END Microsoft Specific

Storage and Alignment of Structures

Microsoft Specific →

Structure members are stored sequentially in the order in which they are declared: the first member has the lowest memory address and the last member the highest.

Every data object has an *alignment-requirement*. For structures, the requirement is the largest of its members. Every object is allocated an *offset* so that

offset % alignment-requirement == 0

Adjacent bit fields are packed into the same 1-, 2-, or 4-byte allocation unit if the integral types are the same size and if the next bit field fits into the current allocation unit without crossing the boundary imposed by the common alignment requirements of the bit fields.

To conserve space or to conform to existing data structures, you may want to store structures more or less compactly. The /Zp [*n*] compiler option and the **#pragma pack** control how structure data is "packed" into memory. When you use the /Zp[*n*] option, where *n* is 1, 2, 4, 8, or 16, each structure member after the first is stored on byte boundaries that are either the alignment requirement of the field or the packing size (*n*), whichever is smaller. Expressed as a formula, the byte boundaries are the

min(*n*, **sizeof**(*item*))

where *n* is the packing size expressed with the /Zp[*n*] option and *item* is the structure member. The default packing size is /Zp8.

To use the **pack** pragma to specify packing other than the packing specified on the command line for a particular structure, give the **pack** pragma, where the packing size is 1, 2, 4, 8, or 16, before the structure. To reinstate the packing given on the command line, specify the **pack** pragma with no arguments.

Bit fields default to size **long** for the Microsoft C compiler. Structure members are aligned on the size of the type or the /Zp[*n*] size, whichever is smaller. The default size is 4.

END Microsoft Specific

Union Declarations

A "union declaration" specifies a set of variable values and, optionally, a tag naming the union. The variable values are called "members" of the union and can have different types. Unions are similar to "variant records" in other languages.

Syntax

struct-or-union-specifier :
        struct-or-union identifier ₒₚₜ { *struct-declaration-list* }
        struct-or-union identifier

struct-or-union :
        struct
        union

struct-declaration-list :
        struct-declaration
        struct-declaration-list struct-declaration

The union content is defined to be

struct-declaration :
        specifier-qualifier-list struct-declarator-list ;

specifier-qualifier-list :
        type-specifier specifier-qualifier-list ₒₚₜ
        type-qualifier specifier-qualifier-list ₒₚₜ

struct-declarator-list :
        struct-declarator
        struct-declarator-list , *struct-declarator*

A variable with **union** type stores one of the values defined by that type. The same rules govern structure and union declarations. Unions can also have bit fields.

Members of unions cannot have an incomplete type, type **void,** or function type. Therefore members cannot be an instance of the union but can be pointers to the union type being declared.

A union type declaration is a template only. Memory is not reserved until the variable is declared.

Note   If a union of two types is declared and one value is stored, but the union is accessed with the other type, the results are unreliable. For example, a union of **float** and **int** is declared. A **float** value is stored, but the program later accesses the value as an **int**. In such a situation, the value would depend on the internal storage of **float** values. The integer value would not be reliable.

Examples

The following are examples of unions:

```
union sign    /* A definition and a declaration */
{
   int svar;
   unsigned uvar;
} number;
```

This example defines a union variable with sign type and declares a variable named number that has two members: svar, a signed integer, and uvar, an unsigned integer.

This declaration allows the current value of number to be stored as either a signed or an unsigned value. The tag associated with this union type is sign.

```
union                  /* Defines a two-dimensional */
{                      /*  array named screen */
   struct
   {
      unsigned int icon : 8;
      unsigned color : 4;
   } window1;
   int screenval;
} screen[25][80];
```

The screen array contains 2,000 elements. Each element of the array is an individual union with two members: window1 and screenval. The window1 member is a structure with two bit-field members, icon and color. The screenval member is an **int**. At any given time, each union element holds either the **int** represented by screenval or the structure represented by window1.

Microsoft Specific →

Nested unions can be declared anonymously when they are members of another structure or union. This is an example of a nameless union:

```
struct str
{
   int a, b;
   union              / * Unnamed union */
   {
      char c[4];
      long l;
      float f;
   };
   char c_array[10];
} my_str;
   .
   .
   .
my_str.l == 0L;  /* A reference to a field in the my_str union */
```

Unions are often nested within a structure that includes a field giving the type of data contained in the union at any particular time. This is an example of a declaration for such a union:

```
struct x
{
   int type_tag;
   union
   {
      int x;
      float y;
   }
}
```

See "Structure and Union Members" on page 106 in Chapter 4 for information about referencing unions.

END Microsoft Specific

Storage of Unions

The storage associated with a union variable is the storage required for the largest
member of the union. When a smaller member is stored, the union variable can
contain unused memory space. All members are stored in the same memory space
and start at the same address. The stored value is overwritten each time a value is
assigned to a different member. For example:

```
union            /* Defines a union named x */
{
   char *a, b;
   float f[20];
} x;
```

The members of the x union are, in order of their declaration, a pointer to a **char**
value, a **char** value, and an array of **float** values. The storage allocated for x is the
storage required for the 20-element array f, since f is the longest member of the
union. Because no tag is associated with the union, its type is unnamed or
"anonymous."

Array Declarations

An "array declaration" names the array and specifies the type of its elements. It can
also define the number of elements in the array. A variable with array type is
considered a pointer to the type of the array elements.

Syntax

declaration :
> *declaration-specifiers init-declarator-list* opt **;**

init-declarator-list :
> *init-declarator*
> *init-declarator-list* **,** *init-declarator*

init-declarator :
> *declarator*
> *declarator* = *initializer*

declarator :
> *pointer* opt *direct-declarator*

direct-declarator :
> *direct-declarator* [*constant-expression* opt]

Because *constant-expression* is optional, the syntax has two forms:

- The first form defines an array variable. The *constant-expression* argument within
  the brackets specifies the number of elements in the array. The *constant-expression*,
  if present, must have integral type, and a value larger than zero. Each element has
  the type given by *type-specifier*, which can be any type except **void**. An array
  element cannot be a function type.

- The second form declares a variable that has been defined elsewhere. It omits the *constant-expression* argument in brackets, but not the brackets. You can use this form only if you previously have initialized the array, declared it as a parameter, or declared it as a reference to an array explicitly defined elsewhere in the program.

In both forms, *direct-declarator* names the variable and can modify the variable's type. The brackets ([ ]) following *direct-declarator* modify the declarator to an array type.

Type qualifiers can appear in the declaration of an object of array type, but the qualifiers apply to the elements rather than the array itself.

You can declare an array of arrays (a "multidimensional" array) by following the array declarator with a list of bracketed constant expressions in this form:

type-specifier declarator [*constant-expression*] [*constant-expression*] ...

Each *constant-expression* in brackets defines the number of elements in a given dimension: two-dimensional arrays have two bracketed expressions, three-dimensional arrays have three, and so on. You can omit the first constant expression if you have initialized the array, declared it as a parameter, or declared it as a reference to an array explicitly defined elsewhere in the program.

You can define arrays of pointers to various types of objects by using complex declarators, as described in "Interpreting More Complex Declarators" on page 72.

Arrays are stored by row. For example, the following array consists of two rows with three columns each:

```
char A[2][3];
```

The three columns of the first row are stored first, followed by the three columns of the second row. This means that the last subscript varies most quickly.

To refer to an individual element of an array, use a subscript expression, as described in "Postfix Operators" on page 103 in Chapter 4.

Examples

These examples illustrate array declarations:

```
float matrix[10][15];
```

The two-dimensional array named matrix has 150 elements, each having **float** type.

```
struct {
    float x, y;
} complex[100];
```

This is a declaration of an array of structures. This array has 100 elements; each element is a structure containing two members.

```
extern char *name[];
```

This statement declares the type and name of an array of pointers to **char**. The actual definition of name occurs elsewhere.

Microsoft Specific →

The type of integer required to hold the maximum size of an array is the size of **size_t**. Defined in the header file STDDEF.H, **size_t** is an **unsigned int** with the range 0x00000000 to 0x7CFFFFFF.

END Microsoft Specific

Storage of Arrays

The storage associated with an array type is the storage required for all of its elements. The elements of an array are stored in contiguous and increasing memory locations, from the first element to the last.

Pointer Declarations

A "pointer declaration" names a pointer variable and specifies the type of the object to which the variable points. A variable declared as a pointer holds a memory address.

Syntax
declarator :
>   *pointer* opt *direct-declarator*

direct-declarator :
>   *identifier*
>   (*declarator*)
>   *direct-declarator* [*constant-expression* opt]
>   *direct-declarator* (*parameter-type-list*)
>   *direct-declarator* (*identifier-list* opt)

pointer :
>   * *type-qualifier-list* opt
>   * *type-qualifier-list* opt *pointer*

type-qualifier-list :
>   *type-qualifier*
>   *type-qualifier-list type-qualifier*

The *type-specifier* gives the type of the object, which can be any basic, structure, or union type. Pointer variables can also point to functions, arrays, and other pointers. (For information on declaring and interpreting more complex pointer types, refer to "Interpreting More Complex Declarators" on page 72.)

By making the *type-specifier* **void**, you can delay specification of the type to which the pointer refers. Such an item is referred to as a "pointer to **void**" and is written as void *. A variable declared as a pointer to **void** can be used to point to an object of any type. However, to perform most operations on the pointer or on the object to which it points, the type to which it points must be explicitly specified for each operation. (Variables of type **char** * and type **void** * are assignment-compatible without a type cast.) Such conversion can be accomplished with a type cast (see "Type-Cast Conversions" on page 132 in Chapter 4 for more information).

The *type-qualifier* can be either **const** or **volatile**, or both. These specify, respectively, that the pointer cannot be modified by the program itself (**const**), or that the pointer can legitimately be modified by some process beyond the control of the program (**volatile**). (See "Type Qualifiers" on page 51 for more information on **const** and **volatile**.)

The *declarator* names the variable and can include a type modifier. For example, if *declarator* represents an array, the type of the pointer is modified to be a pointer to an array.

You can declare a pointer to a structure, union, or enumeration type before you define the structure, union, or enumeration type. You declare the pointer by using the structure or union tag as shown in the examples below. Such declarations are allowed because the compiler does not need to know the size of the structure or union to allocate space for the pointer variable.

Examples

The following examples illustrate pointer declarations.

```
char *message; /* Declares a pointer variable named message */
```

The message pointer points to a variable with **char** type.

```
int *pointers[10];  /* Declares an array of pointers */
```

The pointers array has 10 elements; each element is a pointer to a variable with **int** type.

```
int (*pointer)[10]; /* Declares a pointer to an array of 10 elements */
```

The pointer variable points to an array with 10 elements. Each element in this array has **int** type.

```
int const *x;       /* Declares a pointer variable, x,
                       to a constant value */
```

The pointer x can be modified to point to a different **int** value, but the value to which it points cannot be modified.

```
const int some_object = 5 ;
int other_object = 37;
int *const y = &fixed_object;
const volatile *const z = &some_object;
int *const volatile w = &some_object;
```

The variable y in these declarations is declared as a constant pointer to an **int** value. The value it points to can be modified, but the pointer itself must always point to the same location: the address of fixed_object. Similarly, z is a constant pointer, but it is also declared to point to an **int** whose value cannot be modified by the program. The additional specifier volatile indicates that although the value of the **const int** pointed to by z cannot be modified by the program, it could legitimately be modified by a process running concurrently with the program. The declaration of w specifies that the program cannot change the value pointed to and that the program cannot modify the pointer.

```
struct list *next, *previous; /* Uses the tag for list */
```

This example declares two pointer variables, next and previous, that point to the structure type list. This declaration can appear before the definition of the list structure type (see the next example), as long as the list type definition has the same visibility as the declaration.

```
struct list
{
    char *token;
    int count;
    struct list *next;
} line;
```

The variable line has the structure type named list. The list structure type has three members: the first member is a pointer to a **char** value, the second is an **int** value, and the third is a pointer to another list structure.

```
struct id
{
    unsigned int id_no;
    struct name *pname;
} record;
```

The variable record has the structure type id. Note that pname is declared as a pointer to another structure type named name. This declaration can appear before the name type is defined.

Storage of Addresses

The amount of storage required for an address and the meaning of the address depend on the implementation of the compiler. Pointers to different types are not guaranteed to have the same length. Therefore, **sizeof(char *)** is not necessarily equal to **sizeof(int *)**.

Microsoft Specific →

For the Microsoft C compiler, **sizeof(char *)** is equal to **sizeof(int *)**.

END Microsoft Specific

Based Pointers

Microsoft Specific →

For the Microsoft 32-bit C compiler, a based pointer is a 32-bit offset from a 32-bit pointer base. Based addressing is useful for exercising control over sections where objects are allocated, thereby decreasing the size of the executable file and increasing execution speed. In general, the form for specifying a based pointer is

type __**based**(*base*) *declarator*

The "based on pointer" variant of based addressing enables specification of a pointer as a base. The based pointer, then, is an offset into the memory section starting at the beginning of the pointer on which it is based. Pointers based on pointer addresses are the only form of the __based keyword valid in 32-bit compilations. In such compilations, they are 32-bit displacements from a 32-bit base.

One use for pointers based on pointers is for persistent identifiers that contain pointers. A linked list that consists of pointers based on a pointer can be saved to disk, then reloaded to another place in memory, with the pointers remaining valid.

The following example shows a pointer based on a pointer.

```
void *vpBuffer;

struct llist_t
{
   void __based( vpBuffer ) *vpData;
   struct llist_t __based( vpBuffer ) *llNext;
};
```

The pointer vpBuffer is assigned the address of memory allocated at some later point in the program. The linked list is relocated relative to the value of vpBuffer.

END Microsoft Specific

Abstract Declarators

An abstract declarator is a declarator without an identifier, consisting of one or more pointer, array, or function modifiers. The pointer modifier (*) always precedes the identifier in a declarator; array ([ ]) and function (( )) modifiers follow the identifier. Knowing this, you can determine where the identifier would appear in an abstract declarator and interpret the declarator accordingly. See "Interpreting More Complex Declarators" on page 72 for additional information and examples of complex declarators. Generally **typedef** can be used to simplify declarators. See "Typedef Declarations" on page 86.

Abstract declarators can be complex. Parentheses in a complex abstract declarator specify a particular interpretation, just as they do for the complex declarators in declarations.

These examples illustrate abstract declarators:

```
int *          /* The type name for a pointer to type int:   */

int *[3]       /* An array of three pointers to int           */

int (*) [5]    /* A pointer to an array of five int           */

int *()        /* A function with no parameter specification */
               /* returning a pointer to int                 */
```

```
/* A pointer to a function taking no arguments and
 * returning an int
 */

int (*) ( void )

/* An array of an unspecified number of constant pointers to
 * functions each with one parameter that has type unsigned int
 * and an unspecified number of other parameters returning an int
 */

int (*const []) ( unsigned int, ... )
```

Note The abstract declarator consisting of a set of empty parentheses, **( )**, is not allowed because it is ambiguous. It is impossible to determine whether the implied identifier belongs inside the parentheses (in which case it is an unmodified type) or before the parentheses (in which case it is a function type).

Interpreting More Complex Declarators

You can enclose any declarator in parentheses to specify a particular interpretation of a "complex declarator." A complex declarator is an identifier qualified by more than one array, pointer, or function modifier. You can apply various combinations of array, pointer, and function modifiers to a single identifier. Generally **typedef** may be used to simplify declarations. See "Typedef Declarations" on page 86.

In interpreting complex declarators, brackets and parentheses (that is, modifiers to the right of the identifier) take precedence over asterisks (that is, modifiers to the left of the identifier). Brackets and parentheses have the same precedence and associate from left to right. After the declarator has been fully interpreted, the type specifier is applied as the last step. By using parentheses you can override the default association order and force a particular interpretation. Never use parentheses, however, around an identifier name by itself. This could be misinterpreted as a parameter list.

A simple way to interpret complex declarators is to read them "from the inside out," using the following four steps:

1. Start with the identifier and look directly to the right for brackets or parentheses (if any).

2. Interpret these brackets or parentheses, then look to the left for asterisks.

3. If you encounter a right parenthesis at any stage, go back and apply rules 1 and 2 to everything within the parentheses.

4. Apply the type specifier.

```
char *( *(*var)() )[10];
     ^   ^ ^ ^ ^     ^
     7   6 4 2 1     3   5
```

In this example, the steps are numbered in order and can be interpreted as follows:

1. The identifier `var` is declared as
2. a pointer to
3. a function returning
4. a pointer to
5. an array of 10 elements, which are
6. pointers to
7. **char** values.

Examples

The following examples illustrate other complex declarations and show how parentheses can affect the meaning of a declaration.

```
int *var[5]; /* Array of pointers to int values */
```

The array modifier has higher priority than the pointer modifier, so `var` is declared to be an array. The pointer modifier applies to the type of the array elements; therefore, the array elements are pointers to **int** values.

```
int (*var)[5]; /* Pointer to array of int values */
```

In this declaration for `var`, parentheses give the pointer modifier higher priority than the array modifier, and `var` is declared to be a pointer to an array of five **int** values.

```
long *var( long, long ); /* Function returning pointer to long */
```

Function modifiers also have higher priority than pointer modifiers, so this declaration for `var` declares `var` to be a function returning a pointer to a **long** value. The function is declared to take two **long** values as arguments.

```
long (*var)( long, long ); /* Pointer to function returning long */
```

This example is similar to the previous one. Parentheses give the pointer modifier higher priority than the function modifier, and `var` is declared to be a pointer to a function that returns a **long** value. Again, the function takes two **long** arguments.

```
struct both        /* Array of pointers to functions */
{                  /*   returning structures          */
    int a;
    char b;
} ( *var[5] )( struct both, struct both );
```

The elements of an array cannot be functions, but this declaration demonstrates how to declare an array of pointers to functions instead. In this example, `var` is declared to be an array of five pointers to functions that return structures with two members. The arguments to the functions are declared to be two structures with the same structure type, `both`. Note that the parentheses surrounding `*var[5]` are required. Without them, the declaration is an illegal attempt to declare an array of functions, as shown below:

```
/* ILLEGAL */
struct both *var[5]( struct both, struct both );
```

The following statement declares an array of pointers.

```
unsigned int *(* const *name[5][10] ) ( void );
```

The `name` array has 50 elements organized in a multidimensional array. The elements are pointers to a pointer that is a constant. This constant pointer points to a function that has no parameters and returns a pointer to an unsigned type.

This next example is a function returning a pointer to an array of three **double** values.

```
double ( *var( double (*)[3] ) )[3];
```

In this declaration, a function returns a pointer to an array, since functions returning arrays are illegal. Here `var` is declared to be a function returning a pointer to an array of three **double** values. The function `var` takes one argument. The argument, like the return value, is a pointer to an array of three **double** values. The argument type is given by a complex *abstract-declarator*. The parentheses around the asterisk in the argument type are required; without them, the argument type would be an array of three pointers to **double** values. For a discussion and examples of abstract declarators, see "Abstract Declarators" on page 71.

```
union sign         /* Array of arrays of pointers */
{                  /* to pointers to unions       */
   int x;
   unsigned y;
} **var[5][5];
```

As the above example shows, a pointer can point to another pointer, and an array can contain arrays as elements. Here `var` is an array of five elements. Each element is a five-element array of pointers to pointers to unions with two members.

```
union sign *(*var[5])[5]; /* Array of pointers to arrays
                             of pointers to unions       */
```

This example shows how the placement of parentheses changes the meaning of the declaration. In this example, `var` is a five-element array of pointers to five-element arrays of pointers to unions. For examples of how to use **typedef** to avoid complex declarations, see "Typedef Declarations" on page 86.

Initialization

An "initializer" is a value or a sequence of values to be assigned to the variable being declared. You can set a variable to an initial value by applying an initializer to the declarator in the variable declaration. The value or values of the initializer are assigned to the variable.

The following sections describe how to initialize variables of scalar, aggregate, and string types. "Scalar types" include all the arithmetic types, plus pointers. "Aggregate types" include arrays, structures, and unions.

Initializing Scalar Types

When initializing scalar types, the value of the *assignment-expression* is assigned to the variable. The conversion rules for assignment apply. (See "Type Conversions" on page 126 in Chapter 4 for information on conversion rules.)

Syntax

declaration :
        declaration-specifiers init-declarator-list opt **;**

declaration-specifiers :
        storage-class-specifier declaration-specifiers opt
        type-specifier declaration-specifiers opt
        type-qualifier declaration-specifiers opt

init-declarator-list :
        init-declarator
        init-declarator-list **,** *init-declarator*

init-declarator :
        declarator
        declarator = initializer   /* For scalar initialization */

initializer :
        assignment-expression

You can initialize variables of any type, provided that you obey the following rules:

- Variables declared at the file-scope level can be initialized. If you do not explicitly initialize a variable at the external level, it is initialized to 0 by default.

- A constant expression can be used to initialize any global variable declared with the **static** *storage-class-specifier*. Variables declared to be **static** are initialized when program execution begins. If you do not explicitly initialize a global **static** variable, it is initialized to 0 by default, and every member that has pointer type is assigned a null pointer.

- Variables declared with the **auto** or **register** storage-class specifier are initialized each time execution control passes to the block in which they are declared. If you omit an initializer from the declaration of an **auto** or **register** variable, the initial value of the variable is undefined. For automatic and register values, the initializer is not restricted to being a constant; it can be any expression involving previously defined values, even function calls.

- The initial values for external variable declarations and for all **static** variables, whether external or internal, must be constant expressions. (For more information, see "Constant Expressions" on page 96 in Chapter 4.) Since the address of any externally declared or static variable is constant, it can be used to initialize an internally declared **static** pointer variable. However, the address of an **auto** variable cannot be used as a static initializer because it may be different for each execution of the block. You can use either constant or variable values to initialize **auto** and **register** variables.

- If the declaration of an identifier has block scope, and the identifier has external linkage, the declaration cannot have an initialization.

Examples

The following examples illustrate initializations:

```
int x = 10;
```

The integer variable x is initialized to the constant expression 10.

```
register int *px = 0;
```

The pointer px is initialized to 0, producing a "null" pointer.

```
const int c = (3 * 1024);
```

This example uses a constant expression (3 * 1024) to initialize c to a constant value that cannot be modified because of the **const** keyword.

```
int *b = &x;
```

This statement initializes the pointer b with the address of another variable, x.

```
int *const a = &z;
```

The pointer a is initialized with the address of a variable named z. However, since it is specified to be a **const**, the variable a can only be initialized, never modified. It always points to the same location.

```
int GLOBAL ;

int function( void )
{
    int LOCAL ;
    static int *lp = &LOCAL;    /* Illegal initialization */
    static int *gp = &GLOBAL;   /* Legal initialization   */
    register int *rp = &LOCAL;  /* Legal initialization   */
}
```

The global variable GLOBAL is declared at the external level, so it has global lifetime. The local variable LOCAL has **auto** storage class and only has an address during the execution of the function in which it is declared. Therefore, attempting to initialize the **static** pointer variable lp with the address of LOCAL is not permitted. The **static** pointer variable gp can be initialized to the address of GLOBAL because that address is always the same. Similarly, *rp can be initialized because rp is a local variable and can have a nonconstant initializer. Each time the block is entered, LOCAL has a new address, which is then assigned to rp.

Initializing Aggregate Types

An "aggregate" type is a structure, union, or array type. If an aggregate type contains members of aggregate types, the initialization rules apply recursively.

Syntax

initializer :
  { *initializer-list* }   /* For aggregate initialization */
  { *initializer-list* , }

initializer-list :
  initializer
  initializer-list , *initializer*

The *initializer-list* is a list of initializers separated by commas. Each initializer in the list is either a constant expression or an initializer list. Therefore, initializer lists can be nested. This form is useful for initializing aggregate members of an aggregate type, as shown in the examples in this section. However, if the initializer for an automatic identifier is a single expression, it need not be a constant expression; it merely needs to have appropriate type for assignment to the identifier.

For each initializer list, the values of the constant expressions are assigned, in order, to the corresponding members of the aggregate variable.

If *initializer-list* has fewer values than an aggregate type, the remaining members or elements of the aggregate type are initialized to 0 for external and static variables. The initial value of an automatic identifier not explicitly initialized is undefined. If *initializer-list* has more values than an aggregate type, an error results. These rules apply to each embedded initializer list, as well as to the aggregate as a whole.

A structure's initializer is either an expression of the same type, or a list of initializers for its members enclosed in curly braces ({ }). Unnamed bit-field members are not initialized.

When a union is initialized, *initializer-list* must be a single constant expression. The value of the constant expression is assigned to the first member of the union.

If an array has unknown size, the number of initializers determines the size of the array, and its type becomes complete. There is no way to specify repetition of an initializer in C, or to initialize an element in the middle of an array without providing all preceding values as well. If you need this operation in your program, write the routine in assembly language.

Note that the number of initializers can set the size of the array:

```
int x[ ] = { 0, 1, 2 }
```

If you specify the size and give the wrong number of initializers, however, the compiler generates an error.

The maximum size for an array is defined by **size_t**. Defined in the header file STDDEF.H, **size_t** is an **unsigned int** with the range 0x00000000 to 0x7CFFFFFF.

Examples

This example shows initializers for an array.

```
int P[4][3] =
{
    { 1, 1, 1 },
    { 2, 2, 2 },
    { 3, 3, 3,},
    { 4, 4, 4,},
};
```

This statement declares P as a four-by-three array and initializes the elements of its first row to 1, the elements of its second row to 2, and so on through the fourth row. Note that the initializer list for the third and fourth rows contains commas after the last constant expression. The last initializer list ({4, 4, 4,},) is also followed by a comma. These extra commas are permitted but are not required; only commas that separate constant expressions from one another, and those that separate one initializer list from another, are required.

If an aggregate member has no embedded initializer list, values are simply assigned, in order, to each member of the subaggregate. Therefore, the initialization in the previous example is equivalent to the following:

```
int P[4][3] =
{
    1, 1, 1, 2, 2, 2, 3, 3, 3, 4, 4, 4
};
```

Braces can also appear around individual initializers in the list and would help to clarify the example above.

When you initialize an aggregate variable, you must be careful to use braces and initializer lists properly. The following example illustrates the compiler's interpretation of braces in more detail:

```
typedef struct
{
    int n1, n2, n3;
} triplet;

triplet nlist[2][3] =
{
    { { 1, 2, 3 }, { 4, 5, 6 }, { 7, 8, 9 } },   /* Row 1 */
    { { 10,11,12 }, { 13,14,15 }, { 16,17,18 } }   /* Row 2 */
};
```

In this example, nlist is declared as a 2-by-3 array of structures, each structure having three members. Row 1 of the initialization assigns values to the first row of nlist, as follows:

1. The first left brace on row 1 signals the compiler that initialization of the first aggregate member of nlist (that is, nlist[0]) is beginning.

2. The second left brace indicates that initialization of the first aggregate member of nlist[0] (that is, the structure at nlist[0][0]) is beginning.

3. The first right brace ends initialization of the structure nlist[0][0]; the next left brace starts initialization of nlist[0][1].

4. The process continues until the end of the line, where the closing right brace ends initialization of nlist[0].

Row 2 assigns values to the second row of nlist in a similar way. Note that the outer sets of braces enclosing the initializers on rows 1 and 2 are required. The following construction, which omits the outer braces, would cause an error:

```
triplet nlist[2][3] =  /* THIS CAUSES AN ERROR */
{
    { 1, 2, 3 },{ 4, 5, 6 },{ 7, 8, 9 },   /* Line 1 */
    { 10,11,12 },{ 13,14,15 },{ 16,17,18 } /* Line 2 */
};
```

In this construction, the first left brace on line 1 starts the initialization of nlist[0], which is an array of three structures. The values 1, 2, and 3 are assigned to the three members of the first structure. When the next right brace is encountered (after the value 3), initialization of nlist[0] is complete, and the two remaining structures in the three-structure array are automatically initialized to 0. Similarly, { 4,5,6 } initializes the first structure in the second row of nlist. The remaining two structures of nlist[1] are set to 0. When the compiler encounters the next initializer list ({ 7,8,9 }), it tries to initialize nlist[2]. Since nlist has only two rows, this attempt causes an error.

In this next example, the three **int** members of x are initialized to 1, 2, and 3, respectively.

```
struct list
{
    int i, j, k;
    float m[2][3];
} x = {
        1,
        2,
        3,
        {4.0, 4.0, 4.0}
    };
```

In the list structure above, the three elements in the first row of m are initialized to 4.0; the elements of the remaining row of m are initialized to 0.0 by default.

```
union
{
    char x[2][3];
    int i, j, k;
} y = { {
            {'1'},
            {'4'}
        }
    };
```

The union variable y, in this example, is initialized. The first element of the union is an array, so the initializer is an aggregate initializer. The initializer list { '1' } assigns values to the first row of the array. Since only one value appears in the list, the element in the first column is initialized to the character 1, and the remaining two elements in the row are initialized to the value 0 by default. Similarly, the first element of the second row of x is initialized to the character 4, and the remaining two elements in the row are initialized to the value 0.

Initializing Strings

You can initialize an array of characters (or wide characters) with a string literal (or wide string literal). For example:

```
char code[ ] = "abc";
```

initializes code as a four-element array of characters. The fourth element is the null character, which terminates all string literals.

An identifier list can only be as long as the number of identifiers to be initialized. If you specify an array size that is shorter than the string, the extra characters are ignored. For example, the following declaration initializes code as a three-element character array:

```
char code[3] = "abcd";
```

Only the first three characters of the initializer are assigned to code. The character d and the string-terminating null character are discarded. Note that this creates an unterminated string (that is, one without a 0 value to mark its end) and generates a diagnostic message indicating this condition.

The declaration

```
char s[] = "abc", t[3] = "abc";
```

is identical to

```
char s[]  = {'a', 'b', 'c', '\0'},
     t[3] = {'a', 'b', 'c' };
```

If the string is shorter than the specified array size, the remaining elements of the array are initialized to 0.

Microsoft Specific →

In Microsoft C, string literals can be up to 2048 bytes in length.

END Microsoft Specific

Storage of Basic Types

Table 3.2 summarizes the storage associated with each basic type.

Table 3.2   Sizes of Fundamental Types

Type	Storage
char, unsigned char, signed char	1 byte
short, unsigned short	2 bytes
int, unsigned int	4 bytes
long, unsigned long	4 bytes
float	4 bytes
double	8 bytes
long double	8 bytes

The C data types fall into general categories. The "integral types" include **char**, **int**, **short**, **long**, **signed**, **unsigned**, and **enum**. The "floating types" include **float**, **double**, and **long double**. The "arithmetic types" include all floating and integral types.

Type char

The **char** type is used to store the integer value of a member of the representable character set. That integer value is the ASCII code corresponding to the specified character.

Microsoft Specific →

Character values of type **unsigned char** have a range from 0 to 0xFF hexadecimal. A **signed char** has range 0x80 to 0x7F. These ranges translate to 0 to 255 decimal, and −128 to +127 decimal, respectively. The /J compiler option changes the default from **signed** to **unsigned**.

END Microsoft Specific

Type int

The size of a signed or unsigned **int** item is the standard size of an integer on a particular machine. For example, in 16-bit operating systems, the **int** type is usually 16 bits, or 2 bytes. In 32-bit operating systems, the **int** type is usually 32 bits, or 4 bytes. Thus, the **int** type is equivalent to either the **short int** or the **long int** type, and the **unsigned int** type is equivalent to either the **unsigned short** or the **unsigned long** type, depending on the target environment. The **int** types all represent signed values unless specified otherwise.

The type specifiers **int** and **unsigned int** (or simply **unsigned**) define certain features of the C language (for instance, the **enum** type). In these cases, the definitions of **int** and **unsigned int** for a particular implementation determine the actual storage.

Microsoft Specific →

Signed integers are represented in two's-complement form. The most-significant bit holds the sign: 1 for negative, 0 for positive and zero. The range of values is given in Table 1.3, which is taken from the LIMITS.H header file.

END Microsoft Specific

Note The **int** and **unsigned int** type specifiers are widely used in C programs because they allow a particular machine to handle integer values in the most efficient way for that machine. However, since the sizes of the **int** and **unsigned int** types vary, programs that depend on a specific **int** size may not be portable to other machines. To make programs more portable, you can use expressions with the **sizeof** operator (as discussed in "The sizeof Operator" on page 111 in Chapter 4) instead of hard-coded data sizes.

Sized Integer Types

Microsoft Specific →

Microsoft C features support for sized integer types. You can declare 8-, 16-, 32-, or 64-bit integer variables by using the __int*n* type specifier, where *n* is the size, in bits, of the integer variable. The value of *n* can be 8, 16, 32, or 64. The following example declares one variable of each of the four types of sized integers:

```
__int8 nSmall;     // Declares 8-bit integer
__int16 nMedium;   // Declares 16-bit integer
__int32 nLarge;    // Declares 32-bit integer
__int64 nHuge;     // Declares 64-bit integer
```

The first three types of sized integers are synonyms for the ANSI types that have the same size, and are useful for writing portable code that behaves identically across multiple platforms. Note that the **__int8** data type is synonymous with type **char,** **__int16** is synonymous with type **short,** and **__int32** is synonymous with type **int.** The **__int64** type has no equivalent ANSI counterpart.

END Microsoft Specific

Type float

Floating-point numbers use the IEEE (Institute of Electrical and Electronics Engineers) format. Single-precision values with **float** type have 4 bytes, consisting of a sign bit, an 8-bit excess-127 binary exponent, and a 23-bit mantissa. The mantissa represents a number between 1.0 and 2.0. Since the high-order bit of the mantissa is always 1, it is not stored in the number. This representation gives a range of approximately 3.4E–38 to 3.4E+38 for type **float**.

You can declare variables as **float** or **double**, depending on the needs of your application. The principal differences between the two types are the significance they can represent, the storage they require, and their range. Table 3.3 shows the relationship between significance and storage requirements.

Table 3.3   Floating-Point Types

Type	Significant digits	Number of bytes
float	6–7	4
double	15–16	8

Floating-point variables are represented by a mantissa, which contains the value of the number, and an exponent, which contains the order of magnitude of the number.

Table 3.4 shows the number of bits allocated to the mantissa and the exponent for each floating-point type. The most significant bit of any **float** or **double** is always the sign bit. If it is 1, the number is considered negative; otherwise, it is considered a positive number.

Table 3.4   Lengths of Exponents and Mantissas

Type	Exponent length	Mantissa length
float	8 bits	23 bits
double	11 bits	52 bits

Because exponents are stored in an unsigned form, the exponent is biased by half its possible value. For type **float**, the bias is 127; for type **double**, it is 1023. You can compute the actual exponent value by subtracting the bias value from the exponent value.

The mantissa is stored as a binary fraction greater than or equal to 1 and less than 2. For types **float** and **double**, there is an implied leading 1 in the mantissa in the most-significant bit position, so the mantissas are actually 24 and 53 bits long, respectively, even though the most-significant bit is never stored in memory.

Instead of the storage method just described, the floating-point package can store binary floating-point numbers as denormalized numbers. "Denormalized numbers" are nonzero floating-point numbers with reserved exponent values in which the most-significant bit of the mantissa is 0. By using the denormalized format, the range of a floating-point number can be extended at the cost of precision. You cannot control whether a floating-point number is represented in normalized or denormalized form; the floating-point package determines the representation. The floating-point package never uses a denormalized form unless the exponent becomes less than the minimum that can be represented in a normalized form.

Table 3.5 shows the minimum and maximum values you can store in variables of each floating-point type. The values listed in this table apply only to normalized floating-point numbers; denormalized floating-point numbers have a smaller minimum value. Note that numbers retained in 80x87 registers are always represented in 80-bit normalized form; numbers can only be represented in denormalized form when stored in 32-bit or 64-bit floating-point variables (variables of type **float** and type **long**).

Table 3.5   Range of Floating-Point Types

Type	Minimum value	Maximum value
float	1.175494351 E − 38	3.402823466 E + 38
double	2.2250738585072014 E − 308	1.7976931348623158 E + 308

If precision is less of a concern than storage, consider using type **float** for floating-point variables. Conversely, if precision is the most important criterion, use type **double**.

Floating-point variables can be promoted to a type of greater significance (from type **float** to type **double**). Promotion often occurs when you perform arithmetic on floating-point variables. This arithmetic is always done in as high a degree of precision as the variable with the highest degree of precision. For example, consider the following type declarations:

```
float f_short;
double f_long;
long double f_longer;

f_short = f_short * f_long;
```

In the preceding example, the variable f_short is promoted to type **double** and multiplied by f_long; then the result is rounded to type **float** before being assigned to f_short.

In the following example (which uses the declarations from the preceding example), the arithmetic is done in **float** (32-bit) precision on the variables; the result is then promoted to type **double**:

```
f_longer = f_short * f_short;
```

Type double

Double precision values with **double** type have 8 bytes. The format is similar to the **float** format except that it has an 11-bit excess-1023 exponent and a 52-bit mantissa, plus the implied high-order 1 bit. This format gives a range of approximately 1.7E–308 to 1.7E+308 for type **double**.

Microsoft Specific →

The **double** type contains 64 bits: 1 for sign, 11 for the exponent, and 52 for the mantissa. Its range is +/–1.7E308 with at least 15 digits of precision.

END Microsoft Specific

Type long double

The range of values for a variable is bounded by the minimum and maximum values that can be represented *internally* in a given number of bits. However, because of C's conversion rules (discussed in detail in "Type Conversions" on page 126 in Chapter 4) you cannot always use the maximum or minimum value for a constant of a particular type in an expression.

For example, the constant expression -32768 consists of the arithmetic negation operator (–) applied to the constant value 32,768. Since 32,768 is too large to represent as a **short int**, it is given the **long** type. Consequently, the constant expression -32768 has **long** type. You can only represent –32,768 as a **short int** by type-casting it to the **short** type. No information is lost in the type cast, since –32,768 can be represented internally in 2 bytes.

The value 65,000 in decimal notation is considered a signed constant. It is given the **long** type because 65,000 does not fit into a **short**. A value such as 65,000 can only be represented as an **unsigned short** by type-casting the value to **unsigned short** type, by giving the value in octal or hexadecimal notation, or by specifying it as 65000U. You can cast this **long** value to the **unsigned short** type without loss of information, since 65,000 can fit in 2 bytes when it is stored as an unsigned number.

Microsoft Specific →

The **long double** contains 80 bits: 1 for sign, 15 for exponent, and 64 for mantissa. Its range is +/–1.2E4932 with at least 19 digits of precision. Although **long double** and **double** are separate types, the representation of **long double** and **double** is identical.

END Microsoft Specific

Incomplete Types

An incomplete type is a type that describes an identifier but lacks information needed to determine the size of the identifier. An "incomplete type" can be:

- A structure type whose members you have not yet specified.

- A union type whose members you have not yet specified.

- An array type whose dimension you have not yet specified.

The **void** type is an incomplete type that cannot be completed. To complete an incomplete type, specify the missing information. The following examples show how to create and complete the incomplete types.

- To create an incomplete structure type, declare a structure type without specifying its members. In this example, the ps pointer points to an incomplete structure type called student.

```
struct student *ps;
```

- To complete an incomplete structure type, declare the same structure type later in the same scope with its members specified, as in

```
struct student
{
    int num;
}                        /* student structure now completed */
```

- To create an incomplete array type, declare an array type without specifying its repetition count. For example:

```
char a[];  /* a has incomplete type */
```

- To complete an incomplete array type, declare the same name later in the same scope with its repetition count specified, as in

```
char a[25]; /* a now has complete type */
```

Typedef Declarations

A typedef declaration is a declaration with **typedef** as the storage class. The declarator becomes a new type. You can use **typedef** declarations to construct shorter or more meaningful names for types already defined by C or for types that you have declared. Typedef names allow you to encapsulate implementation details that may change.

A **typedef** declaration is interpreted in the same way as a variable or function declaration, but the identifier, instead of assuming the type specified by the declaration, becomes a synonym for the type.

Syntax

declaration :
        declaration-specifiers init-declarator-list opt **;**

declaration-specifiers :
        storage-class-specifier declaration-specifiers opt
        type-specifier declaration-specifiers opt
        type-qualifier declaration-specifiers opt

storage-class-specifier :
        typedef

type-specifier :
        void
        char
        short
        int
        long
        float
        double
        signed
        unsigned
        struct-or-union-specifier
        enum-specifier
        typedef-name

typedef-name :
        identifier

Note that a **typedef** declaration does not create types. It creates synonyms for existing types, or names for types that could be specified in other ways. When a **typedef** name is used as a type specifier, it can be combined with certain type specifiers, but not others. Acceptable modifiers include **const** and **volatile**.

Typedef names share the name space with ordinary identifiers (see "Name Spaces" on page 37 in Chapter 2 for more information). Therefore, a program can have a typedef name and a local-scope identifier by the same name. For example:

```
typedef char FlagType;

int main()
{
}

int myproc( int )
{
    int FlagType;
}
```

When declaring a local-scope identifier by the same name as a typedef, or when declaring a member of a structure or union in the same scope or in an inner scope, the type specifier must be specified. This example illustrates this constraint:

```
typedef char FlagType;
const FlagType x;
```

To reuse the FlagType name for an identifier, a structure member, or a union member, the type must be provided:

```
const int FlagType;  /* Type specifier required */
```

It is not sufficient to say

```
const FlagType;      /* Incomplete specification */
```

because the FlagType is taken to be part of the type, not an identifier that is being redeclared. This declaration is taken to be an illegal declaration like

```
int;  /* Illegal declaration */
```

You can declare any type with **typedef**, including pointer, function, and array types. You can declare a **typedef** name for a pointer to a structure or union type before you define the structure or union type, as long as the definition has the same visibility as the declaration.

Typedef names can be used to improve code readability. All three of the following declarations of signal specify exactly the same type, the first without making use of any typedef names.

```
typedef void fv( int ), (*pfv)( int );  /* typedef declarations */

void ( *signal( int, void (*) (int)) ) ( int );
fv *signal( int, fv * );   /* Uses typedef type */
pfv signal( int, pfv );    /* Uses typedef type */
```

Examples

The following examples illustrate **typedef** declarations:

```
typedef int WHOLE;  /* Declares WHOLE to be a synonym for int */
```

Note that WHOLE could now be used in a variable declaration such as WHOLE i; or const WHOLE i;. However, the declaration long WHOLE i; would be illegal.

```
typedef struct club
{
    char name[30];
    int size, year;
} GROUP;
```

This statement declares GROUP as a structure type with three members. Since a structure tag, club, is also specified, either the **typedef** name (GROUP) or the structure tag can be used in declarations. You must use the **struct** keyword with the tag, and you cannot use the **struct** keyword with the **typedef** name.

```
typedef GROUP *PG;  /* Uses the previous typedef name
                       to declare a pointer        */
```

The type PG is declared as a pointer to the GROUP type, which in turn is defined as a structure type.

```
typedef void DRAWF( int, int );
```

This example provides the type DRAWF for a function returning no value and taking two **int** arguments. This means, for example, that the declaration

```
DRAWF box;
```

is equivalent to the declaration

```
void box( int, int );
```

Extended Storage-Class Attributes

Microsoft Specific →

Extended attribute syntax simplifies and standardizes the Microsoft-specific extensions to the C language. The storage-class attributes that use extended attribute syntax include **thread**, **naked**, **dllimport**, and **dllexport**.

The extended attribute syntax for specifying storage-class information uses the **__declspec** keyword, which specifies that an instance of a given type is to be stored with a Microsoft-specific storage-class attribute (**thread**, **naked**, **dllimport**, or **dllexport**). Examples of other storage-class modifiers include the **static** and **extern** keywords. However, these keywords are part of the ANSI C standard and as such are not covered by extended attribute syntax.

Syntax

storage-class-specifier :

    __declspec (*extended-decl-modifier-seq*)   /* Microsoft Specific */

extended-decl-modifier-seq :

    extended-decl-modifier _{opt}

    extended-decl-modifier-seq extended-decl-modifier

extended-decl-modifier :

    thread

    naked

    dllimport

    dllexport

White space separates the declaration modifiers. Note that *extended-decl-modifier-seq* can be empty; in this case, **__declspec** has no effect.

The **thread, naked, dllimport**, and **dllexport** storage-class attributes are a property only of the declaration of the data or function to which they are applied; they do not redefine the type attributes of the function itself. The **thread** attribute affects data only. The **naked** attribute affects functions only. The **dllimport** and **dllexport** attributes affect functions and data.

END Microsoft Specific

DLL Import and Export

Microsoft Specific →

The **dllimport** and **dllexport** storage-class modifiers are Microsoft-specific extensions to the C language. These modifiers define the DLL's interface to its client (the executable file or another DLL). For specific information about using these modifiers, see "DLL Import and Export Functions" on page 158 in Chapter 6.

END Microsoft Specific

Naked

Microsoft Specific →

The **naked** storage-class attribute is a Microsoft-specific extension to the C language. The compiler generates code without prolog and epilog code for functions declared with the **naked** storage-class attribute. Naked functions are useful when you need to write your own prolog/epilog code sequences using inline assembler code. Naked functions are useful for writing virtual device drivers.

For specific information about using the **naked** attribute, see "Naked Functions" on page 162 in Chapter 6.

END Microsoft Specific

Thread Local Storage

Microsoft Specific →

Thread Local Storage (TLS) is the mechanism by which each thread in a given multithreaded process allocates storage for thread-specific data. In standard multithreaded programs, data is shared among all threads of a given process, whereas thread local storage is the mechanism for allocating per-thread data. For a complete discussion of threads, see "Processes and Threads" in the Microsoft Win32® Software Development Kit online documentation.

The Microsoft C language includes the extended storage-class attribute, **thread**, which is used with the **__declspec** keyword to declare a thread local variable. For example, the following code declares an integer thread local variable and initializes it with a value:

```
__declspec( thread ) int tls_i = 1;
```

These guidelines must be observed when you are declaring statically bound thread local variables:

- You can apply the **thread** attribute only to data declarations and definitions. It cannot be used on function declarations or definitions. For example, the following code generates a compiler error:

```
#define Thread __declspec( thread )
Thread void func();       /* Error */
```

- You can specify the **thread** attribute only on data items with static storage duration. This includes global data (both **static** and **extern**) and local static data. You cannot declare automatic data with the **thread** attribute. For example, the following code generates compiler errors:

```
#define Thread __declspec( thread )
void func1()
{
    Thread int tls_i;            /* Error */
}

int func2( Thread int tls_i )    /* Error */
{
    return tls_i;
}
```

- You must use the **thread** attribute for the declaration and the definition of thread local data, regardless of whether the declaration and definition occur in the same file or separate files. For example, the following code generates an error:

```
#define Thread __declspec( thread )
extern int tls_i;    /* This generates an error, because the   */
int Thread tls_i;    /* declaration and the definition differ. */
```

- You cannot use the **thread** attribute as a type modifier. For example, the following code generates a compiler error:

```
char *ch __declspec( thread );               /* Error */
```

- The address of a thread local variable is not considered constant, and any expression involving such an address is not considered a constant expression. This means that you cannot use the address of a thread local variable as an initializer for a pointer. For example, the compiler flags the following code as an error:

```
#define Thread __declspec( thread )
Thread int tls_i;
int *p = &tls_i;      /* Error */
```

- C permits initialization of a variable with an expression involving a reference to itself, but only for objects of nonstatic extent. For example:

```
#define Thread __declspec( thread )
Thread int tls_i = tls_i;               /* Error */
int j = j;                              /* Error */
Thread int tls_i = sizeof( tls_i )     /* Okay  */
```

Note that a **sizeof** expression that includes the variable being initialized does not constitute a reference to itself and is allowed.

For more information about using the **thread** attribute, see "Multithreading Topics" in *Visual C++ Programmer's Guide* online.

END Microsoft Specific

CHAPTER 4

Expressions and Assignments

This chapter describes how to form expressions and to assign values in the C language. Constants, identifiers, strings, and function calls are all operands that are manipulated in expressions. The C language has all the usual language operators. This chapter covers those operators as well as operators that are unique to C or Microsoft C. The topics discussed include:

- L-value and r-value expressions
- Constant expressions
- Side effects
- Sequence points
- Operators
- Operator precedence
- Type conversions
- Type casts

Operands and Expressions

An "operand" is an entity on which an operator acts. An "expression" is a sequence of operators and operands that performs any combination of these actions:

- Computes a value
- Designates an object or function
- Generates side effects

Operands in C include constants, identifiers, strings, function calls, subscript expressions, member-selection expressions, and complex expressions formed by combining operands with operators or by enclosing operands in parentheses. The syntax for these operands is given in "Primary Expressions" on page 94.

Primary Expressions

The operands in expressions are called "primary expressions."

Syntax

primary-expression :
    identifier
    constant
    string-literal
    (*expression*)

expression :
    assignment-expression
    expression , *assignment-expression*

Identifiers in Primary Expressions

Identifiers can have integral, **float**, **enum**, **struct**, **union**, array, pointer, or function type. An identifier is a primary expression provided it has been declared as designating an object (in which case it is an l-value) or as a function (in which case it is a function designator). See "L-Value and R-Value Expressions" on page 95 for a definition of l-value.

The pointer value represented by an array identifier is not a variable, so an array identifier cannot form the left-hand operand of an assignment operation and therefore is not a modifiable l-value.

An identifier declared as a function represents a pointer whose value is the address of the function. The pointer addresses a function returning a value of a specified type. Thus, function identifiers also cannot be l-values in assignment operations. For more information, see "Identifiers" on page 5 in Chapter 1.

Constants in Primary Expressions

A constant operand has the value and type of the constant value it represents. A character constant has **int** type. An integer constant has **int**, **long**, **unsigned int**, or **unsigned long** type, depending on the integer's size and on the way the value is specified. See "Constants" on page 9 in Chapter 1 for more information.

String Literals in Primary Expressions

A "string literal" is a character, wide character, or sequence of adjacent characters enclosed in double quotation marks. Since they are not variables, neither string literals nor any of their elements can be the left-hand operand in an assignment operation. The type of a string literal is an array of **char** (or an array of **wchar_t** for wide-string literals). Arrays in expressions are converted to pointers. See "String Literals" on page 18 in Chapter 1 for more information about strings.

Expressions in Parentheses

You can enclose any operand in parentheses without changing the type or value of the enclosed expression. For example, in the expression

```
( 10 + 5 ) / 5
```

the parentheses around 10 + 5 mean that the value of 10 + 5 is evaluated first and it becomes the left operand of the division (/) operator. The result of (10 + 5) / 5 is 3. Without the parentheses, 10 + 5 / 5 would evaluate to 11.

Although parentheses affect the way operands are grouped in an expression, they cannot guarantee a particular order of evaluation in all cases. For example, neither the parentheses nor the left-to-right grouping of the following expression guarantees what the value of i will be in either of the subexpressions:

```
( i++ +1 ) * ( 2 + i )
```

The compiler is free to evaluate the two sides of the multiplication in any order. If the initial value of i is zero, the whole expression could be evaluated as either of these two statements:

```
( 0 + 1 + 1 ) * ( 2 + 1 )
( 0 + 1 + 1 ) * ( 2 + 0 )
```

Exceptions resulting from side effects are discussed in "Side Effects" on page 97.

L-Value and R-Value Expressions

Expressions that refer to memory locations are called "l-value" expressions. An l-value represents a storage region's "locator" value, or a "left" value, implying that it can appear on the left of the equal sign (=). L-values are often identifiers.

Expressions referring to modifiable locations are called "modifiable l-values." A modifiable l-value cannot have an array type, an incomplete type, or a type with the **const** attribute. For structures and unions to be modifiable l-values, they must not have any members with the **const** attribute. The name of the identifier denotes a storage location, while the value of the variable is the value stored at that location.

An identifier is a modifiable l-value if it refers to a memory location and if its type is arithmetic, structure, union, or pointer. For example, if ptr is a pointer to a storage region, then *ptr is a modifiable l-value that designates the storage region to which ptr points.

Any of the following C expressions can be l-value expressions:

- An identifier of integral, floating, pointer, structure, or union type
- A subscript ([ ]) expression that does not evaluate to an array
- A member-selection expression (–> or **.**)
- A unary-indirection (*) expression that does not refer to an array

- An l-value expression in parentheses
- A **const** object (a nonmodifiable l-value)

The term "r-value" is sometimes used to describe the value of an expression and to distinguish it from an l-value. All l-values are r-values but not all r-values are l-values.

Microsoft Specific →

Microsoft C includes an extension to the ANSI C standard that allows casts of l-values to be used as l-values, as long as the size of the object is not lengthened through the cast. (See "Type-Cast Conversions" on page 132 for more information.) The following example illustrates this feature:

```
char *p ;
short  i;
long l;

(long *) p = &l ;        /* Legal cast   */
(long) i = l ;           /* Illegal cast */
```

The default for Microsoft C is that the Microsoft extensions are enabled. Use the /Za compiler option to disable these extensions.

END Microsoft Specific

Constant Expressions

A constant expression is evaluated at compile time, not run time, and can be used in any place that a constant can be used. The constant expression must evaluate to a constant that is in the range of representable values for that type. The operands of a constant expression can be integer constants, character constants, floating-point constants, enumeration constants, type casts, **sizeof** expressions, and other constant expressions.

Syntax

constant-expression :
    conditional-expression

conditional-expression :
    logical-OR-expression
    logical-OR-expression **?** *expression* **:** *conditional-expression*

expression :
    assignment-expression
    expression **,** *assignment-expression*

assignment-expression :
    conditional-expression
    unary-expression assignment-operator assignment-expression

assignment-operator : one of
    = *= /= %= += –= <<= >>= &= ^= |=

The nonterminals for struct declarator, enumerator, direct declarator, direct-abstract declarator, and labeled statement contain the *constant-expression* nonterminal.

An integral constant expression must be used to specify the size of a bit-field member of a structure, the value of an enumeration constant, the size of an array, or the value of a **case** constant.

Constant expressions used in preprocessor directives are subject to additional restrictions. Consequently, they are known as "restricted constant expressions." A restricted constant expression cannot contain **sizeof** expressions, enumeration constants, type casts to any type, or floating-type constants. It can, however, contain the special constant expression **defined** (*identifier*).

Expression Evaluation

Expressions involving assignment, unary increment, unary decrement, or calling a function may have consequences incidental to their evaluation (side effects). When a "sequence point" is reached, everything preceding the sequence point, including any side effects, is guaranteed to have been evaluated before evaluation begins on anything following the sequence point.

"Side effects" are changes caused by the evaluation of an expression. Side effects occur whenever the value of a variable is changed by an expression evaluation. All assignment operations have side effects. Function calls can also have side effects if they change the value of an externally visible item, either by direct assignment or by indirect assignment through a pointer.

Side Effects

The order of evaluation of expressions is defined by the specific implementation, except when the language guarantees a particular order of evaluation (as outlined in "Precedence and Order of Evaluation" on page 100). For example, side effects occur in the following function calls:

```
add( i + 1, i = j + 2 );
myproc( getc(), getc() );
```

The arguments of a function call can be evaluated in any order. The expression i + 1 may be evaluated before i = j + 2, or i = j + 2 may be evaluated before i + 1. The result is different in each case. Likewise, it is not possible to guarantee what characters are actually passed to the myproc. Since unary increment and decrement operations involve assignments, such operations can cause side effects, as shown in the following example:

```
x[i] = i++;
```

In this example, the value of x that is modified is unpredictable. The value of the subscript could be either the new or the old value of i. The result can vary under different compilers or different optimization levels.

Since C does not define the order of evaluation of side effects, both evaluation methods discussed above are correct and either may be implemented. To make sure that your code is portable and clear, avoid statements that depend on a particular order of evaluation for side effects.

Sequence Points

Between consecutive "sequence points" an object's value can be modified only once by an expression. The C language defines the following sequence points:

- Left operand of the logical-AND operator (**&&**). The left operand of the logical-AND operator is completely evaluated and all side effects complete before continuing. If the left operand evaluates to false (0), the other operand is not evaluated.

- Left operand of the logical-OR operator (||). The left operand of the logical-OR operator is completely evaluated and all side effects complete before continuing. If the left operand evaluates to true (nonzero), the other operand is not evaluated.

- Left operand of the comma operator. The left operand of the comma operator is completely evaluated and all side effects complete before continuing. Both operands of the comma operator are always evaluated. Note that the comma operator in a function call does not guarantee an order of evaluation.

- Function-call operator. All arguments to a function are evaluated and all side effects complete before entry to the function. No order of evaluation among the arguments is specified.

- First operand of the conditional operator. The first operand of the conditional operator is completely evaluated and all side effects complete before continuing.

- The end of a full initialization expression (that is, an expression that is not part of another expression such as the end of an initialization in a declaration statement).

- The expression in an expression statement. Expression statements consist of an optional expression followed by a semicolon (**;**). The expression is evaluated for its side effects and there is a sequence point following this evaluation.

- The controlling expression in a selection (**if** or **switch**) statement. The expression is completely evaluated and all side effects complete before the code dependent on the selection is executed.

- The controlling expression of a **while** or **do** statement. The expression is completely evaluated and all side effects complete before any statements in the next iteration of the **while** or **do** loop are executed.

- Each of the three expressions of a **for** statement. The expressions are completely evaluated and all side effects complete before any statements in the next iteration of the **for** loop are executed.

- The expression in a **return** statement. The expression is completely evaluated and all side effects complete before control returns to the calling function.

Operators

There are three types of operators. A unary expression consists of either a unary operator prepended to an operand, or the **sizeof** keyword followed by an expression. The expression can be either the name of a variable or a cast expression. If the expression is a cast expression, it must be enclosed in parentheses. A binary expression consists of two operands joined by a binary operator. A ternary expression consists of three operands joined by the conditional-expression operator.

C includes the following unary operators:

Symbol	Name
− ~ !	Negation and complement operators
* &	Indirection and address-of operators
sizeof	Size operator
+	Unary plus operator
++ −−	Unary increment and decrement operators

Binary operators associate from left to right. C provides the following binary operators:

Symbol	Name
* / %	Multiplicative operators
+ −	Additive operators
<< >>	Shift operators
< > <= >= == !=	Relational operators
& | ^	Bitwise operators
&& ||	Logical operators
,	Sequential-evaluation operator

The conditional-expression operator has lower precedence than binary expressions and differs from them in being right associative.

Expressions with operators also include assignment expressions, which use unary or binary assignment operators. The unary assignment operators are the increment (++) and decrement (−−) operators; the binary assignment operators are the simple-assignment operator (=) and the compound-assignment operators. Each compound-assignment operator is a combination of another binary operator with the simple-assignment operator.

Precedence and Order of Evaluation

The precedence and associativity of C operators affect the grouping and evaluation of operands in expressions. An operator's precedence is meaningful only if other operators with higher or lower precedence are present. Expressions with higher-precedence operators are evaluated first. Precedence can also be described by the word "binding." Operators with a higher precedence are said to have tighter binding.

Table 4.1 summarizes the precedence and associativity (the order in which the operands are evaluated) of C operators, listing them in order of precedence from highest to lowest. Where several operators appear together, they have equal precedence and are evaluated according to their associativity. The operators in the table are described in the sections beginning with "Postfix Operators" on page 103. The rest of this section gives general information about precedence and associativity.

Table 4.1 Precedence and Associativity of C Operators

Symbol[1]	Type of Operation	Associativity
[ ] ( ) . -> postfix ++ and postfix --	Expression	Left to right
prefix ++ and prefix -- sizeof & * + - ~ !	Unary	Right to left
typecasts	Unary	Right to left
* / %	Multiplicative	Left to right
+ -	Additive	Left to right
<< >>	Bitwise shift	Left to right
< > <= >=	Relational	Left to right
== !=	Equality	Left to right
&	Bitwise-AND	Left to right
^	Bitwise-exclusive-OR	Left to right
|	Bitwise-inclusive-OR	Left to right
&&	Logical-AND	Left to right
||	Logical-OR	Left to right
? :	Conditional-expression	Right to left
= *= /= %= += -= <<= >>= &= ^= |=	Simple and compound assignment[2]	Right to left
,	Sequential evaluation	Left to right

[1] Operators are listed in descending order of precedence. If several operators appear on the same line or in a group, they have equal precedence.

[2] All simple and compound-assignment operators have equal precedence.

An expression can contain several operators with equal precedence. When several such operators appear at the same level in an expression, evaluation proceeds according to the associativity of the operator, either from right to left or from left to right. The direction of evaluation does not affect the results of expressions that include more than one multiplication (*), addition (+), or binary-bitwise (**&** **|** **^**) operator at the same level. Order of operations is not defined by the language. The compiler is free to evaluate such expressions in any order, if the compiler can guarantee a consistent result.

Only the sequential-evaluation (,), logical-AND (**&&**), logical-OR (**||**), conditional-expression (**? :**), and function-call operators constitute sequence points and therefore guarantee a particular order of evaluation for their operands. The function-call operator is the set of parentheses following the function identifier. The sequential-evaluation operator (,) is guaranteed to evaluate its operands from left to right. (Note that the comma operator in a function call is not the same as the sequential-evaluation operator and does not provide any such guarantee.) For more information, see "Sequence Points" on page 98.

Logical operators also guarantee evaluation of their operands from left to right. However, they evaluate the smallest number of operands needed to determine the result of the expression. This is called "short-circuit" evaluation. Thus, some operands of the expression may not be evaluated. For example, in the expression

```
x && y++
```

the second operand, y++, is evaluated only if x is true (nonzero). Thus, y is not incremented if x is false (0).

Examples

The following list shows how the compiler automatically binds several sample expressions:

Expression	Automatic Binding
a & b || c	(a & b) || c
a = b || c	a = (b || c)
q && r || s--	(q && r) || s--

In the first expression, the bitwise-AND operator (&) has higher precedence than the logical-OR operator (||), so a & b forms the first operand of the logical-OR operation.

In the second expression, the logical-OR operator (||) has higher precedence than the simple-assignment operator (=), so b || c is grouped as the right-hand operand in the assignment. Note that the value assigned to a is either 0 or 1.

The third expression shows a correctly formed expression that may produce an unexpected result. The logical-AND operator (&&) has higher precedence than the logical-OR operator (||), so q && r is grouped as an operand. Since the logical operators guarantee evaluation of operands from left to right, q && r is evaluated before s--. However, if q && r evaluates to a nonzero value, s-- is not evaluated, and s is not decremented. If not decrementing s would cause a problem in your program, s-- should appear as the first operand of the expression, or s should be decremented in a separate operation.

The following expression is illegal and produces a diagnostic message at compile time:

Illegal Expression	Default Grouping
p == 0 ? p += 1: p += 2	(p == 0 ? p += 1 : p) += 2

In this expression, the equality operator (==) has the highest precedence, so p == 0 is grouped as an operand. The conditional-expression operator (? :) has the next-highest precedence. Its first operand is p == 0, and its second operand is p += 1. However, the last operand of the conditional-expression operator is considered to be p rather than p += 2, since this occurrence of p binds more closely to the conditional-expression operator than it does to the compound-assignment operator. A syntax error occurs because += 2 does not have a left-hand operand. You should use parentheses to prevent errors of this kind and produce more readable code. For example, you could use parentheses as shown below to correct and clarify the preceding example:

(p == 0) ? (p += 1) : (p += 2)

Usual Arithmetic Conversions

Most C operators perform type conversions to bring the operands of an expression to a common type or to extend short values to the integer size used in machine operations. The conversions performed by C operators depend on the specific operator and the type of the operand or operands. However, many operators perform similar conversions on operands of integral and floating types. These conversions are known as "arithmetic conversions." Conversion of an operand value to a compatible type causes no change to its value.

The arithmetic conversions summarized below are called "usual arithmetic conversions." These steps are applied only for binary operators that expect arithmetic type and only if the two operands do not have the same type. The purpose is to yield a common type which is also the type of the result. To determine which conversions actually take place, the compiler applies the following algorithm to binary operations in the expression. The steps below are not a precedence order.

1. If either operand is of type **long double**, the other operand is converted to type **long double**.

2. If the above condition is not met and either operand is of type **double**, the other operand is converted to type **double**.

3. If the above two conditions are not met and either operand is of type **float**, the other operand is converted to type **float**.

4. If the above three conditions are not met (none of the operands are of floating types), then integral conversions are performed on the operands as follows:

   - If either operand is of type **unsigned long**, the other operand is converted to type **unsigned long**.

   - If the above condition is not met and either operand is of type **long** and the other of type **unsigned int**, both operands are converted to type **unsigned long**.

   - If the above two conditions are not met, and either operand is of type **long**, the other operand is converted to type **long**.

   - If the above three conditions are not met, and either operand is of type **unsigned int**, the other operand is converted to type **unsigned int**.

   - If none of the above conditions are met, both operands are converted to type **int**.

The following code illustrates these conversion rules:

```
float    fVal;
double   dVal;
int    iVal;
unsigned long ulVal;

dVal = iVal * ulVal; /* iVal converted to unsigned long
                      * Uses step 4.
                      * Result of multiplication converted to double
                      */
dVal = ulVal + fVal; /* ulVal converted to float
                      * Uses step 3.
                      * Result of addition converted to double
                      */
```

Postfix Operators

The postfix operators have the highest precedence (the tightest binding) in expression evaluation.

Syntax
postfix-expression :
  primary-expression
  postfix-expression [*expression*]
  postfix-expression (*argument-expression-list* opt)
  postfix-expression **.** *identifier*
  postfix-expression –> *identifier*
  postfix-expression **++**
  postfix-expression ––

Operators in this precedence level are the array subscripts, function calls, structure and union members, and postfix increment and decrement operators.

One-Dimensional Arrays

A postfix expression followed by an expression in square brackets ([ ]) is a subscripted representation of an element of an array object. A subscript expression represents the value at the address that is *expression* positions beyond *postfix-expression* when expressed as

postfix-expression [*expression*]

Usually, the value represented by *postfix-expression* is a pointer value, such as an array identifier, and *expression* is an integral value. However, all that is required syntactically is that one of the expressions be of pointer type and the other be of integral type. Thus the integral value could be in the *postfix-expression* position and the pointer value could be in the brackets in the *expression*, or "subscript," position. For example, this code is legal:

```
int sum, *ptr, a[10];

int main()
{
    ptr = a;
    sum = 4[ptr];
}
```

Subscript expressions are generally used to refer to array elements, but you can apply a subscript to any pointer. Whatever the order of values, *expression* must be enclosed in brackets ([ ]).

The subscript expression is evaluated by adding the integral value to the pointer value, then applying the indirection operator (*) to the result. (See "Indirection and Address-of Operators" on page 109 for a discussion of the indirection operator.) In effect, for a one-dimensional array, the following four expressions are equivalent, assuming that a is a pointer and b is an integer:

```
a[b]
*(a + b)
*(b + a)
b[a]
```

According to the conversion rules for the addition operator (given in "Additive Operators" on page 114), the integral value is converted to an address offset by multiplying it by the length of the type addressed by the pointer.

For example, suppose the identifier line refers to an array of **int** values. The following procedure is used to evaluate the subscript expression line[i]:

1. The integer value i is multiplied by the number of bytes defined as the length of an **int** item. The converted value of i represents i **int** positions.

2. This converted value is added to the original pointer value (line) to yield an address that is offset i **int** positions from line.

3. The indirection operator is applied to the new address. The result is the value of the array element at that position (intuitively, line [i]).

The subscript expression line[0] represents the value of the first element of line, since the offset from the address represented by line is 0. Similarly, an expression such as line[5] refers to the element offset five positions from line, or the sixth element of the array.

Multidimensional Arrays

A subscript expression can also have multiple subscripts, as follows:

expression1 [*expression2*] [*expression3*]...

Subscript expressions associate from left to right. The leftmost subscript expression, *expression1*[*expression2*], is evaluated first. The address that results from adding *expression1* and *expression2* forms a pointer expression; then *expression3* is added to this pointer expression to form a new pointer expression, and so on until the last subscript expression has been added. The indirection operator (*) is applied after the last subscripted expression is evaluated, unless the final pointer value addresses an array type (see examples below).

Expressions with multiple subscripts refer to elements of "multidimensional arrays." A multidimensional array is an array whose elements are arrays. For example, the first element of a three-dimensional array is an array with two dimensions.

Examples

For the following examples, an array named prop is declared with three elements, each of which is a 4-by-6 array of **int** values.

```
int prop[3][4][6];
int i, *ip, (*ipp)[6];
```

A reference to the prop array looks like this:

```
i = prop[0][0][1];
```

The example above shows how to refer to the second individual **int** element of prop. Arrays are stored by row, so the last subscript varies most quickly; the expression prop[0][0][2] refers to the next (third) element of the array, and so on.

```
i = prop[2][1][3];
```

This statement is a more complex reference to an individual element of prop. The expression is evaluated as follows:

1. The first subscript, 2, is multiplied by the size of a 4-by-6 **int** array and added to the pointer value prop. The result points to the third 4-by-6 array of prop.

2. The second subscript, 1, is multiplied by the size of the 6-element **int** array and added to the address represented by prop[2].

3. Each element of the 6-element array is an **int** value, so the final subscript, 3, is multiplied by the size of an **int** before it is added to `prop[2][1]`. The resulting pointer addresses the fourth element of the 6-element array.

4. The indirection operator is applied to the pointer value. The result is the **int** element at that address.

These next two examples show cases where the indirection operator is not applied.

```
ip = prop[2][1];

ipp = prop[2];
```

In the first of these statements, the expression `prop[2][1]` is a valid reference to the three-dimensional array `prop`; it refers to a 6-element array (declared above). Since the pointer value addresses an array, the indirection operator is not applied.

Similarly, the result of the expression `prop[2]` in the second statement `ipp = prop[2];` is a pointer value addressing a two-dimensional array.

Function Call

A "function call" is an expression that includes the name of the function being called or the value of a function pointer and, optionally, the arguments being passed to the function.

Syntax

postfix-expression :
      postfix-expression (*argument-expression-list* _{opt})

argument-expression-list :
      assignment-expression
      argument-expression-list , *assignment-expression*

The *postfix-expression* must evaluate to a function address (for example, a function identifier or the value of a function pointer), and *argument-expression-list* is a list of expressions (separated by commas) whose values (the "arguments") are passed to the function. The *argument-expression-list* argument can be empty.

A function-call expression has the value and type of the function's return value. A function cannot return an object of array type. If the function's return type is **void** (that is, the function has been declared never to return a value), the function-call expression also has **void** type. (See "Function Calls" on page 171 in Chapter 6 for more information.)

Structure and Union Members

A "member-selection expression" refers to members of structures and unions. Such an expression has the value and type of the selected member.

Syntax

postfix-expression **.** *identifier*
   postfix-expression –> *identifier*

This list describes the two forms of the member-selection expressions:

1. In the first form, *postfix-expression* represents a value of **struct** or **union** type, and *identifier* names a member of the specified structure or union. The value of the operation is that of *identifier* and is an l-value if *postfix-expression* is an l-value. See "L-Value and R-Value Expressions" on page 95 for more information.

2. In the second form, *postfix-expression* represents a pointer to a structure or union, and *identifier* names a member of the specified structure or union. The value is that of *identifier* and is an l-value.

The two forms of member-selection expressions have similar effects.

In fact, an expression involving the member-selection operator (–>) is a shorthand version of an expression using the period (.) if the expression before the period consists of the indirection operator (*) applied to a pointer value. Therefore,

expression –> identifier

is equivalent to

(**expression*) . *identifier*

when *expression* is a pointer value.

Examples

The following examples refer to this structure declaration. For information about the indirection operator (*) used in these examples, see "Indirection and Address-of Operators" on page 109.

```
struct pair
{
    int a;
    int b;
    struct pair *sp;
} item, list[10];
```

A member-selection expression for the item structure looks like this:

```
item.sp = &item;
```

In the example above, the address of the item structure is assigned to the sp member of the structure. This means that item contains a pointer to itself.

```
(item.sp)->a = 24;
```

In this example, the pointer expression item.sp is used with the member-selection operator (–>) to assign a value to the member a.

```
list[8].b = 12;
```

This statement shows how to select an individual structure member from an array of structures.

Postfix Increment and Decrement Operators

Operands of the postfix increment and decrement operators are scalar types that are modifiable l-values.

Syntax

postfix-expression :
  postfix-expression **++**
  postfix-expression **−−**

The result of the postfix increment or decrement operation is the value of the operand. After the result is obtained, the value of the operand is incremented (or decremented). The following code illustrates the postfix increment operator.

```
if( var++ > 0 )
   *p++ = *q++;
```

In this example, the variable var is compared to 0, then incremented. If var was positive before being incremented, the next statement is executed. First, the value of the object pointed to by q is assigned to the object pointed to by p. Then, q and p are incremented.

Unary Operators

Unary operators appear before their operand and associate from right to left.

Syntax

unary-expression :
  postfix-expression
  ++ *unary-expression*
  −− *unary-expression*
  unary-operator cast-expression
  sizeof *unary-expression*
  sizeof (*type-name*)

unary-operator : one of
  & * + − ~ !

Prefix Increment and Decrement Operators

The unary operators (**++** and **−−**) are called "prefix" increment or decrement operators when the increment or decrement operators appear before the operand. Postfix increment and decrement has higher precedence than prefix increment and decrement. The operand must have integral, floating, or pointer type and must be a modifiable l-value expression (an expression without the **const** attribute). The result is an l-value.

When the operator appears before its operand, the operand is incremented or decremented and its new value is the result of the expression.

An operand of integral or floating type is incremented or decremented by the integer value 1. The type of the result is the same as the operand type. An operand of pointer type is incremented or decremented by the size of the object it addresses. An incremented pointer points to the next object; a decremented pointer points to the previous object.

Example

This example illustrates the unary prefix decrement operator:

```
if( line[--i] != '\n' )
    return;
```

In this example, the variable i is decremented before it is used as a subscript to line.

Indirection and Address-of Operators

The indirection operator (*) accesses a value indirectly, through a pointer. The operand must be a pointer value. The result of the operation is the value addressed by the operand; that is, the value at the address to which its operand points. The type of the result is the type that the operand addresses.

If the operand points to a function, the result is a function designator. If it points to a storage location, the result is an l-value designating the storage location.

If the pointer value is invalid, the result is undefined. The following list includes some of the most common conditions that invalidate a pointer value.

- The pointer is a null pointer.
- The pointer specifies the address of a local item that is not visible at the time of the reference.
- The pointer specifies an address that is inappropriately aligned for the type of the object pointed to.
- The pointer specifies an address not used by the executing program.

The address-of operator (&) gives the address of its operand. The operand of the address-of operator can be either a function designator or an l-value that designates an object that is not a bit field and is not declared with the **register** storage-class specifier.

The result of the address operation is a pointer to the operand. The type addressed by the pointer is the type of the operand.

The address-of operator can only be applied to variables with fundamental, structure, or union types that are declared at the file-scope level, or to subscripted array references. In these expressions, a constant expression that does not include the address-of operator can be added to or subtracted from the address expression.

Examples

The following examples use these declarations:

```
int *pa, x;
int a[20];
double d;
```

This statement uses the address-of operator:

```
pa = &a[5];
```

The address-of operator (**&**) takes the address of the sixth element of the array a. The result is stored in the pointer variable pa.

```
x = *pa;
```

The indirection operator (*) is used in this example to access the **int** value at the address stored in pa. The value is assigned to the integer variable x.

```
if( x == *&x )
    printf( "True\n" );
```

This example prints the word True, demonstrating that the result of applying the indirection operator to the address of x is the same as x.

```
int roundup( void );      /* Function declaration */

int  *proundup  = roundup;
int  *pround  = &roundup;
```

Once the function roundup is declared, two pointers to roundup are declared and initialized. The first pointer, proundup, is initialized using only the name of the function, while the second, pround, uses the address-of operator in the initialization. The initializations are equivalent.

Unary Arithmetic Operators

The C unary plus, arithmetic-negation, complement, and logical-negation operators are discussed in the following list:

Operator	Description
+	The unary plus operator preceding an expression in parentheses forces the grouping of the enclosed operations. It is used with expressions involving more than one associative or commutative binary operator. The operand must have arithmetic type. The result is the value of the operand. An integral operand undergoes integral promotion. The type of the result is the type of the promoted operand.
−	The arithmetic-negation operator produces the negative (two's complement) of its operand. The operand must be an integral or floating value. This operator performs the usual arithmetic conversions.

(continued)

Operator	Description
~	The bitwise-complement (or bitwise-NOT) operator produces the bitwise complement of its operand. The operand must be of integral type. This operator performs usual arithmetic conversions; the result has the type of the operand after conversion.
!	The logical-negation (logical-NOT) operator produces the value 0 if its operand is true (nonzero) and the value 1 if its operand is false (0). The result has **int** type. The operand must be an integral, floating, or pointer value.

Unary arithmetic operations on pointers are illegal.

Examples

The following examples illustrate the unary arithmetic operators:

```
short x = 987;
   x = -x;
```

In the example above, the new value of x is the negative of 987, or –987.

```
unsigned short y = 0xAAAA;
   y = ~y;
```

In this example, the new value assigned to y is the one's complement of the unsigned value 0xAAAA, or 0x5555.

```
if( !(x < y) )
```

If x is greater than or equal to y, the result of the expression is 1 (true). If x is less than y, the result is 0 (false).

The sizeof Operator

The **sizeof** operator gives the amount of storage, in bytes, required to store an object of the type of the operand. This operator allows you to avoid specifying machine-dependent data sizes in your programs.

Syntax

sizeof *unary-expression*

sizeof (*type-name*)

The operand is either an identifier that is a *unary-expression*, or a type-cast expression (that is, a type specifier enclosed in parentheses). The *unary-expression* cannot represent a bit-field object, an incomplete type, or a function designator. The result is an unsigned integral constant. The standard header STDDEF.H defines this type as **size_t**.

When you apply the **sizeof** operator to an array identifier, the result is the size of the entire array rather than the size of the pointer represented by the array identifier.

When you apply the **sizeof** operator to a structure or union type name, or to an identifier of structure or union type, the result is the number of bytes in the structure or union, including internal and trailing padding. This size may include internal and trailing padding used to align the members of the structure or union on memory boundaries. Thus, the result may not correspond to the size calculated by adding up the storage requirements of the individual members.

If an unsized array is the last element of a structure, the **sizeof** operator returns the size of the structure without the array.

```
buffer = calloc(100, sizeof (int) );
```

This example uses the **sizeof** operator to pass the size of an **int**, which varies among machines, as an argument to a run-time function named **calloc**. The value returned by the function is stored in `buffer`.

```
static char *strings[] ={
        "this is string one",
        "this is string two",
        "this is string three",
        };
const int string_no = ( sizeof strings ) / ( sizeof strings[0] );
```

In this example, `strings` is an array of pointers to **char**. The number of pointers is the number of elements in the array, but is not specified. It is easy to determine the number of pointers by using the **sizeof** operator to calculate the number of elements in the array. The **const** integer value `string_no` is initialized to this number. Because it is a **const** value, `string_no` cannot be modified.

Cast Operators

A type cast provides a method for explicit conversion of the type of an object in a specific situation.

Syntax

cast-expression :
    unary-expression
    (*type-name*) *cast-expression*

The compiler treats *cast-expression* as type *type-name* after a type cast has been made. Casts can be used to convert objects of any scalar type to or from any other scalar type. Explicit type casts are constrained by the same rules that determine the effects of implicit conversions, discussed in "Assignment Conversions" on page 126. Additional restraints on casts may result from the actual sizes or representation of specific types. See "Storage of Basic Types" on page 81 in Chapter 3 for information on actual sizes of integral types. For more information on type casts, see "Type-Cast Conversions" on page 132.

Multiplicative Operators

The multiplicative operators perform multiplication (*), division (/), and remainder (%) operations.

Syntax

multiplicative-expression :
    cast-expression
    multiplicative-expression * *cast-expression*
    multiplicative-expression / *cast-expression*
    multiplicative-expression % *cast-expression*

The operands of the remainder operator (%) must be integral. The multiplication (*) and division (/) operators can take integral- or floating-type operands; the types of the operands can be different.

The multiplicative operators perform the usual arithmetic conversions on the operands. The type of the result is the type of the operands after conversion.

Note   Since the conversions performed by the multiplicative operators do not provide for overflow or underflow conditions, information may be lost if the result of a multiplicative operation cannot be represented in the type of the operands after conversion.

The C multiplicative operators are described below:

Operator	Description
*	The multiplication operator causes its two operands to be multiplied.
/	The division operator causes the first operand to be divided by the second. If two integer operands are divided and the result is not an integer, it is truncated according to the following rules:
	• The result of division by 0 is undefined according to the ANSI C standard. The Microsoft C compiler generates an error at compile time or run time.
	• If both operands are positive or unsigned, the result is truncated toward 0.
	• If either operand is negative, whether the result of the operation is the largest integer less than or equal to the algebraic quotient or is the smallest integer greater than or equal to the algebraic quotient is implementation defined. (See the Microsoft Specific section below.)
%	The result of the remainder operator is the remainder when the first operand is divided by the second. When the division is inexact, the result is determined by the following rules:
	• If the right operand is zero, the result is undefined.
	• If both operands are positive or unsigned, the result is positive.
	• If either operand is negative and the result is inexact, the result is implementation defined. (See the Microsoft Specific section below.)

In division where either operand is negative, the direction of truncation is toward 0.

If either operation is negative in division with the remainder operator, the result has the same sign as the dividend (the first operand in the expression).

Examples

The declarations shown below are used for the following examples:

```
int i = 10, j = 3, n;
double x = 2.0, y;
```

This statement uses the multiplication operator:

```
y = x * i;
```

In this case, x is multiplied by i to give the value 20.0. The result has **double** type.

```
n = i / j;
```

In this example, 10 is divided by 3. The result is truncated toward 0, yielding the integer value 3.

```
n = i % j;
```

This statement assigns n the integer remainder, 1, when 10 is divided by 3.

The sign of the remainder is the same as the sign of the dividend. For example:

```
50 % -6 = 2
-50 % 6 = -2
```

In each case, 50 and 2 have the same sign.

Additive Operators

The additive operators perform addition (**+**) and subtraction (**−**).

Syntax

additive-expression :
    multiplicative-expression
    additive-expression **+** *multiplicative-expression*
    additive-expression **−** *multiplicative-expression*

Note Although the syntax for *additive-expression* includes *multiplicative-expression*, this does not imply that expressions using multiplication are required. See the syntax in Appendix A, "C Language Syntax Summary," for *multiplicative-expression*, *cast-expression*, and *unary-expression*.

The operands can be integral or floating values. Some additive operations can also be performed on pointer values, as outlined under the discussion of each operator.

The additive operators perform the usual arithmetic conversions on integral and floating operands. The type of the result is the type of the operands after conversion. Since the conversions performed by the additive operators do not provide for overflow or underflow conditions, information may be lost if the result of an additive operation cannot be represented in the type of the operands after conversion.

Addition (+)

The addition operator (+) causes its two operands to be added. Both operands can be either integral or floating types, or one operand can be a pointer and the other an integer.

When an integer is added to a pointer, the integer value (*i*) is converted by multiplying it by the size of the value that the pointer addresses. After conversion, the integer value represents *i* memory positions, where each position has the length specified by the pointer type. When the converted integer value is added to the pointer value, the result is a new pointer value representing the address *i* positions from the original address. The new pointer value addresses a value of the same type as the original pointer value and therefore is the same as array indexing (see "One-Dimensional Arrays" on page 104 and "Multidimensional Arrays" on page 105). If the sum pointer points outside the array, except at the first location beyond the high end, the result is undefined. For more information, see "Pointer Arithmetic" on page 116.

Subtraction (–)

The subtraction operator (–) subtracts the second operand from the first. Both operands can be either integral or floating types, or one operand can be a pointer and the other an integer.

When two pointers are subtracted, the difference is converted to a signed integral value by dividing the difference by the size of a value of the type that the pointers address. The size of the integral value is defined by the type **ptrdiff_t** in the standard include file STDDEF.H. The result represents the number of memory positions of that type between the two addresses. The result is only guaranteed to be meaningful for two elements of the same array, as discussed in "Pointer Arithmetic" on page 116.

When an integer value is subtracted from a pointer value, the subtraction operator converts the integer value (*i*) by multiplying it by the size of the value that the pointer addresses. After conversion, the integer value represents *i* memory positions, where each position has the length specified by the pointer type. When the converted integer value is subtracted from the pointer value, the result is the memory address *i* positions before the original address. The new pointer points to a value of the type addressed by the original pointer value.

Using the Additive Operators

The following examples, which illustrate the addition and subtraction operators, use these declarations:

```
int i = 4, j;
float x[10];
float *px;
```

These statements are equivalent:

```
px = &x[4 + i];
px = &x[4] + i;
```

The value of i is multiplied by the length of a **float** and added to &x[4]. The resulting pointer value is the address of x[8].

```
j = &x[i] - &x[i-2];
```

In this example, the address of the third element of x (given by x[i-2]) is subtracted from the address of the fifth element of x (given by x[i]). The difference is divided by the length of a **float**; the result is the integer value 2.

Pointer Arithmetic

Additive operations involving a pointer and an integer give meaningful results only if the pointer operand addresses an array member and the integer value produces an offset within the bounds of the same array. When the integer value is converted to an address offset, the compiler assumes that only memory positions of the same size lie between the original address and the address plus the offset.

This assumption is valid for array members. By definition, an array is a series of values of the same type; its elements reside in contiguous memory locations. However, storage for any types except array elements is not guaranteed to be filled by the same type of identifiers. That is, blanks can appear between memory positions, even positions of the same type. Therefore, the results of adding to or subtracting from the addresses of any values but array elements are undefined.

Similarly, when two pointer values are subtracted, the conversion assumes that only values of the same type, with no blanks, lie between the addresses given by the operands.

Bitwise Shift Operators

The shift operators shift their first operand left (<<) or right (>>) by the number of positions the second operand specifies.

Syntax

shift-expression :
    additive-expression
    shift-expression **<<** *additive-expression*
    shift-expression **>>** *additive-expression*

Both operands must be integral values. These operators perform the usual arithmetic conversions; the type of the result is the type of the left operand after conversion.

For leftward shifts, the vacated right bits are set to 0. For rightward shifts, the vacated left bits are filled based on the type of the first operand after conversion. If the type is **unsigned**, they are set to 0. Otherwise, they are filled with copies of the sign bit. For left-shift operators without overflow, the statement

```
expr1 << expr2
```

is equivalent to multiplication by 2^{expr2}. For right-shift operators,

```
expr1 >> expr2
```

is equivalent to division by 2^{expr2} if expr1 is unsigned or has a nonnegative value.

The result of a shift operation is undefined if the second operand is negative, or if the right operand is greater than or equal to the width in bits of the promoted left operand.

Since the conversions performed by the shift operators do not provide for overflow or underflow conditions, information may be lost if the result of a shift operation cannot be represented in the type of the first operand after conversion.

```
unsigned int x, y, z;

x = 0x00AA;
y = 0x5500;

z = ( x << 8 ) + ( y >> 8 );
```

In this example, x is shifted left eight positions and y is shifted right eight positions. The shifted values are added, giving 0xAA55, and assigned to z.

Shifting a negative value to the right yields half the absolute value, rounded down. For example, –253 (binary 11111111 00000011) shifted right one bit produces –127 (binary 11111111 10000001). A *positive* 253 shifts right to produce +126.

Right shifts preserve the sign bit. When a signed integer shifts right, the most-significant bit remains set. When an unsigned integer shifts right, the most-significant bit is cleared.

If 0xF000 is unsigned, the result is 0x7800. If 0xF0000000 is signed, a right shift produces 0xF8000000. Shifting a positive number right 32 times produces 0xF0000000. Shifting a negative number right 32 times produces 0xFFFFFFFF.

Relational and Equality Operators

The binary relational and equality operators compare their first operand to their second operand to test the validity of the specified relationship. The result of a relational expression is 1 if the tested relationship is true and 0 if it is false. The type of the result is **int**.

Syntax

relational-expression :
        shift-expression
        relational-expression < *shift-expression*
        relational-expression > *shift-expression*
        relational-expression <= *shift-expression*
        relational-expression >= *shift-expression*

equality-expression :
        relational-expression
        equality-expression == *relational-expression*
        equality-expression != *relational-expression*

The relational and equality operators test the following relationships:

Operator	Relationship Tested
<	First operand less than second operand
>	First operand greater than second operand
<=	First operand less than or equal to second operand
>=	First operand greater than or equal to second operand
==	First operand equal to second operand
!=	First operand not equal to second operand

The first four operators in the list above have a higher precedence than the equality operators (== and !=). See the precedence information in Table 4.1.

The operands can have integral, floating, or pointer type. The types of the operands can be different. Relational operators perform the usual arithmetic conversions on integral and floating type operands. In addition, you can use the following combinations of operand types with the relational and equality operators:

- Both operands of any relational or equality operator can be pointers to the same type. For the equality (==) and inequality (!=) operators, the result of the comparison indicates whether the two pointers address the same memory location. For the other relational operators (<, >, <=, and >=), the result of the comparison indicates the relative position of the two memory addresses of the objects pointed to. Relational operators compare only offsets.

  Pointer comparison is defined only for parts of the same object. If the pointers refer to members of an array, the comparison is equivalent to comparison of the corresponding subscripts. The address of the first array element is "less than" the address of the last element. In the case of structures, pointers to structure members declared later are "greater than" pointers to members declared earlier in the structure. Pointers to the members of the same union are equal.

- A pointer value can be compared to the constant value 0 for equality (==) or inequality (!=). A pointer with a value of 0 is called a "null" pointer; that is, it does not point to a valid memory location.

- The equality operators follow the same rules as the relational operators, but permit additional possibilities: a pointer can be compared to a constant integral expression with value 0, or to a pointer to **void**. If two pointers are both null pointers, they compare as equal. Equality operators compare both segment and offset.

Examples

The examples below illustrate relational and equality operators.

```
int x = 0, y = 0;
if ( x < y )
```

Because x and y are equal, the expression in this example yields the value 0.

```
char array[10];
char *p;

for ( p = array; p < &array[10]; p++ )
    *p = '\0';
```

The fragment in this example sets each element of array to a null character constant.

```
enum color { red, white, green } col;
    .
    .
    .
    if ( col == red )
    .
    .
    .
```

These statements declare an enumeration variable named col with the tag color. At any time, the variable may contain an integer value of 0, 1, or 2, which represents one of the elements of the enumeration set color: the color red, white, or green, respectively. If col contains 0 when the **if** statement is executed, any statements depending on the **if** will be executed.

Bitwise Operators

The bitwise operators perform bitwise-AND (**&**), bitwise-exclusive-OR (**^**), and bitwise-inclusive-OR (l) operations.

Syntax

AND-expression :
>   *equality-expression*
>   *AND-expression* **&** *equality-expression*

exclusive-OR-expression :
>   *AND-expression*
>   *exclusive-OR-expression* **^** *AND-expression*

inclusive-OR-expression :
> *exclusive-OR-expression*
> *inclusive-OR-expression* | *exclusive-OR-expression*

The operands of bitwise operators must have integral types, but their types can be different. These operators perform the usual arithmetic conversions; the type of the result is the type of the operands after conversion.

The C bitwise operators are described below:

Operator	Description
&	The bitwise-AND operator compares each bit of its first operand to the corresponding bit of its second operand. If both bits are 1, the corresponding result bit is set to 1. Otherwise, the corresponding result bit is set to 0.
^	The bitwise-exclusive-OR operator compares each bit of its first operand to the corresponding bit of its second operand. If one bit is 0 and the other bit is 1, the corresponding result bit is set to 1. Otherwise, the corresponding result bit is set to 0.
|	The bitwise-inclusive-OR operator compares each bit of its first operand to the corresponding bit of its second operand. If either bit is 1, the corresponding result bit is set to 1. Otherwise, the corresponding result bit is set to 0.

Examples

These declarations are used for the following three examples:

```
short i = 0xAB00;
short j = 0xABCD;
short n;

n = i & j;
```

The result assigned to n in this first example is the same as i (0xAB00 hexadecimal).

```
n = i | j;

n = i ^ j;
```

The bitwise-inclusive OR in the second example results in the value 0xABCD (hexadecimal), while the bitwise-exclusive OR in the third example produces 0xCD (hexadecimal).

Microsoft Specific →

The results of bitwise operation on signed integers is implementation-defined according to the ANSI C standard. For the Microsoft C compiler, bitwise operations on signed integers work the same as bitwise operations on unsigned integers. For example, -16 & 99 can be expressed in binary as

```
  11111111 11110000
& 00000000 01100011
  ─────────────────
  00000000 01100000
```

The result of the bitwise AND is 96 decimal.

END Microsoft Specific

Logical Operators

The logical operators perform logical-AND (**&&**) and logical-OR (**||**) operations.

Syntax

logical-AND-expression :
> *inclusive-OR-expression*
> *logical-AND-expression* **&&** *inclusive-OR-expression*

logical-OR-expression :
> *logical-AND-expression*
> *logical-OR-expression* **||** *logical-AND-expression*

Logical operators do not perform the usual arithmetic conversions. Instead, they evaluate each operand in terms of its equivalence to 0. The result of a logical operation is either 0 or 1. The result's type is **int**.

The C logical operators are described below:

Operator	Description
&&	The logical-AND operator produces the value 1 if both operands have nonzero values. If either operand is equal to 0, the result is 0. If the first operand of a logical-AND operation is equal to 0, the second operand is not evaluated.
||	The logical-OR operator performs an inclusive-OR operation on its operands. The result is 0 if both operands have 0 values. If either operand has a nonzero value, the result is 1. If the first operand of a logical-OR operation has a nonzero value, the second operand is not evaluated.

The operands of logical-AND and logical-OR expressions are evaluated from left to right. If the value of the first operand is sufficient to determine the result of the operation, the second operand is not evaluated. This is called "short-circuit evaluation." There is a sequence point after the first operand. See "Sequence Points" on page 98 for more information.

Examples

The following examples illustrate the logical operators:

```
int w, x, y, z;

if ( x < y && y < z )
   printf( "x is less than z\n" );
```

In this example, the `printf` function is called to print a message if x is less than y and y is less than z. If x is greater than y, the second operand (y < z) is not evaluated and nothing is printed. Note that this could cause problems in cases where the second operand has side effects that are being relied on for some other reason.

```
printf( "%d" , (x == w || x == y || x == z) );
```

In this example, if x is equal to either w, y, or z, the second argument to the `printf` function evaluates to true and the value 1 is printed. Otherwise, it evaluates to false and the value 0 is printed. As soon as one of the conditions evaluates to true, evaluation ceases.

Conditional-Expression Operator

C has one ternary operator: the conditional-expression operator (**? :**).

Syntax

conditional-expression :
    logical-OR-expression
    logical-OR-expression **?** *expression* **:** *conditional-expression*

The *logical-OR-expression* must have integral, floating, or pointer type. It is evaluated in terms of its equivalence to 0. A sequence point follows *logical-OR-expression*. Evaluation of the operands proceeds as follows:

- If *logical-OR-expression* is not equal to 0, *expression* is evaluated. The result of evaluating the expression is given by the nonterminal *expression*. (This means *expression* is evaluated only if *logical-OR-expression* is true.)

- If *logical-OR-expression* equals 0, *conditional-expression* is evaluated. The result of the expression is the value of *conditional-expression*. (This means *conditional-expression* is evaluated only if *logical-OR-expression* is false.)

Note that either *expression* or *conditional-expression* is evaluated, but not both.

The type of the result of a conditional operation depends on the type of the *expression* or *conditional-expression* operand, as follows:

- If *expression* or *conditional-expression* has integral or floating type (their types can be different), the operator performs the usual arithmetic conversions. The type of the result is the type of the operands after conversion.

- If both *expression* and *conditional-expression* have the same structure, union, or pointer type, the type of the result is the same structure, union, or pointer type.

- If both operands have type **void**, the result has type **void**.

- If either operand is a pointer to an object of any type, and the other operand is a pointer to **void**, the pointer to the object is converted to a pointer to **void** and the result is a pointer to **void**.

- If either *expression* or *conditional-expression* is a pointer and the other operand is a constant expression with the value 0, the type of the result is the pointer type.

In the type comparison for pointers, any type qualifiers (**const** or **volatile**) in the type to which the pointer points are insignificant, but the result type inherits the qualifiers from both components of the conditional.

Examples

The following examples show uses of the conditional operator:

```
j = ( i < 0 ) ? ( -i ) : ( i );
```

This example assigns the absolute value of i to j. If i is less than 0, -i is assigned to j. If i is greater than or equal to 0, i is assigned to j.

```
void f1( void );
void f2( void );
int x;
int y;
    .
    .
    .
( x == y ) ? ( f1() ) : ( f2() );
```

In this example, two functions, f1 and f2, and two variables, x and y, are declared. Later in the program, if the two variables have the same value, the function f1 is called. Otherwise, f2 is called.

Assignment Operators

An assignment operation assigns the value of the right-hand operand to the storage location named by the left-hand operand. Therefore, the left-hand operand of an assignment operation must be a modifiable l-value. After the assignment, an assignment expression has the value of the left operand but is not an l-value.

Syntax

assignment-expression :
>   *conditional-expression*
>   *unary-expression assignment-operator assignment-expression*

assignment-operator : one of
>   = *= /= %= += −= <<= >>= &= ^= |=

The assignment operators in C can both transform and assign values in a single operation. C provides the following assignment operators:

Operator	Operation Performed
=	Simple assignment
*=	Multiplication assignment
/=	Division assignment
%=	Remainder assignment
+=	Addition assignment
−=	Subtraction assignment
<<=	Left-shift assignment
>>=	Right-shift assignment
&=	Bitwise-AND assignment
^=	Bitwise-exclusive-OR assignment
|=	Bitwise-inclusive-OR assignment

In assignment, the type of the right-hand value is converted to the type of the left-hand value, and the value is stored in the left operand after the assignment has taken place. The left operand must not be an array, a function, or a constant. The specific conversion path, which depends on the two types, is outlined in detail in "Type Conversions" on page 126.

Simple Assignment

The simple-assignment operator assigns its right operand to its left operand. The value of the right operand is converted to the type of the assignment expression and replaces the value stored in the object designated by the left operand. The conversion rules for assignment apply (see "Assignment Conversions" on page 126).

```
double x;
int y;

x = y;
```

In this example, the value of y is converted to type **double** and assigned to x.

Compound Assignment

The compound-assignment operators combine the simple-assignment operator with another binary operator. Compound-assignment operators perform the operation specified by the additional operator, then assign the result to the left operand. For example, a compound-assignment expression such as

expression1 += *expression2*

can be understood as

expression1 = *expression1* + *expression2*

However, the compound-assignment expression is not equivalent to the expanded version because the compound-assignment expression evaluates *expression1* only once, while the expanded version evaluates *expression1* twice: in the addition operation and in the assignment operation.

The operands of a compound-assignment operator must be of integral or floating type. Each compound-assignment operator performs the conversions that the corresponding binary operator performs and restricts the types of its operands accordingly. The addition-assignment (+=) and subtraction-assignment (−=) operators can also have a left operand of pointer type, in which case the right-hand operand must be of integral type. The result of a compound-assignment operation has the value and type of the left operand.

```
#define MASK 0xff00

n &= MASK;
```

In this example, a bitwise-inclusive-AND operation is performed on n and MASK, and the result is assigned to n. The manifest constant MASK is defined with a **#define** preprocessor directive.

Sequential-Evaluation Operator

The sequential-evaluation operator, also called the "comma operator," evaluates its two operands sequentially from left to right.

Syntax

expression :
>   *assignment-expression*
>   *expression* **,** *assignment-expression*

The left operand of the sequential-evaluation operator is evaluated as a **void** expression. The result of the operation has the same value and type as the right operand. Each operand can be of any type. The sequential-evaluation operator does not perform type conversions between its operands, and it does not yield an l-value. There is a sequence point after the first operand, which means all side effects from the evaluation of the left operand are completed before beginning evaluation of the right operand. See "Sequence Points" on page 98 for more information.

The sequential-evaluation operator is typically used to evaluate two or more expressions in contexts where only one expression is allowed.

Commas can be used as separators in some contexts. However, you must be careful not to confuse the use of the comma as a separator with its use as an operator; the two uses are completely different.

Example

This example illustrates the sequential-evaluation operator:

```
for ( i = j = 1; i + j < 20; i += i, j-- );
```

In this example, each operand of the **for** statement's third expression is evaluated independently. The left operand i += i is evaluated first; then the right operand, j--, is evaluated.

```
func_one( x, y + 2, z );
func_two( (x--, y + 2), z );
```

In the function call to func_one, three arguments, separated by commas, are passed: x, y + 2, and z. In the function call to func_two, parentheses force the compiler to interpret the first comma as the sequential-evaluation operator. This function call passes two arguments to func_two. The first argument is the result of the sequential-evaluation operation (x--, y + 2), which has the value and type of the expression y + 2; the second argument is z.

Type Conversions

Type conversions depend on the specified operator and the type of the operand or operators. Type conversions are performed in the following cases:

- When a value of one type is assigned to a variable of a different type or an operator converts the type of its operand or operands before performing an operation
- When a value of one type is explicitly cast to a different type
- When a value is passed as an argument to a function or when a type is returned from a function

A character, a short integer, or an integer bit field, all either signed or not, or an object of enumeration type, can be used in an expression wherever an integer can be used. If an **int** can represent all the values of the original type, then the value is converted to **int**; otherwise, it is converted to **unsigned int**. This process is called "integral promotion." Integral promotions preserve value. That is, the value after promotion is guaranteed to be the same as before the promotion. See "Usual Arithmetic Conversions" on page 102 for more information.

Assignment Conversions

In assignment operations, the type of the value being assigned is converted to the type of the variable that receives the assignment. C allows conversions by assignment between integral and floating types, even if information is lost in the conversion. The conversion method used depends on the types involved in the assignment, as described in "Usual Arithmetic Conversions" on page 102 and in the following sections.

Type qualifiers do not affect the allowability of the conversion although a **const** l-value cannot be used on the left side of the assignment.

Conversions from Signed Integral Types

When a signed integer is converted to an unsigned integer with equal or greater size and the value of the signed integer is not negative, the value is unchanged. The conversion is made by sign-extending the signed integer. A signed integer is converted to a shorter signed integer by truncating the high-order bits. The result is interpreted as an unsigned value, as shown in this example.

```
int i = -3;
unsigned short u;

u = i;
printf( "%hu\n", u );   /* Prints 65533 */
```

No information is lost when a signed integer is converted to a floating value, except that some precision may be lost when a **long int** or **unsigned long int** value is converted to a **float** value.

Table 4.2 summarizes conversions from signed integral types. This table assumes that the **char** type is signed by default. If you use a compile-time option to change the default for the **char** type to unsigned, the conversions given in Table 4.3 for the **unsigned char** type apply instead of the conversions in Table 4.2.

Table 4.2   Conversions from Signed Integral Types

From	To	Method
char[1]	short	Sign-extend
char	long	Sign-extend
char	unsigned char	Preserve pattern; high-order bit loses function as sign bit
char	unsigned short	Sign-extend to **short**; convert **short** to **unsigned short**
char	unsigned long	Sign-extend to **long**; convert **long** to **unsigned long**
char	float	Sign-extend to **long**; convert **long** to **float**
char	double	Sign-extend to **long**; convert **long** to **double**
char	long double	Sign-extend to **long**; convert **long** to **double**
short	char	Preserve low-order byte
short	long	Sign-extend
short	unsigned char	Preserve low-order byte
short	unsigned short	Preserve bit pattern; high-order bit loses function as sign bit
short	unsigned long	Sign-extend to **long**; convert **long** to **unsigned long**
short	float	Sign-extend to **long**; convert **long** to **float**
short	double	Sign-extend to **long**; convert **long** to **double**
short	long double	Sign-extend to **long**; convert **long** to **double**
long	char	Preserve low-order byte
long	short	Preserve low-order word
long	unsigned char	Preserve low-order byte
long	unsigned short	Preserve low-order word
long	unsigned long	Preserve bit pattern; high-order bit loses function as sign bit
long	float	Represent as **float**. If **long** cannot be represented exactly, some precision is lost.
long	double	Represent as **double**. If **long** cannot be represented exactly as a **double**, some precision is lost.
long	long double	Represent as **double**. If **long** cannot be represented exactly as a **double**, some precision is lost.

[1] All **char** entries assume that the **char** type is signed by default.

C Language Reference

For the Microsoft 32-bit C compiler, an integer is equivalent to a **long**. Conversion of an **int** value proceeds the same as for a **long**.

END Microsoft Specific

Conversions from Unsigned Integral Types

An unsigned integer is converted to a shorter unsigned or signed integer by truncating the high-order bits, or to a longer unsigned or signed integer by zero-extending (see Table 4.3).

When the value with integral type is demoted to a signed integer with smaller size, or an unsigned integer is converted to its corresponding signed integer, the value is unchanged if it can be represented in the new type. However, the value it represents changes if the sign bit is set, as in the following example.

```
int j;
unsigned short k = 65533;

j = k;
printf( "%hd\n", j );   /* Prints -3 */
```

If it cannot be represented, the result is implementation-defined. See "Type-Cast Conversions" on page 132 for information on the Microsoft C compiler's handling of demotion of integers. The same behavior results from integer conversion or from type casting the integer.

Unsigned values are converted in a way that preserves their value and is not representable directly in C. The only exception is a conversion from **unsigned long** to **float**, which loses at most the low-order bits. Otherwise, value is preserved, signed or unsigned. When a value of integral type is converted to floating, and the value is outside the range representable, the result is undefined. (See "Storage of Basic Types" on page 81 in Chapter 3 for information about the range for integral and floating-point types.)

Table 4.3 summarizes conversions from unsigned integral types.

Table 4.3 Conversions from Unsigned Integral Types

From	To	Method
unsigned char	**char**	Preserve bit pattern; high-order bit becomes sign bit
unsigned char	**short**	Zero-extend
unsigned char	**long**	Zero-extend
unsigned char	**unsigned short**	Zero-extend
unsigned char	**unsigned long**	Zero-extend
unsigned char	**float**	Convert to **long**; convert **long** to **float**
unsigned char	**double**	Convert to **long**; convert **long** to **double**
unsigned char	**long double**	Convert to **long**; convert **long** to **double**

Table 4.3   Conversions from Unsigned Integral Types *(continued)*

From	To	Method
unsigned short	**char**	Preserve low-order byte
unsigned short	**short**	Preserve bit pattern; high-order bit becomes sign bit
unsigned short	**long**	Zero-extend
unsigned short	**unsigned char**	Preserve low-order byte
unsigned short	**unsigned long**	Zero-extend
unsigned short	**float**	Convert to **long**; convert **long** to **float**
unsigned short	**double**	Convert to **long**; convert **long** to **double**
unsigned short	**long double**	Convert to **long**; convert **long** to **double**
unsigned long	**char**	Preserve low-order byte
unsigned long	**short**	Preserve low-order word
unsigned long	**long**	Preserve bit pattern; high-order bit becomes sign bit
unsigned long	**unsigned char**	Preserve low-order byte
unsigned long	**unsigned short**	Preserve low-order word
unsigned long	**float**	Convert to **long**; convert **long** to **float**
unsigned long	**double**	Convert directly to **double**
unsigned long	**long double**	Convert to **long**; convert **long** to **double**

Microsoft Specific →

For the Microsoft 32-bit C compiler, the **unsigned int** type is equivalent to the **unsigned long** type. Conversion of an **unsigned int** value proceeds in the same way as conversion of an **unsigned long**. Conversions from **unsigned long** values to **float** are not accurate if the value being converted is larger than the maximum positive signed **long** value.

END Microsoft Specific

Conversions from Floating-Point Types

A **float** value converted to a **double** or **long double**, or a **double** converted to a **long double**, undergoes no change in value. A **double** value converted to a **float** value is represented exactly, if possible. Precision may be lost if the value cannot be represented exactly. If the result is out of range, the behavior is undefined. See "Limits on Floating-Point Constants" on page 10 in Chapter 1 for the range of floating-point types.

A floating value is converted to an integral value by first converting to a **long**, then from the **long** value to the specific integral value, as described below in Table 4.4. The decimal portion of the floating value is discarded in the conversion to a **long**. If the result is still too large to fit into a **long**, the result of the conversion is undefined.

Microsoft Specific →

When converting a **double** or **long double** floating-point number to a smaller floating-point number, the value of the floating-point variable is truncated toward zero when an underflow occurs. An overflow causes a run-time error. Note that the Microsoft C compiler maps **long double** to type **double**.

END Microsoft Specific

Table 4.4 summarizes conversions from floating types.

Table 4.4 Conversions from Floating-Point Types

From	To	Method
float	char	Convert to **long**; convert **long** to **char**
float	short	Convert to **long**; convert **long** to **short**
float	long	Truncate at decimal point. If result is too large to be represented as **long**, result is undefined.
float	unsigned short	Convert to **long**; convert **long** to **unsigned short**
float	unsigned long	Convert to **long**; convert **long** to **unsigned long**
float	double	Change internal representation
float	long double	Change internal representation
double	char	Convert to **float**; convert **float** to **char**
double	short	Convert to **float**; convert **float** to **short**
double	long	Truncate at decimal point. If result is too large to be represented as **long**, result is undefined.
double	unsigned short	Convert to **long**; convert **long** to **unsigned short**
double	unsigned long	Convert to **long**; convert **long** to **unsigned long**
double	float	Represent as a **float**. If **double** value cannot be represented exactly as **float**, loss of precision occurs. If value is too large to be represented as **float**, the result is undefined.
long double	char	Convert to **float**; convert **float** to **char**
long double	short	Convert to **float**; convert **float** to **short**
long double	long	Truncate at decimal point. If result is too large to be represented as **long**, result is undefined.
long double	unsigned short	Convert to **long**; convert **long** to **unsigned short**
long double	unsigned long	Convert to **long**; convert **long** to **unsigned long**
long double	float	Represent as a **float**. If **double** value cannot be represented exactly as **float**, loss of precision occurs. If value is too large to be represented as **float**, the result is undefined.
long double	double	The **long double** value is treated as **double**.

Conversions from **float**, **double**, or **long double** values to **unsigned long** are not accurate if the value being converted is larger than the maximum positive **long** value.

Conversions to and from Pointer Types

A pointer to one type of value can be converted to a pointer to a different type. However, the result may be undefined because of the alignment requirements and sizes of different types in storage. A pointer to an object can be converted to a pointer to an object whose type requires less or equally strict storage alignment, and back again without change.

A pointer to **void** can be converted to or from a pointer to any type, without restriction or loss of information. If the result is converted back to the original type, the original pointer is recovered.

If a pointer is converted to another pointer with the same type but having different or additional qualifiers, the new pointer is the same as the old except for restrictions imposed by the new qualifier.

A pointer value can also be converted to an integral value. The conversion path depends on the size of the pointer and the size of the integral type, according to the following rules:

- If the size of the pointer is greater than or equal to the size of the integral type, the pointer behaves like an unsigned value in the conversion, except that it cannot be converted to a floating value.

- If the pointer is smaller than the integral type, the pointer is first converted to a pointer with the same size as the integral type, then converted to the integral type.

Conversely, an integral type can be converted to a pointer type according to the following rules:

- If the integral type is the same size as the pointer type, the conversion simply causes the integral value to be treated as a pointer (an unsigned integer).

- If the size of the integral type is different from the size of the pointer type, the integral type is first converted to the size of the pointer, using the conversion paths given in Table 4.2 and Table 4.3. It is then treated as a pointer value.

An integral constant expression with value 0 or such an expression cast to type **void *** can be converted by a type cast, by assignment, or by comparison to a pointer of any type. This produces a null pointer that is equal to another null pointer of the same type, but this null pointer is not equal to any pointer to a function or to an object. Integers other than the constant 0 can be converted to pointer type, but the result is not portable.

Conversions from Other Types

Since an **enum** value is an **int** value by definition, conversions to and from an **enum** value are the same as those for the **int** type. For the Microsoft C compiler, an integer is the same as a **long**.

No conversions between structure or union types are allowed.

Any value can be converted to type **void**, but the result of such a conversion can be used only in a context where an expression value is discarded, such as in an expression statement.

The **void** type has no value, by definition. Therefore, it cannot be converted to any other type, and other types cannot be converted to **void** by assignment. However, you can explicitly cast a value to type **void**, as discussed in "Type-Cast Conversions."

Type-Cast Conversions

You can use type casts to explicitly convert types.

Syntax

cast-expression :
> *unary expression*
> (*type-name*) *cast-expression*

type-name :
> *specifier-qualifier-list abstract-declarator* opt

The *type-name* is a type and *cast-expression* is a value to be converted to that type. An expression with a type cast is not an l-value. The *cast-expression* is converted as though it had been assigned to a variable of type *type-name*. The conversion rules for assignments (outlined in "Assignment Conversions" on page 126) apply to type casts as well. Table 4.5 shows the types that can be cast to any given type.

Table 4.5 Legal Type Casts

Destination Types	Potential Sources
Integral types	Any integer type or floating-point type, or pointer to an object
Floating-point	Any arithmetic type
A pointer to an object, or (**void ***)	Any integer type, (**void ***), a pointer to an object, or a function pointer
Function pointer	Any integral type, a pointer to an object, or a function pointer
A structure, union, or array	None
Void type	Any type

Any identifier can be cast to **void** type. However, if the type specified in a type-cast expression is not **void**, then the identifier being cast to that type cannot be a **void** expression. Any expression can be cast to **void**, but an expression of type **void** cannot be cast to any other type. For example, a function with **void** return type cannot have its return cast to another type.

Note that a **void** * expression has a type pointer to **void**, not type **void**. If an object is cast to **void** type, the resulting expression cannot be assigned to any item. Similarly, a type-cast object is not an acceptable l-value, so no assignment can be made to a type-cast object.

Microsoft Specific →

A type cast can be an l-value expression as long as the size of the identifier does not change. For information on l-value expressions, see "L-Value and R-Value Expressions" on page 95.

END Microsoft Specific

You can convert an expression to type **void** with a cast, but the resulting expression can be used only where a value is not required. An object pointer converted to **void** * and back to the original type will return to its original value.

Function-Call Conversions

The type of conversion performed on the arguments in a function call depends on the presence of a function prototype (forward declaration) with declared argument types for the called function.

If a function prototype is present and includes declared argument types, the compiler performs type checking (see Chapter 6, "Functions").

If no function prototype is present, only the usual arithmetic conversions are performed on the arguments in the function call. These conversions are performed independently on each argument in the call. This means that a **float** value is converted to a **double**; a **char** or **short** value is converted to an **int**; and an **unsigned char** or **unsigned short** is converted to an **unsigned int**.

CHAPTER 5

Statements

The statements of a C program control the flow of program execution. In C, as in other programming languages, several kinds of statements are available to perform loops, to select other statements to be executed, and to transfer control. Following a brief overview of statement syntax, this chapter describes the C statements in alphabetical order:

break statement	**if** statement
compound statement	null statement
continue statement	**return** statement
do-while statement	**switch** statement
expression statement	**try-except** statement
for statement	**try-finally** statement
goto and labeled statements	**while** statement

Overview of Statements

C statements consist of tokens, expressions, and other statements. A statement that forms a component of another statement is called the "body" of the enclosing statement. Each statement type given by the following syntax is discussed in this chapter.

Syntax

statement :
    labeled-statement
    compound-statement
    expression-statement
    selection-statement
    iteration-statement
    jump-statement
    try-except-statement /* Microsoft Specific */
    try-finally-statement /* Microsoft Specific */

Frequently the statement body is a "compound statement." A compound statement consists of other statements that can include keywords. The compound statement is delimited by braces ({ }). All other C statements end with a semicolon (;). The semicolon is a statement terminator.

The expression statement contains a C expression that can contain the arithmetic or logical operators introduced in Chapter 4, "Expressions and Assignments." The null statement is an empty statement.

Any C statement can begin with an identifying label consisting of a name and a colon. Since only the **goto** statement recognizes statement labels, statement labels are discussed with **goto**. See "The goto and Labeled Statements" on page 141 for more information.

The break Statement

The **break** statement terminates the execution of the nearest enclosing **do, for, switch**, or **while** statement in which it appears. Control passes to the statement that follows the terminated statement.

Syntax

jump-statement :
    break;

The **break** statement is frequently used to terminate the processing of a particular case within a **switch** statement. Lack of an enclosing iterative or **switch** statement generates an error.

Within nested statements, the **break** statement terminates only the **do, for, switch**, or **while** statement that immediately encloses it. You can use a **return** or **goto** statement to transfer control elsewhere out of the nested structure.

This example illustrates the **break** statement:

```
for ( i = 0; i < LENGTH; i++ )    /* Execution returns here when */
{                                 /* break statement is executed */
   for ( j = 0; j < WIDTH; j++)
   {
      if ( lines[i][j] == '\0' )
      {
         lengths[i] = j;
         break;
      }
   }
}
```

The example processes an array of variable-length strings stored in `lines`. The **break** statement causes an exit from the interior **for** loop after the terminating null character ('\0') of each string is found and its position is stored in `lengths[i]`.

The variable j is not incremented when **break** causes the exit from the interior loop. Control then returns to the outer **for** loop. The variable i is incremented and the process is repeated until i is greater than or equal to LENGTH.

The Compound Statement

A compound statement (also called a "block") typically appears as the body of another statement, such as the **if** statement. Chapter 3, "Declarations and Types," describes the form and meaning of the declarations that can appear at the head of a compound statement.

Syntax

compound-statement :

       { *declaration-list* _{opt} *statement-list* _{opt} **}**

declaration-list :

      declaration

      declaration-list declaration

statement-list :

      statement

      statement-list statement

If there are declarations, they must come before any statements. The scope of each identifier declared at the beginning of a compound statement extends from its declaration point to the end of the block. It is visible throughout the block unless a declaration of the same identifier exists in an inner block.

Identifiers in a compound statement are presumed **auto** unless explicitly declared otherwise with **register**, **static**, or **extern**, except functions, which can only be **extern**. You can leave off the **extern** specifier in function declarations and the function will still be **extern**.

Storage is not allocated and initialization is not permitted if a variable or function is declared in a compound statement with storage class **extern**. The declaration refers to an external variable or function defined elsewhere.

Variables declared in a block with the **auto** or **register** keyword are reallocated and, if necessary, initialized each time the compound statement is entered. These variables are not defined after the compound statement is exited. If a variable declared inside a block has the **static** attribute, the variable is initialized when program execution begins and keeps its value throughout the program. See "Storage Classes" on page 42 in Chapter 3 for information about **static**.

This example illustrates a compound statement:

```
if ( i > 0 )
{
    line[i] = x;
    x++;
    i--;
}
```

In this example, if i is greater than 0, all statements inside the compound statement are executed in order.

The continue Statement

The **continue** statement passes control to the next iteration of the **do**, **for**, or **while** statement in which it appears, bypassing any remaining statements in the **do**, **for**, or **while** statement body. A typical use of the **continue** statement is to return to the start of a loop from within a deeply nested loop.

Syntax

jump-statement :
      continue;

The next iteration of a **do**, **for**, or **while** statement is determined as follows:

- Within a **do** or a **while** statement, the next iteration starts by reevaluating the expression of the **do** or **while** statement.

- A **continue** statement in a **for** statement causes the first expression of the **for** statement to be evaluated. Then the compiler reevaluates the conditional expression and, depending on the result, either terminates or iterates the statement body. See "The for Statement" on page 140 for more information on the **for** statement and its nonterminals.

This is an example of the **continue** statement:

```
while ( i-- > 0 )
{
    x = f( i );
    if ( x == 1 )
        continue;
    y += x * x;
}
```

In this example, the statement body is executed while i is greater than 0. First f(i) is assigned to x; then, if x is equal to 1, the **continue** statement is executed. The rest of the statements in the body are ignored, and execution resumes at the top of the loop with the evaluation of the loop's test.

The do-while Statement

The **do-while** statement lets you repeat a statement or compound statement until a specified expression becomes false.

Syntax

iteration-statement :
> **do** *statement* **while** (*expression*) **;**

The *expression* in a **do-while** statement is evaluated after the body of the loop is executed. Therefore, the body of the loop is always executed at least once.

The *expression* must have arithmetic or pointer type. Execution proceeds as follows:

1. The statement body is executed.
2. Next, *expression* is evaluated. If *expression* is false, the **do-while** statement terminates and control passes to the next statement in the program. If *expression* is true (nonzero), the process is repeated, beginning with step 1.

The **do-while** statement can also terminate when a **break**, **goto**, or **return** statement is executed within the statement body.

This is an example of the **do-while** statement:

```
do
{
    y = f( x );
    x--;
} while ( x > 0 );
```

In this **do-while** statement, the two statements y = f(x); and x--; are executed, regardless of the initial value of x. Then x > 0 is evaluated. If x is greater than 0, the statement body is executed again and x > 0 is reevaluated. The statement body is executed repeatedly as long as x remains greater than 0. Execution of the **do-while** statement terminates when x becomes 0 or negative. The body of the loop is executed at least once.

The Expression Statement

When an expression statement is executed, the expression is evaluated according to the rules outlined in Chapter 4, "Expressions and Assignments."

Syntax

expression-statement :
> *expression* opt **;**

All side effects from the expression evaluation are completed before the next statement is executed. An empty expression statement is called a null statement. See "The Null Statement" on page 143 for more information.

These examples demonstrate expression statements.

```
x = ( y + 3 );          /* x is assigned the value of y + 3  */
x++;                    /* x is incremented                  */
x = y = 0;              /* Both x and y are initialized to 0 */
proc( arg1, arg2 );     /* Function call returning void      */
y = z = ( f( x ) + 3 ); /* A function-call expression        */
```

In the last statement, the function-call expression, the value of the expression, which includes any value returned by the function, is increased by 3 and then assigned to both the variables y and z.

The for Statement

The **for** statement lets you repeat a statement or compound statement a specified number of times. The body of a **for** statement is executed zero or more times until an optional condition becomes false. You can use optional expressions within the **for** statement to initialize and change values during the **for** statement's execution.

Syntax

iteration-statement :
    for (*init-expression* $_{opt}$; *cond-expression* $_{opt}$; *loop-expression* $_{opt}$) *statement*

Execution of a **for** statement proceeds as follows:

1. The *init-expression*, if any, is evaluated. This specifies the initialization for the loop. There is no restriction on the type of *init-expression*.

2. The *cond-expression*, if any, is evaluated. This expression must have arithmetic or pointer type. It is evaluated before each iteration. Three results are possible:

   - If *cond-expression* is true (nonzero), *statement* is executed; then *loop-expression*, if any, is evaluated. The *loop-expression* is evaluated after each iteration. There is no restriction on its type. Side effects will execute in order. The process then begins again with the evaluation of *cond-expression*.

   - If *cond-expression* is omitted, *cond-expression* is considered true, and execution proceeds exactly as described in the previous paragraph. A **for** statement without a *cond-expression* argument terminates only when a **break** or **return** statement within the statement body is executed, or when a **goto** (to a labeled statement outside the **for** statement body) is executed.

   - If *cond-expression* is false (0), execution of the **for** statement terminates and control passes to the next statement in the program.

A **for** statement also terminates when a **break**, **goto**, or **return** statement within the statement body is executed. A **continue** statement in a **for** loop causes *loop-expression* to be evaluated. When a **break** statement is executed inside a **for** loop, *loop-expression* is not evaluated or executed. This statement

```
for( ;; );
```

is the customary way to produce an infinite loop which can only be exited with a **break**, **goto**, or **return** statement.

This example illustrates the **for** statement:

```
for ( i = space = tab = 0; i < MAX; i++ )
{
    if ( line[i] == ' ' )
        space++;
    if ( line[i] == '\t' )
    {
        tab++;
        line[i] = ' ';
    }
}
```

This example counts space (' ') and tab ('\t') characters in the array of characters named `line` and replaces each tab character with a space. First `i`, `space`, and `tab` are initialized to 0. Then `i` is compared with the constant `MAX`; if `i` is less than `MAX`, the statement body is executed. Depending on the value of `line[i]`, the body of one or neither of the **if** statements is executed. Then `i` is incremented and tested against `MAX`; the statement body is executed repeatedly as long as `i` is less than `MAX`.

The goto and Labeled Statements

The **goto** statement transfers control to a label. The given label must reside in the same function and can appear before only one statement in the same function.

Syntax

statement :
> *labeled-statement*
> *jump-statement*

jump-statement :
> **goto** *identifier* **;**

labeled-statement :
> *identifier* **:** *statement*

A statement label is meaningful only to a **goto** statement; in any other context, a labeled statement is executed without regard to the label.

A *jump-statement* must reside in the same function and can appear before only one statement in the same function. The set of *identifier* names following a **goto** has its own name space so the names do not interfere with other identifiers. Labels cannot be redeclared. See "Name Spaces" on page 37 in Chapter 2 for more information.

It is good programming style to use the **break**, **continue**, and **return** statement in preference to **goto** whenever possible. Since the **break** statement only exits from one level of the loop, a **goto** may be necessary for exiting a loop from within a deeply nested loop.

This example demonstrates the **goto** statement:

```
void main()
{
    int i, j;

    for ( i = 0; i < 10; i++ )
    {
        printf( "Outer loop executing. i = %d\n", i );
        for ( j = 0; j < 3; j++ )
        {
            printf( " Inner loop executing. j = %d\n", j );
            if ( i == 5 )
                goto stop;
        }
    }
    /* This message does not print: */
    printf( "Loop exited. i = %d\n", i );
    stop: printf( "Jumped to stop. i = %d\n", i );
}
```

In this example, a **goto** statement transfers control to the point labeled stop when I equals 5.

The if Statement

The **if** statement controls conditional branching. The body of an **if** statement is executed if the value of the expression is nonzero. The syntax for the **if** statement has two forms.

Syntax

selection-statement :
> **if** (*expression*) *statement*
> **if** (*expression*) *statement* **else** *statement*

In both forms of the **if** statement, the expressions, which can have any value except a structure, are evaluated, including all side effects.

In the first form of the syntax, if *expression* is true (nonzero), *statement* is executed. If *expression* is false, *statement* is ignored. In the second form of syntax, which uses **else**, the second *statement* is executed if *expression* is false. With both forms, control then passes from the **if** statement to the next statement in the program unless one of the statements contains a **break**, **continue**, or **goto**.

The following are examples of the **if** statement:

```
if ( i > 0 )
    y = x / i;
else
{
    x = i;
    y = f( x );
}
```

In this example, the statement `y = x/i;` is executed if `i` is greater than 0. If `i` is less than or equal to 0, `i` is assigned to `x` and `f( x )` is assigned to `y`. Note that the statement forming the **if** clause ends with a semicolon.

When nesting **if** statements and **else** clauses, use braces to group the statements and clauses into compound statements that clarify your intent. If no braces are present, the compiler resolves ambiguities by associating each **else** with the closest **if** that lacks an **else**.

```
if ( i > 0 )              /* Without braces */
    if ( j > i )
        x = j;
    else
        x = i;
```

The **else** clause is associated with the inner **if** statement in this example. If `i` is less than or equal to 0, no value is assigned to `x`.

```
if ( i > 0 )
{                         /* With braces */
    if ( j > i )
        x = j;
}
else
    x = i;
```

The braces surrounding the inner **if** statement in this example make the **else** clause part of the outer **if** statement. If `i` is less than or equal to 0, `i` is assigned to `x`.

The Null Statement

A "null statement" is a statement containing only a semicolon; it can appear wherever a statement is expected. Nothing happens when a null statement is executed. The correct way to code a null statement is:

Syntax

```
;
```

Statements such as **do**, **for**, **if**, and **while** require that an executable statement appear as the statement body. The null statement satisfies the syntax requirement in cases that do not need a substantive statement body.

As with any other C statement, you can include a label before a null statement. To label an item that is not a statement, such as the closing brace of a compound statement, you can label a null statement and insert it immediately before the item to get the same effect.

This example illustrates the null statement:

```
for ( i = 0; i < 10; line[i++] = 0 )
    ;
```

In this example, the loop expression of the **for** statement `line[i++] = 0` initializes the first 10 elements of `line` to 0. The statement body is a null statement, since no further statements are necessary.

The return Statement

The **return** statement terminates the execution of a function and returns control to the calling function. Execution resumes in the calling function at the point immediately following the call. A **return** statement can also return a value to the calling function. See "Return Type" on page 166 in Chapter 6 for more information.

Syntax

jump-statement :
        return *expression* _{opt} **;**

The value of *expression*, if present, is returned to the calling function. If *expression* is omitted, the return value of the function is undefined. The expression, if present, is converted to the type returned by the function. If the function was declared with return type **void**, a **return** statement containing an expression generates a warning and the expression is not evaluated.

If no **return** statement appears in a function definition, control automatically returns to the calling function after the last statement of the called function is executed. In this case, the return value of the called function is undefined. If a return value is not required, declare the function to have **void** return type; otherwise, the default return type is **int**.

Many programmers use parentheses to enclose the *expression* argument of the **return** statement. However, C does not require the parentheses.

This example demonstrates the **return** statement:

```
void draw( int I, long L );
long sq( int s );
int main()
{
    long y;
    int x;

    y = sq( x );
    draw( x, y );
    return();
}
```

```
long sq( int s )
{
    return( s * s );
}

void draw( int I, long L )
{
    /* Statements defining the draw function here */
    return;
}
```

In this example, the main function calls two functions: sq and draw. The sq function returns the value of x * x to main, where the return value is assigned to y. The draw function is declared as a **void** function and does not return a value. An attempt to assign the return value of draw would cause a diagnostic message to be issued.

The switch Statement

The **switch** and **case** statements help control complex conditional and branching operations. The **switch** statement transfers control to a statement within its body.

Syntax
selection-statement :
> **switch** (*expression*) *statement*

labeled-statement :
> **case** *constant-expression* **:** *statement*
> **default** **:** *statement*

Control passes to the statement whose **case** *constant-expression* matches the value of **switch** (*expression*). The **switch** statement can include any number of **case** instances, but no two case constants within the same **switch** statement can have the same value. Execution of the statement body begins at the selected statement and proceeds until the end of the body or until a **break** statement transfers control out of the body.

Use of the **switch** statement usually looks something like this:

switch (*expression*)
{
> *declarations*
> .
> .
> .
> **case** *constant-expression* **:**

>   *statements executed if the expression equals the*
>   *value of this constant-expression*

.

.

.

break;
default :
>   *statements executed if expression does not equal*
>   *any case constant-expression*

}

You can use the **break** statement to end processing of a particular case within the **switch** statement and to branch to the end of the **switch** statement. Without **break**, the program continues to the next case, executing the statements until a **break** or the end of the statement is reached. In some situations, this continuation may be desirable.

The **default** statement is executed if no **case** *constant-expression* is equal to the value of **switch** (*expression*). If the **default** statement is omitted, and no **case** match is found, none of the statements in the **switch** body are executed. There can be at most one **default** statement. The **default** statement need not come at the end; it can appear anywhere in the body of the **switch** statement. In fact it is often more efficient if it appears at the beginning of the **switch** statement. A **case** or **default** label can only appear inside a **switch** statement.

The type of **switch** *expression* and **case** *constant-expression* must be integral. The value of each **case** *constant-expression* must be unique within the statement body.

The **case** and **default** labels of the **switch** statement body are significant only in the initial test that determines where execution starts in the statement body. Switch statements can be nested. Any static variables are initialized before executing into any **switch** statements.

Note Declarations can appear at the head of the compound statement forming the **switch** body, but initializations included in the declarations are not performed. The **switch** statement transfers control directly to an executable statement within the body, bypassing the lines that contain initializations.

The following examples illustrate **switch** statements:

```
switch( c )
{
    case 'A':
        capa++;
    case 'a':
        lettera++;
    default :
        total++;
}
```

All three statements of the **switch** body in this example are executed if c is equal to 'A' since a **break** statement does not appear before the following case. Execution control is transferred to the first statement (capa++;) and continues in order through the rest of the body. If c is equal to 'a', lettera and total are incremented. Only total is incremented if c is not equal to 'A' or 'a'.

```
switch( i )
{
   case -1:
      n++;
      break;
   case 0 :
      z++;
      break;
   case 1 :
      p++;
      break;
}
```

In this example, a **break** statement follows each statement of the **switch** body. The **break** statement forces an exit from the statement body after one statement is executed. If i is equal to –1, only n is incremented. The **break** following the statement n++; causes execution control to pass out of the statement body, bypassing the remaining statements. Similarly, if i is equal to 0, only z is incremented; if i is equal to 1, only p is incremented. The final **break** statement is not strictly necessary, since control passes out of the body at the end of the compound statement, but it is included for consistency.

A single statement can carry multiple **case** labels, as the following example shows:

```
case 'a' :
case 'b' :
case 'c' :
case 'd' :
case 'e' :
case 'f' :  hexcvt(c);
```

In this example, if *constant-expression* equals any letter between 'a' and 'f', the hexcvt function is called.

Microsoft Specific →

Microsoft C does not limit the number of case values in a **switch** statement. The number is limited only by the available memory. ANSI C requires at least 257 case labels be allowed in a **switch** statement.

The default for Microsoft C is that the Microsoft extensions are enabled. Use the /Za compiler option to disable these extensions.

END Microsoft Specific

The try-except Statement

Microsoft Specific →

The **try-except** statement is a Microsoft extension to the C language that enables applications to gain control of a program when events that normally terminate execution occur. Such events are called exceptions, and the mechanism that deals with exceptions is called structured exception handling.

Exceptions can be either hardware- or software-based. Even when applications cannot completely recover from hardware or software exceptions, structured exception handling makes it possible to display error information and trap the internal state of the application to help diagnose the problem. This is especially useful for intermittent problems that cannot be reproduced easily.

Syntax

try-except-statement :
    __**try** *compound-statement*
    __**except** (*expression*) *compound-statement*

The compound statement after the __**try** clause is the guarded section. The compound statement after the __**except** clause is the exception handler. The handler specifies a set of actions to be taken if an exception is raised during execution of the guarded section. Execution proceeds as follows:

1. The guarded section is executed.

2. If no exception occurs during execution of the guarded section, execution continues at the statement after the __**except** clause.

3. If an exception occurs during execution of the guarded section or in any routine the guarded section calls, the__**except** expression is evaluated and the value returned determines how the exception is handled. There are three values:

   EXCEPTION_CONTINUE_SEARCH Exception is not recognized. Continue to search up the stack for a handler, first for containing **try-except** statements, then for handlers with the next highest precedence.

   EXCEPTION_CONTINUE_EXECUTION Exception is recognized but dismissed. Continue execution at the point where the exception occurred.

   EXCEPTION_EXECUTE_HANDLER Exception is recognized. Transfer control to the exception handler by executing the __**except** compound statement, then continue execution at the point the exception occurred.

Because the __**except** expression is evaluated as a C expression, it is limited to a single value, the conditional-expression operator, or the comma operator. If more extensive processing is required, the expression can call a routine that returns one of the three values listed above.

Note Structured exception handling works with C and C++ source files. However, it is not specifically designed for C++. You can ensure that your code is more portable by using C++ exception handling. Also, the C++ exception handling mechanism is much more flexible, in that it can handle exceptions of any type.

For C++ programs, C++ exception handling should be used instead of structured exception handling. For more information, see "Exception Handling" in the *C++ Language Reference*.

Each routine in an application can have its own exception handler. The **__except** expression executes in the scope of the **__try** body. This means it has access to any local variables declared there.

The **__leave** keyword is valid within a **try-except** statement block. The effect of **__leave** is to jump to the end of the **try-except** block. Execution resumes after the end of the exception handler. Although a **goto** statement can be used to accomplish the same result, a **goto** statement causes stack unwinding. The **__leave** statement is more efficient because it does not involve stack unwinding.

Exiting a **try-except** statement using the **longjmp** run-time function is considered abnormal termination. It is illegal to jump into a **__try** statement, but legal to jump out of one. The exception handler is not called if a process is killed in the middle of executing a **try-except** statement.

Example

Following is an example of an exception handler and a termination handler. See "The try-finally Statement" on page 150 for more information about termination handlers.

```
.
.
.
puts("hello");
__try{
   puts("in try");
   __try{
      puts("in try");
      RAISE_AN_EXCEPTION();
   }__finally{
      puts("in finally");
   }
}__except( puts("in filter"), EXCEPTION_EXECUTE_HANDLER ){
   puts("in except");
}
puts("world");
```

This is the output from the example, with commentary added on the right:

```
hello
in try          /* fall into try                          */
in try          /* fall into nested try                   */
in filter       /* execute filter; returns 1 so accept    */
in finally      /* unwind nested finally                  */
in except       /* transfer control to selected handler   */
world           /* flow out of handler                    */
```

END Microsoft Specific

The try-finally Statement

Microsoft Specific →

The **try-finally** statement is a Microsoft extension to the C language that enables applications to guarantee execution of cleanup code when execution of a block of code is interrupted. Cleanup consists of such tasks as deallocating memory, closing files, and releasing file handles. The **try-finally** statement is especially useful for routines that have several places where a check is made for an error that could cause premature return from the routine.

Syntax

try-finally-statement :

    __**try** *compound-statement*
    __**finally** *compound-statement*

The compound statement after the __**try** clause is the guarded section. The compound statement after the __**finally** clause is the termination handler. The handler specifies a set of actions that execute when the guarded section is exited, whether the guarded section is exited by an exception (abnormal termination) or by standard fall through (normal termination).

Control reaches a __**try** statement by simple sequential execution (fall through). When control enters the __**try** statement, its associated handler becomes active. Execution proceeds as follows:

1. The guarded section is executed.

2. The termination handler is invoked.

3. When the termination handler completes, execution continues after the __**finally** statement. Regardless of how the guarded section ends (for example, via a **goto** statement out of the guarded body or via a **return** statement), the termination handler is executed before the flow of control moves out of the guarded section.

The __leave keyword is valid within a **try-finally** statement block. The effect of __leave is to jump to the end of the **try-finally** block. The termination handler is immediately executed. Although a **goto** statement can be used to accomplish the same result, a **goto** statement causes stack unwinding. The __leave statement is more efficient because it does not involve stack unwinding.

Exiting a **try-finally** statement using a **return** statement or the **longjmp** run-time function is considered abnormal termination. It is illegal to jump into a __try statement, but legal to jump out of one. All __finally statements that are active between the point of departure and the destination must be run. This is called a "local unwind."

The termination handler is not called if a process is killed while executing a **try-finally** statement.

Note   Structured exception handling works with C and C++ source files. However, it is not specifically designed for C++. You can ensure that your code is more portable by using C++ exception handling. Also, the C++ exception handling mechanism is much more flexible, in that it can handle exceptions of any type.

For C++ programs, C++ exception handling should be used instead of structured exception handling. For more information, see "Exception Handling" in the *C++ Language Reference*.

See the example for the "try-except statement" on page 149 to see how the **try-finally** statement works.

END Microsoft Specific

The while Statement

The **while** statement lets you repeat a statement until a specified expression becomes false.

Syntax

iteration-statement :
    while (*expression*) *statement*

The *expression* must have arithmetic or pointer type. Execution proceeds as follows:

1. The *expression* is evaluated.

2. If *expression* is initially false, the body of the **while** statement is never executed, and control passes from the **while** statement to the next statement in the program.

    If *expression* is true (nonzero), the body of the statement is executed and the process is repeated beginning at step 1.

The **while** statement can also terminate when a **break, goto,** or **return** within the statement body is executed. Use the **continue** statement to terminate an iteration without exiting the **while** loop. The **continue** statement passes control to the next iteration of the **while** statement.

This is an example of the **while** statement:

```
while ( i >= 0 )
{
    string1[i] = string2[i];
    i--;
}
```

This example copies characters from string2 to string1. If i is greater than or equal to 0, string2[i] is assigned to string1[i] and i is decremented. When i reaches or falls below 0, execution of the **while** statement terminates.

CHAPTER 6

Functions

The function is the fundamental modular unit in C. A function is usually designed to perform a specific task, and its name often reflects that task. A function contains declarations and statements. This chapter describes how to declare, define, and call C functions. Other topics discussed are:

- Overview of functions
- Function attributes
- Specifying calling conventions
- Inline functions
- DLL export and import functions
- Naked functions
- Storage class
- Return type
- Arguments
- Parameters

Overview of Functions

Functions must have a definition and should have a declaration, although a definition can serve as a declaration if the declaration appears before the function is called. The function definition includes the function body—the code that executes when the function is called.

A function declaration establishes the name, return type, and attributes of a function that is defined elsewhere in the program. A function declaration must precede the call to the function. This is why the header files containing the declarations for the run-time functions are included in your code before a call to a run-time function. If the declaration has information about the types and number of parameters, the declaration is a prototype. See "Function Prototypes" on page 169 for more information.

The compiler uses the prototype to compare the types of arguments in subsequent calls to the function with the function's parameters and to convert the types of the arguments to the types of the parameters whenever necessary.

A function call passes execution control from the calling function to the called function. The arguments, if any, are passed by value to the called function. Execution of a **return** statement in the called function returns control and possibly a value to the calling function.

Obsolete Forms of Function Declarations and Definitions

The old-style function declarations and definitions use slightly different rules for declaring parameters than the syntax recommended by the ANSI C standard. First, the old-style declarations don't have a parameter list. Second, in the function definition, the parameters are listed, but their types are not declared in the parameter list. The type declarations precede the compound statement constituting the function body. The old-style syntax is obsolete and should not be used in new code. Code using the old-style syntax is still supported, however. This example illustrates the obsolete forms of declarations and definitions:

```
double old_style();          /* Obsolete function declaration */

double alt_style( a , real ) /* Obsolete function definition */
    double *real;
    int a;
{
    return ( *real + a ) ;
}
```

Functions returning an integer or pointer with the same size as an **int** are not required to have a declaration although the declaration is recommended.

To comply with the ANSI C standard, old-style function declarations using an ellipsis now generate an error when compiling with the /Za option and a level 4 warning when compiling with /Ze. For example:

```
void funct1( a, ... )        /* Generates a warning under /Ze or */
int a;                       /* an error when compiling with /Za */
{
}
```

You should rewrite this declaration as a prototype:

```
void funct1( int a, ... )
{
}
```

Old-style function declarations also generate warnings if you subsequently declare or define the same function with either an ellipsis or a parameter with a type that is not the same as its promoted type.

The next section, "Function Definitions," shows the syntax for function definitions, including the old-style syntax. The nonterminal for the list of parameters in the old-style syntax is *identifier-list*.

Function Definitions

A function definition specifies the name of the function, the types and number of parameters it expects to receive, and its return type. A function definition also includes a function body with the declarations of its local variables, and the statements that determine what the function does.

Syntax

translation-unit :
> *external-declaration*
> *translation-unit external-declaration*

external-declaration :   /* Allowed only at external (file) scope */
> *function-definition*
> *declaration*

function-definition :   /* Declarator here is the function declarator */
> *declaration-specifiers*$_{opt}$ *attribute-seq*$_{opt}$ *declarator declaration-list*$_{opt}$
> *compound-statement*   /* *attribute-seq* is Microsoft Specific */

Prototype parameters are:

declaration-specifiers :
> *storage-class-specifier declaration-specifiers* $_{opt}$
> *type-specifier declaration-specifiers* $_{opt}$
> *type-qualifier declaration-specifiers* $_{opt}$

declaration-list
> *declaration*
> *declaration-list declaration*

declarator
> *pointer* $_{opt}$ *direct-declarator*

direct-declarator :   /* A function declarator */
> *direct-declarator* (*parameter-type-list*)   /* New-style declarator */
> *direct-declarator* (*identifier-list* $_{opt}$)   /* Obsolete-style declarator */

The parameter list in a definition uses this syntax:

parameter-type-list :   /* The parameter list */
> *parameter-list*
> *parameter-list* , ...

parameter-list :
      parameter-declaration
      parameter-list **,** *parameter-declaration*

parameter-declaration :
      declaration-specifiers declarator
      declaration-specifiers abstract-declarator opt

The parameter list in an old-style function definition uses this syntax:

identifier-list: /* Used in obsolete-style function definitions and declarations */
      identifier
      identifier-list **,** *identifier*

The syntax for the function body is:

compound-statement :   /* The function body */
      { *declaration-list* opt *statement-list* opt }

The only storage-class specifiers that can modify a function declaration are **extern** and **static**. The **extern** specifier signifies that the function can be referenced from other files; that is, the function name is exported to the linker. The **static** specifier signifies that the function cannot be referenced from other files; that is, the name is not exported by the linker. If no storage class appears in a function definition, **extern** is assumed. In any case, the function is always visible from the definition point to the end of the file.

The optional *declaration-specifiers* and mandatory *declarator* together specify the function's return type and name. The *declarator* is a combination of the identifier that names the function and the parentheses following the function name. The optional *attribute-seq* nonterminal is a Microsoft-specific feature defined in "Function Attributes" on page 157.

The *direct-declarator* (in the *declarator* syntax) specifies the name of the function being defined and the identifiers of its parameters. If the *direct-declarator* includes a *parameter-type-list*, the list specifies the types of all the parameters. Such a declarator also serves as a function prototype for later calls to the function.

A *declaration* in the *declaration-list* in function definitions cannot contain a *storage-class-specifier* other than **register**. The *type-specifier* in the *declaration-specifiers* syntax can be omitted only if the **register** storage class is specified for a value of **int** type.

The *compound-statement* is the function body containing local variable declarations, references to externally declared items, and statements.

The sections "Function Attributes," "Storage Class," "Return Type," "Parameters," and "Function Body" on pages 157 through 169 describe the components of the function definition in detail.

Function Attributes

Microsoft Specific →

The optional *attribute-seq* nonterminal allows you to select a calling convention on a per-function basis. You can also specify functions as **__fastcall** or **__inline**.

END Microsoft Specific

Specifying Calling Conventions

Microsoft Specific →

For information on calling conventions, see "Calling Conventions Topics" in *Visual C++ Programmer's Guide* online.

END Microsoft Specific

Inline Functions

Microsoft Specific →

The **__inline** keyword tells the compiler to substitute the code within the function definition for every instance of a function call. However, substitution occurs only at the compiler's discretion. For example, the compiler does not inline a function if its address is taken or if it is too large to inline.

For a function to be considered as a candidate for inlining, it must use the new-style function definition.

Use this form to specify an inline function:

__inline *type* opt *function-definition*;

The use of inline functions generates faster code and can sometimes generate smaller code than the equivalent function call generates for the following reasons:

- It saves the time required to execute function calls.

- Small inline functions, perhaps three lines or less, create less code than the equivalent function call because the compiler doesn't generate code to handle arguments and a return value.

- Functions generated inline are subject to code optimizations not available to normal functions because the compiler does not perform interprocedural optimizations.

Functions using **__inline** should not be confused with inline assembler code. See "Inline Assembler" on page 158 for more information.

END Microsoft Specific

The Inline Assembler

The inline assembler lets you embed assembly-language instructions directly in your C source programs without extra assembly and link steps. The inline assembler is built into the compiler—you don't need a separate assembler such as the Microsoft Macro Assembler (MASM).

Because the inline assembler doesn't require separate assembly and link steps, it is more convenient than a separate assembler. Inline assembly code can use any C variable or function name that is in scope, so it is easy to integrate it with your program's C code. And because the assembly code can be mixed with C statements, it can do tasks that are cumbersome or impossible in C alone.

The **__asm** keyword invokes the inline assembler and can appear wherever a C statement is legal. It cannot appear by itself. It must be followed by an assembly instruction, a group of instructions enclosed in braces, or, at the very least, an empty pair of braces. The term "**__asm** block" here refers to any instruction or group of instructions, whether or not in braces.

The code below is a simple **__asm** block enclosed in braces. (The code is a custom function prolog sequence.)

```
__asm
{
    push ebp
    mov  ebp, esp
    sub  esp, __LOCAL_SIZE
}
```

Alternatively, you can put **__asm** in front of each assembly instruction:

```
__asm push ebp
__asm mov  ebp, esp
__asm sub  esp, __LOCAL_SIZE
```

Since the **__asm** keyword is a statement separator, you can also put assembly instructions on the same line:

```
__asm push ebp   __asm mov  ebp, esp   __asm sub  esp, __LOCAL_SIZE
```

DLL Import and Export Functions

The **dllimport** and **dllexport** storage-class modifiers are Microsoft-specific extensions to the C language. These modifiers explicitly define the DLL's interface to its client (the executable file or another DLL). Declaring functions as **dllexport** eliminates the need for a module-definition (.DEF) file. You can also use the **dllimport** and **dllexport** modifiers with data and objects.

The **dllimport** and **dllexport** storage-class modifiers must be used with the extended attribute syntax keyword, **__declspec**, as shown in this example:

```
#define DllImport __declspec( dllimport )
#define DllExport __declspec( dllexport )

DllExport void func();
DllExport int i = 10;
DllExport int j;
DllExport int n;
```

For specific information about the syntax for extended storage-class modifiers, see "Extended Storage-Class Attributes" on page 88 in Chapter 3.

END Microsoft Specific

Definitions and Declarations

Microsoft Specific →

The DLL interface refers to all items (functions and data) that are known to be exported by some program in the system; that is, all items that are declared as **dllimport** or **dllexport**. All declarations included in the DLL interface must specify either the **dllimport** or **dllexport** attribute. However, the definition can specify only the **dllexport** attribute. For example, the following function definition generates a compiler error:

```
#define DllImport __declspec( dllimport )
#define DllExport __declspec( dllexport )

DllImport int func()     /* Error: dllimport prohibited in */
                         /* definition. */
{
   return 1;
}
```

This code also generates an error:

```
#define DllImport __declspec( dllimport )
#define DllExport __declspec( dllexport )

DllImport int i = 10;    /* Error; this is a definition. */
```

However, this is correct syntax:

```
#define DllImport __declspec( dllimport )
#define DllExport __declspec( dllexport )

DllExport int i = 10;    /* Okay: this is an export definition. */
```

The use of **dllexport** implies a definition, while **dllimport** implies a declaration. You must use the **extern** keyword with **dllexport** to force a declaration; otherwise, a definition is implied.

```
#define DllImport __declspec( dllimport )
#define DllExport __declspec( dllexport )

extern DllImport int k;   /* These are correct and imply */
Dllimport int j;          /* a declaration. */
```

END Microsoft Specific

Defining Inline Functions with dllexport and dllimport

Microsoft Specific →

You can define as inline a function with the **dllexport** attribute. In this case, the function is always instantiated and exported, whether or not any module in the program references the function. The function is presumed to be imported by another program.

You can also define as inline a function declared with the **dllimport** attribute. In this case, the function can be expanded (subject to the /Ob (inline) compiler option specification) but never instantiated. In particular, if the address of an inline imported function is taken, the address of the function residing in the DLL is returned. This behavior is the same as taking the address of a non-inline imported function.

Static local data and strings in inline functions maintain the same identities between the DLL and client as they would in a single program (that is, an executable file without a DLL interface).

Exercise care when providing imported inline functions. For example, if you update the DLL, don't assume that the client will use the changed version of the DLL. To ensure that you are loading the proper version of the DLL, rebuild the DLL's client as well.

END Microsoft Specific

Rules and Limitations for dllimport/dllexport

Microsoft Specific →

- If you declare a function without the **dllimport** or **dllexport** attribute, the function is not considered part of the DLL interface. Therefore, the definition of the function must be present in that module or in another module of the same program. To make the function part of the DLL interface, you must declare the definition of the function in the other module as **dllexport**. Otherwise, a linker error is generated when the client is built.

- If a single module in your program contains **dllimport** and **dllexport** declarations for the same function, the **dllexport** attribute takes precedence over the **dllimport** attribute. However, a compiler warning is generated. For example:

```
#define DllImport __declspec( dllimport )
#define DllExport __declspec( dllexport )

    DllImport void func1( void );
    DllExport void func1( void );   /* Warning; dllexport */
                                    /* takes precedence. */
```

- You cannot initialize a static function pointer with the address of a function declared with the **dllimport** attribute, or initialize a static data pointer with the address of a data object declared with the **dllimport** attribute. For example, the following code generates errors:

```
#define DllImport __declspec( dllimport )
#define DllExport __declspec( dllexport )

    DllImport void func1( void );
    DllImport int i;
    .
    .
    .
    int *pi = &i;                              /* Error */
    static void ( *pf )( void ) = &func1;      /* Error */

    void func2()
    {
        static int *pi = &i;                   /* Error */
        static void ( *pf )( void ) = &func1;  /* Error */
    }
```

However, because a program that includes the **dllexport** attribute in the declaration of an object must provide the definition for that object somewhere in the program, you can initialize a global or local static function pointer with the address of a **dllexport** function. Similarly, you can initialize a global or local static data pointer with the address of a **dllexport** data object. For example, the following code does not generate errors:

```
#define DllImport __declspec( dllimport )
#define DllExport __declspec( dllexport )

    DllImport void func1( void );
    DllImport int i;

    DllExport void func1( void );
    DllExport int i;
    .
    .
    .
    int *pi = &i;                              /* Okay */
    static void ( *pf )( void ) = &func1;      /* Okay */

    void func2()
    {
        static int                             /* Okay */
        static void ( *pf )( void ) = &func1;  /* Okay */
    }
```

END Microsoft Specific

Naked Functions

Microsoft Specific →

The **naked** storage-class attribute is a Microsoft-specific extension to the C language. For functions declared with the **naked** storage-class attribute, the compiler generates code without prolog and epilog code. You can use this feature to write your own prolog/epilog code sequences using inline assembler code. Naked functions are particularly useful in writing virtual device drivers.

Because the **naked** attribute is only relevant to the definition of a function and is not a type modifier, naked functions use the extended attribute syntax, described in "Extended Storage-Class Attributes" on page 88 in Chapter 3.

The following example defines a function with the **naked** attribute:

```
__declspec( naked ) int func( formal_parameters )
{
   /* Function body */
}
```

Or, alternatively:

```
#define Naked   __declspec( naked )

Naked int func( formal_parameters )
{
   /* Function body */
}
```

The **naked** attribute affects only the nature of the compiler's code generation for the function's prolog and epilog sequences. It does not affect the code that is generated for calling such functions. Thus, the **naked** attribute is not considered part of the function's type, and function pointers cannot have the **naked** attribute. Furthermore, the **naked** attribute cannot be applied to a data definition. For example, the following code generates errors:

```
__declspec( naked ) int i;    /* Error--naked attribute not */
                              /* permitted on data declarations. */
```

The **naked** attribute is relevant only to the definition of the function and cannot be specified in the function's prototype. The following declaration generates a compiler error:

```
__declspec( naked ) int func(); /* Error--naked attribute not */
                               /* permitted on function declarations. */
```

END Microsoft Specific

Rules and Limitations for Using Naked Functions

Microsoft Specific →

- The **return** statement is not permitted in a naked function. However, you can return an **int** by moving the return value into the EAX register before the **RET** instruction.

- Structured exception handling constructs are not permitted in a naked function, because the constructs must unwind across the stack frame.

- The **setjmp** run-time function is not permitted in a naked function, because it too must unwind across the stack frame. However, the **longjmp** run-time function is permitted.

- The **_alloca** function is not permitted in a naked function.

- To ensure that no initialization code for local variables appears before the prolog sequence, initialized local variables are not permitted at function scope.

- Frame pointer optimization (the /Oy compiler option) is not recommended, but it is automatically suppressed for a naked function.

END Microsoft Specific

Considerations when Writing Prolog/Epilog Code

Microsoft Specific →

Before writing your own prolog and epilog code sequences, it is important to understand how the stack frame is laid out. It is also useful to know how to use the **__LOCAL_SIZE** predefined constant.

Stack Frame Layout

This example shows the standard prolog code that might appear in a 32-bit function:

```
push    ebp              ; Save ebp
mov     ebp, esp         ; Set stack frame pointer
sub     esp, localbytes  ; Allocate space for locals
push    <registers>      ; Save registers
```

The localbytes variable represents the number of bytes needed on the stack for local variables, and the registers variable is a placeholder that represents the list of registers to be saved on the stack. After pushing the registers, you can place any other appropriate data on the stack. The following is the corresponding epilog code:

```
pop     <registers>      ; Restore registers
mov     esp, ebp         ; Restore stack pointer
pop     ebp              ; Restore ebp
ret                      ; Return from function
```

The stack always grows down (from high to low memory addresses). The base pointer (ebp) points to the pushed value of ebp. The local variables area begins at ebp-2. To access local variables, calculate an offset from ebp by subtracting the appropriate value from ebp.

The __LOCAL_SIZE Constant

The compiler provides a constant, **__LOCAL_SIZE**, for use in the inline assembler block of function prolog code. This constant is used to allocate space for local variables on the stack frame in custom prolog code.

The compiler determines the value of **__LOCAL_SIZE**. The value is the total number of bytes of all user-defined local variables and compiler-generated temporary variables. **__LOCAL_SIZE** can be used only as an immediate operand; it cannot be used in an expression. You must not change or redefine the value of this constant. For example:

```
mov   eax, __LOCAL_SIZE        ;Immediate operand--Okay
mov   eax, [ebp - __LOCAL_SIZE]  ;Error
```

The following example of a naked function containing custom prolog and epilog sequences uses **__LOCAL_SIZE** in the prolog sequence:

```
__declspec ( naked ) func()
{
   int i;
   int j;

   __asm    /* prolog */
     {
     push  ebp
     mov   ebp, esp
     sub   esp, __LOCAL_SIZE
     }

   /* Function body */

   __asm    /* epilog */
     {
     mov   esp, ebp
     pop   ebp
     ret
     }
}
```

END Microsoft Specific

Storage Class

The storage-class specifier in a function definition gives the function either **extern** or **static** storage class.

Syntax

function-definition :
    declaration-specifiers opt *attribute-seq* opt *declarator declaration-list* opt
        compound-statement /* *attribute-seq* is Microsoft Specific */

declaration-specifiers :
  storage-class-specifier declaration-specifiers opt
  type-specifier declaration-specifiers opt
  type-qualifier declaration-specifiers opt

storage-class-specifier :   /* For function definitions */
  extern
  static

If a function definition does not include a *storage-class-specifier*, the storage class defaults to **extern**. You can explicitly declare a function as **extern**, but it is not required.

If the declaration of a function contains the *storage-class-specifier* **extern**, the identifier has the same linkage as any visible declaration of the identifier with file scope. If there is no visible declaration with file scope, the identifier has external linkage. If an identifier has file scope and no *storage-class-specifier*, the identifier has external linkage. External linkage means that each instance of the identifier denotes the same object or function. See "Lifetime, Scope, Visibility, and Linkage" on page 32 in Chapter 2 for more information about linkage and file scope.

Block-scope function declarations with a storage-class specifier other than **extern** generate errors.

A function with **static** storage class is visible only in the source file in which it is defined. All other functions, whether they are given **extern** storage class explicitly or implicitly, are visible throughout all source files in the program. If **static** storage class is desired, it must be declared on the first occurrence of a declaration (if any) of the function, and on the definition of the function.

Microsoft Specific →

When the Microsoft extensions are enabled, a function originally declared without a storage class (or with **extern** storage class) is given **static** storage class if the function definition is in the same source file and if the definition explicitly specifies **static** storage class.

When compiling with the /Ze compiler option, functions declared within a block using the **extern** keyword have global visibility. This is not true when compiling with /Za. This feature should not be relied upon if portability of source code is a consideration.

END Microsoft Specific

Return Type

The return type of a function establishes the size and type of the value returned by the function and corresponds to the type-specifier in the syntax below:

Syntax

function-definition :
    declaration-specifiers opt *attribute-seq* opt *declarator declaration-list* opt
        compound-statement /* *attribute-seq* is Microsoft Specific */

declaration-specifiers :
    storage-class-specifier declaration-specifiers opt
    type-specifier declaration-specifiers opt
    type-qualifier declaration-specifiers opt

type-specifier :
    void
    char
    short
    int
    long
    float
    double
    signed
    unsigned
    struct-or-union-specifier
    enum-specifier
    typedef-name

The *type-specifier* can specify any fundamental, structure, or union type. If you do not include *type-specifier*, the return type **int** is assumed.

The return type given in the function definition must match the return type in declarations of the function elsewhere in the program. A function returns a value when a **return** statement containing an expression is executed. The expression is evaluated, converted to the return value type if necessary, and returned to the point at which the function was called. If a function is declared with return type **void**, a return statement containing an expression generates a warning and the expression is not evaluated.

The following examples illustrate function return values.

```
typedef struct
{
    char name[20];
    int id;
    long class;
} STUDENT;
```

```
/* Return type is STUDENT: */

STUDENT sortstu( STUDENT a, STUDENT b )
{
    return ( (a.id < b.id) ? a : b );
}
```

This example defines the STUDENT type with a **typedef** declaration and defines the function sortstu to have STUDENT return type. The function selects and returns one of its two structure arguments. In subsequent calls to the function, the compiler checks to make sure the argument types are STUDENT.

Note   Efficiency would be enhanced by passing pointers to the structure, rather than the entire structure.

```
char *smallstr( char s1[], char s2[] )
{
    int i;

    i = 0;
    while ( s1[i] != '\0' && s2[i] != '\0' )
        i++;
    if ( s1[i] == '\0' )
        return ( s1 );
    else
        return ( s2 );
}
```

This example defines a function returning a pointer to an array of characters. The function takes two character arrays (strings) as arguments and returns a pointer to the shorter of the two strings. A pointer to an array points to the first of the array elements and has its type; thus, the return type of the function is a pointer to type **char**.

You need not declare functions with **int** return type before you call them, although prototypes are recommended so that correct type checking for arguments and return values is enabled.

Parameters

Arguments are names of values passed to a function by a function call. Parameters are the values the function expects to receive. In a function prototype, the parentheses following the function name contain a complete list of the function's parameters and their types. Parameter declarations specify the types, sizes, and identifiers of values stored in the parameters.

Syntax

function-definition :
    declaration-specifiers ~opt~ *attribute-seq* ~opt~ *declarator declaration-list* ~opt~
        compound-statement   /* *attribute-seq* is Microsoft Specific */

declarator :
    pointer _{opt} *direct-declarator*

direct-declarator :   /* A function declarator */
    direct-declarator (*parameter-type-list*)   /* New-style declarator */

parameter-type-list :   /* A parameter list */
    parameter-list
    parameter-list , ...

parameter-list :
    parameter-declaration
    parameter-list , *parameter-declaration*

parameter-declaration :
    declaration-specifiers declarator
    declaration-specifiers abstract-declarator _{opt}

The *parameter-type-list* is a sequence of parameter declarations separated by commas. The form of each parameter in a parameter list looks like this:

[**register**] *type-specifier* [*declarator*]

Function parameters declared with the **auto** attribute generate errors. The identifiers of the parameters are used in the function body to refer to the values passed to the function. You can name the parameters in a prototype, but the names go out of scope at the end of the declaration. Therefore parameter names can be assigned the same way or differently in the function definition. These identifiers cannot be redefined in the outermost block of the function body, but they can be redefined in inner, nested blocks as though the parameter list were an enclosing block.

Each identifier in *parameter-type-list* must be preceded by its appropriate type specifier, as shown in this example:

```
void new( double x, double y, double z )
{
    /* Function body here */
}
```

If at least one parameter occurs in the parameter list, the list can end with a comma followed by three periods (, ...). This construction, called the "ellipsis notation," indicates a variable number of arguments to the function. (See "Calls with a Variable Number of Arguments" on page 175 for more information.) However, a call to the function must have at least as many arguments as there are parameters before the last comma.

If no arguments are to be passed to the function, the list of parameters is replaced by the keyword **void**. This use of **void** is distinct from its use as a type specifier.

The order and type of parameters, including any use of the ellipsis notation, must be the same in all the function declarations (if any) and in the function definition. The types of the arguments after usual arithmetic conversions must be assignment-compatible with the types of the corresponding parameters. (See "Usual Arithmetic Conversions" on page 102 in Chapter 4 for information on arithmetic conversions.) Arguments following the ellipsis are not checked. A parameter can have any fundamental, structure, union, pointer, or array type.

The compiler performs the usual arithmetic conversions independently on each parameter and on each argument, if necessary. After conversion, no parameter is shorter than an **int**, and no parameter has **float** type unless the parameter type is explicitly specified as **float** in the prototype. This means, for example, that declaring a parameter as a **char** has the same effect as declaring it as an **int**.

Function Body

A "function body" is a compound statement containing the statements that specify what the function does.

Syntax

function-definition :
    declaration-specifiers opt *attribute-seq* opt *declarator declaration-list* opt
        compound-statement   /* *attribute-seq* is Microsoft Specific */

compound-statement :   /* The function body */
    { *declaration-list* opt *statement-list* opt }

Variables declared in a function body, "local variables," have **auto** storage class unless otherwise specified. When the function is called, storage is created for the local variables and local initializations are performed. Execution control passes to the first statement in *compound-statement* and continues until a **return** statement is executed or the end of the function body is encountered. Control then returns to the point at which the function was called.

A **return** statement containing an expression must be executed if the function is to return a value. The return value of a function is undefined if no **return** statement is executed or if the **return** statement does not include an expression.

Function Prototypes

A function declaration precedes the function definition and specifies the name, return type, storage class, and other attributes of a function. To be a prototype, the function declaration must also establish types and identifiers for the function's arguments.

Syntax

declaration :
        declaration-specifiers attribute-seq opt *init-declarator-list* opt **;**
    /* *attribute-seq*opt is Microsoft Specific */

declaration-specifiers :
  storage-class-specifier declaration-specifiers _{opt}
  type-specifier declaration-specifiers _{opt}
  type-qualifier declaration-specifiers _{opt}

init-declarator-list :
  init-declarator
  init-declarator-list **,** *init-declarator*

init-declarator :
  declarator
  declarator = initializer

declarator :
  pointer _{opt} *direct-declarator*

direct-declarator :   /* A function declarator */
  direct-declarator (*parameter-type-list*)   /* New-style declarator */
  direct-declarator (*identifier-list* _{opt})   /* Obsolete-style declarator */

The prototype has the same form as the function definition, except that it is terminated by a semicolon immediately following the closing parenthesis and therefore has no body. In either case, the return type must agree with the return type specified in the function definition.

Function prototypes have the following important uses:

- They establish the return type for functions that return types other than **int**. Although functions that return **int** values do not require prototypes, prototypes are recommended.

- Without complete prototypes, standard conversions are made, but no attempt is made to check the type or number of arguments with the number of parameters.

- Prototypes are used to initialize pointers to functions before those functions are defined.

- The parameter list is used for checking the correspondence of arguments in the function call with the parameters in the function definition.

The converted type of each parameter determines the interpretation of the arguments that the function call places on the stack. A type mismatch between an argument and a parameter may cause the arguments on the stack to be misinterpreted. For example, on a 16-bit computer, if a 16-bit pointer is passed as an argument, then declared as a **long** parameter, the first 32 bits on the stack are interpreted as a **long** parameter. This error creates problems not only with the **long** parameter, but with any parameters that follow it. You can detect errors of this kind by declaring complete function prototypes for all functions.

A prototype establishes the attributes of a function so that calls to the function that precede its definition (or occur in other source files) can be checked for argument-type and return-type mismatches. For example, if you specify the **static** storage-class specifier in a prototype, you must also specify the **static** storage class in the function definition.

Complete parameter declarations (`int a`) can be mixed with abstract declarators (`int`) in the same declaration. For example, the following declaration is legal:

```
int add( int a, int );
```

The prototype can include both the type of, and an identifier for, each expression that is passed as an argument. However, such identifiers have scope only until the end of the declaration. The prototype can also reflect the fact that the number of arguments is variable, or that no arguments are passed. Without such a list, mismatches may not be revealed, so the compiler cannot generate diagnostic messages concerning them. See "Arguments" on page 173 for more information on type checking.

Prototype scope in the Microsoft C compiler is now ANSI-compliant when compiling with the /Za compiler option. This means that if you declare a **struct** or **union** tag within a prototype, the tag is entered at that scope rather than at global scope. For example, when compiling with /Za for ANSI compliance, you can never call this function without getting a type mismatch error:

```
void func1( struct S * );
```

To correct your code, define or declare the **struct** or **union** at global scope before the function prototype:

```
struct S;
void func1( struct S * );
```

Under /Ze, the tag is still entered at global scope.

Function Calls

A function call is an expression that passes control and arguments (if any) to a function and has the form

expression (*expression-list* opt)

where *expression* is a function name or evaluates to a function address and *expression-list* is a list of expressions (separated by commas). The values of these latter expressions are the arguments passed to the function. If the function does not return a value, then you declare it to be a function that returns **void**.

If a declaration exists before the function call, but no information is given concerning the parameters, any undeclared arguments simply undergo the usual arithmetic conversions.

Note The expressions in the function argument list can be evaluated in any order, so arguments whose values may be changed by side effects from another argument have undefined values. The sequence point defined by the function-call operator guarantees only that all side effects in the argument list are evaluated before control passes to the called function. (Note that the order in which arguments are pushed on the stack is a separate matter.) See "Sequence Points" on page 98 in Chapter 4 for more information.

The only requirement in any function call is that the expression before the parentheses must evaluate to a function address. This means that a function can be called through any function-pointer expression.

Example

This example illustrates function calls called from a **switch** statement:

```
void main()
{
    /* Function prototypes */

    long lift( int ), step( int ), drop( int );
    void work( int number, long (*function)(int i) );

    int select, count;
    .
    .
    .
    select = 1;
    switch( select )
    {
        case 1: work( count, lift );
                break;

        case 2: work( count, step );
                break;

        case 3: work( count, drop );
                /* Fall through to next case */
        default:
                break;
    }
}

/* Function definition */

void work( int number, long (*function)(int i) )
{
    int i;
    long j;

    for ( i = j = 0; i < number; i++ )
            j += ( *function )( i );
}
```

In this example, the function call in `main`,

```
work( count, lift );
```

passes an integer variable, `count`, and the address of the function `lift` to the function `work`. Note that the function address is passed simply by giving the function identifier, since a function identifier evaluates to a pointer expression. To use a function identifier in this way, the function must be declared or defined before the identifier is used; otherwise, the identifier is not recognized. In this case, a prototype for `work` is given at the beginning of the `main` function.

The parameter `function` in `work` is declared to be a pointer to a function taking one **int** argument and returning a **long** value. The parentheses around the parameter name are required; without them, the declaration would specify a function returning a pointer to a **long** value.

The function `work` calls the selected function from inside the **for** loop by using the following function call:

```
( *function )( i );
```

One argument, `i`, is passed to the called function.

Arguments

The arguments in a function call have this form:

expression (*expression-list* ₒₚₜ) /* Function call */

In a function call, *expression-list* is a list of expressions (separated by commas). The values of these latter expressions are the arguments passed to the function. If the function takes no arguments, *expression-list* should contain the keyword **void**.

An argument can be any value with fundamental, structure, union, or pointer type. All arguments are passed by value. This means a copy of the argument is assigned to the corresponding parameter. The function does not know the actual memory location of the argument passed. The function uses this copy without affecting the variable from which it was originally derived.

Although you cannot pass arrays or functions as arguments, you can pass pointers to these items. Pointers provide a way for a function to access a value by reference. Since a pointer to a variable holds the address of the variable, the function can use this address to access the value of the variable. Pointer arguments allow a function to access arrays and functions, even though arrays and functions cannot be passed as arguments.

The order in which arguments are evaluated can vary under different compilers and different optimization levels. However, the arguments and any side effects are completely evaluated before the function is entered. See "Side Effects" on page 97 in Chapter 4 for information on side effects.

The *expression-list* in a function call is evaluated and the usual arithmetic conversions are performed on each argument in the function call. If a prototype is available, the resulting argument type is compared to the prototype's corresponding parameter. If they do not match, either a conversion is performed, or a diagnostic message is issued. The parameters also undergo the usual arithmetic conversions.

The number of expressions in *expression-list* must match the number of parameters, unless the function's prototype or definition explicitly specifies a variable number of arguments. In this case, the compiler checks as many arguments as there are type names in the list of parameters and converts them, if necessary, as described above. See "Calls with a Variable Number of Arguments" on page 175 for more information.

If the prototype's parameter list contains only the keyword **void**, the compiler expects zero arguments in the function call and zero parameters in the definition. A diagnostic message is issued if it finds any arguments.

Example

This example uses pointers as arguments:

```
void main()
{
    /* Function prototype */

    void swap( int *num1, int *num2 );
    int x, y;
    .
    .
    .
    swap( &x, &y );  /* Function call */
}

/* Function definition */

void swap( int *num1, int *num2 )
{
    int t;

    t = *num1;
    *num1 = *num2;
    *num2 = t;
}
```

In this example, the swap function is declared in main to have two arguments, represented respectively by identifiers num1 and num2, both of which are pointers to **int** values. The parameters num1 and num2 in the prototype-style definition are also declared as pointers to **int** type values.

In the function call

```
swap( &x, &y )
```

the address of x is stored in num1 and the address of y is stored in num2. Now two names, or "aliases," exist for the same location. References to *num1 and *num2 in swap are effectively references to x and y in main. The assignments within swap actually exchange the contents of x and y. Therefore, no **return** statement is necessary.

The compiler performs type checking on the arguments to swap because the prototype of swap includes argument types for each parameter. The identifiers within the parentheses of the prototype and definition can be the same or different. What is important is that the types of the arguments match those of the parameter lists in both the prototype and the definition.

Calls with a Variable Number of Arguments

A partial parameter list can be terminated by the ellipsis notation, a comma followed by three periods (, ...), to indicate that there may be more arguments passed to the function, but no more information is given about them. Type checking is not performed on such arguments. At least one parameter must precede the ellipsis notation and the ellipsis notation must be the last token in the parameter list. Without the ellipsis notation, the behavior of a function is undefined if it receives parameters in addition to those declared in the parameter list.

To call a function with a variable number of arguments, simply specify any number of arguments in the function call. An example is the **printf** function from the C run-time library. The function call must include one argument for each type name declared in the parameter list or the list of argument types.

All the arguments specified in the function call are placed on the stack unless the __**fastcall** calling convention is specified. The number of parameters declared for the function determines how many of the arguments are taken from the stack and assigned to the parameters. You are responsible for retrieving any additional arguments from the stack and for determining how many arguments are present. The STDARGS.H file contains ANSI-style macros for accessing arguments of functions which take a variable number of arguments. Also, the XENIX®- style macros in VARARGS.H are still supported.

This sample declaration is for a function that calls a variable number of arguments:

```
int average( int first, ...);
```

Microsoft Specific →

To maintain compatibility with previous versions of Microsoft C, a Microsoft extension to the ANSI C standard allows a comma without trailing periods (,) at the end of the list of parameters to indicate a variable number of arguments. However, it is recommended that code be changed to incorporate the ellipsis notation.

END Microsoft Specific

Recursive Functions

Any function in a C program can be called recursively; that is, it can call itself. The number of recursive calls is limited to the size of the stack. See the "Stack Allocations" (/STACK) linker option in the *Visual C++ Programmer's Guide* online for information about linker options that set stack size. Each time the function is called, new storage is allocated for the parameters and for the **auto** and **register** variables so that their values in previous, unfinished calls are not overwritten. Parameters are only directly accessible to the instance of the function in which they are created. Previous parameters are not directly accessible to ensuing instances of the function.

Note that variables declared with **static** storage do not require new storage with each recursive call. Their storage exists for the lifetime of the program. Each reference to such a variable accesses the same storage area.

Example

This example illustrates recursive calls:

```
int factorial( int num );        /* Function prototype */

void main()
{
    int result, number;
    .
    .
    .
    result = factorial( number );
}

int factorial( int num )        /* Function definition */
{
    .
    .
    .
    if ( ( num > 0 ) || ( num <= 10 ) )
        return( num * factorial( num - 1 ) );
}
```

C Language Syntax Summary

This appendix gives the full description of the C language and the Microsoft-specific C language features. You can use the syntax notation in this appendix to determine the exact syntax for any language component. The explanation for the syntax appears in the section of this manual where a topic is discussed.

Note This syntax summary is not part of the ANSI C standard, but is included for information only. Microsoft-specific syntax is noted in comments following the syntax.

Definitions and Conventions

Terminals are endpoints in a syntax definition. No other resolution is possible. Terminals include the set of reserved words and user-defined identifiers.

Nonterminals are placeholders in the syntax and are defined elsewhere in this syntax summary. Definitions can be recursive.

An optional component is indicated by the subscripted $_{opt}$. For example,

{ *expression* $_{opt}$ }

indicates an optional expression enclosed in curly braces.

The syntax conventions use different font attributes for different components of the syntax. The symbols and fonts are as follows:

Attribute	Description
nonterminal	Italic type indicates nonterminals.
const	Terminals in bold type are literal reserved words and symbols that must be entered as shown. Characters in this context are always case sensitive.
$_{opt}$	Nonterminals followed by $_{opt}$ are always optional.
default typeface	Characters in the set described or listed in this typeface can be used as terminals in C statements.

A colon (:) following a nonterminal introduces its definition. Alternative definitions are listed on separate lines, except when prefaced with the words "one of."

Lexical Grammar

Tokens

token :
>*keyword*
>*identifier*
>*constant*
>*string-literal*
>*operator*
>*punctuator*

preprocessing-token :
>*header-name*
>*identifier*
>*pp-number*
>*character-constant*
>*string-literal*
>*operator*
>*punctuator*
>each nonwhite-space character that cannot be one of the above

header-name :
>*< path-spec >*
>*"path spec"*

path-spec :
>Legal file path

pp-number :
>*digit*
>*. digit*
>*pp-number digit*
>*pp-number nondigit*
>*pp-number* **e** *sign*
>*pp-number* **E** *sign*
>*pp-number* **.**

Keywords

keyword : one of

auto	**double**	**int**	**struct**
break	**else**	**long**	**switch**
case	**enum**	**register**	**typedef**
char	**extern**	**return**	**union**
const	**float**	**short**	**unsigned**
continue	**for**	**signed**	**void**
default	**goto**	**sizeof**	**volatile**
do	**if**	**static**	**while**

Identifiers

identifier :
>   *nondigit*
>   *identifier nondigit*
>   *identifier digit*

nondigit : one of
>   **_ a b c d e f g h i j k l m**
>   **n o p q r s t u v w x y z**
>   **A B C D E F G H I J K L M**
>   **N O P Q R S T U V W X Y Z**

digit : one of
>   **0 1 2 3 4 5 6 7 8 9**

Constants

constant :
>   *floating-point-constant*
>   *integer-constant*
> *enumeration-constant*
>   *character-constant*

floating-point-constant :
>   *fractional-constant exponent-part* $_{opt}$ *floating-suffix* $_{opt}$
>   *digit-sequence exponent-part floating-suffix* $_{opt}$

fractional-constant :
>   *digit-sequence* $_{opt}$ **.** *digit-sequence*
>   *digit-sequence* **.**

exponent-part :
>   **e** *sign* $_{opt}$ *digit-sequence*
>   **E** *sign* $_{opt}$ *digit-sequence*

sign : one of
   + −
digit-sequence :
   digit
   digit-sequence digit
floating-suffix : one of
   f l F L
integer-constant :
   decimal-constant integer-suffix _{opt}
   octal-constant integer-suffix _{opt}
   hexadecimal-constant integer-suffix _{opt}
decimal-constant :
   nonzero-digit
   decimal-constant digit
octal-constant :
   0
   octal-constant octal-digit
hexadecimal-constant :
   0x *hexadecimal-digit*
   0X *hexadecimal-digit*
   hexadecimal-constant hexadecimal-digit
nonzero-digit : one of
   1 2 3 4 5 6 7 8 9
octal-digit : one of
   0 1 2 3 4 5 6 7
hexadecimal-digit : one of
   0 1 2 3 4 5 6 7 8 9
   a b c d e f
   A B C D E F
unsigned-suffix : one of
   u U
long-suffix : one of
   l L
character-constant :
   '*c-char-sequence***'**
   L'*c-char-sequence***'**
integer-suffix :
   unsigned-suffix long-suffix _{opt}
   long-suffix unsigned-suffix _{opt}
c-char-sequence :
   c-char
   c-char-sequence c-char

c-char :

> Any member of the source character set except the single quotation mark ('),
>> backslash (\), or newline character
>
> *escape-sequence*

escape-sequence :

> *simple-escape-sequence*
> *octal-escape-sequence*
> *hexadecimal-escape-sequence*

simple-escape-sequence : one of

> **\a \b \f \n \r \t \v**
> **\' \" \\ \?**

octal-escape-sequence :

> \ *octal-digit*
> \ *octal-digit octal-digit*
> \ *octal-digit octal-digit octal-digit*

hexadecimal-escape-sequence :

> **\x** *hexadecimal-digit*
> *hexadecimal-escape-sequence hexadecimal-digit*

String Literals

string-literal :

> "*s-char-sequence* opt"
> **L**"*s-char-sequence* opt"

s-char-sequence :

> *s-char*
> *s-char-sequence s-char*

s-char :

> any member of the source character set except the double-quotation mark ("),
>> backslash (\), or newline character
>
> *escape-sequence*

Operators

operator : one of

> **[ ] ( ) . ->**
> **++ -- & * + - ~ ! sizeof**
> **/ % << >> < > <= >= == != ^ | && !!**
> **? :**
> **= *= /= %= += -= <<= >>= &= ^= |=**
> **, # ##**

assignment-operator : one of

> **= *= /= %= += -= <<= >>= &= ^= |=**

Punctuators

punctuator : one of
    [ ] ( ) { } * , : = ; ... #

Phrase Structure Grammar

Expressions

primary-expression :
    identifier
    constant
    string-literal
    (*expression*)

expression :
    assignment-expression
    expression , *assignment-expression*

constant-expression :
    conditional-expression

conditional-expression :
    logical-OR-expression
    logical-OR-expression **?** *expression* **:** *conditional-expression*

assignment-expression :
    conditional-expression
    unary-expression assignment-operator assignment-expression

postfix-expression :
    primary-expression
    postfix-expression [*expression*]
    postfix-expression (*argument-expression-list* opt)
    postfix-expression **.** *identifier*
    postfix-expression **–>** *identifier*
    postfix-expression **++**
    postfix-expression **– –**

argument-expression-list :
    assignment-expression
    argument-expression-list , *assignment-expression*

unary-expression :
>   *postfix-expression*
>   **++** *unary-expression*
>   **– –** *unary-expression*
>   *unary-operator cast-expression*
>   **sizeof** *unary-expression*
>   **sizeof** (*type-name*)

unary-operator : one of
>   **& * + – ~ !**

cast-expression :
>   *unary-expression*
>   (*type-name*) *cast-expression*

multiplicative-expression :
>   *cast-expression*
>   *multiplicative-expression* ***** *cast-expression*
>   *multiplicative-expression* **/** *cast-expression*
>   *multiplicative-expression* **%** *cast-expression*

additive-expression :
>   *multiplicative-expression*
>   *additive-expression* **+** *multiplicative-expression*
>   *additive-expression* **–** *multiplicative-expression*

shift-expression :
>   *additive-expression*
>   *shift-expression* **<<** *additive-expression*
>   *shift-expression* **>>** *additive-expression*

relational-expression :
>   *shift-expression*
>   *relational-expression* **<** *shift-expression*
>   *relational-expression* **>** *shift-expression*
>   *relational-expression* **<=** *shift-expression*
>   *relational-expression* **>=** *shift-expression*

equality-expression :
>   *relational-expression*
>   *equality-expression* **==** *relational-expression*
>   *equality-expression* **!=** *relational-expression*

AND-expression :
>   *equality-expression*
>   *AND-expression* **&** *equality-expression*

exclusive-OR-expression :
>   *AND-expression*
>   *exclusive-OR-expression* **^** *AND-expression*

inclusive-OR-expression :
>   *exclusive-OR-expression*
>   *inclusive-OR-expression* **|** *exclusive-OR-expression*

logical-AND-expression :
    inclusive-OR-expression
    logical-AND-expression **&&** *inclusive-OR-expression*
logical-OR-expression :
    logical-AND-expression
    logical-OR-expression **||** *logical-AND-expression*

Declarations

declaration :
    declaration-specifiers attribute-seq $_{opt}$ *init-declarator-list* $_{opt}$ **;**
                              /* *attribute-seq* is Microsoft Specific */

declaration-specifiers :
    storage-class-specifier declaration-specifiers $_{opt}$
    type-specifier declaration-specifiers $_{opt}$
    type-qualifier declaration-specifiers $_{opt}$
attribute-seq :   /* *attribute-seq* is Microsoft Specific */
    attribute attribute-seq $_{opt}$
    attribute : one of   /* Microsoft Specific */

__asm	**__fastcall**
__based	**__inline**
__cdecl	**__stdcall**

init-declarator-list :
    init-declarator
    init-declarator-list **,** *init-declarator*
init-declarator :
    declarator
    declarator **=** *initializer*   /* For scalar initialization */
storage-class-specifier :
    auto
    register
    static
    extern
    typedef
    __declspec (*extended-decl-modifier-seq*)   /* Microsoft Specific */
type-specifier :
    void
    char
    short
    int
    __int8   /* Microsoft Specific */
    __int16   /* Microsoft Specific */
    __int32   /* Microsoft Specific */
    __int64   /* Microsoft Specific */

      long
      float
      double
      signed
      unsigned
      struct-or-union-specifier
      enum-specifier
      typedef-name
type-qualifier :
      const
      volatile
declarator :
      pointer $_{opt}$ *direct-declarator*
direct-declarator :
      identifier
      (*declarator*)
      direct-declarator [*constant-expression* $_{opt}$]
      direct-declarator (*parameter-type-list*) /* New-style declarator */
      direct-declarator (*identifier-list* $_{opt}$)   /* Obsolete-style declarator */
pointer :
      * *type-qualifier-list* $_{opt}$
      * *type-qualifier-list* $_{opt}$ *pointer*
parameter-type-list :   /* The parameter list */
      parameter-list
      parameter-list , ...
parameter-list :
      parameter-declaration
      parameter-list , *parameter-declaration*
type-qualifier-list :
      type-qualifier
      type-qualifier-list type-qualifier
enum-specifier :
      enum *identifier* $_{opt}$ { *enumerator-list* }
      enum *identifier*
enumerator-list :
      enumerator
      enumerator-list , *enumerator*
enumerator :
      enumeration-constant
      enumeration-constant = *constant-expression*
enumeration-constant :
      identifier
struct-or-union-specifier :
      struct-or-union identifier $_{opt}$ { *struct-declaration-list* }
      struct-or-union identifier

struct-or-union :
> **struct**
> **union**

struct-declaration-list :
> *struct-declaration*
> *struct-declaration-list struct-declaration*

struct-declaration :
> *specifier-qualifier-list struct-declarator-list* **;**

specifier-qualifier-list :
> *type-specifier specifier-qualifier-list* $_{opt}$
> *type-qualifier specifier-qualifier-list* $_{opt}$

struct-declarator-list :
> *struct-declarator*
> *struct-declarator-list* **,** *struct-declarator*

struct-declarator :
> *declarator*
> *type-specifier declarator* $_{opt}$ **:** *constant-expression*

parameter-declaration :
> *declaration-specifiers declarato r*   /* Named declarator */
> *declaration-specifiers abstract-declarator* $_{opt}$ /* Anonymous declarator */

identifier-list :   /* For old-style declarator */
> *identifier*
> *identifier-list* **,** *identifier*

abstract-declarator :   /* Used with anonymous declarators */
> *pointer*
> *pointer* $_{opt}$ *direct-abstract-declarator*

direct-abstract-declarator :
> **(** *abstract-declarator* **)**
> *direct-abstract-declarator* $_{opt}$ **[** *constant-expression* $_{opt}$ **]**
> *direct-abstract-declarator* $_{opt}$ **(** *parameter-type-list* $_{opt}$ **)**

initializer :
> *assignment-expression*
> **{** *initializer-list* **}**   /* For aggregate initialization */
> **{** *initializer-list* **, }**

initializer-list :
> *initializer*
> *initializer-list* **,** *initializer*

type-name :
> *specifier-qualifier-list abstract-declarator* $_{opt}$

typedef-name :
> *identifier*

extended-decl-modifier-seq :   /* Microsoft Specific */
> *extended-decl-modifier* $_{opt}$
> *extended-decl-modifier-seq extended-decl-modifier*

extended-decl-modifier :   /* Microsoft Specific */
    thread
    naked
    dllimport
    dllexport

Statements

statement :
    labeled-statement
    compound-statement
    expression-statement
    selection-statement
    iteration-statement
    jump-statement
    try-except-statement   /* Microsoft Specific */
    try-finally-statement   /* Microsoft Specific */
jump-statement :
    goto *identifier* ;
    continue;
    break;
    return *expression* $_{opt}$;
compound-statement :
    { *declaration-list* $_{opt}$ *statement-list* $_{opt}$ }
declaration-list :
    declaration
    declaration-list declaration
statement-list :
    statement
    statement-list statement
expression-statement :
    expression $_{opt}$;
iteration-statement :
    while (*expression*) *statement*
    do *statement* **while** (*expression*);
    for (*expression* $_{opt}$; *expression* $_{opt}$; *expression* $_{opt}$) *statement*
selection-statement :
    if (*expression*) *statement*
    if (*expression*) *statement* **else** *statement*
    switch (*expression*) *statement*
labeled-statement :
    identifier **:** *statement*
    case *constant-expression* **:** *statement*
    default : *statement*

try-except-statement :   /* Microsoft Specific */
    __**try** *compound-statement*
    __**except** (*expression*) *compound-statement*
try-finally-statement :   /* Microsoft Specific */
    __**try** *compound-statement*
    __**finally** *compound-statement*

External Definitions

translation-unit :
    external-declaration
    translation-unit external-declaration
external-declaration :   /* Allowed only at external (file) scope */
    function-definition
    declaration
function-definition :   /* Declarator here is the function declarator */
    declaration-specifiers $_{opt}$ *declarator declaration-list* $_{opt}$ *compound-statement*

Implementation-Defined Behavior

ANSI X3.159-1989, *American National Standard for Information Systems–Programming Language–C*, contains an appendix called "Portability Issues." The ANSI appendix lists areas of the C language that ANSI leaves open to each particular implementation. This appendix describes how Microsoft C handles these implementation-defined areas of the C language.

This appendix follows the same order as the ANSI appendix. Each item covered includes references to the ANSI chapter and section that explains the implementation-defined behavior.

Note This appendix describes the U.S. English-language version of the C compiler only. Implementations of Microsoft C for other languages may differ slightly.

Translation: Diagnostics

ANSI 2.1.1.3 How a diagnostic is identified

Microsoft C produces error messages in the form:

filename(*line-number*) : *diagnostic* C*number message*

where *filename* is the name of the source file in which the error was encountered; *line-number* is the line number at which the compiler detected the error; *diagnostic* is either "error" or "warning"; *number* is a unique four-digit number (preceded by a **C**, as noted in the syntax) that identifies the error or warning; *message* is an explanatory message.

Environment

Arguments to main

ANSI 2.1.2.2.1 The semantics of the arguments to main

In Microsoft C, the function called at program startup is called **main**. There is no prototype declared for **main**, and it can be defined with zero, two, or three parameters:

```
int main( void )
int main( int argc, char *argv[] )
int main( int argc, char *argv[], char *envp[] )
```

The third line above, where **main** accepts three parameters, is a Microsoft extension to the ANSI C standard. The third parameter, **envp**, is an array of pointers to environment variables. The **envp** array is terminated by a null pointer. See "The main Function and Program Execution" on page 27 in Chapter 2 for more information about **main** and **envp**.

The variable **argc** never holds a negative value.

The array of strings ends with **argv[argc]**, which contains a null pointer.

All elements of the **argv** array are pointers to strings.

A program invoked with no command-line arguments will receive a value of one for **argc**, as the name of the executable file is placed in **argv[0]**. (In MS-DOS versions prior to 3.0, the executable-file name is not available. The letter "C" is placed in **argv[0]**.) Strings pointed to by **argv[1]** through **argv[argc – 1]** represent program parameters.

The parameters **argc** and **argv** are modifiable and retain their last-stored values between program startup and program termination.

Interactive Devices

ANSI 2.1.2.3 What constitutes an interactive device

Microsoft C defines the keyboard and the display as interactive devices.

Identifiers

Significant Characters Without External Linkage

ANSI 3.1.2 The number of significant characters without external linkage

Identifiers are significant to 247 characters. The compiler does not restrict the number of characters you can use in an identifier; it simply ignores any characters beyond the limit.

Significant Characters with External Linkage

ANSI 3.1.2 The number of significant characters with external linkage

Identifiers declared **extern** in programs compiled with Microsoft C are significant to 247 characters. You can modify this default to a smaller number using the /H (restrict length of external names) option.

Uppercase and Lowercase

ANSI 3.1.2 Whether case distinctions are significant

Microsoft C treats identifiers within a compilation unit as case sensitive.

The Microsoft linker is case sensitive. You must specify all identifiers consistently according to case.

Characters

The ASCII Character Set

ANSI 2.2.1 Members of source and execution character sets

The source character set is the set of legal characters that can appear in source files. For Microsoft C, the source character set is the standard ASCII character set.

Warning Because keyboard and console drivers can remap the character set, programs intended for international distribution should check the country code.

Multibyte Characters

ANSI 2.2.1.2 Shift states for multibyte characters

Multibyte characters are used by some implementations, including Microsoft C, to represent foreign-language characters not represented in the base character set. However, Microsoft C does not support any state-dependent encodings. Therefore, there are no shift states. See "Multibyte and Wide Characters" on page 7 in Chapter 1 for more information.

Bits per Character

ANSI 2.2.4.2.1 Number of bits in a character

The number of bits in a character is represented by the manifest constant **CHAR_BIT**. The LIMITS.H file defines **CHAR_BIT** as 8.

Character Sets

ANSI 3.1.3.4 Mapping members of the source character set

The source character set and execution character set include the ASCII characters listed in Table B.1. Escape sequences are also shown in the table.

Table B.1 Escape Sequences

Escape Sequence	Character	ASCII Value
\a	Alert/bell	7
\b	Backspace	8
\f	Formfeed	12
\n	Newline	10
\r	Carriage return	13
\t	Horizontal tab	9
\v	Vertical tab	11
\"	Double quotation	34
\'	Single quotation	39
\\	Backslash	92

Unrepresented Character Constants

ANSI 3.1.3.4 The value of an integer character constant that contains a character or escape sequence not represented in the basic execution character set or the extended character set for a wide character constant

All character constants or escape sequences can be represented in the extended character set.

Wide Characters

ANSI 3.1.3.4 The value of an integer character constant that contains more than one character or a wide character constant that contains more than one multibyte character

The regular character constant, "ab" has the integer value (int)0x6162. When there is more than one byte, previously read bytes are shifted left by the value of **CHAR_BIT** and the next byte is compared using the bitwise-OR operator with the low **CHAR_BIT** bits. The number of bytes in the multibyte character constant cannot exceed sizeof(int), which is 4 for 32-bit target code.

The multibyte character constant is read as above and this is converted to a wide-character constant using the **mbtowc** run-time function. If the result is not a valid wide-character constant, an error is issued. In any event, the number of bytes examined by the **mbtowc** function is limited to the value of **MB_CUR_MAX**.

Converting Multibyte Characters

ANSI 3.1.3.4 The current locale used to convert multibyte characters into corresponding wide characters (codes) for a wide character constant

The current locale is the "C" locale by default. It can be changed with the setlocale library routine. The **LC_CTYPE** category of the current locale sets the current working code page, which determines correspondence and conversion between the multibyte and wide-character sets. The **mbstowcs**, **wcstombs**, **mbtowc**, and **wctomb** library routines provide direct mappings between the multibyte and wide-character sets. Also, many of the stream routines, such as the print, scan, get, and put families, automatically provide mappings between these two character sets.

Range of char Values

ANSI 3.2.1.1 Whether a "plain" **char** has the same range of values as a **signed char** or an **unsigned char**

All signed character values range from −128 to 127. All unsigned character values range from 0 to 255.

The /J compiler option changes the default from **signed** to **unsigned**.

Integers

Range of Integer Values

ANSI 3.1.2.5 The representations and sets of values of the various types of integers

Integers contain 32 bits (four bytes). Signed integers are represented in two's-complement form. The most-significant bit holds the sign: 1 for negative, 0 for positive and zero. The values are listed below:

Type	Minimum and Maximum
unsigned short	0 to 65535
signed short	−32768 to 32767
unsigned long	0 to 4294967295
signed long	−2147483648 to 2147483647

Demotion of Integers

ANSI 3.2.1.2 The result of converting an integer to a shorter signed integer, or the result of converting an unsigned integer to a signed integer of equal length, if the value cannot be represented

When a **long** integer is cast to **a short**, or a **short** is cast to a **char**, the least-significant bytes are retained.

For example, this line

```
short x = (short)0x12345678L;
```

assigns the value 0x5678 to x, and this line

```
char y = (char)0x1234;
```

assigns the value 0x34 to y.

When signed variables are converted to unsigned and vice versa, the bit patterns remain the same. For example, casting −2 (0xFE) to an unsigned value yields 254 (also 0xFE).

Signed Bitwise Operations

ANSI 3.3 The results of bitwise operations on signed integers

Bitwise operations on signed integers work the same as bitwise operations on unsigned integers. For example, -16 & 99 can be expressed in binary as

```
  11111111 11110000
& 00000000 01100011
  ─────────────────
  00000000 01100000
```

The result of the bitwise AND is 96.

Remainders

ANSI 3.3.5   The sign of the remainder on integer division

The sign of the remainder is the same as the sign of the dividend. For example,

```
 50 / -6 == -8
 50 % -6 ==  2
-50 /  6 == -8
-50 %  6 == -2
```

Right Shifts

ANSI 3.3.7   The result of a right shift of a negative-value signed integral type

Shifting a negative value to the right yields half the absolute value, rounded down. For example, –253 (binary 11111111 00000011) shifted right one bit produces –127 (binary 11111111 10000001). A *positive* 253 shifts right to produce +126.

Right shifts preserve the sign bit. When a signed integer shifts right, the most-significant bit remains set. When an unsigned integer shifts right, the most-significant bit is cleared.

If 0xF000 is unsigned, the result is 0x7800.

If 0xF0000000 is signed, a right shift produces 0xF8000000. Shifting a positive number right 32 times produces 0xF0000000. Shifting a negative number right 32 times produces 0xFFFFFFFF.

Floating-Point Math

Values

ANSI 3.1.2.5   The representations and sets of values of the various types of floating-point numbers

The **float** type contains 32 bits: 1 for the sign, 8 for the exponent, and 23 for the mantissa. Its range is +/– 3.4E38 with at least 7 digits of precision.

The **double** type contains 64 bits: 1 for the sign, 11 for the exponent, and 52 for the mantissa. Its range is +/– 1.7E308 with at least 15 digits of precision.

The **long double** type contains 80 bits: 1 for the sign, 15 for the exponent, and 64 for the mantissa. Its range is +/– 1.2E4932 with at least 19 digits of precision. With the Microsoft C compiler, the representation of type **long double** is identical to type **double**.

Casting Integers to Floating-Point Values

ANSI 3.2.1.3 The direction of truncation when an integral number is converted to a floating-point number that cannot exactly represent the original value

When an integral number is cast to a floating-point value that cannot exactly represent the value, the value is rounded (up or down) to the nearest suitable value.

For example, casting an **unsigned long** (with 32 bits of precision) to a **float** (whose mantissa has 23 bits of precision) rounds the number to the nearest multiple of 256. The **long** values 4,294,966,913 to 4,294,967,167 are all rounded to the **float** value 4,294,967,040.

Truncation of Floating-Point Values

ANSI 3.2.1.4 The direction of truncation or rounding when a floating-point number is converted to a narrower floating-point number

When an underflow occurs, the value of a floating-point variable is rounded down to zero. An overflow may cause a run-time error or it may produce an unpredictable value, depending on the optimizations specified.

Arrays and Pointers

Largest Array Size

ANSI 3.3.3.4, 4.1.1 The type of integer required to hold the maximum size of an array—that is, the size of **size_t**

The **size_t** typedef is an **unsigned int** with the range 0x00000000 to 0x7CFFFFFF.

Pointer Subtraction

ANSI 3.3.6, 4.1.1 The type of integer required to hold the difference between two pointers to elements of the same array, **ptrdiff_t**

A **ptrdiff_t** is a **signed int** in the range –4,294,967,296 to 4,294,967,295.

Registers: Availability of Registers

ANSI 3.5.1 The extent to which objects can actually be placed in registers by use of the register storage-class specifier

The 32-bit compiler does not honor user requests for register variables. Instead, it makes it own choices when optimizing.

Structures, Unions, Enumerations, and Bit Fields

Improper Access to a Union

ANSI 3.3.2.3   A member of a union object is accessed using a member of a different type

If a union of two types is declared and one value is stored, but the union is accessed with the other type, the results are unreliable.

For example, a union of **float** and **int** is declared. A **float** value is stored, but the program later accesses the value as an **int**. In such a situation, the value would depend on the internal storage of **float** values. The integer value would not be reliable.

Padding and Alignment of Structure Members

ANSI 3.5.2.1   The padding and alignment of members of structures and whether a bit field can straddle a storage-unit boundary

Structure members are stored sequentially in the order in which they are declared: the first member has the lowest memory address and the last member the highest.

Every data object has an alignment-requirement. The alignment-requirement for all data except structures, unions, and arrays is either the size of the object or the current packing size (specified with either /Zp or the **pack** pragma, whichever is less). For structures, unions, and arrays, the alignment-requirement is the largest alignment-requirement of its members. Every object is allocated an offset so that

offset % alignment-requirement == 0

Adjacent bit fields are packed into the same 1-, 2-, or 4-byte allocation unit if the integral types are the same size and if the next bit field fits into the current allocation unit without crossing the boundary imposed by the common alignment requirements of the bit fields.

Sign of Bit Fields

ANSI 3.5.2.1   Whether a "plain" **int** field is treated as a **signed int** bit field or as an unsigned int bit field

Bit fields can be signed or unsigned. Plain bit fields are treated as signed.

Storage of Bit Fields

ANSI 3.5.2.1 The order of allocation of bit fields within an int

Bit fields are allocated within an integer from least-significant to most-significant bit. In the following code

```
struct mybitfields
{
    unsigned a : 4;
    unsigned b : 5;
    unsigned c : 7;
} test;

void main( void )
{
    test.a = 2;
    test.b = 31;
    test.c = 0;
}
```

the bits would be arranged as follows:

```
00000001 11110010
ccccccccb bbbbaaaa
```

Since the 80x86 processors store the low byte of integer values before the high byte, the integer 0x01F2 above would be stored in physical memory as 0xF2 followed by 0x01.

The enum type

ANSI 3.5.2.2 The integer type chosen to represent the values of an enumeration type

A variable declared as **enum** is an **int**.

Qualifiers: Access to Volatile Objects

ANSI 3.5.5.3 What constitutes an access to an object that has volatile-qualified type

Any reference to a volatile-qualified type is an access.

Declarators: Maximum number

ANSI 3.5.4 The maximum number of declarators that can modify an arithmetic, structure, or union type

Microsoft C does not limit the number of declarators. The number is limited only by available memory.

Statements: Limits on Switch Statements

ANSI 3.6.4.2   The maximum number of **case** values in a **switch** statement

Microsoft C does not limit the number of **case** values in a **switch** statement. The number is limited only by available memory.

Preprocessing Directives

Character Constants and Conditional Inclusion

ANSI 3.8.1   Whether the value of a single-character character constant in a constant expression that controls conditional inclusion matches the value of the same character constant in the execution character set. Whether such a character constant can have a negative value

The character set used in preprocessor statements is the same as the execution character set. The preprocessor recognizes negative character values.

Including Bracketed Filenames

ANSI 3.8.2   The method for locating includable source files

For file specifications enclosed in angle brackets, the preprocessor does not search directories of the parent files. A "parent" file is the file that has the **#include** directive in it. Instead, it begins by searching for the file in the directories specified on the compiler command line following /I. If the /I option is not present or fails, the preprocessor uses the INCLUDE environment variable to find any include files within angle brackets. The INCLUDE environment variable can contain multiple paths separated by semicolons (;). If more than one directory appears as part of the /I option or within the INCLUDE environment variable, the preprocessor searches them in the order in which they appear.

Including Quoted Filenames

ANSI 3.8.2   The support for quoted names for includable source files

If you specify a complete, unambiguous path specification for the include file between two sets of double quotation marks (" "), the preprocessor searches only that path specification and ignores the standard directories.

For include files specified as **#include** "path-spec", directory searching begins with the directories of the parent file, then proceeds through the directories of any grandparent files. Thus, searching begins relative to the directory containing the source file currently being processed. If there is no grandparent file and the file has not been found, the search continues as if the filename were enclosed in angle brackets.

Character Sequences

ANSI 3.8.2 The mapping of source file character sequences

Preprocessor statements use the same character set as source file statements with the exception that escape sequences are not supported.

Thus, to specify a path for an include file, use only one backslash:

```
#include "path1/path2/myfile"
```

Within source code, two backslashes are necessary:

```
fil = fopen( "path1\\path2\\myfile", "rt" );
```

Pragmas

ANSI 3.8.6 The behavior on each recognized #pragma directive

The following pragmas are defined for the Microsoft C compiler:

alloc_text	data_seg	include_alias	setlocale
auto_inline	function	intrinsic	warning
check_stack	hdrstop	message	
code_seg	inline_depth	optimize	
comment	inline_recursion	pack	

Default Date and Time

ANSI 3.8.8 The definitions for _DATE_ and _TIME_ when, respectively, the date and time of translation are not available

When the operating system does not provide the date and time of translation, the default values for _DATE_ and _TIME_ are May 03 1957 and 17:00:00".

Library Functions

NULL Macro

ANSI 4.1.5 The null pointer constant to which the macro NULL expands

Several include files define the NULL macro as ((void *)0).

Diagnostic Printed by the assert Function

ANSI 4.2 The diagnostic printed by and the termination behavior of the **assert** function

The **assert** function prints a diagnostic message and calls the **abort** routine if the expression is false (0). The diagnostic message has the form

Assertion failed: *expression*, **file** *filename*, **line** *linenumber*

where filename is the name of the source file and linenumber is the line number of the assertion that failed in the source file. No action is taken if expression is true (nonzero).

Character Testing

ANSI 4.3.1 The sets of characters tested for by the **isalnum**, **isalpha**, **iscntrl**, **islower**, **isprint**, and **isupper** functions

The following list describes these functions as they are implemented by the Microsoft C compiler.

Function	Tests For
isalnum	Characters 0–9, A–Z, a–z ASCII 48–57, 65–90, 97–122
isalpha	Characters A–Z, a–z ASCII 65–90, 97–122
iscntrl	ASCII 0–31, 127
islower	Characters a–z ASCII 97–122
isprint	Characters A–Z, a–z, 0–9, punctuation, space ASCII 32–126
isupper	Characters A–Z ASCII 65–90

Domain Errors

ANSI 4.5.1 The values returned by the mathematics functions on domain errors

The ERRNO.H file defines the domain error constant **EDOM** as 33.

Underflow of Floating-Point Values

ANSI 4.5.1 Whether the mathematics functions set the integer expression **errno** to the value of the macro **ERANGE** on underflow range errors

A floating-point underflow does not set the expression **errno** to **ERANGE**. When a value approaches zero and eventually underflows, the value is set to zero.

The fmod Function

ANSI 4.5.6.4 Whether a domain error occurs or zero is returned when the **fmod** function has a second argument of zero

When the **fmod** function has a second argument of zero, the function returns zero.

The signal Function

ANSI 4.7.1.1 The set of signals for the **signal** function

The first argument passed to **signal** must be one of the symbolic constants described in the *Run-Time Library Reference* for the **signal** function. The information in the *Run-Time Library Reference* also lists the operating mode support for each signal. The constants are also defined in SIGNAL.H.

Default Signals

ANSI 4.7.1.1 If the equivalent of **signal** (*sig*, **SIG_DFL**) is not executed prior to the call of a signal handler, the blocking of the signal that is performed

Signals are set to their default status when a program begins running.

Terminating Newline Characters

ANSI 4.9.2 Whether the last line of a text stream requires a terminating newline character

Stream functions recognize either new line or end of file as the terminating character for a line.

Blank Lines

ANSI 4.9.2 Whether space characters that are written out to a text stream immediately before a newline character appear when read in

Space characters are preserved.

Null Characters

ANSI 4.9.2 The number of null characters that can be appended to data written to a binary stream

Any number of null characters can be appended to a binary stream.

File Position in Append Mode

ANSI 4.9.3 Whether the file position indicator of an append mode stream is initially positioned at the beginning or end of the file

When a file is opened in append mode, the file-position indicator initially points to the end of the file.

Truncation of Text Files

ANSI 4.9.3 Whether a write on a text stream causes the associated file to be truncated beyond that point

Writing to a text stream does not truncate the file beyond that point.

File Buffering

ANSI 4.9.3 The characteristics of file buffering

Disk files accessed through standard I/O functions are fully buffered. By default, the buffer holds 512 bytes.

Zero-Length Files

ANSI 4.9.3 Whether a zero-length file actually exists

Files with a length of zero are permitted.

Filenames

ANSI 4.9.3 The rules for composing valid file names

A file specification can include an optional drive letter (always followed by a colon), a series of optional directory names (separated by backslashes), and a filename.

Filenames and directory names can contain up to eight characters followed by a period and a three-character extension. Case is ignored. The wildcards * and ? are not permitted within the name or extension.

File Access Limits

ANSI 4.9.3 Whether the same file can be open multiple times

Opening a file that is already open is not permitted.

Deleting Open Files

ANSI 4.9.4.1   The effect of the remove function on an open file

The remove function deletes a file, even if the file is open.

Renaming with a Name That Exists

ANSI 4.9.4.2   The effect if a file with the new name exists prior to a call to the **rename** function

If you attempt to rename a file using a name that exists, the **rename** function fails and returns an error code.

Reading Pointer Values

ANSI 4.9.6.2   The input for **%p** conversion in the **fscanf** function

When the **%p** format character is specified, the **fscanf** function converts pointers from hexadecimal ASCII values into the correct address.

Reading Ranges

ANSI 4.9.6.2   The interpretation of a dash (–) character that is neither the first nor the last character in the scanlist for % [conversion in the **fscanf** function

The following line

```
fscanf( fileptr, "%[A-Z]", strptr);
```

reads any number of characters in the range A–Z into the string to which `strptr` points.

File Position Errors

ANSI 4.9.9.1, 4.9.9.4   The value to which the macro **errno** is set by the **fgetpos** or **ftell** function on failure

When **fgetpos** or **ftell** fails, **errno** is set to the manifest constant **EINVAL** if the position is invalid or EBADF if the file number is bad. The constants are defined in ERRNO.H.

Messages Generated by the perror Function

ANSI 4.9.10.4   The messages generated by the **perror** function

The **perror** function generates these messages:

```
0   Error 0
1
2   No such file or directory
3
4
5
6
7   Arg list too long
8   Exec format error
9   Bad file number
10
11
12  Not enough core
13  Permission denied
14
15
16
17  File exists
18  Cross-device link
19
20
21
22  Invalid argument
23
24  Too many open files
25
26
27
28  No space left on device
29
30
31
32
33  Math argument
34  Result too large
35
36  Resource deadlock would occur
```

Allocating Zero Memory

ANSI 4.10.3   The behavior of the **calloc**, **malloc**, or **realloc** function if the size requested is zero

The **calloc**, **malloc**, and **realloc** functions accept zero as an argument. No actual memory is allocated, but a valid pointer is returned and the memory block can be modified later by realloc.

The abort Function

ANSI 4.10.4.1 The behavior of the **abort** function with regard to open and temporary files

The **abort** function does not close files that are open or temporary. It does not flush stream buffers.

The atexit Function

ANSI 4.10.4.3 The status returned by the **atexit** function if the value of the argument is other than zero, EXIT_SUCCESS, or EXIT_FAILURE

The **atexit** function returns zero if successful, or a nonzero value if unsuccessful.

Environment Names

ANSI 4.10.4.4 The set of environment names and the method for altering the environment list used by the **getenv** function

The set of environment names is unlimited.

To change environment variables from within a C program, call the **_putenv** function. To change environment variables from the command line in Windows 95 or Windows NT, use the SET command (for example, SET LIB = D:\ LIBS).

Environment variables set from within a C program exist only as long as their host copy of the operating system command shell is running (CMD.EXE in Windows NT and COMMAND.COM in Windows 95). For example, the line

```
system( SET LIB = D:\LIBS );
```

would run a copy of the Windows NT command shell (CMD.EXE), set the environment variable LIB, and return to the C program, exiting the secondary copy of CMD.EXE. Exiting that copy of CMD.EXE removes the temporary environment variable LIB.

This example also runs on the Windows 95 platform.

Likewise, changes made by the **_putenv** function last only until the program ends.

The system Function

ANSI 4.10.4.5 The contents and mode of execution of the string by the **system** function

The **system** function executes an internal operating system command, or an .EXE, .COM (.CMD in Windows NT) or .BAT file from within a C program rather than from the command line.

The system function finds the command interpreter, which is typically CMD.EXE in the Windows NT operating system or COMMAND.COM in Windows 95. The system function then passes the argument string to the command interpreter.

The strerror Function

ANSI 4.11.6.2   The contents of the error message strings returned by the **strerror** function

The **strerror** function generates these messages:

```
0     Error 0
1
2     No such file or directory
3
4
5
6
7     Arg list too long
8     Exec format error
9     Bad file number
10
11
12    Not enough core
13    Permission denied
14
15
16
17    File exists
18    Cross-device link
19
20
21
22    Invalid argument
23
24    Too many open files
25
26
27
28    No space left on device
29
30
31
32
33    Math argument
34    Result too large
35
36    Resource deadlock would occur
```

The Time Zone

ANSI 4.12.1   The local time zone and Daylight Savings Time

The local time zone is Pacific Standard Time. Microsoft C supports Daylight
Savings Time.

The clock Function

ANSI 4.12.2.1   The era for the **clock** function

The **clock** function's era begins (with a value of 0) when the C program starts
to execute. It returns times measured in 1/**CLOCKS_PER_SEC** (which equals
1/1000 for Microsoft C).

Index

Q

Contributors to *C Language Reference*

Richard Carlson, Index Editor

David Adam Edelstein, Art Director

Seth Manheim, Writer

Rod Wilkinson, Editor

WASSER*Studios*, Production

Quick.
Explain COM, OLE, and ActiveX.™

UNDERSTANDING

ActiveX
AND
OLE

A GUIDE FOR
DEVELOPERS &
MANAGERS

DAVID CHAPPELL

Microsoft Press

U.S.A.	**$22.95**
U.K.	£20.99
Canada	$30.95
ISBN 1-57231-216-5	

When it comes to strategic technologies like these, what decision makers need first is a good explanation—one that gives them a quick, clear understanding of the parts and the greater whole. And that's exactly what UNDERSTANDING ACTIVEX AND OLE does. Here you'll learn the strategic significance of the Component Object Model (COM) as the foundation for Microsoft's object technology. You'll understand the evolution of OLE. You'll discover the powerful ActiveX technology for the Internet. And in all these subjects and more, you'll gain a firm conceptual grounding without extraneous details or implementing specifics. UNDERSTANDING ACTIVEX AND OLE is also easy to browse, with colorful illustrations and "fast track" margin notes. Get it quick. And get up to speed on a fundamental business technology.

The *Strategic Technology* series is for executives, business planners, software designers, and technical managers who need a quick, comprehensive introduction to important technologies and their implications for business.

Microsoft ® Press

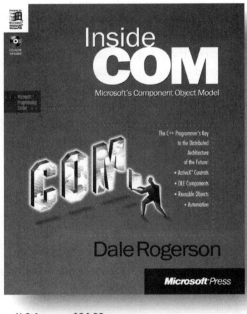

C++ Language Reference

Microsoft®
Visual C++®
Language Reference

Contents

Chapter 4   Expressions   65

Chapter 5   Statements   125

Contents

Chapter 9   Derived Classes   257

Appendixes

Appendix D   Charts   403

Index   411

Figures and Tables

Figures

Tables

Introduction

Scope of this Manual

C++, like C, is a language that is heavily reliant on a rich set of library functions to provide the following:

- Portable operating-system interface (file and screen I/O)
- String and buffer manipulation
- Floating-point math transformations
- Other supporting functionality

For information about the run-time library functions, see the *Run-Time Library Reference*. For information on the Microsoft Foundation classes or the iostream classes, see the *Class Library Reference* or the *iostream Class Library Reference*, respectively.

Organization

This manual is organized as follows:

Chapter 1, "Lexical Conventions," introduces the fundamental elements of a C++ program as they are meaningful to the compiler. These elements, called "lexical elements," are used to construct statements, definitions, declarations, and so on, which are used to construct complete programs.

Chapter 2, "Basic Concepts," explains concepts such as scope, linkage, program startup and termination, storage classes, and types. These concepts are key to understanding C++. Terminology used in this book is also introduced.

Chapter 3, "Standard Conversions," describes the type conversions the compiler performs between built-in, or "fundamental," types. It also explains how the compiler performs conversions among pointer, reference, and pointer-to-member types.

Chapter 4, "Expressions," describes C++ expressions—sequences of operators and operands that are used for computing values, designating objects or functions, or generating other side effects.

Chapter 5, "Statements," explains the C++ program elements that control how and in what order programs are executed. Among the statements covered are expression statements, null statements, compound statements, selection statements, iteration statements, jump statements, and declaration statements.

Chapter 6, "Declarations," is one of three chapters devoted to how complete declarations are used to form declaration statements. This chapter describes such topics as storage-class specifiers, function definitions, initializations, enumerations, class, struct, and union declarations, and typedef declarations. Related information can be found in Chapter 7, "Declarators," and Appendix B, "Microsoft-Specific Modifiers."

Chapter 7, "Declarators," explains the portion of a declaration statement that names an object, type, or function.

Chapter 8, "Classes," introduces C++ classes. C++ treats an object declared with the **class**, **struct**, or **union** keyword as a class type. This chapter explains how to use these class types.

Chapter 9, "Derived Classes," covers the details of inheritance—a process by which you can define a new type as having all the attributes of an existing type, plus any new attributes you add.

Chapter 10, "Member-Access Control," explains how you can control access to class members. Use of access-control specifiers can help produce more robust code because you can limit the number of ways an object's state can be changed.

Chapter 11, "Special Member Functions," describes special functions unique to class types. These special functions perform initialization (constructor functions), cleanup (destructor functions), and conversions. This chapter also describes the **new** and **delete** operators, which are used for dynamic memory allocation.

Chapter 12, "Overloading," explains a C++ feature that enables you to define a group of functions with the same name but different arguments. Which function in the group is called depends on the argument list in the actual function call. In addition, this chapter covers overloaded operators, a mechanism for defining your own behavior for C++ operators.

Appendix A, "Grammar Summary," is a summary of the C++ grammar with the Microsoft extensions. Portions of this grammar are shown throughout this manual in "Syntax" sections.

Appendix B, "Microsoft-Specific Modifiers," describes the modifiers specific to Microsoft C++. These modifiers control memory addressing, calling conventions, and so on.

Appendix C, "Microsoft-Specific Compiler COM Support Classes," is a reference to four Microsoft-specific classes used to support some Component Object Model types.

Appendix D, "Charts," contains the following charts: ASCII Character Codes, ASCII Multilingual Codes, ANSI Character Codes, and Key Codes.

Note For information on Microsoft product support, see the technical support help file, PSS.HLP.

Special Terminology in this Manual

In this manual, the term "argument" refers to the entity that is passed to a function. In some cases, it is modified by "actual" or "formal," which mean the argument expression specified in the function call and the argument declaration specified in the function definition, respectively.

The term "variable" refers to a simple C-type data object. The term "object" refers to both C++ objects and variables; it is an inclusive term.

For more information on terminology, see "Terms" on page 19 in Chapter 2.

CHAPTER 1

Lexical Conventions

This chapter introduces the fundamental elements of a C++ program. You use these elements, called "lexical elements" or "tokens" to construct statements, definitions, declarations, and so on, which are used to construct complete programs. The following lexical elements are discussed in this chapter:

- Tokens
- Comments
- Identifiers
- C++ keywords
- Punctuators
- Operators
- Literals

This chapter also includes Table 1.1, which shows the precedence and associativity of C++ operators (from highest to lowest precedence). For a complete discussion of operators, see Chapter 4, "Expressions."

Overview of File Translation

C++ programs, like C programs, consist of one or more files. Each of these files is translated in the following conceptual order (the actual order follows the "as if" rule: translation must occur as if these steps had been followed):

1. Lexical tokenizing. Character mapping and trigraph processing, line splicing, and tokenizing are performed in this translation phase.

2. Preprocessing. This translation phase brings in ancillary source files referenced by **#include** directives, handles "stringizing" and "charizing" directives, and performs token pasting and macro expansion (see "Preprocessor Directives" in the *Preprocessor Reference* for more information). The result of the preprocessing phase is a sequence of tokens that, taken together, define a "translation unit."

Preprocessor directives always begin with the number-sign (#) character (that is, the first nonwhite-space character on the line must be a number sign). Only one preprocessor directive can appear on a given line.

For example:

```
#include <iostream.h>    // Include text of iostream.h in
                         //  translation unit.
#define NDEBUG           // Define NDEBUG (NDEBUG contains empty
                         //  text string).
```

3. Code generation. This translation phase uses the tokens generated in the preprocessing phase to generate object code.

During this phase, syntactic and semantic checking of the source code is performed.

See "Phases of Translation" in the *Preprocessor Reference* for more information.

The C++ preprocessor is a strict superset of the ANSI C preprocessor, but the C++ preprocessor differs in a few instances. The following list describes several differences between the ANSI C and the C++ preprocessors:

- Single-line comments are supported. See "Comments" for more information.

- One predefined macro, **__cplusplus**, is defined only for C++. See "Predefined Macros" in the *Preprocessor Reference* for more information.

- The C preprocessor does not recognize the C++ operators: .*, ->*, and ::. See "Operators" on page 7 and Chapter 4, "Expressions," for more information about operators.

Tokens

A token is the smallest element of a C++ program that is meaningful to the compiler. The C++ parser recognizes these kinds of tokens: identifiers, keywords, literals, operators, punctuators, and other separators. A stream of these tokens makes up a translation unit.

Tokens are usually separated by "white space." White space can be one or more:

- Blanks
- Horizontal or vertical tabs
- New lines
- Formfeeds
- Comments

Syntax

token:

> *keyword*
> *identifier*
> *constant*
> *operator*
> *punctuator*

preprocessing-token:

> *header-name*
> *identifier*
> *pp-number*
> *character-constant*
> *string-literal*
> *operator*
> *punctuator*
> each nonwhite-space character that cannot be one of the above

The parser separates tokens from the input stream by creating the longest token possible using the input characters in a left-to-right scan. Consider this code fragment:

```
a = i+++j;
```

The programmer who wrote the code might have intended either of these two statements:

```
a = i + (++j)
```

```
a = (i++) + j
```

Because the parser creates the longest token possible from the input stream, it chooses the second interpretation, making the tokens i++, +, and j.

Comments

A comment is text that the compiler ignores but that is useful for programmers. Comments are normally used to annotate code for future reference. The compiler treats them as white space. You can use comments in testing to make certain lines of code inactive; however, **#if/#endif** preprocessor directives work better for this because you can surround code that contains comments but you cannot nest comments.

A C++ comment is written in one of the following ways:

- The /* (slash, asterisk) characters, followed by any sequence of characters (including new lines), followed by the */ characters. This syntax is the same as ANSI C.

- The // (two slashes) characters, followed by any sequence of characters. A new line not immediately preceded by a backslash terminates this form of comment. Therefore, it is commonly called a "single-line comment."

The comment characters (/*, */, and //) have no special meaning within a character constant, string literal, or comment. Comments using the first syntax, therefore, cannot be nested. Consider this example:

```
/* Intent:  Comment out this block of code.
   Problem: Nested comments on each line of code are illegal.
FileName = String( "hello.dat" ); /* Initialize file string */
cout << "File: " << FileName << "\n"; /* Print status message */
*/
```

The preceding code will not compile because the compiler scans the input stream from the first /* to the first */ and considers it a comment. In this case, the first */ occurs at the end of the Initialize file string comment. The last */, then, is no longer paired with an opening /*.

Note that the single-line form (//) of a comment followed by the line-continuation token (\) can have surprising effects. Consider this code:

```
#include <stdio.h>

void main()
{
    printf( "This is a number %d", // \
            5 );
}
```

After preprocessing, the preceding code contains errors and appears as follows:

```
#include <stdio.h>

void main()
{
    printf( "This is a number %d",
}
```

Identifiers

An identifier is a sequence of characters used to denote one of the following:

- Object or variable name
- Class, structure, or union name
- Enumerated type name
- Member of a class, structure, union, or enumeration
- Function or class-member function
- **typedef** name
- Label name
- Macro name
- Macro parameter

Syntax

identifier:

> *nondigit*
> *identifier nondigit*
> *identifier digit*

nondigit: one of

> **_ a b c d e f g h i j k l m**
> **n o p q r s t u v w x y z**
> **A B C D E F G H I J K L M**
> **N O P Q R S T U V W X Y Z**

digit: one of

> **0 1 2 3 4 5 6 7 8 9**

Microsoft Specific →

Only the first 247 characters of Microsoft C++ identifiers are significant. This restriction is complicated by the fact that names for user-defined types are "decorated" by the compiler to preserve type information. The resultant name, including the type information, cannot be longer than 247 characters. (See "Decorated Names" in the *Visual C++ Programmer's Guide* online for more information.) Factors that can influence the length of a decorated identifier are:

- Whether the identifier denotes an object of user-defined type or a type derived from a user-defined type.

- Whether the identifier denotes a function or a type derived from a function.

- The number of arguments to a function.

END Microsoft Specific

The first character of an identifier must be an alphabetic character, either uppercase or lowercase, or an underscore (_). Because C++ identifiers are case sensitive, `fileName` is different from `FileName`.

Identifiers cannot be exactly the same spelling and case as keywords. Identifiers that contain keywords are legal. For example, `Pint` is a legal identifier, even though it contains **int**, which is a keyword.

Use of two sequential underscore characters (__) at the beginning of an identifier, or a single leading underscore followed by a capital letter, is reserved for C++ implementations in all scopes. You should avoid using one leading underscore followed by a lowercase letter for names with file scope because of possible conflicts with current or future reserved identifiers.

Keywords

Keywords are predefined reserved identifiers that have special meanings. They cannot be used as identifiers in your program. The following keywords are reserved for C++:

Syntax

keyword: one of

asm[1]	auto	bad_cast	bad_typeid
bool	break	case	catch
char	class	const	const_cast
continue	default	delete	do
double	dynamic_cast	else	enum
except	explicit	extern	false
finally	float	for	friend
goto	if	inline	int
long	mutable	namespace	new
operator	private	protected	public
register	reinterpret_cast	return	short
signed	sizeof	static	static_cast
struct	switch	template	this
throw	true	try	type_info
typedef	typeid	typename	union
unsigned	using	virtual	void
volatile	while	xalloc	

[1] Reserved for compatibility with other C++ implementations, but not implemented. Use __asm.

Microsoft Specific →

In Microsoft C++, identifiers with two leading underscores are reserved for compiler implementations. Therefore, the Microsoft convention is to precede Microsoft-specific keywords with double underscores. These words cannot be used as identifier names.

allocate[3]	__except	__int64	__single_inheritance
__asm[1]	__fastcall	__leave	__stdcall
__based[2]	__finally	__multiple_inheritance	thread[3]
__cdecl	__inline	naked[3]	__try
__declspec	__int8	nothrow[3]	uuid[3]
dllexport[3]	__int16	property[3]	__uuidof
dllimport[3]	__int32	selectany[3]	__virtual_inheritance

[1] Replaces C++ **asm** syntax.

[2] The __**based** keyword has limited uses for 32-bit target compilations.

[3] These are special identifiers when used with __**declspec**; their use in other contexts is not restricted.

Microsoft extensions are enabled by default. To ensure that your programs are fully portable, you can disable Microsoft extensions by specifying the ANSI-compatible /Za command-line option (compile for ANSI compatibility) during compilation. When you do this, Microsoft-specific keywords are disabled.

When Microsoft extensions are enabled, you can use the previously-listed keywords in your programs. For ANSI compliance, these keywords are prefaced by a double underscore. For backward compatibility, single-underscore versions of all the keywords except __except, __finally, __leave, and __try are supported. In addition, __cdecl is available with no leading underscore.

END Microsoft Specific

Punctuators

Punctuators in C++ have syntactic and semantic meaning to the compiler but do not, of themselves, specify an operation that yields a value. Some punctuators, either alone or in combination, can also be C++ operators or be significant to the preprocessor.

Syntax

punctuator: one of
>   ! % ^ & * ( ) – + = { } | ~
>   [ ] \ ; ' : " < > ? . , . / #

The punctuators [ ], ( ), and { } must appear in pairs after translation phase 4.

Operators

Operators specify an evaluation to be performed on one of the following:

- One operand (unary operator)
- Two operands (binary operator)
- Three operands (ternary operator)

The C++ language includes all C operators and adds several new operators. Table 1.1 lists the operators available in Microsoft C++.

Operators follow a strict precedence which defines the evaluation order of expressions containing these operators. Operators associate with either the expression on their left or the expression on their right; this is called "associativity." Operators in the same group have equal precedence and are evaluated left to right in an expression unless explicitly forced by a pair of parentheses, ( ). Table 1.1 shows the precedence and associativity of C++ operators (from highest to lowest precedence).

Table 1.1 C++ Operator Precedence and Associativity

Operator	Name or Meaning	Associativity
::	Scope resolution	None
::	Global	None
[ ]	Array subscript	Left to right
( )	Function call	Left to right
( )	Conversion	None
.	Member selection (object)	Left to right
->	Member selection (pointer)	Left to right
++	Postfix increment	None
- -	Postfix decrement	None
new	Allocate object	None
delete	Deallocate object	None
delete[ ]	Deallocate object	None
++	Prefix increment	None
- -	Prefix decrement	None
*	Dereference	None
&	Address-of	None
+	Unary plus	None
-	Arithmetic negation (unary)	None
!	Logical NOT	None
~	Bitwise complement	None
sizeof	Size of object	None
sizeof ( )	Size of type	None
typeid( )	type name	None
(*type*)	Type cast (conversion)	Right to left
const_cast	Type cast (conversion)	None
dynamic_cast	Type cast (conversion)	None
reinterpret_cast	Type cast (conversion)	None
static_cast	Type cast (conversion)	None
.*	Apply pointer to class member (objects)	Left to right
->*	Dereference pointer to class member	Left to right
*	Multiplication	Left to right
/	Division	Left to right
%	Remainder (modulus)	Left to right
+	Addition	Left to right
-	Subtraction	Left to right
<<	Left shift	Left to right

Table 1.1   C++ Operator Precedence and Associativity *(continued)*

Operator	Name or Meaning	Associativity
>>	Right shift	Left to right
<	Less than	Left to right
>	Greater than	Left to right
<=	Less than or equal to	Left to right
>=	Greater than or equal to	Left to right
==	Equality	Left to right
!=	Inequality	Left to right
&	Bitwise AND	Left to right
^	Bitwise exclusive OR	Left to right
|	Bitwise OR	Left to right
&&	Logical AND	Left to right
||	Logical OR	Left to right
e1?e2:e3	Conditional	Right to left
=	Assignment	Right to left
*=	Multiplication assignment	Right to left
/=	Division assignment	Right to left
%=	Modulus assignment	Right to left
+=	Addition assignment	Right to left
-=	Subtraction assignment	Right to left
<<=	Left-shift assignment	Right to left
>>=	Right-shift assignment	Right to left
&=	Bitwise AND assignment	Right to left
|=	Bitwise inclusive OR assignment	Right to left
^=	Bitwise exclusive OR assignment	Right to left
,	Comma	Left to right

Literals

Invariant program elements are called "literals" or "constants." The terms "literal" and "constant" are used interchangeably here. Literals fall into four major categories: integer, character, floating-point, and string literals.

Syntax
literal:
      integer-constant
      character-constant
      floating-constant
      string-literal

Integer Constants

Integer constants are constant data elements that have no fractional parts or exponents. They always begin with a digit. You can specify integer constants in decimal, octal, or hexadecimal form. They can specify signed or unsigned types and long or short types.

Syntax

integer-constant:

> *decimal-constant integer-suffix*$_{opt}$
> *octal-constant integer-suffix*$_{opt}$
> *hexadecimal-constant integer-suffix*$_{opt}$
> **'***c-char-sequence***'**

decimal-constant:

> *nonzero-digit*
> *decimal-constant digit*

octal-constant:

> **0**
> *octal-constant octal-digit*

hexadecimal-constant:

> **0x** *hexadecimal-digit*
> **0X** *hexadecimal-digit*
> *hexadecimal-constant hexadecimal-digit*

nonzero-digit: one of

> **1 2 3 4 5 6 7 8 9**

octal-digit: one of

> **0 1 2 3 4 5 6 7**

hexadecimal-digit: one of

> **0 1 2 3 4 5 6 7 8 9**
> **a b c d e f**
> **A B C D E F**

integer-suffix:

> *unsigned-suffix long-suffix*$_{opt}$
> *long-suffix unsigned-suffix*$_{opt}$

unsigned-suffix: one of

> **u U**

long-suffix: one of

> **l L**

64-bit integer-suffix:

> **i64**

To specify integer constants using octal or hexadecimal notation, use a prefix that denotes the base. To specify an integer constant of a given integral type, use a suffix that denotes the type.

To specify a decimal constant, begin the specification with a nonzero digit. For example:

```
int i = 157;      // Decimal constant
int j = 0198;     // Not a decimal number; erroneous octal constant
int k = 0365;     // Leading zero specifies octal constant, not decimal
```

To specify an octal constant, begin the specification with 0, followed by a sequence of digits in the range 0 through 7. The digits 8 and 9 are errors in specifying an octal constant. For example:

```
int i = 0377;     // Octal constant
int j = 0397;     // Error: 9 is not an octal digit
```

To specify a hexadecimal constant, begin the specification with 0x or 0X (the case of the "x" does not matter), followed by a sequence of digits in the range 0 through 9 and a (or A) through f (or F). Hexadecimal digits a (or A) through f (or F) represent values in the range 10 through 15. For example:

```
int i = 0x3fff;   // Hexadecimal constant
int j = 0X3FFF;   // Equal to i
```

To specify an unsigned type, use either the **u** or **U** suffix. To specify a long type, use either the **l** or **L** suffix. For example:

```
unsigned uVal = 328u;             // Unsigned value
long lVal = 0x7FFFFFL;            // Long value specified
                                  //   as hex constant
unsigned long ulVal = 0776745ul;  // Unsigned long value
```

Character Constants

Character constants are one or more members of the "source character set," the character set in which a program is written, surrounded by single quotation marks ('). They are used to represent characters in the "execution character set," the character set on the machine where the program executes.

Microsoft Specific →

For Microsoft C++, the source and execution character sets are both ASCII.

END Microsoft Specific

There are three kinds of character constants:

- Normal character constants
- Multicharacter constants
- Wide-character constants

Note Use wide-character constants in place of multicharacter constants to ensure portability. Character constants are specified as one or more characters enclosed in single quotation marks. For example:

```
char ch = 'x';          // Specify normal character constant.
int mbch = 'ab';        // Specify system-dependent
                        //  multicharacter constant.
wchar_t wcch = L'ab';   // Specify wide-character constant.
```

Note that mbch is of type **int**. If it were declared as type **char**, the second byte would not be retained. A multicharacter constant has four meaningful characters; specifying more than four generates an error message.

Syntax

character-constant:
> '*c-char-sequence*'
> **L**'*c-char-sequence*'

c-char-sequence:
> *c-char*
> *c-char-sequence c-char*

c-char:
> any member of the source character set except the single quotation mark ('),
>> backslash (\), or newline character
> *escape-sequence*

escape-sequence:
> *simple-escape-sequence*
> *octal-escape-sequence*
> *hexadecimal-escape-sequence*

simple-escape-sequence: one of
> \' \" \? \\
> \a \b \f \n \r \t \v

octal-escape-sequence:
> *octal-digit*
> *octal-digit octal-digit*
> *octal-digit octal-digit octal-digit*

hexadecimal-escape-sequence:
> **x***hexadecimal-digit*
> *hexadecimal-escape-sequence hexadecimal-digit*

Microsoft C++ supports normal, multicharacter, and wide-character constants. Use wide-character constants to specify members of the extended execution character set (for example, to support an international application). Normal character constants have type **char**, multicharacter constants have type **int**, and wide-character constants have type **wchar_t**. (The type **wchar_t** is defined in the standard include files STDDEF.H, STDLIB.H, and STRING.H. The wide-character functions, however, are prototyped only in STDLIB.H.)

The only difference in specification between normal and wide-character constants is that wide-character constants are preceded by the letter L. For example:

```
char schar = 'x';              // Normal character constant
wchar_t wchar = L'\x81\x19';   // Wide-character constant
```

Table 1.2 shows reserved or nongraphic characters that are system dependent or not allowed within character constants. These characters should be represented with escape sequences.

Table 1.2   C++ Reserved or Nongraphic Characters

Character	ASCII Representation	ASCII Value	Escape Sequence
Newline	NL (LF)	10 or 0x0a	\n
Horizontal tab	HT	9	\t
Vertical tab	VT	11 or 0x0b	\v
Backspace	BS	8	\b
Carriage return	CR	13 or 0x0d	\r
Formfeed	FF	12 or 0x0c	\f
Alert	BEL	7	\a
Backslash	\	92 or 0x5c	\\
Question mark	?	63 or 0x3f	\?
Single quotation mark	'	39 or 0x27	\'
Double quotation mark	"	34 or 0x22	\"
Octal number	*ooo*	—	*ooo*
Hexadecimal number	*hhh*	—	\x*hhh*
Null character	NUL	0	\0

If the character following the backslash does not specify a legal escape sequence, the result is implementation defined. In Microsoft C++, the character following the backslash is taken literally, as though the escape were not present, and a level 1 warning ("unrecognized character escape sequence") is issued.

Octal escape sequences, specified in the form *ooo*, consist of a backslash and one, two, or three octal characters. Hexadecimal escape sequences, specified in the form \x*hhh*, consist of the characters \x followed by a sequence of hexadecimal digits. Unlike octal escape constants, there is no limit on the number of hexadecimal digits in an escape sequence.

Octal escape sequences are terminated by the first character that is not an octal digit, or when three characters are seen. For example:

```
wchar_t och = L'\076a';   // Sequence terminates at a
char    ch = '\233';      // Sequence terminates after 3 characters
```

Similarly, hexadecimal escape sequences terminate at the first character that is not a hexadecimal digit. Because hexadecimal digits include the letters a through f (and A through F), make sure the escape sequence terminates at the intended digit.

Because the single quotation mark (') encloses character constants, use the escape sequence \' to represent enclosed single quotation marks. The double quotation mark (") can be represented without an escape sequence. The backslash character (\) is a line-continuation character when placed at the end of a line. If you want a backslash character to appear within a character constant, you must type two backslashes in a row (\\). (See "Phases of Translation" in the *Preprocessor Reference* for more information about line continuation.)

Floating-Point Constants

Floating-point constants specify values that must have a fractional part. These values contain decimal points (.) and can contain exponents.

Syntax

floating-constant:
        fractional-constant exponent-part$_{opt}$ *floating-suffix*$_{opt}$
        digit-sequence exponent-part floating-suffix$_{opt}$

fractional-constant:
        digit-sequence$_{opt}$. *digit-sequence*
        digit-sequence .

exponent-part:
        e *sign*$_{opt}$ *digit-sequence*
        E *sign*$_{opt}$ *digit-sequence*

sign: one of
        + −

digit-sequence:
        digit
        digit-sequence digit

floating-suffix: one of
        f l F L

Floating-point constants have a "mantissa," which specifies the value of the number, an "exponent," which specifies the magnitude of the number, and an optional suffix that specifies the constant's type. The mantissa is specified as a sequence of digits followed by a period, followed by an optional sequence of digits representing the fractional part of the number. For example:

```
18.46
38.
```

The exponent, if present, specifies the magnitude of the number as a power of 10, as shown in the following example:

```
18.46e0    // 18.46
18.46e1    // 184.6
```

If an exponent is present, the trailing decimal point is unnecessary in whole numbers such as 18E0.

Floating-point constants default to type **double**. By using the suffixes **f** or **l** (or **F** or **L**—the suffix is not case sensitive), the constant can be specified as **float** or **long double**, respectively.

Although **long double** and **double** have the same representation, they are not the same type. For example, you can have overloaded functions like

```
void func( double );
```

and

```
void func( long double );
```

String Literals

A string literal consists of zero or more characters from the source character set surrounded by double quotation marks ("). A string literal represents a sequence of characters that, taken together, form a null-terminated string.

Syntax

string-literal:
>   "*s-char-sequence*$_{opt}$"
>   **L**"*s-char-sequence*$_{opt}$"

s-char-sequence:
>   *s-char*
>   *s-char-sequence s-char*

s-char:
>   any member of the source character set except the double quotation mark ("),
>   backslash (\\), or newline character
>   *escape-sequence*

C++ strings have these types:

- Array of **char**[*n*], where *n* is the length of the string (in characters) plus 1 for the terminating '\0' that marks the end of the string

- Array of **wchar_t**, for wide-character strings

The result of modifying a string constant is undefined. For example:

```
char *szStr = "1234";
szStr[2] = 'A';    // Results undefined
```

Microsoft Specific →

In some cases, identical string literals can be "pooled" to save space in the executable file. In string-literal pooling, the compiler causes all references to a particular string literal to point to the same location in memory, instead of having each reference point to a separate instance of the string literal. The /Gf compiler option enables string pooling.

END Microsoft Specific

When specifying string literals, adjacent strings are concatenated. Therefore, this declaration:

```
char szStr[] = "12" "34";
```

is identical to this declaration:

```
char szStr[] = "1234";
```

This concatenation of adjacent strings makes it easy to specify long strings across multiple lines:

```
cout << "Four score and seven years "
        "ago, our forefathers brought forth "
        "upon this continent a new nation.";
```

In the preceding example, the entire string Four score and seven years ago, our forefathers brought forth upon this continent a new nation. is spliced together. This string can also be specified using line splicing as follows:

```
cout << "Four score and seven years \
ago, our forefathers brought forth \
upon this continent a new nation.";
```

After all adjacent strings in the constant have been concatenated, the **NULL** character, '\0', is appended to provide an end-of-string marker for C string-handling functions.

When the first string contains an escape character, string concatenation can yield surprising results. Consider the following two declarations:

```
char szStr1[] = "\01" "23";
char szStr2[] = "\0123";
```

Although it is natural to assume that szStr1 and szStr2 contain the same values, the values they actually contain are shown in Figure 1.1.

Figure 1.1 Escapes and String Concatenation

The maximum length of a string literal is approximately 2,048 bytes. This limit applies to strings of type **char[]** and **wchar_t[]**. If a string literal consists of parts enclosed in double quotation marks, the preprocessor concatenates the parts into a single string, and for each line concatenated, it adds an extra byte to the total number of bytes.

For example, suppose a string consists of 40 lines with 50 characters per line (2,000 characters), and one line with 7 characters, and each line is surrounded by double quotation marks. This adds up to 2,007 bytes plus one byte for the terminating null character, for a total of 2,008 bytes. On concatenation, an extra character is added to the total number of bytes for each of the first 40 lines. This makes a total of 2,048 bytes. (The extra characters are not actually written to the string.) Note, however, that if line continuations (\) are used instead of double quotation marks, the preprocessor does not add an extra character for each line.

END Microsoft Specific

Determine the size of string objects by counting the number of characters and adding 1 for the terminating '\0' or 2 for type **wchar_t**.

Because the double quotation mark (") encloses strings, use the escape sequence (\") to represent enclosed double quotation marks. The single quotation mark (') can be represented without an escape sequence. The backslash character (\) is a line-continuation character when placed at the end of a line. If you want a backslash character to appear within a string, you must type two backslashes (\\). (See "Phases of Translation" in the *Preprocessor Reference* for more information about line continuation.)

To specify a string of type wide-character (**wchar_t[]**), precede the opening double quotation mark with the character **L**. For example:

```
wchar_t wszStr[] = L"1a1g";
```

All normal escape codes listed in "Character Constants" on page 11 are valid in string constants. For example:

```
cout << "First line\nSecond line";
cout << "Error! Take corrective action\a";
```

Because the escape code terminates at the first character that is not a hexadecimal digit, specification of string constants with embedded hexadecimal escape codes can cause unexpected results. The following example is intended to create a string literal containing ASCII 5, followed by the characters five:

```
\x05five"
```

The actual result is a hexadecimal 5F, which is the ASCII code for an underscore, followed by the characters ive. The following example produces the desired results:

```
"\005five"    // Use octal constant.
"\x05" "five"  // Use string splicing.
```

CHAPTER 2

Basic Concepts

This chapter explains concepts that are critical to understanding C++. C programmers will be familiar with many of these concepts, but there are some subtle differences that can cause unexpected program results. The following topics are included:

- Terms
- Declarations and definitions
- Scope of a C++ object or function
- Program definition and linkage rules
- Startup and termination
- Storage classes
- Types

Additional topics include l-values, r-values, and numerical limits.

Terms

C++ terms used in this book are defined in Table 2.1:

Table 2.1   C++ Terminology

Term	Meaning
Declaration	A declaration introduces names and their types into a program without necessarily defining an associated object or function. However, many declarations serve as definitions.
Definition	A definition provides information that allows the compiler to allocate memory for objects or generate code for functions.
Lifetime	The lifetime of an object is the period during which an object exists, including its creation and destruction.

(continued)

Table 2.1   C++ Terminology *(continued)*

Term	Meaning
Linkage	Names can have external linkage, internal linkage, or no linkage. Within a program (a set of translation units), only names with external linkage denote the same object or function. Within a translation unit, names with either internal or external linkage denote the same object or function (except when functions are overloaded). (For more information on translation units, see "Phases of Translation", in the *Preprocessor Reference*.) Names with no linkage denote unique objects or functions.
Name	A name denotes an object, function, set of overloaded functions, enumerator, type, class member, template, value, or label. C++ programs use names to refer to their associated language element. Names can be type names or identifiers.
Object	An object is an instance (a data item) of a user-defined type (a class type). The difference between an object and a variable is that variables retain state information, whereas objects can also have behavior.
	This manual draws a distinction between objects and variables: "object" means instance of a user-defined type, whereas "variable" means instance of a fundamental type.
	In cases where either object or variable is applicable, the term "object" is used as the inclusive term, meaning "object or variable."
Scope	Names can be used only within specific regions of program text. These regions are called the scope of the name.
Storage class	The storage class of a named object determines its lifetime, initialization, and, in certain cases, its linkage.
Type	Names have associated types that determine the meaning of the value or values stored in an object or returned by a function.
Variable	A variable is a data item of a fundamental type (for example, **int**, **float**, or **double**). Variables store state information but define no behavior for how that information is handled. See the preceding list item "Object" for information about how the terms "variable" and "object" are used in this documentation.

Declarations and Definitions

Declarations tell the compiler that a program element or name exists. Definitions specify what code or data the name describes. A name must be declared before it can be used.

Declarations

A declaration introduces one or more names into a program. Declarations can occur more than once in a program. Therefore, classes, structures, enumerated types, and other user-defined types can be declared for each compilation unit. The constraint on this multiple declaration is that all declarations must be identical. Declarations also serve as definitions, except when the declaration:

- Is a function prototype (a function declaration with no function body).

- Contains the **extern** specifier but no initializer (objects and variables) or function body (functions). This signifies that the definition is not necessarily in the current translation unit and gives the name external linkage.

- Is of a static data member inside a class declaration.

  Because static class data members are discrete variables shared by all objects of the class, they must be defined and initialized outside the class declaration. (For more information about classes and class members, see Chapter 8, "Classes.")

- Is a class name declaration with no following definition, such as class T;.

- Is a **typedef** statement.

Examples of declarations that are also definitions are:

```
// Declare and define int variables i and j.
int i;
int j = 10;

// Declare enumeration suits.
enum suits { Spades = 1, Clubs, Hearts, Diamonds };

// Declare class CheckBox.
class CheckBox : public Control
{
public:
            Boolean IsChecked();
   virtual int      ChangeState() = 0;
};
```

Some declarations that are not definitions are:

```
extern int i;
char *strchr( const char *Str, const char Target );
```

Definitions

A definition is a unique specification of an object or variable, function, class, or enumerator. Because definitions must be unique, a program can contain only one definition for a given program element.

There can be a many-to-one correspondence between declarations and definitions. There are two cases in which a program element can be declared and not defined:

- A function is declared but never referenced with a function call or with an expression that takes the function's address.

- A class is used only in a way that does not require its definition be known. However, the class must be declared. The following code illustrates such a case:

```
class WindowCounter;     // Forward reference; no definition

class Window
{
    static WindowCounter windowCounter;  // Definition of
                                         //  WindowCounter
                                         //  not required.
};
```

Scope

C++ names can be used only in certain regions of a program. This area is called the "scope" of the name. Scope determines the "lifetime" of a name that does not denote an object of static extent. Scope also determines the visibility of a name, when class constructors and destructors are called, and when variables local to the scope are initialized. (For more information, see "Constructors" and "Destructors" on pages 292 and 297 in Chapter 11.) There are five kinds of scope:

- Local scope. A name declared within a block is accessible only within that block and blocks enclosed by it, and only after the point of declaration. The names of formal arguments to a function in the scope of the outermost block of the function have local scope, as if they had been declared inside the block enclosing the function body. Consider the following code fragment:

```
{
    int i;
}
```

Because the declaration of i is in a block enclosed by curly braces, i has local scope and is never accessible because no code accesses it before the closing curly brace.

- Function scope. Labels are the only names that have function scope. They can be used anywhere within a function but are not accessible outside that function.

- File scope. Any name declared outside all blocks or classes has file scope. It is accessible anywhere in the translation unit after its declaration. Names with file scope that do not declare static objects are often called "global" names.

- Class scope. Names of class members have class scope. Class member functions can be accessed only by using the member-selection operators (. or –>) or pointer-to-member operators (.* or –>*) on an object or pointer to an object of that class; nonstatic class member data is considered local to the object of that class. Consider the following class declaration:

```
class Point
{
    int x;
    int y;
};
```

The class members x and y are considered to be in the scope of class `Point`.

- Prototype scope. Names declared in a function prototype are visible only until the end of the prototype. The following prototype declares two names (`szDest`, `szSource`); these names go out of scope at the end of the prototype:

```
char *strcpy( char *szDest, const char *szSource );
```

Point of Declaration

A name is considered to be declared immediately after its declarator but before its (optional) initializer. (For more information on declarators, see Chapter 7, "Declarators.") An enumerator is considered to be declared immediately after the identifier that names it but before its (optional) initializer.

Consider this example:

```
double dVar = 7.0;

void main()
{
    double dVar = dVar;
}
```

If the point of declaration were *after* the initialization, then the local dVar would be initialized to 7.0, the value of the global variable dVar. However, since that is not the case, dVar is initialized to an undefined value.

Enumerators follow the same rule. However, enumerators are exported to the enclosing scope of the enumeration. In the following example, the enumerators Spades, Clubs, Hearts, and Diamonds are declared. Because the enumerators are exported to the enclosing scope, they are considered to have global scope. The identifiers in the example are already defined in global scope.

Consider the following code:

```
const int Spades = 1, Clubs = 2, Hearts = 3, Diamonds = 4;

enum Suits
{
    Spades = Spades,    // error
    Clubs,              // error
    Hearts,             // error
    Diamonds            // error
};
```

Because the identifiers in the preceding code are already defined in global scope, an error message is generated.

Note Using the same name to refer to more than one program element—for example, an enumerator and an object—is considered poor programming practice and should be avoided. In the preceding example, this practice causes an error.

Hiding Names

You can hide a name by declaring it in an enclosed block. In Figure 2.1, i is redeclared within the inner block, thereby hiding the variable associated with i in the outer block scope.

Figure 2.1 Block Scope and Name Hiding

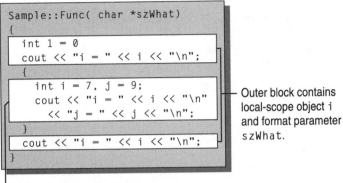

```
Sample::Func( char *szWhat)
{
    int 1 = 0
    cout << "i = " << i << "\n";
    {
        int i = 7, j = 9;
        cout << "i = " << i << "\n"
            << "j = " << j << "\n";
    }
    cout << "i = " << i << "\n";
}
```

— Outer block contains local-scope object i and format parameter szWhat.

— Inner block contains local-scope objects i and j.

The output from the program shown in Figure 2.1 is:

```
i = 0
i = 7
j = 9
i = 0
```

Note The argument szWhat is considered to be in the scope of the function. Therefore, it is treated as if it had been declared in the outermost block of the function.

Hiding Names with File Scope

You can hide names with file scope by explicitly declaring the same name in block scope. However, file-scope names can be accessed using the scope-resolution operator (::). For example:

```
#include <iostream.h>

int i = 7;        // i has file scope--declared
                  // outside all blocks

void main( int argc, char *argv[] )
{
    int i = 5;    // i has block scope--hides
                  // the i with file scope
```

```
    cout << "Block-scoped i has the value: " << i << "\n";
    cout << "File-scoped i has the value: " << ::i << "\n";
}
```

The result of the preceding code is:

```
Block-scoped i has the value: 5
File-scoped i has the value: 7
```

Hiding Class Names

You can hide class names by declaring a function, object or variable, or enumerator in the same scope. However, the class name can still be accessed when prefixed by the keyword **class**.

```
// Declare class Account at file scope.
class Account
{
public:
    Account( double InitialBalance )
        { balance = InitialBalance; }
    double GetBalance()
        { return balance; }
private:
    double balance;
};

double Account = 15.37;                // Hides class name Account

void main()
{
    class Account Checking( Account ); // Qualifies Account as
                                       //  class name

    cout << "Opening account with balance of: "
        << Checking.GetBalance() << "\n";
}
```

Note that any place the class name (Account) is called for, the keyword **class** must be used to differentiate it from the file-scoped variable Account. This rule does not apply when the class name occurs on the left side of the scope-resolution operator (::). Names on the left side of the scope-resolution operator are always considered class names. The following example demonstrates how to declare a pointer to an object of type Account using the **class** keyword:

```
class Account *Checking = new class Account( Account );
```

The Account in the initializer (in parentheses) in the preceding statement has file scope; it is of type **double**.

Note The reuse of identifier names as shown in this example is considered poor programming style.

For more information about pointers, see "Derived Types" on page 44. For information about declaration and initialization of class objects, see Chapter 8, "Classes." For information about using the **new** and **delete** free-store operators, see Chapter 11, "Special Member Functions."

Scope of Formal Arguments to Functions

Formal arguments (arguments specified in function definitions) to functions are considered to be in the scope of the outermost block of the function body.

Program and Linkage

A program consists of one or more translation units linked together. Execution (conceptually) begins in the translation unit that contains the function **main**. (For more information on translation units, see "Phases of Translation," in the *Preprocessor Reference*.) For more information about the **main** function, see "Program Startup: the main Function.")

Types of Linkage

The way the names of objects and functions are shared between translation units is called "linkage." These names can have:

- Internal linkage, in which case they refer only to program elements inside their own translation units; they are not shared with other translation units.

  The same name in another translation unit may refer to a different object or a different class. Names with internal linkage are sometimes referred to as being "local" to their translation units.

  An example declaration of a name with internal linkage is:

  ```
  static int i;    // The static keyword ensures internal linkage.
  ```

- External linkage, in which case they can refer to program elements in any translation unit in the program—the program element is shared among the translation units.

  The same name in another translation unit is guaranteed to refer to the same object or class. Names with external linkage are sometimes referred to as being "global."

  An example declaration of a name with external linkage is:

  ```
  extern int i;
  ```

- No linkage, in which case they refer to unique entities. The same name in another scope may not refer to the same object. An example is an enumeration. (Note, however, that you can pass a pointer to an object with no linkage. This makes the object accessible in other translation units.)

Linkage in Names with File Scope

The following linkage rules apply to names (other than **typedef** and enumerator names) with file scope:

- If a name is explicitly declared as **static**, it has internal linkage and identifies a program element inside its own translation unit.
- Enumerator names and **typedef** names have no linkage.
- All other names with file scope have external linkage.

Microsoft Specific →

- If a function name with file scope is explicitly declared as **inline**, it has external linkage if it is instantiated or its address is referenced. Therefore, it is possible for a function with file scope to have either internal or external linkage.

END Microsoft Specific

A class has internal linkage if it:

- Uses no C++ functionality (for example, member-access control, member functions, constructors, destructors, and so on).
- Is not used in the declaration of another name that has external linkage. This constraint means that objects of class type that are passed to functions with external linkage cause the class to have external linkage.

Linkage in Names with Class Scope

The following linkage rules apply to names with class scope:

- Static class members have external linkage.
- Class member functions have external linkage.
- Enumerators and **typedef** names have no linkage.

Microsoft Specific →

- Functions declared as **friend** functions must have external linkage. Declaring a static function as a **friend** generates an error.

END Microsoft Specific

Linkage in Names with Block Scope

The following linkage rules apply to names with block scope (local names):

- Names declared as **extern** have external linkage unless they were previously declared as **static**.
- All other names with block scope have no linkage.

Names with No Linkage

The only names that have no linkage are:

- Function parameters.

- Block-scoped names not declared as **extern** or **static**.

- Enumerators.

- Names declared in a **typedef** statement. An exception is when the **typedef** statement is used to provide a name for an unnamed class type. The name may then have external linkage if the class has external linkage. The following example shows a situation in which a **typedef** name has external linkage:

```
typedef struct
{
    short x;
    short y;
} POINT;
extern int MoveTo( POINT pt );
```

The **typedef** name, POINT, becomes the class name for the unnamed structure. It is then used to declare a function with external linkage.

Because **typedef** names have no linkage, their definitions can differ between translation units. Because the compilations take place discretely, there is no way for the compiler to detect these differences. As a result, errors of this kind are not detected until link time. Consider the following case:

```
// Translation unit 1
typedef int INT

INT myInt;
...

// Translation unit 2
typedef short INT

extern INT myInt;
...
```

The preceding code generates an "unresolved external" error at link time.

C++ functions can be defined only in file or class scope. The following example illustrates how to define functions and shows an erroneous function definition:

```
#include <iostream.h>

void ShowChar( char ch );      // Declare function ShowChar.

void ShowChar( char ch )       // Define function ShowChar.
{                              // Function has file scope.
    cout << ch;
}
```

```
struct Char                    // Define class Char.
{
   char Show();                // Declare Show function.
   char Get();                 // Declare Get function.
   char ch;
};

char Char::Show()              // Define Show function
{                              //  with class scope.
   cout << ch;
   return ch;
}

void GoodFuncDef( char ch )  // Define GoodFuncDef
{                            //  with file scope.
   int BadFuncDef( int i )   // Erroneous attempt to
   {                         //  nest functions.
      return i * 7;
   }
   for( int i = 0; i < BadFuncDef( 2 ); ++i )
      cout << ch;
   cout << "\n";
}
```

Linkage to Non-C++ Functions

C functions and data can be accessed only if they are previously declared as having C linkage. However, they must be defined in a separately compiled translation unit.

Syntax

linkage-specification:

> **extern** *string-literal* { *declaration-list*_{opt} }
> **extern** *string-literal declaration*

declaration-list:

> *declaration*
> *declaration-list declaration*

Microsoft C++ supports the strings **"C"** and **"C++"** in the *string-literal* field. The following example shows alternative ways to declare names that have C linkage:

```
// Declare printf with C linkage.
extern "C" int printf( const char *fmt, ... );

//  Cause everything in the header file "cinclude.h"
//    to have C linkage.
extern "C"
{
#include <cinclude.h>
}
```

```
//  Declare the two functions ShowChar and GetChar
//   with C linkage.
extern "C"
{
   char ShowChar( char ch );
   char GetChar( void );
}

//  Define the two functions ShowChar and GetChar
//   with C linkage.
extern "C" char ShowChar( char ch )
{
   putchar( ch );
   return ch;
}

extern "C" char GetChar( void )
{
   char ch;

   ch = getchar();
   return ch;
}

// Declare a global variable, errno, with C linkage.
extern "C" int errno;
```

Startup and Termination

Program startup and termination is facilitated by using two functions: **main** and **exit**. Other startup and termination code may be executed.

Program Startup: the main Function

A special function called **main** is the entry point to all C++ programs. This function is not predefined by the compiler; rather, it must be supplied in the program text. If you are writing code that adheres to the Unicode programming model, you can use the wide-character version of **main**, **wmain**. The declaration syntax for **main** is:

int main( );

or, optionally:

int main(int *argc*[**, char** **argv*[ ] [, **char** **envp*[ ]]] **);**

The declaration syntax for **wmain** is as follows:

int wmain( );

or, optionally:

int wmain(int *argc*[**, wchar_t** **argv*[ ] [, **wchar_t** **envp*[ ]]] **);**

Alternatively, the **main** and **wmain** functions can be declared as returning **void** (no return value). If you declare **main** or **wmain** as returning **void**, you cannot return an exit code to the parent process or operating system using a **return** statement; to return an exit code when **main** or **wmain** are declared as **void**, you must use the **exit** function.

Using wmain Instead of main

In the Unicode programming model, you can define a wide-character version of the **main** function. Use **wmain** instead of **main** if you want to write portable code that adheres to the Unicode specification.

You declare formal parameters to **wmain** using a similar format to **main**. You can then pass wide-character arguments and, optionally, a wide-character environment pointer to the program. The *argv* and *envp* parameters to **wmain** are of type **wchar_t***.

If your program uses a **main** function, the multibyte-character environment is created by the operating system at program startup. A wide-character copy of the environment is created only when needed (for example, by a call to the **_wgetenv** or **_wputenv** functions). On the first call to **_wputenv**, or on the first call to **_wgetenv** if an MBCS environment already exists, a corresponding wide-character string environment is created and is then pointed to by the **_wenviron** global variable, which is a wide-character version of the **_environ** global variable. At this point, two copies of the environment (MBCS and Unicode) exist simultaneously and are maintained by the operating system throughout the life of the program.

Similarly, if your program uses a **wmain** function, an MBCS (ASCII) environment is created on the first call to **_putenv** or **getenv**, and is pointed to by the **_environ** global variable.

For more information on the MBCS environment, see "Single-byte and Multibyte Character Sets" in Chapter 1 of the *Run-Time Library Reference*.

Argument Definitions

The arguments in the prototype

int main(int *argc*[**, char ****argv*[ ] [**, char ****envp*[ ]]] **);**

or

int wmain(int *argc*[**, wchar_t ****argv*[ ] [**, wchar_t ****envp*[ ]]] **);**

allow convenient command-line parsing of arguments and, optionally, access to environment variables. The argument definitions are as follows:

argc   An integer that contains the count of arguments that follow in *argv*. The *argc* parameter is always greater than or equal to 1.

argv   An array of null-terminated strings representing command-line arguments entered by the user of the program. By convention, *argv*[0] is the command with which the program is invoked, *argv*[1] is the first command-line argument, and so on, until *argv*[*argc*], which is always **NULL**. See "Customizing Command Line Processing" on page 34 for information on suppressing command-line processing.

The first command-line argument is always *argv*[1] and the last one is *argv*[*argc* − 1].

Microsoft Specific →

envp   The *envp* array, which is a common extension in many UNIX® systems, is used in Microsoft C++. It is an array of strings representing the variables set in the user's environment. This array is terminated by a **NULL** entry. See "Customizing Command Line Processing" on page 34 for information on suppressing environment processing.

END Microsoft Specific

The following example shows how to use the *argc*, *argv*, and *envp* arguments to **main**:

```
#include <iostream.h>
#include <string.h>

void main( int argc, char *argv[], char *envp[] )
{
    int iNumberLines = 0;     // Default is no line numbers.

    // If more than .EXE filename supplied, and if the
    // /n command-line option is specified, the listing
    // of environment variables is line-numbered.

    if( argc == 2 && stricmp( argv[1], "/n" ) == 0 )
        iNumberLines = 1;

    // Walk through list of strings until a NULL is encountered.
    for( int i = 0; envp[i] != NULL; ++i )
    {
        if( iNumberLines )
            cout << i << ": " << envp[i] << "\n";
    }
}
```

Wildcard Expansion

Microsoft Specific →

You can use wildcards—the question mark (?) and asterisk (*)—to specify filename and path arguments on the command line.

Command-line arguments are handled by a routine called **_setargv**. By default, **_setargv** expands wildcards into separate strings in the `argv` string array. If no matches are found for the wildcard argument, the argument is passed literally.

END Microsoft Specific

Parsing Command-Line Arguments

Microsoft Specific →

Microsoft C/C++ startup code uses the following rules when interpreting arguments given on the operating system command line:

- Arguments are delimited by white space, which is either a space or a tab.

- The caret character (^) is not recognized as an escape character or delimiter. The character is handled completely by the command-line parser in the operating system before being passed to the argv array in the program.

- A string surrounded by double quotation marks ("*string*") is interpreted as a single argument, regardless of white space contained within. A quoted string can be embedded in an argument.

- A double quotation mark preceded by a backslash (\") is interpreted as a literal double quotation mark character (").

- Backslashes are interpreted literally, unless they immediately precede a double quotation mark.

- If an even number of backslashes is followed by a double quotation mark, one backslash is placed in the argv array for every pair of backslashes, and the double quotation mark is interpreted as a string delimiter.

- If an odd number of backslashes is followed by a double quotation mark, one backslash is placed in the argv array for every pair of backslashes, and the double quotation mark is "escaped" by the remaining backslash, causing a literal double quotation mark (") to be placed in argv.

The following program demonstrates how command-line arguments are passed:

```
include <iostream.h>

void main( int argc,      // Number of strings in array argv
           char *argv[],  // Array of command-line argument strings
           char *envp[] )  // Array of environment variable strings
{
    int count;

    // Display each command-line argument.
    cout << "\nCommand-line arguments:\n";
    for( count = 0; count < argc; count++ )
      cout << "  argv[" << count << "]   "
           << argv[count] << "\n";
}
```

Table 2.2 shows example input and expected output, demonstrating the rules in the preceding list.

Table 2.2 Results of Parsing Command Lines

Command-Line Input	argv[1]	argv[2]	argv[3]
"abc" d e	abc	d	e
a\\\b d"e f"g h	a\\\b	de fg	h
a\\\"b c d	a\"b	c	d
a\\\\"b c" d e	a\\b c	d	e

END Microsoft Specific

Customizing Command-Line Processing

Microsoft Specific →

If your program does not take command-line arguments, you can save a small amount of space by suppressing use of the library routine that performs command-line processing. This routine is called **_setargv** and is described in "Wildcard Expansion" on page 32. To suppress its use, define a routine that does nothing in the file containing the **main** function, and name it **_setargv**. The call to _setargv is then satisfied by your definition of **_setargv**, and the library version is not loaded.

Similarly, if you never access the environment table through the *envp* argument, you can provide your own empty routine to be used in place of **_setenvp**, the environment-processing routine. Just as with the **_setargv** function, _setenvp must be declared as **extern "C"**.

Your program might make calls to the **spawn** or **exec** family of routines in the C run-time library. If this is the case, you should not suppress the environment-processing routine, since this routine is used to pass an environment from the parent process to the child process.

END Microsoft Specific

main Function Restrictions

Several restrictions apply to the **main** function that do not apply to any other C++ functions. The **main** function:

- Cannot be overloaded (see Chapter 12, "Overloading").
- Cannot be declared as **inline**.
- Cannot be declared as **static**.
- Cannot have its address taken.
- Cannot be called.

Program Termination

In C++, there are several ways to exit a program:

- Call the **exit** function.
- Call the **abort** function.
- Execute a **return** statement from **main**.

exit Function

The **exit** function, declared in the standard include file STDLIB.H, terminates a C++ program.

The value supplied as an argument to **exit** is returned to the operating system as the program's return code or exit code. By convention, a return code of zero means that the program completed successfully.

Note You can use the constants **EXIT_FAILURE** and **EXIT_SUCCESS**, defined in STDLIB.H, to indicate success or failure of your program.

Issuing a **return** statement from the **main** function is equivalent to calling the **exit** function with the return value as its argument.

For more information, see "exit" in the *Run-Time Library Reference*.

abort Function

The **abort** function, also declared in the standard include file STDLIB.H, terminates a C++ program. The difference between **exit** and **abort** is that **exit** allows the C++ run-time termination processing to take place (global object destructors will be called), whereas **abort** terminates the program immediately. For more information, see **abort** in the *Run-Time Library Reference*.

return Statement

Issuing a **return** statement from **main** is functionally equivalent to calling the **exit** function. Consider the following example:

```
int main()
{
   exit( 3 );
   return 3;
}
```

The **exit** and **return** statements in the preceding example are functionally identical. However, C++ requires that functions that have return types other than **void** return a value. The **return** statement allows you to return a value from **main**.

Additional Startup Considerations

In C++, object construction and destruction can involve executing user code. Therefore, it is important to understand which initializations happen before entry to **main** and which destructors are invoked after exit from **main**. (For detailed information about construction and destruction of objects, see "Constructors" and "Destructors" on pages 292 and 297 in Chapter 11.)

The following initializations take place prior to entry to **main**:

- Default initialization of static data to zero. All static data without explicit initializers are set to zero prior to executing any other code, including run-time initialization. Static data members must still be explicitly defined.

- Initialization of global static objects in a translation unit. This may occur either before entry to **main** or before the first use of any function or object in the object's translation unit.

Microsoft Specific →

In Microsoft C++, global static objects are initialized before entry to **main**.

END Microsoft Specific

Global static objects that are mutually interdependent but in different translation units may cause incorrect behavior.

Additional Termination Considerations

You can terminate a C++ program by using **exit**, **return**, or **abort**. You can add exit processing using the **atexit** function. These are discussed in the following sections.

Using exit or return

When you call **exit** or execute a **return** statement from **main**, static objects are destroyed in the reverse order of their initialization. This example shows how such initialization and cleanup works:

```
#include <stdio.h>

class ShowData
{
public:
    // Constructor opens a file.
    ShowData( const char *szDev )
    {
        OutputDev = fopen( szDev, "w" );
    }

    // Destructor closes the file.
    ~ShowData() { fclose( OutputDev ); }
```

```
   // Disp function shows a string on the output device.
   void Disp( char *szData )
   {
      fputs( szData, OutputDev );
   }
private:
   FILE *OutputDev;
};

//  Define a static object of type ShowData. The output device
//    selected is "CON" -- the standard output device.
ShowData sd1 = "CON";
//  Define another static object of type ShowData. The output
//    is directed to a file called "HELLO.DAT"
ShowData sd2 = "hello.dat";

int main()
{
   sd1.Disp( "hello to default device\n" );
   sd2.Disp( "hello to file hello.dat\n" );

   return 0;
}
```

In the preceding example, the static objects sd1 and sd2 are created and initialized
before entry to main. After this program terminates using the return statement, first
sd2 is destroyed and then sd1. The destructor for the ShowData class closes the files
associated with these static objects. (For more information about initialization,
constructors, and destructors, see Chapter 11, "Special Member Functions.")

Another way to write this code is to declare the ShowData objects with block scope,
allowing them to be destroyed when they go out of scope:

```
int main()
{
   ShowData sd1, sd2( "hello.dat" );

   sd1.Disp( "hello to default device\n" );
   sd2.Disp( "hello to file hello.dat\n" );

   return 0;
}
```

Using atexit

With the **atexit** function, you can specify an exit-processing function that executes
prior to program termination. No global static objects initialized prior to the call to
atexit are destroyed prior to execution of the exit-processing function.

Using abort

Calling the **abort** function causes immediate termination. It bypasses the normal destruction process for initialized global static objects. It also bypasses any special processing that was specified using the **atexit** function.

Storage Classes

Storage classes govern the lifetime, linkage, and treatment of objects and variables in C++. A given object can have only one storage class. This section discusses the C++ storage classes for data:

- Automatic
- Static
- Register
- External

Automatic

Objects and variables with automatic storage are local to a given instance of a block. In recursive or multithreaded code, automatic objects and variables are guaranteed to have different storage in different instances of a block. Microsoft C++ stores automatic objects and variables on the program's stack.

Objects and variables defined within a block have **auto** storage unless otherwise specified using the **extern** or **static** keyword. Automatic objects and variables can be specified using the **auto** keyword, but explicit use of **auto** is unnecessary. Automatic objects and variables have no linkage.

Automatic objects and variables persist only until the end of the block in which they are declared.

Static

Objects and variables declared as **static** retain their values for the duration of the program's execution. In recursive code, a static object or variable is guaranteed to have the same state in different instances of a block of code.

Objects and variables defined outside all blocks have static lifetime and external linkage by default. A global object or variable that is explicitly declared as **static** has internal linkage.

Static objects and variables persist for the duration of the program's execution.

Register

Only function arguments and local variables can be declared with the register storage class.

Like automatic variables, register variables persist only until the end of the block in which they are declared.

The compiler does not honor user requests for register variables; instead, it makes its own register choices when global optimizations are on. However, all other semantics associated with the **register** keyword are honored by the compiler.

External

Objects and variables declared as **extern** declare an object that is defined in another translation unit or in an enclosing scope as having external linkage.

Declaration of **const** variables with the **extern** storage class forces the variable to have external linkage. An initialization of an **extern const** variable is allowed in the defining translation unit. Initializations in translation units other than the defining translation unit produce undefined results.

The following code shows two **extern** declarations, `DefinedElsewhere` (which refers to a name defined in a different translation unit) and `DefinedHere` (which refers to a name defined in an enclosing scope):

```
extern int DefinedElsewhere;        // Defined in another translation
                                    //  unit.
void main()
{
   int DefinedHere;
   {
      extern int DefinedHere;       // Refers to DefinedHere in
                                    //  the enclosing scope.
   }
}
```

Initialization of Objects

A local automatic object or variable is initialized every time the flow of control reaches its definition. A local static object or variable is initialized the first time the flow of control reaches its definition. Consider the following example, which defines a class that logs initialization and destruction of objects and then defines three objects, I1, I2, and I3:

```
#include <iostream.h>
#include <string.h>

// Define a class that logs initializations and destructions.
class InitDemo
{
```

```cpp
public:
    InitDemo( const char *szWhat );
    ~InitDemo();
private:
    char *szObjName;
};

// Constructor for class InitDemo
InitDemo::InitDemo( const char *szWhat )
{
    if( szWhat != 0 && strlen( szWhat ) > 0 )
    {
        // Allocate storage for szObjName, then copy
        //  initializer szWhat into szObjName.
        szObjName = new char[ strlen( szWhat ) + 1 ];
        strcpy( szObjName, szWhat );
            cout << "Initializing: " << szObjName << "\n";
    }
    else
        szObjName = 0;
}

// Destructor for InitDemo
InitDemo::~InitDemo()
{
    if( szObjName != 0 )
    {
        cout << "Destroying: " << szObjName << "\n";
        delete szObjName;
    }
}

// Enter main function
void main()
{
    InitDemo I1( "Auto I1" );
    {
        cout << "In block.\n";
        InitDemo I2( "Auto I2" );
        static InitDemo I3( "Static I3" );
    }
    cout << "Exited block.\n";
}
```

The preceding code demonstrates how and when the objects I1, I2, and I3 are initialized and when they are destroyed. The output from the program is:

```
Initializing: Auto I1
In block.
Initializing: Auto I2
Initializing: Static I3
Destroying: Auto I2
Exited block.
Destroying: Auto I1
Destroying: Static I3
```

There are several points to note about the program.

First, I1 and I2 are automatically destroyed when the flow of control exits the block in which they are defined.

Second, in C++, it is not necessary to declare objects or variables at the beginning of a block. Furthermore, these objects are initialized only when the flow of control reaches their definitions. (I2 and I3 are examples of such definitions.) The output shows exactly when they are initialized.

Finally, static local variables such as I3 retain their values for the duration of the program but are destroyed as the program terminates.

Types

C++ supports three kinds of object types:

- Fundamental types are built into the language (such as **int**, **float**, or **double**). Instances of these fundamental types are often called "variables."

- Derived types are new types derived from built-in types. See page 44.

- Class types are new types created by combining existing types. These are discussed in Chapter 8, "Classes."

Fundamental Types

Fundamental types in C++ are divided into three categories: "integral," "floating," and "void." Integral types are capable of handling whole numbers. Floating types are capable of specifying values that may have fractional parts.

The **void** type describes an empty set of values. No variable of type **void** can be specified—it is used primarily to declare functions that return no values or to declare "generic" pointers to untyped or arbitrarily typed data. Any expression can be explicitly converted or cast to type **void**. However, such expressions are restricted to the following uses:

- An expression statement. (See Chapter 4, "Expressions," for more information.)

- The left operand of the comma operator. (See "Comma Operator" on page 101 in Chapter 4 for more information.)

- The second or third operand of the conditional operator (**? :**). (See "Expressions with the Conditional Operator" on page 102 in Chapter 4 for more information.)

Table 2.3 explains the restrictions on type sizes. These restrictions are independent of the Microsoft implementation.

Table 2.3   Fundamental Types of the C++ Language

Category	Type	Contents
Integral	**char**	Type **char** is an integral type that usually contains members of the execution character set—in Microsoft C++, this is ASCII.
		The C++ compiler treats variables of type **char**, **signed char**, and **unsigned char** as having different types. Variables of type **char** are promoted to **int** as if they are type **signed char** by default, unless the /J compilation option is used. In this case they are treated as type **unsigned char** and are promoted to **int** without sign extension.
	short	Type **short int** (or simply **short**) is an integral type that is larger than or equal to the size of type **char**, and shorter than or equal to the size of type **int**.
		Objects of type **short** can be declared as **signed short** or **unsigned short**. **Signed short** is a synonym for **short**.
	int	Type **int** is an integral type that is larger than or equal to the size of type **short int**, and shorter than or equal to the size of type **long**.
		Objects of type **int** can be declared as **signed int** or **unsigned int**. **Signed int** is a synonym for **int**.
	__int$n$	Sized integer, where n is the size, in bits, of the integer variable. The value of n can be 8, 16, 32, or 64.
	long	Type **long** (or **long int**) is an integral type that is larger than or equal to the size of type **int**.
		Objects of type **long** can be declared as **signed long** or **unsigned long**. **Signed long** is a synonym for **long**.
Floating	**float**	Type **float** is the smallest floating type.
	double	Type **double** is a floating type that is larger than or equal to type **float**, but shorter than or equal to the size of type **long double**.[1]
	long double[1]	Type **long double** is a floating type that is equal to type **double**.

[1] The representation of **long double** and **double** is identical. However, **long double** and **double** are separate types.

Table 2.4 lists the amount of storage required for fundamental types in Microsoft C++.

Table 2.4 Sizes of Fundamental Types

Type	Size
char, **unsigned char**, **signed char**	1 byte
short, **unsigned short**	2 bytes
int, **unsigned int**	4 bytes
long, **unsigned long**	4 bytes
float	4 bytes
double	8 bytes
long double[1]	8 bytes

[1] The representation of **long double** and **double** is identical. However, **long double** and **double** are separate types.

For more information about type conversion, see Chapter 3, "Standard Conversions."

Sized Integer Types

Microsoft C++ also supports sized integer types. You can declare 8-, 16-, 32-, or 64-bit integer variables by using the __int*n* type specifier, where *n* is the size, in bits, of the integer variable. The value of *n* can be 8, 16, 32, or 64. The following example declares one variable for each of these types of sized integers:

```
__int8 nSmall;    // Declares 8-bit integer
__int16 nMedium;  // Declares 16-bit integer
__int32 nLarge;   // Declares 32-bit integer
__int64 nHuge;    // Declares 64-bit integer
```

The types **__int8**, **__int16**, and **__int32**, are synonyms for the ANSI types that have the same size, and are useful for writing portable code that behaves identically across multiple platforms. Note that the **__int8** data type is synonymous with type **char**, **__int16** is synonymous with type **short**, and **__int32** is synonymous with type **int**. The **__int64** data type has no ANSI equivalent.

Since **__int8**, **__int16**, and **__int32** are considered synonyms by the compiler, care should be taken when using these types as arguments to overloaded function calls. For example, the following C++ code will generate a compiler error:

```
void MyFunc( __int8 ) {}
void MyFunc( char ) {}

void main()
{
   __int8 newVal;
   char MyChar;
   MyFunc( MyChar );    // Ambiguous function calls;
   MyFunc( newVal );    // char is synonymous with __int8.
}
```

Derived Types

Derived types are new types that can be used in a program, and can include directly derived types and composed derivative types.

Directly Derived Types

New types derived directly from existing types are types that point to, refer to, or (in the case of functions) transform type data to return a new type.

- Arrays of Variables or Objects
- Functions
- Pointers of a Given Type
- References to Objects
- Constants
- Pointers to Class Members

Arrays of Variables or Objects

Arrays of variables or objects can contain a specified number of a particular type. For example, an array derived from integers is an array of type **int**. The following code sample declares and defines an array of 10 **int** variables and an array of 5 objects of class `SampleClass`:

```
int         ArrayOfInt[10];
SampleClass aSampleClass[5];
```

Functions

Functions take zero or more arguments of given types and return objects of a specified type (or return nothing, if the function has a **void return** type).

Pointers of a Given Type

Pointers to variables or objects select an object in memory. The object can be global, local (or stack-frame), or dynamically allocated. Pointers to functions of a given type allow a program to defer selection of the function used on a particular object or objects until run time. The following example shows a definition of a pointer to a variable of type **char**:

```
char *szPathStr;
```

References to Objects

References to objects provide a convenient way to access objects by reference but use the same syntax required to access objects by value. The following example demonstrates how to use references as arguments to functions and as return types of functions:

```
BigClassType &func( BigClassType &objname )
{
    objname.DoSomething();    // Note that member-of operator(.)
                              //  is used.
    objname.SomeData = 7;     // Data passed by non-const
                              //  reference is modifiable.
    return objname;
}
```

The important points about passing objects to a function by reference are:

- The syntax for accessing members of **class**, **struct**, and **union** objects is the same as if they were passed by value: the member-of operator (.).

- The objects are not copied prior to the function call; their addresses are passed. This can reduce the overhead of the function call.

Additionally, functions that return a reference need only accept the address of the object to which they refer, instead of a copy of the whole object.

Although the preceding example describes references only in the context of communication with functions, references are not constrained to this use. Consider, for example, a case where a function needs to be an l-value—a common requirement for overloaded operators:

```
class Vector
{
public:
    Point &operator[]( int nSubscript ); // Function returns a
                                          //  reference type
    ...
};
```

The preceding declaration specifies a user-defined subscript operator for class
Vector. In an assignment statement, two possible conditions occur:

```
Vector v1;
int    i;
Point p;
v1[7] = p;    // Vector used as an l-value
p = v1[7];    // Vector used as an r-value
```

The latter case, where v1[7] is used as an r-value, can be implemented without use of references. However, the former case, where v1[7] is used as an l-value, cannot be implemented easily without functions that are of reference type. Conceptually, the last two statements in the preceding example translate to the following code:

```
v1.operator[]( 7 ) = 3;    // Vector used as an l-value
i = v1.operator[]( 7 );    // Vector used as an r-value
```

When viewed in this way, it is easier to see that the first statement must be an l-value to be semantically correct on the left side of the assignment statement.

For more information about overloading, and about overloaded operators in particular, see "Overloaded Operators" on page 336 in Chapter 12.

You can also use references to declare a **const** reference to a variable or object. A reference declared as **const** retains the efficiency of passing an argument by reference, while preventing the called function from modifying the original object. Consider the following code:

```
// IntValue is a const reference.
void PrintInt( const int &IntValue )
{
    printf( "%d\n", IntValue );
}
```

Reference initialization is different from assignment to a variable of reference type. Consider the following code:

```
int i = 7;
int j = 5;

// Reference initialization
int &ri = i;  // Initialize ri to refer to i.
int &rj = j;  // Initialize rj to refer to j.

// Assignment
ri = 3;       // i now equal to 3.
rj = 12;      // j now equal to 12.
ri = rj;      // i now equals j (12).
```

Constants

See "Literals" in Chapter 1 for more information about the various kinds of constants allowed in C++.

Pointers to Class Members

These pointers define a type that points to a class member of a particular type. Such a pointer can be used by any object of the class type or any object of a type derived from the class type.

Use of pointers to class members enhances the type safety of the C++ language. Three new operators and constructs are used with pointers to members, as shown in Table 2.5.

Table 2.5 Operators and Constructs Used with Pointers to Members

Operator or Construct	Syntax	Use
::*	*type*::**ptr-name*	Declaration of pointer to member. The *type* specifies the class name, and *ptr-name* specifies the name of the pointer to member. Pointers to members can be initialized. For example: `MyType::*pMyType = &MyType::i;`
.*	*obj-name*.**ptr-name*	Dereference a pointer to a member using an object or object reference. For example: `int j = Object.*pMyType;`

Table 2.5 Operators and Constructs Used with Pointers to Members *(continued)*

Operator or Construct	Syntax	Use
–>*	*obj-ptr–>*ptr-name*	Dereference a pointer to a member using a pointer to an object. For example: `int j = pObject->*pMyType;`

Consider this example that defines a class `AClass` and the derived type `pDAT`, which points to the member `I1`:

```
#include <iostream.h>

// Define class AClass.
class AClass
{
public:
    int I1;
    Show() { cout << I1 << "\n"; }
};

// Define a derived type pDAT that points to I1 members of
// objects of type AClass.
int AClass::*pDAT = &AClass::I1;

void main()
{
    AClass aClass;              // Define an object of type AClass.
    AClass *paClass = &aClass;  // Define a pointer to that object.

    int i;

    aClass.*pDAT = 7777;        // Assign to aClass::I1 using .* operator.
    aClass.Show();

    i = paClass->*pDAT;         // Dereference a pointer using ->* operator.
    cout << i << "\n";
}
```

The pointer to member `pDAT` is a new type derived from class `AClass`. It is more strongly typed than a "plain" pointer to **int** because it points only to **int** members of class `AClass` (in this case, `I1`). Pointers to static members are plain pointers rather than pointers to class members. Consider the following example:

```
class HasStaticMember
{
public:
    static int SMember;
};
int HasStaticMember::SMember = 0;

int *pSMember = &HasStaticMember::SMember;
```

Note that the type of the pointer is "pointer to **int**," not "pointer to `HasStaticMember::int`."

Pointers to members can refer to member functions as well as member data. Consider the following code:

```
#include <stdio.h>

// Declare a base class, A, with a virtual function, Identify.
// (Note that in this context, struct is the same as class.)
struct A
{
    virtual void Identify() = 0; // No definition for class A.
};

// Declare a pointer to the Identify member function.
void (A::*pIdentify)() = &A::Identify;

// Declare class B derived from class A.
struct B : public A
{
    void Identify();
};

// Define Identify functions for classe B
void B::Identify()
{
    printf( "Identification is B::Identify\n" );
}

void main()
{
    B  BObject;          // Declare objects of type B
    A *pA;               // Declare pointer to type A.

    pA = &BObject;       // Make pA point to an object of type B.
    (pA->*pIdentify)();  // Call Identify function through pointer
                         //  to member pIdentify.
}
```

The output from this program is:

```
Identification is B::Identify
```

The function is called through a pointer to type A. However, because the function is a virtual function, the correct function for the object to which pA refers is called.

Composed Derivative Types

This section describes the following composed derivative types:

- Classes
- Structures
- Unions

Information about aggregate types and initialization of aggregate types can be found in "Initializing Aggregates" on page 224 in Chapter 7.

Classes

Classes are a composite group of member objects, functions to manipulate these members, and (optionally) access-control specifications to member objects and functions.

By grouping composite groups of objects and functions in classes, C++ enables programmers to create derivative types that define not only data but also the behavior of objects.

Class members default to private access and private inheritance. Classes are covered in Chapter 8, "Classes," access control is covered in Chapter 10, "Member-Access Control."

Structures

C++ structures are the same as classes, except that all member data and functions default to public access, and inheritance defaults to public inheritance.

For more information about access control, see Chapter 10, "Member-Access Control."

Unions

Unions enable programmers to define types capable of containing different kinds of variables in the same memory space. The following code shows how you can use a union to store several different types of variables:

```
//  Declare a union that can hold data of types char, int,
//    or char *.
union ToPrint
{
   char   chVar;
   int    iVar;
   char  *szVar;
};
// Declare an enumerated type that describes what type to print.
enum PrintType { CHAR_T, INT_T, STRING_T };

void Print( ToPrint Var, PrintType Type )
{
   switch( Type )
   {
   case CHAR_T:
      printf( "%c", Var.chVar );
      break;
   case INT_T:
      printf( "%d", Var.iVar );
      break;
   case STRING_T:
      printf( "%s", Var.szVar );
      break;
   }
}
```

Type Names

Synonyms for both fundamental and derived types can be defined using the **typedef** keyword. The following code illustrates the use of **typedef**:

```
typedef unsigned char BYTE;    // 8-bit unsigned entity.
typedef BYTE *       PBYTE;    // Pointer to BYTE.

BYTE Ch;                       // Declare a variable of type BYTE.
PBYTE pbCh;                    // Declare a pointer to a BYTE
                               //  variable.
```

The preceding example shows uniform declaration syntax for the fundamental type **unsigned char** and its derivative type **unsigned char ***. The **typedef** construct is also helpful in simplifying declarations. A **typedef** declaration defines a synonym, not a new independent type. The following example declares a type name (PVFN) representing a pointer to a function that returns type **void**. The advantage of this declaration is that, later in the program, an array of these pointers is declared very simply.

```
// Prototype two functions.
void func1();
void func2();

//  Define PVFN to represent a pointer to a function that
//   returns type void.
typedef void (*PVFN)();

...

// Declare an array of pointers to functions.
PVFN pvfn[] = { func1, func2 };

// Invoke one of the functions.
(*pvfn[1])();
```

L-Values and R-Values

Expressions in C++ can evaluate to "l-values" or "r-values." L-values are expressions that evaluate to a type other than **void** and that designate a variable.

L-values appear on the left side of an assignment statement (hence the "l" in l-value). Variables that would normally be l-values can be made nonmodifiable by using the **const** keyword; these cannot appear on the left of an assignment statement. Reference types are always l-values.

The term r-value is sometimes used to describe the value of an expression and to distinguish it from an l-value. All l-values are r-values but not all r-values are l-values.

Some examples of correct and incorrect usages are:

```
i = 7;              // Correct. A variable name, i, is an l-value.
7 = i;              // Error. A constant, 7, is an r-value.
j * 4 = 7;          // Error. The expression j * 4 yields an r-value.
*p = i;             // Correct. A dereferenced pointer is an l-value.
const int ci = 7;   // Declare a const variable.
ci = 9;             // ci is a nonmodifiable l-value, so the
                    //  assignment causes an error message to
                    //  be generated.
((i < 3) ? i : j) = 7; // Correct. Conditional operator (? :)
                    //  returns an l-value.
```

Note The examples in this section illustrate correct and incorrect usage when operators are not overloaded. By overloading operators, you can make an expression such as j * 4 an l-value.

Numerical Limits

The two standard include files, LIMITS.H and FLOAT.H, define the "numerical limits," or minimum and maximum values that a variable of a given type can hold. These minimums and maximums are guaranteed to be portable to any C++ compiler that uses the same data representation as ANSI C. The LIMITS.H include file defines the numerical limits for integral types, and FLOAT.H defines the numerical limits for floating types.

Integer Limits

Microsoft Specific →

The limits for integer types are listed in Table 2.6. These limits are also defined in the standard header file LIMITS.H.

Table 2.6 Limits on Integer Constants

Constant	Meaning	Value
CHAR_BIT	Number of bits in the smallest variable that is not a bit field.	8
SCHAR_MIN	Minimum value for a variable of type **signed char**.	−128
SCHAR_MAX	Maximum value for a variable of type **signed char**.	127
UCHAR_MAX	Maximum value for a variable of type **unsigned char**.	255 (0xff)
CHAR_MIN	Minimum value for a variable of type **char**.	−128; 0 if /J option used
CHAR_MAX	Maximum value for a variable of type **char**.	127; 255 if /J option used

(continued)

Table 2.6   Limits on Integer Constants *(continued)*

Constant	Meaning	Value
MB_LEN_MAX	Maximum number of bytes in a multicharacter constant.	2
SHRT_MIN	Minimum value for a variable of type **short**.	–32768
SHRT_MAX	Maximum value for a variable of type **short**.	32767
USHRT_MAX	Maximum value for a variable of type **unsigned short**.	65535 (0xffff)
INT_MIN	Minimum value for a variable of type **int**.	–2147483647–1
INT_MAX	Maximum value for a variable of type **int**.	2147483647
UINT_MAX	Maximum value for a variable of type **unsigned int**.	4294967295 (0xffffffff)
LONG_MIN	Minimum value for a variable of type **long**.	–2147483647–1
LONG_MAX	Maximum value for a variable of type **long**.	2147483647
ULONG_MAX	Maximum value for a variable of type **unsigned long**.	4294967295 (0xffffffff)

If a value exceeds the largest integer representation, the Microsoft compiler generates an error.

END Microsoft Specific

Floating Limits

Microsoft Specific →

Table 2.7 lists the limits on the values of floating-point constants. These limits are also defined in the standard header file FLOAT.H.

Table 2.7   Limits on Floating-Point Constants

Constant	Meaning	Value
FLT_DIG	Number of digits, q, such that	6
DBL_DIG	a floating-point number with q	15
LDBL_DIG	decimal digits can be rounded into a floating-point representation and back without loss of precision.	15
FLT_EPSILON	Smallest positive number x, such	1.192092896e–07F
DBL_EPSILON	that x + 1.0 is not equal to 1.0.	2.2204460492503131e–016
LDBL_EPSILON		2.2204460492503131e–016
FLT_GUARD		0
FLT_MANT_DIG	Number of digits in the radix	24
DBL_MANT_DIG	specified by FLT_RADIX in the	53
LDBL_MANT_DIG	floating-point significand. The radix is 2; hence these values specify bits.	53

Table 2.7 Limits on Floating-Point Constants *(continued)*

Constant	Meaning	Value
FLT_MAX DBL_MAX LDBL_MAX	Maximum representable floating-point number.	3.402823466e+38F 1.7976931348623158e+308 1.7976931348623158e+308
FLT_MAX_10_EXP DBL_MAX_10_EXP LDBL_MAX_10_EXP	Maximum integer such that 10 raised to that number is a representable floating-point number.	38 308 308
FLT_MAX_EXP DBL_MAX_EXP LDBL_MAX_EXP	Maximum integer such that FLT_RADIX raised to that number is a representable floating-point number.	128 1024 1024
FLT_MIN DBL_MIN LDBL_MIN	Minimum positive value.	1.175494351e–38F 2.2250738585072014e–308 2.2250738585072014e–308
FLT_MIN_10_EXP DBL_MIN_10_EXP LDBL_MIN_10_EXP	Minimum negative integer such that 10 raised to that number is a representable floating-point number.	–37 –307 –307
FLT_MIN_EXP DBL_MIN_EXP LDBL_MIN_EXP	Minimum negative integer such that FLT_RADIX raised to that number is a representable floating-point number.	–125 –1021 –1021
FLT_NORMALIZE		0
FLT_RADIX _DBL_RADIX _LDBL_RADIX	Radix of exponent representation.	2 2 2
FLT_ROUNDS _DBL_ROUNDS _LDBL_ROUNDS	Rounding mode for floating-point addition.	1 (near) 1 (near) 1 (near)

Note that the information in Table 2.7 may differ in future versions of the product.

END Microsoft Specific

CHAPTER 3

Standard Conversions

The C++ language defines conversions between its fundamental types. It also defines conversions for pointer, reference, and pointer-to-member derived types. These conversions are called "standard conversions." (For more information about types, standard types, and derived types, see "Types" on page 41 in Chapter 2.)

This chapter discusses the following standard conversions:

- Integral promotions
- Integral conversions
- Floating conversions
- Floating and integral conversions
- Arithmetic conversions
- Pointer conversions
- Reference conversions
- Pointer-to-member conversions

Note   User-defined types can specify their own conversions. Conversion of user-defined types is covered in "Constructors" and "Conversions" on pages 292 and 302 in Chapter 11.

The following code causes conversions (in this example, integral promotions):

```
long   lnum1, lnum2;
int    inum;

// inum promoted to type long prior to assignment.
lnum1 = inum;

// inum promoted to type long prior to multiplication.
lnum2 = inum * lnum2;
```

Note The result of a conversion is an l-value only if it produces a reference type. For example, a user-defined conversion declared as

```
operator int&()
```

returns a reference and is an l-value. However, a conversion declared as

```
operator int()
```

returns an object and is not an l-value.

Integral Promotions

Objects of an integral type can be converted to another wider integral type (that is, a type that can represent a larger set of values). This widening type of conversion is called "integral promotion." With integral promotion, you can use the following in an expression wherever another integral type can be used:

- Objects, literals, and constants of type **char** and **short int**
- Enumeration types
- **int** bit fields
- Enumerators

C++ promotions are "value-preserving." That is, the value after the promotion is guaranteed to be the same as the value before the promotion. In value-preserving promotions, objects of shorter integral types (such as bit fields or objects of type **char**) are promoted to type **int** if **int** can represent the full range of the original type. If **int** cannot represent the full range of values, then the object is promoted to type **unsigned int**. Although this strategy is the same as that used by ANSI C, value-preserving conversions do not preserve the "signedness" of the object.

Value-preserving promotions and promotions that preserve signedness normally produce the same results. However, they can produce different results if the promoted object is one of the following:

- An operand of /, %, /=, %=, <, <=, >, or >=

  These operators rely on sign for determining the result. Therefore, value-preserving and sign-preserving promotions produce different results when applied to these operands.

- The left operand of >> or >>=

  These operators treat signed and unsigned quantities differently when performing a shift operation. For signed quantities, shifting a quantity right causes the sign bit to be propagated into the vacated bit positions. For unsigned quantities, the vacated bit positions are zero-filled.

- An argument to an overloaded function or operand of an overloaded operator that depends on the signedness of the type of that operand for argument matching. (See "Overloaded Operators" on page 336 in Chapter 12 for more about defining overloaded operators.)

Integral Conversions

Integral conversions are performed between integral types. The integral types are **char**, **int**, and **long** (and the **short**, **signed**, and **unsigned** versions of these types).

This section describes the following types of integral conversions:

- Converting signed to unsigned
- Converting unsigned to signed
- Standard conversion

Converting Signed to Unsigned

Objects of signed integral types can be converted to corresponding unsigned types. When these conversions occur, the actual bit pattern does not change; however, the interpretation of the data changes. Consider this code:

```
#include <iostream.h>

void main()
{
    short   i = -3;
    unsigned short u;

    cout << (u = i) << "\n";
}
```

The following output results:

```
65533
```

In the preceding example, a **signed short**, i, is defined and initialized to a negative number. The expression (u = i) causes i to be converted to an **unsigned short** prior to the assignment to u.

Converting Unsigned to Signed

Objects of unsigned integral types can be converted to corresponding signed types. However, such a conversion can cause misinterpretation of data if the value of the unsigned object is outside the range representable by the signed type, as demonstrated in the following example:

```
#include <iostream.h>

void main()
{
 short   i;
 unsigned short u = 65533;

 cout << (i = u) << "\n";
}
```

The following output results:

```
-3
```

In the preceding example, u is an **unsigned short** integral object that must be converted to a signed quantity to evaluate the expression (i = u). Because its value cannot be properly represented in a **signed short**, the data is misinterpreted as shown.

Standard Conversion

Objects of integral types can be converted to shorter signed or unsigned integral types. Such a conversion is called "standard conversion." It can result in loss of data if the value of the original object is outside the range representable by the shorter type.

Note The compiler issues a high-level warning when a conversion to a shorter type takes place.

Floating Conversions

An object of a floating type can be safely converted to a more precise floating type—that is, the conversion causes no loss of significance. For example, conversions from **float** to **double** or from **double** to **long double** are safe, and the value is unchanged.

An object of a floating type can also be converted to a less precise type, if it is in a range representable by that type. (See "Floating Limits" on page 52 in Chapter 2 for the ranges of floating types.) If the original value cannot be represented precisely, it can be converted to either the next higher or the next lower representable value. If no such value exists, the result is undefined. Consider the following example:

```
cout << (float)1E300 << endl;
```

The maximum value representable by type **float** is 3.402823466E38—a much smaller number than 1E300. Therefore, the number is converted to infinity, and the result is 1.#INF.

Floating and Integral Conversions

Certain expressions can cause objects of floating type to be converted to integral types, or vice versa.

This section describes the following types of floating and integral conversions:

- Floating to integral
- Integral to floating

Floating to Integral

When an object of floating type is converted to an integral type, the fractional part is truncated. No rounding takes place in the conversion process. Truncation means that a number like 1.3 is converted to 1, and –1.3 is converted to –1.

Integral to Floating

When an object of integral type is converted to a floating type and the original value cannot be represented exactly, the result is either the next higher or the next lower representable value.

Arithmetic Conversions

Many binary operators (discussed in "Expressions with Binary Operators" on page 88 in Chapter 4) cause conversions of operands and yield results the same way. The way these operators cause conversions is called "usual arithmetic conversions." Arithmetic conversions of operands of different types are performed as shown in Table 3.1.

Table 3.1   Conditions for Type Conversion

Conditions Met	Conversion
Either operand is of type **long double**.	Other operand is converted to type **long double**.
Preceding condition not met and either operand is of type **double**.	Other operand is converted to type **double**.
Preceding conditions not met and either operand is of type **float**.	Other operand is converted to type **float**.
Preceding conditions not met (none of the operands are of floating types).	Integral promotions are performed on the operands as follows: <ul><li>If either operand is of type **unsigned long**, the other operand is converted to type **unsigned long**.</li><li>If preceding condition not met, and if either operand is of type **long** and the other of type **unsigned int**, both operands are converted to type **unsigned long**.</li><li>If the preceding two conditions are not met, and if either operand is of type **long**, the other operand is converted to type **long**.</li><li>If the preceding three conditions are not met, and if either operand is of type **unsigned int**, the other operand is converted to type **unsigned int**.</li><li>If none of the preceding conditions are met, both operands are converted to type **int**.</li></ul>

The following code illustrates the conversion rules described in Table 3.1:

```
float    fVal;
double   dVal;
int      iVal;
unsigned long ulVal;

dVal = iVal * ulVal; // iVal converted to unsigned long;
                     // result of multiplication converted to double.

dVal = ulVal + fVal; // ulVal converted to float;
                     // result of addition converted to double.
```

The first statement in the preceding example shows multiplication of two integral types, iVal and ulVal. The condition met is that neither operand is of floating type and one operand is of type **unsigned int**. Therefore, the other operand, iVal, is converted to type **unsigned int**. The result is assigned to dVal. The condition met is that one operand is of type **double**; therefore, the **unsigned int** result of the multiplication is converted to type **double**.

The second statement in the preceding example shows addition of a **float** and an integral type, fVal and ulVal. The ulVal variable is converted to type **float** (third condition in Table 3.1). The result of the addition is converted to type **double** (second condition in Table 3.1) and assigned to dVal.

Pointer Conversions

Pointers can be converted during assignment, initialization, comparison, and other expressions. This section describes the following pointer conversion:

- Null pointers
- Pointers to type void
- Pointers to objects
- Pointers to functions
- Pointers to classes
- Expressions
- Pointers modified by const or volatile

Null Pointers

An integral constant expression that evaluates to zero, or such an expression cast to type **void ***, is converted to a pointer called the "null pointer." This pointer is guaranteed to compare unequal to a pointer to any valid object or function (except for pointers to based objects, which can have the same offset and still point to different objects).

Pointers to Type void

Pointers to type **void** can be converted to pointers to any other type, but only with an explicit type cast (unlike in C). (See "Expressions with Explicit Type Conversions" on page 103 in Chapter 4 for more information about type casts.) A pointer to any type can be converted implicitly to a pointer to type **void**.

A pointer to an incomplete object of a type can be converted to a pointer to **void** (implicitly) and back (explicitly). The result of such a conversion is equal to the value of the original pointer. An object is considered incomplete if it is declared, but there is insufficient information available to determine its size or base class.

Pointers to Objects

A pointer to any object that is not **const** or **volatile** can be implicitly converted to a pointer of type **void ***.

Pointers to Functions

A pointer to a function can be converted to type **void ***, if type **void *** is large enough to hold that pointer.

Pointers to Classes

There are two cases in which a pointer to a class can be converted to a pointer to a base class.

The first case is when the specified base class is accessible and the conversion is unambiguous. (See "Multiple Base Classes" on page 264 in Chapter 9 for more information about ambiguous base-class references.)

Whether a base class is accessible depends on the kind of inheritance used in derivation. Consider the inheritance illustrated in Figure 3.1.

Figure 3.1   Inheritance Graph for Illustration of Base-Class Accessibility

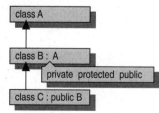

Table 3.2 shows the base-class accessibility for the situation illustrated in Figure 3.1.

Table 3.2 Base-Class Accessibility

Type of Function	Derivation	Conversion from B* to A* Legal?
External (not class-scoped) function	Private	No
	Protected	No
	Public	Yes
B member function (in B scope)	Private	Yes
	Protected	Yes
	Public	Yes
C member function (in C scope)	Private	No
	Protected	Yes
	Public	Yes

The second case in which a pointer to a class can be converted to a pointer to a base class is when you use an explicit type conversion. (See "Expressions with Explicit Type Conversions" on page 103 in Chapter 4 for more information about explicit type conversions.)

The result of such a conversion is a pointer to the "subobject," the portion of the object that is completely described by the base class.

The following code defines two classes, A and B, where B is derived from A. (For more information on inheritance, see Chapter 9, "Derived Classes.") It then defines bObject, an object of type B, and two pointers (pA and pB) that point to the object.

```
class A
{
public:
    int AComponent;
    int AMemberFunc();
};

class B : public A
{
public:
    int BComponent;
    int BMemberFunc();
};
B bObject;
A *pA = &bObject;
B *pB = &bObject;

pA->AMemberFunc();   // OK in class A
pB->AMemberFunc();   // OK: inherited from class A
pA->BMemberFunc();   // Error: not in class A
```

The pointer pA is of type A *, which can be interpreted as meaning "pointer to an object of type A." Members of bObject (such as BComponent and BMemberFunc) are unique to type B and are therefore inaccessible through pA. The pA pointer allows access only to those characteristics (member functions and data) of the object that are defined in class A.

Pointer Expressions

Any expression with an array type can be converted to a pointer of the same type. The result of the conversion is a pointer to the first array element. The following example demonstrates such a conversion:

```
char szPath[_MAX_PATH]; // Array of type char.
char *pszPath = szPath; // Equals &szPath[0].
```

An expression that results in a function returning a particular type is converted to a pointer to a function returning that type, except when:

- The expression is used as an operand to the address-of operator (**&**).

- The expression is used as an operand to the function-call operator.

Pointers Modified by const or volatile

C++ does not supply a standard conversion from a **const** or **volatile** type to a type that is not **const** or **volatile**. However, any sort of conversion can be specified using explicit type casts (including conversions that are unsafe).

Note   C++ pointers to members, except pointers to static members, are different from normal pointers and do not have the same standard conversions. Pointers to static members are normal pointers and have the same conversions as normal pointers. (See "Pointers to Class Members" page 46 in Chapter 2 for more information.)

Reference Conversions

A reference to a class can be converted to a reference to a base class in the following cases:

- The specified base class is accessible (as defined in "Pointers to Classes" on page 61).

- The conversion is unambiguous. (See "Multiple Base Classes" on page 264 in Chapter 9 for more information about ambiguous base-class references.)

The result of the conversion is a pointer to the subobject that represents the base class.

For more information about references, see "References to Objects" on page 44 in Chapter 2.

Pointer-to-Member Conversions

Pointers to class members can be converted during assignment, initialization, comparison, and other expressions. This section describes the following pointer-to-member conversions:

- Integral constant expressions
- Pointers to base-class members

Integral Constant Expressions

An integral constant expression that evaluates to zero is converted to a pointer called the "null pointer." This pointer is guaranteed to compare unequal to a pointer to any valid object or function (except for pointers to based objects, which can have the same offset and still point to different objects).

The following code illustrates the definition of a pointer to member i in class A. The pointer, pai, is initialized to 0, which is the null pointer.

```
class A
{
public:
 int i;
};

int A::*pai = 0;
```

Pointers to Base-Class Members

A pointer to a member of a base class can be converted to a pointer to a member of a class derived from it, when the following conditions are met:

- The inverse conversion, from pointer to derived class to base-class pointer, is accessible.
- The derived class does not inherit virtually from the base class.

When the left operand is a pointer to member, the right operand must be of pointer-to-member type or be a constant expression that evaluates to 0. This assignment is valid only in the following cases:

- The right operand is a pointer to a member of the same class as the left operand.
- The left operand is a pointer to a member of a class derived publicly and unambiguously from the class of the right operand.

CHAPTER 4

Expressions

This chapter describes C++ expressions. Expressions are sequences of operators and operands that are used for one or more of these purposes:

- Computing a value from the operands.

- Designating objects or functions.

- Generating "side effects." (Side effects are any actions other than the evaluation of the expression — for example, modifying the value of an object.)

In C++, operators can be overloaded and their meanings can be user-defined. However, their precedence and the number of operands they take cannot be modified. This chapter describes the syntax and semantics of operators as they are supplied with the language, not overloaded. The following topics are included:

- Types of expressions

- Semantics of expressions

(For more information about overloaded operators, see "Overloaded Operators" on page 336 in Chapter 12.)

Note Operators for built-in types cannot be overloaded; their behavior is predefined.

Types of Expressions

C++ expressions are divided into several categories:

- Primary expressions. These are the building blocks from which all other expressions are formed.

- Postfix expressions. These are primary expressions followed by an operator — for example, the array subscript or postfix increment operator.

- Expressions formed with unary operators. Unary operators act on only one operand in an expression.

- Expressions formed with binary operators. Binary operators act on two operands in an expression.

- Expressions with the conditional operator. The conditional operator is a ternary operator — the only such operator in the C++ language — and takes three operands.

- Constant expressions. Constant expressions are formed entirely of constant data.

- Expressions with explicit type conversions. Explicit type conversions, or "casts," can be used in expressions.

- Expressions with pointer-to-member operators.

- Casting. Type-safe "casts" can be used in expressions.

- Run-Time Type Information. Determine the type of an object during program execution.

Primary Expressions

Primary expressions are the building blocks of more complex expressions. They are literals, names, and names qualified by the scope-resolution operator (::).

Syntax

primary-expression:
> *literal*
> **this**
> :: *identifier*
> :: *operator-function-name*
> :: *qualified-name*
> (*expression*)
> *name*

A *literal* is a constant primary expression. Its type depends on the form of its specification. See "Literals" on page 9 in Chapter 1 for complete information about specifying literals.

The **this** keyword is a pointer to a class object. It is available within nonstatic member functions and points to the instance of the class for which the function was invoked. The **this** keyword cannot be used outside the body of a class-member function.

The type of the **this** pointer is *type* ***const** (where *type* is the class name) within functions not specifically modifying the **this** pointer. The following example shows member function declarations and the types of **this**:

```
class Example
{
public:
    void Func();        //  * const this
    void Func() const;  //  const * const this
    void Func() volatile; //  volatile * const this
};
```

See "Type of this Pointer" on page 245 in Chapter 8 for more information about modifying the type of the **this** pointer.

The scope-resolution operator (::) followed by an *identifier*, *operator-function-name*, or *qualified-name* constitutes a primary expression. The type of this expression is determined by the declaration of the *identifier*, *operator-function-name*, or *name*. It is an l-value if the declaring name is an l-value. The scope-resolution operator allows a global name to be referred to, even if that name is hidden in the current scope. See "Scope" on page 22 in Chapter 2 for an example of how to use the scope-resolution operator.

An expression enclosed in parentheses is a primary expression whose type and value are identical to those of the unparenthesized expression. It is an l-value if the unparenthesized expression is an l-value.

Names

In the C++ syntax for *primary-expression*, a *name* is a primary expression that can appear only after the member-selection operators (. or –>), and names the member of a class.

Syntax

name:
>   *identifier*
>   *operator-function-name*
>   *conversion-function-name*
>   ~ *class-name*
>   *qualified-name*

Any *identifier* that has been declared is a *name*.

An *operator-function-name* is a name that is declared in the form

operator *operator-name*(*argument1* [, *argument2*]);

See "Overloaded Operators" on page 336 in Chapter 12 for more information about declaration of *operator-function-name*.

A *conversion-function-name* is a name that is declared in the form

operator type-name( )

Note You can supply a derivative type name such as **char *** in place of the *type-name* when declaring a conversion function.

Conversion functions supply conversions to and from user-defined types. For more information about user-supplied conversions, see "Conversion Functions" on page 305 in Chapter 11.

A name declared as ~ *class-name* is taken as the "destructor" for objects of a class type. Destructors typically perform cleanup operations at the end of an object's lifetime. For information on destructors, see "Destructors" on page 297 in Chapter 11.

Qualified Names

Syntax

qualified-name:

    qualified-class-name **::** *name*

If a *qualified-class-name* is followed by the scope-resolution operator (**::**) and then the name of a member of either that class or a base of that class, then the scope-resolution operator is considered a *qualified-name*. The type of a *qualified-name* is the same as the type of the member, and the result of a *qualified-name* expression is the member. If the member is an l-value, then the *qualified-name* is also an l-value. For information about declaring *qualified-class-name*, see "Type Specifiers" on page 162 in Chapter 6 or "Class Names" on page 236 in Chapter 8.

The *class-name* part of a *qualified-class-name* can be hidden by redeclaration of the same name in the current or enclosing scope; the *class-name* is still found and used. See "Scope" on page 22 in Chapter 2 for an example of how to use a *qualified-class-name* to access a hidden *class-name*.

Note Class constructors and destructors of the form *class-name* **::** *class-name* and *class-name* **::** ~ *class-name*, respectively, must refer to the same *class-name*.

A name with more than one qualification, such as the following, designates a member of a nested class:

class-name **::** *class-name* **::** *name*

Postfix Expressions

Postfix expressions consist of primary expressions or expressions in which postfix operators follow a primary expression. The postfix operators are listed in Table 4.1.

Table 4.1 Postfix Operators

Operator Name	Operator Notation
Subscript operator	[ ]
Function-call operator	( )
Explicit type conversion operator	*type-name*( )
Member-selection operator	**.** or **->**
Postfix increment operator	**++**
Postfix decrement operator	**– –**

Syntax

postfix-expression:

    primary-expression

    postfix-expression [*expression*]

    postfix-expression (*expression-list*$_{opt}$)

    simple-type-name (*expression-list*$_{opt}$)

    postfix-expression **.** *name*

```
        postfix-expression -> name
        postfix-expression ++
        postfix-expression —
expression-list:
        assignment-expression
        expression-list , assignment-expression
```

Subscript Operator

A *postfix-expression* followed by the subscript operator, [ ], specifies array indexing. One of the expressions must be of pointer or array type — that is, it must have been declared as *type** or type[ ]. The other expression must be of an integral type (including enumerated types). In common usage, the expression enclosed in the brackets is the one of integral type, but that is not strictly required. Consider the following example:

```
MyType m[10];      // Declare an array of a user-defined type.

MyType n1 = m[2]; // Select third element of array.
MyType n2 = 2[m]; // Select third element of array.
```

In the preceding example, the expression m[2] is identical to 2[m]. Although m is not of an integral type, the effect is the same. The reason that m[2] is equivalent to 2[m] is that the result of a subscript expression *e1*[*e2*] is given by:

$$*((e2) + (e1))$$

The address yielded by the expression is not *e2* bytes from the address *e1*. Rather, the address is scaled to yield the next object in the array *e2*. For example:

```
double aDbl[2];
```

The addresses of aDb[0] and aDb[1] are 8 bytes apart — the size of an object of type **double**. This scaling according to object type is done automatically by the C++ language and is defined in "Additive Operators" on page 90 where addition and subtraction of operands of pointer type is discussed.

Positive and Negative Subscripts

The first element of an array is element 0. The range of a C++ array is from *array*[0] to *array*[*size* – 1]. However, C++ supports positive and negative subscripts. Negative subscripts must fall within array boundaries or results are unpredictable. The following code illustrates this concept:

```
#include <iostream.h>

void main()
{
    int iNumberArray[1024];
    int *iNumberLine = &iNumberArray[512];
```

```
        cout << iNumberArray[-256] << "\n";        // Unpredictable
        cout << iNumberLine[-256] << "\n";         // OK
}
```

The negative subscript in iNumberArray can produce a run-time error because it yields an address 256 bytes lower in memory than the origin of the array. The object iNumberLine is initialized to the middle of iNumberArray; it is therefore possible to use both positive and negative array indexes on it. Array subscript errors do not generate compile-time errors, but they yield unpredictable results.

The subscript operator is commutative. Therefore, the expressions *array*[*index*] and *index*[*array*] are guaranteed to be equivalent as long as the subscript operator is not overloaded (see "Overloaded Operators" on page 336 in Chapter 12). The first form is the most common coding practice, but either works.

Function-Call Operator

A *postfix-expression* followed by the function-call operator, ( ), specifies a function call. The arguments to the function-call operator are zero or more expressions separated by commas — the actual arguments to the function.

The *postfix-expression* must be of one of these types:

- Function returning type T. An example declaration is

  ```
  T func( int i )
  ```

- Pointer to a function returning type T. An example declaration is

  ```
  T (*func)( int i )
  ```

- Reference to a function returning type T. An example declaration is

  ```
  T (&func)(int i)
  ```

- Pointer-to-member function dereference returning type T. Example function calls are

  ```
  (pObject->*pmf)();
  (Object.*pmf)();
  ```

Formal and Actual Arguments

Calling programs pass information to called functions in "actual arguments." The called functions access the information using corresponding "formal arguments."

When a function is called, the following tasks are performed:

- All actual arguments (those supplied by the caller) are evaluated. There is no implied order in which these arguments are evaluated, but all arguments are evaluated and all side effects completed prior to entry to the function.

- Each formal argument is initialized with its corresponding actual argument in the expression list. (A formal argument is an argument that is declared in the function header and used in the body of a function.) Conversions are done as if by initialization — both standard and user-defined conversions are performed in converting an actual argument to the correct type. The initialization performed is illustrated conceptually by the following code:

```
void Func( int i ); // Function prototype

Func( 7 );          // Execute function call
```

The conceptual initializations prior to the call are:

```
int Temp_i = 7;
Func( Temp_i );
```

Note that the initialization is performed as if using the equal-sign syntax instead of the parentheses syntax. A copy of i is made prior to passing the value to the function. (For more information, see "Initializers" on page 223 in Chapter 7, and "Conversions," "Initialization Using Special Member Functions," and "Explicit Initialization" in Chapter 11 on pages 302, 314, and 315, respectively.

Therefore, if the function prototype (declaration) calls for an argument of type **long**, and if the calling program supplies an actual argument of type **int**, the actual argument is promoted using a standard type conversion to type **long** (see Chapter 3, "Standard Conversions").

It is an error to supply an actual argument for which there is no standard or user-defined conversion to the type of the formal argument.

For actual arguments of class type, the formal argument is initialized by calling the class's constructor. (See "Constructors" on page 292 in Chapter 11 for more about these special class member functions.)

- The function call is executed.

The following program fragment demonstrates a function call:

```
void func( long param1, double param2 );

void main()
{
    int i, j;

    // Call func with actual arguments i and j.
    func( i, j );
    ...
}

// Define func with formal parameters param1 and param2.
void func( long param1, double param2 )
{
    ...
}
```

When func is called from main, the formal parameter param1 is initialized with the value of i (i is converted to type **long** to correspond to the correct type using a standard conversion), and the formal parameter param2 is initialized with the value of j (j is converted to type **double** using a standard conversion).

Treatment of Argument Types

Formal arguments declared as const types cannot be changed within the body of a function. Functions can change any argument that is not of type **const**. However, the change is local to the function and does not affect the actual argument's value unless the actual argument was a reference to an object not of type **const**.

The following functions illustrate some of these concepts:

```
int func1( const int i, int j, char *c )
{
   i = 7;          // Error: i is const.
   j = i;          // OK, but value of j is
                   //  lost at return.
   *c = 'a' + j;   // OK: changes value of c
                   //  in calling function.

   return i;
}

double& func2( double& d, const char *c )
{
   d = 14.387;     // OK: changes value of d
                   //  in calling function.
   *c = 'a';       // Error: c is a pointer to
                   //  a const object.

   return d;
}
```

Ellipses and Default Arguments

Functions can be declared to accept fewer arguments than specified in the function definition, using one of two methods: ellipsis (. . .) or default arguments.

Ellipses denote that arguments may be required but that the number and types are not specified in the declaration. This is normally poor C++ programming practice because it defeats one of the benefits of C++: type safety. Different conversions are applied to functions declared with ellipses than to those functions for which the formal and actual argument types are known:

- If the actual argument is of type **float**, it is promoted to type **double** prior to the function call.

- Any signed or unsigned **char**, **short**, enumerated type, or bit field is converted to either a signed or an unsigned **int** using integral promotion.

- Any argument of class type is passed by value as a data structure; the copy is created by binary copying instead of by invoking the class's copy constructor (if one exists).

Ellipses, if used, must be declared last in the argument list. For more information about passing a variable number of arguments, see the discussion of **va_arg**, **va_start**, and **va_list** in the *Run-Time Library Reference*.

Default arguments enable you to specify the value an argument should assume if none is supplied in the function call. The following code fragment shows how default arguments work. For more information about restrictions on specifying default arguments, see "Default Arguments" on page 218 in Chapter 7.

```
#include <iostream.h>

// Declare the function print that prints a string,
// then a terminator.
void print( const char *string,
            const char *terminator = "\n" );

void main()
{
    print( "hello," );
    print( "world!" );

    print( "good morning", ", " );
    print( "sunshine." );
}

// Define print.
void print( char *string, char *terminator )
{
    if( string != NULL )
        cout << string;

    if( terminator != NULL )
        cout << terminator;
}
```

The preceding program declares a function, `print`, that takes two arguments. However, the second argument, `terminator`, has a default value, `"\n"`. In **main**, the first two calls to `print` allow the default second argument to supply a new line to terminate the printed string. The third call specifies an explicit value for the second argument. The output from the program is

```
hello,
world!
good morning, sunshine.
```

Function-Call Results

A function call evaluates to an r-value unless the function is declared as a reference type. Functions with reference return type evaluate to l-values, and can be used on the left side of an assignment statement as follows:

```
#include <iostream.h>

class Point
{
```

```
public:
    // Define "accessor" functions as
    // reference types.
    unsigned& x() { return _x; }
    unsigned& y() { return _y; }
private:
    unsigned _x;
    unsigned _y;
};

void main()
{
    Point ThePoint;

    ThePoint.x() = 7;              // Use x() as an l-value.
    unsigned y = ThePoint.y();     // Use y() as an r-value.

    // Use x() and y() as r-values.
    cout << "x = " << ThePoint.x() << "\n"
         << "y = " << ThePoint.y() << "\n";
}
000000
```

The preceding code defines a class called Point, which contains private data objects that represent *x* and *y* coordinates. These data objects must be modified and their values retrieved. This program is only one of several designs for such a class; use of the GetX and SetX or GetY and SetY functions is another possible design.

Functions that return class types, pointers to class types, or references to class types can be used as the left operand to member-selection operators. Therefore, the following code is legal:

```
class A
{
public:
    int SetA( int i ) { return (I = i); }
    int GetA()        { return I; }

private:
    int I;
};

// Declare three functions:
//   func1, which returns type A
//   func2, which returns a pointer to type A
//   func3, which returns a reference to type A
A func1();
A* func2();
A& func3();

int iResult = func1().GetA();
func2()->SetA( 3 );
func3().SetA( 7 );
```

Functions can be called recursively. For more information about function declarations, see "Function Specifiers" and "Member Functions." Related material is in "Program and Linkage."

Member-Selection Operator

A *postfix-expression* followed by the member-selection operator (**.**) and a *name* is another example of a *postfix-expression*. The first operand of the member-selection operator must have class or class reference type, and the second operand must identify a member of that class.

The result of the expression is the value of the member, and it is an l-value if the named member is an l-value.

A *postfix-expression* followed by the member-selection operator (**–>**) and a *name* is a *postfix-expression*. The first operand of the member-selection operator must have type pointer to a class object (an object declared as **class**, **struct**, or **union** type), and the second operand must identify a member of that class.

The result of the expression is the value of the member, and it is an l-value if the named member is an l-value. The **–>** operator dereferences the pointer. Therefore, the expressions *e–>member* and (***e**).*member* (where *e* represents an expression) yield identical results (except when the operators **–>** or ***** are overloaded).

When a value is stored through one member of a union but retrieved through another member, no conversion is performed. The following program stores data into the object U as **int** but retrieves the data as two separate bytes of type **char**:

```
#include <iostream.h>

void main()
{
    struct ch
    {
        char b1;
        char b2;
    };
    union u
    {
        struct ch uch;
        short  i;
    };

    u U;

    U.i = 0x6361;  // Bit pattern for "ac"
    cout << U.uch.b1 << U.uch.b2 << "\n";
}
```

Postfix Increment and Decrement Operators

C++ provides prefix and postfix increment and decrement operators; this section describes only the postfix increment and decrement operators. (For more information, see "Increment and Decrement Operators." The difference between the two is that in the postfix notation, the operator appears after *postfix-expression*, whereas in the prefix notation, the operator appears before *expression*. The following example shows a postfix-increment operator:

```
i++
```

The effect of applying the postfix increment, or "postincrement," operator (**++**) is that the operand's value is increased by one unit of the appropriate type. Similarly, the effect of applying the postfix decrement, or "postdecrement," operator (**− −**) is that the operand's value is decreased by one unit of the appropriate type.

For example, applying the postincrement operator to a pointer to an array of objects of type **long** actually adds four to the internal representation of the pointer. This behavior causes the pointer, which previously referred to the *n*th element of the array, to refer to the (*n*+1)th element.

The operands to postincrement and postdecrement operators must be modifiable (not **const**) l-values of arithmetic or pointer type. The result of the postincrement or postdecrement expression is the value of the *postfix-expression* prior to application of the increment operator. The type of the result is the same as that of the *postfix-expression*, but it is no longer an l-value.

The following code illustrates the postfix increment operator.

```
if( var++ > 0 )
    *p++ = *q++;
```

In this example, the variable `var` is compared to 0, then incremented. If `var` was positive before being incremented, the next statement is executed. First, the value of the object pointed to by q is assigned to the object pointed to by p. Then, q and p are incremented.

Postincrement and postdecrement, when used on enumerated types, yield integral values. Therefore, the following code is illegal:

```
enum Days {
    Sunday = 1,
    Monday,
    Tuesday,
    Wednesday,
    Thursday,
    Friday,
    Saturday
};
```

```
void main()
{
    Days Today = Tuesday;
    Days SaveToday;

    SaveToday = Today++;   // error
}
```

The intent of this code is to save today's day and then move to tomorrow. However, the result is that the expression Today++ yields an **int**—an error when assigned to an object of the enumerated type Days.

Expressions with Unary Operators

Unary operators act on only one operand in an expression. The unary operators are:

- Indirection operator (*)
- Address-of operator (&)
- Unary plus operator (+)
- Unary negation operator (–)
- Logical NOT operator (!)
- One's complement operator
- Prefix increment operator (++)
- Prefix decrement operator (––)
- sizeof operator
- new operator
- delete operator

These operators have right-to-left associativity.

Syntax

unary-expression:
> *postfix-expression*
> **++***unary-expression*
> *– –unary-expression*
> *unary-operator cast-expression*
> **sizeof** *.unary-expression*
> **sizeof** (*type-name*)
> *allocation-expression*
> *deallocation-expression*

unary-operator: one of
> * & + – ! ~

Indirection Operator (*)

The unary indirection operator (*) "dereferences" a pointer; that is, it converts a pointer value to an l-value. The operand of the indirection operator must be a pointer to a type. The result of the indirection expression is the type from which the pointer type is derived. The use of the * operator in this context is different from its meaning as a binary operator, which is multiplication.

If the operand points to a function, the result is a function designator. If it points to a storage location, the result is an l-value designating the storage location.

If the pointer value is invalid, the result is undefined. The following list includes some of the most common conditions that invalidate a pointer value.

- The pointer is a null pointer.
- The pointer specifies the address of a local item that is not visible at the time of the reference.
- The pointer specifies an address that is inappropriately aligned for the type of the object pointed to.
- The pointer specifies an address not used by the executing program.

Address-Of Operator (&)

The unary address-of operator (**&**) takes the address of its operand. The address-of operator can be applied only to the following:

- Functions (although its use for taking the address of a function is unnecessary)
- L-values
- Qualified names

In the first two cases listed above, the result of the expression is a pointer type (an r-value) derived from the type of the operand. For example, if the operand is of type **char**, the result of the expression is of type pointer to **char**. The address-of operator, applied to **const** or **volatile** objects, evaluates to **const** *type* * or **volatile** *type* *, where *type* is the type of the original object.

The result produced by the third case, applying the address-of operator to a *qualified-name*, depends on whether the *qualified-name* specifies a static member. If so, the result is a pointer to the type specified in the declaration of the member. If the member is not static, the result is a pointer to the member *name* of the class indicated by *qualified-class-name*. (See "Primary Expressions" on page 66 for more about *qualified-class-name*.) The following code fragment shows how the result differs, depending on whether the member is static:

```
class PTM
{
public:
        int    iValue;
   static float fValue;
};
```

```
int   PTM::*piValue = &PTM::iValue;  // OK: non-static
float PTM::*pfValue = &PTM::fValue;  // Error: static
float *spfValue     = &PTM::fValue;  // OK
```

In this example, the expression &PTM::fValue yields type float * instead of type float PTM::* because fValue is a static member.

The address of an overloaded function can be taken only when it is clear which version of the function is being referenced. See "Address of Overloaded Functions" on page 335 in Chapter 12 for information about how to obtain the address of a particular overloaded function.

Applying the address-of operator to a reference type gives the same result as applying the operator to the object to which the reference is bound. The following program demonstrates this concept:

```
#include <iostream.h>

void main()
{
   double d;        // Define an object of type double.
   double& rd = d;  // Define a reference to the object.

   // Compare the address of the object to the address
   //  of the reference to the object.
   if( &d == &rd )
      cout << "&d equals &rd" << "\n";
   else
      cout << "&d is not equal to &rd" << "\n";
}
```

The output from the program is always &d equals &rd.

Unary Plus Operator (+)

The result of the unary plus operator (+) is the value of its operand. The operand to the unary plus operator must be of an arithmetic type.

Integral promotion is performed on integral operands. The resultant type is the type to which the operand is promoted. Thus, the expression +ch, where ch is of type **char**, results in type **int**; the value is unmodified. See "Integral Promotions" on page 56 in Chapter 3 for more information about how the promotion is done.

Unary Negation Operator (-)

The unary negation operator (–) produces the negative of its operand. The operand to the unary negation operator must be an arithmetic type.

Integral promotion is performed on integral operands, and the resultant type is the type to which the operand is promoted. See "Integral Promotions" on page 56 in Chapter 3 for more information on how the promotion is done.

Microsoft Specific →

Unary negation of unsigned quantities is performed by subtracting the value of the operand from 2^n, where n is the number of bits in an object of the given unsigned type. (Microsoft C++ runs on processors that utilize two's-complement arithmetic. On other processors, the algorithm for negation can differ.)

END Microsoft Specific

Logical NOT Operator (!)

The result of the logical NOT operator (!) is 0 if its operand evaluates to a nonzero value; the result is 1 only if the operand is equal to 0. The operand must be of arithmetic or pointer type. The result is of type **int**.

For an expression e, the unary expression $!e$ is equivalent to the expression ($e == 0$), except where overloaded operators are involved.

The following example illustrates the logical NOT operator (!):

```
if( !(x < y) )
```

If x is greater than or equal to y, the result of the expression is 1 (true). If x is less than y, the result is 0 (false).

Unary arithmetic operations on pointers are illegal.

One's Complement Operator (~)

The one's complement operator (~), sometimes called the "bitwise complement" operator, yields a bitwise one's complement of its operand. That is, every bit that is set in the operand is 0 in the result. Conversely, every bit that is 0 in the operand is set in the result. The operand to the one's complement operator must be an integral type.

```
unsigned short y = 0xAAAA;
    y = ~y;
```

In this example, the new value assigned to y is the one's complement of the unsigned value 0xAAAA, or 0x5555.

Integral promotion is performed on integral operands, and the resultant type is the type to which the operand is promoted. See "Integral Promotions" on page 56 in Chapter 3 for more information on how the promotion is done.

Increment and Decrement Operators (++, --)

The prefix increment operator (++), also called the "preincrement" operator, adds one to its operand; this incremented value is the result of the expression. The operand must be an l-value not of type **const**. The result is an l-value of the same type as the operand.

The prefix decrement operator (--), also called the "predecrement" operator, is analogous to the preincrement operator, except that the operand is decremented by one and the result is this decremented value.

Both the prefix and postfix increment and decrement operators affect their operands. The key difference between them is when the increment or decrement takes place in the evaluation of an expression. (For more information, see "Postfix Increment and Decrement Operators" on page 76.) In the prefix form, the increment or decrement takes place before the value is used in expression evaluation, so the value of the expression is different from the value of the operand. In the postfix form, the increment or decrement takes place after the value is used in expression evaluation, so the value of the expression is the same as the value of the operand.

An operand of integral or floating type is incremented or decremented by the integer value 1. The type of the result is the same as the operand type. An operand of pointer type is incremented or decremented by the size of the object it addresses. An incremented pointer points to the next object; a decremented pointer points to the previous object.

This example illustrates the unary decrement operator:

```
if( line[--i] != '\n' )
    return;
```

In this example, the variable i is decremented before it is used as a subscript to line.

Because increment and decrement operators have side effects, using expressions with increment or decrement operators in a macro can have undesirable results (see "Macros" in the *Preprocessor Reference* for more information about macros). Consider this example:

```
#define max(a,b) ((a)<(b))?(b):(a)
```

```
int i, j, k;
```

```
k = max( ++i, j );
```

The macro expands to:

```
k = ((++i)<(j))?(j):(++i);
```

If i is greater than or equal to j, it will be incremented twice.

Note   C++ inline functions are preferable to macros in many cases because they eliminate side effects such as those described here, and allow the language to perform more complete type checking.

sizeof Operator

The **sizeof** operator yields the size of its operand with respect to the size of type **char**. The result of the **sizeof** operator is of type **size_t**, an integral type defined in the include file STDDEF.H. The operand to **sizeof** can be one of the following:

- A type name. To use **sizeof** with a type name, the name must be enclosed in parentheses.

- An expression. When used with an expression, **sizeof** can be specified with or without the parentheses. The expression is not evaluated.

When the **sizeof** operator is applied to an object of type **char**, it yields 1. When the **sizeof** operator is applied to an array, it yields the total number of bytes in that array. For example:

```
#include <iostream.h>

void main()
{
    char szHello[] = "Hello, world!";

    cout << "The size of the type of " << szHello << " is: "
        << sizeof( char ) << "\n";
    cout << "The length of " << szHello << " is: "
        << sizeof szHello << "\n";
}
```

The program output is:

```
The size of the type of Hello, world! is: 1
The length of Hello, world! is: 14
```

When the **sizeof** operator is applied to a **class**, **struct**, or **union** type, the result is the number of bytes in an object of that **class**, **struct**, or **union** type, plus any padding added to align members on word boundaries. (The /Zp [pack structure members] compiler option and the **pack** pragma affect alignment boundaries for members.) The **sizeof** operator never yields 0, even for an empty class.

The **sizeof** operator cannot be used with the following operands:

- Functions. (However, **sizeof** can be applied to pointers to functions.)
- Bit fields.
- Undefined classes.
- The type **void**.
- Incomplete types.
- Parenthesized names of incomplete types.

When the **sizeof** operator is applied to a reference, the result is the same as if **sizeof** had been applied to the object itself.

The **sizeof** operator is often used to calculate the number of elements in an array using an expression of the form:

```
sizeof array / sizeof array[0]
```

new Operator

The **new** operator attempts to dynamically allocate (at run time) one or more objects of *type-name*. The **new** operator cannot be used to allocate a function; however, it can be used to allocate a pointer to a function.

Syntax

allocation-expression:
>> $::_{opt}$ **new** *nmodel*$_{opt}$ *placement*$_{opt}$ *new-type-name* *new-initializer*$_{opt}$
>> $::_{opt}$ **new** *nmodel*$_{opt}$ *placement*$_{opt}$ (*type-name*) *new-initializer*$_{opt}$

placement:
>>   (*expression-list*)

new-type-name:
>>   *type-specifier-list new-declarator*$_{opt}$

The **new** operator is used to allocate objects and arrays of objects. The **new** operator allocates from a program memory area called the "free store." In C, the free store is often referred to as the "heap."

When **new** is used to allocate a single object, it yields a pointer to that object; the resultant type is *new-type-name* * or *type-name* *. When **new** is used to allocate a singly dimensioned array of objects, it yields a pointer to the first element of the array, and the resultant type is *new-type-name* * or *type-name* *. When **new** is used to allocate a multidimensional array of objects, it yields a pointer to the first element of the array, and the resultant type preserves the size of all but the leftmost array dimension. For example:

```
new float[10][25][10]
```

yields type `float (*)[25][10]`. Therefore, the following code will not work because it attempts to assign a pointer to an array of `float` with the dimensions `[25][10]` to a pointer to type `float`:

```
float *fp;
fp = new float[10][25][10];
```

The correct expression is:

```
float (*cp)[25][10];
cp = new float[10][25][10];
```

The definition of `cp` allocates a pointer to an array of type `float` with dimensions `[25][10]` — it does not allocate an array of pointers.

All but the leftmost array dimensions must be constant expressions that evaluate to positive values; the leftmost array dimension can be any expression that evaluates to a positive value. When allocating an array using the **new** operator, the first dimension can be zero — the **new** operator returns a unique pointer.

The *type-specifier-list* cannot contain **const**, **volatile**, class declarations, or enumeration declarations. Therefore, the following expression is illegal:

```
volatile char *vch = new volatile char[20];
```

The **new** operator does not allocate reference types because they are not objects.

If there is insufficient memory for the allocation request, by default **operator new** returns **NULL**. You can change this default behavior by writing a custom exception-handling routine and calling the **_set_new_handler** run-time library function with your function name as its argument. Alternately, you can choose to have **new** throw a C++ exception (of type **xalloc**) in the event of a memory allocation failure. For more details on these two recovery schemes, see "The operator new Function" on page 307 in Chapter 11.

Lifetime of Objects Allocated with new

Objects allocated with the **new** operator are not destroyed when the scope in which they are defined is exited. Because the **new** operator returns a pointer to the objects it allocates, the program must define a pointer with suitable scope to access those objects. For example:

```
void main()
{
    // Use new operator to allocate an array of 20 characters.
    char *AnArray = new char[20];

    for( int i = 0; i < 20; ++i )
    {
        // On the first iteration of the loop, allocate
        //  another array of 20 characters.
        if( i == 0 )
        {
            char *AnotherArray = new char[20];
        }
        ...
    }

    delete AnotherArray; // Error: pointer out of scope.
    delete AnArray;      // OK: pointer still in scope.
}
```

Once the pointer AnotherArray goes out of scope in the example, the object can no longer be deleted.

Initializing Objects Allocated with new

An optional *new-initializer* field is included in the syntax for the **new** operator. This allows new objects to be initialized with user-defined constructors. For more information about how initialization is done, see "Initializers" on page 223 in Chapter 7.

The following example illustrates how to use an initialization expression with the **new** operator:

```
#include <iostream.h>

class Acct
{
public:
    // Define default constructor and a constructor that accepts
    //  an initial balance.
    Acct() { balance = 0.0; }
    Acct( double init_balance ) { balance = init_balance; }
private:
    double balance;
};

void main()
{
    Acct *CheckingAcct = new Acct;
    Acct *SavingsAcct = new Acct ( 34.98 );
    double *HowMuch = new double ( 43.0 );
    ...
}
```

In this example, the object CheckingAcct is allocated using the **new** operator, but no default initialization is specified. Therefore, the default constructor for the class, Acct(), is called. Then the object SavingsAcct is allocated the same way, except that it is explicitly initialized to 34.98. Because 34.98 is of type **double**, the constructor that takes an argument of that type is called to handle the initialization. Finally, the nonclass type HowMuch is initialized to 43.0.

If an object is of a class type and that class has constructors (as in the preceding example), the object can be initialized by the **new** operator only if one of these conditions is met:

- The arguments provided in the initializer agree with those of a constructor.

- The class has a default constructor (a constructor that can be called with no arguments).

Access control and ambiguity control are performed on **operator new** and on the constructors according to the rules set forth in "Ambiguity" on page 276 in Chapter 9 and "Initialization Using Special Member Functions" on page 314 in Chapter 11.

No explicit per-element initialization can be done when allocating arrays using the **new** operator; only the default constructor, if present, is called. See "Default Arguments" on page 218 in Chapter 7 for more information.

If the memory allocation fails (**operator new** returns a value of 0), no initialization is performed. This protects against attempts to initialize data that does not exist.

As with function calls, the order in which initialized expressions are evaluated is not defined. Furthermore, you should not rely on these expressions being completely evaluated before the memory allocation is performed. If the memory allocation fails and the **new** operator returns zero, some expressions in the initializer may not be completely evaluated.

How new Works

The *allocation-expression* — the expression containing the **new** operator — does three things:

- Locates and reserves storage for the object or objects to be allocated. When this stage is complete, the correct amount of storage is allocated, but it is not yet an object.

- Initializes the object(s). Once initialization is complete, enough information is present for the allocated storage to be an object.

- Returns a pointer to the object(s) of a pointer type derived from *new-type-name* or *type-name*. The program uses this pointer to access the newly allocated object.

The **new** operator invokes the function **operator new**. For arrays of any type, and for objects that are not of **class**, **struct**, or **union** types, a global function, **::operator new**, is called to allocate storage. Class-type objects can define their own **operator new** static member function on a per-class basis.

When the compiler encounters the **new** operator to allocate an object of type *type*, it issues a call to *type***::operator new(sizeof(** *type* **))** or, if no user-defined **operator new** is defined, **::operator new(sizeof(** *type* **))**. Therefore, the **new** operator can allocate the correct amount of memory for the object.

Note The argument to **operator new** is of type **size_t**. This type is defined in DIRECT.H, MALLOC.H, MEMORY.H, SEARCH.H, STDDEF.H, STDIO.H, STDLIB.H, STRING.H, and TIME.H.

An option in the syntax allows specification of *placement* (see Syntax for "new Operator" on page 83). The *placement* parameters can be used only for user-defined implementations of **operator new**; it allows extra information to be passed to **operator new**. An expression with a *placement* field such as

```
T *TObject = new ( 0x0040 ) T;
```

is translated to

```
T *TObject = T::operator new( sizeof( T ), 0x0040 );
```

The original intention of the *placement* field was to allow hardware-dependent objects to be allocated at user-specified addresses.

Note Although the preceding example shows only one argument in the *placement* field, there is no restriction on how many extra arguments can be passed to **operator new** this way.

Even when **operator new** has been defined for a class type, the global operator can be used by using the form of this example:

```
T *TObject =::new TObject;
```

The scope-resolution operator (**::**) forces use of the global **new** operator.

delete Operator

The **delete** operator deallocates an object created with the **new** operator. The **delete** operator has a result of type **void** and therefore does not return a value. The operand to **delete** must be a pointer returned by the **new** operator.

Using **delete** on a pointer to an object not allocated with **new** gives unpredictable results. You can, however, use **delete** on a pointer with the value 0. This provision means that, because **new** always returns 0 on failure, deleting the result of a failed **new** operation is harmless.

Syntax

deallocation-expression:
> **::**_{opt} **delete** *cast-expression*
> **::**_{opt} **delete** [ ] *cast-expression*

Using the **delete** operator on an object deallocates its memory. A program that dereferences a pointer after the object is deleted can have unpredictable results or crash.

If the operand to the **delete** operator is a modifiable l-value, its value is undefined after the object is deleted.

Pointers to **const** objects cannot be deallocated with the **delete** operator.

How delete Works

The **delete** operator invokes the function **operator delete**. For objects of class types (**class**, **struct**, and **union**), the **delete** operator invokes the destructor for an object prior to deallocating memory (if the pointer is not null). For objects not of class type, the global **delete** operator is invoked. For objects of class type, the **delete** operator can be defined on a per-class basis; if there is no such definition for a given class, the global operator is invoked.

Using delete

There are two syntactic variants for the **delete** operator: one for single objects and the other for arrays of objects. The following code fragment shows how these differ:

```
void main()
{
    // Allocate a user-defined object, UDObject, and an object
    //  of type double on the free store using the
    //  new operator.
    UDType *UDObject = new UDType;
    double *dObject = new double;
    ...
    // Delete the two objects.
    delete UDObject;
    delete dObject;
    ...
    // Allocate an array of user-defined objects on the
    // free store using the new operator.
    UDType (*UDArr)[7] = new UDType[5][7];
    ...
    // Use the array syntax to delete the array of objects.
    delete [] UDArr;
}
```

These two cases produce undefined results: using the array form of **delete** (**delete [ ]**) on an object and using the nonarray form of **delete** on an array.

Expressions with Binary Operators

Binary operators act on two operands in an expression. The binary operators are:

- Multiplicative operators
  - Multiplication (*)
  - Division (/)
  - Modulus (%)
- Additive operators
  - Addition (+)
  - Subtraction (−)
- Shift operators
  - Right shift (>>)
  - Left shift (<<)
- Relational and equality operators
  - Less than (<)
  - Greater than (>)

- Less than or equal to (**<=**)
- Greater than or equal to (**>=**)
- Equal to (**==**)
- Not equal to (**!=**)
- Bitwise operators
  - Bitwise AND (**&**)
  - Bitwise exclusive OR (**^**)
  - Bitwise inclusive OR (**|**)
  - Logical AND (**&&**)
  - Logical OR (**||**)

Multiplicative Operators

The multiplicative operators are:

- Multiplication (*)
- Division (/)
- Modulus or "remainder from division" (%)

These binary operators have left-to-right associativity.

Syntax

multiplicative-expression:
>   *pm-expression*
>   *multiplicative-expression * pm-expression*
>   *multiplicative-expression / pm-expression*
>   *multiplicative-expression % pm-expression*

The multiplicative operators take operands of arithmetic types. The modulus operator (%) has a stricter requirement in that its operands must be of integral type. (To get the remainder of a floating-point division, use the run-time function, **fmod.**) The conversions covered in "Arithmetic Conversions" on page 59 in Chapter 3 are applied to the operands, and the result is of the converted type.

The multiplication operator yields the result of multiplying the first operand by the second.

The division operator yields the result of dividing the first operand by the second.

The modulus operator yields the remainder given by the following expression, where *e1* is the first operand and *e2* is the second: $e1 - (e1 / e2) * e2$, where both operands are of integral types.

Division by 0 in either a division or a modulus expression is undefined and causes a run-time error. Therefore, the following expressions generate undefined, erroneous results:

```
i % 0
f / 0.0
```

If both operands to a multiplication, division, or modulus expression have the same sign, the result is positive. Otherwise, the result is negative. The result of a modulus operation's sign is implementation-defined.

Microsoft Specific →

In Microsoft C++, the result of a modulus expression is always the same as the sign of the first operand.

END Microsoft Specific

If the computed division of two integers is inexact and only one operand is negative, the result is the largest integer (in magnitude, disregarding the sign) that is less than the exact value the division operation would yield. For example, the computed value of –11 / 3 is –3.666666666. The result of that integral division is –3.

The relationship between the multiplicative operators is given by the identity
(e1 / e2) * e2 + e1 % e2 == e1.

Additive Operators

The additive operators are:

- Addition (+)
- Subtraction (–)

These binary operators have left-to-right associativity.

Syntax

additive-expression:
    multiplicative-expression
    additive-expression + *multiplicative-expression*
    additive-expression – *multiplicative-expression*

The additive operators take operands of arithmetic or pointer types. The result of the addition (+) operator is the sum of the operands. The result of the subtraction (–) operator is the difference between the operands. If one or both of the operands are pointers, they must be pointers to objects, not to functions.

Additive operators take operands of *arithmetic*, *integral*, and *scalar* types. These are defined in Table 4.2.

Table 4.2 Types Used with Additive Operators

Type	Meaning
arithmetic	Integral and floating types are collectively called "arithmetic" types.
integral	Types **char** and **int** of all sizes (**long**, **short**) and enumerations are "integral" types.
scalar	Scalar operands are operands of either arithmetic or pointer type.

The legal combinations for these operators are:

arithmetic + arithmetic
scalar + integral
integral + scalar
arithmetic − arithmetic
scalar − scalar

Note that addition and subtraction are not equivalent operations.

If both operands are of arithmetic type, the conversions covered in "Arithmetic Conversions" on page 59 in Chapter 3 are applied to the operands, and the result is of the converted type.

Addition of Pointer Types

If one of the operands in an addition operation is a pointer to an array of objects, the other must be of integral type. The result is a pointer that is of the same type as the original pointer and that points to another array element. The following code fragment illustrates this concept:

```
short IntArray[10]; // Objects of type short occupy 2 bytes
short *pIntArray = IntArray;

for( int i = 0; i < 10; ++i )
{
   *pIntArray = i;
   cout << *pIntArray << "\n";
   pIntArray = pIntArray + 1;
}
```

Although the integral value 1 is added to `pIntArray`, it does not mean "add 1 to the address"; rather it means "adjust the pointer to point to the next object in the array" that happens to be 2 bytes (or `sizeof( int )`) away.

Note Code of the form `pIntArray = pIntArray + 1` is rarely found in C++ programs; to perform an increment, these forms are preferable: `pIntArray++` or `pIntArray += 1`.

Subtraction of Pointer Types

If both operands are pointers, the result of subtraction is the difference (in array elements) between the operands. The subtraction expression yields a signed integral result of type **ptrdiff_t** (defined in the standard include file STDDEF.H).

One of the operands can be of integral type, as long as it is the second operand. The result of the subtraction is of the same type as the original pointer. The value of the subtraction is a pointer to the $(n - i)$th array element, where n is the element pointed to by the original pointer and i is the integral value of the second operand.

Shift Operators

The bitwise shift operators are:

- Right shift (>>)
- Left shift (<<)

These binary operators have left-to-right associativity.

Syntax

shift-expression:
    additive-expression
    shift-expression << *additive-expression*
    shift-expression >> *additive-expression*

Both operands of the shift operators must be of integral types. Integral promotions are performed according to the rules described in "Integral Promotions" on page 56 in Chapter 3. The type of the result is the same as the type of the left operand. The value of a right-shift expression *e1* >> *e2* is *e1* / 2^{e2}, and the value of a left-shift expression *e1* << *e2* is *e1* * 2^{e2}.

The results are undefined if the right operand of a shift expression is negative or if the right operand is greater than or equal to the number of bits in the (promoted) left operand.

The left-shift operator causes the bit pattern in the first operand to be shifted left the number of bits specified by the second operand. Bits vacated by the shift operation are zero-filled. This is a logical shift, as opposed to a shift-and-rotate operation.

The right-shift operator causes the bit pattern in the first operand to be shifted right the number of bits specified by the second operand. Bits vacated by the shift operation are zero-filled for unsigned quantities. For signed quantities, the sign bit is propagated into the vacated bit positions. The shift is a logical shift if the left operand is an unsigned quantity; otherwise, it is an arithmetic shift.

Microsoft Specific →

The result of a right shift of a signed negative quantity is implementation dependent. Although Microsoft C++ propagates the most-significant bit to fill vacated bit positions, there is no guarantee that other implementations will do likewise.

END Microsoft Specific

Relational and Equality Operators

The relational and equality operators determine equality, inequality, or relative values of their operands. The relational operators are shown in Table 4.3.

Table 4.3 Relational and Equality Operators

Operator	Meaning
==	Equal to
!=	Not equal to
<	Less than
>	Greater than
<=	Less than or equal to
>=	Greater than or equal to

Relational Operators

The binary relational operators determine the following relationships:

- Less than
- Greater than
- Less than or equal to
- Greater than or equal to

Syntax
relational-expression:
 shift-expression
 relational-expression < *shift-expression*
 relational-expression > *shift-expression*
 relational-expression <= *shift-expression*
 relational-expression >= *shift-expression*

The relational operators have left-to-right associativity. Both operands of relational operators must be of arithmetic or pointer type. They yield values of type **int**. The value returned is 0 if the relationship in the expression is false; otherwise, it is 1. Consider the following code, which demonstrates several relational expressions:

```
#include <iostream.h>

void main()
{
    cout << "The true expression 3 > 2 yields: "
        << (3 > 2) << "\n";
    cout << "The false expression 20 < 10 yields: "
        << (20 < 10) << "\n";
    cout << "The expression 10 < 20 < 5 yields: "
        << (10 < 20 < 5) << "\n";
}
```

The output from this program is:

```
The true expression 3 > 2 yields 1
The false expression 20 < 10 yields 0
The expression 10 < 20 < 5 yields 1
```

The expressions in the preceding example must be enclosed in parentheses because the insertion operator (<<) has higher precedence than the relational operators. Therefore, the first expression without the parentheses would be evaluated as:

```
(cout << "The true expression 3 > 2 yields: " << 3) < (2 << "\n");
```

Note that the third expression evaluates to 1 — because of the left-to-right associativity of relational operators, the explicit grouping of the expression 10 < 20 < 5 is:

```
(10 < 20) < 5
```

Therefore, the test performed is:

```
1 < 5
```

and the result is 1 (or true).

The usual arithmetic conversions covered in "Arithmetic Conversions" on page 59 in Chapter 3 are applied to operands of arithmetic types.

Comparing Pointers Using Relational Operators

When two pointers to objects of the same type are compared, the result is determined by the location of the objects pointed to in the program's address space. Pointers can also be compared to a constant expression that evaluates to 0 or to a pointer of type **void ***. If a pointer comparison is made against a pointer of type **void ***, the other pointer is implicitly converted to type **void ***. Then the comparison is made.

Two pointers of different types cannot be compared unless:

- One type is a class type derived from the other type.
- At least one of the pointers is explicitly converted (cast) to type **void ***. (The other pointer is implicitly converted to type **void *** for the conversion.)

Two pointers of the same type that point to the same object are guaranteed to compare equal. If two pointers to nonstatic members of an object are compared, the following rules apply:

- If the class type is not a union, and if the two members are not separated by an *access-specifier*, such as **public**, **protected**, or **private**, the pointer to the member declared last will compare greater than the pointer to the member declared earlier. (For information on *access-specifier*, see the Syntax section in "Access Specifiers" on page 280 in Chapter 10.)
- If the two members are separated by an *access-specifier*, the results are undefined.
- If the class type is a union, pointers to different data members in that union compare equal.

If two pointers point to elements of the same array or to the element one beyond the end of the array, the pointer to the object with the higher subscript compares higher. Comparison of pointers is guaranteed valid only when the pointers refer to objects in the same array or to the location one past the end of the array.

Equality Operators

The binary equality operators compare their operands for strict equality or inequality.

Syntax

equality-expression:
> *relational-expression*
> *equality-expression* **==** *relational-expression*
> *equality-expression* **!=** *relational-expression*

The equality operators, equal to (==) and not equal to (!=), have lower precedence than the relational operators, but they behave similarly.

The equal-to operator (==) returns true if both operands have the same value; otherwise, it returns false. The not-equal-to operator (!=) returns true if the operands do not have the same value; otherwise, it returns false.

Equality operators can compare pointers to members of the same type. In such a comparison, pointer-to-member conversions, as discussed in "Pointer-to-Member Conversions" on page 64 in Chapter 3 are performed. Pointers to members can also be compared to a constant expression that evaluates to 0.

Bitwise Operators

The bitwise operators are:

- Bitwise AND (&)
- Bitwise exclusive OR (^)
- Bitwise inclusive OR (|)

These operators return bitwise combinations of their operands.

Bitwise AND Operator

The bitwise AND operator (&) returns the bitwise AND of the two operands. All bits that are on (1) in both the left and right operand are on in the result; bits that are off (0) in either the left or the right operand are off in the result.

Syntax

and-expression:
> *relational-expression*
> *and-expression* **&** *equality-expression*

Both operands to the bitwise AND operator must be of integral types. The usual arithmetic conversions covered in "Arithmetic Conversions" on page 59 in Chapter 3, are applied to the operands.

Bitwise Exclusive OR Operator

The bitwise exclusive OR operator (^) returns the bitwise exclusive OR of the two operands. All bits that are on (1) in either the left or right operand, but not both, are on in the result. Bits that are the same (either on or off) in both operands are off in the result.

Syntax

exclusive-or-expression:
    and-expression
    exclusive-or-expression ^ *and-expression*

Both operands to the bitwise exclusive OR operator must be of integral types. The usual arithmetic conversions covered in "Arithmetic Conversions" on page 59 in Chapter 3 are applied to the operands.

Bitwise Inclusive OR Operator

The bitwise inclusive OR operator (|) returns the bitwise inclusive OR of the two operands. All bits that are on (1) in either the left or right operand are on in the result. Bits that are off (0) in both operands are off in the result.

Syntax

inclusive-or-expression:
    exclusive-or-expression
    inclusive-or-expression | *exclusive-or-expression*

Both operands to the bitwise inclusive OR operator must be of integral types. The usual arithmetic conversions covered in "Arithmetic Conversions" on page 59 in Chapter 3 are applied to the operands.

Logical Operators

The logical operators, logical AND (**&&**) and logical OR (**||**), are used to combine multiple conditions formed using relational or equality expressions.

Logical AND Operator

The logical AND operator (**&&**) returns the integral value 1 if both operands are nonzero; otherwise, it returns 0. Logical AND has left-to-right associativity.

Syntax

logical-and-expression:
    inclusive-or-expression
    logical-and-expression **&&** *inclusive-or-expression*

The operands to the logical AND operator need not be of the same type, but they must be of integral or pointer type. The operands are commonly relational or equality expressions.

The first operand is completely evaluated and all side effects are completed before continuing evaluation of the logical AND expression.

The second operand is evaluated only if the first operand evaluates to true (nonzero). This evaluation eliminates needless evaluation of the second operand when the logical AND expression is false. You can use this short-circuit evaluation to prevent null-pointer dereferencing, as shown in the following example:

```
char *pch = 0;
...
(pch) && (*pch = 'a');
```

If pch is null (0), the right side of the expression is never evaluated. Therefore, the assignment through a null pointer is impossible.

Logical OR Operator

The logical OR operator (||) returns the integral value 1 if either operand is nonzero; otherwise, it returns 0. Logical OR has left-to-right associativity.

Syntax

logical-or-expression:
    logical-and-expression
    logical-or-expression || *logical-and-expression*

The operands to the logical OR operator need not be of the same type, but they must be of integral or pointer type. The operands are commonly relational or equality expressions.

The first operand is completely evaluated and all side effects are completed before continuing evaluation of the logical OR expression.

The second operand is evaluated only if the first operand evaluates to false (0). This eliminates needless evaluation of the second operand when the logical OR expression is true.

```
printf( "%d" , (x == w || x == y || x == z) );
```

In this example, if x is equal to either w, y, or z, the second argument to the printf function evaluates to true and the value 1 is printed. Otherwise, it evaluates to false and the value 0 is printed. As soon as one of the conditions evaluates to true, evaluation ceases.

Assignment Operators

Assignment operators store a value in the object designated by the left operand. There are two kinds of assignment operations: "simple assignment," in which the value of the second operand is stored in the object specified by the first operand, and "compound assignment," in which an arithmetic, shift, or bitwise operation is performed prior to storing the result. All assignment operators in Table 4.4 except the = operator are compound assignment operators.

Table 4.4 Assignment Operators

Operator	Meaning
=	Store the value of the second operand in the object specified by the first operand ("simple assignment").
*=	Multiply the value of the first operand by the value of the second operand; store the result in the object specified by the first operand.
/=	Divide the value of the first operand by the value of the second operand; store the result in the object specified by the first operand.
%=	Take modulus of the first operand specified by the value of the second operand; store the result in the object specified by the first operand.
+=	Add the value of the second operand to the value of the first operand; store the result in the object specified by the first operand.
-=	Subtract the value of the second operand from the value of the first operand; store the result in the object specified by the first operand.
<<=	Shift the value of the first operand left the number of bits specified by the value of the second operand; store the result in the object specified by the first operand.
>>=	Shift the value of the first operand right the number of bits specified by the value of the second operand; store the result in the object specified by the first operand.
&=	Obtain the bitwise AND of the first and second operands; store the result in the object specified by the first operand.
^=	Obtain the bitwise exclusive OR of the first and second operands; store the result in the object specified by the first operand.
|=	Obtain the bitwise inclusive OR of the first and second operands; store the result in the object specified by the first operand.

Syntax

assignment-expression:
        conditional-expression
        unary-expression assignment-operator assignment-expression

assignment-operator: one of
        = *= /= %= += -= <<= >>= &= ^= |=

Result of Assignment Operators

The assignment operators return the value of the object specified by the left operand after the assignment. The resultant type is the type of the left operand. The result of an assignment expression is always an l-value. These operators have right-to-left associativity. The left operand must be a modifiable l-value.

Note In ANSI C, the result of an assignment expression is not an l-value. Therefore, the legal C++ expression (a += b) += c is illegal in C.

Simple Assignment

The simple assignment operator (=) causes the value of the second operand to be stored in the object specified by the first operand. If both objects are of arithmetic types, the right operand is converted to the type of the left, prior to storing the value.

Objects of **const** and **volatile** types can be assigned to l-values of types that are just **volatile** or that are neither **const** nor **volatile**.

Assignment to objects of class type (**struct**, **union**, and **class** types) is performed by a function named **operator=**. The default behavior of this operator function is to perform a bitwise copy; however, this behavior can be modified using overloaded operators. (See "Overloaded Operators" on page 336 in Chapter 12 for more information.)

An object of any unambiguously derived class from a given base class can be assigned to an object of the base class. The reverse is not true because there is an implicit conversion from derived class to base class but not from base class to derived class. For example:

```
#include <iostream.h>

class ABase
{
public:
    ABase() { cout << "constructing ABase\n"; }
};
class ADerived : public ABase
{
public:
    ADerived() { cout << "constructing ADerived\n"; }
};

void main()
{
    ABase aBase;
    ADerived aDerived;

    aBase = aDerived; // OK
    aDerived = aBase; // Error
}
```

Assignments to reference types behave as if the assignment were being made to the object to which the reference points.

For class-type objects, assignment is different from initialization. To illustrate how different assignment and initialization can be, consider the code

```
UserType1 A;
UserType2 B = A;
```

The preceding code shows an initializer; it calls the constructor for UserType1 that takes an argument of type UserType1. Given the code

```
UserType1 A;
UserType2 B;

B = A;
```

the assignment statement

```
B = A;
```

can have one of the following effects:

- Call the function **operator=** for UserType2, provided **operator=** is provided with a UserType1 argument.
- Call the explicit conversion function UserType1::operator UserType2, if such a function exists.
- Call a constructor UserType2::UserType2, provided such a constructor exists, that takes a UserType1 argument and copies the result.

Compound Assignment

The compound assignment operators, shown in Table 4.4, are specified in the form *e1 op= e2*, where *e1* is a modifiable l-value not of **const** type and *e2* is one of the following:

- An arithmetic type
- A pointer, if *op* is + or −

The *e1 op= e2* form behaves as *e1 = e1 op e2*, but *e1* is evaluated only once.

Compound assignment to an enumerated type generates an error message. If the left operand is of a pointer type, the right operand must be of a pointer type or it must be a constant expression that evaluates to 0. If the left operand is of an integral type, the right operand must not be of a pointer type.

Comma Operator

The comma operator allows grouping two statements where one is expected.

Syntax

expression:

  assignment-expression

  expression **,** *assignment-expression*

The comma operator has left-to-right associativity. Two expressions separated by a comma are evaluated left to right. The left operand is always evaluated, and all side effects are completed before the right operand is evaluated.

Consider the expression

e1 , *e2*

The type and value of the expression are the type and value of *e2*; the result of evaluating *e1* is discarded. The result is an l-value if the right operand is an l-value.

Where the comma has special meaning (for example in actual arguments to functions or aggregate initializers), the comma operator and its operands must be enclosed in parentheses. Therefore, the following function calls are not equivalent:

```
// Declare functions:
void Func( int, int );
void Func( int );

Func( arg1, arg2 );    // Call Func( int, int )
Func( (arg1, arg2) );  // Call Func( int )
```

This example illustrates the comma operator:

```
for ( i = j = 1; i + j < 20; i += i, j-- );
```

In this example, each operand of the **for** statement's third expression is evaluated independently. The left operand i += i is evaluated first; then the right operand, j--, is evaluated.

```
func_one( x, y + 2, z );
func_two( (x--, y + 2), z );
```

In the function call to func_one, three arguments, separated by commas, are passed: x, y + 2, and z. In the function call to func_two, parentheses force the compiler to interpret the first comma as the sequential-evaluation operator. This function call passes two arguments to func_two. The first argument is the result of the sequential-evaluation operation (x--, y + 2), which has the value and type of the expression y + 2; the second argument is z.

Expressions with the Conditional Operator

The conditional operator (**? :**) is a ternary operator (it takes three operands). The conditional operator works as follows:

- The first operand is evaluated and all side effects are completed before continuing.
- If the first operand evaluates to true (a nonzero value), the second operand is evaluated.
- If the first operand evaluates to false (0), the third operand is evaluated.

The result of the conditional operator is the result of whichever operand is evaluated —the second or the third. Only one of the last two operands is evaluated in a conditional expression.

Syntax

conditional-expression:
    logical-or-expression
    logical-or-expression **?** *expression* **:** *conditional-expression*

Conditional expressions have no associativity. The first operand must be of integral or pointer type. The following rules apply to the second and third expressions:

- If both expressions are of the same type, the result is of that type.
- If both expressions are of arithmetic types, usual arithmetic conversions (covered in "Arithmetic Conversions" on page 59 in Chapter 3) are performed to convert them to a common type.
- If both expressions are of pointer types or if one is a pointer type and the other is a constant expression that evaluates to 0, pointer conversions are performed to convert them to a common type.
- If both expressions are of reference types, reference conversions are performed to convert them to a common type.
- If both expressions are of type **void**, the common type is type **void**.
- If both expressions are of a given class type, the common type is that class type.

Any combinations of second and third operands not in the preceding list are illegal. The type of the result is the common type, and it is an l-value if both the second and third operands are of the same type and both are l-values.

For example:

```
(val >= 0) ? val : -val
```

If the condition is true, the expression evaluates to `val`. If not, the expression equals `-val`.

Constant Expressions

C++ requires constant expressions — expressions that evaluate to a constant — for declarations of:

- Array bounds
- Selectors in **case** statements
- Bit-field length specification
- Enumeration initializers

Syntax

constant-expression:
  conditional-expression

The only operands that are legal in constant expressions are:

- Literals
- Enumeration constants
- Values declared as **const** that are initialized with constant expressions
- **sizeof** expressions

Nonintegral constants must be converted (either explicitly or implicitly) to integral types to be legal in a constant expression. Therefore, the following code is legal:

```
const double Size = 11.0;

char chArray[(int)Size];
```

Explicit conversions to integral types are legal in constant expressions; all other types and derived types are illegal except when used as operands to the **sizeof** operator.

The comma operator and assignment operators cannot be used in constant expressions.

Expressions with Explicit Type Conversions

C++ provides implicit type conversion, as described in Chapter 3, "Standard Conversions." You can also specify explicit type conversions when you need more precise control of the conversions applied.

Explicit Type Conversion Operator

C++ allows explicit type conversion using a syntax similar to the function-call syntax. A *simple-type-name* followed by an *expression-list* enclosed in parentheses constructs an object of the specified type using the specified expressions. The following example shows an explicit type conversion to type **int**:

```
int i = int( d );
```

The following example uses a modified version of the `Point` class defined in "Function-Call Results."

```cpp
#include <iostream.h>

class Point
{
public:
    // Define default constructor.
    Point() { _x = _y = 0; }
    // Define another constructor.
    Point( int X, int Y ) { _x = X; _y = Y; }

    // Define "accessor" functions as
    // reference types.
    unsigned& x() { return _x; }
    unsigned& y() { return _y; }
    void Show()    { cout << "x = " << _x << ", "
                         << "y = " << _y << "\n"; }
private:
    unsigned _x;
    unsigned _y;
};

void main()
{
    Point Point1, Point2;

    // Assign Point1 the explicit conversion
    //   of ( 10, 10 ).
    Point1 = Point( 10, 10 );

    // Use x() as an l-value by assigning an explicit
    //   conversion of 20 to type unsigned.
    Point1.x() = unsigned( 20 );
    Point1.Show();

    // Assign Point2 the default Point object.
    Point2 = Point();
    Point2.Show();
}
```

The output from this program is:

```
x = 20, y = 10
x = 0, y = 0
```

Although the preceding example demonstrates explicit type conversion using constants, the same technique works to perform these conversions on objects. The following code fragment demonstrates this:

```cpp
int i = 7;
float d;

d = float( i );
```

Explicit type conversions can also be specified using the "cast" syntax. The previous example, rewritten using the cast syntax, is:

```
d = (float)i;
```

Both cast and function-style conversions have the same results when converting from single values. However, in the function-style syntax, you can specify more than one argument for conversion. This difference is important for user-defined types. Consider a `Point` class and its conversions:

```
struct Point
{
    Point( short x, short y ) { _x = x; _y = y; }
    ...
    short _x, _y;
};
...
Point pt = Point( 3, 10 );
```

The preceding example, which uses function-style conversion, shows how to convert two values (one for *x* and one for *y*) to the user-defined type `Point`.

Important   Use the explicit type conversions with care, since they override the C++ compiler's built-in type checking.

Syntax
cast-expression:
> *unary-expression*
> (*type-name*) *cast-expression*

The cast notation must be used for conversions to types that do not have a *simple-type-name* (pointer or reference types, for example). Conversion to types that can be expressed with a *simple-type-name* can be written in either form. See "Type Specifiers" on page 162 in Chapter 6 for more information about what constitutes a *simple-type-name*.

Type definition within casts is illegal.

Legal Conversions

You can do explicit conversions from a given type to another type if the conversion can be done using standard conversions. The results are the same. The conversions described in this section are legal; any other conversions not explicitly defined by the user (for a class type) are illegal.

A value of integral type can be explicitly converted to a pointer if the pointer is large enough to hold the integral value. A pointer that is converted to an integral value can be converted back to a pointer; its value is the same. This identity is given by the following (where *p* represents a pointer of any type):

p == (*type* *) *integral-conversion*(*p*)

With explicit conversions, the compiler does not check whether the converted value fits in the new type except when converting from pointer to integral type or vice versa.

This section describes the following conversions:

- Converting pointer types
- Converting the null pointer
- Converting to a forward reference class type
- Converting to reference types
- Converting among pointer to member types

Converting Pointer Types

A pointer to one object type can be explicitly converted to a pointer of another object type. A pointer declared as **void *** is considered a pointer to any object type.

A pointer to a base class can be explicitly converted to a pointer to a derived class as long as these conditions are met:

- There is an unambiguous conversion.
- The base class is not declared as **virtual** at any point.

Because conversion to type **void *** can change the representation of an object, there is no guarantee that the conversion *type1** **void *** *type2** is equivalent to the conversion *type1* type2** (which is a change in value only).

When such a conversion is performed, the result is a pointer to the subobject of the original object representing the base class.

See Chapter 9, "Derived Classes," for more information about ambiguity and virtual base classes.

C++ allows explicit conversions of pointers to objects or functions to type **void ***.

Pointers to object types can be explicitly converted to pointers to functions if the function pointer type has enough bits to accommodate the pointer to object type.

A pointer to a **const** object can be explicitly converted to a pointer not of **const** type. The result of this conversion points to the original object. An object of **const** type, or a reference to an object of **const** type, can be cast to a reference to a type that is not **const**. The result is a reference to the original object. The original object was probably declared as **const** because it was to remain constant across the duration of the program. Therefore, an explicit conversion defeats this safeguard, allowing modification of such objects. The behavior in such cases is undefined.

A pointer to an object of **volatile** type can be cast to a pointer to a type that is not **volatile**. The result of this conversion refers to the original object. Similarly, an object of **volatile** type can be cast to a reference to a type that is not **volatile**.

Converting the Null Pointer

The null pointer (0) is converted into itself.

Converting to a Forward-Reference Class Type

A class that has been declared but not yet defined (a forward reference) can be used in a pointer cast. In this case, the compiler returns a pointer to the original object, not to a subobject as it might if the class's relationships were known.

Converting to Reference Types

Any object whose address can be converted to a given pointer type can also be converted to the analogous reference type. For example, any object whose address can be converted to type **char *** can also be converted to type **char &**. No constructors or class conversion functions are called to make a conversion to a reference type.

Objects or values can be converted to class-type objects only if a constructor or conversion operator has been provided specifically for this purpose. For more information about these user-defined functions, see "Conversion Constructors" on page 303 in Chapter 11.

Conversion of a reference to a base class, to a reference to a derived class (and vice versa) is done the same way as for pointers.

A cast to a reference type results in an l-value. The results of casts to other types are not l-values. Operations performed on the result of a pointer or reference cast are still performed on the original object.

Converting Among Pointer-to-Member Types

A pointer to a member can be converted to a different pointer-to-member type subject to these rules: Either the pointers must both be pointers to members in the same class or they must be pointers to members of classes, one of which is derived unambiguously from the other. When converting pointer-to-member functions, the return and argument types must match.

Expressions with Pointer-to-Member Operators

The pointer-to-member operators, .* and –>*, return the value of a specific class member for the object specified on the left side of the expression. The following example shows how to use these operators:

```
#include <iostream.h>

class Window
{
public:
    void Paint(); // Causes window to repaint.
    int WindowId;
};
```

107

```
// Define derived types pmfnPaint and pmWindowId.
// These types are pointers to members Paint() and
// WindowId, respectively.
void (Window::*pmfnPaint)() = &Window::Paint;
int Window::*pmWindowId = &Window::WindowId;

void main()
{
    Window AWindow;
    Window *pWindow = new Window;
// Invoke the Paint function normally, then use pointer to member.
    AWindow.Paint();
    (AWindow.*pmfnPaint)();

    pWindow->Paint();
    (pWindow->*pmfnPaint)(); // Parentheses required since * binds
                             //  less tightly than the function call.

    int Id;
    // Retrieve window id.
    Id = AWindow.*pmWindowId;
    Id = pWindow->*pmWindowId;
}
```

In the preceding example, a pointer to a member, `pmfnPaint`, is used to invoke the member function `Paint`. Another pointer to a member, `pmWindowId`, is used to access the `WindowId` member.

Syntax

pm-expression:
> *cast-expression*
> *pm-expression* .* *cast-expression*
> *pm-expression* –>* *cast-expression*

The binary operator .* combines its first operand, which must be an object of class type, with its second operand, which must be a pointer-to-member type.

The binary operator –>* combines its first operand, which must be a pointer to an object of class type, with its second operand, which must be a pointer-to-member type.

In an expression containing the .* operator, the first operand must be of the class type of, and be accessible to, the pointer to member specified in the second operand or of an accessible type unambiguously derived from and accessible to that class.

In an expression containing the –>* operator, the first operand must be of the type "pointer to the class type" of the type specified in the second operand, or it must be of a type unambiguously derived from that class.

Consider the following classes and program fragment:

```
class BaseClass
{
public:
   BaseClass(); // Base class constructor.
   void Func1();
};

// Declare a pointer to member function Func1.
void (BaseClass::*pmfnFunc1)() = &BaseClass::Func1;

class Derived : public BaseClass
{
public:
   Derived();  // Derived class constructor.
   void Func2();
};

// Declare a pointer to member function Func2.
void (Derived::*pmfnFunc2)() = &Derived::Func2;

void main()
{
   BaseClass ABase;
   Derived ADerived;

   (ABase.*pmfnFunc1)();      // OK: defined for BaseClass.
   (ABase.*pmfnFunc2)();      // Error: cannot use base class to
                              //  access pointers to members of
                              //  derived classes.
   (ADerived.*pmfnFunc1)();   // OK: Derived is unambiguously
                              //  derived from BaseClass.
   (ADerived.*pmfnFunc2)();   // OK: defined for Derived.
}
```

The result of the .* or –>* pointer-to-member operators is an object or function of the type specified in the declaration of the pointer to member. So, in the preceding example, the result of the expression ADerived.*pmfnFunc1() is a pointer to a function that returns **void**. This result is an l-value if the second operand is an l-value.

Note If the result of one of the pointer-to-member operators is a function, then the result can be used only as an operand to the function call operator.

Semantics of Expressions

This section explains when, and in what order, expressions are evaluated. It includes descriptions of certain expression that are ambiguous in their meaning, and compatible types that can be used in expressions. In addition, it describes certain expressions that are ambiguous in their meaning and compatible types that can be used in expressions.

The following topics are included:

- Order of evaluation
- Sequence points
- Ambiguous expressions
- Notation in expressions

Order of Evaluation

This section discusses the order in which expressions are evaluated but does not explain the syntax or the semantics of the operators in these expressions. The earlier sections in this chapter provide a complete reference for each of these operators.

Expressions are evaluated according to the precedence and grouping of their operators. (Table 1.1 in Chapter 1, "Lexical Conventions," shows the relationships the C++ operators impose on expressions.) Consider this example:

```
#include <iostream.h>

void main()
{
    int a = 2, b = 4, c = 9;

    cout << a + b * c << "\n";
    cout << a + (b * c) << "\n";
    cout << (a + b) * c << "\n";
}
```

The output from the preceding code is:

```
38
38
54
```

Figure 4.1 Expression-Evaluation Order

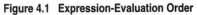
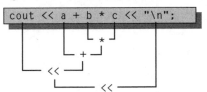

The order in which the expression shown in Figure 4.1 is evaluated is determined by the precedence and associativity of the operators:

1. Multiplication (*) has the highest precedence in this expression; hence the subexpression b * c is evaluated first.

2. Addition (+) has the next highest precedence, so a is added to the product of b and c.

3. Left shift (<<) has the lowest precedence in the expression, but there are two occurrences. Because the left-shift operator groups left-to-right, the left subexpression is evaluated first and then the right one.

When parentheses are used to group the subexpressions, they alter the precedence and also the order in which the expression is evaluated, as shown in Figure 4.2.

Figure 4.2 Expression-Evaluation Order with Parentheses

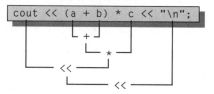

Expressions such as those in Figure 4.2 are evaluated purely for their side effects — in this case, to transfer information to the standard output device.

Note The left-shift operator is used to insert an object in an object of class **ostream**. It is sometimes called the "insertion" operator when used with iostream. For more about the iostream library, see the *iostream Class Library Reference*.

Sequence Points

An expression can modify an object's value only once between consecutive "sequence points."

Microsoft Specific →

The C++ language definition does not currently specify sequence points. Microsoft C++ uses the same sequence points as ANSI C for any expression involving C operators and not involving overloaded operators. When operators are overloaded, the semantics change from operator sequencing to function-call sequencing. Microsoft C++ uses the following sequence points:

- Left operand of the logical AND operator (**&&**). The left operand of the logical AND operator is completely evaluated and all side effects completed before continuing. There is no guarantee that the right operand of the logical AND operator will be evaluated.

- Left operand of the logical OR operator (||). The left operand of the logical OR operator is completely evaluated and all side effects completed before continuing. There is no guarantee that the right operand of the logical OR operator will be evaluated.

- Left operand of the comma operator. The left operand of the comma operator is completely evaluated and all side effects completed before continuing. Both operands of the comma operator are always evaluated.

- Function-call operator. The function-call expression and all arguments to a function, including default arguments, are evaluated and all side effects completed prior to entry to the function. There is no specified order of evaluation among the arguments or the function-call expression.

- First operand of the conditional operator. The first operand of the conditional operator is completely evaluated and all side effects completed before continuing.

- The end of a full initialization expression, such as the end of an initialization in a declaration statement.

- The expression in an expression statement. Expression statements consist of an optional expression followed by a semicolon (;). The expression is completely evaluated for its side effects.

- The controlling expression in a selection (**if** or **switch**) statement. The expression is completely evaluated and all side effects completed before the code dependent on the selection is executed.

- The controlling expression of a **while** or **do** statement. The expression is completely evaluated and all side effects completed before any statements in the next iteration of the **while** or **do** loop are executed.

- Each of the three expressions of a **for** statement. Each expression is completely evaluated and all side effects completed before moving to the next expression.

- The expression in a **return** statement. The expression is completely evaluated and all side effects completed before control returns to the calling function.

END Microsoft Specific

Ambiguous Expressions

Certain expressions are ambiguous in their meaning. These expressions occur most frequently when an object's value is modified more than once in the same expression. These expressions rely on a particular order of evaluation where the language does not define one. Consider the following example:

```
int i = 7;

func( i, ++i );
```

The C++ language does not guarantee the order in which arguments to a function call are evaluated. Therefore, in the preceding example, func could receive the values 7 and 8, or 8 and 8 for its parameters, depending on whether the parameters are evaluated from left to right or from right to left.

Notation in Expressions

The C++ language specifies certain compatibilities when specifying operands. Table 4.5 shows the types of operands acceptable to operators that require operands of type *type*.

Table 4.5   Operand Types Acceptable to Operators

Type Expected	Types Allowed
type	**const** *type* **volatile** *type* *type***&** **const** *type***&** **volatile** *type***&** **volatile const** *type* **volatile const** *type***&**
type*	*type** **const** *type** **volatile** *type** **volatile const**
const *type*	*type* **const** *type* **const** *type***&**
volatile *type*	*type* **volatile** *type* **volatile** *type***&**

Because the preceding rules can always be used in combination, a **const** pointer to a **volatile** object can be supplied where a pointer is expected.

Casting

The C++ language provides that if a class is derived from a base class containing virtual functions, a pointer to that base class type can be used to call the implementations of the virtual functions residing in the derived class object. A class containing virtual functions is sometimes called a "polymorphic class."

Since a derived class completely contains the definitions of all the base classes from which it is derived, it is safe to cast a pointer up the class hierarchy to any of these base classes. Given a pointer to a base class, it might be safe to cast the pointer down the hierarchy. It is safe if the object being pointed to is actually of a type derived from the base class. In this case, the actual object is said to be the "complete object." The pointer to the base class is said to point to a "subobject" of the complete object. For example, consider the class hierarchy shown in Figure 4.3:

Figure 4.3   Class Hierarchy

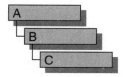

An object of type C could be visualized as shown in Figure 4.4:

Figure 4.4 Class C with B Subobject and A Subobject

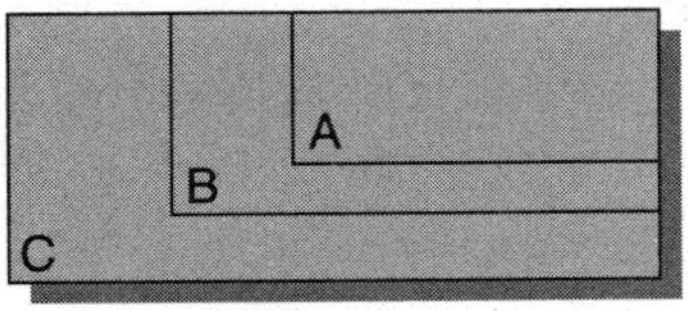

Given an instance of class C, there is a B subobject and an A subobject. The instance of C, including the A and B subobjects, is the "complete object."

Using run-time type information, it is possible to check whether a pointer actually points to a complete object and can be safely cast to point to another object in its hierarchy. The **dynamic_cast** operator can be used to make these types of casts. It also performs the run-time check necessary to make the operation safe.

Casting Operators

There are several casting operators specific to the C++ language. These operators are intended to remove some of the ambiguity and danger inherent in old style C language casts. These operators are:

- **dynamic_cast** Used for conversion of polymorphic types.
- **static_cast** Used for conversion of nonpolymorphic types.
- **const_cast** Used to remove the **const**, **volatile**, and **__unaligned** attributes.
- **reinterpret_cast** Used for simple reinterpretation of bits.

Use **const_cast** and **reinterpret_cast** as a last resort, since these operators present the same dangers as old style casts. However, they are still necessary in order to completely replace old style casts.

dynamic_cast Operator

The expression **dynamic_cast**<*type-id*>(*expression*) converts the operand *expression* to an object of type *type-id*. The *type-id* must be a pointer or a reference to a previously defined class type or a "pointer to **void**". The type of *expression* must be a pointer if *type-id* is a pointer, or an l-value if *type-id* is a reference.

Syntax
dynamic_cast < *type-id* > (*expression*)

If *type-id* is a pointer to an unambiguous accessible direct or indirect base class of *expression*, a pointer to the unique subobject of type *type-id* is the result. For example:

```
class B { ... };
class C : public B { ... };
class D : public C { ... };

void f(D* pd)
{
    C* pc = dynamic_cast<C*>(pd);    // ok: C is a direct base class
                                     // pc points to C subobject of pd

    B* pb = dynamic_cast<B*>(pd);    // ok: B is an indirect base class
                                     // pb points to B subobject of pd
    ...
}
```

This type of conversion is called an "upcast" because it moves a pointer up a class hierarchy, from a derived class to a class it is derived from. An upcast is an implicit conversion.

If *type-id* is **void***, a run-time check is made to determine the actual type of *expression*. The result is a pointer to the complete object pointed to by *expression*. For example:

```
class A { ... };

class B { ... };

void f()
{
    A* pa = new A;
    B* pb = new B;
    void* pv = dynamic_cast<void*>(pa);
    // pv now points to an object of type A
    ...
    pv = dynamic_cast<void*>(pb);
    // pv now points to an object of type B
}
```

If *type-id* is not **void***, a run-time check is made to see if the object pointed to by *expression* can be converted to the type pointed to by *type-id*.

If the type of *expression* is a base class of the type of *type-id*, a run-time check is made to see if *expression* actually points to a complete object of the type of *type-id*. If this is true, the result is a pointer to a complete object of the type of *type-id*. For example:

```
class B { ... };
class D : public B { ... };

void f()
{
    B* pb = new D;                   // unclear but ok
    B* pb2 = new B;

    D* pd = dynamic_cast<D*>(pb);    // ok: pb actually points to a D
    ...
    D* pd2 = dynamic_cast<D*>(pb2);  //error: pb2 points to a B, not a D
                                     // pd2 == NULL
    ...
}
```

This type of conversion is called a "downcast" because it moves a pointer down a class hierarchy, from a given class to a class derived from it.

In cases of multiple inheritance, possibilities for ambiguity are introduced. Consider the class hierarchy shown in Figure 4.5:

Figure 4.5 Class Hierarchy Showing Multiple Inheritance

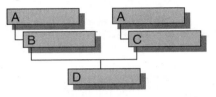

A pointer to an object of type D can be safely cast to B or C. However, if D is cast to point to an A object, which instance of A would result? This would result in an ambiguous casting error. To get around this problem, you can perform two unambiguous casts. For example:

```
void f()
{
    D* pd = new D;
    A* pa = dynamic_cast<A*>(pd);      // error: ambiguous
    B* pb = dynamic_cast<B*>(pd);      // first cast to B
    A* pa2 = dynamic_cast<A*>(pb);     // ok: unambiguous
}
```

Further ambiguities can be introduced when you use virtual base classes. Consider the class hierarchy shown in Figure 4.6:

Figure 4.6 Class Hierarchy Showing Virtual Base Classes

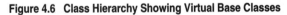
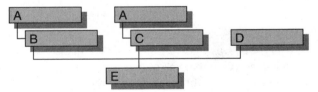

In this hierarchy, A is a virtual base class. See "Virtual Base Classes" on page 265 in Chapter 9 for the definition of a virtual base class. Given an instance of class E and a pointer to the A subobject, a **dynamic_cast** to a pointer to B will fail due to ambiguity. You must first cast back to the complete E object, then work your way back up the hierarchy, in an unambiguous manner, to reach the correct B object.

Consider the class hierarchy shown in Figure 4.7:

Figure 4.7   Class Hierarchy Showing Duplicate Base Classes

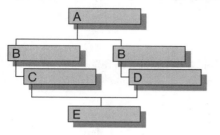

Given an object of type E and a pointer to the D subobject, to navigate from the
D subobject to the left-most A subobject, three conversions can be made. You
can perform a **dynamic_cast** conversion from the D pointer to an E pointer, then
a conversion (either **dynamic_cast** or an implicit conversion) from E to B, and
finally an implicit conversion from B to A. For example:

```
void f(D* pd)
{
   E* pe = dynamic_cast<E*>(pd);
   B* pb = pe;    // upcast, implicit conversion
   A* pa = pb;    // upcast, implicit conversion
}
```

The **dynamic_cast** operator can also be used to perform a "cross cast." Using the
same class hierarchy, it is possible to cast a pointer, for example, from the B subobject
to the D subobject, as long as the complete object is of type E.

Considering cross casts, it is actually possible to do the conversion from a pointer to
D to a pointer to the left-most A subobject in just two steps. You can perform a cross
cast from D to B, then an implicit conversion from B to A. For example:

```
void f(D* pd)
{
   B* pb = dynamic_cast<B*>(pd);    // cross cast
   A* pa = pb;                      // upcast, implicit conversion
}
```

A **null** pointer value is converted to the **null** pointer value of the destination type
by **dynamic_cast**.

When you use **dynamic_cast** < *type-id* > (*expression*), if *expression* cannot
be safely converted to type *type-id*, the run-time check causes the cast to fail.
For example:

```
class A { ... };

class B { ... };
```

```
void f()
{
   A* pa = new A;
   B* pb = dynamic_cast<B*>(pa);        // fails, not safe;
                                        // B not derived from A

   ...
}
```

The value of a failed cast to pointer type is the **null** pointer. A failed cast to reference type throws a **bad_cast** exception.

bad_cast Exception

The **dynamic_cast** operator throws a **bad_cast** exception as the result of a failed cast to a reference type. The interface for **bad_cast** is:

```
class bad_cast : public logic {
public:
   bad_cast(const __exString& what_arg) : logic(what_arg) {}
   void raise() { handle_raise(); throw *this; }
   // virtual __exString what() const;        //inherited
};
```

static_cast Operator

The expression **static_cast** < *type-id* > (*expression*) converts *expression* to the type of *type-id* based solely on the types present in the expression. No run-time type check is made to ensure the safety of the conversion.

Syntax
static_cast < *type-id* > (*expression*)

The **static_cast** operator can be used for operations such as converting a pointer to a base class to a pointer to a derived class. Such conversions are not always safe. For example:

```
class B { ... };

class D : public B { ... };

void f(B* pb, D* pd)
{
   D* pd2 = static_cast<D*>(pb);        // not safe, pb may
                                        // point to just B

   B* pb2 = static_cast<B*>(pd);        // safe conversion
   ...
}
```

In contrast to **dynamic_cast**, no run-time check is made on the **static_cast** conversion of pb. The object pointed to by pb may not be an object of type D, in which case the use of *pd2 could be disastrous. For instance, calling a function that is a member of the D class, but not the B class, could result in an access violation.

The **dynamic_cast** and **static_cast** operators move a pointer throughout a class hierarchy. However, **static_cast** relies exclusively on the information provided in the cast statement and can therefore be unsafe. For example:

```
class B { ... };
class D : public B { ... };

void f(B* pb)
{
    D* pd1 = dynamic_cast<D*>(pb);
    D* pd2 = static_cast<D*>(pb);
}
```

If pb really points to an object of type D, then pd1 and pd2 will get the same value. They will also get the same value if pb == 0.

If pb points to an object of type B and not to the complete D class, then **dynamic_cast** will know enough to return zero. However, **static_cast** relies on the programmer's assertion that pb points to an object of type D and simply returns a pointer to that supposed D object.

Consequently, **static_cast** can do the inverse of implicit conversions, in which case the results are undefined. It is left to the programmer to ensure that the results of a **static_cast** conversion are safe.

This behavior also applies to types other than class types. For instance, **static_cast** can be used to convert from an **int** to a **char**. However, the resulting **char** may not have enough bits to hold the entire **int** value. Again, it is left to the programmer to ensure that the results of a **static_cast** conversion are safe.

The **static_cast** operator can also be used to perform any implicit conversion, including standard conversions and user-defined conversions. For example:

```
typedef unsigned char BYTE

void f()
{
    char ch;
    int i = 65;
    float f = 2.5;
    double dbl;

    ch = static_cast<char>(i);              // int to char
    dbl = static_cast<double>(f);               // float to double
    ...
    i = static_cast<BYTE>(ch);
    ...
}
```

The **static_cast** operator can explicitly convert an integral value to an enumeration type. If the value of the integral type does not fall within the range of enumeration values, the resulting enumeration value is undefined.

The **static_cast** operator converts a **null** pointer value to the **null** pointer value of the destination type.

Any expression can be explicitly converted to type **void** by the **static_cast** operator. The destination **void** type can optionally include the **const**, **volatile**, or **__unaligned** attribute.

The **static_cast** operator cannot cast away the **const**, **volatile**, or **__unaligned** attributes. See "const_cast Operator" for information on removing these attributes.

const_cast Operator

The **const_cast** operator can be used to remove the **const, volatile,** and **__unaligned** attribute(s) from a class.

Syntax
const_cast < *type-id* > (*expression*)

A pointer to any object type or a pointer to a data member can be explicitly converted to a type that is identical except for the **const**, **volatile**, and **__unaligned** qualifiers. For pointers and references, the result will refer to the original object. For pointers to data members, the result will refer to the same member as the original (uncast) pointer to data member. Depending on the type of the referenced object, a write operation through the resulting pointer, reference, or pointer to data member might produce undefined behavior.

The **const_cast** operator converts a **null** pointer value to the **null** pointer value of the destination type.

reinterpret_cast Operator

The **reinterpret_cast** operator allows any pointer to be converted into any other pointer type. It also allows any integral type to be converted into any pointer type and vice versa. Misuse of the **reinterpret_cast** operator can easily be unsafe. Unless the desired conversion is inherently low-level, you should use one of the other cast operators.

Syntax
reinterpret_cast < *type-id* > (*expression*)

The **reinterpret_cast** operator can be used for conversions such as `char*` to `int*`, or `One_class*` to `Unrelated_class*`, which are inherently unsafe.

The result of a **reinterpret_cast** cannot safely be used for anything other than being cast back to its original type. Other uses are, at best, nonportable.

The **reinterpret_cast** operator cannot cast away the **const**, **volatile**, or **__unaligned** attributes. See "const_cast Operator" for information on removing these attributes.

The **reinterpret_cast** operator converts a **null** pointer value to the **null** pointer value of the destination type.

Run-Time Type Information

Run-time type information (RTTI) is a mechanism that allows the type of an object to be determined during program execution. RTTI was added to the C++ language because many vendors of class libraries were implementing this functionality themselves. This caused incompatibilities between libraries. Thus, it became obvious that support for run-time type information was needed at the language level.

For the sake of clarity, this discussion of RTTI is almost completely restricted to pointers. However, the concepts discussed also apply to references.

There are three main C++ language elements to run-time type information:

- The **dynamic_cast** operator.
  Used for conversion of polymorphic types. See "dynamic_cast Operator" on page 114 for more information.

- The **typeid** operator.
  Used for identifying the exact type of an object.

- The **type_info** class.
  Used to hold the type information returned by the **typeid** operator.

typeid Operator

The **typeid** operator allows the type of an object to be determined at run time.

Syntax
typeid(*type-id*)
typeid(*expression*)

The result of a **typeid** expression is a **const type_info&**. The value is a reference to a **type_info** object that represents either the *type-id* or the type of the *expression*, depending on which form of **typeid** is used. See "type_info Class" on page 122 for more information.

The **typeid** operator does a run-time check when applied to an l-value of a polymorphic class type, where the true type of the object cannot be determined by the static information provided. Such cases are:

- A reference to a class

- A pointer, dereferenced with *

- A subscripted pointer (i.e. [ ]). (Note that it is generally not safe to use a subscript with a pointer to a polymorphic type.)

If the *expression* points to a base class type, yet the object is actually of a type derived from that base class, a **type_info** reference for the derived class is the result. The *expression* must point to a polymorphic type, that is, a class with virtual functions. Otherwise, the result is the **type_info** for the static class referred to in the *expression*. Further, the pointer must be dereferenced so that the object it points to is used. Without dereferencing the pointer, the result will be the **type_info** for the pointer, not what it points to. For example:

```
class Base { ... };

class Derived : public Base { ... };

void f()
{
    Derived* pd = new Derived;
    Base* pb = pd;
    ...
    const type_info& t = typeid(pb);    // t holds pointer type_info
    const type_info& t1 = typeid(*pb);  // t1 holds Derived info
    ...
}
```

If the *expression* is dereferencing a pointer, and that pointer's value is zero, **typeid** throws a **bad_typeid** exception. If the pointer does not point to a valid object, a **__non_rtti_object** exception is thrown.

If the *expression* is neither a pointer nor a reference to a base class of the object, the result is a **type_info** reference representing the static type of the *expression*.

bad_typeid Exception

Under some circumstances, the **typeid** operator throws a **bad_typeid** exception. The interface for **bad_typeid** is:

```
class bad_typeid : public logic {
public:
    bad_typeid(const char * what_arg) : logic(what_arg) {}
    void raise()    { handle_raise(); throw *this; }
    // virtual __exString what() const;    //inherited
};
```

See "typeid Operator" on page 121 for more information.

type_info Class

The **type_info** class describes type information generated within the program by the compiler. Objects of this class effectively store a pointer to a name for the type. The **type_info** class also stores an encoded value suitable for comparing two types for equality or collating order. The encoding rules and collating sequence for types are unspecified and may differ between programs.

The `typeinfo.h` header file must be included in order to use the **type_info** class.

```
class type_info {
public:
    virtual ~type_info();
    int operator==(const type_info& rhs) const;
    int operator!=(const type_info& rhs) const;
    int before(const type_info& rhs) const;
    const char* name() const;
    const char* raw_name() const;
private:
    ...
};
```

The operators `==` and `!=` can be used to compare for equality and inequality with other **type_info** objects, respectively.

There is no link between the collating order of types and inheritance relationships. Use the **type_info::before** member function to determine the collating sequence of types. There is no guarantee that **type_info::before** will yield the same result in different programs or even different runs of the same program. In this manner, **type_info::before** is similar to the address-of (&) operator.

The **type_info::name** member function returns a **const char*** to a null-terminated string representing the human-readable name of the type. The memory pointed to is cached and should never be directly deallocated.

The **type_info::raw_name** member function returns a **const char*** to a null-terminated string representing the decorated name of the object type. The name is actually stored in its decorated form to save space. Consequently, this function is faster than **type_info::name** because it doesn't need to undecorate the name. The string returned by the **type_info::raw_name** function is useful in comparison operations but is not readable. If you need a human-readable string, use the **type_info::name** function instead.

Type information is generated for polymorphic classes only if the /GR (Enable Run-Time Type Information) compiler option is specified.

CHAPTER 5

Statements

C++ statements are the program elements that control how and in what order objects are manipulated. This chapter includes:

- Overview
- Labeled Statements
- Categories of Statements
  - Expression statements. These statements evaluate an expression for its side effects or for its return value.
  - Null statements. These statements can be provided where a statement is required by the C++ syntax but where no action is to be taken.
  - Compound statements. These statements are groups of statements enclosed in curly braces ({ }). They can be used wherever the grammar calls for a single statement.
  - Selection statements. These statements perform a test; they then execute one section of code if the test evaluates to true (nonzero). They may execute another section of code if the test evaluates to false.
  - Iteration statements. These statements provide for repeated execution of a block of code until a specified termination criterion is met.
  - Jump statements. These statements either transfer control immediately to another location in the function or return control from the function.
  - Declaration statements. Declarations introduce a name into a program. (Chapter 6, "Declarations," provides more detailed information about declarations.)
  - Exception handling statements, which include C++ exception handling (**try**, **throw**, **catch**) and structured exception handling (**__try/__except**, **__try/__finally**). The **try-except** statement provides a method to gain control of a program when events that normally terminate execution occur. The **try-finally** and **leave** statements provide a method to guarantee execution of cleanup code when execution of a block of code is interrupted.

Overview of Statements

C++ statements are executed sequentially, except when an expression statement, a selection statement, an iteration statement, or a jump statement specifically modifies that sequence.

Syntax

statement:
>*labeled-statement*
>*expression-statement*
>*compound-statement*
>*selection-statement*
>*iteration-statement*
>*jump-statement*
>*declaration-statement*
>*try-throw-catch*

In most cases, the C++ statement syntax is identical to that of ANSI C. The primary difference between the two is that in C, declarations are allowed only at the start of a block; C++ adds the *declaration-statement*, which effectively removes this restriction. This enables you to introduce variables at a point in the program where a precomputed initialization value can be calculated.

Declaring variables inside blocks also allows you to exercise precise control over the scope and lifetime of those variables.

Labeled Statements

To transfer program control directly to a given statement, the statement must be labeled.

Syntax

labeled-statement:
>*identifier* **:** *statement*
>**case** *constant-expression* **:** *statement*
>**default** **:** *statement*

Using Labels with the goto Statement

The appearance of an *identifier* label in the source program declares a label. Only a **goto** statement can transfer control to an *identifier* label. The following code fragment illustrates use of the **goto** statement and an *identifier* label to escape a tightly nested loop:

```
for( p = 0; p < NUM_PATHS; ++p )
{
    NumFiles = FillArray( pFileArray, pszFNames )
    for( i = 0; i < NumFiles; ++i )
    {
        if( (pFileArray[i] = fopen( pszFNames[i], "r" )) == NULL )
            goto FileOpenError;
        // Process the files that were opened.
    }
}

FileOpenError:
    cerr << "Fatal file open error. Processing interrupted.\n" );
```

In the preceding example, the **goto** statement transfers control directly to the statement that prints an error message if an unknown file-open error occurs.

A label cannot appear by itself but must always be attached to a statement. If a label is needed by itself, place a null statement after the label.

The label has function scope and cannot be redeclared within the function. However, the same name can be used as a label in different functions.

Using Labels in the case Statement

Labels that appear after the **case** keyword cannot also appear outside a **switch** statement. (This restriction also applies to the **default** keyword.) The following code fragment shows the correct use of **case** labels:

```
// Sample Microsoft Windows message processing loop.
switch( msg )
{
case WM_TIMER:     // Process timer event.
    SetClassWord( hWnd, GCW_HICON, ahIcon[nIcon++] );
    ShowWindow( hWnd, SW_SHOWNA );
    nIcon %= 14;
    Yield();
    break;

case WM_PAINT:
    // Obtain a handle to the device context.
    // BeginPaint will send WM_ERASEBKGND if appropriate.

    memset( &ps, 0x00, sizeof(PAINTSTRUCT) );
    hDC = BeginPaint( hWnd, &ps );

    // Inform Windows that painting is complete.

    EndPaint( hWnd, &ps );
    break;

case WM_CLOSE:
    // Close this window and all child windows.
```

```
    KillTimer( hWnd, TIMER1 );
    DestroyWindow( hWnd );
    if( hWnd == hWndMain )
       PostQuitMessage( 0 );   // Quit the application.
    break;

default:
    // This choice is taken for all messages not specifically
    //  covered by a case statement.

    return DefWindowProc( hWnd, Message, wParam, lParam );
    break;
```

Expression Statement

Expression statements cause expressions to be evaluated. No transfer of control or iteration takes place as a result of an expression statement.

Syntax

expression-statement:
    *expression*_{opt} ;

All expressions in an expression statement are evaluated and all side effects are completed before the next statement is executed. The most common expression statements are assignments and function calls. C++ also provides a null statement.

The Null Statement

The "null statement" is an expression statement with the *expression* missing. It is useful when the syntax of the language calls for a statement but no expression evaluation. It consists of a semicolon.

Null statements are commonly used as placeholders in iteration statements or as statements on which to place labels at the end of compound statements or functions.

The following code fragment shows how to copy one string to another and incorporates the null statement:

```
char *strcpy( char *Dest, const char *Source )
{
   char *DestStart = Dest;

   // Assign value pointed to by Source to
   //  Dest until the end-of-string 0 is
   //  encountered.
   while( *Dest++ = *Source++ )
       ;                       // Null statement.

   return DestStart;
}
```

Compound Statements (Blocks)

A compound statement consists of zero or more statements enclosed in curly braces
({ }). A compound statement can be used anywhere a statement is expected.
Compound statements are commonly called "blocks."

Syntax

compound-statement:
>   { *statement-list*_{opt} }

statement-list:
>   *statement*
>   *statement-list* *statement*

The following example uses a compound statement as the *statement* part of the **if**
statement (see "The if Statement" on page 129 for details about the syntax):

```
if( Amount > 100 )
{
    cout << "Amount was too large to handle\n";
    Alert();
}
else
    Balance -= Amount;
```

Note   Because a declaration is a statement, a declaration can be one of the statements in the
statement-list. As a result, names declared inside a compound statement, but not explicitly
declared as static, have local scope and (for objects) lifetime. See "Scope" on page 22 in
Chapter 2 for details about treatment of names with local scope.

Selection Statements

The C++ selection statements, **if** and **switch**, provide a means to conditionally execute
sections of code.

Syntax

selection-statement:
>   **if** (*expression*) *statement*
>   **if** (*expression*) *statement* **else** *statement*
>   **switch** (*expression*) *statement*

The if Statement

The **if** statement evaluates the expression enclosed in parentheses. The expression
must be of arithmetic or pointer type, or it must be of a class type that defines an
unambiguous conversion to an arithmetic or pointer type. (For information about
conversions, see Chapter 3, "Standard Conversions.")

In both forms of the **if** syntax, if the expression evaluates to a nonzero value (true), the statement dependent on the evaluation is executed; otherwise, it is skipped.

In the **if...else** syntax, the second statement is executed if the result of evaluating the expression is zero.

The **else** clause of an **if...else** statement is associated with the closest previous **if** statement that does not have a corresponding **else** statement. The following code fragment demonstrates how this works:

```
if( condition1 == true )
    if( condition2 == true )
        cout << "condition1 true; condition2 true\n";
    else
        cout << "condition1 true; condition2 false\n";
else
    cout << "condition 1 false\n";
```

Many programmers use curly braces ({ }) to explicitly clarify the pairing of complicated **if** and **else** clauses, such as in the following example:

```
if( condition1 == true )
{
    if( condition1 == true )
        cout << "condition1 true; condition2 true\n";
    else
        cout << "condition1 true; condition2 false\n";
}
else
    cout << "condition 1 false\n";
```

Although the braces are not strictly necessary, they clarify the pairing between **if** and **else** statements.

The switch Statement

The C++ **switch** statement allows selection among multiple sections of code, depending on the value of an expression. The expression enclosed in parentheses, the "controlling expression," must be of an integral type or of a class type for which there is an unambiguous conversion to integral type. Integral promotion is performed as described in "Integral Promotions" on page 56 in Chapter 3.

The **switch** statement causes an unconditional jump to, into, or past the statement that is the "switch body," depending on the value of the controlling expression, the values of the **case** labels, and the presence or absence of a **default** label. The switch body is normally a compound statement (although this is not a syntactic requirement). Usually, some of the statements in the switch body are labeled with **case** labels or with the **default** label. Labeled statements are not syntactic requirements, but the **switch** statement is meaningless without them. The **default** label can appear only once.

Syntax

case *constant-expression* **:** *statement*

default **:** *statement*

The *constant-expression* in the **case** label is converted to the type of the controlling expression and is then compared for equality. In a given **switch** statement, no two constant expressions in **case** statements can evaluate to the same value. The behavior is shown in Table 5.1.

Table 5.1   Switch Statement Behavior

Condition	Action
Converted value matches that of the promoted controlling expression.	Control is transferred to the statement following that label.
None of the constants match the constants in the **case** labels; **default** label is present.	Control is transferred to the **default** label.
None of the constants match the constants in the **case** labels; **default** label is not present.	Control is transferred to the statement after the **switch** statement.

An inner block of a **switch** statement can contain definitions with initializations as long as they are reachable — that is, not bypassed by all possible execution paths. Names introduced using these declarations have local scope. The following code fragment shows how the **switch** statement works:

```
switch( tolower( *argv[1] ) )
{
    // Error. Unreachable declaration.
    char szChEntered[] = "Character entered was: ";

case 'a' :
    {
    // Declaration of szChEntered OK. Local scope.
    char szChEntered[] = "Character entered was: ";
    cout << szChEntered << "a\n";
    }
    break;

case 'b' :
    // Value of szChEntered undefined.
    cout << szChEntered << "b\n";
    break;

default:
    // Value of szChEntered undefined.
    cout << szChEntered << "neither a nor b\n";
    break;
}
```

A **switch** statement can be nested. In such cases, **case** or **default** labels associate with the most deeply nested **switch** statements that enclose them. For example:

```
switch( msg )
{
case WM_COMMAND:      // Windows command. Find out more.
   switch( wParam )
   {
   case IDM_F_NEW:    // File New menu command.
      delete wfile;
      wfile = new WinAppFile;
      break;
   case IDM_F_OPEN:   // File Open menu command.
      wfile->FileOpenDlg();
      break;
   ...
   }
case WM_CREATE:       // Create window.
   ...
   break;
case WM_PAINT:        // Window needs repainting.
   ...
   break;
default:
   return DefWindowProc( hWnd, Message, wParam, lParam );
}
```

The preceding code fragment from a Microsoft Windows® message loop shows how **switch** statements can be nested. The **switch** statement that selects on the value of wParam is executed only if msg is **WM_COMMAND**. The **case** labels for menu selections, IDM_F_NEW and IDM_F_OPEN, associate with the inner **switch** statement.

Control is not impeded by **case** or **default** labels. To stop execution at the end of a part of the compound statement, insert a **break** statement. This transfers control to the statement after the **switch** statement. This example demonstrates how control "drops through" unless a **break** statement is used:

```
BOOL fClosing = FALSE;

...

switch( wParam )
{
case IDM_F_CLOSE:         // File close command.
   fClosing = TRUE;
   // fall through

case IDM_F_SAVE:          // File save command.
   if( document->IsDirty() )
      if( document->Name() == "UNTITLED" )
         FileSaveAs( document );
      else
         FileSave( document );
```

```
if( fClosing )
    document->Close();

break;
}
```

The preceding code shows how to take advantage of the fact that **case** labels do not impede the flow of control. If the switch statement transfers control to IDM_F_SAVE, fClosing is FALSE. Therefore, after the file is saved, the document is not closed. However, if the **switch** statement transfers control to IDM_F_CLOSE, fClosing is set to TRUE, and the code to save a file is executed.

Iteration Statements

Iteration statements cause statements (or compound statements) to be executed zero or more times, subject to some loop-termination criteria. When these statements are compound statements, they are executed in order, except when either the **break** statement or the **continue** statement is encountered. (For a description of these statements, see "The break Statement" and "The continue Statement" on page 137.)

C++ provides three iteration statements — **while**, **do**, and **for**. Each of these iterates until its termination expression evaluates to zero (false), or until loop termination is forced with a **break** statement. Table 5.2 summarizes these statements and their actions; each is discussed in detail in the sections that follow.

Table 5.2   C++ Iteration Statements

Statement	Evaluated At	Initialization	Increment
while	Top of loop	No	No
do	Bottom of loop	No	No
for	Top of loop	Yes	Yes

Syntax

iteration-statement:

> **while** (*expression*) *statement*
> **do** *statement* **while** (*expression*) **;**
> **for** (*for-init-statement* *expression*_{opt} **;** *expression*_{opt}) *statement*

for-init-statement:

> *expression-statement*
> *declaration-statement*

The statement part of an iteration statement cannot be a declaration. However, it can be a compound statement containing a declaration.

The while Statement

The **while** statement executes a *statement* repeatedly until the termination condition (the *expression*) specified evaluates to zero. The test of the termination condition takes place before each execution of the loop; therefore, a **while** loop executes zero or more times, depending on the value of the termination expression. The following code uses a **while** loop to trim trailing spaces from a string:

```
char *trim( char *szSource )
{
    char *pszEOS;

    // Set pointer to end of string to point to the character just
    //  before the 0 at the end of the string.
    pszEOS = szSource + strlen( szSource ) - 1;

    while( pszEOS >= szSource && *pszEOS == ' ' )
        *pszEOS-- = '\0';

    return szSource;
}
```

The termination condition is evaluated at the top of the loop. If there are no trailing spaces, the loop never executes.

The expression must be of an integral type, a pointer type, or a class type with an unambiguous conversion to an integral or pointer type.

The do Statement

The **do** statement executes a *statement* repeatedly until the specified termination condition (the *expression*) evaluates to zero. The test of the termination condition is made after each execution of the loop; therefore, a **do** loop executes one or more times, depending on the value of the termination expression. The following function uses the **do** statement to wait for the user to press a specific key:

```
void WaitKey( char ASCIICode )
{
    char chTemp;

    do
    {
        chTemp = _getch();
    }
    while( chTemp != ASCIICode );
}
```

A **do** loop rather than a **while** loop is used in the preceding code — with the **do** loop, the **_getch** function is called to get a keystroke before the termination condition is evaluated. This function can be written using a **while** loop, but not as concisely:

```
void WaitKey( char ASCIICode )
{
   char chTemp;

   chTemp = _getch();

   while( chTemp != ASCIICode )
   {
      chTemp = _getch();
   }
}
```

The expression must be of an integral type, a pointer type, or a class type with an unambiguous conversion to an integral or pointer type.

The for Statement

The **for** statement can be divided into three separate parts, as shown in Table 5.3.

Table 5.3   for Loop Elements

Syntax Name	When Executed	Contents
for-init-statement	Before any other element of the **for** statement or the substatement.	Often used to initialize loop indices. It can contain expressions or declarations.
expression1	Before execution of a given iteration of the loop, including the first iteration.	An expression that evaluates to an integral type or a class type that has an unambiguous conversion to an integral type.
expression2	At the end of each iteration of the loop; *expression1* is tested after *expression2* is evaluated.	Normally used to increment loop indices.

The *for-init-statement* is commonly used to declare and initialize loop-index variables. The *expression1* is often used to test for loop-termination criteria. The *expression2* is commonly used to increment loop indices.

The **for** statement executes the *statement* repeatedly until *expression1* evaluates to zero. The *for-init-statement*, *expression1*, and *expression2* fields are all optional.

The following **for** loop:

```
for( for-init-statement; expression1; expression2 )
{
   // Statements
}
```

is equivalent to the following **while** loop:

```
for-init-statement;
while( expression1 )
{
   // Statements
   expression2;
}
```

A convenient way to specify an infinite loop using the **for** statement is:

```
for( ; ; )
{
    // Statements to be executed.
}
```

This is equivalent to:

```
while( 1 )
{
    // Statements to be executed.
}
```

The initialization part of the **for** loop can be a declaration statement or an expression statement, including the null statement. The initializations can include any sequence of expressions and declarations, separated by commas. Any object declared inside a *for-init-statement* has local scope, as if it had been declared immediately prior to the **for** statement. Although the name of the object can be used in more than one **for** loop in the same scope, the declaration can appear only once. For example:

```
#include <iostream.h>

void main()
{
    for( int i = 0; i < 100; ++i )
        cout << i << "\n";

    // The loop index, i, cannot be declared in the
    //  for-init-statement here because it is still in scope.
    for( i = 100; i >= 0; --i )
        cout << i << "\n";
}
```

Although the three fields of the **for** statement are normally used for initialization, testing for termination, and incrementing, they are not restricted to these uses. For example, the following code prints the numbers 1 to 100. The substatement is the null statement:

```
#include <iostream.h>

void main()
{
    for( int i = 0; i < 100; cout << ++i << endl )
        ;
}
```

Jump Statements

The C++ jump statements perform an immediate local transfer of control.

Syntax

jump-statement:
>   **break** ;
>   **continue** ;
>   **return** *expression*~opt~ ;
>   **goto** *identifier*   ;

The break Statement

The **break** statement is used to exit an iteration or **switch** statement. It transfers control to the statement immediately following the iteration substatement or **switch** statement.

The **break** statement terminates only the most tightly enclosing loop or **switch** statement. In loops, **break** is used to terminate before the termination criteria evaluate to 0. In the **switch** statement, **break** is used to terminate sections of code — normally before a **case** label. The following example illustrates the use of the **break** statement in a **for** loop:

```
for( ; ; )      // No termination condition.
{
    if( List->AtEnd() )
        break;

    List->Next();
}

cout << "Control transfers to here.\n";
```

Note There are other simple ways to escape a loop. It is best to use the **break** statement in more complex loops, where it can be difficult to tell whether the loop should be terminated before several statements have been executed.

For an example of using the **break** statement within the body of a **switch** statement, see "The switch Statement" on page 130.

The continue Statement

The **continue** statement forces immediate transfer of control to the loop-continuation statement of the smallest enclosing loop. (The "loop-continuation" is the statement that contains the controlling expression for the loop.) Therefore, the **continue** statement can appear only in the dependent *statement* of an iteration statement (although it may be the sole statement in that *statement*). In a **for** loop, execution of a **continue** statement causes evaluation of *expression2* and then *expression1*.

The following example shows how the **continue** statement can be used to bypass sections of code and skip to the next iteration of a loop:

```
#include <conio.h>

// Get a character that is a member of the zero-terminated
//  string, szLegalString. Return the index of the character
//  entered.
int GetLegalChar( char *szLegalString )
{
    char *pch;

    do
    {
        char ch = _getch();

        // Use strchr library function to determine if the
        //  character read is in the string. If not, use the
        //  continue statement to bypass the rest of the
        //  statements in the loop.
        if( (pch = strchr( szLegalString, ch )) == NULL )
            continue;

        // A character that was in the string szLegalString
        //  was entered. Return its index.
        return (pch - szLegalString);

        // The continue statement transfers control to here.
    } while( 1 );

    return 0;
}
```

The return Statement

The **return** statement allows a function to immediately transfer control back to the calling function (or, in the case of the main function, transfer control back to the operating system). The **return** statement accepts an expression, which is the value passed back to the calling function. Functions of type **void**, constructors, and destructors cannot specify expressions in the **return** statement; functions of all other types must specify an expression in the **return** statement.

The expression, if specified, is converted to the type specified in the function declaration, as if an initialization were being performed. Conversion from the type of the expression to the **return** type of the function can cause temporary objects to be created. See "Temporary Objects" on page 301 in Chapter 11 for more information about how and when temporaries are created.

When the flow of control exits the block enclosing the function definition, the result is the same as it would be if a **return** statement with no expression had been executed. This is illegal for functions that are declared as returning a value.

A function can have any number of **return** statements.

The goto Statement

The **goto** statement performs an unconditional transfer of control to the named label. The label must be in the current function.

For more information about labels and the **goto** statement, see "Labeled Statements" and "Using Labels with the goto Statement" on page 126.

Declaration Statements

Declaration statements introduce new names into the current scope. These names can be:

- Type names (**class**, **struct**, **union**, **enum**, **typedef**, and pointer-to-member).
- Object names.
- Function names.

Syntax

declaration-statement:
    declaration

If a declaration within a block introduces a name that is already declared outside the block, the previous declaration is hidden for the duration of the block. After termination of the block, the previous declaration is again visible.

Multiple declarations of the same name in the same block are illegal.

For more information about declarations and name hiding, see "Declarations and Definitions" and "Scope" in Chapter 2 on pages 20 and 22, respectively.

Declaration of Automatic Objects

In C++, objects can be declared with automatic storage class using the **auto** or **register** keyword. If no storage-class keyword is used for a local object (an object declared inside a function), **auto** is assumed. C++ initializes and declares these objects differently than objects declared with static storage classes.

Initialization of Automatic Objects

Each time declaration statements for objects of storage class **auto** or **register** are executed, initialization takes place. The following example, from The continue Statement, shows initialization of the automatic object ch inside the do loop.

```
#include <conio.h>

// Get a character that is a member of the zero-terminated string,
//   szLegalString. Return the index of the character entered.
int GetLegalChar( char *szLegalString )
{
    char *pch;
```

```
    do
    {
        // This declaration statement is executed once for each
        //   execution of the loop.
        char ch = _getch();

        if( (pch = strchr( szLegalString, ch )) == NULL )
            continue;

        // A character that was in the string szLegalString
        //   was entered. Return its index.
        return (pch - szLegalString);
    } while( 1 );
}
```

For each iteration of the loop (each time the declaration is encountered), the macro _getch is evaluated and ch is initialized with the results. When control is transferred outside the block using the return statement, ch is destroyed (in this case, the storage is deallocated).

See "Storage Classes" on page 38 in Chapter 2 for another example of initialization.

Destruction of Automatic Objects

Objects defined in a loop are destroyed once per iteration of the loop, on exit from the block, or when control transfers to a point prior to the declaration. Objects declared in a block that is not a loop are destroyed on exit from the block or when control transfers to a point prior to the declaration.

Note Destruction can mean simply deallocating the object or, for class-type objects, invoking the object's destructor.

When a jump statement transfers control out of a loop or block, objects declared in the block transferred from are destroyed; objects in the block transferred to are not destroyed.

When control is transferred to a point prior to a declaration, the object is destroyed.

Transfers of Control

You can use the **goto** statement or a **case** label in a **switch** statement to specify a program that branches past an initializer. Such code is illegal unless the declaration that contains the initializer is in a block enclosed by the block in which the jump statement occurs.

The following example shows a loop that declares and initializes the objects total, ch, and i. There is also an erroneous goto statement that transfers control past an initializer.

```
// Read input until a nonnumeric character is entered.
while( 1 )
{
   int total = 0;

   char ch = _getch();

   if( ch >= '0' || ch <= '9' )
   {
      goto Label1;    // Error: transfers past initialization
                      //  of i.

      int i = ch - '0';
Label1:
      total += i;
   } // i would be destroyed here if the
     //  goto error were not present.
   else
      // Break statement transfers control out of loop,
      //  destroying total and ch.
      break;
}
```

In the preceding example, the goto statement tries to transfer control past the initialization of i. However, if i were declared but not initialized, the transfer would be legal.

The objects total and ch, declared in the block that serves as the *statement* of the while statement, are destroyed when that block is exited using the break statement.

Declaration of Static Objects

An object can be declared with static storage class using the **static** or **extern** keyword. Local objects must be explicitly declared as **static** or **extern** to have static storage class. All global objects (objects declared outside all functions) have static storage class. You cannot declare static instances in a tiny-model program.

Initialization of Static Objects

Global objects are initialized at program startup. (For more information about construction and destruction of global objects, see "Additional Startup Considerations" and "Additional Termination Considerations" on page 36 in Chapter 2.)

Local objects declared as **static** are initialized the first time their declarations are encountered in the program flow. The following class, introduced in Chapter 2, "Basic Concepts", shows how this works:

```
#include <iostream.h>
#include <string.h>

// Define a class that logs initializations and destructions.
class InitDemo
{
```

```
public:
    InitDemo( char *szWhat );
    ~InitDemo();
private:
    char *szObjName;
};

// Constructor for class InitDemo.
InitDemo::InitDemo( char *szWhat )
{
    if( szWhat != 0 && strlen( szWhat ) > 0 )
    {
        szObjName = new char[ strlen( szWhat ) + 1 ];
        strcpy( szObjName, szWhat );
    }
    else
        szObjName = 0;

    clog << "Initializing: " << szObjName << "\n";
}

// Destructor for InitDemo.
InitDemo::~InitDemo()
{
    if( szObjName != 0 )
    {
        clog << "Destroying: " << szObjName << "\n";
        delete szObjName;
    }
}

// Main function.
void main( int argc, char *argv[] )
{
    if( argc < 2 )
    {
        cerr << "Supply a one-letter argument.\n";
        return -1;
    }

    if( *argv[1] == 'a' )
    {
        cout << "*argv[1] was an 'a'\n";

        // Declare static local object.
        static InitDemo I1( "static I1" );
    }
    else
        cout << "*argv[1] was not an 'a'\n";
}
```

If the command-line argument supplied to this program starts with the lowercase letter "a," the declaration of I1 is executed, the initialization takes place, and the result is:

```
*argv[1] was an 'a'
Initializing: static I1
Destroying: static I1
```

Otherwise, the flow of control bypasses the declaration of I1 and the result is:

```
*argv[1] was not an 'a'
```

When a static local object is declared with an initializer that does not evaluate to a constant expression, the object is given the value 0 (converted to the appropriate type) at the point before execution enters the block for the first time. However, the object is not visible and no constructors are called until the actual point of declaration.

At the point of declaration, the object's constructor (if the object is of a class type) is called as expected. (Static local objects are only initialized the first time they are seen.)

Destruction of Static Objects

Local static objects are destroyed during termination specified by **atexit**.

If a static object was not constructed because the program's flow of control bypassed its declaration, no attempt is made to destroy that object.

Exception Handling

Microsoft C++ supports two kinds of exception handling, C++ exception handling (**try, throw, catch**) and structured exception handling (__**try**/__**except**, __**try**/__**finally**). If possible, you should use C++ exception handling rather than structured exception handling.

Note   In this section, the terms "structured exception handling" and "structured exception" (or "C exception") refer exclusively to the structured exception handling mechanism provided by Win32®. All other references to exception handling (or "C++ exception") refer to the C++ exception handling mechanism.

Although structured exception handling works with C and C++ source files, it is not specifically designed for C++. For C++ programs, you should use C++ exception handling.

The try, catch, and throw Statements

The C++ language provides built-in support for handling anomalous situations, known as "exceptions," which may occur during the execution of your program. The **try, throw,** and **catch** statements have been added to the C++ language to implement exception handling. With C++ exception handling, your program can communicate unexpected events to a higher execution context that is better able to recover from such abnormal events. These exceptions are handled by code which is outside the normal flow of control. The Microsoft C++ compiler implements the C++ exception handling model based on the ISO WG21/ANSI X3J16 working papers towards the evolving standard for C++.

Syntax

try-block :
   try *compound-statement handler-list*

handler-list :
   handler handler-list$_{opt}$

handler :
   catch (*exception-declaration*) *compound-statement*

exception-declaration :
   type-specifier-list declarator
   type-specifier-list abstract-declarator
   type-specifier-list
   ...

throw-expression :
   throw *assignment-expression*$_{opt}$

The *compound-statement* after the **try** clause is the guarded section of code. The *throw-expression* "throws" (raises) an exception. The *compound-statement* after the **catch** clause is the exception handler, and "catches" (handles) the exception thrown by the throw-expression. The *exception-declaration* statement indicates the type of exception the clause handles. The type can be any valid data type, including a C++ class. If the exception-declaration statement is an ellipsis (**...**), the **catch** clause handles any type of exception, including a C exception. Such a handler must be the last handler for its **try** block.

The operand of **throw** is syntactically similar to the operand of a **return** statement.

Note Microsoft C++ does not support the function **throw** signature mechanism, as described in section 15.5 of the ANSI C++ draft.

Execution proceeds as follows:

1. Control reaches the **try** statement by normal sequential execution. The guarded section (within the **try** block) is executed.

2. If no exception is thrown during execution of the guarded section, the **catch** clauses that follow the **try** block are not executed. Execution continues at the statement after the last **catch** clause following the **try** block in which the exception was thrown.

3. If an exception is thrown during execution of the guarded section or in any routine the guarded section calls (either directly or indirectly), an exception object is created from the object created by the **throw** operand. (This implies that a copy constructor may be involved.) At this point, the compiler looks for a **catch** clause

in a higher execution context that can handle an exception of the type thrown (or a **catch** handler that can handle any type of exception). The **catch** handlers are examined in order of their appearance following the **try** block. If no appropriate handler is found, the next dynamically enclosing **try** block is examined. This process continues until the outermost enclosing **try** block is examined.

4. If a matching handler is still not found, or if an exception occurs while unwinding, but before the handler gets control, the predefined run-time function `terminate` is called. If an exception occurs after throwing the exception, but before the unwind begins, `terminate` is called.

5. If a matching **catch** handler is found, and it catches by value, its formal parameter is initialized by copying the exception object. If it catches by reference, the parameter is initialized to refer to the exception object. After the formal parameter is initialized, the process of "unwinding the stack" begins. This involves the destruction of all automatic objects that were constructed (but not yet destructed) between the beginning of the **try** block associated with the **catch** handler and the exception's throw site. Destruction occurs in reverse order of construction. The **catch** handler is executed and the program resumes execution following the last handler (that is, the first statement or construct which is not a **catch** handler). Control can only enter a **catch** handler through a thrown exception; never via a `goto` statement or a `case` label in a `switch` statement.

The following is a simple example of a **try** block and its associated **catch** handler. This example detects failure of a memory allocation operation using the **new** operator. If **new** is successful, the **catch** handler is never executed:

```cpp
#include <iostream.h>

int main()
{
    char *buf;
    try
    {
        buf = new char[512];
        if( buf == 0 )
            throw "Memory allocation failure!";
    }
    catch( char * str )
    {
        cout << "Exception raised: " << str << '\n';
    }
    // ...
    return 0;
}
```

The operand of the **throw** expression specifies that an exception of type `char *` is being thrown. It is handled by a **catch** handler that expresses the ability to catch an exception of type `char *`. In the event of a memory allocation failure, this is the output from the preceding example:

```
Exception raised: Memory allocation failure!
```

The real power of C++ exception handling lies not only in its ability to deal with exceptions of varying types, but also in its ability to automatically call destructor functions during stack unwinding, for all local objects constructed before the exception was thrown.

The following example demonstrates C++ exception handling using classes with destructor semantics:

```
#include <iostream.h>

void MyFunc( void );

class CTest
{
public:
    CTest(){};
    ~CTest(){};
    const char *ShowReason() const { return "Exception in CTest class."; }

};

class CDtorDemo
{
public:
    CDtorDemo();
    ~CDtorDemo();
};

CDtorDemo::CDtorDemo()
{
    cout << "Constructing CDtorDemo.\n";
}

CDtorDemo::~CDtorDemo()
{
    cout << "Destructing CDtorDemo.\n";
}

void MyFunc()
{

    CDtorDemo D;
    cout<< "In MyFunc(). Throwing CTest exception.\n";
    throw CTest();
}

int main()
{
    cout << "In main.\n";
    try
    {
        cout << "In try block, calling MyFunc().\n";
        MyFunc();
    }
```

```
catch( CTest E )
{
   cout << "In catch handler.\n";
   cout << "Caught CTest exception type: ";
   cout << E.ShowReason() << "\n";
}
catch( char *str )
{
   cout << "Caught some other exception: " << str << "\n";
}
cout << "Back in main. Execution resumes here.\n";
return 0;
}
```

This is the output from the preceding example:

```
In main.
In try block, calling MyFunc().
Constructing CDtorDemo.
In MyFunc(). Throwing CTest exception.
Destructing CDtorDemo.
In catch handler.
Caught CTest exception type: Exception in CTest class.
Back in main. Execution resumes here.
```

Note that in this example, the exception parameter (the argument to the **catch** clause) is declared in both **catch** handlers:

```
catch( CTest E )
// ...
catch( char *str )
// ...
```

You do not need to declare this parameter; in many cases it may be sufficient to notify the handler that a particular type of exception has occurred. However, if you do not declare an exception object in the exception-declaration, you will not have access to that object in the **catch** handler clause.

A throw-expression with no operand re-throws the exception currently being handled. Such an expression should appear only in a **catch** handler or in a function called from within a **catch** handler. The re-thrown exception object is the original exception object (not a copy). For example:

```
try
{
   throw CSomeOtherException();
}
catch(...)     // Handle all exceptions
{
   // Respond (perhaps only partially) to exception
   // ...

   throw;      // Pass exception to some other handler
}
```

Unhandled Exceptions

If a matching handler (or ellipsis **catch** handler) cannot be found for the current exception, the predefined `terminate` function is called. (You can also explicitly call `terminate` in any of your handlers.) The default action of `terminate` is to call `abort`. If you want `terminate` to call some other function in your program before exiting the application, call the `set_terminate` function with the name of the function to be called as its single argument. You can call `set_terminate` at any point in your program. The `terminate` routine always calls the last function given as an argument to `set_terminate`. For example:

```
#include <eh.h>      // For function prototypes
//...
void term_func() { // ... }
int main()
{
   try
   {
      // ...
      set_terminate( term_func );
      // ...
      throw "Out of memory!"; // No catch handler for this exception
   }
   catch( int )
   {
      cout << "Integer exception raised.";
   }
   return 0;
}
```

The `term_func` function should terminate the program or current thread, ideally by calling `exit`. If it doesn't, and instead returns to its caller, `abort` is called.

For more information about C++ exception handling, see the *C++ Annotated Reference Manual* by Margaret Ellis and Bjarne Stroustrup.

Structured Exception Handling

The **__try/__except** and **__try/__finally** statements are a Microsoft extension to the C language that enables applications to gain control of a program after events that would normally terminate execution.

Note Structured exception handling works with C and C++ source files. However, it is not specifically designed for C++. Although destructors for local objects will be called if you use structured exception handling in a C++ program (if you use the /GX compiler option), you can ensure that your code is more portable by using C++ exception handling. The C++ exception handling mechanism is more flexible, in that it can handle exceptions of any type.

For more information, see "The try-except Statement" and "The try-finally Statement" in the *C Language Reference*.

Syntax

try-except-statement :

>__**try** *compound-statement*
>__**except** (*expression*) *compound-statement*

try-finally-statement :

>__**try** *compound-statement*
>__**finally** *compound-statement*

If you have C modules that use structured exception handling, they can be mixed with C++ modules that use C++ exception handling. When a C (structured) exception is raised, it can be handled by the C handler, or it can be caught by a C++ **catch** handler, whichever is dynamically closest to the exception context. One of the major differences between the two models is that when a C exception is raised, it is always of type unsigned int, whereas a C++ exception can be of any type. That is, C exceptions are identified by an unsigned integer value, whereas C++ exceptions are identified by data type. However, while a C++ **catch** handler can catch a C exception (for example, via an "ellipsis" **catch** handler), a C exception can also be handled as a typed exception by using a C exception wrapper class. By deriving from this class, each C exception can be attributed a specific derived class.

To use a C exception wrapper class, you install a custom C exception translator function which is called by the internal exception handling mechanism each time a C exception is thrown. Within your translator function, you can throw any typed exception, which can be caught by an appropriate matching C++ **catch** handler. To specify a custom translation function, call the _set_se_translator function with the name of your translation function as its single argument.

Declarations

Declarations introduce new names into a program. Topics covered in this chapter include the following uses for declarations:

- Specify storage class, type, and linkage for an object.
- Specify storage class, type, and linkage for a function.
- Define a function.
- Provide an initial value for an object.
- Associate a name with a constant (enumerated type declaration).
- Declare a new type (**class**, **struct**, or **union** declaration).
- Specify a synonym for a type (**typedef** declaration).
- Specify a family of classes or functions (**template** declaration).
- Specify a **namespace**.

In addition to introducing a new name, a declaration specifies how an identifier is to be interpreted by the compiler. Declarations do not automatically reserve storage associated with the identifier—reserving storage is done by definitions.

Note   Most declarations are also definitions.

Syntax
declaration:
> *decl-specifiers*$_{opt}$ *declarator-list*$_{opt}$ **;**
> *function-definition*
> *linkage-specification*
> *template-specification*

The declarators in *declarator-list* contain the names being declared. Although the *declarator-list* is shown as optional, it can be omitted only in declarations or definitions of a function.

Note   The declaration of a function is often called a "prototype." This declaration provides type information about arguments and the function's return type that allows the compiler to perform correct conversions and to ensure type safety.

The *decl-specifiers* part of a declaration is also shown as optional; however, it can be omitted only in declarations of class types or enumerations.

Declarations occur in a scope. This controls the visibility of the name declared and the duration of the object defined (if any). For more information about how scope rules interact with declarations, see "Scope" on page 22 in Chapter 2.

An object declaration is also a definition unless it contains the **extern** storage-class specifier described in "Storage-Class Specifiers" on page 153. A function declaration is also a definition unless it is a prototype—a function header with no defining function body. An object's definition causes allocation of storage and appropriate initializations for that object.

Specifiers

This section explains the *decl-specifiers* portion of declarations. (The syntax for declarations is given at the beginning of this chapter.)

Syntax

decl-specifiers:
        *decl-specifiers*opt *decl-specifier*

decl-specifier:
        storage-class-specifier
        type-specifier
        fct-specifier
        friend
        typedef
        __declspec (*extended-decl-modifier-seq*)

The Microsoft-specific keyword, **__declspec**, is discussed in "Extended Attribute Syntax" on page 367 in Appendix B.

The *decl-specifiers* portion of a declaration is the longest sequence of *decl-specifiers* that can be construed to be a type name. The remainder of the declaration is the name or names introduced. The examples in the following list illustrates this concept:

Declaration	decl-specifiers	name
char *lpszAppName;	char *	lpszAppName
typedef char * LPSTR;	char *	LPSTR
LPSTR strcpy(LPSTR, LPSTR);	LPSTR	strcpy
volatile void *pvvObj;	volatile void *	pvvObj

Because **signed, unsigned, long**, and **short** all imply **int**, a **typedef** name following one of these keywords is taken to be a member of *declarator-list,* not of *decl-specifiers*.

Note Because a name can be redeclared, its interpretation is subject to the most recent declaration in the current scope. Redeclaration can affect how names are interpreted by the compiler, particularly **typedef** names.

Storage-Class Specifiers

The C++ storage-class specifiers tell the compiler the duration and visibility of the object or function they declare, as well as where an object should be stored.

Syntax

storage-class-specifier:
    auto
    register
    static
    extern

Automatic Storage-Class Specifiers

The **auto** and **register** storage-class specifiers can be used only to declare names used in blocks or to declare formal arguments to functions. The term "auto" comes from the fact that storage for these objects is automatically allocated at run time (normally on the program's stack).

The auto Keyword

Few programmers use the **auto** keyword in declarations because all block-scoped objects not explicitly declared with another storage class are implicitly automatic. Therefore, the following two declarations are equivalent:

```
{
auto int i;    // Explicitly declared as auto.
int     j;    // Implicitly auto.
}
```

The register Keyword

Microsoft Specific →

The compiler does not accept user requests for register variables; instead, it makes its own register choices when global register-allocation optimization (/Oe option) is on. However, all other semantics associated with the **register** keyword are honored.

END Microsoft Specific

ANSI C does not allow for taking the address of a register object; this restriction does not apply to C++. However, if the address-of operator (**&**) is used on an object, the compiler must put the object in a location for which an address can be represented—in practice, this means in memory instead of in a register.

Static Storage-Class Specifiers

The static storage-class specifiers, **static** and **extern**, can be applied to objects and functions. Table 6.1 shows where the keywords **static** and **extern** can and cannot be used.

Table 6.1   Use of static and extern

Construct	Can static be Used?	Can extern be Used?
Function declarations within a block	No	Yes
Formal arguments to a function	No	No
Objects in a block	Yes	Yes
Objects outside a block	Yes	Yes
Functions	Yes	Yes
Class member functions	Yes	No
Class member data	Yes	No
typedef names	No	No

A name specified using the **static** keyword has internal linkage except for the static members of a class that have external linkage. That is, it is not visible outside the current translation unit. A name specified using the **extern** keyword has external linkage unless previously defined as having internal linkage. For more information about the visibility of names, see "Scope" and "Program and Linkage" in Chapter 2, on pages 22 and 26, respectively.

Note Functions that are declared as **inline** and that are not class member functions are given the same linkage characteristics as functions declared as **static**.

A class name whose declaration has not yet been encountered by the compiler can be used in an **extern** declaration. The name introduced with such a declaration cannot be used until the class declaration has been encountered.

Names Without Storage-Class Specifiers

File-scope names with no explicit storage-class specifiers have external linkage unless they are:

- Declared using the **const** keyword.
- Previously declared with internal linkage.

Function Specifiers

You can use the **inline** and **virtual** keywords as specifiers in function declarations. This use of **virtual** differs from its use in the base-class specifier of a class definition.

inline Specifier

The **inline** specifier instructs the compiler to replace function calls with the code of the function body. This substitution is "inline expansion" (sometimes called "inlining"). Inline expansion alleviates the function-call overhead at the potential cost of larger code size.

The **inline** keyword tells the compiler that inline expansion is preferred. However, the compiler can create a separate instance of the function (instantiate) and create standard calling linkages instead of inserting the code inline. Two cases where this can happen are:

- Recursive functions.
- Functions that are referred to through a pointer elsewhere in the translation unit.

Note that for a function to be considered as a candidate for inlining, it must use the new-style function definition. Functions that are declared as **inline** and that are not class member functions have internal linkage unless otherwise specified.

Microsoft Specific →

The **__inline** keyword is equivalent to **inline**.

END Microsoft Specific

As with normal functions, there is no defined order of evaluation of the arguments to an inline function. In fact, it could be different from the order in which the arguments are evaluated when passed using normal function call protocol.

Microsoft Specific →

Recursive functions can be substituted inline to a depth specified by the **inline_depth** pragma. After that depth, recursive function calls are treated as calls to an instance of the function. The **inline_recursion** pragma controls the inline expansion of a function currently under expansion.

END Microsoft Specific

Inline Class Member Functions

A function defined in the body of a class declaration is an inline function. Consider the following class declaration:

```
class Account
{
public:
    Account(double initial_balance) { balance = initial_balance; }
    double GetBalance();
    double Deposit( double Amount );
    double Withdraw( double Amount );
private:
    double balance;
};
```

The `Account` constructor is an inline function. The member functions `GetBalance`, `Deposit`, and `Withdraw` are not specified as **inline** but can be implemented as inline functions using code such as the following:

```
inline double Account::GetBalance()
{
    return balance;
}

inline double Account::Deposit( double Amount )
{
    return ( balance += Amount );
}

inline double Account::Withdraw( double Amount )
{
    return ( balance -= Amount );
}
```

Note In the class declaration, the functions were declared without the **inline** keyword. The **inline** keyword can be specified in the class declaration; the result is the same.

A given inline member function must be declared the same way in every compilation unit. This constraint causes inline functions to behave as if they were instantiated functions. Additionally, there must be exactly one definition of an inline function.

A class member function defaults to external linkage unless a definition for that function contains the **inline** specifier. The preceding example shows that these functions need not be explicitly declared with the **inline** specifier; using **inline** in the function definition causes it to be an inline function. However, it is illegal to redeclare a function as **inline** after a call to that function.

Inline Functions versus Macros

Although inline functions are similar to macros (because the function code is expanded at the point of the call at compile time), inline functions are parsed by the compiler, whereas macros are expanded by the preprocessor. As a result, there are several important differences:

- Inline functions follow all the protocols of type safety enforced on normal functions.

- Inline functions are specified using the same syntax as any other function except that they include the **inline** keyword in the function declaration.

- Expressions passed as arguments to inline functions are evaluated once. In some cases, expressions passed as arguments to macros can be evaluated more than once. The following example shows a macro that converts lowercase letters to uppercase:

```
#include <stdio.h>
#include <conio.h>

#define toupper(a) ((a) >= 'a' && ((a) <= 'z') ? ((a)-('a'-'A')):(a))

void main()
{
    char ch = toupper( _getch() );
    printf( "%c", ch );
}
```

The intent of the expression `toupper( _getch() )` is that a character should be read from the console device (**stdin**) and, if necessary, converted to uppercase.

Because of the implementation, **_getch** is executed once to determine whether the character is greater than or equal to "a," and once to determine whether it is less than or equal to "z." If it is in that range, **_getch** is executed again to convert the character to uppercase. This means the program waits for two or three characters when, ideally, it should wait for only one.

Inline functions remedy this problem:

```
#include <stdio.h>
#include <conio.h>

inline char toupper( char a )
{
    return ((a >= 'a' && a <= 'z') ? a-('a'-'A') : a );
}

void main()
{
    char ch = toupper( _getch() );
    printf( "%c", ch );
}
```

When to Use Inline Functions

Inline functions are best used for small functions such as accessing private data members. The main purpose of these one- or two-line "accessor" functions is to return state information about objects; short functions are sensitive to the overhead of function calls. Longer functions spend proportionally less time in the calling/returning sequence and benefit less from inlining.

The `Point` class, introduced in "Function-Call Results" on page 73 in Chapter 4 can be optimized as follows:

```
class Point
{
public:
    // Define "accessor" functions as
    //   reference types.
    unsigned& x();
    unsigned& y();
```

```
private:
    unsigned _x;
    unsigned _y;
};

inline unsigned& Point::x()
{
    return _x;
}
inline unsigned& Point::y()
{
    return _y;
}
```

Assuming coordinate manipulation is a relatively common operation in a client of such a class, specifying the two accessor functions (x and y in the preceding example) as **inline** typically saves the overhead on:

- Function calls (including parameter passing and placing the object's address on the stack)

- Preservation of caller's stack frame

- New stack-frame setup

- Return-value communication

- Old stack-frame restore

- Return

virtual Specifier

The **virtual** keyword can be applied only to nonstatic class member functions. It signifies that binding of calls to the function is deferred until run time. For more information, see "Virtual Functions" on page 270 in Chapter 9.

typedef Specifier

The **typedef** specifier defines a name that can be used as a synonym for a type or derived type. You cannot use the **typedef** specifier inside a function definition.

Syntax

typedef-name:
    identifier

A **typedef** declaration introduces a name that, within its scope, becomes a synonym for the type given by the *decl-specifiers* portion of the declaration. In contrast to the **class**, **struct**, **union**, and **enum** declarations, **typedef** declarations do not introduce new types—they introduce new names for existing types.

One use of **typedef** declarations is to make declarations more uniform and compact. For example:

```
typedef char CHAR;          // Character type.
typedef CHAR * PSTR;        // Pointer to a string (char *).
...
LPSTR strchr( LPSTR source, CHAR target );
```

The names introduced by the preceding declarations are synonyms for:

Name	Synonymous Type
CHAR	**char**
PSTR	**char ***

The preceding example code declares a type name, CHAR, which is then used to define the derived type name PSTR (a pointer to a string). Finally, the names are used in declaring the function **strchr**. To see how the **typedef** keyword can be used to clarify declarations, contrast the preceding declaration of **strchr** with the following declaration:

```
char * strchr( char * source, char target );
```

To use **typedef** to specify fundamental and derived types in the same declaration, you can separate declarators with commas. For example:

```
typedef char CHAR, *PSTR;
```

A particularly complicated use of **typedef** is to define a synonym for a "pointer to a function that returns type *T*." For example, a **typedef** declaration that means "pointer to a function that takes no arguments and returns type **void**" uses this code:

```
typedef void (*PVFN)();
```

The synonym can be handy in declaring arrays of functions that are to be invoked through a pointer:

```
#include <iostream.h>
#include <stdlib.h>

extern void func1();        // Declare 4 functions.
extern void func2();        // These functions are assumed to be
extern void func3();        //  defined elsewhere.
extern void func4();

                            // Declare synonym for pointer to
typedef void (*PVFN)();     //  function that takes no arguments
                            //  and returns type void.

void main( int argc, char * argv[] )
{
    // Declare an array of pointers to functions.
    PVFN pvfn1[] = { func1, func2, func3, func4 };

    // Invoke the function specified on the command line.
    if( argc > 0 && *argv[1] > '0' && *argv[1] <= '4' )
    (*pvfn1[atoi( argv[1] ) - 1])();
}
```

Redeclaration of typedef Names

The **typedef** declaration can be used to redeclare the same name to refer to the same type. For example:

```
// FILE1.H
typedef char CHAR;

// FILE2.H
typedef char CHAR;

// PROG.CPP
#include "file1.h"
#include "file2.h"      // OK
...
```

The program PROG.CPP includes two header files, both of which contain **typedef** declarations for the name CHAR. As long as both declarations refer to the same type, such redeclaration is acceptable.

A **typedef** cannot redefine a name that was previously declared as a different type. Therefore, if FILE2.H contains

```
// FILE2.H
typedef int CHAR;       // Error
```

the compiler issues an error because of the attempt to redeclare the name CHAR to refer to a different type. This extends to constructs such as:

```
typedef char CHAR;
typedef CHAR CHAR;      // OK: redeclared as same type

typedef union REGS      // OK: name REGS redeclared
{                       //  by typedef name with the
    struct wordregs x;  //  same meaning.
    struct byteregs h;
} REGS;
```

Use of typedef with Class Types

Use of the **typedef** specifier with class types is supported largely because of the ANSI C practice of declaring unnamed structures in **typedef** declarations. For example, many C programmers use the following:

```
typedef struct          // Declare an unnamed structure and give it
{                       //  the typedef name POINT.
    unsigned x;
    unsigned y;
} POINT;
```

The advantage of such a declaration is that it enables declarations like:

```
POINT ptOrigin;
```

instead of:

```
struct point_t ptOrigin;
```

In C++, the difference between **typedef** names and real types (declared with the **class**, **struct**, **union**, and **enum** keywords) is more distinct. Although the C practice of declaring a nameless structure in a **typedef** statement still works, it provides no notational benefits as it does in C.

In the following code, the POINT function is not a type constructor. It is interpreted as a function declarator with an **int** return type.

```
typedef struct
{
   POINT();              // Not a constructor.
   unsigned x;
   unsigned y;
} POINT;
```

The preceding example declares a class named POINT using the unnamed class **typedef** syntax. POINT is treated as a class name; however, the following restrictions apply to names introduced this way:

- The name (the synonym) cannot appear after a **class**, **struct**, or **union** prefix.
- The name cannot be used as constructor or destructor names within a class declaration.

In summary, this syntax does not provide any mechanism for inheritance, construction, or destruction.

Name Space of typedef Names

Names declared using **typedef** occupy the same name space as other identifiers (except statement labels). Therefore, they cannot use the same identifier as a previously declared name, except in a class-type declaration. Consider the following example:

```
typedef unsigned long UL;  // Declare a typedef name, UL.
int UL;                    // Error: redefined.
```

The name-hiding rules that pertain to other identifiers also govern the visibility of names declared using **typedef**. Therefore, the following example is legal in C++:

```
typedef unsigned long UL;  // Declare a typedef name, UL.
...
long Beep
{
   unsigned int UL;        // Redeclaration hides typedef name.
   ...
}
// typedef name "unhidden" here.
```

friend Specifier

The **friend** specifier is used to designate functions or classes that have the same access privileges as class member functions. Friend functions and classes are covered in detail in "Friends" on page 283 in Chapter 10.

Type Specifiers

Type specifiers determine the type of the name being declared.

Syntax

type-specifier:
>   *simple-type-name*
>   *class-specifier*
>   *enum-specifier*
>   *elaborated-type-specifier*
>   :: *class-name*
>   **const**
>   **volatile**

The following sections discuss simple type names, elaborated type specifiers, and nested type names.

Simple Type Names

A simple type name is the name of a complete type.

Syntax

simple-type-name:
>   *complete-class-name*
>   *qualified-type-name*
>   **char**
>   **short**
>   **int**
>   **long**
>   **signed**
>   **unsigned**
>   **float**
>   **double**
>   **void**

Table 6.2 shows how the simple type names can be used together.

Table 6.2 Type Name Combinations

Type	Can Appear With	Comments
int	**long** or **short**, but not both	Type **int** implies type **long int**.
long	**int** or **double**	Type **long** implies type **long int**.

Table 6.2   Type Name Combinations *(continued)*

Type	Can Appear With	Comments
short	**int**	Type **short** implies type **short int**.
signed	**char**, **short**, **int**, or **long**	Type **signed** implies **signed int**. The most-significant bit of objects of type **signed char** and bit fields of signed integral types is taken to be the sign bit.
unsigned	**char**, **short**, **int**, or **long**	Type **unsigned** implies **unsigned int**. The most-significant bit of objects of type **unsigned char** and bit fields of unsigned integral types is not treated as the sign bit.

Elaborated Type Specifiers

Elaborated type specifiers are used to declare user-defined types. These can be either class- or enumerated-types.

Syntax

elaborated-type-specifier:
> *class-key class-name*
> *class-key identifier*
> **enum** *enum-name*

class-key:
> **class**
> **struct**
> **union**

If *identifier* is specified, it is taken to be a class name. For example:

```
class Window;
```

This statement declares the `Window` identifier as a class name. This syntax is used for forward declaration of classes. For more information about class names, see "Class Names" on page 236 in Chapter 8.

If a name is declared using the **union** keyword, it must also be defined using the **union** keyword. Names that are defined using the **class** keyword can be declared using the **struct** keyword (and vice versa). Therefore, the following code samples are legal:

```
// Legal example 1
struct A;    // Forward declaration of A.

class A      // Define A.
{
public:
   int i;
};
```

```
// Legal example 2
class A;     // Forward declaration of A.

struct A     // Define A.
{
private:
   int i;
};

// Legal example 3
union A;     // Forward declaration of A.

union A      // Define A.
{
   int  i;
   char ch[2];
};
```

These examples, however, are illegal:

```
// Illegal example 1
union A;     // Forward declaration of A.

struct A     // Define A.
{
   int i;
};
// Illegal example 2
union A;     // Forward declaration of A.

class A      // Define A.
{
public:
   int i;
};
// Illegal example 3
struct A;    // Forward declaration of A.

union A      // Define A.
{
   int  i;
   char ch[2];
};
```

Nested Type Names

Microsoft C++ supports declaration of nested types —both named and anonymous.

Syntax

qualified-type-name:
>   *typedef-name*
>   *class-name* **::** *qualified-type-name*

complete-class-name:
>   *qualified-class-name*
>   **::** *qualified-class-name*

qualified-class-name:
>   *class-name*
>   *class-name* :: *qualified-class-name*

In some programming situations, it makes sense to define nested types. These types are visible only to member functions of the class type in which they are defined. They can also be made visible by constructing a qualified type name using the scope-resolution operator (::).

Note One commonly used class hierarchy that employs nested types is iostream. In the iostream header files, the definition of class **ios** includes a series of enumerated types, which are packaged for use only with the iostream library.

The following example defines nested classes:

```
class WinSystem
{
public:
    class Window
    {
    public:
        Window();          // Default constructor.
        ~Window();         // Destructor.
        int NumberOf();    // Number of objects of class.
        int Count();       // Count number of objects of class.
    private:
        static int CCount;
    };
    class CommPort
    {
    public:
        CommPort();        // Default constructor.
        ~CommPort();       // Destructor.
        int NumberOf();    // Number of objects of class.
        int Count();       // Count number of objects of class.
    private:
        static int CCount;
    };
};

// Initialize WinSystem static members.
int WinSystem::Window::CCount = 0;
int WinSystem::CommPort::CCount = 0;
```

To access a name defined in a nested class, use the scope-resolution operator (::) to construct a complete class name. Use of this operator is shown in the initializations of the **static** members in the preceding example. To use a nested class in your program, use code such as:

```
WinSystem::Window Desktop;
WinSystem::Window AppWindow;

cout << "Number of active windows: " << Desktop.Count() << "\n";
```

Nested anonymous classes or structures can be defined as:

```
class Ledger
{
   class
   {
   public:
      double   PayableAmt;
      unsigned PayableDays;
   } Payables;

   class
   {
   public:
      double   RecvableAmt;
      unsigned RecvableDays;
   } Receivables;
};
```

An anonymous class must be an aggregate that has no member functions and no static members.

Note Although an enumerated type can be defined inside a class declaration, the reverse is not true; class types cannot be defined inside enumeration declarations.

Enumeration Declarations

An enumeration is a distinct integral type that defines named constants. Enumerations are declared using the **enum** keyword.

Syntax

enum-name:
>   *identifier*

enum-specifier:
>   **enum** *identifier*$_{opt}$ { *enum-list*$_{opt}$ }

enum-list:
>   *enumerator*
>   *enum-list* , *enumerator*

enumerator:
>   *identifier*
>   *identifier* = *constant-expression*

Enumerated types are valuable when an object can assume a known and reasonably limited set of values. Consider the example of the suits from a deck of cards:

```
class Card
{
public:
    enum Suit
    {
        Diamonds,
        Hearts,
        Clubs,
        Spades
    };
    // Declare two constructors: a default constructor,
    //  and a constructor that sets the cardinal and
    //  suit value of the new card.
    Card();
    Card( int CardInit, Suit SuitInit );

    // Get and Set functions.
    int   GetCardinal();            // Get cardinal value of card.
    int   SetCardinal();            // Set cardinal value of card.
    Suit  GetSuit();                // Get suit of card.
    void  SetSuit(Suit new_suit);   // Set suit of card.
    char *NameOf();                 // Get string representation of card.
private:
    Suit  suit;
    int   cardinalValue;
};

// Define a postfix increment operator for Suit.
inline Card::Suit operator++( Card::Suit &rs, int )
{
    return rs = (Card::Suit)(rs + 1);
}
```

The preceding example defines a class, Card, that contains a nested enumerated
type, Suit. To create a pack of cards in a program, use code such as:

```
Card *Deck[52];
int   j = 0;

for( Card::Suit curSuit = Card::Diamonds; curSuit <= Card::Spades;
    curSuit++ )
    for( int i = 1; i <= 13; ++i )
        Deck[j++] = new Card( i, curSuit );
```

In the preceding example, the type Suit is nested; therefore, the class name
(Card) must be used explicitly in public references. In member functions, however,
the class name can be omitted.

In the first segment of code, the postfix increment operator for Card::Suit is
defined. Without a user-defined increment operator, curSuit could not be
incremented. For more information about user-defined operators, see
"Overloaded Operators" on page 336 in Chapter 12.

Consider the code for the NameOf member function (a better implementation is presented later):

```
char* Card::NameOf() // Get the name of a card.
{
    static char szName[20];
    static char *Numbers[] =
    { "1", "2", "3", "4", "5", "6", "7", "8", "9",
        "10", "Jack", "Queen", "King"
    };
    static char *Suits[] =
    { "Diamonds", "Hearts", "Clubs", "Spades" };

    if( GetCardinal() < 13)
        strcpy( szName, Numbers[GetCardinal()] );

    strcat( szName, " of " );

    switch( GetSuit() )
    {
    // Diamonds, Hearts, Clubs, and Spades do not need explicit
    //   class qualifier.
    case Diamonds: strcat( szName, "Diamonds" ); break;
    case Hearts:   strcat( szName, "Hearts" );   break;
    case Clubs:    strcat( szName, "Clubs" );    break;
    case Spades:   strcat( szName, "Spades" );   break;
    }

    return szName;
}
```

An enumerated type is an integral type. The identifiers introduced with the **enum** declaration can be used wherever constants appear. Normally, the first identifier's value is 0 (Diamonds, in the preceding example), and the values increase by one for each succeeding identifier. Therefore, the value of Spades is 3.

Any enumerator in the list, including the first one, can be initialized to a value other than its default value. Suppose the declaration of Suit had been the following:

```
enum Suit
{
    Diamonds = 5,
    Hearts,
    Clubs = 4,
    Spades
};
```

Then the values of Diamonds, Hearts, Clubs, and Spades would have been 5, 6, 4, and 5, respectively. Note that 5 is used more than once.

The default values for these enumerators simplify implementation of the NameOf function:

```
char* Card::NameOf() // Get the name of a card.
{
    static char szName[20];
    static char *Numbers[] =
    { "1", "2", "3", "4", "5", "6", "7", "8", "9",
       "10", "Jack", "Queen", "King"
    };
    static char *Suits[] =
    { "Diamonds", "Hearts", "Clubs", "Spades"};

    if( GetCardinal() < 13)
        strcpy( szName, Numbers[GetCardinal()] );

    strcat( szName, " of " );

    strcat( szName, Suits[GetSuit()] );

    return szName;
}
```

The accessor function GetSuit returns type Suit, an enumerated type.
Because enumerated types are integral types, they can be used as arguments to
the array subscript operator. (For more information, see "Subscript Operator"
on page 69 in Chapter 4.)

Enumerator Names

The names of enumerators must be different from any other enumerator or
variable in the same scope. However, the values can be duplicated.

Definition of Enumerator Constants

Enumerators are considered defined immediately after their initializers; therefore,
they can be used to initialize succeeding enumerators. The following example
defines an enumerated type that ensures that any two enumerators can be
combined with the OR operator:

```
enum FileOpenFlags
{
    OpenReadOnly  = 1,
    OpenReadWrite = OpenReadOnly << 1,
    OpenBinary    = OpenReadWrite << 1,
    OpenText      = OpenBinary   << 1,
    OpenShareable = OpenText     << 1
};
```

In this example, the preceding enumerator initializes each succeeding
enumerator.

Conversions and Enumerated Types

Because enumerated types are integral types, any enumerator can be converted to another integral type by integral promotion. Consider this example:

```
enum Days
{
    Sunday,
    Monday,
    Tuesday,
    Wednesday,
    Thursday,
    Friday,
    Saturday
};

int  i;
Days d = Thursday;

i = d;        // Converted by integral promotion.
cout << "i = " << i << "\n";
```

However, there is no implicit conversion from any integral type to an enumerated type. Therefore (continuing with the preceding example), the following statement is in error:

```
d = 6;        // Erroneous attempt to set d to Saturday.
```

Assignments such as this, where no implicit conversion exists, must use a cast to perform the conversion:

```
d = (Days)6;    // Explicit cast-style conversion to type Days.
d = Days( 4 );  // Explicit function-style conversion to type Days.
```

The preceding example shows conversions of values that coincide with the enumerators. There is no mechanism that protects you from converting a value that does not coincide with one of the enumerators. For example:

```
d = Days( 967 );
```

Some such conversions may work. However, there is no guarantee that the resultant value will be one of the enumerators. Additionally, if the size of the enumerator is too small to hold the value being converted, the value stored may not be what you expect.

Linkage Specifications

The term "linkage specification" refers to the protocol for linking functions (or procedures) written in different languages. The following calling conventions are affected:

- Case sensitivity of names.

- Decoration of names. In C, the compiler prefixes names with an underscore. This is often called "decoration." In C++, name decoration is used to retain type information through the linkage phase. (See "Decorated Names" in *Visual C++ Programmer's Guide* online.)

- Order in which arguments are expected on the stack.
- Responsibility for adjusting the stack on function return. Either the called function or the calling function is responsible.
- Passing of hidden arguments (whether any hidden arguments are passed).

Syntax

linkage-specification:
>>> **extern** *string-literal* { *declaration-list*_{opt} }
>>> **extern** *string-literal declaration*

declaration-list:
>> *declaration*
>> *declaration-list*

Linkage specification facilitates gradually porting C code to C++ by allowing the use of existing code.

Microsoft Specific →

The only linkage specifications currently supported by Microsoft C++ are **"C"** and **"C++"**.

END Microsoft Specific

The following example declares the functions `atoi` and `atol` with C linkage:

```
extern "C"
{
   int  atoi( char *string );
   long atol( char *string );
}
```

Calls to these functions are made using C linkage. The same result could be achieved with these two declarations:

```
extern "C" int  atoi( char *string );
extern "C" long atol( char *string );
```

Microsoft Specific →

All Microsoft C standard include files use conditional compilation directives to detect C++ compilation. When a C++ compilation is detected, the prototypes are enclosed in an **extern "C"** directive as follows:

```
// Sample.h
#if defined(__cplusplus)
extern "C"
{
#endif
```

```
// Function declarations

#if defined(__cplusplus)
}
#endif
```

END Microsoft Specific

You do not need to declare the functions in the standard include files as **extern "C"**.

If a function is overloaded, no more than one of the functions of the same name can have a linkage specifier. (For more information, see "Function Overloading" on page 214 in Chapter 7.)

Table 6.3 shows how various linkage specifications work.

Table 6.3   Effects of Linkage Specifications

Specification	Effect
On an object	Affects linkage of that object only
On a function	Affects linkage of that function and all functions or objects declared within it
On a class	Affects linkage of all nonmember functions and objects declared within the class

If a function has more than one linkage specification, they must agree; it is an error to declare functions as having both C and C++ linkage. Furthermore, if two declarations for a function occur in a program—one with a linkage specification and one without—the declaration with the linkage specification must be first. Any redundant declarations of functions that already have linkage specification are given the linkage specified in the first declaration. For example:

```
extern "C" int CFunc1();
...
int CFunc1();          // Redeclaration is benign; C linkage is
                       //   retained.

int CFunc2();
...
extern "C" int CFunc2(); // Error: not the first declaration of
                         //   CFunc2;  cannot contain linkage
                         //   specifier.
```

Functions and objects explicitly declared as **static** within the body of a compound linkage specifier ({ }) are treated as static functions or objects; the linkage specifier is ignored. Other functions and objects behave as if declared using the **extern** keyword. (See "Storage-Class Specifiers" on page 153 for details about the **extern** keyword.)

Template Specifications

The **template** declaration specifies a set of parameterized classes or functions.

Note   For more information, see "Template Topics" in *Visual C++ Programmer's Guide* online.

Syntax

template-declaration:
> **template** < *template-argument-list* > *declaration*

template-argument-list:
> *template-argument*
> *template-argument-list* **,** *template-argument*

template-argument:
> *type-argument*
> *argument-declaration*

type-argument:
> **class** *identifier*
> **typename** *identifier*

The *declaration* declares a function or a class. With function templates, each *template-argument* must appear at least once in the *template-argument-list* of the function being declared.

The *template-argument-list* is a list of arguments used by the template function that specifies which parts of the following code will vary. For example:

```
template< class T, int i > class MyStack...
```

In this case the template can receive a type (class T) and a constant parameter (int I). The template will use type T and the constant integer i upon construction. Within the body of the MyStack declaration, you must refer to the T identifier.

The **typename** keyword can be used in the *template-argument-list*. The following template declarations are identical:

```
template< class T1, class T2 > class X...
template< typename T1, typename T2 > class X...
```

Template arguments of the following form are allowed:

```
template<typename Type> class allocator {};
template<typename Type,
   typename Allocator = allocator<Type> > class stack {};
stack<int> MyStack;
```

Visual C++ 5.0 now supports the reuse of template parameters in the template parameter list. For example, the following code is now legal:

```
class Y {...};
template<class T, T* pT> class X1 {...};
template<class T1, class T2 = T1> class X2 {...};

Y aY;

X1<Y, &aY> x1;
X2<int> x2;
```

A template declaration itself does not generate code; it specifies a family of classes or functions, one or more of which will be generated when referenced by other code.

Template declarations have global or namespace scope.

Visual C++ 5.0 now performs syntax checking of template definitions. This version of Visual C++ can detect errors that previous versions cannot. The compiler can now detect syntax errors of templates that are defined but never instantiated.

Here is a list of common errors which could compile with the Visual C++ 4.0 compiler, but not the Visual C++ 5.0 compiler:

- A user-defined type is used in a template declaration before it is declared, but it is declared before the first instantiation or use of the template.
  For example:

```
template<class T> class X {\
    //...
    Data m_data;    //Error Visual C++ 5.0, Data not defined
};

class Data {...};

void g() { X<int> x1; }
```

- Move the declaration of Data before the class template X to fix this problem.

- A member function is declared outside a class template, whereas it is never declared inside the class. For example:

```
template<class T> class X {
    //no mf declared here
};

// This definition did not cause an error with Visual
//   C++ 4.0, but it will cause an error with Visual
//   C++ 5.0
//
template<class T> void X<T>::mf() {...};
```

- A class identifier is considered to be a normal class unless declared to be a class template. For example, the following code generates an error with Visual C++ 5.0 but not with Visual C++ 4.0:

```
template<class T> class X {
    friend class Y<T>;      // Parsed as Y 'less-than'
                            //  T 'greater-than';
    Z<T> mf( );             // Parsed as Z 'less-than'
                            //  T 'greater-than';
};

template<class T> class Y {...};
template<class T> class Z {...};

X<int> x;
```

To fix the problem, forward declare Y and Z before the definition of X.

```
template<class T> class Y {...};
template<class T> class Z {...};

template<class T> class X {...};
```

Referencing a Template

To reference a template class or function use the following syntax:

Syntax

template-class-name:
>   *template-name* < *template-arg-list* >

template-arg-list:
>   *template-arg*
>   *template-arg-list* , *template-arg*

template-arg:
>   *expression*
>   *type-name*

All *template-arg* arguments must be constant expressions. The compiler creates a new instance (called an instantiation) of the templated class or function if there is no exact match to a previously generated template. For example:

```
MyStack< unsigned long, 5 > stack1;   // creates a stack of
                                      //  unsigned longs
MyStack< DWORD, 5 >  stack2;          // uses code created above
MyStack< char, 6 > stack3;            // generates new code
MyStack< MyClass, 6 > stack4;         // generates stack of
                                      //  MyClass objects
```

Each generated template function creates its own static variables and members.

Function Templates

Class templates define a family of related classes that are based on the parameters passed to the class upon instantiation. Function templates are similar to class templates, but define a family of functions. Here is a function template that swaps two items:

```
template< class T > void MySwap( T& a, T& b )
{
    T c;
    c = a; a = b; b = c;
}
```

Although this function could be performed by a nontemplated function, using void pointers, the template version is type-safe. Consider the following calls:

```
int j = 10;
int k = 18;
CString Hello = "Hello, Windows!";
MySwap( j, k );          //OK
MySwap( j, Hello );      //error
```

The second MySwap call triggers a compile-time error, since the compile cannot generate a MySwap function with parameters of different types. If void pointers were used, both function calls would compile correctly, but the function would not work properly at run time.

Explicit specification of the template arguments for a function template is allowed. For example:

```
template<class T> void f(T) {...}
void g(char j) {
    f<int>(j);   //generate the specialization f(int)
}
```

When the template argument is explicitly specified, normal implicit conversions are done to convert the function argument to the type of the corresponding function template parameters. In the above example, the compiler will convert (char j) to type int.

Member Function Templates

After declaring a templated class, define member functions as function templates. For example:

```
template<class T, int i> class MyStack
{
    T*  pStack;
    T StackBuffer[i];
    int cItems = i * sizeof(T);
public:
    MyStack( void );
    void push( const T item );
    T& pop( void );
};
```

```
template< class T, int i > MyStack< T, i >::MyStack( void )
{ ... } ;
template< class T, int i > void MyStack< T, i >::push( const T item )
{ ... } ;
template< class T, int i > T& MyStack< T, i >::pop( void )
{ ... } ;
```

Note that the definition of the constructor function does not include the template argument list twice.

Explicit Instantiation

Explicit instantiation lets you create an instantiation of a templated class or function without actually using it in your code. Since this is useful when you are creating library (.LIB) files that use templates for distribution, uninstantiated template definitions are not put into object (.OBJ) files.

The following explicitly instantiates MyStack for int variables and six items:

```
template class MyStack<int, 6>;
```

This statement creates an instantiation of MyStack without reserving any storage for an object; code is generated for all members.

The following explicitly instantiates only the constructor member function:

```
template MyStack<int, 6>::MyStack( void );
```

Visual C++ 5.0 now supports explicit instantiation of function templates. Previous versions only supported the explicit instantiation of class templates. For example, the following code is now legal:

```
template<class T> void f(T) {...}

//Instantiate f with the explicitly specified template
//argument 'int'
//
template void f<int> (int);

//Instantiate f with the deduced template argument 'char'
//
template void f(char);
```

Microsoft Specific →

You can use the **extern** keyword to prevent the automatic instantiation of members. For example:

```
extern template class MyStack<int, 6>;
```

Similarly, you can mark specific members as being external and not instantiated as follows:

```
extern template MyStack<int, 6>::MyStack( void );
```

Note The **extern** keyword in the specialization only applies to member functions defined outside of the body of the class. Functions defined inside the class declaration are considered inline functions and are always instantiated.

END Microsoft Specific

Differences from Other Implementations

Microsoft Specific →

Templates are not officially standardized and, as a result, different C++ compiler vendors have implemented them differently. The following list shows some differences between this version of Visual C++ and other compilers. Note that this list will change in future versions of the compiler.

- The compiler cannot instantiate a template outside of the module in which it is defined.

- Templates cannot be used with functions declared with **__declspec (dllimport)** or **__declspec (dllexport)**.

- All template arguments must be of an unambiguous type that exactly matches that of the template parameter list. For example:

```
template< class T > T check( T );
template< class S > void watch( int (*)(S) );
watch( check );      //error
```

The compiler should instantiate the `check` templated function in the form `int check( int )`, but the inference can not be followed.

- Friend functions must be declared before they are used in a templated class. You cannot have a friend function defined within a class definition. This is because the friend function could be a templated function, which would cause an illegal nested template definition.

END Microsoft Specific

Namespaces

The C++ language provides a single global namespace. This can cause problems with global name clashes. For instance, consider these two C++ header files:

```
// one.h
char func(char);
class String { ... };

// somelib.h
class String { ... };
```

With these definitions, it is impossible to use both header files in a single program; the `String` classes will clash.

A namespace is a declarative region that attaches an additional identifier to any names declared inside it. The additional identifier makes it less likely that a name will conflict with names declared elsewhere in the program. It is possible to use the same name in separate namespaces without conflict even if the names appear in the same translation unit. As long as they appear in separate namespaces, each name will be unique because of the addition of the namespace identifier. For example:

```
// one.h
namespace one
{
    char func(char);
    class String { ... };
}

// somelib.h
namespace SomeLib
{
    class String { ... };
}
```

Now the class names will not clash because they become `one::String` and `SomeLib::String`, respectively.

Declarations in the file scope of a translation unit, outside all namespaces, are still members of the global namespace.

namespace Declaration

A **namespace** declaration identifies and assigns a name to a declarative region.

Syntax

original-namespace-name :
    identifier

namespace-definition :
    original-namespace-definition
    extension-namespace-definition
    unnamed-namespace-definition

original-namespace-definition :
    namespace *identifier* { *namespace-body* }

extension-namespace-definition :
    namespace *original-namespace-name* { *namespace-body* }

unnamed-namespace-definition :
    namespace { *namespace-body* }

namespace-body :
    *declaration-seq*opt

The *identifier* in an *original-namespace-definition* must be unique in the declarative region in which it is used. The *identifier* is the name of the namespace and is used to reference its members. Subsequently, in that declarative region, it is treated as an *original-namespace-name*.

The declarative region of a *namespace-definition* is its *namespace-body*.

A namespace can contain data and function declarations. The *declaration-seq* is a list of these declarations which are said to be members of the namespace.

Unnamed namespaces

An *unnamed-namespace-definition* behaves as if it were replaced by:

namespace *unique* { *namespace-body* }
using namespace *unique*;

Each unnamed namespace has an identifier, represented by *unique*, that differs from all other identifiers in the entire program. For example:

```
namespace { int i; }     // unique::i
void f() { i++; }         // unique::i++

namespace A {
    namespace {
        int I;            // A::unique::i
        int j;            // A::unique::j
    }
}

using namespace A;

void h()
{
    I++;                  // error: unique::i or A::unique::i
    A::i++;               // error: A::i undefined
    j++;                  // A::unique::j++
}
```

Unnamed namespaces are a superior replacement for the static declaration of variables. They allow variables and functions to be visible within an entire translation unit, yet not visible externally. Although entities in an unnamed namespace might have external linkage, they are effectively qualified by a name unique to their translation unit and therefore can never be seen from any other translation unit.

namespace Definition

A *namespace-definition* can be nested within another *namespace-definition*. Every *namespace-definition* must appear either at file scope or immediately within another *namespace-definition*.

For example:

```
namespace A {
    int j = 3;
    int f(int k);
}

namespace Outer {
    int n = 6;
    int func(int num);

    namespace Inner {
        float f = 9.993;
    }
}

void main()
{
    namespace local { ... }    // error: not at global scope
    .
    .
    .
}
```

Unlike other declarative regions, the definition of a namespace can be split over several parts of a single translation unit.

```
namespace A {
    // declare namespace A variables
    int i;
    int j;
}

namespace B {
    ...
}
    .
    .
    .
namespace A {
    // declare namespace A functions
    void func(void);
    int int_func(int i);
}
```

When a namespace is continued in this manner, after its initial definition, the continuation is called an *extension-namespace-definition*.

Defining namespace Members

Members of a namespace may be defined within that namespace. For example:

```
namespace X { void f() { } }
```

Members of a named namespace can be defined outside the namespace in which they are declared by explicit qualification of the name being defined. However, the entity being defined must already be declared in the namespace. In addition, the definition must appear after the point of declaration in a namespace that encloses the declaration's namespace. For example:

```
namespace Q {
    namespace V {
        void f();
    }

    void V::f() { }      // ok
    void V::g() { }      // error, g() is not yet a member of V

    namespace V {
        void g();
    }
}
```

Namespace Alias

A *namespace-alias* is an alternative name for a **namespace**.

Syntax

namespace-alias :
      identifier

namespace-alias-definition :
      namespace *identifier = qualified-namespace-specifier;*

qualified-namespace-specifier :
      ::opt *nested-name-specifier*opt *class-or-namespace-name*

A *namespace-alias-definition* declares an alternate name for a namespace. The *identifier* is a synonym for the *qualified-namespace-specifier* and becomes a *namespace-alias*. For example:

```
namespace a_very_long_namespace_name { ... }
namespace AVLNN = a_very_long_namespace_name;
// AVLNN is now a namespace-alias for a_very_long_namespace_name.
```

A *namespace-name* cannot be identical to any other entity in the same declarative region. In addition, a global *namespace-name* cannot be the same as any other global entity name in a given program.

using Declaration

The **using** declaration introduces a name into the declarative region in which the **using** declaration appears. The name becomes a synonym for an entity declared elsewhere. It allows an *individual* name from a specific namespace to be used without explicit qualification. This is in contrast to the **using** directive, which allows *all* the names in a namespace to be used without qualification. See "using Directive" on page 187 for more information.

Syntax

using-declaration :
> **using ::**_{opt} *nested-name-specifier unqualified-id*
> **using ::** *unqualified-id*

A *using-declaration* can be used in a class definition. For example:

```
class B
{
   void f(char);
   void g(char);
};

class D : B
{
   using B::f;
   void f(int) { f('c'); }    // calls B::f(char)
   void g(int) { g('c'); }    // recursively calls D::g(int)
                              //   only B::f is being used
};
```

When used to declare a member, a *using-declaration* must refer to a member of a base class. For example:

```
class C
{
   int g();
};

class D2 : public B
{
   using B::f;    // ok: B is a base of D2
   using C::g;    // error: C isn't a base of D2
};
```

Members declared with a *using-declaration* can be referenced using explicit qualification. The **::** prefix refers to the global namespace. For example:

```
void f();

namespace A
{
   void g();
}
```

```
namespace X
{
    using ::f;      // global f
    using A::g;     // A's g
}

void h()
{
    X::f();         // calls ::f
    X::g();         // calls A::g
}
```

Just as with any declaration, a *using-declaration* can be used repeatedly only where multiple declarations are allowed. For example:

```
namespace A
{
    int i;
}

void f()
{
    using A::i;
    using A::i;     // ok: double declaration
}

class B
{
protected:
    int i;
};

class X : public B
{
public:
    using B::i;
    using B::i;  // error: class members cannot be multipally declared
};
```

When a *using-declaration* is made, the synonym created by the declaration refers only to definitions that are valid at the point of the *using-declaration*. Definitions added to a namespace after the *using-declaration* are not valid synonyms. For example:

```
namespace A
{
    void f(int);
}

using A::f;         // f is a synonym for A::f(int) only

namespace A
{
    void f(char);
}
```

```
void f()
{
   f('a');          // refers to A::f(int), even though A::f(char) exists
}

void b()
{
   using A::f;     // refers to A::f(int) AND A::f(char)
   f('a');          // calls A::f(char);
}
```

A name defined by a *using-declaration* is an alias for its original name. It does not affect the type, linkage or other attributes of the original declaration.

If a set of local declarations and *using-declaration*s for a single name are given in a declarative region, they must all refer to the same entity, or they must all refer to functions. For example:

```
namespace B
{
   int i;
   void f(int);
   void f(double);
}

void g()
{
   int i;
   using B::i;     // error: i declared twice
   void f(char);
   using B::f;     // ok: each f is a function
}
```

In the example above, the using B::i statement causes a second int i to be declared in the g() function. The using B::f statement does not conflict with the f(char) function because the function names introduced by B::f have different parameter types.

A local function declaration cannot have the same name and type as a function introduced by a *using-declaration*. For example:

```
namespace B
{
   void f(int);
   void f(double);
}

namespace C
{
   void f(int);
   void f(double);
   void f(char);
}
```

```
void h()
{
   using B::f;      // introduces B::f(int) and B::f(double)
   using C::f;      // C::f(int), C::f(double), and C::f(char)
   f('h');          // calls C::f(char)
   f(1);            // error: ambiguous: B::f(int) or C::f(int)?
   void f(int);     // error: conflicts with B::f(int) and C::f(int)
}
```

When a *using-declaration* introduces a name from a base class into a derived class scope, member functions in the derived class override virtual member functions with the same name and argument types in the base class. For example:

```
struct B
{
   virtual void f(int);
   virtual void f(char);
   void g(int);
   void h(int);
};

struct D : B
{
   using B::f;
   void f(int);        // ok: D::f(int) overrides B::f(int)

   using B::g;
   void g(char);       // ok: there is no B::g(char)

   using B::h;
   void h(int);        // error: D::h(int) conflicts with B::h(int)
                       //   B::h(int) is not virtual
};

void f(D* pd)
{
   pd->f(1);           // calls D::f(int)
   pd->f('a');         // calls B::f(char)
   pd->g(1);           // calls B::g(int)
   pd->g('a');         // calls D::g(char)
}
```

All instances of a name mentioned in a *using-declaration* must be accessible. In particular, if a derived class uses a *using-declaration* to access a member of a base class, the member name must be accessible. If the name is that of an overloaded member function, then all functions named must be accessible. For example:

```
class A
{
private:
   void f(char);
public:
   void f(int);
protected:
   void g();
};
```

```
class B : public A
{
    using A::f;       // error: A::f(char) is inaccessible
public:
    using A::g;       // B::g is a public synonym for A::g
};
```

See Chapter 10, "Member-Access Control" for more information on accessibility of members.

using Directive

The *using-directive* allows the names in a **namespace** to be used without the *namespace-name* as an explicit qualifier. In contrast to a **using** declaration, which allows an *individual* name to be used without qualification, the **using** directive allows *all* the names in a namespace to be used without qualification. See "using Declaration" on page 183 for more information.

Syntax

using-directive :
    using namespace ::opt *nested-name-specifier*opt *namespace-name*

The intent of the *using-directive* is to allow unique, descriptive names to be used when declaring functions and variables, without requiring the complete name every time access to the functions or variables is needed. Of course, the complete, qualified name can still be used to retain clarity.

The unqualified names can be used from the point of the **using** directive on. If a namespace is extended after a *using-directive* is given, the additional members of the namespace can be used, without qualification, after the *extended-namespace-definition*. For example:

```
namespace M
{
    int i;
}

using namespace M;

namespace N
{
    int j;
    double f() { return M::d; }    // error: M::d does not yet exist
}

namespace M           // namespace extension
{
    double d;
}
                      // now M::d can be used
```

It is possible for a *using-directive* to introduce conflicting names when used in another namespace. For example:

```
namespace M
{
    int i;
}

namespace N
{
    int i;
    using namespace M;    // no error here
}
        .
        .
        .
void f()
{
    using namespace N;
    i = 7;                // error: ambiguous: M::i or N::i?
}
```

In this example, bringing M::i into namespace N does not hide the declaration of N::i, but instead creates an ambiguity when N::i is used. In this manner, the *using-directive* can easily introduce unintended ambiguities. Consider the following code fragment:

```
namespace D
{
    int d1;
    void f(int);
    void f(char);
}

using namespace D;

int d1;         // no conflict with D::d1

namespace E
{
    int e;
    void f(int);
}

namespace D        // namespace extension
{
    int d2;
    using namespace E;
    void f(int);
}

void f()
{
```

```
    d1++;              // error: ambiguous: ::d1 or D::d1?
    ::d1++;            // ok
    D::d1++;           // ok
    d2++;              // ok: D::d2
    e++;               // ok: E::e
    f(1);              // error: ambiguous: D::f(int) or E::f(int)?
    f('a');            // ok D::f(char)
}
```

When a variable is referenced after a *using-directive*, the local variable of the same name takes precedence over the one declared in the specified namespace. For example:

```
namespace N {
    int data = 4;
}

void f(bool flag) {
    int data = 0;

    if (flag) {
        using namespace N;

        prinf("data=%d\n", data);
    }
}

void main() {
    f(true);
}
```

In the above code, the variable data referenced in the **printf** statement is the local variable initialized to 0, instead of the variable initialized in namespace N. The output is data=0 instead of data=4.

In the presence of namespace *using-directives*, the way qualified names are looked up is shown in the following example:

```
namespace A {
    int flat = 0;
}

namespace B {
    using namespace A;
}

namespace C {
    using namespace A;
    using namespace B;
}

void main() {
    printf("C::flag = %d\n", C::flag);
}
```

The qualified name (C::flag) is resolved to (A::flag) due to the namespace *using-directives* in namespace C.

Explicit Qualification

A name in a class or namespace can be accessed using an explicit qualifier.

Syntax

id-expression :
>   *unqualified-id*
>   *qualified-id*

nested-name-specifier :
>   *class-or-namespace-name* **::** *nested-name-specifier*_{opt}

class-or-namespace-name :
>   *class-name*
>   *namespace-name*

namespace-name :
>   *original-namespace-name*
>   *namespace-alias*

This is very similar to using the scope operator to resolve access to a member of a class. For more information, see "Qualified Names" on page 68 in Chapter 4.

CHAPTER 7

Declarators

A "declarator" is the part of a declaration that names an object, type, or function. Declarators appear in a declaration as one or more names separated by commas; each name can have an associated initializer.

Syntax

declarator-*list:*
> *init-declarator*
> *declarator-list* , *init-declarator*

init-declarator*:*
> *declarator initializer*_{opt}

This chapter includes the following topics:

- Overview
- Type names
- Abstract declarators
- Function definitions
- Initializers

Overview of Declarators

Declarators are the components of a declaration that specify names. Declarators can also modify basic type information to cause names to be functions or pointers to objects or functions. (Specifiers, discussed on page 152 in Chapter 6, "Declarations," convey properties such as type and storage class. Modifiers, discussed in this chapter and in Appendix B, "Microsoft-Specific Modifiers," modify declarators.) Figure 7.1 shows a complete declaration of two names, szBuf and strcpy, and calls out the components of the declaration.

Figure 7.1 Specifiers, Modifiers, and Declarators

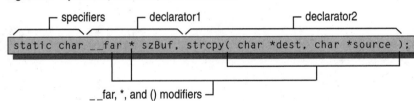

Microsoft Specific →

Most Microsoft extended keywords can be used as modifiers to form derived types; they are not specifiers or declarators. (See Appendix B, "Microsoft-Specific Modifiers.")

END Microsoft Specific

Syntax

declarator:
    dname
    ptr-operator declarator
    declarator (*argument-declaration-list*) *cv-mod-list*
    declarator [*constant-expression*opt]
    (*declarator*)

ptr-operator:
    * *cv-qualifier-list*opt
    & *cv-qualifier-list*opt
    complete-class-name :: * *cv-qualifier-list*opt

cv-qualifier-list:
    *cv-qualifier cv-qualifier-list*opt

cv-qualifier:
    const
    volatile

cv-mod-list:
    *cv-qualifier cv-mod-list*opt
    *pmodel cv-mod-list*opt

dname:
    name
    class-name
    ~ *class-name*
    typedef-name
    qualified-type-name

Declarators appear in the declaration syntax after an optional list of specifiers (*decl-specifiers*). These specifiers are discussed in Chapter 6, "Declarations." A declaration can contain more than one declarator, but each declarator declares only one name. The following sample declaration shows how specifiers and declarators are combined to form a complete declaration:

```
const char *pch, ch;
```

In this preceding declaration, the keywords **const** and **char** make up the list of specifiers. Two declarators are listed: `*pch` and `ch`. The simplified syntax of a declaration, then, is the following, where `const char` is the type and `*pch` and `ch` are the declarators:

type declarator$_1$[, *declarator*$_2$[...,*declarator*$_n$]] ;

When the binding of elements in a declarator list does not yield the desired result, you can use parentheses for clarification. A better technique, however, is to use a **typedef** or a combination of parentheses and the **typedef** keyword. Consider declaring an array of pointers to functions. Each function must obey the same protocol so that the arguments and return values are known:

```
//  Function returning type int that takes one
//    argument of type char *.
typedef int (*PIFN)( char * );

//  Declare an array of 7 pointers to functions
//    returning int and taking one argument of type
//    char *.
PIFN pifnDispatchArray[7];
```

The equivalent declaration can be written without the **typedef** declaration, but it is so complicated that the potential for error exceeds any benefits:

```
int ( *pifnDispatchArray[7] )( char * );
```

Type Names

Type names are used in some declarators in the following ways:

- In explicit conversions
- As arguments to the **sizeof** operator
- As arguments to the **new** operator
- In function prototypes
- In **typedef** statements

A type name consists of type specifiers, as described in Chapter 6, "Declarations," and the next section, "Abstract Declarators."

In the following example, the arguments to the function **strcpy** are supplied using their type names. In the case of the `source` argument, `const char` is the specifier and `*` is the abstract declarator:

```
static char *szBuf, *strcpy( char *dest, const char *source );
```

Syntax

type-name:

    *type-specifier-list abstract-declarator*_{opt}

type-specifier-list:

    *type-specifier type-specifier-list*_{opt}

abstract-declarator:

    *ptr-operator abstract-declarator*_{opt}

    *abstract-declarator*_{opt} (*argument-declaration-list*) *cv-qualifier-list*_{opt}

    *abstract-declarator*_{opt} [*constant-expression*_{opt}]

    (*abstract-declarator*)

Abstract Declarators

An abstract declarator is a declarator in which the identifier is omitted. (For related information, see the previous section, "Type Names.")

The following abstract declarators are discussed in this section:

- Pointers
- References
- Pointers to members
- Arrays
- Functions
- Default arguments

An abstract declarator is a declarator that does not declare a name— the identifier is left out. For example,

```
char *
```

declares the type "pointer to type **char**." This abstract declarator can be used in a function prototype as follows:

```
char *strcmp( char *, char * );
```

In this prototype (declaration), the function's arguments are specified as abstract declarators. The following is a more complicated abstract declarator that declares the type "pointer to a function that takes two arguments, both of type **char ***," and returns type **char ***:

```
char * (*)( char *, char * )
```

Since abstract declarators completely declare a type, it is legal to form expressions of the form:

```
// Get the size of array of 10 pointers to type char.
size_t nSize = sizeof( char *[10] );
```

```
// Allocate a pointer to a function that has no
//  return value and takes no arguments.
typedef void (PVFN *)();
PVFN *pvfn = new PVFN;

// Allocate an array of pointers to functions that
//  return type WinStatus, and take one argument of
//  type WinHandle.
typedef WinStatus (PWSWHFN *)( WinHandle );
PWSWHFN pwswhfnArray[] = new PWSWHFN[10];
```

Ambiguity Resolution

To perform explicit conversions from one type to another, you must use casts, specifying the desired type name. Some type casts result in syntactic ambiguity. The following function-style type cast is ambiguous:

```
char *aName( String( s ) );
```

It is unclear whether it is a function declaration or an object declaration with a function-style cast as the initializer: It could declare a function returning type **char *** that takes one argument of type String, or it could declare the object aName and initialize it with the value of s cast to type String.

If a declaration can be considered a valid function declaration, it is treated as such. Only if it cannot possibly be a function declaration—that is, if it would be syntactically incorrect—is a statement examined to see if it is a function-style type cast. Therefore, the compiler considers the statement to be a declaration of a function and ignores the parentheses around the identifier s. On the other hand, the statements:

```
char *aName( (String)s );
```

and

```
char *aName = String( s );
```

are clearly declarations of objects, and a user-defined conversion from type String to type **char *** is invoked to perform the initialization of aName.

Pointers

Pointers are declared using the declarator syntax:

* *cv-qualifier-list*_{opt} *dname*

A pointer holds the address of an object. The full declaration, then, is:

decl-specifiers * *cv-qualifier-list*_{opt} *dname* ;

A simple example of such a declaration is:

```
char *pch;
```

The preceding declaration specifies that pch points to an object of type **char**.

const and volatile Pointers

The **const** and **volatile** keywords change how pointers are treated. The **const** keyword specifies that the pointer cannot be modified after initialization; the pointer is protected from modification thereafter.

The **volatile** keyword specifies that the value associated with the name that follows can be modified by actions other than those in the user application. Therefore, the **volatile** keyword is useful for declaring objects in shared memory that can be accessed by multiple processes or global data areas used for communication with interrupt service routines.

When a name is declared as **volatile**, the compiler reloads the value from memory each time it is accessed by the program. This dramatically reduces the possible optimizations. However, when the state of an object can change unexpectedly, it is the only way to ensure predictable program performance.

To declare the object pointed to by the pointer as **const** or **volatile**, use a declaration of the form:

```
const    char *cpch;
volatile char *vpch;
```

To declare the value of the pointer—that is, the actual address stored in the pointer—as **const** or **volatile**, use a declaration of the form:

```
char * const    pchc;
char * volatile pchv;
```

The C++ language prevents assignments that would allow modification of an object or pointer declared as **const**. Such assignments would remove the information that the object or pointer was declared with, thereby violating the intent of the original declaration. Consider the following declarations:

```
const char cch = 'A';
char       ch = 'B';
```

Given the preceding declarations of two objects (cch, of type **const char**, and ch, of type **char**), the following declaration/initializations are valid:

```
const char        *pch1 = &cch;
const char *const pch4 = &cch;
const char        *pch5 = &ch;
char              *pch6 = &ch;
char       *const pch7 = &ch;
const char *const pch8 = &ch;
```

The following declaration/initializations are erroneous.

```
char *pch2 = &cch;        // Error
char *const pch3 = &cch;  // Error
```

The declaration of pch2 declares a pointer through which a constant object might be modified and is therefore disallowed. The declaration of pch3 specifies that the *pointer* is constant, not the object; the declaration is disallowed for the same reason the pch2 declaration is disallowed.

The following eight assignments show assigning through pointer and changing of pointer value for the preceding declarations; for now, assume that the initialization was correct for pch1 through pch8.

```
*pch1 = 'A';    // Error: object declared const
pch1 = &ch;     // OK: pointer not declared const
*pch2 = 'A';    // OK: normal pointer
pch2 = &ch;     // OK: normal pointer
*pch3 = 'A';    // OK: object not declared const
pch3 = &ch;     // Error: pointer declared const
*pch4 = 'A';    // Error: object declared const
pch4 = &ch;     // Error: pointer declared const
```

Pointers declared as **volatile** or as a mixture of **const** and **volatile** obey the same rules.

Pointers to **const** objects are often used in function declarations as follows:

```
char *strcpy( char *szTarget, const char *szSource );
```

The preceding statement declares a function, **strcpy**, that takes two arguments of type "pointer to **char**" and returns a pointer to type **char**. Because the arguments are passed by reference and not by value, the function would be free to modify both szTarget and szSource if szSource were not declared as **const**. The declaration of szSource as **const** assures the caller that szSource cannot be changed by the called function.

Note Because there is a standard conversion from *typename* * to **const** *typename* *, it is legal to pass an argument of type **char** * to **strcpy**. However, the reverse is not true; no implicit conversion exists to remove the **const** attribute from an object or pointer.

A **const** pointer of a given type can be assigned to a pointer of the same type. However, a pointer that is not **const** cannot be assigned to a **const** pointer. The following code shows correct and incorrect assignments:

```
int *const cpObject = 0;
int *pObject;

void main()
{
    pObject = cpObject; // OK
    cpObject = pObject; // Error
}
```

References

References are declared using the declarator syntax:

Syntax

& *cv-qualifier-list*_{opt} *dname*

& $cv\text{-}qualifier\text{-}list_{opt}$ $dname$

A reference holds the address of an object but behaves syntactically like an object. A reference declaration consists of an (optional) list of specifiers followed by a reference declarator.

Syntax

decl-specifiers **&** $cv\text{-}qualifier\text{-}list_{opt}$ $dname$ **;**

Consider the user-defined type Date:

```
struct Date
{
    short DayOfWeek;
    short Month;
    short Day;
    short Year;
};
```

The following statements declare an object of type Date and a reference to that object:

```
Date  Today;              // Declare the object.
Date& TodayRef = Today;   // Declare the reference.
```

The name of the object, Today, and the reference to the object, TodayRef, can be used identically in programs:

```
Today.DayOfWeek = 3;     // Tuesday
TodayRef.Month  = 7;     // July
```

Reference-Type Function Arguments

It is often more efficient to pass references, rather than functions, to large objects. This allows the compiler to pass the address of the object while maintaining the syntax that would have been used to access the object. Consider the following example that uses the Date structure:

```
// Create a Julian date of the form DDDYYYY
// from a Gregorian date.
long JulianFromGregorian( Date& GDate )
{
    static int cDaysInMonth[] = {
    31, 28, 31, 30, 31, 30, 31, 31, 30, 31, 30, 31
    };
    long JDate;
```

```
   // Add in days for months already elapsed.
   for( int i = 0; i < GDate.Month - 1; ++i )
      JDate += cDaysInMonth[i];

   // Add in days for this month.
   JDate += GDate.Day;

   // Check for leap year.
   if( GDate.Year % 100 != 0 && GDate.Year % 4 == 0 )
      JDate++;

   // Add in year.
   JDate *= 10000;
   JDate += GDate.Year;

   return JDate;
}
```

The preceding code shows that members of a structure passed by reference are accessed using the member-selection operator (.) instead of the pointer member-selection operator (–>).

Although arguments passed as reference types observe the syntax of nonpointer types, they retain one important characteristic of pointer types: they are modifiable unless declared as **const**. Because the intent of the preceding code is not to modify the object GDate, a more appropriate function prototype is:

```
long JulianFromGregorian( const Date& GDate );
```

This prototype guarantees that the function JulianFromGregorian will not change its argument.

Any function prototyped as taking a reference type can accept an object of the same type in its place because there is a standard conversion from *typename* to *typename***&**.

Reference-Type Function Returns

Functions can be declared to return a reference type. There are two reasons to make such a declaration:

- The information being returned is a large enough object that returning a reference is more efficient than returning a copy.

- The type of the function must be an l-value.

Just as it can be more efficient to pass large objects *to* functions by reference, it also can be more efficient to return large objects *from* functions by reference. Reference-return protocol eliminates the necessity of copying the object to a temporary location prior to returning.

Reference-return types can also be useful when the function must evaluate to an l-value. Most overloaded operators fall into this category, particularly the assignment operator. Overloaded operators are covered in "Overloaded Operators" on page 336 in Chapter 12. Consider the `Point` example from Chapter 4:

```
class Point
{
public:
    // Define "accessor" functions as
    //  reference types.
    unsigned& x();
    unsigned& y();
private:
    unsigned obj_x;
    unsigned obj_y;
};

unsigned& Point :: x()
{
    return obj_x;
}
unsigned& Point :: y()
{
    return obj_y;
}

void main()
{
    Point ThePoint;

    // Use x() and y() as l-values.
    ThePoint.x() = 7;
    ThePoint.y() = 9;

    // Use x() and y() as r-values.
    cout << "x = " << ThePoint.x() << "\n"
        << "y = " << ThePoint.y() << "\n";
}
```

Notice that the functions x and y are declared as returning reference types. These functions can be used on either side of an assignment statement.

Declarations of reference types must contain initializers except in the following cases:

- Explicit **extern** declaration
- Declaration of a class member
- Declaration within a class
- Declaration of an argument to a function or the return type for a function

References to Pointers

References to pointers can be declared in much the same way as references to objects. Declaring a reference to a pointer yields a modifiable value that is used like a normal pointer. The following code samples illustrate the difference between using a pointer to a pointer and a reference to a pointer:

```cpp
#include <iostream.h>
#include <string.h>

// Define a binary tree structure.
struct BTree
{
    char    *szText;
    BTree *Left;
    BTree *Right;
};
// Define a pointer to the root of the tree.
BTree *btRoot = 0;

int Add1( BTree **Root, char *szToAdd );
int Add2( BTree*& Root, char *szToAdd );
void PrintTree( BTree* btRoot );

int main( int argc, char *argv[] )
{
    if( argc < 2 )
    {
        cerr << "Usage: Refptr [1 | 2]" << "\n";
        cerr << "\n\twhere:\n";
        cerr << "\t1 uses double indirection\n";
        cerr << "\t2 uses a reference to a pointer.\n";
        cerr << "\n\tInput is from stdin.\n";
        return 1;
    }

    char *szBuf = new char[132];

    // Read a text file from the standard input device and
    //   build a binary tree.
    while( !cin.eof() )
    {
        cin.get( szBuf, 132, '\n' );
        cin.get();
        if( strlen( szBuf ) )
            switch( *argv[1] )
            {
            // Method 1: Use double indirection.
            case '1':
                Add1( &btRoot, szBuf );
                break;
```

```cpp
            // Method 2: Use reference to a pointer.
            case '2':
                Add2( btRoot, szBuf );
                break;
            default:
                cerr << "Illegal value '" << *argv[1]
                     << "' supplied for add method.\n"
                     << "Choose 1 or 2.\n";
                return -1;
            }
    }

    // Display the sorted list.
    PrintTree( btRoot );
    return 0;
}

// PrintTree: Display the binary tree in order.
void PrintTree( BTree* btRoot )
{
    // Traverse the left branch of the tree recursively.
    if( btRoot->Left )
        PrintTree( btRoot->Left );

    // Print the current node.
    cout << btRoot->szText << "\n";

    // Traverse the right branch of the tree recursively.
    if( btRoot->Right )
        PrintTree( btRoot->Right );
}

// Add1: Add a node to the binary tree.
//     Uses double indirection.
int Add1( BTree **Root, char *szToAdd )
{
    if( (*Root) == 0 )
    {
        (*Root) = new BTree;
        (*Root)->Left = 0;
        (*Root)->Right = 0;
        (*Root)->szText = new char[strlen( szToAdd ) + 1];
        strcpy( (*Root)->szText, szToAdd );
        return 1;
    }
    else if( strcmp( (*Root)->szText, szToAdd ) > 0 )
        return Add1( &((*Root)->Left), szToAdd );
    else
        return Add1( &((*Root)->Right), szToAdd );
}
```

```
// Add2: Add a node to the binary tree.
//       Uses reference to pointer
int Add2( BTree*& Root, char *szToAdd )
{
    if( Root == 0 )
    {
        Root = new BTree;
        Root->Left = 0;
        Root->Right = 0;
        Root->szText = new char[strlen( szToAdd ) + 1];
        strcpy( Root->szText, szToAdd );
        return 1;
    }
    else if( strcmp( Root->szText, szToAdd ) > 0 )
        return Add2( Root->Left, szToAdd );
    else
        return Add2( Root->Right, szToAdd );
}
```

In the preceding program, functions Add1 and Add2 are functionally equivalent (although they are not called the same way). The difference is that Add1 uses double indirection whereas Add2 uses the convenience of a reference to a pointer.

Pointers to Members

Declarations of pointers to members are special cases of pointer declarations.

Syntax

decl-specifiers class-name **::** ***** *cv-qualifier-list*$_{opt}$ *dname* **;**

A pointer to a member of a class differs from a normal pointer because it has type information for the type of the member and for the class to which the member belongs. A normal pointer identifies (has the address of) only a single object in memory. A pointer to a member of a class identifies that member in any instance of the class. The following example declares a class, Window, and some pointers to member data.

```
class Window
{
public:
    Window();                            // Default constructor.
    Window( int x1, int y1,              // Constructor specifying
        int x2, int y2 );                //  window size.
    BOOL SetCaption( const char *szTitle ); // Set window caption.
    const char *GetCaption();            // Get window caption.
    char *szWinCaption;                  // Window caption.
};

// Declare a pointer to the data member szWinCaption.
char * Window::* pwCaption = &Window::szWinCaption;
```

In the preceding example, pwCaption is a pointer to any member of class Window that has type **char***. The type of pwCaption is char * Window::*. The next code fragment declares pointers to the SetCaption and GetCaption member functions.

```
const char * (Window::*pfnwGC)() = &Window::GetCaption;
BOOL (Window::*pfnwSC)( const char * ) = &Window::SetCaption;
```

The pointers pfnwGC and pfnwSC point to GetCaption and SetCaption of the Window class, respectively. The code copies information to the window caption directly using the pointer to member pwCaption:

```
Window wMainWindow;
Window *pwChildWindow = new Window;
char   *szUntitled    = "Untitled - ";
int    cUntitledLen   = strlen( szUntitled );

strcpy( wMainWindow.*pwCaption, szUntitled );
(wMainWindow.*pwCaption)[cUntitledLen - 1] = '1';     //same as
//wMainWindow.SzWinCaption [ ] = '1';
strcpy( pwChildWindow->*pwCaption, szUntitled );
(pwChildWindow->*pwCaption)[szUntitledLen - 1] = '2'; //same as
//pwChildWindow->szWinCaption[ ] = '2';
```

The difference between the **.*** and **–>*** operators (the pointer-to-member operators) is that the **.*** operator selects members given an object or object reference, while the **–>*** operator selects members through a pointer. (For more about these operators, see "Expressions with Pointer-to-Member Operators" on page 107 in Chapter 4.)

The result of the pointer-to-member operators is the type of the member—in this case, **char ***.

The following code fragment invokes the member functions GetCaption and SetCaption using pointers to members:

```
// Allocate a buffer.
char szCaptionBase[100];

// Copy the main window caption into the buffer
//  and append " [View 1]".
strcpy( szCaptionBase, (wMainWindow.*pfnwGC)() );
strcat( szCaptionBase, " [View 1]" );

// Set the child window's caption.
(pwChildWindow->*pfnwSC)( szCaptionBase );
```

Restrictions on Pointers to Members

The address of a static member is not a pointer to member. It is a regular pointer to the one instance of the static member. Because only one instance of a static member exists for all objects of a given class, the ordinary address-of (**&**) and dereference (*****) operators can be used.

Pointers to Members and Virtual Functions

Invoking a virtual function through a pointer-to-member function works as if the function had been called directly: the correct function is looked up in the v-table and invoked. The following code shows how this is done:

```
class Base
{
public:
    virtual void Print();
};
void (Base ::* bfnPrint)() = &Base :: Print;

void Base :: Print()
{
    cout << "Print function for class 'Base'\n";
}

class Derived : public Base
{
public:
    void Print();   // Print is still a virtual function.
};

void Derived :: Print()
{
    cout << "Print function for class 'Derived'\n";
}

void main()
{
    Base    *bPtr;
    Base     bObject;
    Derived dObject;

    bPtr = &bObject;    // Set pointer to address of bObject.
    (bPtr->*bfnPrint)();

    bPtr = &dObject;    // Set pointer to address of dObject.
    (bPtr->*bfnPrint)();
}
```

The output from this program is:

```
Print function for class 'Base'
Print function for class 'Derived'
```

The key to virtual functions working, as always, is invoking them through a pointer to a base class. (For more information about virtual functions, see "Virtual Functions" on page 270 in Chapter 9.)

Representing Pointers to Members of Classes Using Inheritance

Declaring a pointer to a member of a class prior to the class definition impacts the size and speed of the resulting executable file. The number of bytes required to represent a pointer to a member of a class and the code required to interpret the representation may depend on whether the class is defined with no, single, multiple, or virtual inheritance.

In general, the more complex the inheritance used by a class, the greater the number of bytes required to represent a pointer to a member of the class and the larger the code required to interpret the pointer.

If you need to declare a pointer to a member of a class prior to defining the class, you must use either the /vmg command-line option or the related **pointers_to_members** pragma. Or you can specify the inheritance used in the class declaration using the __**single_inheritance**, __**multiple_inheritance**, or __**virtual_inheritance** keywords, thus allowing control of the code generated on a per-class basis. These options are explained in the following.

Note If you always declare a pointer to a member of a class after defining the class, you don't need to use any of these options.

Microsoft attempts to optimize the representation and code generated for pointers to members by selecting the most compact representation possible. This requires defining the class the pointer to member is based upon at the point where the pointer to member is declared. The **pointers_to_members** pragma allows you to relax this restriction and to control the pointer size and the code required to interpret the pointer.

Syntax
#pragma pointers_to_members(*pointer-declaration*, [*most-general-representation*] **)**

The *pointer-declaration* argument specifies whether you have declared a pointer to a member before or after the associated function definition. The *pointer-declaration* argument can be either **full_generality** or **best_case**.

The *most-general-representation* argument specifies the smallest pointer representation that the compiler can safely use to reference any pointer to a member of a class in a translation unit. This argument can be **single_inheritance**, **multiple_inheritance**, or **virtual_inheritance**.

The **pointers_to_members** pragma with the **best_case** argument is the compiler default. You can use this default if you always define a class before declaring a pointer to a member of the class. When the compiler encounters the declaration of a pointer to a member of a class, it already has knowledge of the kind of inheritance used by the class. Thus, the compiler can use the smallest possible representation of a pointer and generate the smallest amount of code required to operate on the pointer for each kind of inheritance. This is equivalent to using /vmb on the command-line to specify best-case representation for all classes in the compilation unit.

Use the **pointers_to_members** pragma with the **full_generality** argument if you need to declare a pointer to a member of a class before defining the class. (This need can arise if you define members in two different classes that reference each other using pointers to members. For such mutually referencing classes, one class must be referenced before it is defined.) The compiler uses the most general representation for the pointer to the member. This is equivalent to the /vmg compiler option. If you specify **full-generality**, you must also specify **single-inheritance**, **multiple-inheritance**, or **virtual-inheritance**. This is equivalent to using the **/vmg** compiler option with the /vms, /vmm, or /vmv option.

The **pointers_to_members** pragma with the **full_generality, single_inheritance** arguments (/vms option with the /vmg option) specifies that the most general representation of a pointer to a member of a class is one that uses no inheritance or single inheritance. This is the smallest possible representation of a pointer to a member of a class. The compiler generates an error if the inheritance model of a class definition for which a pointer to a member is declared is multiple or virtual. For example, placing this statement

```
#pragma pointers_to_members(full_generality, single_inheritance)
```

before a class definition declares that all class definitions that follow use only single inheritance. Once specified, the option specified with the **pointers_to_members** pragma cannot be changed.

The **pointers_to_members** pragma with the **full_generality, multiple_inheritance** arguments (/vmm option with the /vmg option) specifies that the most general representation of a pointer to a member of a class is one that uses multiple inheritance. This representation is larger than that required for single inheritance. The compiler generates an error if the inheritance model of a class definition for which a pointer to a member is declared is virtual.

The **pointers_to_members** pragma with the **full_generality, virtual_inheritance** arguments (/vmv option with the /vmg option) specifies that the most general representation of a pointer to a member of a class is one that uses virtual inheritance. In terms of pointer size and the code required to interpret the pointer, this is the most expensive option. However, this option never causes an error and is the default when the **full_generality** argument to the **pointers_to_members** pragma is specified or when the /vmg command-line option is used.

Syntax
The equivalent language construction uses this syntax:

class-declaration:
    class *inheritance-type*_{opt} *class-name*;
inheritance-type:
    __single_inheritance
    __multiple_inheritance
    __virtual_inheritance

As shown in this example,

```
class __single_inheritance S;
int S::p;
```

regardless of compiler options or pragmas, pointers to members of class S will use the smallest possible representation.

You can also explicitly give a forward declaration to the pointer-to-member representation of a class that has a forward declaration.

Note The same forward declaration of a class pointer-to-member representation should occur in every translation unit that declares pointers to members of that class, and the declaration should occur before the pointers to members are declared.

Array

An array is a collection of like objects. The simplest case of an array is a vector. C++ provides a convenient syntax for declaration of fixed-size arrays:

Syntax
decl-specifiers dname [*constant-expression*_{opt}] ;

The number of elements in the array is given by the *constant-expression*. The first element in the array is the 0th element, and the last element is the (n-1th) element, where n is the size of the array. The *constant-expression* must be of an integral type and must be greater than 0. A zero-sized array is legal only when the array is the last field in a **struct** or **union** and when the Microsoft extensions (/Ze) are enabled.

Arrays are derived types and can therefore be constructed from any other derived or fundamental type except functions, references, and **void**.

Arrays constructed from other arrays are multidimensional arrays. These multidimensional arrays are specified by placing multiple [*constant-expression*] specifications in sequence. For example, consider this declaration:

```
int i2[5][7];
```

It specifies an array of type **int**, conceptually arranged in a two-dimensional matrix of five rows and seven columns, as shown in Figure 7.2.

Figure 7.2   Conceptual Layout of Multidimensional Array

0, 0	0, 1	0, 2	0, 3	0, 4	0, 5	0, 6
1, 0	1, 1	1, 2	1, 3	1, 4	1, 5	1, 6
2, 0	2, 1	2, 2	2, 3	2, 4	2, 5	2, 6
3, 0	3, 1	3, 2	3, 3	3, 4	3, 5	3, 6
4, 0	4, 1	4, 2	4, 3	4, 4	4, 5	4, 6

In declarations of multidimensioned arrays that have an *initializer-list* (as described in "Initializers" on page 223), the *constant-expression* that specifies the bounds for the first dimension can be omitted. For example:

```
const int cMarkets = 4;

// Declare a float that represents the transportation costs.
double TransportCosts[][cMarkets] =
{ { 32.19, 47.29, 31.99, 19.11 },
  { 11.29, 22.49, 33.47, 17.29 },
  { 41.97, 22.09,  9.76, 22.55 }  };
```

The preceding declaration defines an array that is three rows by four columns. The rows represent factories and the columns represent markets to which the factories ship. The values are the transportation costs from the factories to the markets. The first dimension of the array is left out, but the compiler fills it in by examining the initializer.

The technique of omitting the bounds specification for the first dimension of a multidimensioned array can also be used in function declarations as follows:

```
#include <float.h>        // Includes DBL_MAX.
#include <iostream.h>

const int     cMkts = 4;

// Declare a float that represents the transportation costs.
double TransportCosts[][cMkts] =
{ { 32.19, 47.29, 31.99, 19.11 },
  { 11.29, 22.49, 33.47, 17.29 },
  { 41.97, 22.09,  9.76, 22.55 }  };
// Calculate size of unspecified dimension.
const int cFactories = sizeof TransportCosts / sizeof( double[cMkts] );

double FindMinToMkt( int Mkt, double TransportCosts[][cMkts],
                     int cFacts );

void main( int argc, char *argv[] )
{
    double MinCost;
    MinCost = FindMinToMkt( *argv[1] - '0', TransportCosts, cFacts );
    cout << "The minimum cost to Market " << argv[1] << " is: "
        << MinCost << "\n";
}
```

```
double FindMinToMkt( int Mkt, double TransportCosts[][cMkts],
                int cFacts )
{
    double MinCost = DBL_MAX;
    for( int i = 0; i < cFacts; ++i )
        MinCost = (MinCost < TransportCosts[i][Mkt]) ?
                    MinCost : TransportCosts[i][Mkt];
    return MinCost;
}
```

The function FindMinToMkt is written such that adding new factories does not require any code changes, just a recompilation.

Using Arrays

Individual elements of arrays are accessed using the array subscript operator ([ ]). If a singly dimensioned array is used in an expression with no subscript, the array name evaluates to a pointer to the first element in the array. For example:

```
char chArray[10];
```

```
...
```

```
char *pch = chArray;       // Pointer to first element.
char   ch = chArray[0];    // Value of first element.
       ch = chArray[3];    // Value of fourth element.
```

When using multidimensioned arrays, various combinations are acceptable in expressions. The following example illustrates this:

```
double multi[4][4][3];       // Declare the array.

double (*p2multi)[3];
double (*p1multi);

cout << multi[3][2][3] << "\n";  // Use three subscripts.
p2multi = multi[3];              // Make p2multi point to
                                 //  fourth "plane" of multi.
p1multi = multi[3][2];           // Make p1multi point to fourth
                                 //  plane, second row of multi.
```

In the preceding code, multi is a three-dimensional array of type **double**. The p2multi pointer points to an array of type **double** of size three. The array is used with one, two, and three subscripts in this example. Although it is more common to specify all the subscripts, as in the **cout** statement, it is sometimes useful to select a specific subset of array elements as shown in the succeeding statements.

Arrays in Expressions

When an identifier of an array type appears in an expression other than **sizeof**, address-of (**&**), or initialization of a reference, it is converted to a pointer to the first array element. For example:

```
char szError1[] = "Error: Disk drive not ready.";
char *psz = szError1;
```

The pointer `psz` points to the first element of the array `szError1`. Note that arrays, unlike pointers, are not modifiable l-values. Therefore, the following assignment is illegal:

```
szError1 = psz;
```

Interpretation of Subscript Operator

Like other operators, the subscript operator ([ ]) can be redefined by the user. The default behavior of the subscript operator, if not overloaded, is to combine the array name and the subscript using the following method:

*((*array-name*) + (*subscript*))

As in all addition that involves pointer types, scaling is performed automatically to adjust for the size of the type. Therefore, the resultant value is not *subscript* bytes from the origin of *array-name*; rather, it is the *subscript*th element of the array. (For more information about this conversion, see "Additive Operators" on page 90 in Chapter 4.)

Similarly, for multidimensional arrays, the address is derived using the following method:

$$*((\textit{array-name}) + (\textit{subscript}_1 * \textit{max}_2 * \textit{max}_3...\textit{max}_n)$$
$$+ \textit{subscript}_2 * \textit{max}_3...\textit{max}_n)$$
$$... + \textit{subscript}_n))$$

Indirection on Array Types

Use of the indirection operator (*) on an n-dimensional array type yields an $n-1$ dimensional array. If n is 1, a scalar (or array element) is yielded.

Ordering of C++ Arrays

C++ arrays are stored in row-major order. Row-major order means the last subscript varies the fastest.

Function Declarations

This section includes the following topics:

- Function declaration syntax
  - Variable argument lists
  - Declaring functions that take no arguments
  - Function overloading
  - Restrictions on functions
  - The argument declaration list
  - Argument lists in function prototypes (nondefining declaration)
  - Argument lists in function definitions

- Default arguments
  - Default argument expressions
  - Other considerations

Function definition is covered in "Function Definitions" on page 220.

Function Declaration Syntax

Syntax

decl-specifiers dname (*argument-declaration-list*) *cv-mod-list*_{opt}
argument-declaration-list:
    arg-declaration-list , ...
arg-declaration-list:
    argument-declaration
    arg-declaration-list , *argument-declaration*
argument-declaration:
    decl-specifiers declarator
    decl-specifiers declarator = *expression*
    *decl-specifiers abstract-declarator*_{opt}
    *decl-specifiers abstract-declarator*_{opt} = *expression*

The identifier given by *dname* has the type "*cv-mod-list* function, taking *argument-declaration-list*, and returning type *decl-specifiers*."

Note that **const**, **volatile**, and many of the Microsoft-specific keywords can appear in *cv-mod-list* and in the declaration of the name. The following example shows two simple function declarations:

```
char *strchr( char *dest, char *src );
static int atoi( const char *ascnum ) const;
```

The following syntax explains the details of a function declaration:

Syntax

argument-declaration-list:
    *arg-declaration-list*_{opt} ..._{opt}
    arg-declaration-list , ...
arg-declaration-list:
    argument-declaration
    arg-declaration-list , *argument-declaration*
argument-declaration:
    decl-specifiers declarator
    decl-specifiers declarator , *expression*
    *decl-specifiers abstract-declarator*_{opt}
    *decl-specifiers abstract-declarator*_{opt} , *expression*

Variable Argument Lists

Function declarations in which the last member of *argument-declaration-list* is the ellipsis (...) can take a variable number of arguments. In these cases, C++ provides type checking only for the explicitly declared arguments. You can use variable argument lists when you need to make a function so general that even the number and types of arguments can vary. The **printf** family of functions is an example of functions that use variable argument lists.

To access arguments after those declared, use the macros contained in the standard include file STDARG.H as described in "Functions with Variable Argument Lists" on page 221.

Microsoft Specific →

Microsoft C++ allows the ellipsis to be specified as an argument if the ellipsis is the first argument and the ellipsis is preceded by a comma. Therefore, the declaration int Func(int i, ...); is legal, but int Func(int i ...); is not.

END Microsoft Specific

Declaration of a function that takes a variable number of arguments requires at least one "placeholder" argument, even if it is not used. If this place-holder argument is not supplied, there is no way to access the remaining arguments.

When arguments of type **char** are passed as variable arguments, they are converted to type **int**. Similarly, when arguments of type **float** are passed as variable arguments, they are converted to type **double**. Arguments of other types are subject to the usual integral and floating-point promotions. See "Integral Promotions" on page 56 in Chapter 3 for more information.

Declaring Functions That Take No Arguments

A function declared with the single keyword **void** in *argument-declaration-list* takes no arguments, as long as the keyword **void** is the first and only member of *argument-declaration list*. Arguments of type **void** elsewhere in *argument-declaration-list* produce errors. For example:

```
long GetTickCount( void );            // OK
long GetTickCount( int Reset, void ); // Error
long GetTickCount( void, int Reset ); // Error
```

In C++, explicitly specifying that a function requires no arguments is the same as declaring a function with no *argument-declaration-list*. Therefore, the following two statements are identical:

```
long GetTickCount();
long GetTickCount( void );
```

Note that, while it is illegal to specify a **void** argument except as outlined here, types derived from type **void** (such as pointers to **void** and arrays of **void**) can appear anywhere in *argument-declaration-list*.

Function Overloading

C++ allows specification of more than one function of the same name in the same scope. These are called "overloaded functions" and are described in detail in Chapter 12, "Overloading." Overloaded functions enable programmers to supply different semantics for a function, depending on the types and number of arguments.

For example, a **print** function that takes a string (or **char ***) argument performs very different tasks than one that takes an argument of type **double**. Overloading permits uniform naming and prevents programmers from having to invent names such as `print_sz` or `print_d`. Table 7.1 shows what parts of a function declaration C++ uses to differentiate between groups of functions with the same name in the same scope.

Table 7.1 Overloading Considerations

Function Declaration Element	Used for Overloading?
Function return type	No
Number of arguments	Yes
Type of arguments	Yes
Presence or absence of ellipsis	Yes
Use of **typedef** names	No
Unspecified array bounds	No
const or **volatile** (in *cv-mod-list*)	Yes

Although functions can be distinguished on the basis of return type, they cannot be overloaded on this basis.

The following example illustrates how overloading can be used. Another way to solve the same problem is presented in "Default Arguments" on page 218.

```
#include <iostream.h>
#include <math.h>
#include <stdlib.h>

// Prototype three print functions.
int print( char *s );                   // Print a string.
int print( double dvalue );             // Print a double.
int print( double dvalue, int prec );   // Print a double with a
                                        //  given precision.
void main( int argc, char *argv[] )
{
    const double d = 893094.2987;

    if( argc < 2 )
    {
        // These calls to print invoke print( char *s ).
        print( "This program requires one argument." );
        print( "The argument specifies the number of" );
        print( "digits precision for the second number" );
        print( "printed." );
    }
```

```
    // Invoke print( double dvalue ).
    print( d );

    // Invoke print( double dvalue, int prec ).
    print( d, atoi( argv[1] ) );
}

// Print a string.
int print( char *s )
{
    cout << s << endl;
    return cout.good();
}

// Print a double in default precision.
int print( double dvalue )
{
    cout << dvalue << endl;
    return cout.good();
}

// Print a double in specified precision.
//   Positive numbers for precision indicate how many digits'
//   precision after the decimal point to show. Negative
//   numbers for precision indicate where to round the number
//   to the left of the decimal point.
int print( double dvalue, int prec )
{
    // Use table-lookup for rounding/truncation.
    static const double rgPow10[] = {
        10E-7, 10E-6, 10E-5, 10E-4, 10E-3, 10E-2, 10E-1, 10E0,
        10E1,  10E2,  10E3,  10E4,  10E5,  10E6
    };
    const int iPowZero = 6;

    // If precision out of range, just print the number.
    if( prec < -6 || prec > 7 )
        return print( dvalue );

    // Scale, truncate, then rescale.
    dvalue = floor( dvalue / rgPow10[iPowZero - prec] ) *
                            rgPow10[iPowZero - prec];

    cout << dvalue << endl;
    return cout.good();
}
```

The preceding code shows overloading of the print function in file scope.

For restrictions on overloading and information on how overloading affects other elements of C++, see Chapter 12, "Overloading."

Restrictions on Functions

Functions cannot return arrays or functions. They can, however, return references or pointers to arrays or functions. Another way to return an array is to declare a structure with only that array as a member:

```
struct Address
{ char szAddress[31]; };

Address GetAddress();
```

It is illegal to define a type in either the return-type portion of a function declaration or in the declaration of any argument to a function. The following legal C code is illegal in C++:

```
enum Weather { Cloudy, Rainy, Sunny } GetWeather( Date Today )
```

The preceding code is disallowed because the type Weather has function scope local to GetWeather and the return value cannot be properly used. Because arguments to functions have function scope, declarations made within the argument list would have the same problem if not allowed.

C++ does not support arrays of functions. However, arrays of pointers to functions can be useful. In parsing a Pascal-like language, the code is often separated into a lexical analyzer that parses tokens and a parser that attaches semantics to the tokens. If the analyzer returns a particular ordinal value for each token, code can be written to perform appropriate processing as shown in this example:

```
int ProcessFORToken( char *szText );
int ProcessWHILEToken( char *szText );
int ProcessBEGINToken( char *szText );
int ProcessENDToken( char *szText );
int ProcessIFToken( char *szText );
int ProcessTHENToken( char *szText );
int ProcessELSEToken( char *szText );
int (*ProcessToken[])( char * ) = {
    ProcessFORToken, ProcessWHILEToken, ProcessBEGINToken,
    ProcessENDToken, ProcessIFToken, ProcessTHENToken,
    ProcessELSEToken };
const int MaxTokenID = sizeof ProcessToken / sizeof( int (*)() );

...
int DoProcessToken( int TokenID, char *szText )
{
    if( TokenID < MaxTokenID )
        return (*ProcessToken[TokenID])( szText );
    else
        return Error( szText );
}
```

The Argument Declaration List

The *argument-declaration-list* portion of a function declaration:

- Allows the compiler to check type consistency among the arguments the function requires and the arguments supplied in the call.

- Enables conversions, either implicit or user-defined, to be performed from the supplied argument type to the required argument type.

- Checks initializations of, or assignments to, pointers to functions.

- Checks initializations of, or assignments to, references to functions.

Argument Lists in Function Prototypes (Nondefining Declaration)

The form *argument-declaration-list* is a list of the type names of the arguments. Consider an *argument-declaration-list* for a function, func, that takes these three arguments: pointer to type **char**, **char**, and **int**.

The code for such an *argument-declaration-list* can be written:

```
char *, char, int
```

The function declaration (the prototype) might therefore be written:

```
void func( char *, char, int );
```

Although the preceding declaration contains enough information for the compiler to perform type checking and conversions, it does not provide much information about what the arguments are. A good way to document function declarations is to include identifiers as they would appear in the function definition, as in the following:

```
void func( char *szTarget, char chSearchChar, int nStartAt );
```

These identifiers in prototypes are useful only for default arguments, because they go out of scope immediately. However, they provide meaningful program documentation.

Argument Lists in Function Definitions

The argument list in a function definition differs from that of a prototype only in that the identifiers, if present, represent formal arguments to the function. The identifier names need not match those in the prototype (if there are any).

Note It is possible to define functions with unnamed arguments. However, these arguments are inaccessible to the functions for which they are defined.

Default Arguments

In many cases, functions have arguments that are used so infrequently that a default value would suffice. To address this, the default-argument facility allows for specifying only those arguments to a function that are meaningful in a given call. To illustrate this concept, consider the example presented in "Function Overloading" on page 214.

```
// Prototype three print functions.
int print( char *s );              // Print a string.
int print( double dvalue );        // Print a double.
int print( double dvalue, int prec );  // Print a double with a
                                   //  given precision.
```

In many applications, a reasonable default can be supplied for `prec`, eliminating the need for two functions:

```
// Prototype two print functions.
int print( char *s );              // Print a string.
int print( double dvalue, int prec=2 );  // Print a double with a
                                   //  given precision.
```

The implementation of the `print` function is changed slightly to reflect the fact that only one such function exists for type **double**:

```
// Print a double in specified precision.
//  Positive numbers for precision indicate how many digits'
//  precision after the decimal point to show. Negative
//  numbers for precision indicate where to round the number
//  to the left of the decimal point.
int print( double dvalue, int prec )
{
    // Use table-lookup for rounding/truncation.
    static const double rgPow10[] = {
        10E-7, 10E-6, 10E-5, 10E-4, 10E-3, 10E-2, 10E-1, 10E0,
        10E1,  10E2,  10E3,  10E4, 10E5,  10E6
    };
    const int iPowZero = 6;
// If precision out of range, just print the number.
    if( prec >= -6 || prec <= 7 )
        // Scale, truncate, then rescale.
        dvalue = floor( dvalue / rgPow10[iPowZero - prec] ) *
                            rgPow10[iPowZero - prec];

    cout << dvalue << endl;

    return cout.good();
}
```

To invoke the new `print` function, use code such as the following:

```
print( d );          // Precision of 2 supplied by default argument.
print( d, 0 );       // Override default argument to achieve other
                     //  results.
```

Note these points when using default arguments:

- Default arguments are used only in function calls where trailing arguments are omitted —they must be the last argument(s). Therefore, the following code is illegal:

  ```
  int print( double dvalue = 0.0, int prec );
  ```

- A default argument cannot be redefined in later declarations even if the redefinition is identical to the original. Therefore, the following code produces an error:

  ```
  // Prototype for print function.
  int print( double dvalue, int prec = 2 );

  ...

  // Definition for print function.
  int print( double dvalue, int prec = 2 )
  {
  ...
  }
  ```

  The problem with this code is that the function declaration in the definition redefines the default argument for `prec`.

- Additional default arguments can be added by later declarations.

- Default arguments can be provided for pointers to functions. For example:

  ```
  int (*pShowIntVal)( int i = 0 );
  ```

Default Argument Expressions

The expressions used for default arguments are often constant expressions, but this is not a requirement. The expression can combine functions that are visible in the current scope, constant expressions, and global variables. The expression cannot contain local variables or nonstatic class-member variables. The following code illustrates this:

```
BOOL CreateVScrollBar( HWND hWnd, short nWidth =
                       GetSystemMetrics( SM_CXVSCROLL ) );
```

The preceding declaration specifies a function that creates a vertical scroll bar of a given width for a window. If no width argument is supplied, the Windows API function, **GetSystemMetrics**, is called to find the default width for a scroll bar.

The default expression is evaluated after the function call, but the evaluation is completed before the function call actually takes place.

Because formal arguments to a function are in function scope, and because the evaluation of default arguments takes place prior to entry to this scope, you cannot use formal arguments, or local variables in default argument expressions.

Note that any formal argument declared before a default argument expression can hide a global name in the function scope, which can cause errors. The following code is illegal:

```
const int Categories = 9;

void EnumCategories( char *Categories[], int n = Categories );
```

In the preceding code, the global name Categories is hidden at function scope, making the default argument expression invalid.

Other Considerations

The default argument is not considered part of the function type. Therefore, it is not used in selecting overloaded functions. Two functions that differ only in their default arguments are considered multiple definitions rather than overloaded functions.

Default arguments cannot be supplied for overloaded operators.

Function Definitions

Function definitions differ from function declarations in that they supply function bodies —the code that makes up the function.

Syntax

function-definition:
    *decl-specifiers*opt *declarator ctor-initializer*opt *fct-body*
fct-body:
    compound-statement

As discussed in "Functions," the form of the declarator in the syntax is:

dname (*argument-declaration-list*) *cv-mod-list*opt

The formal arguments declared in *argument-declaration-list* are in the scope of the function body.

Figure 7.3 shows the parts of a function definition. The shaded area is the function body.

Figure 7.3   Parts of a Function Definition

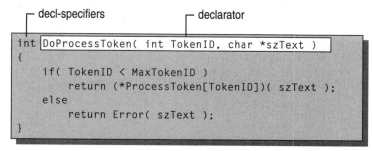

The *cv-mod-list* element of the declarator syntax specifies how the **this** pointer is to be treated; it is only for use with class member functions.

The *ctor-initializer* element of the syntax is used only in constructors. Its purpose is to allow initialization of base classes and contained objects. (For more information about use of *ctor-initializer*, see "Initializing Bases and Members" on page 317 in Chapter 11.)

Functions with Variable Argument Lists

Functions that require variable lists are declared using the ellipsis (...) in the argument list, as described in "Variable Argument Lists" on page 213. To access arguments passed to functions using this method, use the types and macros described in the STDARG.H standard include file.

The following example shows how the **va_start**, **va_arg**, and **va_end** macros, along with the **va_list** type (declared in STDARG.H), work together:

```
#include <stdio.h>
#include <stdarg.h>

//  Declaration, but not definition, of ShowVar.
int ShowVar( char *szTypes, ... );

void main()
{
    ShowVar( "fcsi", 32.4f, 'a', "Test string", 4 );
}
//  ShowVar takes a format string of the form
//   "ifcs", where each character specifies the
//   type of the argument in that position.
//
//  i = int
//  f = float
//  c = char
//  s = string (char *)
//
//  Following the format specification is a list
//   of n arguments, where n == strlen( szTypes ).
```

```
void ShowVar( char *szTypes, ... )
{
   va_list vl;
   int i;

   //  szTypes is the last argument specified; all
   //    others must be accessed using the variable-
   //    argument macros.
   va_start( vl, szTypes );

   // Step through the list.
   for( i = 0; szTypes[i] != '\0'; ++i )
   {
      union Printable_t
      {
         int      i;
         float    f;
         char     c;
         char     *s;
      } Printable;

      switch( szTypes[i] )     // Type to expect.
      {
      case 'i':
         Printable.i = va_arg( vl, int );
         printf( "%i\n", Printable.i );
         break;

      case 'f':
         Printable.f = va_arg( vl, float );
         printf( "%f\n", Printable.f );
         break;

      case 'c':
         Printable.c = va_arg( vl, char );
         printf( "%c\n", Printable.c );
         break;

      case 's':
         Printable.s = va_arg( vl, char * );
         printf( "%s\n", Printable.s );
         break;

      default:
         break;
      }
   }
   va_end( vl );
}
```

The preceding example illustrates these important concepts:

- A list marker must be established as a variable of type **va_list** before any variable arguments are accessed. In the preceding example, the marker is called vl.

- The individual arguments are accessed using the **va_arg** macro. The **va_arg** macro needs to be told the type of argument to retrieve so it can transfer the correct number of bytes from the stack. If an incorrect type of a size different than that supplied by the calling program is specified to **va_arg**, the results are unpredictable.

- The result obtained using the **va_arg** macro should be explicitly cast to the desired type.

- The **va_end** macro must be called to terminate variable-argument processing.

Initializers

Declarators can specify the initial value for objects. The only way to specify a value for objects of **const** type is in the declarator. The part of the declarator that specifies this initial value is called the "initializer."

Syntax

initializer:
>   = *assignment-expression*
>   = { *initializer-list* ,opt }
>   (*expression-list*)

initializer-list:
>   *expression*
>   *initializer-list* , *expression*
>   { *initializer-list* ,opt }

There are two fundamental types of initializers:

- The initializer invoked using the equal-sign syntax

- The initializer invoked using function-style syntax

Only objects of classes with constructors can be initialized with the function-style syntax. The two syntax forms also differ in access control and in the potential use of temporary objects. Consider the following code, which illustrates some declarators with initializers:

```
int      i = 7;                     // Uses equal-sign syntax.
Customer Cust( "Taxpayer, Joe",     // Uses function-style
               "14 Cherry Lane",    //   syntax. Requires presence
               "Manteca", "CA" );   //   of a constructor.
```

Declarations of automatic, register, static, and external variables can contain initializers. However, declarations of external variables can contain initializers only if the variables are not declared as **extern**.

These initializers can contain expressions involving constants and variables in the current scope. The initializer expression is evaluated at the point the declaration is encountered in program flow, or, for global static objects and variables, at program startup. (For more information about initialization of global static objects, see "Additional Startup Considerations" on page 36 in Chapter 2.)

Initializing Pointers to const Objects

A pointer to a **const** object can be initialized with a pointer to an object that is not **const**, but not vice versa. For example, the following initialization is legal:

```
Window StandardWindow;
const Window* pStandardWindow( &StandardWindow );
```

In the preceding code, the pointer `pStandardWindow` is declared as a pointer to a **const** object. Although `StandardWindow` is not declared as **const**, the declaration is acceptable because it does not allow an object not declared as **const** access to a **const** object. The reverse of this is as follows:

```
const Window StandardWindow;
Window* pStandardWindow( &StandardWindow );
```

The preceding code explicitly declares `StandardWindow` as a **const** object. Initializing the nonconstant pointer `pStandardWindow` with the address of `StandardWindow` generates an error because it allows access to the **const** object through the pointer. That is, it allows removal of the **const** attribute from the object.

Uninitialized Objects

Objects and simple variables of storage class **static** that are declared with no initializer are guaranteed to be initialized to a bit pattern of zeros. No such special processing takes place for uninitialized objects of automatic or register storage classes. They have undefined values.

Initializing Static Members

Static member initialization occurs in class scope. Therefore, they can access other member data or functions. For example:

```
class DialogWindow
{
public:
    static short   GetTextHeight();
private:
    static short nTextHeight;
};

short DialogWindow :: nTextHeight = GetTextHeight();
```

Note that in the preceding definition of the static member `nTextHeight`, `GetTextHeight` is implicitly known to be `DialogWindow :: GetTextHeight`.

Initializing Aggregates

An aggregate type is an array, class, or structure type which:

- Has no constructors

- Has no nonpublic members
- Has no base classes
- Has no virtual functions

Initializers for aggregates can be specified as a comma-separated list of values enclosed in curly braces. For example, this code declares an **int** array of 10 and initializes it:

```
int rgiArray[10] = { 9, 8, 4, 6, 5, 6, 3, 5, 6, 11 };
```

The initializers are stored in the array elements in increasing subscript order. Therefore, `rgiArray[0]` is 9, `rgiArray[1]` is 8, and so on, until `rgiArray[9]`, which is 11. To initialize a structure, use code such as:

```
struct RCPrompt
{
    short nRow;
    short nCol;
    char *szPrompt;
};
RCPrompt rcContinueYN = { 24, 0, "Continue (Y/N?)" };
```

Length of Aggregate-Initializer Lists

If an aggregate initializer list is shorter than the array or class type that is being initialized, zeros are stored in the elements for which no initializer is specified. Therefore, the following two declarations are equivalent:

```
// Explicitly initialize all elements.
int rgiArray[5] = { 3, 2, 0, 0, 0 };

// Allow remaining elements to be zero-initialized.
int rgiArray[5] = { 3, 2 };
```

As this shows, initializer lists can be truncated but supplying too many initializers generates an error.

Initializing Aggregates That Contain Aggregates

Some aggregates contain other aggregates—for example, arrays of arrays, arrays of structures, or structures that are composed of other structures. Initializers can be supplied for such constructs by initializing each one in the order it occurs with a brace-enclosed list. For example:

```
// Declare an array of type RCPrompt.
RCPrompt rgRCPrompt[4] =
{ { 4,  7, "Options Are:" },
  { 6,  7, "1. Main Menu" },
  { 8,  7, "2. Print Menu" },
  { 10, 7, "3. File Menu"  } };
```

Note that `rgRCPrompt` is initialized with a brace-enclosed list of brace-enclosed lists. The enclosed braces are not syntactically required, but they lend clarity to the declaration. The following example program shows how a two-dimensional array is filled by such an initializer:

```
#include <iostream.h>

void main()
{
    int rgI[2][4] = { 1, 2, 3, 4, 5, 6, 7, 8 };

    for( int i = 0; i < 2; ++i )
        for( int j = 0; j < 4; ++j )
            cout << "rgI[" << i << "][" << j << "] = "
                << rgI[i][j] << endl;
}
```

The output from this program is:

```
rgI[0][0] = 1
rgI[0][1] = 2
rgI[0][2] = 3
rgI[0][3] = 4
rgI[1][0] = 5
rgI[1][1] = 6
rgI[1][2] = 7
rgI[1][3] = 8
```

Short initialization lists can be used only with explicit subaggregate initializers and enclosed in braces. If `rgI` had been declared as:

```
int rgI[2][4] = { { 1, 2 }, { 3, 4 } };
```

the program output would have been:

```
rgI[0][0] = 1
rgI[0][1] = 2
rgI[0][2] = 0
rgI[0][3] = 0
rgI[1][0] = 3
rgI[1][1] = 4
rgI[1][2] = 0
rgI[1][3] = 0
```

Initializing Incomplete Types

Incomplete types, such as unbounded array types, can be initialized as follows:

```
char HomeRow[] = { 'a', 's', 'd', 'f', 'g', 'h', 'j', 'k', 'l' };
```

The compiler computes the size of the array from the number of initializers provided.

Incomplete types, such as pointers to class types that are declared but not defined, are declared as follows:

```
class DefinedElsewhere;          // Class definition elsewhere.
class DefinedHere
{
   ...
   friend class DefinedElsewhere;
};
```

Initializing Using Constructors

Objects of class type are initialized by calling the appropriate constructor for the class. For complete information about initializing class types, see "Explicit Initialization" on page 315 in Chapter 11.

Initializers and Unions

Objects of **union** type are initialized with a single value (if the union does not have a constructor). This is done in one of two ways:

- Initialize the union with another object of the same **union** type. For example:
  ```
  struct Point
  {
      unsigned x;
      unsigned y;
  };
  union PtLong
  {
      long  l;
      Point pt;
  };

      ...

  PtLong ptOrigin;
  PtLong ptCurrent = ptOrigin;
  ```

  In the preceding code, ptCurrent is initialized with the value of ptOrigin — an object of the same type.

- Initialize the union with a brace-enclosed initializer for the first member. For example:
  ```
  PtLong ptCurrent = { 0x0a000aL };
  ```

Initializing Character Arrays

Character arrays can be initialized in one of two ways:

- Individually, as follows:
  ```
  char chABCD[4] = { 'a', 'b', 'c', 'd' };
  ```
- With a string, as follows:
  ```
  char chABCD[5] = "abcd";
  ```

In the second case, where the character array is initialized with a string, the compiler appends a trailing '\0' (end-of-string character). Therefore, the array must be at least one larger than the number of characters in the string.

Because most string handling uses the standard library functions or relies on the presence of the trailing end-of-string character, it is common to see unbounded array declarations initialized with strings:

```
char chABCD[] = "ABCD";
```

Initializing References

Variables of reference type must be initialized with an object of the type from which the reference type is derived, or with an object of a type that can be converted to the type from which the reference type is derived. For example:

```
int   iVar;
long  lVar;

long& LongRef1 = lVar;      // No conversion required.
long& LongRef2 = iVar;      // Error.
const long& LongRef3 = iVar // OK

LongRef1 = 23L;             // Change lVar through a reference.
LongRef2 = 11L;             // Change iVar through a reference.
LongRef3 = 11L;             // Error.
```

The only way to initialize a reference with a temporary object is to initialize a constant temporary object. Once initialized, a reference-type variable always points to the same object; it cannot be modified to point to another object.

Although the syntax can be the same, initialization of reference-type variables and assignment to reference-type variables are semantically different. In the preceding example, the assignments that change iVar and lVar look similar to the initializations but have different effects. The initialization specifies the object to which the reference-type variable points; the assignment assigns to the referred-to object through the reference.

Because both passing an argument of reference type to a function and returning a value of reference type from a function are initializations, the formal arguments to a function are initialized correctly, as are the references returned.

Reference-type variables can be declared without initializers only in the following:

- Function declarations (prototypes). For example:
  ```
  int func( int& );
  ```
- Function-return type declarations. For example:
  ```
  int& func( int& );
  ```

- Declaration of a reference-type class member. For example:

```
class c
{
public:
    int& i;
};
```

- Declaration of a variable explicitly specified as **extern**. For example:

```
extern int& iVal;
```

When initializing a reference-type variable, the compiler uses the decision graph shown in Figure 7.4 to select between creating a reference to an object or creating a temporary object to which the reference points.

References to **volatile** types (declared as **volatile** *typename& identifier*) can be initialized with **volatile** objects of the same type or with objects that have not been declared as **volatile**. They cannot, however, be initialized with **const** objects of that type. Similarly, references to **const** types (declared as **const** *typename& identifier*) can be initialized with **const** objects of the same type (or anything that has a conversion to that type or with objects that have not been declared as **const**). They cannot, however, be initialized with **volatile** objects of that type.

References that are not qualified with either the **const** or **volatile** keyword can be initialized only with objects declared as neither **const** nor **volatile**.

Figure 7.4 Decision Graph for Initialization of Reference Types

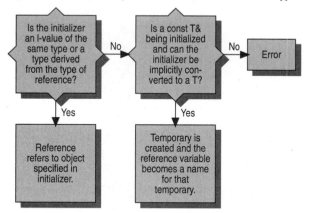

CHAPTER 8

Classes

This chapter introduces C++ classes. Classes, which can contain data and functions, introduce user-defined types into a program. User-defined types in traditional programming languages are collections of data which, taken together, describe an object's attributes and state. Class types in C++ enable you to describe attributes and state, and to define behavior.

The following topics are included:

- Overview
- Class names
- Class members
- Member functions
- Static data members
- Unions
- Bit fields
- Nested class declarations
- Type names in class scope

Overview of Classes

Class types are defined using the **class**, **struct**, and **union** keywords. For simplicity, types defined with these keywords are called class declarations, except in discussions of language elements that behave differently depending on which keyword is used.

Names of classes defined within another class ("nested") have class scope of the enclosing class.

Syntax
class-name:
    identifier

The variables and functions of a class are called members. When defining a class, it is common practice to supply the following members (although all are optional):

- Class data members, which define the state and attributes of an object of the class type.
- One or more "constructor" functions, which initialize an object of the class type. Constructors are described in "Constructors" on page 292 in Chapter 11.
- One or more "destructor" functions, which perform cleanup functions such as deallocating dynamically allocated memory or closing files. Destructors are described in "Destructors" on page 297 in Chapter 11.
- One or more member functions that define the object's behavior.

Defining Class Types

Class types are defined using *class-specifiers*. Class types can be declared using *elaborated-type-specifiers* as shown in "Type Specifiers" on page 162 in Chapter 6.

Syntax

class-specifier:
    class-head { *member-list*opt }

class-head:
    *class-key imodel*opt *identifier*opt *base-spec*opt
    *class-key imodel*opt *class-name*opt *base-spec*opt

class-key:
    class
    struct
    union

imodel:
    __declspec

Class names are introduced as identifiers immediately after the compiler processes them (before entry into the class body); they can be used to declare class members. This allows declaration of self-referential data structures, such as the following:

```
class Tree
{
public:
    void *Data;
    Tree *Left;
    Tree *Right;
};
```

Structures, Classes, and Unions

The three class types are structure, class, and union. They are declared using the **struct**, **class**, and **union** keywords (see *class-key* syntax). Table 8.1 shows the differences among the three class types.

Table 8.1   Access Control and Constraints of Structures, Classes, and Unions

Structures	Classes	Unions
class-key is **struct**	*class-key* is **class**	*class-key* is **union**
Default access is public	Default access is private	Default access is public
No usage constraints	No usage constraints	Use only one member at a time

Anonymous Class Types

Classes can be anonymous — that is, they can be declared without an *identifier*. This is useful when you replace a class name with a **typedef** name, as in the following:

```
typedef struct
{
    unsigned x;
    unsigned y;
} POINT;
```

Note   The use of anonymous classes shown in the previous example is useful for preserving compatibility with existing C code. In some C code, the use of **typedef** in conjunction with anonymous structures is prevalent.

Anonymous classes are also useful when you want a reference to a class member to appear as though it were not contained in a separate class, as in the following:

```
struct PTValue
{
    POINT ptLoc;
    union
    {
        int  iValue;
        long lValue;
    };
};

PTValue ptv;
```

In the preceding code, iValue can be accessed using the object member-selection operator (.) as follows:

```
int i = ptv.iValue;
```

Anonymous classes are subject to certain restrictions. (For more information about anonymous unions, see "Unions" on page 248.) Anonymous classes:

- Cannot have a constructor or destructor.
- Cannot be passed as arguments to functions (unless type checking is defeated using ellipses).
- Cannot be returned as return values from functions.

Point of Class Definition

A class is defined at the end of its *class-specifier*. Member functions need not be defined in order for the class to be considered defined. Consider the following:

```
class Point               // Point class
{                         //   considered defined.
public:
   Point()
      { cx = cy = 0; }     // Constructor defined.
   Point( int x, int y )
      { cx = X, cy = Y; }  // Constructor defined.
   unsigned &x( unsigned ); // Accessor declared.
   unsigned &y( unsigned ); // Accessor declared.
private:
   unsigned  cx, cy;
};
```

Even though the two accessor functions (x and y) are not defined, the class Point is considered defined. (Accessor functions are functions provided to give safe access to member data.)

Class-Type Objects

An object is a typed region of storage in the execution environment; in addition to retaining state information, it also defines behavior. Class-type objects are defined using *class-name*. Consider the following code fragment:

```
class Account             // Class name is Account.
{
public:
        Account();        // Default constructor.
        Account( double ); // Construct from double.
   double& Deposit( double );
   double& Withdraw( double, int );
   ...
}:

Account CheckingAccount;  // Define object of class type.
```

The preceding code declares a class (a new type) called Account. It then uses this new type to define an object called CheckingAccount.

The following operations are defined by C++ for objects of class type:

- Assignment. One object can be assigned to another. The default behavior for this operation is a memberwise copy. This behavior can be modified by supplying a user-defined assignment operator.

- Initialization using copy constructors.

The following are examples of initialization using user-defined copy constructors:

- Explicit initialization of an object. For example:

```
Point myPoint = thatPoint;
```

declares myPoint as an object of type Point and initializes it to the value of thatPoint.

- Initialization caused by passing as an argument. Objects can be passed to functions by value or by reference. If they are passed by value, a copy of each object is passed to the function. The default method for creating the copy is memberwise copy; this can be modified by supplying a user-defined copy constructor (a constructor that takes a single argument of the type "reference to class").

- Initialization caused by the initialization of return values from functions. Objects can be returned from functions by value or by reference. The default method for returning an object by value is a memberwise copy; this can be modified by supplying a user-defined copy constructor. An object returned by reference (using pointer or reference types) should not be both automatic and local to the called function. If it is, the object referred to by the return value will have gone out of scope before it can be used.

"Overloaded Operators" on page 336 in Chapter 12 explains how to redefine other operators on a class-by-class basis.

Empty Classes

You can declare empty classes, but objects of such types still have nonzero size. The following example illustrates this:

```
#include <iostream.h>

class NoMembers
{
};

void main()
{
    NoMembers n;        // Object of type NoMembers.

    cout << "The size of an object of empty class is: "
        << sizeof n << endl;
}
```

This is the output of the preceding program:

```
The size of an object of empty class is: 1.
```

The memory allocated for such objects is of nonzero size; therefore, the objects have different addresses. Having different addresses makes it possible to compare pointers to objects for identity. Also, in arrays, each member array must have a distinct address.

Microsoft Specific →

An empty base class typically contributes zero bytes to the size of a derived class.

END Microsoft Specific

Class Names

Class declarations introduce new types, called class names, into programs. These class declarations also act as definitions of the class for a given translation unit. There may be only one definition for a given class type per translation unit. Using these new class types, you can declare objects, and the compiler can perform type checking to verify that no operations incompatible with the types are performed on the objects.

An example of such type checking is:

```
class Point
{
public:
    unsigned x, y;
};

class Rect
{
public:
    unsigned x1, y1, x2, y2;
};

// Prototype a function that takes two arguments, one of type
//  Point and the other of type pointer to Rect.
int PtInRect( Point, Rect & );

...

Point pt;
Rect  rect;

rect = pt;      // Error. Types are incompatible.
pt = rect;      // Error. Types are incompatible.

// Error. Arguments to PtInRect are reversed.
cout << "Point is " << PtInRect( rect, pt ) ? "" : "not"
    << " in rectangle" << endl;
```

As the preceding code illustrates, operations (such as assignment and argument passing) on class-type objects are subject to the same type checking as objects of built-in types.

Because the compiler distinguishes between class types, functions can be overloaded on the basis of class-type arguments as well as built-in type arguments. For more information about overloaded functions, see "Function Overloading" on page 214 in Chapter 7 and Chapter 12, "Overloading."

Declaring and Accessing Class Names

Class names can be declared in global or class scope. If they are declared in class scope, they are referred to as "nested" classes.

Microsoft Specific →

Function definitions are not permitted in local class declarations in Microsoft C++.

END Microsoft Specific

Any class name introduced in class scope hides other elements of the same name in an enclosing scope. Names hidden by such a declaration can then be referred to only by using an *elaborated-type-specifier*. The following example shows an example of using an *elaborated-type-specifier* to refer to a hidden name:

```
struct A          // Global scope definition of A.
{
    int a;
};

void main()
{
    char A = 'a';  // Redefine the name A as an object.

    struct A AObject;
    ...
}
```

Because the name A that refers to the structure is hidden by the A that refers to the char object, **struct** (a *class-key*) must be used to declare AObject as type A.

You can use the *class-key* to declare a class without providing a definition. This nondefining declaration of a class introduces a class name for forward reference. This technique is useful when designing classes that refer to one another in **friend** declarations. It is also useful when class names must be present in header files but the definition is not required. For example:

```
// RECT.H
class Point;       // Nondefining declaration of class Point.
class Line
{
public:
    int Draw( Point &ptFrom, Point &ptTo );
    ...
};
```

In the preceding sample, the name Point must be present, but it need not be a defining declaration that introduces the name.

typedef Statements and Classes

Using the **typedef** statement to name a class type causes the **typedef** name to become a *class-name*. For more information, see "typedef Specifier" on page 158 in Chapter 6.

Class Members

Classes can have these kinds of members:

- Member functions.

- Data members.

- Classes, which include classes, structures, and unions. (See "Nested Class Declarations" on page 253 and "Unions" on page 248.)

- Enumerations.

- Bit fields.

- Friends.

- Type names.

Note Friends are included in the preceding list because they are contained in the class declaration. However, they are not true class members, because they are not in the scope of the class.

Syntax

member-list:
> *member-declaration member-list*$_{opt}$
> *access-specifier* : *member-list*$_{opt}$

member-declaration:
> *decl-specifiers*$_{opt}$ *member-declarator-list*$_{opt}$;
> *function-definition*$_{opt}$;
> *qualified-name* ;

member-declarator-list:
> *member-declarator*
> *member-declarator-list* , *member-declarator*

member-declarator:
> *declarator pure-specifier*$_{opt}$
> *identifier*$_{opt}$: *constant-expression*

pure-specifier:
> **= 0**

The purpose of the *member-list* is to:

- Declare the complete set of members for a given class.

- Specify the access (public, private, or protected) associated with various class members.

In the declaration of a member list, you can declare members only once; redeclaration of members produces an error message. Because a member list is a complete set of the members, you cannot add members to a given class with subsequent class declarations.

Member declarators cannot contain initializers. Supplying an initializer produces an error message as illustrated in the following code:

```
class CantInit
{
public:
   long l = 7;        // Error: attempt to initialize class member.
   static int i = 9;  // Error: must be defined and initialized
                      //        outside of class declaration.
};
```

Because a separate instance of nonstatic member data is created for each object of a given class type, the correct way to initialize member data is to use the class's constructor. (Constructors are covered in "Constructors" on page 292 in Chapter 11.) There is only one shared copy of static data members for all objects of a given class type. Static data members must be defined and can be initialized at file scope. (For more information about static data members, see "Static Data Members" on page 247.) The following example shows how to perform these initializations:

```
class CanInit
{
public:
   CanInit() { l = 7; } // Initializes l when new objects of type
                        //   CanInit are created.
   long     l;
   static int i;
   static int j;
};

int CanInit::i = 15;   // i is defined at file scope and
                       //   initialized to 15. The initializer
                       //   is evaluated in the scope of CanInit.
int CanInit::j = i;    // The right side of the initializer is in
                       //   the scope of the object being initialized.
```

Note The class name, CanInit, must precede i to specify that the i being defined is a member of class CanInit.

Class-Member Declaration Syntax

Member data cannot be declared as **auto**, **extern**, or **register** storage class. They can, however, be declared as having **static** storage class.

The *decl-specifiers* specifiers can be omitted in member-function declarations. (For information on *decl-specifiers*, see "Specifiers" on page 152 in Chapter 6 and "Member Functions" on page 242; see also "Functions" on page 211 in Chapter 7.) The following code is therefore legal and declares a function that returns type **int**:

```
class NoDeclSpec
{
public:
   NoSpecifiers();
};
```

When you declare a **friend** class in a member list, you can omit the *member-declarator-list*. For more information on friends, see "friend Specifier" on page 162 in Chapter 6, and "Friends" on page 283 in Chapter 10. Even if a class name has not been introduced, it can be used in a **friend** declaration. This **friend** declaration introduces the name. However, in member declarations for such classes, the *elaborated-type-specifier* syntax must be used, as shown in the following example:

```
class HasFriends
{
public:
    friend class NotDeclaredYet;
};
```

In the preceding example, there is no *member-declarator-list* after the class declaration. Because the declaration for NotDeclaredYet has not yet been processed, the *elaborated-type-specifier* form is used: class NotDeclaredYet. A type that has been declared can be specified in a **friend** member declaration using a normal type specifier:

```
class AlreadyDeclared
{
    ...
};

class HasFriends
{
public:
    friend AlreadyDeclared;
};
```

The *pure-specifier* (shown in the following example) indicates that no implementation is supplied for the virtual function being declared. Therefore, the *pure-specifier* can be specified only on virtual functions. Consider this example:

```
class StrBase   // Base class for strings.
{
public:
    virtual int IsLessThan( StrBase& ) = 0;
    virtual int IsEqualTo( StrBase& ) = 0;
    virtual StrBase& CopyOf( StrBase& ) = 0;
    ...
};
```

The preceding code declares an abstract base class — that is, a class designed to be used only as the base class for more specific classes. Such base classes can enforce a particular protocol, or set of functionality, by declaring one or more virtual functions as "pure" virtual functions, using the *pure-specifier*.

Classes that inherit from the StrBase class must provide implementations for the pure virtual functions; otherwise, they, too, are considered abstract base classes.

Abstract base classes cannot be used to declare objects. For example, before an object of a type inherited from `StrBase` can be declared, the functions `IsLessThan`, `IsEqualTo`, and `CopyOf` must be implemented. (For more information about abstract base classes, see "Abstract Classes" on page 274 in Chapter 9.)

Declaring Unsized Arrays in Member Lists

Microsoft Specific →

Unsized arrays can be declared as the last data member in class member lists if the program is not compiled with the ANSI-compatibility option (/Za). Because this is a Microsoft extension, using unsized arrays in this way can make your code less portable. To declare an unsized array, omit the first dimension. For example:

```
class Symbol
{
public:
   int  SymbolType;
   char SymbolText[];
};
```

END Microsoft Specific

Restrictions

If a class contains an unsized array, it cannot be used as the base class for another class. In addition, a class containing an unsized array cannot be used to declare any member except the last member of another class. A class containing an unsized array cannot have a direct or indirect virtual base class.

The **sizeof** operator, when applied to a class containing an unsized array, returns the amount of storage required for all members except the unsized array. Implementors of classes that contain unsized arrays should provide alternate methods for obtaining the correct size of the class.

You cannot declare arrays of objects that have unsized array components. Also, performing pointer arithmetic on pointers to such objects generates an error message.

Storage of Class-Member Data

Nonstatic class-member data is stored in such a way that items falling between access specifiers are stored at successively higher memory addresses. No ordering across access specifiers is guaranteed.

Microsoft Specific →

Depending on the /Zp compiler option or the **pack** pragma, intervening space can be introduced to align member data on word or doubleword boundaries.

In Microsoft C++, class-member data is stored at successively higher memory addresses, even though the C++ language does not require it. Basing assumptions on this ordering can lead to nonportable code.

END Microsoft Specific

Member Naming Restrictions

A function with the same name as the class in which it is declared is a constructor. A constructor is implicitly called when an object of this class type is created. (For more information about constructors, see "Constructors" on page 292 in Chapter 11.)

The following items cannot have the same name as the classes in whose scope they are declared: data members (both static and nonstatic), enclosed enumerators, members of anonymous unions, and nested class types.

Member Functions

Classes can contain data and functions. These functions are referred to as "member functions." Any nonstatic function declared inside a class declaration is considered a member function and is called using the member-selection operators (. and –>). When calling member functions from other member functions of the same class, the object and member-selection operator can be omitted. For example:

```
class Point
{
public:
    short x() { return _x; }
    short y() { return _y; }
    void  Show() { cout << x() << ", " << y() << "\n"; }
private:
    short _x, _y;
};

void main()
{
    Point pt;

    pt.Show();
}
```

Note that in the member function, Show, calls to the other member functions, x and y, are made without member-selection operators. These calls implicitly mean this->x() and this->y(). However, in **main**, the member function, Show, must be selected using the object pt and the member-selection operator (.).

Static functions declared inside a class can be called using the member-selection operators or by specifying the fully qualified function name (including the class name).

Note A function declared using the **friend** keyword is not considered a member of the class in which it is declared a **friend** (although it can be a member of another class). A **friend** declaration controls the access a nonmember function has to class data.

The following class declaration shows how member functions are declared:

```
class Point
{
public:
    unsigned GetX();
    unsigned GetY();
    unsigned SetX( unsigned x );
    unsigned SetY( unsigned y );
private:
    unsigned ptX, ptY;
};
```

In the preceding class declaration, four functions are declared: GetX, GetY, SetX, and SetY. The next example shows how such functions are called in a program:

```
void main()
{
    // Declare a new object of type Point.
    Point ptOrigin;

    // Member function calls use the . member-selection operator.
    ptOrigin.SetX( 0 );
    ptOrigin.SetY( 0 );

    // Declare a pointer to an object of type Point.
    Point *pptCurrent = new Point;
// Member function calls use the -> member-selection operator.
    pptCurrent->SetX( ptOrigin.GetX() + 10 );
    pptCurrent->SetY( ptOrigin.GetY() + 10 );
}
```

In the preceding code, the member functions of the object ptOrigin are called using the member-selection operator (.). However, the member functions of the object pointed to by pptCurrent are called using the –> member-selection operator.

Overview of Member Functions

Member functions are either static or nonstatic. The behavior of static member functions differs from other member functions because static member functions have no implicit **this** argument. Nonstatic member functions have a **this** pointer. Member functions, whether static or nonstatic, can be defined either in or outside the class declaration.

If a member function is defined inside a class declaration, it is treated as an inline function, and there is no need to qualify the function name with its class name. Although functions defined inside class declarations are already treated as inline functions, you can use the **inline** keyword to document code.

An example of declaring a function within a class declaration follows:

```
class Account
{
public:
    // Declare the member function Deposit within the declaration
    //  of class Account.
    double Deposit( double HowMuch )
    {
        balance += HowMuch;
        return balance;
    }
private:
    double balance;
};
```

If a member function's definition is outside the class declaration, it is treated as an inline function only if it is explicitly declared as **inline**. In addition, the function name in the definition must be qualified with its class name using the scope-resolution operator (::).

The following example is identical to the previous declaration of class `Account`, except that the `Deposit` function is defined outside the class declaration:

```
class Account
{
public:
    // Declare the member function Deposit but do not define it.
    double Deposit( double HowMuch );
private:
    double balance;
};

inline double Account::Deposit( double HowMuch )
{
    balance += HowMuch;
    return balance;
}
```

Note Although member functions can be defined either inside a class declaration or separately, no member functions can be added to a class after the class is defined.

Classes containing member functions can have many declarations, but the member functions themselves must have only one definition in a program. Multiple definitions cause an error message at link time. If a class contains inline function definitions, the function definitions must be identical to observe this "one definition" rule.

Nonstatic Member Functions

Nonstatic member functions have an implied argument, **this**, that points to the object through which the function is invoked. The type of **this** is *type* * **const**. These functions are considered to have class scope and can use class data and other member functions in the same class scope directly. In the preceding example, the expression `balance += HowMuch` adds the value of HowMuch to the class member `balance`. Consider the following statements:

```
Account Checking;

Checking.Deposit( 57.00 );
```

The preceding code declares an object of type `Account` and then invokes the member function `Deposit` to add $57.00 to it. In the function `Account::Deposit`, balance is taken to mean `Checking.balance` (the balance member for this object).

Nonstatic member functions are intended to operate on objects of their class type. Calling such a function on objects of different types (using explicit type conversions) causes undefined behavior.

The this Pointer

All nonstatic member functions can use the **this** keyword, which is a **const** (nonmodifiable) pointer to the object for which the function was called. Member data is addressed by evaluating the expression **this–>***member-name* (although this technique is seldom used). In member functions, using a member name in an expression implicitly uses **this–>***member-name* to select the correct function or data member.

Note   Because the **this** pointer is nonmodifiable, assignments to **this** are not allowed. Earlier implementations of C++ allowed assignments to **this**.

Occasionally, the **this** pointer is used directly — for example, to manipulate self-referential data structures, where the address of the current object is required.

Type of this Pointer

The **this** pointer's type can be modified in the function declaration by the **const** and **volatile** keywords. To declare a function as having the attributes of one or more of these keywords, use the *cv-mod-list* grammar.

Syntax

cv-mod-list:
>   *cv-qualifier cv-mod-list*_{opt}

cv-qualifier:
>   **const**
>   **volatile**

Consider this example:

```
class Point
{
    unsigned X() const;
};
```

The preceding code declares a member function, X, in which the **this** pointer is treated as a **const** pointer to a **const** object. Combinations of *cv-mod-list* options can be used, but they always modify the object pointed to by **this**, not the **this** pointer itself. Therefore, the following declaration declares function X; the **this** pointer is a **const** pointer to a **const** object:

```
class Point
{
    unsigned X() __far const;
};
```

The type of **this** is described by the following syntax, where *cv-qualifier-list* can be **const** or **volatile**, *class-type* is the name of the class:

cv-qualifier-list$_{opt}$ *class-type* * **const this**

Table 8.2 explains more about how these modifiers work.

Table 8.2 Semantics of this Modifiers

Modifier	Meaning
const	Cannot change member data; cannot invoke member functions that are not **const**.
volatile	Member data is loaded from memory each time it is accessed; disables certain optimizations.

It is an error to pass a **const** object to a member function that is not **const**. Similarly, it is an error to pass a **volatile** object to a member function that is not **volatile**.

Member functions declared as **const** cannot change member data—in such functions, the **this** pointer is a pointer to a **const** object.

Note Constructors and destructors cannot be declared as **const** or **volatile**. They can, however, be invoked on **const** or **volatile** objects.

Static Member Functions

Static member functions are considered to have class scope. In contrast to nonstatic member functions, these functions have no implicit **this** argument; therefore, they can use only static data members, enumerators, or nested types directly. Static member functions can be accessed without using an object of the corresponding class type. Consider this example:

```
class WindowManager
{
public:
    static int  CountOf();              // Return count of open windows.
          void Minimize();              // Minimize current window.
          WindowManager SideEffects();  // Function with side effects.
    ...
```

```
private:
    static int wmWindowCount;
};
int WindowManager::wmWindowCount = 0;
```

`...`

```
// Minimize (show iconic) all windows
for( int i = 0; i < WindowManager::CountOf(); ++i )
    rgwmWin[i].Minimize();
```

In the preceding code, the class `WindowManager` contains the static member function `CountOf`. This function returns the number of windows open but is not necessarily associated with a given object of type `WindowManager`. This concept is demonstrated in the loop where the `CountOf` function is used in the controlling expression; because `CountOf` is a static member function, it can be called without reference to an object.

Static member functions have external linkage. These functions do not have **this** pointers (covered in the next section). As a result, the following restrictions apply to such functions:

- They cannot access nonstatic class member data using the member-selection operators (. or –>).

- They cannot be declared as **virtual**.

- They cannot have the same name as a nonstatic function that has the same argument types.

Note   The left side of a member-selection operator (. or –>) that selects a static member function is not evaluated. This can be important if the function is used for its side effects. For example, the expression `SideEffects().CountOf()` does not call the function `SideEffects`.

Static Data Members

Classes can contain static member data and member functions. When a data member is declared as **static**, only one copy of the data is maintained for all objects of the class. (For more information, see "Static Member Functions" on page 246.)

Static data members are not part of objects of a given class type; they are separate objects. As a result, the declaration of a static data member is not considered a definition. The data member is declared in class scope, but definition is performed at file scope. These static members have external linkage. The following example illustrates this:

```
class BufferedOutput
{
public:
    // Return number of bytes written by any object of this class.
    short BytesWritten() { return bytecount; }
```

```
        // Reset the counter.
        static void ResetCount() { bytecount = 0; }

        // Static member declaration.
        static long bytecount;
};

// Define bytecount in file scope.
long BufferedOutput::bytecount;
```

In the preceding code, the member bytecount is declared in class BufferedOutput, but it must be defined outside the class declaration.

Static data members can be referred to without referring to an object of class type. The number of bytes written using BufferedOutput objects can be obtained as follows:

```
long nBytes = BufferedOutput::bytecount;
```

For the static member to exist, it is not necessary that any objects of the class type exist. Static members can also be accessed using the member-selection (. and –>) operators. For example:

```
BufferedOutput Console;

long nBytes = Console.bytecount;
```

In the preceding case, the reference to the object (Console) is not evaluated; the value returned is that of the static object bytecount.

Static data members are subject to class-member access rules, so private access to static data members is allowed only for class-member functions and friends. These rules are described in Chapter 10, "Member-Access Control." The exception is that static data members must be defined in file scope regardless of their access restrictions. If the data member is to be explicitly initialized, an initializer must be provided with the definition.

The type of a static member is not qualified by its class name. Therefore, the type of BufferedOutput::bytecount is long.

Unions

Unions are class types that can contain only one data element at a time (although the data element can be an array or a class type). The members of a union represent the kinds of data the union can contain. An object of union type requires enough storage to hold the largest member in its *member-list*. Consider the following example:

```
#include <stdlib.h>
#include <string.h>
#include <limits.h>
```

```
union NumericType    // Declare a union that can hold the following:
{
    int      iValue; // int value
    long     lValue; // long value
    double   dValue; // double value
};

void main( int argc, char *argv[] )
{
    NumericType *Values = new NumericType[argc - 1];

    for( int i = 1; i < argc; ++i )
        if( strchr( argv[i], '.' ) != 0 )
            // Floating type. Use dValue member for assignment.
            Values[i].dValue = atof( argv[i] );
        else
            // Not a floating type.
            {
                    // If data is bigger than largest int, store it
                    //  in lValue member.
                if( atol( argv[i] ) >  INT_MAX )
                    Values[i].lValue = atol( argv[i] );
                else
                    // Otherwise, store it in iValue member.
                    Values[i].iValue = atoi( argv[i] );
            }
}
```

The NumericType union is arranged in memory (conceptually) as shown in Figure 8.1.

Figure 8.1   Storage of Data in NumericType Union

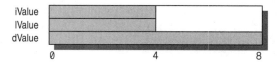

Member Functions in Unions

In addition to member data, unions can have member functions, as described in "Member Functions" on page 242. Although unions can have special functions such as constructors and destructors, unions cannot contain virtual functions. (For more information, see "Constructors" and "Destructors" on pages 292 and 297 in Chapter 11.)

Unions as Class Types

Unions cannot have base classes; that is, they cannot inherit the attributes of other unions, structures, or classes. Unions also cannot be used as base classes for further inheritance.

Inheritance is covered in detail in Chapter 9, "Derived Classes."

Union Member Data

Unions can contain most types in their member lists, except for the following:

- Class types that have constructors or destructors
- Class types that have user-defined assignment operators
- Static data members

Anonymous Unions

Anonymous unions are unions that are declared without a *class-name* or *declarator-list*.

Syntax

union { *member-list* } ;

Such union declarations do not declare types — they declare objects. The names declared in an anonymous union cannot conflict with other names declared in the same scope.

Names declared in an anonymous union are used directly, like nonmember variables. The following example illustrates this:

```
#include <iostream.h>

struct DataForm
{
    enum DataType { CharData = 1, IntData, StringData };
    DataType type;

    // Declare an anonymous union.
    union
    {
        char   chCharMem;
        char  *szStrMem;
        int    iIntMem;
    };
    void print();
};

void DataForm::print()
{
    // Based on the type of the data, print the
    // appropriate data type.
    switch( type )
    {
    case CharData:
        cout << chCharMem;
        break;
```

```
      case IntData:
         cout << szStrMem;
         break;
      case StringData:
         cout << iIntMem;
         break;
   }
}
```

In the function `DataForm::print`, the three members (`chCharMem`, `szStrMem`, and `iIntMem`) are accessed as though they were declared as members (without the **union** declaration). However, the three union members share the same memory.

In addition to the restrictions listed in "Union Member Data" on page 250, anonymous unions are subject to additional restrictions:

- They must also be declared as **static** if declared in file scope.
- They can have only public members; private and protected members in anonymous unions generate errors.
- They cannot have function members.

Note   Simply omitting the *class-name* portion of the syntax does not make a union an anonymous union. For a union to qualify as an anonymous union, the declaration must not declare an object.

Bit Fields

Classes and structures can contain members that occupy less storage than an integral type. These members are specified as bit fields. The syntax for bit-field *member-declarator* specification follows:

Syntax

*declarator*_{opt} : *constant-expression*

The *declarator* is the name by which the member is accessed in the program. It must be an integral type (including enumerated types). The *constant-expression* specifies the number of bits the member occupies in the structure. Anonymous bit fields — that is, bit-field members with no identifier — can be used for padding.

Note   An unnamed bit field of width 0 forces alignment of the next bit field to the next *type* boundary, where *type* is the type of the member.

The following example declares a structure that contains bit fields:

```
struct Date
{
   unsigned nWeekDay  : 3;    // 0..7    (3 bits)
   unsigned nMonthDay : 6;    // 0..31   (6 bits)
   unsigned nMonth    : 5;    // 0..12   (5 bits)
   unsigned nYear     : 8;    // 0..100  (8 bits)
};
```

The conceptual memory layout of an object of type Date is shown in Figure 8.2.

Figure 8.2 Memory Layout of Date Object

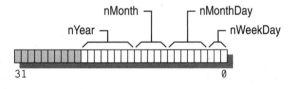

Note that nYear is 8 bits long and would overflow the word boundary of the declared type, **unsigned int**. Therefore, it is begun at the beginning of a new **unsigned int**. It is not necessary that all bit fields fit in one object of the underlying type; new units of storage are allocated, according to the number of bits requested in the declaration.

Microsoft Specific →

The ordering of data declared as bit fields is from low to high bit, as shown in Figure 8.2.

END Microsoft Specific

If the declaration of a structure includes an unnamed field of length 0, as shown in the following example,

```
struct Date
{
    unsigned nWeekDay  : 3;    // 0..7   (3 bits)
    unsigned nMonthDay : 6;    // 0..31  (6 bits)
    unsigned           : 0;    // Force alignment to next boundary.
    unsigned nMonth    : 5;    // 0..12  (5 bits)
    unsigned nYear     : 8;    // 0..100 (8 bits)
};
```

the memory layout is as shown in Figure 8.3.

Figure 8.3 Layout of Date Object with Zero-Length Bit Field

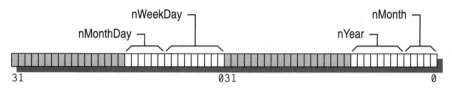

The underlying type of a bit field must be an integral type, as described in "Fundamental Types" on page 41 in Chapter 2.

Restrictions on Use of Bit Fields

The following list details erroneous operations on bit fields:

- Taking the address of a bit field
- Initializing a reference with a bit field

Nested Class Declarations

A class can be declared within the scope of another class. Such a class is called a "nested class." Nested classes are considered to be within the scope of the enclosing class and are available for use within that scope. To refer to a nested class from a scope other than its immediate enclosing scope, you must use a fully qualified name.

The following example shows how to declare nested classes:

```
class BufferedIO
{
public:
    enum IOError { None, Access, General };

    // Declare nested class BufferedInput.
    class BufferedInput
    {
    public:
        int read();
        int good() { return _inputerror == None; }
    private:
        IOError _inputerror;
    };

    // Declare nested class BufferedOutput.
    class BufferedOutput
    {
        // Member list
    };
};
```

`BufferedIO::BufferedInput` and `BufferedIO::BufferedOutput` are declared within `BufferedIO`. These class names are not visible outside the scope of class `BufferedIO`. However, an object of type `BufferedIO` does not contain any objects of types `BufferedInput` or `BufferedOutput`.

Nested classes can directly use names, type names, names of static members, and enumerators only from the enclosing class. To use names of other class members, you must use pointers, references, or object names.

In the preceding `BufferedIO` example, the enumeration `IOError` can be accessed directly by member functions in the nested classes, `BufferedIO::BufferedInput` or `BufferedIO::BufferedOutput`, as shown in function good.

Note Nested classes declare only types within class scope. They do not cause contained objects of the nested class to be created. The preceding example declares two nested classes but does not declare any objects of these class types.

Access Privileges and Nested Classes

Nesting a class within another class does not give special access privileges to member functions of the nested class. Similarly, member functions of the enclosing class have no special access to members of the nested class.

For more information about access privileges, see Chapter 10, "Member-Access Control."

Member Functions in Nested Classes

Member functions declared in nested classes can be defined in file scope. The preceding example could have been written:

```
class BufferedIO
{
public:
    enum IOError { None, Access, General };
    class BufferedInput
    {
    public:
        int read(); // Declare but do not define member
        int good(); //  functions read and good.
    private:
        IOError _inputerror;
    };

    class BufferedOutput
    {
        // Member list.
    };
};
// Define member functions read and good in
//  file scope.
int BufferedIO::BufferedInput::read()
{
    ...
}

int BufferedIO::BufferedInput::good()
{
    return _inputerror == None;
}
```

In the preceding example, the *qualified-type-name* syntax is used to declare the function name. The declaration:

```
BufferedIO::BufferedInput::read()
```

means "the `read` function that is a member of the `BufferedInput` class that is in the scope of the `BufferedIO` class." Because this declaration uses the *qualified-type-name* syntax, constructs of the following form are possible:

```
typedef BufferedIO::BufferedInput BIO_INPUT;

int BIO_INPUT::read()
```

The preceding declaration is equivalent to the previous one, but it uses a **typedef** name in place of the class names.

Friend Functions and Nested Classes

Friend functions declared in a nested class are considered to be in the scope of the nested class, not the enclosing class. Therefore, the friend functions gain no special access privileges to members or member functions of the enclosing class. If you want to use a name that is declared in a nested class in a friend function and the friend function is defined in file scope, use qualified type names as follows:

```
extern char *rgszMessage[];

class BufferedIO
{
public:
    ...
class BufferedInput
    {
    public:
        friend int GetExtendedErrorStatus();
        ...
        static char *message;
        int          iMsgNo;
    };
};
char *BufferedIO::BufferedInput::message;

int GetExtendedErrorStatus()
{
    ...
    strcpy( BufferedIO::BufferedInput::message,
        rgszMessage[iMsgNo] );
    return iMsgNo;
}
```

The preceding code shows the function `GetExtendedErrorStatus` declared as a friend function. In the function, which is defined in file scope, a message is copied from a static array into a class member. Note that a better implementation of `GetExtendedErrorStatus` is to declare it as:

```
int GetExtendedErrorStatus( char *message )
```

With the preceding interface, several classes can use the services of this function by passing a memory location where they want the error message copied.

Type Names in Class Scope

Type names defined within class scope are considered local to their class. They cannot be used outside that class. The following example demonstrates this concept:

```
class Tree
{
public:
    typedef Tree * PTREE;
    PTREE  Left;
    PTREE  Right;
    void   *vData;
};

PTREE pTree;  // Error: not in class scope.
```

CHAPTER 9

Derived Classes

This chapter explains how to use derived classes to produce extensible programs.

The following topics are included:

- Overview
- Multiple base classes
- Virtual functions
- Abstract classes
- Summary of scope rules

Overview of Derived Classes

New classes can be derived from existing classes using a mechanism called "inheritance" (see the information beginning in "Single Inheritance" on page 258). Classes that are used for derivation are called "base classes" of a particular derived class. A derived class is declared using the following syntax:

Syntax
base-spec:
    : *base-list*
base-list:
    base-specifier
    base-list **,** *base-specifier*
base-specifier:
    complete-class-name
    virtual *access-specifier*$_{opt}$ *complete-class-name*
    access-specifier **virtual**$_{opt}$ *complete-class-name*
access-specifier:
    private
    protected
    public

Single Inheritance

In "single inheritance," a common form of inheritance, classes have only one base class. Consider the relationship illustrated in Figure 9.1.

Figure 9.1 Simple Single-Inheritance Graph

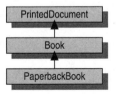

Note the progression from general to specific in Figure 9.1. Another common attribute found in the design of most class hierarchies is that the derived class has a "kind of" relationship with the base class. In Figure 9.1, a Book is a kind of a PrintedDocument, and a PaperbackBook is a kind of a book.

One other item of note in Figure 9.1: Book is both a derived class (from PrintedDocument) and a base class (PaperbackBook is derived from Book). A skeletal declaration of such a class hierarchy is shown in the following example:

```
class PrintedDocument
{
    // Member list.
};

// Book is derived from PrintedDocument.
class Book : public PrintedDocument
{
    // Member list.
};

// PaperbackBook is derived from Book.
class PaperbackBook : public Book
{
    // Member list.
};
```

PrintedDocument is considered a "direct base" class to Book; it is an "indirect base" class to PaperbackBook. The difference is that a direct base class appears in the base list of a class declaration and an indirect base does not.

The base class from which each class is derived is declared before the declaration of the derived class. It is not sufficient to provide a forward-referencing declaration for a base class; it must be a complete declaration.

In the preceding example, the access specifier **public** is used. The meaning of public, protected, and private inheritance is described in Chapter 10, "Member-Access Control."

A class can serve as the base class for many specific classes, as illustrated in Figure 9.2.

Figure 9.2 Sample of Directed Acyclic Graph

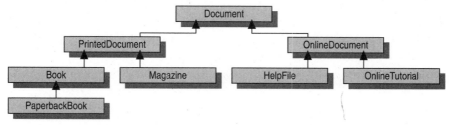

In the diagram in Figure 9.2, called a "directed acyclic graph" (or "DAG"), some of the classes are base classes for more than one derived class. However, the reverse is not true: there is only one direct base class for any given derived class. The graph in Figure 9.2 depicts a "single inheritance" structure.

Note Directed acyclic graphs are not unique to single inheritance. They are also used to depict multiple-inheritance graphs. This topic is covered in "Multiple Inheritance" on page 262.

In inheritance, the derived class contains the members of the base class plus any new members you add. As a result, a derived class can refer to members of the base class (unless those members are redefined in the derived class). The scope-resolution operator (::) can be used to refer to members of direct or indirect base classes when those members have been redefined in the derived class. Consider this example:

```
class Document
{
public:
    char *Name;         // Document name.
    void  PrintNameOf(); // Print name.
};

// Implementation of PrintNameOf function from class Document.
void Document::PrintNameOf()
{
    cout << Name << endl;
}

class Book : public Document
{
public:
    Book( char *name, long pagecount );
private:
    long  PageCount;
};

// Constructor from class Book.
Book::Book( char *name, long pagecount )
```

```
{
    Name = new char[ strlen( name ) + 1 ];
    strcpy( Name, name );
    PageCount = pagecount;
};
```

Note that the constructor for Book, (Book::Book), has access to the data member, Name. In a program, an object of type Book can be created and used as follows:

```
//  Create a new object of type Book. This invokes the
//    constructor Book::Book.
Book LibraryBook( "Programming Windows, 2nd Ed", 944 );

...

//  Use PrintNameOf function inherited from class Document.
LibraryBook.PrintNameOf();
```

As the preceding example demonstrates, class-member and inherited data and functions are used identically. If the implementation for class Book calls for a reimplementation of the PrintNameOf function, the function that belongs to the Document class can be called only by using the scope-resolution (::) operator:

```
class Book : public Document
{
    Book( char *name, long pagecount );
    void PrintNameOf();
    long  PageCount;
};
void Book::PrintNameOf()
{
    cout << "Name of book: ";
    Document::PrintNameOf();
}
```

Pointers and references to derived classes can be implicitly converted to pointers and references to their base classes if there is an accessible, unambiguous base class. The following code demonstrates this concept using pointers (the same principle applies to references):

```
#include <iostream.h>

void main()
{
    Document *DocLib[10];  // Library of ten documents.

    for( int i = 0; i < 10; ++i )
    {
        cout << "Type of document: "
            << "P)aperback, M)agazine, H)elp File, C)BT"
            << endl;
```

```
    char cDocType;
    cin >> cDocType;

    switch( tolower( cDocType ) )
    {
    case 'p':
        DocLib[i] = new PaperbackBook;
        break;

    case 'm':
        DocLib[i] = new Magazine;
        break;

    case 'h':
        DocLib[i] = new HelpFile;
        break;

    case 'c':
        DocLib[i] = new ComputerBasedTraining;
        break;

    default:
        --i;
        break;
    }
}

for( i = 0; i < 10; ++i )
    DocLib[i]->PrintNameOf();
}
```

In the SWITCH statement in the preceding example, objects of different types are created, depending on what the user specified for cDocType. However, because these types are all derived from the Document class, there is an implicit conversion to Document *. As a result, DocLib is a "heterogeneous list" (a list in which not all objects are of the same type) containing different kinds of objects.

Because the Document class has a PrintNameOf function, it can print the name of each book in the library, although it may omit some of the information specific to the type of document (page count for Book, number of bytes for HelpFile, and so on).

Note   Forcing the base class to implement a function such as PrintNameOf is often not the best design. "Virtual Functions" on page 270 offers other design alternatives.

Multiple Inheritance

Later versions of C++ introduced a "multiple inheritance" model for inheritance. In a multiple-inheritance graph, the derived classes may have a number of direct base classes. Consider the graph in Figure 9.3.

Figure 9.3 Simple Multiple-Inheritance Graph

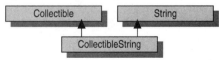

The diagram in Figure 9.3 shows a class, `CollectibleString`. It is like a `Collectible` (something that can be contained in a collection), and it is like a `String`. Multiple inheritance is a good solution to this kind of problem (where a derived class has attributes of more than one base class) because it is easy to form a `CollectibleCustomer`, `CollectibleWindow`, and so on.

If the properties of either class are not required for a particular application, either class can be used alone or in combination with other classes. Therefore, given the hierarchy depicted in Figure 9.3 as a basis, you can form noncollectible strings and collectibles that are not strings. This flexibility is not possible using single inheritance.

Virtual Base Class Hierarchies

Some class hierarchies are broad but have many things in common. The common code is implemented in a base class, whereas the specific code is in the derived classes.

It is important for the base classes to establish a protocol through which the derived classes can attain maximum functionality. These protocols are commonly implemented using virtual functions. Sometimes the base class provides a default implementation for such functions. In a class hierarchy such as the `Document` hierarchy in Figure 9.2, two useful functions are `Identify` and `WhereIs`.

When called, the `Identify` function returns a correct identification, appropriate to the kind of document: For a `Book`, a function call such as `doc->Identify()` must return the ISBN number; however, for a `HelpFile`, a product name and revision number are probably more appropriate. Similarly, `WhereIs` should return a row and shelf for a `Book`, but for a `HelpFile` it should return a disk location—perhaps a directory and filename.

It is important that all implementations of the `Identify` and `WhereIs` functions return the same kind of information. In this case, a character string is appropriate.

These functions are implemented as virtual functions and then invoked using a pointer to a base class. The binding to the actual code occurs at run time, selecting the correct `Identify` or `WhereIs` function.

Class Protocol Implementation

Classes can be implemented to enforce a protocol. These classes are called "abstract classes" because no object of the class type can be created. They exist solely for derivation.

Classes are abstract classes if they contain pure virtual functions or if they inherit pure virtual functions and do not provide an implementation for them. Pure virtual functions are virtual functions declared with the *pure-specifier* (= 0), as follows:

```
virtual char *Identify() = 0;
```

The base class, Document, might impose the following protocol on all derived classes:

- An appropriate Identify function must be implemented.

- An appropriate WhereIs function must be implemented.

By specifying such a protocol when designing the Document class, the class designer can be assured that no nonabstract class can be implemented without Identify and WhereIs functions. The Document class, therefore, contains these declarations:

```
class Document
{
public:
    ...
    //  Requirements for derived classes: They must implement
    //   these functions.
    virtual char *Identify() = 0;
    virtual char *WhereIs() = 0;
    ...
};
```

Base Classes

As discussed previously, the inheritance process creates a new derived class that is made up of the members of the base class(es) plus any new members added by the derived class. In a multiple-inheritance, it is possible to construct an inheritance graph where the same base class is part of more than one of the derived classes. Figure 9.4 shows such a graph.

In Figure 9.4, pictorial representations of the components of CollectibleString and CollectibleSortable are shown. However, the base class, Collectible, is in CollectibleSortableString through the CollectibleString path and the CollectibleSortable path. To eliminate this redundancy, such classes can be declared as virtual base classes when they are inherited.

For information about declaring virtual base classes and how objects with virtual base classes are composed, see "Virtual Base Classes" on page 265.

Figure 9.4 Multiple Instances of a Single Base Class

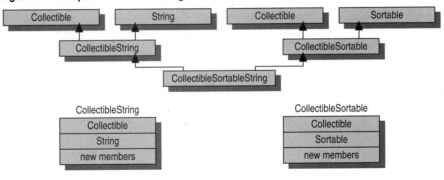

Multiple Base Classes

As described in "Multiple Inheritance" on page 262, a class can be derived from more than one base class. In a multiple-inheritance model (where classes are derived from more than one base class), the base classes are specified using the *base-list* grammar element (see Syntax in "Overview of Derived Classes" on page 257). For example, the class declaration for CollectionOfBook, derived from Collection and Book, can be specified:

```
class CollectionOfBook : public Book, public Collection
{
    // New members
};
```

The order in which base classes are specified is not significant except in certain cases where constructors and destructors are invoked. In these cases, the order in which base classes are specified affects the following:

- The order in which initialization by constructor takes place. If your code relies on the Book portion of CollectionOfBook to be initialized before the Collection part, the order of specification is significant. Initialization takes place in the order the classes are specified in the *base-list*.

- The order in which destructors are invoked to clean up. Again, if a particular "part" of the class must be present when the other part is being destroyed, the order is significant. Destructors are called in the reverse order of the classes specified in the *base-list*.

Note The order of specification of base classes can affect the memory layout of the class. Do not make any programming decisions based on the order of base members in memory.

When specifying the *base-list*, you cannot specify the same class name more than once. However, it is possible for a class to be an indirect base to a derived class more than once.

Virtual Base Classes

Because a class can be an indirect base class to a derived class more than once, C++ provides a way to optimize the way such base classes work. Consider the class hierarchy in Figure 9.5, which illustrates a simulated lunch line.

Figure 9.5   Simulated Lunch-Line Graph

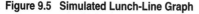
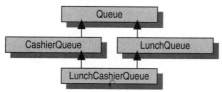

In Figure 9.5, Queue is the base class for both CashierQueue and LunchQueue. However, when both classes are combined to form LunchCashierQueue, the following problem arises: the new class contains two subobjects of type Queue, one from CashierQueue and the other from LunchQueue. Figure 9.6 shows the conceptual memory layout (the actual memory layout might be optimized).

Figure 9.6   Simulated Lunch-Line Object

Note that there are two Queue subobjects in the LunchCashierQueue object. The following code declares Queue to be a virtual base class:

```
class Queue
{
    // Member list
};

class CashierQueue : virtual public Queue
{
    // Member list
};

class LunchQueue : virtual public Queue
{
    // Member list
};

class LunchCashierQueue : public LunchQueue, public CashierQueue
{
    // Member list
};
```

The `virtual` keyword ensures that only one copy of the subobject `Queue` is included (see Figure 9.7).

Figure 9.7 Simulated Lunch-Line Object with Virtual Base Classes

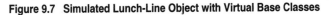

A class can have both a virtual component and a nonvirtual component of a given type. This happens in the conditions illustrated in Figure 9.8.

Figure 9.8 Virtual and Nonvirtual Components of the Same Class

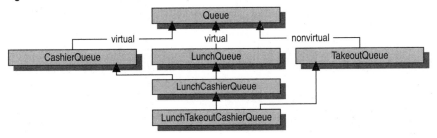

In Figure 9.8., `CashierQueue` and `LunchQueue` use `Queue` as a virtual base class. However, `TakeoutQueue` specifies `Queue` as a base class, not a virtual base class. Therefore, `LunchTakeoutCashierQueue` has two subobjects of type `Queue`: one from the inheritance path that includes `LunchCashierQueue` and one from the path that includes `TakeoutQueue`. This is illustrated in Figure 9.9.

Figure 9.9 Object Layout with Virtual and Nonvirtual Inheritance

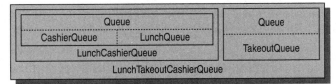

Note Virtual inheritance provides significant size benefits when compared with nonvirtual inheritance. However, it can introduce extra processing overhead.

If a derived class overrides a virtual function that it inherits from a virtual base class, and if a constructor or a destructor for the derived base class calls that function using a pointer to the virtual base class, the compiler may introduce additional hidden "vtordisp" fields into the classes with virtual bases. The /vd0 compiler option suppresses the addition of the hidden vtordisp constructor/destructor displacement member. The /vd1 compiler option, the default, enables them where they are necessary. Turn off vtordisps only if you are sure that all class constructors and destructors call virtual functions virtually.

The /vd compiler option affects an entire compilation module. Use the **vtordisp** pragma to suppress and then reenable vtordisp fields on a class-by-class basis:

```
#pragma vtordisp( off )
class GetReal : virtual public { ... };
#pragma vtordisp( on )
```

Name Ambiguities

Multiple inheritance introduces the possibility for names to be inherited along more than one path. The class-member names along these paths are not necessarily unique. These name conflicts are called "ambiguities."

Any expression that refers to a class member must make an unambiguous reference. The following example shows how ambiguities develop:

```
// Declare two base classes, A and B.
class A
{
public:
   unsigned a;
   unsigned b();
};

class B
{
public:
   unsigned a();   // Note that class A also has a member "a"
   int b();        //  and a member "b".
   char c;
};

// Define class C as derived from A and B.
class C : public A, public B
{
};
```

Given the preceding class declarations, code such as the following is ambiguous because it is unclear whether b refers to the b in A or in B:

```
C *pc = new C;

pc->b();
```

Consider the preceding example. Because the name a is a member of both class A and class B, the compiler cannot discern which a designates the function to be called. Access to a member is ambiguous if it can refer to more than one function, object, type, or enumerator.

The compiler detects ambiguities by performing tests in this order:

1. If access to the name is ambiguous (as just described), an error message is generated.

2. If overloaded functions are unambiguous, they are resolved. (For more information about function overloading ambiguity, see "Argument Matching" on page 329 in Chapter 12.)

3. If access to the name violates member-access permission, an error message is generated. (For more information, see Chapter 10, "Member-Access Control.")

When an expression produces an ambiguity through inheritance, you can manually resolve it by qualifying the name in question with its class name. To make the preceding example compile properly with no ambiguities, use code such as:

```
C *pc = new C;
```

```
pc->B::a( );
```

Note When C is declared, it has the potential to cause errors when B is referenced in the scope of C. No error is issued, however, until an unqualified reference to B is actually made in C's scope.

Ambiguities and Virtual Base Classes

If virtual base classes are used, functions, objects, types, and enumerators can be reached through multiple-inheritance paths. Because there is only one instance of the base class, there is no ambiguity when accessing these names.

Figure 9.10 shows how objects are composed using virtual and nonvirtual inheritance.

Figure 9.10   Virtual vs. Nonvirtual Derivation

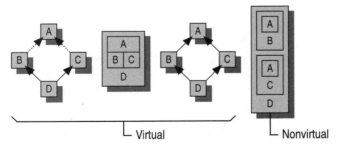
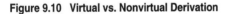

In Figure 9.10, accessing any member of class A through nonvirtual base classes causes an ambiguity; the compiler has no information that explains whether to use the subobject associated with B or the subobject associated with C. However, when A is specified as a virtual base class, there is no question which subobject is being accessed.

Dominance

It is possible for more than one name (function, object, or enumerator) to be reached through an inheritance graph. Such cases are considered ambiguous with nonvirtual base classes. They are also ambiguous with virtual base classes, unless one of the names "dominates" the others.

A name dominates another name if it is defined in both classes and one class is derived from the other. The dominant name is the name in the derived class; this name is used when an ambiguity would otherwise have arisen, as shown in the following example:

```
class A
{
public:
    int a;
};

class B : public virtual A
{
public:
    int a();
};

class C : public virtual A
{
    ...
};

class D : public B, public C
{
public:
    D() { a(); } // Not ambiguous. B::a() dominates A::a.
};
```

Ambiguous Conversions

Explicit and implicit conversions from pointers or references to class types can cause ambiguities. Figure 9.11 shows the following:

- The declaration of an object of type D.

- The effect of applying the address-of operator (**&**) to that object. Note that the address-of operator always supplies the base address of the object.

- The effect of explicitly converting the pointer obtained using the address-of operator to the base-class type A. Note that coercing the address of the object to type A* does not always provide the compiler with enough information as to which subobject of type A to select; in this case, two subobjects exist.

The conversion to type A* (pointer to A) is ambiguous because there is no way to discern which subobject of type A is the correct one. Note that you can avoid the ambiguity by explicitly specifying which subobject you mean to use, as follows:

```
(A *)(B *)&d        // Use B subobject.
(A *)(C *)&d        // Use C subobject.
```

Figure 9.11 Ambiguous Conversion of Pointers to Base Classes

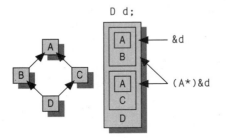

Virtual Functions

"Virtual functions" are functions that ensure that the correct function is called for an object, regardless of the expression used to make the function call.

Suppose a base class contains a function declared as **virtual** and a derived class defines the same function. The function from the derived class is invoked for objects of the derived class, even if it is called using a pointer or reference to the base class. The following example shows a base class that provides an implementation of the PrintBalance function:

```
class Account
{
public:
                   Account( double d );   // Constructor.
   virtual double  GetBalance();          // Obtain balance.
   virtual void    PrintBalance();        // Default implementation.
private:
   double _balance;
};

// Implementation of constructor for Account.
double Account::Account( double d )
{
   _balance = d;
}
// Implementation of GetBalance for Account.
double Account::GetBalance()
{
   return _balance;
}
```

```
// Default implementation of PrintBalance.
void Account::PrintBalance()
{
    cerr << "Error. Balance not available for base type."
        << endl;
}
```

Two derived classes, CheckingAccount and SavingsAccount, can be created as follows:

```
class CheckingAccount : public Account
{
public:
    void PrintBalance();
};

// Implementation of PrintBalance for CheckingAccount.
void CheckingAccount::PrintBalance()
{
    cout << "Checking account balance: " << GetBalance();
}

class SavingsAccount : public Account
{
public:
    void PrintBalance();
};

// Implementation of PrintBalance for SavingsAccount.
void SavingsAccount::PrintBalance()
{
    cout << "Savings account balance: " << GetBalance();
}
```

The PrintBalance function in the derived classes is virtual because it is declared as virtual in the base class, Account. To call virtual functions such as PrintBalance, code such as the following can be used:

```
// Create objects of type CheckingAccount and SavingsAccount.
CheckingAccount *pChecking = new CheckingAccount( 100.00 );
SavingsAccount  *pSavings  = new SavingsAccount( 1000.00 );

// Call PrintBalance using a pointer to Account.
Account *pAccount = pChecking;
pAccount->PrintBalance();

// Call PrintBalance using a pointer to Account.
pAccount = pSavings;
pAccount->PrintBalance();
```

In the preceding code, the calls to PrintBalance are identical, except for the object pAccount points to. Because PrintBalance is virtual, the version of the function defined for each object is called. The PrintBalance function in the derived classes CheckingAccount and SavingsAccount "override" the function in the base class Account.

If a class is declared that does not provide an overriding implementation of the PrintBalance function, the default implementation from the base class Account is used.

Functions in derived classes override virtual functions in base classes only if their type is the same. A function in a derived class cannot differ from a virtual function in a base class in its return type only; the argument list must differ as well.

When calling a function using pointers or references, the following rules apply:

- A call to a virtual function is resolved according to the underlying type of object for which it is called.

- A call to a nonvirtual function is resolved according to the type of the pointer or reference.

The following example shows how virtual and nonvirtual functions behave when called through pointers:

```cpp
#include <iostream.h>

// Declare a base class.
class Base
{
public:
    virtual void NameOf();          // Virtual function.
            void InvokingClass();   // Nonvirtual function.
};

// Implement the two functions.
void Base::NameOf()
{
    cout << "Base::NameOf\n";
}

void Base::InvokingClass()
{
    cout << "Invoked by Base\n";
}

// Declare a derived class.
class Derived : public Base
{
public:
    void NameOf();          // Virtual function.
    void InvokingClass();   // Nonvirtual function.
};

// Implement the two functions.
void Derived::NameOf()
{
    cout << "Derived::NameOf\n";
}
```

```
void Derived::InvokingClass()
{
    cout << "Invoked by Derived\n";
}

void main()
{
    // Declare an object of type Derived.
    Derived aDerived;
    // Declare two pointers, one of type Derived * and the other
    //  of type Base *, and initialize them to point to aDerived.
    Derived *pDerived = &aDerived;
    Base    *pBase    = &aDerived;
    // Call the functions.
    pBase->NameOf();            // Call virtual function.
    pBase->InvokingClass();     // Call nonvirtual function.
    pDerived->NameOf();         // Call virtual function.
    pDerived->InvokingClass(); // Call nonvirtual function.
}
```

The output from this program is:

```
Derived::NameOf
Invoked by Base
Derived::NameOf
Invoked by Derived
```

Note that regardless of whether the NameOf function is invoked through a pointer to Base or a pointer to Derived, it calls the function for Derived. It calls the function for Derived because NameOf is a virtual function, and both pBase and pDerived point to an object of type Derived.

Because virtual functions are called only for objects of class types, you cannot declare global or static functions as **virtual**.

The **virtual** keyword can be used when declaring overriding functions in a derived class, but it is unnecessary; overrides of virtual functions are always virtual.

Virtual functions in a base class must be defined unless they are declared using the *pure-specifier*. (For more information about pure virtual functions, see "Abstract Classes" on page 274.)

The virtual function-call mechanism can be suppressed by explicitly qualifying the function name using the scope-resolution operator (::). Consider the preceding example. To call PrintBalance in the base class, use code such as the following:

```
CheckingAccount *pChecking = new CheckingAccount( 100.00 );

pChecking->Account::PrintBalance();  // Explicit qualification.

Account *pAccount = pChecking;       // Call Account::PrintBalance

pAccount->Account::PrintBalance();   // Explicit qualification.
```

Both calls to PrintBalance in the preceding example suppress the virtual function-call mechanism.

Abstract Classes

Abstract classes act as expressions of general concepts from which more specific classes can be derived. You cannot create an object of an abstract class type; however, you can use pointers and references to abstract class types.

A class that contains at least one pure virtual function is considered an abstract class. Classes derived from the abstract class must implement the pure virtual function or they, too, are abstract classes.

A virtual function is declared as "pure" by using the *pure-specifier* syntax (described in "Class Protocol Implementation" on page 263). Consider the example presented in "Virtual Functions." The intent of class Account is to provide general functionality, but objects of type Account are too general to be useful. Therefore, Account is a good candidate for an abstract class:

```
class Account
{
public:
                    Account( double d );  // Constructor.
    virtual double GetBalance();          // Obtain balance.
    virtual void   PrintBalance() = 0;    // Pure virtual function.
private:
    double _balance;
};
```

The only difference between this declaration and the previous one is that PrintBalance is declared with the pure specifier (= 0).

Restrictions on Using Abstract Classes

Abstract classes cannot be used for:

- Variables or member data
- Argument types
- Function return types
- Types of explicit conversions

Another restriction is that if the constructor for an abstract class calls a pure virtual function, either directly or indirectly, the result is undefined. However, constructors and destructors for abstract classes can call other member functions.

Pure virtual functions can be defined for abstract classes, but they can be called directly only by using the syntax:

abstract-class-name :: *function-name*( )

This helps when designing class hierarchies whose base class(es) include pure virtual destructors, because base class destructors are always called in the process of destroying an object. Consider the following example:

```
#include <iostream.h>

// Declare an abstract base class with a pure virtual destructor.
class base
{
public:
    base() {}
    virtual ~base()=0;
};

// Provide a definition for destructor.
base::~base()
{
}

class derived:public base
{
public:
    derived() {}
    ~derived(){}
};

void main()
{
    derived *pDerived = new derived;

    delete pDerived;
}
```

When the object pointed to by pDerived is deleted, the destructor for class derived is called and then the destructor for class base is called. The empty implementation for the pure virtual function ensures that at least some implementation exists for the function.

Note   In the preceding example, the pure virtual function base::~base is called implicitly from derived::~derived. It is also possible to call pure virtual functions explicitly using a fully qualified member-function name.

Summary of Scope Rules

This section supplements "Scope" on page 22 in Chapter 2 by adding the concepts pertaining to classes. The following topics are included:

- Ambiguity
- Global names
- Names and qualified names
- Function argument names
- Constructor initializers

Ambiguity

The use of a name must be unambiguous within its scope (up to the point where overloading is determined). If the name denotes a function, the function must be unambiguous with respect to number and type of arguments. If the name remains unambiguous, member-access rules are applied.

Global Names

A name of an object, function, or enumerator is global if it is introduced outside any function or class or prefixed by the global unary scope operator (::), and if it is not used in conjunction with any of these binary operators:

- Scope-resolution (::)
- Member-selection for objects and references (.)
- Member-selection for pointers (–>)

Names and Qualified Names

Names used with the binary scope-resolution operator (::) are called "qualified names." The name specified after the binary scope-resolution operator must be a member of the class specified on the left of the operator or a member of its base class(es).

Names specified after the member-selection operator (. or –>) must be members of the class type of the object specified on the left of the operator or members of its base class(es). Names specified on the right of the member-selection operator (–>) can also be objects of another class type, provided that the left-hand side of –> is a class object and that the class defines an overloaded member-selection operator (–>) that evaluates to a pointer to some other class type. (This provision is discussed in more detail in "Class Member Access" on page 347 in Chapter 12.)

The compiler searches for names in the following order, stopping when the name is found:

1. Current block scope if name is used inside a function; otherwise, global scope.
2. Outward through each enclosing block scope, including the outermost function scope (which includes function arguments).
3. If the name is used inside a member function, the class's scope is searched for the name.
4. The class's base classes are searched for the name.
5. The enclosing nested class scope (if any) and its bases are searched. The search continues until the outermost enclosing class scope is searched.
6. Global scope is searched.

However, you can make modifications to this search order as follows:

1. Names preceded by **::** force the search to begin at global scope.

2. Names preceded by the **class**, **struct**, and **union** keywords force the compiler to search only for **class**, **struct**, or **union** names.

3. Names on the left side of the scope-resolution operator (**::**) can be only **class**, **struct**, or **union** names.

If the name refers to a nonstatic member but is used in a static member function, an error message is generated. Similarly, if the name refers to any nonstatic member in an enclosing class, an error message is generated because enclosed classes do not have enclosing-class **this** pointers.

Function Argument Names

Function argument names in function definitions are considered to be in the scope of the outermost block of the function. Therefore, they are local names and go out of scope when the function is exited.

Function argument names in function declarations (prototypes) are in local scope of the declaration and go out of scope at the end of the declaration.

Default arguments are in the scope of the argument for which they are the default, as described in the preceding two paragraphs. However, they cannot access local variables or nonstatic class members. Default arguments are evaluated at the point of the function call, but they are evaluated in the function declaration's original scope. Therefore, the default arguments for member functions are always evaluated in class scope.

Constructor Initializers

Constructor initializers (described in "Initializing Bases and Members" on page 317 in Chapter 11) are evaluated in the scope of the outermost block of the constructor for which they are specified. Therefore, they can use the constructor's argument names.

Member-Access Control

With C++, you can specify the level of access to member data and functions. There are three levels of access: public, protected, and private. This chapter explains how access control applies to objects of class type and to derived classes. This chapter includes the following topics:

- Controlling access to class members
- Access specifiers
- Access specifiers for base classes
- Friends
- Protected member access
- Access to virtual functions
- Multiple access

Controlling Access to Class Members

You can increase the integrity of software built with C++ by controlling access to class member data and functions. Class members can be declared as having private, protected, or public access, as shown in Table 10.1.

Table 10.1 Member-Access Control

Type of Access	Meaning
private	Class members declared as **private** can be used only by member functions and friends (classes or functions) of the class.
protected	Class members declared as **protected** can be used by member functions and friends (classes or functions) of the class. Additionally, they can be used by classes derived from the class.
public	Class members declared as **public** can be used by any function.

Access control prevents you from using objects in ways they were not intended to be used. This protection is lost when explicit type conversions (casts) are performed.

Note Access control is equally applicable to all names: member functions, member data, nested classes, and enumerators.

The default access to class members (members of a class type declared using the **class** keyword) is private; the default access to **struct** and **union** members is public. For either case, the current access level can be changed using the **public**, **private**, or **protected** keyword.

Access Specifiers

In class declarations, members can have access specifiers.

Syntax

access-specifier : *member-list*_{opt}

The *access-specifier* determines the access to the names that follow it, up to the next *access-specifier* or the end of the class declaration. Figure 10.1 illustrates this concept.

Figure 10.1 Access Control in Classes

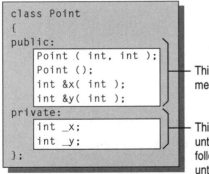

```
class Point
{
public:
    Point ( int, int );
    Point ();
    int &x( int );
    int &y( int );
private:
    int _x;
    int _y;
};
```

This **public** access specifier affects all members until the next access specifier.

This **private** access specifier affects all members until the class end. (If more access specifiers followed, **private** would affect all the members until the next access specifier.)

Although only two access specifiers are shown in Figure 10.1, there is no limit to the number of access specifiers in a given class declaration. For example, the Point class in Figure 10.1 could just as easily be declared using multiple access specifiers as follows:

```
class Point
{
public:                 // Declare public constructor.
    Point( int, int );
private:                // Declare private state variable.
    int _x;
public:                 // Declare public constructor.
    Point();
public:                 // Declare public accessor.
    int &x( int );
```

```
private:                //.Declare private state variable.
    int _y;
public:                 // Declare public accessor.
    int &y( int );
};
```

Note that there is no specific order required for member access, as shown in the preceding example. The allocation of storage for objects of class types is implementation dependent, but members are guaranteed to be assigned successively higher memory addresses between access specifiers.

Access Specifiers for Base Classes

Two factors control which members of a base class are accessible in a derived class; these same factors control access to the inherited members in the derived class:

- Whether the derived class declares the base class using the **public** access specifier in the *class-head* (*class-head* is described in Syntax in "Defining Class Types" on page 232 in Chapter 8).

- What the access to the member is in the base class.

Table 10.2 shows the interaction between these factors and how to determine base-class member access.

Table 10.2   Member Access in Base Class

private	protected	public
Always inaccessible regardless of derivation access	Private in derived class if you use private derivation	Private in derived class if you use private derivation
	Protected in derived class if you use protected derivation	Protected in derived class if you use protected derivation
	Protected in derived class if you use public derivation	Public in derived class if you use public derivation

The following example illustrates this:

```
class BaseClass
{
public:
    int PublicFunc();    // Declare a public member.
protected:
    int ProtectedFunc(); // Declare a protected member.
private:
    int PrivateFunc();   // Declare a private member.
};

// Declare two classes derived from BaseClass.
class DerivedClass1 : public BaseClass
{ };

class DerivedClass2 : private BaseClass
{ };
```

In `DerivedClass1`, the member function `PublicFunc` is a public member and `ProtectedFunc` is a protected member because `BaseClass` is a public base class. `PrivateFunc` is private to `BaseClass`, and it is inaccessible to any derived classes.

In `DerivedClass2`, the functions `PublicFunc` and `ProtectedFunc` are considered private members because `BaseClass` is a private base class. Again, `PrivateFunc` is private to `BaseClass`, and it is inaccessible to any derived classes.

You can declare a derived class without a base-class access specifier. In such a case, the derivation is considered private if the derived class declaration uses the **class** keyword. The derivation is considered public if the derived class declaration uses the **struct** keyword. For example, the following code:

```
class Derived : Base
...
```

is equivalent to:

```
class Derived : private Base
...
```

Similarly, the following code:

```
struct Derived : Base
...
```

is equivalent to:

```
struct Derived : public Base
...
```

Note that members declared as having private access are not accessible to functions or derived classes unless those functions or classes are declared using the **friend** declaration in the base class.

A **union** type cannot have a base class.

Note When specifying a private base class, it is advisable to explicitly use the **private** keyword so users of the derived class understand the member access.

Access Control and Static Members

When you specify a base class as **private**, it affects only nonstatic members. Public static members are still accessible in the derived classes. However, accessing members of the base class using pointers, references, or objects can require a conversion, at which time access control is again applied. Consider the following example:

```
class Base
{
public:
    int Print();            // Nonstatic member.
    static int CountOf();   // Static member.
};
```

```
// Derived1 declares Base as a private base class.
class Derived1 : private Base
{
};
// Derived2 declares Derived1 as a public base class.
class Derived2 : public Derived1
{
    int ShowCount();    // Nonstatic member.
};
// Define ShowCount function for Derived2.
int Derived2::ShowCount()
{
    // Call static member function CountOf explicitly.
    int cCount = Base::CountOf();      // OK.

    // Call static member function CountOf using pointer.
    cCount = this->CountOf();   // Error. Conversion of
                                //  Derived2 * to Base * not
                                //  permitted.
    return cCount;
}
```

In the preceding code, access control prohibits conversion from a pointer to Derived2 to a pointer to Base. The **this** pointer is implicitly of type Derived2 *. To select the CountOf function, **this** must be converted to type Base *. Such a conversion is not permitted because Base is a private indirect base class to Derived2. Conversion to a private base class type is acceptable only for pointers to immediate derived classes. Therefore, pointers of type Derived1 * can be converted to type Base *.

Note that calling the CountOf function explicitly, without using a pointer, reference, or object to select it, implies no conversion. Therefore, the call is allowed.

Members and friends of a derived class, *T*, can convert a pointer to *T* to a pointer to a private direct base class of *T*.

Friends

In some circumstances, it is more convenient to grant member-level access to functions that are not members of a class or to all functions in a separate class. With the **friend** keyword, programmers can designate either the specific functions or the classes whose functions can access not only **public** members but also **protected** and **private** members.

Friend Functions

Friend functions are not considered class members; they are normal external functions that are given special access privileges. Friends are not in the class's scope, and they are not called using the member-selection operators (. and –>) unless they are members of another class. The following example shows a Point class and an overloaded operator, operator+. (This example primarily illustrates friends, not overloaded operators. For more information about overloaded operators, see "Overloaded Operators" on page 336 in Chapter 12.)

```
#include <iostream.h>
// Declare class Point.
class Point
{
public:
    // Constructors
    Point() { _x = _y = 0; }
    Point( unsigned x, unsigned y ) { _x = x; _y = y; }
    // Accessors
    unsigned x() { return _x; }
    unsigned y() { return _y; }
    void      Print() { cout << "Point(" << _x << ", " << _y << ")"
                             << endl; }

    // Friend function declarations
    friend Point operator+( Point& pt, int nOffset );
    friend Point operator+( int nOffset, Point& pt );

private:
    unsigned _x;
    unsigned _y;
};

// Friend-function definitions
//
// Handle Point + int expression.
Point operator+( Point& pt, int nOffset )
{
    Point ptTemp = pt;
    // Change private members _x and _y directly.
    ptTemp._x += nOffset;
    ptTemp._y += nOffset;

    return ptTemp;
}

// Handle int + Point expression.
Point operator+( int nOffset, Point& pt )
{
    Point ptTemp = pt;
    // Change private members _x and _y directly.
    ptTemp._x += nOffset;
    ptTemp._y += nOffset;

    return ptTemp;
}

// Test overloaded operator.
void main()
{
    Point pt( 10, 20 );
    pt.Print();

    pt = pt + 3;       // Point + int
    pt.Print();

    pt = 3 + pt;       // int + Point
    pt.Print();
}
```

When the expression pt + 3 is encountered in the main function, the compiler determines whether an appropriate user-defined operator+ exists. In this case, the function operator+(Point pt, int nOffset) matches the operands, and a call to the function is issued. In the second case (the expression 3 + pt), the function operator+(Point pt, int nOffset) matches the supplied operands. Therefore, supplying these two forms of operator+ preserves the commutative properties of the + operator.

A user-defined operator+ can be written as a member function, but it takes only one explicit argument: the value to be added to the object. As a result, the commutative properties of addition cannot be correctly implemented with member functions; they must use friend functions instead.

Notice that both versions of the overloaded operator+ function are declared as friends in class Point. Both declarations are necessary — when **friend** declarations name overloaded functions or operators, only the particular functions specified by the argument types become friends. Suppose a third operator+ function were declared as follows:

```
Point &operator+( Point &pt, Point &pt );
```

The operator+ function in the preceding example is not a friend of class Point, simply because it has the same name as two other functions that are declared as friends.

Because **friend** declarations are unaffected by access specifiers, they can be declared in any section of the class declaration.

Class Member Functions and Classes as Friends

Class member functions can be declared as friends in other classes. Consider the following example:

```
class A
{
private:
    int _a;
    friend int B::Func1( A );   //  Grant friend access to one
                                //    function in class B.
};

class B
{
public:
    int Func1( A a ) { return a._a; } //  OK: this is a friend.
    int Func2( A a ) { return a._a; } //  Error: _a is a private
                                      //    member.
};
```

In the preceding example, only the function B::Func1(A) is granted friend access to class A. Therefore, access to the private member _a is correct in function b of class B but not in function c.

Suppose the **friend** declaration in class A had been:

```
friend class B;
```

In that case, all member functions in class B would have been granted friend access to class A. Note that "friendship" cannot be inherited, nor is there any "friend of a friend" access. Figure 10.2 shows four class declarations: Base, Derived, aFriend, and anotherFriend. Only class aFriend has direct access to the private members of Base (and to any members Base might have inherited).

Figure 10.2 Implications of friend Relationship

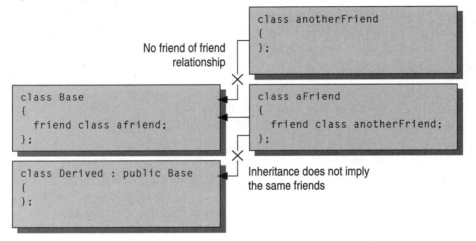

Friend Declarations

If you declare a friend function that was not previously declared, that function is exported to the enclosing nonclass scope.

Functions declared in a friend declaration are treated as if they had been declared using the **extern** keyword. (For more information about **extern**, see "Static Storage-Class Specifiers" on page 153 in Chapter 6.)

Although functions with global scope can be declared as friends prior to their prototypes, member functions cannot be declared as friends before the appearance of their complete class declaration. The following code shows why this fails:

```
class ForwardDeclared;    // Class name is known.

class HasFriends
{
    friend int ForwardDeclared::IsAFriend();    // Error.
};
```

The preceding example enters the class name `ForwardDeclared` into scope, but the complete declaration—specifically, the portion that declares the function `IsAFriend`—is not known. Therefore, the **friend** declaration in class `HasFriends` generates an error.

To declare two classes that are friends of one another, the entire second class must be specified as a friend of the first class. The reason for this restriction is that the compiler has enough information to declare individual friend functions only at the point where the second class is declared.

Note Although the entire second class must be a friend to the first class, you can select which functions in the first class will be friends of the second class.

Defining Friend Functions in Class Declarations

Friend functions can be defined inside class declarations. These functions are inline functions, and like member inline functions they behave as though they were defined immediately after all class members have been seen but before the class scope is closed (the end of the class declaration).

Friend functions defined inside class declarations are not considered in the scope of the enclosing class; they are in file scope.

Protected Member Access

Class members declared as **protected** can be used only by the following:

- Member functions of the class that originally declared these members.
- Friends of the class that originally declared these members.
- Classes derived with public or protected access from the class that originally declared these members.
- Direct privately derived classes that also have private access to protected members.

Protected members are not as private as **private** members, which are accessible only to members of the class in which they are declared, but they are not as public as **public** members, which are accessible in any function.

Protected members that are also declared as **static** are accessible to any friend or member function of a derived class. Protected members that are not declared as **static** are accessible to friends and member functions in a derived class only through a pointer to, reference to, or object of the derived class.

Access to Virtual Functions

The access control applied to virtual functions is determined by the type used to make the function call. Overriding declarations of the function do not affect the access control for a given type. For example:

```
class VFuncBase
{
public:
   virtual int GetState() { return _state; }
protected:
   int _state;
};

class VFuncDerived : public VFuncBase
{
private:
   int GetState() { return _state; }
};

...

VFuncDerived vfd;             // Object of derived type.
VFuncBase *pvfb = &vfd;       // Pointer to base type.
VFuncDerived *pvfd = &vfd;    // Pointer to derived type.
int State;

State = pvfb->GetState();     // GetState is public.
State = pvfd->GetState();     // GetState is private; error.
```

In the preceding example, calling the virtual function GetState using a pointer to type VFuncBase calls VFuncDerived::GetState, and GetState is treated as public. However, calling GetState using a pointer to type VFuncDerived is an access-control violation because GetState is declared private in class VFuncDerived.

Warning   The virtual function GetState can be called using a pointer to the base class VFuncBase. This does not mean that the function called is the base-class version of that function.

Multiple Access

In multiple-inheritance lattices involving virtual base classes, a given name can be reached through more than one path. Because different access control can be applied along these different paths, the compiler chooses the path that gives the most access. See Figure 10.3.

Figure 10.3   Access Along Paths of an Inheritance Graph

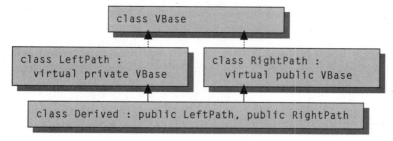

In Figure 10.3, a name declared in class VBase is always reached through class RightPath. The right path is more accessible because RightPath declares VBase as a public base class, whereas LeftPath declares VBase as private.

Special Member Functions

C++ defines several kinds of functions that can be declared only as class members —
these are called "special member functions." These functions affect the way objects of
a given class are created, destroyed, copied, and converted into objects of other types.
Another important property of many of these functions is that they can be called
implicitly (by the compiler).

The special member functions are described briefly in the following list:

- Constructors. These functions enable automatic initialization of
  objects.

- Destructors. These functions perform cleanup after objects are explicitly
  or implicitly destroyed.

- Conversion Functions. These are used to convert between class types
  and other types.

- The **new** operator. This is used to dynamically allocate storage.

- The **delete** operator. This is used to release storage allocated using
  the **new** operator.

- The assignment operator (operator=). This operator is used when an
  assignment takes place.

All of the items in the preceding list can be user-defined for each
class.

Special member functions obey the same access rules as other member functions.
The access rules are described in Chapter 10, "Member-Access Control." Table 11.1
summarizes how member and friend functions behave.

Table 11.1   Summary of Function Behavior

Function Type	Is Function Inherited from Base Class?	Can Function Be Virtual?	Can Function Return a Value?	Is Function a Member or Friend?	Will Compiler Generate Function if User Does Not?
Constructor	No	No	No	Member	Yes
Copy Constructor	No	No	No	Member	Yes
Destructor	No	Yes	No	Member	Yes
Conversion	Yes	Yes	No	Member	No
Assignment (**operator=**)	No	Yes	Yes	Member	Yes
new	Yes	No	**void***	Static member	No
delete	Yes	No	**void**	Static member	No
Other member functions	Yes	Yes	Yes	Member	No
Friend functions	No	No	Yes	Friend	No

Constructors

A member function with the same name as its class is a constructor function. Constructors cannot return values, even if they have **return** statements. Specifying a constructor with a return type is an error, as is taking the address of a constructor.

If a class has a constructor, each object of that type is initialized with the constructor prior to use in a program. (For more information about initialization, see "Initialization Using Special Member Functions" on page 314.)

Constructors are called at the point an object is created. Objects are created as:

- Global (file-scoped or externally linked) objects.
- Local objects, within a function or smaller enclosing block.
- Dynamic objects, using the **new** operator. The **new** operator allocates an object on the program heap or "free store."
- Temporary objects created by explicitly calling a constructor. (For more information, see "Temporary Objects" on page 301.)
- Temporary objects created implicitly by the compiler. (For more information, see "Temporary Objects" on page 301.)
- Data members of another class. Creating objects of class type, where the class type is composed of other class-type variables, causes each object in the class to be created.

- Base class subobject of a class. Creating objects of derived class type causes the base class components to be created.

What a Constructor Does

A constructor performs various tasks that are not visible to you as the programmer, even if you write no code for the constructor. These tasks are all associated with building a complete and correct instance of class type.

In Microsoft C++ (and some other implementations of C++), a constructor:

- Initializes the object's virtual base pointer(s) (vbptr). This step is performed if the class is derived from virtual base classes.

- Calls base class and member constructors in the order of declaration.

- Initializes the object's virtual function pointers (vfptr). This step is performed if the class has or inherits virtual functions. Virtual function pointers point to the class's virtual function table (v-table) and allow correct binding of virtual function calls to code.

- Executes optional code in the body of the constructor function.

When the constructor is finished, the allocated memory is an object of a given class type. Because of the steps the constructor performs, "late binding" in the form of virtual functions can be resolved at the point of a virtual function call. The constructor has also constructed base classes and has constructed composed objects (objects included as data members). Late binding is the mechanism by which C++ implements polymorphic behavior for objects.

Rules for Declaring Constructors

A constructor has the same name as its class. Any number of constructors can be declared, subject to the rules of overloaded functions. (For more information, see Chapter 12, "Overloading.")

Syntax

class-name (*argument-declaration-list*$_{opt}$) *cv-mod-list*$_{opt}$

C++ defines two special kinds of constructors, default and copy constructors, described in Table 11.2.

Table 11.2 Default and Copy Constructors

Kind of Construction	Arguments	Purpose
Default constructor	Can be called with no arguments	Construct a default object of the class type
Copy constructor	Can accept a single argument of reference to same class type	Copy objects of the class type

Default constructors can be called with no arguments. However, you can declare a default constructor with an argument list, provided all arguments have defaults. Similarly, copy constructors must accept a single argument of reference to the same class type. More arguments can be supplied, provided all subsequent arguments have defaults.

If you do not supply any constructors, the compiler attempts to generate a default constructor. If you do not supply a copy constructor, the compiler attempts to generate one. These compiler-generated constructors are considered public member functions. An error is generated if you specify a copy constructor with a first argument that is an object and not a reference.

A compiler-generated default constructor sets up the object (initializes vftables and vbtables, as described previously), and it calls the default constructors for base classes and members, but it takes no other action. Base class and member constructors are called only if they exist, are accessible, and are unambiguous.

A compiler-generated copy constructor sets up a new object and performs a memberwise copy of the contents of the object to be copied. If base class or member constructors exist, they are called; otherwise, bitwise copying is performed.

If all base and member classes of a class *type* have copy constructors that accept a **const** argument, the compiler-generated copy constructor accepts a single argument of type **const** *type***&**. Otherwise, the compiler-generated copy constructor accepts a single argument of type *type***&**.

You can use a constructor to initialize a **const** or **volatile** object, but the constructor itself cannot be declared as **const** or **volatile**. The only legal storage class for a constructor is **inline**; use of any other storage-class modifier, including the **__declspec** keyword, with a constructor causes a compiler error. Constructors and destructors cannot specify a calling convention other than **__stdcall**.

Constructors of base classes are not inherited by derived classes. When an object of derived class type is created, it is constructed starting with the base class components; then it moves to the derived class components. The compiler uses each base class's constructor as that part of the complete object is initialized (except in cases of virtual derivation, as described in "Initializing Base Classes" on page 319).

Explicitly Called Constructors

Constructors can be explicitly called in a program to create objects of a given type. For example, to create two Point objects that describe the ends of a line, the following code can be written:

```
DrawLine( Point( 13, 22 ), Point( 87, 91 ) );
```

Two objects of type Point are created, passed to the function DrawLine, and destroyed at the end of the expression (the function call).

Another context in which a constructor is explicitly called is in an initialization:

```
Point pt = Point( 7, 11 );
```

An object of type Point is created and initialized using the constructor that accepts two arguments of type **int**.

Objects that are created by calling constructors explicitly, as in the preceding two examples, are unnamed and have a lifetime of the expression in which they are created. This is discussed in greater detail in "Temporary Objects" on page 301.

Calling Member Functions and Virtual Functions from Within Constructors

It is usually safe to call any member function from within a constructor because the object has been completely set up (virtual tables have been initialized and so on) prior to the execution of the first line of user code. However, it is potentially unsafe for a member function to call a virtual member function for an abstract base class during construction or destruction.

Constructors can call virtual functions. When virtual functions are called, the function invoked is the function defined for the constructor's own class (or inherited from its bases). The following example shows what happens when a virtual function is called from within a constructor:

```
#include <iostream.h>

class Base
{
public:
    Base();             // Default constructor.
    virtual void f();   // Virtual member function.
};

Base::Base()
{
    cout << "Constructing Base sub-object\n";
    f();                // Call virtual member function
}                       //  from inside constructor.

void Base::f()
{
    cout << "Called Base::f()\n";
}

class Derived : public Base
{
public:
    Derived();          // Default constructor.
    void f();           // Implementation of virtual
};                      //  function f for this class.

Derived::Derived().
{
```

```
        cout << "Constructing Derived object\n";
    }

    void Derived::f()
    {
        cout << "Called Derived::f()\n";
    }

    void main()
    {
        Derived d;
    }
```

When the preceding program is run, the declaration `Derived d` causes the following sequence of events:

1. The constructor for class `Derived` (`Derived::Derived`) is called.

2. Prior to entering the body of the `Derived` class's constructor, the constructor for class `Base` (`Base::Base`) is called.

3. `Base::Base` calls the function `f`, which is a virtual function. Ordinarily, `Derived::f` would be called because the object d is of type `Derived`. Because the `Base::Base` function is a constructor, the object is not yet of the `Derived` type, and `Base::f` is called.

Constructors and Arrays

Arrays are constructed only using the default constructor. Default constructors are constructors that either accept no arguments or for which all arguments have a default. Arrays are always constructed in ascending order. The initialization for each member of the array is done using the same constructor.

Order of Construction

For derived classes and classes that have class-type member data, the order in which construction occurs helps you understand what portions of the object you can use in any given constructor.

Construction and Inheritance

An object of derived type is constructed from the base class to the derived class by calling the constructors for each class in order. Each class's constructor can rely on its base classes being completely constructed.

For a complete description of initialization, including the order of initialization, see "Initializing Bases and Members" on page 317.

Construction and Composed Classes

Classes that contain class-type data members are called "composed classes." When an object of a composed class type is created, the constructors for the contained classes are called before the class's own constructor.

For a more information about this kind of initialization, see "Initializing Bases and Members" on page 317.

Destructors

"Destructor" functions are the inverse of constructor functions. They are called when objects are destroyed (deallocated). Designate a function as a class's destructor by preceding the class name with a tilde (~). For example, the destructor for class String is declared: ~String().

The destructor is commonly used to "clean up" when an object is no longer necessary. Consider the following declaration of a String class:

```
#include <string.h>

class String
{
public:
   String( char *ch );  // Declare constructor
   ~String();           //  and destructor.
private:
   char *_text;
};

// Define the constructor.
String::String( char *ch )
{
   // Dynamically allocate the correct amount of memory.
   _text = new char[strlen( ch ) + 1];

   // If the allocation succeeds, copy the initialization string.
   if( _text )
      strcpy( _text, ch );
}

// Define the destructor.
String::~String()
{
   // Deallocate the memory that was previously reserved
   //  for this string.
   delete[] _text;
}
```

In the preceding example, the destructor String::~String uses the **delete** operator to deallocate the space dynamically allocated for text storage.

Declaring Destructors

Destructors are functions with the same name as the class but preceded by a tilde (~).

Syntax

~class-name()

or

class-name **::** *~class-name*()

The first form of the syntax is used for destructors declared or defined inside a class declaration; the second form is used for destructors defined outside a class declaration.

Several rules govern the declaration of destructors. Destructors:

- Do not accept arguments.

- Cannot specify any return type (including **void**).

- Cannot return a value using the **return** statement.

- Cannot be declared as **const**, **volatile**, or **static**. However, they can be invoked for the destruction of objects declared as **const**, **volatile**, or **static**.

- Can be declared as **virtual**. Using virtual destructors, you can destroy objects without knowing their type—the correct destructor for the object is invoked using the virtual function mechanism. Note that destructors can also be declared as pure virtual functions for abstract classes.

Using Destructors

Destructors are called when one of the following events occurs:

- An object allocated using the **new** operator is explicitly deallocated using the **delete** operator. When objects are deallocated using the **delete** operator, memory is freed for the "most derived object," or the object that is a complete object and not a subobject representing a base class. This "most-derived object" deallocation is guaranteed to work only with virtual destructors. Deallocation may fail in multiple-inheritance situations where the type information does not correspond to the underlying type of the actual object.

- A local (automatic) object with block scope goes out of scope.

- The lifetime of a temporary object ends.

- A program ends and global or static objects exist.

- The destructor is explicitly called using the destructor function's fully qualified name. (For more information, see "Explicit Destructor Calls" on page 301.)

The cases described in the preceding list ensure that all objects can be destroyed with user-defined methods.

If a base class or data member has an accessible destructor, and if a derived class does not declare a destructor, the compiler generates one. This compiler-generated destructor calls the base class destructor and the destructors for members of the derived type. Default destructors are public. (For more information about accessibility, see "Access Specifiers for Base Classes" on page 281 in Chapter 10.)

Destructors can freely call class member functions and access class member data. When a virtual function is called from a destructor, the function called is the function for the class currently being destroyed. (For more information, see the next section, "Order of Destruction.")

There are two restrictions on the use of destructors. The first restriction is that you cannot take the address of a destructor. The second is that derived classes do not inherit their base class's destructors. Instead, as previously explained, they always override the base class's destructors.

Order of Destruction

When an object goes out of scope or is deleted, the sequence of events in its complete destruction is as follows:

1. The class's destructor is called, and the body of the destructor function is executed.

2. Destructors for nonstatic member objects are called in the reverse order in which they appear in the class declaration. The optional member initialization list used in construction of these members does not affect the order of construction or destruction. (For more information about initializing members, see "Initializing Bases and Members" on page 317.)

3. Destructors for nonvirtual base classes are called in the reverse order of declaration.

4. Destructors for virtual base classes are called in the reverse order of declaration.

Destructors for Nonvirtual Base Classes

The destructors for nonvirtual base classes are called in the reverse order in which the base class names are declared. Consider the following class declaration:

```
class MultInherit : public Base1, public Base2
...
```

In the preceding example, the destructor for `Base2` is called before the destructor for `Base1`.

Destructors for Virtual Base Classes

Destructors for virtual base classes are called in the reverse order of their appearance in a directed acyclic graph (depth-first, left-to-right, postorder traversal). Figure 11.1 depicts an inheritance graph.

Figure 11.1 Inheritance Graph Showing Virtual Base Classes

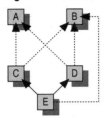

The following lists the class heads for the classes shown in Figure 11.1.

```
class A
class B
class C : virtual public A, virtual public B
class D : virtual public A, virtual public B
class E : public C, public D, virtual public B
```

To determine the order of destruction of the virtual base classes of an object of type E, the compiler builds a list by applying the following algorithm:

1. Traverse the graph left, starting at the deepest point in the graph (in this case, E).

2. Perform leftward traversals until all nodes have been visited. Note the name of the current node.

3. Revisit the previous node (down and to the right) to find out whether the node being remembered is a virtual base class.

4. If the remembered node is a virtual base class, scan the list to see whether it has already been entered. If it is not a virtual base class, ignore it.

5. If the remembered node is not yet in the list, add it to the bottom of the list.

6. Traverse the graph up and along the next path to the right.

7. Go to step 2.

8. When the last upward path is exhausted, note the name of the current node.

9. Go to step 3.

10.Continue this process until the bottom node is again the current node.

Therefore, for class E, the order of destruction is:

1. The nonvirtual base class E.

2. The nonvirtual base class D.

3. The nonvirtual base class C.

4. The virtual base class B.

5. The virtual base class A.

This process produces an ordered list of unique entries. No class name appears twice. Once the list is constructed, it is walked in reverse order, and the destructor for each of the classes in the list from the last to the first is called.

The order of construction or destruction is primarily important when constructors or destructors in one class rely on the other component being created first or persisting longer—for example, if the destructor for A (in the graph in Figure 11.1) relied on B still being present when its code executed, or vice versa.

Such interdependencies between classes in an inheritance graph are inherently dangerous because classes derived later can alter which is the leftmost path, thereby changing the order of construction and destruction.

Explicit Destructor Calls

Calling a destructor explicitly is seldom necessary. However, it can be useful to perform cleanup of objects placed at absolute addresses. These objects are commonly allocated using a user-defined **new** operator that takes a placement argument. The **delete** operator cannot deallocate this memory because it is not allocated from the free store (for more information, see "The **new** and **delete** Operators"). A call to the destructor, however, can perform appropriate cleanup. To explicitly call the destructor for an object, s, of class String, use one of the following statements:

```
s.String::~String();     // Nonvirtual call
ps->String::~String();   // Nonvirtual call

s.~String();             // Virtual call
ps->~String();           // Virtual call
```

The notation for explicit calls to destructors, shown in the preceding, can be used regardless of whether the type defines a destructor. This allows you to make such explicit calls without knowing if a destructor is defined for the type. An explicit call to a destructor where none is defined has no effect.

Temporary Objects

In some cases, it is necessary for the compiler to create temporary objects. These temporary objects can be created for the following reasons:

- To initialize a **const** reference with an initializer of a type different from that of the underlying type of the reference being initialized.
- To store the return value of a function that returns a user-defined type. These temporaries are created only if your program does not copy the return value to an object. For example:
```
UDT Func1();    //  Declare a function that returns a user-defined
                //  type.

...
```

```
Func1();       //  Call Func1, but discard return value.
               //  A temporary object is created to store the
               //   return value.
```

Because the return value is not copied to another object, a temporary object is created. A more common case where temporaries are created is during the evaluation of an expression where overloaded operator functions must be called. These overloaded operator functions return a user-defined type that often is not copied to another object.

Consider the expression `ComplexResult = Complex1 + Complex2 + Complex3`. The expression `Complex1 + Complex2` is evaluated, and the result is stored in a temporary object. Next, the expression *temporary* `+ Complex3` is evaluated, and the result is copied to `ComplexResult` (assuming the assignment operator is not overloaded).

- To store the result of a cast to a user-defined type. When an object of a given type is explicitly converted to a user-defined type, that new object is constructed as a temporary object.

Temporary objects have a lifetime that is defined by their point of creation and the point at which they are destroyed. Any expression that creates more than one temporary object eventually destroys them in the reverse order in which they were created. The points at which destruction occurs are shown in Table 11.3.

Table 11.3 Destruction Points for Temporary Objects

Reason Temporary Created	Destruction Point
Result of expression evaluation	All temporaries created as a result of expression evaluation are destroyed at the end of the expression statement (that is, at the semicolon), or at the end of the controlling expressions for **for**, **if**, **while**, **do**, and **switch** statements.
Result of expressions using the built-in (not overloaded) logical operators (|| and **&&**)	Immediately after the right operand. At this destruction point, all temporary objects created by evaluation of the right operand are destroyed.
Initializing **const** references	If an initializer is not an l-value of the same type as the reference being initialized, a temporary of the underlying object type is created and initialized with the initialization expression. This temporary object is destroyed immediately after the reference object to which it is bound is destroyed.

Conversions

Objects of a given class type can be converted to objects of another type. This is done by constructing an object of the target class type from the source class type and copying the result to the target object. This process is called conversion by constructor. Objects can also be converted by user-supplied conversion functions.

When standard conversions (described in Chapter 3, "Standard Conversions") cannot completely convert from a given type to a class type, the compiler can select user-defined conversions to help complete the job. In addition to explicit type conversions, conversions take place when:

- An initializer expression is not the same type as the object being initialized.

- The type of argument used in a function call does not match the type of argument specified in the function declaration.

- The type of the object being returned from a function does not match the return type specified in the function declaration.

- Two expression operands must be of the same type.

- An expression controlling an iteration or selection statement requires a different type from the one supplied.

A user-defined conversion is applied only if it is unambiguous; otherwise, an error message is generated. Ambiguity is checked at the point of usage. Hence, if the features that cause ambiguity are not used, a class can be designated with potential ambiguities and not generate any errors. Although there are many situations in which ambiguities arise, these are two leading causes of ambiguities:

- A class type is derived using multiple inheritance, and it is unclear from which base class to select the conversion (see "Ambiguity" on page 276 in Chapter 9).

- An explicit type-conversion operator and a constructor for the same conversion exist (see "Conversion Functions" on page 305).

Both conversion by constructor and conversion by conversion functions obey access control rules, as described in Chapter 10, "Member-Access Control." Access control is tested only after the conversion is found to be unambiguous.

Conversion Constructors

A constructor that can be called with a single argument is used for conversions from the type of the argument to the class type. Such a constructor is called a conversion constructor. Consider the following example:

```
class Point
{
public:
    Point();
    Point( int );
    ...
};
```

Sometimes a conversion is required but no conversion constructor exists in the class. These conversions cannot be performed by constructors. The compiler does not look for intermediate types through which to perform the conversion. For example, suppose a conversion exists from type Point to type Rect and a conversion exists from type **int** to type Point. The compiler does not supply a conversion from type **int** to type Rect by constructing an intermediate object of type Point.

Conversions and Constants

Although constants for built-in types such as **int**, **long**, and **double** can appear in expressions, no constants of class types are allowed (this is partly because classes usually describe an object complicated enough to make notation inconvenient). However, if conversion constructors from built-in types are supplied, constants of these built-in types can be used in expressions, and the conversions cause correct behavior. For example, a Money class can have conversions from types **long** and **double**:

```
class Money
{
public:
    Money( long );
    Money( double );
    ...
    Money operator+( const Money& );   // Overloaded addition operator.
};
```

Therefore, expressions such as the following can specify constant values:

```
Money AccountBalance = 37.89;
Money NewBalance = AccountBalance + 14L;
```

The second example involves the use of an overloaded addition operator, which is covered in the next chapter. Both examples cause the compiler to convert the constants to type Money before using them in the expressions.

Drawbacks of Conversion Constructors

Because the compiler can select a conversion constructor implicitly, you relinquish control over what functions are called when. If it is essential to retain full control, do not declare any constructors that take a single argument; instead, define "helper" functions to perform conversions, as in the following example:

```
#include <stdio.h>
#include <stdlib.h>

// Declare Money class.
class Money
{
public:
    Money();
// Define conversion functions that can only be called explicitly.
    static Money Convert( char * ch ) { return Money( ch ); }
    static Money Convert( double d )    { return Money( d ); };
    void   Print() { printf( "\n%f", _amount ); }
private:
    Money( char *ch ) { _amount = atof( ch ); }
    Money( double d ) { _amount = d; }
    double _amount;
};
```

```
void main()
{
    // Perform a conversion from type char * to type Money.
    Money Acct = Money::Convert( "57.29" );
    Acct.Print();
    // Perform a conversion from type double to type Money.
    Acct = Money::Convert( 33.29 );
    Acct.Print();
}
```

In the preceding code, the conversion constructors are private and cannot be used in type conversions. However, they can be invoked explicitly by calling the Convert functions. Because the Convert functions are static, they are accessible without referencing a particular object.

Conversion Functions

In conversion by constructors, described in the previous section, objects of one type can be implicitly converted to a particular class type. This section describes a means by which you can provide explicit conversions from a given class type to another type. Conversion from a class type is often accomplished using conversion functions. Conversion functions use the following syntax:

Syntax

conversion-function-name:
    operator *conversion-type-name* ()
conversion-type-name:
    *type-specifier-list ptr-operator*_{opt}

The following example specifies a conversion function that converts type Money to type double:

```
class Money
{
public:
    Money();
    operator double() { return _amount; }
private:
    double _amount;
};
```

Given the preceding class declaration, the following code can be written:

```
Money Account;
...
double CashOnHand = Account;
```

The initialization of CashOnHand with Account causes a conversion from type Account to type double.

Conversion functions are often called "cast operators" because they (along with constructors) are the functions called when a cast is used. The following example uses a cast, or explicit conversion, to print the current value of an object of type Money:

```
cout << (double)Account << endl;
```

Conversion functions are inherited in derived classes. Conversion operators hide only base-class conversion operators that convert to exactly the same type. Therefore, a user-defined **operator int** function does not hide a user-defined **operator short** function in a base class.

Only one user-defined conversion function is applied when performing implicit conversions. If there is no explicitly defined conversion function, the compiler does not look for intermediate types into which an object can be converted.

If a conversion is required that causes an ambiguity, an error is generated. Ambiguities arise when more than one user-defined conversion is available or when a user-defined conversion and a built-in conversion exist.

The following example illustrates a class declaration with a potential ambiguity:

```
#include <string.h>

class String
{
public:
    // Define constructor that converts from type char *.
    String( char *s ) { strcpy( _text, s ); }
    // Define conversion to type char *.
    operator char *() { return _text; }
    int operator==( const String &s )
    { return !strcmp( _text, s._text ); }
private:
    char _text[80];
};

int main()
{
    String s( "abcd" );
    char   *ch = "efgh";

    // Cause the compiler to select a conversion.
    return s == ch;
}
```

In the expression s == ch, the compiler has two choices and no way of determining which is correct. It can convert ch to an object of type String using the constructor and then perform the comparison using the user-defined operator==. Or it can convert s to a pointer of type char * using the conversion function and then perform a comparison of the pointers.

Because neither choice is "more correct" than the other, the compiler cannot determine the meaning of the comparison expression, and it generates an error.

Rules for Declaring Conversion Functions

The following four rules are used when declaring conversion functions (see "Conversion Functions" on page 305 for syntax):

- Classes, enumerations, and **typedef** names cannot be declared in the *type-specifier-list*. Therefore, the following code generates an error:

```
operator struct String{ char string_storage; }();
```

Instead, declare the String structure prior to the conversion function.

- Conversion functions take no arguments. Specifying arguments generates an error.

- Conversion functions have the return type specified by the *conversion-type-name*; specifying any return type for a conversion function generates an error.

- Conversion functions can be declared as **virtual**.

The new and delete Operators

C++ supports dynamic allocation and deallocation of objects using the **new** and **delete** operators. These operators allocate memory for objects from a pool called the "free store." The **new** operator calls the special function **operator new**, and the **delete** operator calls the special function **operator delete**.

The operator new Function

When a statement such as the following is encountered in a program, it translates into a call to the function **operator new**:

```
char *pch = new char[BUFFER_SIZE];
```

If the request is for zero bytes of storage, **operator new** returns a pointer to a distinct object (that is, repeated calls to **operator new** return different pointers). If there is insufficient memory for the allocation request, by default **operator new** returns **NULL**. You can change this default behavior by writing a custom exception-handling routine and calling the **_set_new_handler** run-time library function with your function name as its argument. Optionally, you can choose to have **new** throw a C++ exception (of type **xalloc**) in the event of a memory allocation failure. For more details on these two recovery schemes, see the following section, "Handling Insufficient Memory Conditions."

The two scopes for **operator new** functions are described in Table 11.4.

Table 11.4 Scope for operator new Functions

Operator	Scope
::operator new	Global
*class-name***::operator new**	Class

The first argument to **operator new** must be of type **size_t** (a type defined in STDDEF.H), and the return type is always **void ***.

The global **operator new** function is called when the **new** operator is used to allocate objects of built-in types, objects of class type that do not contain user-defined **operator new** functions, and arrays of any type. When the **new** operator is used to allocate objects of a class type where an **operator new** is defined, that class's **operator new** is called.

An **operator new** function defined for a class is a static member function (which cannot, therefore, be virtual) that hides the global **operator new** function for objects of that class type. Consider the case where **new** is used to allocate and set memory to a given value:

```
#include <malloc.h>
#include <memory.h>

class Blanks
{
public:
    Blanks(){}
    void *operator new( size_t stAllocateBlock, char chInit );
};
void *Blanks::operator new( size_t stAllocateBlock, char chInit )
{
    void *pvTemp = malloc( stAllocateBlock );
    if( pvTemp != 0 )
        memset( pvTemp, chInit, stAllocateBlock );
    return pvTemp;
}
```

For discrete objects of type Blanks, the global **operator new** function is hidden. Therefore, the following code allocates an object of type Blanks and initializes it to 0xa5:

```
int main()
{
    Blanks *a5 = new( 0xa5 ) Blanks;

    return a5 != 0;
}
```

The argument supplied in parentheses to **new** is passed to Blanks::operator new as the chInit argument. However, the global **operator new** function is hidden, causing code such as the following to generate an error:

```
Blanks *SomeBlanks = new Blanks;
```

For previous versions of the compiler, nonclass types and all arrays (regardless of whether they were of **class** type) allocated using the **new** operator always used the global **operator new** function.

Beginning with Visual C++ 5.0, the compiler supports member array **new** and **delete** operators in a class declaration. For example:

```
class X {
public:
   void* operator new[] (size_t);
   void     operator delete[] (void*);
};

void f() {
   X *pX = new X[5];
   delete [] pX;
}
```

Handling Insufficient Memory Conditions

Testing for failed memory allocation can be done with code such as the following:

```
int *pi = new int[BIG_NUMBER];

if( pi == 0 )
{
   cerr << "Insufficient memory" << endl;
   return -1;
}
```

There are two other ways to handle failed memory allocation requests: write a custom recovery routine to handle such a failure, then register your function by calling the **_set_new_handler** run-time function, or force **operator new** to throw a C++ exception of type **xalloc** (as described in the current ANSI C++ working paper proposal). These methods are described in the following sections.

Using _set_new_handler

In some circumstances, corrective action can be taken during memory allocation and the request can be fulfilled. To gain control when the global **operator new** function fails, use the **_set_new_handler** function (defined in NEW.H) as follows:

```
#include <stdio.h>
#include <new.h>

// Define a function to be called if new fails to allocate memory.
int MyNewHandler( size_t size )
{
   clog << "Allocation failed. Coalescing heap." << endl;

   // Call a fictitious function to recover some heap space.
   return CoalesceHeap();
}

void main()
{
   // Set the failure handler for new to be MyNewHandler.
   _set_new_handler( MyNewHandler );

   int *pi = new int[BIG_NUMBER];
}
```

In the preceding example, the first statement in **main** sets the new handler to
`MyNewHandler`. The second statement tries to allocate a large block of memory using
the **new** operator. When the allocation fails, control is transferred to `MyNewHandler`.
The argument passed to `MyNewHandler` is the number of bytes requested. The value
returned from `MyNewHandler` is a flag indicating whether allocation should be
retried: a nonzero value indicates that allocation should be retried, and a zero value
indicates that allocation has failed.

`MyNewHandler` prints a warning message and takes corrective action. If
`MyNewHandler` returns a nonzero value, the **new** operator retries the allocation.
When `MyNewHandler` returns a 0 the **new** operator stops trying and returns a zero
value to the program.

The **_set_new_handler** function returns the address of the previous new handler.
Therefore, if a new handler needs to be installed for a short time, the previous new
handler can be reinstalled using code such as the following:

```
#include <new.h>

. . .

_PNH old_handler = _set_new_handler( MyNewHandler );
// Code that requires MyNewHandler.
. . .

// Reinstall previous new handler.
_set_new_handler( old_handler );
```

A call to **_set_new_handler** with an argument of 0 causes the new handler to be
removed. There is no default new handler.

The new handler you specify can have any name, but it must be a function returning
type **int** (nonzero indicates the new handler succeeded, and zero indicates that it
failed).

If a user-defined **operator new** is provided, the new handler functions are not
automatically called on failure.

The prototype for **_set_new_handler** and the type **_PNH** is defined in NEW.H:

```
_PNH _set_new_handler( _PNH );
```

The type **_PNH** is a pointer to a function that returns type **int** and takes a single
argument of type **size_t**.

C++ xalloc Exceptions

Microsoft C++ implements an alternate method of handling **new** memory allocation
failure, based on the current ANSI C++ working paper proposal. Using this method,
a new run-time function, **_standard_new_handler**, throws a C++ exception of type
xalloc in the event of a **new** allocation failure. **xalloc** exceptions are based on the
exception class hierarchy defined in STDEXCPT.H.

Using xalloc

If the **new** operator fails to allocate memory for any reason, you can choose to have
your program throw an **xalloc** exception object.

To facilitate using the exception classes, a new run-time function has been added.
The **_standard_new_handler** function, declared in STDEXCPT.H, is prototyped as
follows:

```
int _standard_new_handler( size_t );
```

If you want **new** to throw an **xalloc** exception in the event of a memory allocation
failure, compile with the /GX option (Enable Exception Handling), and in your code,
call **_set_new_handler** with **_standard_new_handler** as its argument. You can then
use **try/catch** exception handling constructs to detect and handle **xalloc** exceptions.
In addition, you must copy the STDEXCPT.H header file and associated .CXX
implementation files to your project subdirectory. Be sure to include STDEXCPT.H
in your code, and add the .CXX files in that subdirectory to your own project.

The **_standard_new_handler** function creates a local static object of the **xalloc** class,
which in turn calls the **raise** member function; thereby throwing an **xalloc** exception.
Note that **_standard_new_handler** does not allocate memory from the free store
(it does not call **new** or **malloc**); thus, it will not recurse.

If you are programming in C++ using the Microsoft Foundation Classes, note that
MFC installs its own **new** exception handler that throws an exception of type
CMemoryException. This will override the **xalloc** exception behavior described
above.

Exception Class Hierarchy

The **xalloc** class defines the type of objects thrown as exceptions to report a failure to
allocate memory. This class, defined in STDEXCPT.H, is part of the **exception** class
hierarchy. This class hierarchy is provided as a general framework for exception
classes.

The base class for the exception object hierarchy is **exception**, defined in
STDEXCPT.H. Note that the name **xmsg** is defined as a synonym for **exception**. If
your code adheres to older working paper standards, the compiler will not generate
an error if you use **xmsg** instead of **exception**. The hierarchy is as follows:

```
class exception
{
    ...
}
    class logic: public exception
    {
        // Defines type of objects thrown as exceptions to
        // report logic errors, such as violated preconditions
        ...
    };
```

```
class  domain: public logic
{
    // Base class for objects thrown as exceptions in
    // response to domain errors
    ...
};
class runtime: public exception
{
    // Base class for objects thrown as exceptions in
    // response to runtime errors
    ...
};
    class range: public runtime
    {
        // Base class for objects thrown as exceptions in
        // response to range errors
        ...
    };
    class alloc: public runtime
    {
        // Base class for objects thrown as exceptions to
        // report memory allocation failure
        ...
    };
        class xalloc: public alloc
        {
            ...
        };
```

Note Because the **xalloc** exception specification in the ANSI working paper proposal is not finalized, Microsoft does not guarantee the same implementation of the **exception** class hierarchy in future releases.

The operator delete Function

Memory that is dynamically allocated using the **new** operator can be freed using the **delete** operator. The delete operator calls the **operator delete** function, which frees memory back to the available pool. Using the **delete** operator also causes the class destructor (if there is one) to be called.

There are global and class-scoped **operator delete** functions. Only one **operator delete** function can be defined for a given class; if defined, it hides the global **operator delete** function. The global **operator delete** function is always called for arrays of any type.

The global **operator delete** function, if declared, takes a single argument of type **void ***, which contains a pointer to the object to deallocate. The return type is **void** (**operator delete** cannot return a value). Two forms exist for class-member **operator delete** functions:

```
void operator delete( void * );
void operator delete( void *, size_t );
```

Only one of the preceding two variants can be present for a given class. The first form works as described for global **operator delete**. The second form takes two arguments, the first of which is a pointer to the memory block to deallocate and the second of which is the number of bytes to deallocate. The second form is particularly useful when an **operator delete** function from a base class is used to delete an object of a derived class.

The **operator delete** function is static; therefore, it cannot be virtual. The **operator delete** function obeys access control, as described in Chapter 10, "Member-Access Control."

The following example shows user-defined **operator new** and **operator delete** functions designed to log allocations and deallocations of memory:

```
#include <iostream.h>
#include <stdlib.h>

int fLogMemory = 0;          // Perform logging (0=no; nonzero=yes)?
int cBlocksAllocated = 0;    // Count of blocks allocated.
// User-defined operator new.
void *operator new( size_t stAllocateBlock )
{
    static fInOpNew = 0;      // Guard flag.

    if( fLogMemory && !fInOpNew )
    {
        fInOpNew = 1;
        clog << "Memory block "   << ++cBlocksAllocated
             << " allocated for " << stAllocateBlock
             << " bytes\n";
        fInOpNew = 0;
    }

    return malloc( stAllocateBlock );
}
// User-defined operator delete.
void operator delete( void *pvMem )
{
    static fInOpDelete = 0;  // Guard flag.
    if( fLogMemory && !fInOpDelete )
    {
        fInOpDelete = 1;
        clog << "Memory block " << --cBlocksAllocated
             << " deallocated\n";
        fInOpDelete = 0;
    }

    free( pvMem );
}

int main( int argc, char *argv[] )
{
    fLogMemory = 1;  // Turn logging on.
```

```
        if( argc > 1 )
        for( int i = 0; i < atoi( argv[1] ); ++i )
        {
            char *pMem = new char[10];
            delete[] pMem;
        }

        return cBlocksAllocated;
}
```

The preceding code can be used to detect "memory leakage"—that is, memory that is allocated on the free store but never freed. To perform this detection, the global **new** and **delete** operators are redefined to count allocation and deallocation of memory.

Beginning with Visual C++ 5.0, the compiler supports member array **new** and **delete** operators in a class declaration. For example:

```
class X {
public:
    void* operator new[] (size_t);
    void    operator delete[] (void*);
};

void f() {
    X *pX = new X[5];
    delete [] pX;
}
```

Initialization Using Special Member Functions

This section describes initialization using special member functions. It expands on the following discussions of initialization:

- "Initializing Aggregates" on page 224 in Chapter 7, which describes how to initialize arrays of nonclass types and objects of simple class types. These simple class types cannot have private or protected members, and they cannot have base classes.

- Constructors, which explains how to initialize class-type objects using special constructor functions.

The default method of initialization is to perform a bit-for-bit copy from the initializer into the object to be initialized. This technique is applicable only to:

- Objects of built-in types. For example:

  ```
  int i = 100;
  ```

- Pointers. For example:

  ```
  int i;
  int *pi = &i;
  ```

- References. For example:

```
String sFileName( "FILE.DAT" );
String &rs = sFileName;
```

- Objects of class type, where the class has no private or protected members, no virtual functions, and no base classes. For example:

```
struct Point
{
    int x, y;
};

Point pt = { 10, 20 };   // Static storage class only
```

Classes can specify more refined initialization by defining constructor functions. (For more information about declaring such functions, see "Constructors" on page 292.) If an object is of a class type that has a constructor, the object must be initialized, or there must be a default constructor. Objects that are not specifically initialized invoke the class's default constructor.

Explicit Initialization

C++ supports two forms of explicit initialization.

- Supplying an initializer list in parentheses:

```
String sFileName( "FILE.DAT" );
```

The items in the parenthesized list are considered arguments to the class constructor. This form of initialization enables initialization of an object with more than one value and can also be used in conjunction with the **new** operator. For example:

```
Rect *pRect = new Rect( 10, 15, 24, 97 );
```

- Supplying a single initializer using the equal-sign initialization syntax. For example:

```
String sFileName = "FILE.DAT";
```

Although the preceding example works the same way as the example shown for String in the first list item, the syntax is not adaptable to use with objects allocated on the free store.

The single expression on the right of the equal sign is taken as the argument to the class's copy constructor; therefore, it must be a type that can be converted to the class type.

Note that because the equal sign (=) in the context of initialization is different from an assignment operator, overloading **operator=** has no effect on initialization.

The equal-sign initialization syntax is different from the function-style syntax, even though the generated code is identical in most cases. The difference is that when the equal-sign syntax is used, the compiler has to behave as if the following sequence of events were taking place:

- Creating a temporary object of the same type as the object being initialized.

- Copying the temporary object to the object.

The constructor must be accessible before the compiler can perform these steps. Even though the compiler can eliminate the temporary creation and copy steps in most cases, an inaccessible copy constructor causes equal-sign initialization to fail. Consider the following example:

```
class anInt
{
    anInt( const anInt& );      //  Private copy constructor.
public:
    anInt( int );               //  Public int constructor.
};
...
anInt myInt = 7;                //  Access-control violation. Attempt to
                                //   reference private copy constructor.
anInt myInt( 7 );               //  Correct; no copy constructor called.
```

When a function is called, class-type arguments passed by value and objects returned by value are conceptually initialized using the form:

type-name name = *value*

For example:

```
String s = "C++";
```

Therefore, it follows that the argument type must be a type that can be converted to the class type being passed as an argument. The class's copy constructor, as well as user-defined conversion operators or constructors that accept the type of the actual argument, must be public.

In expressions that use the **new** operator, the objects allocated on the free store are conceptually initialized using the form:

type-name name(*initializer*$_1$, *initializer*$_2$, ... *initializer*$_n$)

For example:

```
String *ps = new String( "C++" );
```

Initializers for base-class components and member objects of a class are also conceptually initialized this way. (For more information, see "Initializing Bases and Members" on page 317.)

Initializing Arrays

If a class has a constructor, arrays of that class are initialized by a constructor. If there are fewer items in the initializer list than elements in the array, the default constructor is used for the remaining elements. If no default constructor is defined for the class, the initializer list must be complete—that is, there must be one initializer for each element in the array.

Consider the `Point` class that defines two constructors:

```
class Point
{
public:
    Point();            // Default constructor.
    Point( int, int ); // Construct from two ints.
    ...
};
```

An array of `Point` objects can be declared as follows:

```
Point aPoint[3] = {
    Point( 3, 3 )       // Use int, int constructor.
};
```

The first element of `aPoint` is constructed using the constructor `Point( int, int )`; the remaining two elements are constructed using the default constructor.

Static member arrays (whether **const** or not) can be initialized in their definitions (outside the class declaration). For example:

```
class WindowColors
{
public:
    static const char *rgszWindowPartList[7];
    ...
};
const char *WindowColors::rgszWindowPartList[7] = {
    "Active Title Bar", "Inactive Title Bar", "Title Bar Text",
    "Menu Bar", "Menu Bar Text", "Window Background", "Frame"   };
```

Initializing Static Objects

Global static objects are initialized in the order they occur in the source. They are destroyed in the reverse order. Across translation units, however, the order of initialization is dependent on how the object files are arranged by the linker; the order of destruction still takes place in the reverse of that in which objects were constructed.

Local static objects are initialized when they are first encountered in the program flow, and they are destroyed in the reverse order at program termination. Destruction of local static objects occurs only if the object was encountered and initialized in the program flow.

Initializing Bases and Members

An object of a derived class is made up of a component that represents each base class and a component that is unique to the particular class. Objects of classes that have member objects may also contain instances of other classes. This section describes how these component objects are initialized when an object of the class type is created.

To perform the initialization, the constructor-initializer, or *ctor-initializer*, syntax is used.

Syntax

ctor-initializer:
    mem-initializer-list
mem-initializer-list:
    mem-initializer
    mem-initializer **,** *mem-initializer-list*
mem-initializer:
    complete-class-name **(** *expression-list*$_{opt}$ **)**
    identifier **(** *expression-list*$_{opt}$ **)**

This syntax, used in constructors, is described more fully in the next section, "Initializing Member Objects," and in "Initializing Base Classes" on page 319.

Initializing Member Objects

Classes can contain member objects of class type, but to ensure that initialization requirements for the member objects are met, one of the following conditions must be met:

- The contained object's class requires no constructor.

- The contained object's class has an accessible default constructor.

- The containing class's constructors all explicitly initialize the contained object.

The following example shows how to perform such an initialization:

```
// Declare a class Point.
class Point
{
public:
    Point( int x, int y ) { _x = x; _y = y; }
private:
    int _x, _y;
};

// Declare a rectangle class that contains objects of type Point.
class Rect
{
public:
    Rect( int x1, int y1, int x2, int y2 );
private:
    Point _topleft, _bottomright;
};

//  Define the constructor for class Rect. This constructor
//   explicitly initializes the objects of type Point.
Rect::Rect( int x1, int y1, int x2, int y2 ) :
_topleft( x1, y1 ), _bottomright( x2, y2 )
{
}
```

The Rect class, shown in the preceding example, contains two member objects of class Point. Its constructor explicitly initializes the objects _topleft and _bottomright. Note that a colon follows the closing parenthesis of the constructor (in the definition). The colon is followed by the member names and arguments with which to initialize the objects of type Point.

Warning The order in which the member initializers are specified in the constructor does not affect the order in which the members are constructed; the members are constructed in the order in which they are declared in the class.

Reference and **const** member objects must be initialized using the member initialization syntax shown in Syntax in "Initializing Bases and Members" on page 317. There is no other way to initialize these objects.

Initializing Base Classes

Direct base classes are initialized in much the same way as member objects. Consider the following example:

```
//  Declare class Window.
class Window
{
public:
   Window( Rect rSize );
   ...
};

//  Declare class DialogBox, derived from class Window.
class DialogBox : public Window
{
public:
   DialogBox( Rect rSize );
   ...
};

//  Define the constructor for DialogBox. This constructor
//   explicitly initializes the Window subobject.
DialogBox::DialogBox( Rect rSize ) : Window( rSize )
{
}
```

Note that in the constructor for DialogBox, the Window base class is initialized using the argument rSize. This initialization consists of the name of the base class to initialize, followed by a parenthesized list of arguments to the class's constructor.

In initialization of base classes, the object that is not the subobject representing a base class's component is considered a "complete object." The complete object's class is considered the "most derived" class for the object.

The subobjects representing virtual base classes are initialized by the constructor for the most derived class. That means that where virtual derivation is specified, the most derived class must explicitly initialize the virtual base class, or the virtual base class must have a default constructor. Initializations for virtual base classes that appear in constructors for classes other than the most derived class are ignored.

Although initialization of base classes is usually restricted to direct base classes, a class constructor can initialize an indirect virtual base class.

Initialization Order of Bases and Members

Base classes and member objects are initialized in the following order:

1. Virtual base classes are initialized in the order in which they appear in the directed acyclic graph. For information about using the directed acyclic graph to construct a list of unique subobjects, see "Virtual Base Classes" on page 265 in Chapter 9. (Note that these subobjects are destroyed by walking the same list in reverse.) For more information about how the directed acyclic graph is traversed, see "Order of Destruction" on page 299.

2. Nonvirtual base classes are initialized in the order in which they are declared in the class declaration.

3. Member objects are initialized in the order in which the objects are declared in the class.

The order in which base classes and member objects are initialized is not affected by the order in which the member initializers or base-class initializers appear in the *member-initializer-list* of the constructor.

Scope of Initializers

Initializers for base classes and member objects are evaluated in the scope of the constructor with which they are declared. Therefore, they can refer implicitly to class-member data.

Copying Class Objects

Two operations cause objects to be copied:

- Assignment. When one object's value is assigned to another object, the first object is copied to the second object. Therefore:

```
Point a, b;
...
a = b;
```

causes the value of b to be copied to a.

- Initialization. Initialization occurs at the point of declaration of a new object, when arguments are passed to functions by value, and when values are returned from functions by value.

The programmer can define the semantics of "copy" for objects of class type. For example, consider the following code:

```
TextFile a, b;
a.Open( "FILE1.DAT" );
b.Open( "FILE2.DAT" );
b = a;
```

The preceding code could mean "copy the contents of FILE1.DAT to FILE2.DAT," or it could mean "ignore FILE2.DAT and make b a second handle to FILE1.DAT." The programmer is responsible for attaching appropriate copying semantics to each class.

Copying is done in one of two ways:

• Assignment (using the assignment operator, **operator=**).

• Initialization (using the copy constructor). (For more information about the copy constructor, see "Rules for Declaring Constructors" on page 293.)

Any given class can implement one or both copy methods. If neither method is implemented, assignment is handled as a member-by-member ("memberwise") assignment, and initialization is handled as a member-by-member initialization. Memberwise assignment is covered in more detail in "Memberwise Assignment and Initialization" on page 322.

The copy constructor takes a single argument of type *class-name***&**, where *class-name* is the name of the class for which the constructor is defined. For example:

```
class Window
{
public:
    Window( const Window& ); // Declare copy constructor.
    ...
};
```

Note   The type of the copy constructor's argument should be *const class-name*& whenever possible. This prevents the copy constructor from accidentally changing the object from which it is copying. It also allows copying from **const** objects.

Compiler-Generated Copying

Compiler-generated copy constructors, like user-defined copy constructors, have a single argument of type "reference to *class-name*." An exception is when all base classes and member classes have copy constructors declared as taking a single argument of type **const** *class-name***&**. In such a case, the compiler-generated copy constructor's argument is also **const**.

When the argument type to the copy constructor is not **const**, initialization by copying a **const** object generates an error. The reverse is not true: If the argument is **const**, initialization by copying an object that is not **const**.

Compiler-generated assignment operators follow the same pattern with regard to **const.** They take a single argument of type *class-name***&** unless the assignment operators in all base and member classes take arguments of type **const** *class-name***&**. In this case, the class's generated assignment operator takes a **const** argument.

Note When virtual base classes are initialized by copy constructors, compiler-generated or user-defined, they are initialized only once: at the point when they are constructed.

The implications are similar to those of the copy constructor. When the argument type is not **const**, assignment from a **const** object generates an error. The reverse is not true: If a **const** value is assigned to a value that is not **const**, the assignment succeeds.

For more information about overloaded assignment operators, see "Assignment" on page 344 in Chapter 12.

Memberwise Assignment and Initialization

The methods for default assignment and initialization are "memberwise assignment" and "memberwise initialization," respectively. Memberwise assignment consists of copying one object to the other, a member at a time, as if assigning each member individually. Memberwise initialization consists of copying one object to the other, a member at a time, as if initializing each member individually. The primary difference between the two is that memberwise assignment invokes each member's assignment operator (**operator=**), whereas memberwise initialization invokes each member's copy constructor.

Memberwise assignment is performed only by the assignment operator declared in the form:

*type***&** *type* **:: operator=(** [**const** | **volatile**] *type***&)**

Default assignment operators for memberwise assignment cannot be generated if any of the following conditions exist:

- A member class has **const** members.
- A member class has reference members.
- A member class or its base class has a private assignment operator (**operator=**).
- A base class or member class has no assignment operator (**operator=**).

Default copy constructors for memberwise initialization cannot be generated if the class or one of its base classes has a private copy constructor or if any of the following conditions exist:

- A member class has **const** members.
- A member class has reference members.
- A member class or its base class has a private copy constructor.
- A base class or member class has no copy constructor.

The default assignment operators and copy constructors for a given class are always declared, but they are not defined unless both of the following conditions are met:

- The class does not provide a user-defined function for this copy.
- The program requires that the function be present. This requirement exists if an assignment or initialization is encountered that requires memberwise copying or if the address of the class's **operator=** function is taken.

If both of these conditions are not met, the compiler is not required to generate code for the default assignment operator and copy constructor functions (elimination of such code is an optimization performed by the Microsoft C++ compiler). Specifically, if the class declares a user-defined **operator=** that takes an argument of type "reference to *class-name*," no default assignment operator is generated. If the class declares a copy constructor, no default copy constructor is generated.

Therefore, for a given class A, the following declarations are always present:

```
//  Implicit declarations of copy constructor
//   and assignment operator.
A::A( const A& );
A& A::operator=( const A& );
```

The definitions are supplied only if required (according to the preceding criteria). The copy constructor functions shown in the preceding example are considered public member functions of the class.

Default assignment operators allow objects of a given class to be assigned to objects of a public base-class type. Consider the following code:

```
class Account
{
public:
   // Public member functions
   ...
private:
   double _balance;
};

class Checking : public Account
{
private:
   int _fOverdraftProtect;
};

...
```

```
Account account;
Checking checking;

account = checking;
```

In the preceding example, the assignment operator chosen is `Account::operator=`. Because the default `operator=` function takes an argument of type `Account&` (reference to `Account`), the `Account` subobject of `checking` is copied to `account`; `fOverdraftProtect` is not copied.

Overloading

This chapter explains how to use C++ overloaded functions and overloaded operators. The following topics are included:

- Overview
- Declaration matching
- Argument matching
- Address of overloaded functions
- Overloaded operators

Overview of Overloading

With the C++ language, you can overload functions and operators. Overloading is the practice of supplying more than one definition for a given function name in the same scope. The compiler is left to pick the appropriate version of the function or operator based on the arguments with which it is called. For example:

```
double max( double d1, double d2 )
{
    return ( d1 > d2 ) ? d1 : d2;
}

int max( int i1, int i2 )
{
    return ( i1 > i2 ) ? i1 : i2;
}
```

The function max is considered an overloaded function. It can be used in code such as the following:

```
main()
{
    int    i = max( 12, 8 );
    double d = max( 32.9, 17.4 );

    return i + (int)d;
}
```

In the first case, where the maximum value of two variables of type `int` is being requested, the function `max( int, int )` is called. However, in the second case, the arguments are of type `double`, so the function `max( double, double )` is called.

Argument Type Differences

Overloaded functions differentiate between argument types that take different initializers. Therefore, an argument of a given type and a reference to that type are considered the same for the purposes of overloading. They are considered the same because they take the same initializers. For example, `max( double, double )` is considered the same as `max( double &, double & )`. Declaring two such functions causes an error.

For the same reason, function arguments of a type modified by **const** or **volatile** are not treated differently than the base type for the purposes of overloading.

However, the function overloading mechanism can distinguish between references that are qualified by **const** and **volatile** and references to the base type. This makes code such as the following possible:

```
#include <iostream.h>

class Over
{
public:
    Over() { cout << "Over default constructor\n"; }
    Over( Over &o ) { cout << "Over&\n"; }
    Over( const Over &co ) { cout << "const Over&\n"; }
    Over( volatile Over &vo ) { cout << "volatile Over&\n"; }
};

void main()
{
    Over o1;             // Calls default constructor.
    Over o2( o1 );       // Calls Over( Over& ).
    const Over o3;       // Calls default constructor.
    Over o4( o3 );       // Calls Over( const Over& ).
    volatile Over o5;    // Calls default constructor.
    Over o6( o5 );       // Calls Over( volatile Over& ).
}
```

Pointers to **const** and **volatile** objects are also considered different from pointers to the base type for the purposes of overloading.

Restrictions on Overloaded Functions

Several restrictions govern an acceptable set of overloaded functions:

- Any two functions in a set of overloaded functions must have different argument lists.

- Overloading functions with argument lists of the same types, based on return type alone, is an error.

Microsoft Specific →

You can overload **operator new** solely on the basis of return type—specifically, on the basis of the memory-model modifier specified.

END Microsoft Specific

- Member functions cannot be overloaded solely on the basis of one being static and the other nonstatic.

- **typedef** declarations do not define new types; they introduce synonyms for existing types. They do not affect the overloading mechanism. Consider the following code:

```
typedef char * PSTR;

void Print( char *szToPrint );
void Print( PSTR szToPrint );
```

The preceding two functions have identical argument lists. PSTR is a synonym for type **char ***. In member scope, this code generates an error.

- Enumerated types are distinct types and can be used to distinguish between overloaded functions.

- The types "array of" and "pointer to" are considered identical for the purposes of distinguishing between overloaded functions. This is true only for singly dimensioned arrays. Therefore, the following overloaded functions conflict and generate an error message:

```
void Print( char *szToPrint );
void Print( char szToPrint[] );
```

For multiply dimensioned arrays, the second and all succeeding dimensions are considered part of the type. Therefore, they are used in distinguishing between overloaded functions:

```
void Print( char szToPrint[] );
void Print( char szToPrint[][7] );
void Print( char szToPrint[][9][42] );
```

Declaration Matching

Any two function declarations of the same name in the same scope can refer to the same function, or to two discrete functions that are overloaded. If the argument lists of the declarations contain arguments of equivalent types (as described in the previous section), the function declarations refer to the same function. Otherwise, they refer to two different functions that are selected using overloading.

Class scope is strictly observed; therefore, a function declared in a base class is not in the same scope as a function declared in a derived class. If a function in a derived class is declared with the same name as a function in the base class, the derived-class function hides the base-class function instead of causing overloading.

Block scope is strictly observed; therefore, a function declared in file scope is not in the same scope as a function declared locally. If a locally declared function has the same name as a function declared in file scope, the locally declared function hides the file-scoped function instead of causing overloading. For example:

```
#include <iostream.h>

void func( int i )
{
    cout << "Called file-scoped func : " << i << endl;
}

void func( char *sz )
{
    cout << "Called locally declared func : " << sz << endl;
}

void main()
{
    // Declare func local to main.
    extern void func( char *sz );

    func( 3 );      // Error. func( int ) is hidden.
    func( "s" );
}
```

The preceding code shows two definitions from the function func. The definition that takes an argument of type char * is local to main because of the extern statement. Therefore, the definition that takes an argument of type int is hidden, and the first call to func is in error.

For overloaded member functions, different versions of the function can be given different access privileges. They are still considered to be in the scope of the enclosing class and thus are overloaded functions. Consider the following code, in which the member function Deposit is overloaded; one version is public, the other, private:

```
class Account
{
public:
    Account();
    double Deposit( double dAmount, char *szPassword );
private:
    double Deposit( double dAmount );
    int    Validate( char *szPassword );
};
```

The intent of the preceding code is to provide an Account class in which a correct password is required to perform deposits. This is accomplished using overloading. The following code shows how this class can be used and also shows an erroneous call to the private member, Deposit:

```
void main()
{
   // Allocate a new object of type Account.
   Account *pAcct = new Account;

   // Deposit $57.22. Error: calls a private function.
   pAcct->Deposit( 57.22 );

   // Deposit $57.22 and supply a password. OK: calls a
   //  public function.
   pAcct->Deposit( 52.77, "pswd" );
}

double Account::Deposit( double dAmount, char *szPassword )
{
   if( Validate( szPassword ) )
      return Deposit( dAmount );
   else
      return 0.0;
}
```

Note that the call to Deposit in Account::Deposit calls the private member
function. This call is correct because Account::Deposit is a member function and
therefore has access to the private members of the class.

Argument Matching

Overloaded functions are selected for the best match of function declarations in the
current scope to the arguments supplied in the function call. If a suitable function is
found, that function is called. "Suitable" in this context means one of the following:

- An exact match was found.
- A trivial conversion was performed.
- An integral promotion was performed.
- A standard conversion to the desired argument type exists.
- A user-defined conversion (either conversion operator or constructor) to the
  desired argument type exists.
- Arguments represented by an ellipsis were found.

The compiler creates a set of candidate functions for each argument. Candidate
functions are functions in which the actual argument in that position can be converted
to the type of the formal argument.

A set of "best matching functions" is built for each argument, and the selected
function is the intersection of all the sets. If the intersection contains more than one
function, the overloading is ambiguous and generates an error. The function that is
eventually selected is always a better match than every other function in the group for

at least one argument. If this is not the case (if there is no clear winner), the function call generates an error.

Consider the following declarations (the functions are marked Variant 1, Variant 2, and Variant 3, for identification in the following discussion):

```
Fraction &Add( Fraction &f, long 1 );       // Variant 1
Fraction &Add( long 1, Fraction &f );       // Variant 2
Fraction &Add( Fraction &f, Fraction &f );  // Variant 3

Fraction F1, F2;
```

Consider the following statement:

```
F1 = Add( F2, 23 );
```

The preceding statement builds two sets:

Set 1: Candidate Functions That Have First Argument of Type Fraction	Set 2: Candidate Functions Whose Second Argument Can Be Converted to Type int
Variant 1	Variant 1 (**int** can be converted to **long** using a standard conversion)
Variant 3	

Functions in Set 2 are functions for which there are implicit conversions from actual parameter type to formal parameter type, and among such functions there is a function for which the "cost" of converting the actual parameter type to its formal parameter type is the smallest.

The intersection of these two sets is Variant 1. An example of an ambiguous function call is:

```
F1 = Add( 3, 6 );
```

The preceding function call builds the following sets:

Set 1: Candidate Functions That Have First Argument of Type int	Set 2: Candidate Functions That Have Second Argument of Type int
Variant 2 (**int** can be converted to **long** using a standard conversion)	Variant 1 (**int** can be converted to **long** using a standard conversion)

Note that the intersection between these two sets is empty. Therefore, the compiler generates an error message.

For argument matching, a function with n default arguments is treated as $n+1$ separate functions, each with a different number of arguments.

The ellipsis (...) acts as a wildcard; it matches any actual argument. This can lead to many ambiguous sets, if you do not design your overloaded function sets with extreme care.

Note   Ambiguity of overloaded functions cannot be determined until a function call is encountered. At that point, the sets are built for each argument in the function call, and you can determine whether an unambiguous overload exists. This means that ambiguities can remain in your code until they are evoked by a particular function call.

Argument Matching and the this Pointer

Class member functions are treated differently, depending on whether they are declared as **static**. Because nonstatic functions have an implicit argument that supplies the **this** pointer, nonstatic functions are considered to have one more argument than static functions; otherwise, they are declared identically.

These nonstatic member functions require that the implied **this** pointer match the object type through which the function is being called, or, for overloaded operators, they require that the first argument match the object on which the operator is being applied. (For more information about overloaded operators, see "Overloaded Operators" on page 336.)

Unlike other arguments in overloaded functions, no temporary objects are introduced and no conversions are attempted when trying to match the **this** pointer argument.

When the **–>** member-selection operator is used to access a member function, the **this** pointer argument has a type of *class-name* *** const**. If the members are declared as **const** or **volatile**, the types are **const** *class-name* *** const** and **volatile** *class-name* *** const**, respectively.

The **.** member-selection operator works exactly the same way, except that an implicit **&** (address-of) operator is prefixed to the object name. The following example shows how this works:

```
// Expression encountered in code
obj.name

// How the compiler treats it
(&obj)->name
```

The left operand of the **–>*** and **.*** (pointer to member) operators are treated the same way as the **.** and **–>** (member-selection) operators with respect to argument matching.

Argument Matching and Conversions

When the compiler tries to match actual arguments against the arguments in function declarations, it can supply standard or user-defined conversions to obtain the correct type if no exact match can be found. The application of conversions is subject to these rules:

- Sequences of conversions that contain more than one user-defined conversion are not considered.

- Sequences of conversions that can be shortened by removing intermediate conversions are not considered.

The resultant sequence of conversions, if any, is called the best matching sequence. There are several ways to convert an object of type **int** to type **unsigned long** using standard conversions (described in Chapter 3, "Standard Conversions"):

- Convert from **int** to **long** and then from **long** to **unsigned long**.

- Convert from **int** to **unsigned long**.

The first sequence, although it achieves the desired goal, is not the best matching sequence—a shorter sequence exists.

Table 12.1 shows a group of conversions, called trivial conversions, that have a limited effect on determining of which sequence is the best matching. The instances in which trivial conversions affect choice of sequence are discussed in the list following the table.

Table 12.1 Trivial Conversions

Convert from Type	Convert to Type
type-name	*type-name*&
type-name&	*type-name*
type-name[ ]	*type-name**
type-name(*argument-list*)	(**type-name*) (*argument-list*)
type-name	**const** *type-name*
type-name	**volatile** *type-name*
*type-name**	**const** *type-name**
*type-name**	**volatile** *type-name**

The sequence in which conversions are attempted is as follows:

1. Exact match. An exact match between the types with which the function is called and the types declared in the function prototype is always the best match. Sequences of trivial conversions are classified as exact matches. However, sequences that do not make any of these conversions are considered better than sequences that convert:

   - From pointer, to pointer to **const** (*type* * to **const** *type* *).
   - From pointer, to pointer to **volatile** (*type* * to **volatile** *type* *).
   - From reference, to reference to **const** (*type* & to **const** *type* &).
   - From reference, to reference to **volatile** (*type* & to **volatile** *type* &).

2. Match using promotions. Any sequence not classified as an exact match that contains only integral promotions, conversions from **float** to **double**, and trivial conversions is classified as a match using promotions. Although not as good a match as any exact match, a match using promotions is better than a match using standard conversions.

3. Match using standard conversions. Any sequence not classified as an exact match or a match using promotions that contains only standard conversions and trivial conversions is classified as a match using standard conversions. Within this category, the following rules are applied:

- Conversion from a pointer to a derived class, to a pointer to a direct or indirect base class is preferable to converting to **void *** or **const void ***.

- Conversion from a pointer to a derived class, to a pointer to a base class produces a better match the closer the base class is to a direct base class. Suppose the class hierarchy is as shown in Figure 12.1.

Figure 12.1   Graph Illustrating Preferred Conversions

Conversion from type D* to type C* is preferable to conversion from type D* to type B*. Similarly, conversion from type D* to type B* is preferable to conversion from type D* to type A*.

This same rule applies to reference conversions. Conversion from type D& to type C& is preferable to conversion from type D& to type B&, and so on.

This same rule applies to pointer-to-member conversions. Conversion from type T D::* to type T C::* is preferable to conversion from type T D::* to type T B::*, and so on (where T is the type of the member).

The preceding rule applies only along a given path of derivation. Consider the graph shown in Figure 12.2.

Figure 12.2   Multiple-Inheritance Graph Illustrating Preferred Conversions

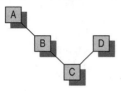

Conversion from type C* to type B* is preferable to conversion from type C* to type A*. The reason is that they are on the same path, and B* is closer. However, conversion from type C* to type D* is not preferable to conversion to type A*; there is no preference because the conversions follow different paths.

4. Match with user-defined conversions. This sequence cannot be classified as an exact match, a match using promotions, or a match using standard conversions. The sequence must contain only user-defined conversions, standard conversions, or trivial conversions to be classified as a match with user-defined conversions. A match with user-defined conversions is considered a better match than a match with an ellipsis but not as good a match as a match with standard conversions.

5. Match with an ellipsis. Any sequence that matches an ellipsis in the declaration is classified as a match with an ellipsis. This is considered the weakest match.

User-defined conversions are applied if no built-in promotion or conversion exists. These conversions are selected on the basis of the type of the argument being matched. Consider the following code:

```
class UDC
{
public:
   operator int();
   operator long();
};

void Print( int i );
...
UDC udc;
Print( udc );
```

The available user-defined conversions for class UDC are from type **int** and type **long**. Therefore, the compiler considers conversions for the type of the object being matched: UDC. A conversion to **int** exists, and it is selected.

During the process of matching arguments, standard conversions can be applied to both the argument and the result of a user-defined conversion. Therefore, the following code works:

```
void LogToFile( long l );
...
UDC udc;
LogToFile( udc );
```

In the preceding example, the user-defined conversion, **operator long**, is invoked to convert udc to type **long**. If no user-defined conversion to type **long** had been defined, the conversion would have proceeded as follows: Type UDC would have been converted to type **int** using the user-defined conversion. Then the standard conversion from type **int** to type **long** would have been applied to match the argument in the declaration.

If any user-defined conversions are required to match an argument, the standard conversions are not used when evaluating the best match. This is true even if more than one candidate function requires a user-defined conversion; in such a case, the functions are considered equal. For example:

```
class UDC1
{
public:
    UDC1( int );  // User-defined conversion from int.
};

class UDC2
{
public:
    UDC2( long ); // User-defined conversion from long.
};

...

void Func( UDC1 );
void Func( UDC2 );

...

Func( 1 );
```

Both versions of Func require a user-defined conversion to convert type **int** to the class type argument. The possible conversions are:

- Convert from type **int** to type UDC1 (a user-defined conversion).

- Convert from type **int** to type **long**; then convert to type UDC2 (a two-step conversion).

Even though the second of these requires a standard conversion, as well as the user-defined conversion, the two conversions are still considered equal.

Note   User-defined conversions are considered conversion by construction or conversion by initialization (conversion function). Both methods are considered equal when considering the best match.

Address of Overloaded Functions

Use of a function name without arguments returns the address of that function. For example:

```
int Func( int i, int j );
int Func( long l );

...

int (*pFunc) ( int, int ) = Func;
```

In the preceding example, the first version of Func is selected, and its address is copied into pFunc.

The compiler determines which version of the function to select by finding a function with an argument list that exactly matches that of the target. The arguments in the overloaded function declarations are matched against one of the following:

- An object being initialized (as shown in the preceding example)
- The left side of an assignment statement
- A formal argument to a function
- A formal argument to a user-defined operator
- A function return type

If no exact match is found, the expression that takes the address of the function is ambiguous and an error is generated.

Note that although a nonmember function, Func, was used in the preceding example, the same rules are applied when taking the address of overloaded member functions.

Overloaded Operators

With C++, you can redefine the function of most built-in operators. These operators can be redefined, or "overloaded," globally or on a class-by-class basis. Overloaded operators are implemented as functions and can be class-member or global functions.

The name of an overloaded operator is **operator**x, where x is the operator as it appears in Table 12.2. For example, to overload the addition operator, you define a function called **operator+**. Similarly, to overload the addition/assignment operator, +=, define a function called **operator+=**.

Although these operators are usually called implicitly by the compiler when they are encountered in code, they can be invoked explicitly the same way as any member or nonmember function is called:

```
Point pt;

pt.operator+( 3 );   // Call addition operator to add 3 to pt.
```

Table 12.2   Redefinable Operators

Operator	Name	Type
,	Comma	Binary
!	Logical NOT	Unary
!=	Inequality	Binary
%	Modulus	Binary
%=	Modulus/assignment	Binary
&	Bitwise AND	Binary
&	Address-of	Unary
&&	Logical AND	Binary

Table 12.2 Redefinable Operators (continued)

Operator	Name	Type
&=	Bitwise AND/assignment	Binary
( )	Function call	—
*	Multiplication	Binary
*	Pointer dereference	Unary
*=	Multiplication/assignment	Binary
+	Addition	Binary
+	Unary Plus	Unary
++	Increment[1]	Unary
+=	Addition/assignment	Binary
–	Subtraction	Binary
–	Unary negation	Unary
– –	Decrement[1]	Unary
–=	Subtraction/assignment	Binary
–>	Member selection	Binary
–>*	Pointer-to-member selection	Binary
/	Division	Binary
/=	Division/assignment	Binary
<	Less than	Binary
<<	Left shift	Binary
<<=	Left shift/assignment	Binary
<=	Less than or equal to	Binary
=	Assignment	Binary
==	Equality	Binary
>	Greater than	Binary
>=	Greater than or equal to	Binary
>>	Right shift	Binary
>>=	Right shift/assignment	Binary
[ ]	Array subscript	—
^	Exclusive OR	Binary
^=	Exclusive OR/assignment	Binary
I	Bitwise inclusive OR	Binary
I=	Bitwise inclusive OR/assignment	Binary
II	Logical OR	Binary
~	One's complement	Unary

(continued)

Table 12.2 Redefinable Operators *(continued)*

Operator	Name	Type
delete	delete	—
new	new	—

[1] Two versions of the unary increment and decrement operators exist: preincrement and postincrement.

The constraints on the various categories of overloaded operators are described in "Unary Operators" on page 340, "Binary Operators" on page 343, "Assignment" on page 344, "Function Call"and "Subscripting" on page 345, "Class-Member Access" on page 347, and "Increment and Decrement" on page 340.

The operators shown in Table 12.3 cannot be overloaded.

Table 12.3 Nonredefinable Operators

Operator	Name
.	Member selection
.*	Pointer-to-member selection
::	Scope resolution
? :	Conditional
#	Preprocessor symbol
##	Preprocessor symbol

General Rules for Operator Overloading

The following rules constrain how overloaded operators are implemented. However, they do not apply to the **new** and **delete** operators, which are covered separately in Chapter 4.

- Operators must either be class member functions or take an argument that is of class or enumerated type or arguments that are references to class or enumerated types. For example:

```
class Point
{
public:
    Point operator<( Point & );  // Declare a member operator
                                 //  overload.
    ...
    // Declare addition operators.
    friend Point operator+( Point&, int );
    friend Point operator+( int, Point& );
};
```

The preceding code sample declares the less-than operator as a member function; however, the addition operators are declared as global functions that have friend access. Note that more than one implementation can be provided for a given operator. In the case of the preceding addition operator, the two implementations are provided to facilitate commutativity. It is just as likely that operators that add a `Point` to a `Point`, `int` to a `Point`, and so on, might be implemented.

- Operators obey the precedence, grouping, and number of operands dictated by their typical use with built-in types. Therefore, there is no way to express the concept "add 2 and 3 to an object of type `Point`," expecting 2 to be added to the x coordinate and 3 to be added to the y coordinate.

- Unary operators declared as member functions take no arguments; if declared as global functions, they take one argument.

- Binary operators declared as member functions take one argument; if declared as global functions, they take two arguments.

- Overloaded operators cannot have default arguments.

- All overloaded operators except assignment (**operator=**) are inherited by derived classes.

- The first argument for member-function overloaded operators is always of the class type of the object for which the operator is invoked (the class in which the operator is declared, or a class derived from that class). No conversions are supplied for the first argument.

Note that the meaning of any of the operators can be changed completely. That includes the meaning of the address-of (**&**), assignment (**=**), and function-call operators. Also, identities that can be relied upon for built-in types can be changed using operator overloading. For example, the following four statements are usually equivalent when completely evaluated:

```
var = var + 1;
var += 1;
var++;
++var;
```

This identity cannot be relied upon for class types that overload operators. Moreover, some of the requirements implicit in the use of these operators for basic types are relaxed for overloaded operators. For example, the addition/assignment operator, **+=**, requires the left operand to be an l-value when applied to basic types; there is no such requirement when the operator is overloaded.

Note For consistency, it is often best to follow the model of the built-in types when defining overloaded operators. If the semantics of an overloaded operator differ significantly from its meaning in other contexts, it can be more confusing than useful.

Unary Operators

The unary operators are shown in Table 12.4.

Table 12.4   Redefinable Unary Operators

Operator	Name
!	Logical NOT
&	Address-of
~	One's complement
*	Pointer dereference
+	Unary plus
++	Increment
–	Unary negation
– –	Decrement

Of the operators shown in Table 12.4, the postfix increment and decrement operators (**++** and **– –**) are treated separately in the next section, "Increment and Decrement."

To declare a unary operator function as a nonstatic member, you must declare it in the form:

ret-type **operator***op*()

where *ret-type* is the return type and *op* is one of the operators listed in Table 12.4.

To declare a unary operator function as a global function, you must declare it in the form:

ret-type **operator***op*(*arg*)

where *ret-type* and *op* are as described for member operator functions and the *arg* is an argument of class type on which to operate.

Note   There is no restriction on the return types of the unary operators. For example, it makes sense for logical NOT (!) to return an integral value, but this is not enforced.

Increment and Decrement

The increment and decrement operators fall into a special category because there are two variants of each:

- Preincrement and postincrement
- Predecrement and postdecrement

When you write overloaded operator functions, it can be useful to implement separate versions for the prefix and postfix versions of these operators. To distinguish between the two, the following rule is observed: The prefix form of the operator is declared exactly the same way as any other unary operator; the postfix form accepts an additional argument of type **int**.

Important   When specifying an overloaded operator for the postfix form of the increment or decrement operator, the additional argument must be of type **int**; specifying any other type generates an error.

The following example shows how to define prefix and postfix increment and decrement operators for the `Point` class:

```
class Point
{
public:
    // Declare prefix and postfix increment operators.
    Point& operator++();        // Prefix increment operator.
    Point operator++(int);      // Postfix increment operator.

    // Declare prefix and postfix decrement operators.
    Point& operator--();        // Prefix decrement operator.
    Point operator--(int);      // Postfix decrement operator.

    // Define default constructor.
    Point() { _x = _y = 0; }

    // Define accessor functions.
    int x() { return _x; }
    int y() { return _y; }
private:
    int _x, _y;
};

// Define prefix increment operator.
Point& Point::operator++()
{
    _x++;
    _y++;
    return *this;
}

// Define postfix increment operator.
Point Point::operator++(int)
{
    Point temp = *this;
    ++*this;
    return temp;
}

// Define prefix decrement operator.
Point& Point::operator--()
{
    _x--;
    _y--;
    return *this;
}
```

```
// Define postfix decrement operator.
Point Point::operator--(int)
{
    Point temp = *this;
    --*this;
    return temp;
}
```

The same operators can be defined in file scope (globally) using the following function heads:

```
friend Point& operator++( Point& )        // Prefix increment
friend Point& operator++( Point&, int ) // Postfix increment
friend Point& operator--( Point& )        // Prefix decrement
friend Point& operator--( Point&, int ) // Postfix decrement
```

The argument of type **int** that denotes the postfix form of the increment or decrement operator is not commonly used to pass arguments. It usually contains the value 0. However, it can be used as follows:

```
class Int
{
public:
    Int &operator++( int n );
private:
    int _i;
};

Int& Int::operator++( int n )
{
    if( n != 0 )      // Handle case where an argument is passed.
        _i += n;
    else
        _i++;          // Handle case where no argument is passed.
    return *this;
}
...

Int i;
i.operator++( 25 ); // Increment by 25.
```

There is no syntax for using the increment or decrement operators to pass these values other than explicit invocation, as shown in the preceding code. A more straightforward way to implement this functionality is to overload the addition/assignment operator (**+=**).

Binary Operators

Table 12.5 shows a list of operators that can be overloaded.

Table 12.5   Redefinable Binary Operators

Operator	Name
,	Comma
!=	Inequality
%	Modulus
%=	Modulus/assignment
&	Bitwise AND
&&	Logical AND
&=	Bitwise AND/assignment
*	Multiplication
*=	Multiplication/assignment
+	Addition
+=	Addition/assignment
−	Subtraction
−=	Subtraction/assignment
–>	Member selection
–>*	Pointer-to-member selection
/	Division
/=	Division/assignment
<	Less than
<<	Left shift
<<=	Left shift/assignment
<=	Less than or equal to
=	Assignment
==	Equality
>	Greater than
>=	Greater than or equal to
>>	Right shift
>>=	Right shift/assignment
^	Exclusive OR
^=	Exclusive OR/assignment
|	Bitwise inclusive OR
|=	Bitwise inclusive OR/assignment
||	Logical OR

To declare a binary operator function as a nonstatic member, you must declare it in the form:

ret-type **operator***op*(*arg*)

where *ret-type* is the return type, *op* is one of the operators listed in Table 12.5, and *arg* is an argument of any type.

To declare a binary operator function as a global function, you must declare it in the form:

ret-type **operator***op*(*arg1*, *arg2*)

where *ret-type* and *op* are as described for member operator functions and *arg1* and *arg2* are arguments. At least one of the arguments must be of class type.

Note There is no restriction on the return types of the binary operators; however, most user-defined binary operators return either a class type or a reference to a class type.

Assignment

The assignment operator (=) is, strictly speaking, a binary operator. Its declaration is identical to any other binary operator, with the following exceptions:

- It must be a nonstatic member function. No **operator=** can be declared as a nonmember function.

- It is not inherited by derived classes.

- A default **operator=** function can be generated by the compiler for class types if none exists. (For more information about default **operator=** functions, see "Memberwise Assignment and Initialization" on page 322 in Chapter 11.)

The following example illustrates how to declare an assignment operator:

```
class Point
{
public:
    Point &operator=( Point & );  // Right side is the argument.
    ...
};

// Define assignment operator.
Point &Point::operator=( Point &ptRHS )
{
    _x = ptRHS._x;
    _y = ptRHS._y;

    return *this;  // Assignment operator returns left side.
}
```

Note that the supplied argument is the right side of the expression. The operator returns the object to preserve the behavior of the assignment operator, which returns the value of the left side after the assignment is complete. This allows writing statements such as:

```
pt1 = pt2 = pt3;
```

Function Call

The function-call operator, invoked using parentheses, is a binary operator. The syntax for a function call is:

Syntax

primary-expression **(** *expression-list*~opt~ **)**

In this context, *primary-expression* is the first operand, and *expression-list*, a possibly empty list of arguments, is the second operand. The function-call operator is used for operations that require a number of parameters. This works because *expression-list* is a list instead of a single operand. The function-call operator must be a nonstatic member function.

The function-call operator, when overloaded, does not modify how functions are called; rather, it modifies how the operator is to be interpreted when applied to objects of a given class type. For example, the following code would usually be meaningless:

```
Point pt;
pt( 3, 2 );
```

Given an appropriate overloaded function-call operator, however, this syntax can be used to offset the *x* coordinate 3 units and the *y* coordinate 2 units. The following code shows such a definition:

```
class Point
{
public:
    Point() { _x = _y = 0; }
    Point &operator()( int dx, int dy )
        { _x += dx; _y += dy; return *this; }
private:
    int _x, _y;
};

...

Point pt;
pt( 3, 2 );
```

Note that the function-call operator is applied to the name of an object, not the name of a function.

Subscripting

The subscript operator ([ ]), like the function-call operator, is considered a binary operator. The subscript operator must be a nonstatic member function that takes a single argument. This argument can be of any type and designates the desired array subscript.

The following example demonstrates how to create a vector of type **int** that implements bounds checking:

```
#include <iostream.h>

class IntVector
{
public:
    IntVector( int cElements );
    ~IntVector() { delete _iElements; }
    int& operator[]( int nSubscript );
private:
    int *_iElements;
    int _iUpperBound;
};

// Construct an IntVector.
IntVector::IntVector( int cElements )
{
    _iElements = new int[cElements];
    _iUpperBound = cElements;
}

// Subscript operator for IntVector.
int& IntVector::operator[]( int nSubscript )
{
    static int iErr = -1;

    if( nSubscript >= 0 && nSubscript < _iUpperBound )
        return _iElements[nSubscript];
    else
    {
        clog << "Array bounds violation." << endl;
        return iErr;
    }
}

// Test the IntVector class.
int main()
{
    IntVector v( 10 );

    for( int i = 0; i <= 10; ++i )
        v[i] = i;

    v[3] = v[9];

    for( i = 0; i <= 10; ++i )
        cout << "Element: [" << i << "] = " << v[i]
                << endl;

    return v[0];
}
```

When i reaches 10 in the preceding program, `operator[]` detects that an out-of-bounds subscript is being used and issues an error message.

Note that the function `operator[]` returns a reference type. This causes it to be an l-value, allowing you to use subscripted expressions on either side of assignment operators.

Class-Member Access

Class-member access can be controlled by overloading the member-selection operator (–>). This operator is considered a unary operator in this usage, and the overloaded operator function must be a class member function. Therefore, the declaration for such a function is:

class-type ***operator–>()**

where *class-type* is the name of the class to which this operator belongs. The member-selection operator function must be a nonstatic member function.

This operator is used (often in conjunction with the pointer-dereference operator) to implement "smart pointers" that validate pointers prior to dereference or count usage.

The **.** member-selector operator cannot be overloaded.

Grammar Summary

This appendix describes the formal grammar of the C++ language, as implemented in the Microsoft C++ compiler. It is loosely organized around the chapter organization of this book as follows:

- The Keywords section describes keywords, covered in Chapter 1, "Lexical Conventions."

- The Expressions section describes the syntax of expressions, described in Chapter 4, "Expressions."

- The Declarations section describes the syntax of declarations, described in Chapter 6, "Declarations."

- The Declarators section describes the syntax of declarators, covered in Chapter 7, "Declarators."

- The Classes section covers the syntax used in declaring classes, as covered in Chapter 8, "Classes."

- The Statements section covers the syntax used in writing statements, as covered in Chapter 5, "Statements."

- The Microsoft Extensions section covers the syntax of features unique to Microsoft C++. Many of these features are covered in Appendix B, "Microsoft-Specific Modifiers."

Keywords

class-name:
   identifier

enum-name:
   identifier

typedef-name:
   identifier

identifier: one of
    nondigit
    identifier nondigit
    identifier digit

nondigit: one of
    _ a b c d e f g h i j k l m
    n o p q r s t u v w x y z
    A B C D E F G H I J K L M
    N O P Q R S T U V W X Y Z

digit: one of
    0 1 2 3 4 5 6 7 8 9

Expressions

expression:
    assignment-expression
    expression , *assignment-expression*

assignment-expression:
    conditional-expression
    unary-expression assignment-operator assignment-expression

assignment-operator: one of
    = *= /= %= += −= >= <= **&=** ^= |=

conditional-expression:
    logical-or-expression
    logical-or-expression **?** *expression* **:** *conditional-expression*

logical-or-expression:
    logical-and-expression
    logical-or-expression **||** *logical-and-expression*

logical-and-expression:
    inclusive-or-expression
    logical-and-expression **&&** *inclusive-or-expression*

inclusive-or-expression:
    exclusive-or-expression
    inclusive-or-expression **|** *exclusive-or-expression*

exclusive-or-expression:
    and-expression
    exclusive-or-expression **^** *and-expression*

and-expression:
    equality-expression
    and-expression **&** *equality-expression*

equality-expression:
    relational-expression
    equality-expression **==** *relational-expression*
    equality-expression **!=** *relational-expression*

relational-expression:
    shift-expression
    relational-expression **<** *shift-expression*
    relational-expression **>** *shift-expression*
    relational-expression **<=** *shift-expression*
    relational-expression **=>** *shift-expression*

shift-expression:
    additive-expression
    shift-expression **<<** *additive-expression*
    shift-expression **>>** *additive-expression*

additive-expression:
    multiplicative-expression
    additive-expression **+** *multiplicative-expression*
    additive-expression **−** *multiplicative-expression*

multiplicative-expression:
    segment-expression
    multiplicative-expression ***** *segment-expression*
    multiplicative-expression **/** *segment-expression*
    multiplicative-expression **%** *segment-expression*

segment-expression:
    pm-expression
    segment-expression **:>** *pm-expression*

pm-expression:
    cast-expression
    pm-expression **.*** *cast-expression*
    pm-expression **−>*** *cast-expression*

cast-expression:
    unary-expression
    (*type-name* **)** *cast-expression*

unary-expression:
    postfix-expression
    ++ *unary-expression*
    −− *unary-expression*
    unary-operator cast-expression
    sizeof *unary-expression*
    sizeof (*type-name*)
    allocation-expression
    deallocation-expression

unary-operator: one of
    * & + − ! ~

allocation-expression:
    ::$_{opt}$ **new** *nmodel*$_{opt}$ *placement*$_{opt}$ *new-type-name new-initializer*$_{opt}$
    ::$_{opt}$ **new** *nmodel*$_{opt}$ *placement*$_{opt}$ (*type-name*) *new-initializer*$_{opt}$

placement:
    (*expression-list*)

new-type-name:
    type-specifier-list new-declarator$_{opt}$

new-declarator:
    ms-modifier-list $_{opt}$ ***** *cv-qualifier-list* $_{opt}$ *new-declarator*$_{opt}$
    ms-modifier-list $_{opt}$ *complete-class-name* **::** ******cv-qualifier-list*$_{opt}$
      new-declarator$_{opt}$
    new-declarator$_{opt}$ [*expression*]

new-initializer:
    (*initializer-list*)

deallocation-expression:
    ::$_{opt}$ **delete** *cast-expression*
    ::$_{opt}$ **delete** [ ] *cast-expression*

postfix-expression:
    primary-expression
    postfix-expression [*expression*]
    postfix-expression (*expression-list*)
    simple-type-name (*expression-list*)
    postfix-expression **.** *name*
    postfix-expression **−>** *name*
    postfix-expression **++**
    postfix-expression **−−**
    dynamic_cast < *type-id* > (*expression*)
    static_cast < *type-id* > (*expression*)
    const_cast < *type-id* > (*expression*)
    reinterpret_cast < *type-id* > (*expression*)

typeid(*expression*)
typeid(*type-id*)

expression-list:
    assignment-expression
    expression-list **,** *assignment-expression*

primary-expression:
    literal
    this
    :: *identifier*
    :: *operator-function-name*
    :: *qualified-name* (*expression*)
    name

name:
    identifier
    operator-function-name
    conversion-function-name
        ~ *class-name*
    qualified-name

qualified-name:
    ms-modifier-list$_{opt}$ *qualified-class-name* **::** *name*

literal:
    integer-constant
    character-constant
    floating-constant
    string-literal

integer-constant:
    decimal-constant integer-suffix$_{opt}$
    octal-constant integer-suffix$_{opt}$
    hexadecimal-constant integer-suffix$_{opt}$
    '*c-char-sequence*'

decimal-constant:
    nonzero-digit
    decimal-constant digit

octal-constant:
    0
    octal-constant octal-digit

hexadecimal-constant:
    0x *hexadecimal-digit*
    0X *hexadecimal-digit*
    hexadecimal-constant hexadecimal-digit

nonzero-digit: one of
    1 2 3 4 5 6 7 8 9

octal-digit: one of
    0 1 2 3 4 5 6 7

hexadecimal-digit: one of
    0 1 2 3 4 5 6 7 8 9
    a b c d e f
    A B C D E F

integer-suffix:
    unsigned-suffix long-suffix$_{opt}$
    long-suffix unsigned-suffix$_{opt}$

unsigned-suffix: one of
    u U

long-suffix: one of
    l L

character-constant:
    '*c-char-sequence*'
    L'*c-char-sequence*'

c-char-sequence:
    c-char
    c-char-sequence c-char

c-char:
    any member of the source character set except the single quote ('),
        backslash (\ ), or newline character
    escape-sequence

escape-sequence:
    simple-escape-sequence
    octal-escape-sequence
    hexadecimal-escape-sequence

simple-escape-sequence: one of
    **\' \" \? **
    \a \b \f \n \r \t \v

octal-escape-sequence:
    \ *octal-digit*
    \ *octal-digit octal-digit*
    \ *octal-digit octal-digit octal-digit*

hexadecimal-escape-sequence:
    \x*hexadecimal-digit*
    hexadecimal-escape-sequence hexadecimal-digit

floating-constant:
> *fractional-constant exponent-part*_{opt} *floating-suffix*_{opt}
> *digit-sequence exponent-part floating-suffix*_{opt}

fractional-constant:
> *digit-sequence*_{opt} **.** *digit-sequence*
> *digit-sequence* **.**

exponent-part:
> **e** *sign*_{opt} *digit-sequence*
> **E** *sign*_{opt} *digit-sequence*

sign: one of
> **+ −**

digit-sequence:
> *digit*
> *digit-sequence digit*

floating-suffix: one of
> **f l F L**

string literal:
> **"***s-char-sequence* _{opt}**"**
> **L "***s-char-sequence* _{opt}**"**

s-char-sequence:
> *s-char*
> *s-char-sequence s-char*

s-char:
> any member of the source character set except double quotation marks ("),
>   backslash (\), or newline character
> *escape-sequence*

Declarations

declaration:
> *decl-specifiers*_{opt} *declarator-list*_{opt} **;**
> *asm-declaration*
> *function-definition*
> *linkage-specification*
> *template-declaration*:

asm-declaration:
> **__asm(** *string-literal* **);**

decl-specifiers:
> *decl-specifiers*_{opt} *decl-specifier*

decl-specifier:
    storage-class-specifier
    type-specifier
    fct-specifier
    friend
    typedef
    __declspec (*extended-decl-modifier-seq*)

storage-class-specifier:
    auto
    register
    static
    extern

fct-specifier:
    inline
    virtual

type-specifier:
    simple-type-name
    class-specifier
    enum-specifier
    elaborated-type-specifier
    const
    volatile

extended-decl-modifier-seq:
    extended-decl-modifier$_{opt}$
    extended-decl-modifier extended-decl-modifier-seq

extended-decl-modifier:
    thread
    naked
    dllimport
    dllexport

simple-type-name:
    complete-class-name
    qualified-type-name
    char
    short
    int
    long
    signed
    unsigned
    float
    double
    void

elaborated-type-specifier:
    class-key *rmodel*_{opt} *identifier*
    class-key *rmodel*_{opt} *class-name*
    enum-name

class-key:
    class
    struct
    union

qualified-type-name:
    typedef-name
    class-name **::** *qualified-type-name*

complete-class-name:
    qualified-class-name
    :: *qualified-class-name*

qualified-class-name:
    class-name
    class-name **::** *qualified-class-name*

enum-specifier:
    enum *identifier*_{opt} **{** *enum-list*_{opt} **}**

enum-list:
    enumerator
    enum-list **,** *enumerator*

enumerator:
    identifier
    identifier **=** *constant-expression*

constant-expression:
    conditional-expression

linkage-specification:
    extern *string-literal* **{** *declaration-list*_{opt} **}**
    extern *string-literal declaration*

declaration-list:
    declaration
    declaration-list declaration

template-declaration:
    template **<** *template-argument-list* **>** *declaration*

template-argument-list:
    template-argument
    template-argument-list **,** *template-argument*

template-argument:
    type-argument
    argument-declaration

type-argument:
    class *identifier*

template-class-name:
    template-name **<** *template-arg-list* **>**

template-arg-list:
    template-arg
    template-arg-list **,** *template-arg*

template-arg:
    expression
    type-name

original-namespace-name :
    identifier

namespace-definition :
    original-namespace-definition
    extension-namespace-definition
    unnamed-namespace-definition

original-namespace-definition :
    namespace *identifier* **{** *namespace-body* **}**

extension-namespace-definition :
    namespace *original-namespace-name* **{** *namespace-body* **}**

unnamed-namespace-definition :
    namespace **{** *namespace-body* **}**

namespace-body :
    declaration-seq$_{opt}$

id-expression :
    unqualified-id
    qualified-id

nested-name-specifier :
    class-or-namespace-name **::** *nested-name-specifier*$_{opt}$

class-or-namespace-name :
    class-name
    namespace-name

namespace-name :
    original-namespace-name
    namespace-alias

namespace-alias :
  identifier

namespace-alias-definition :
  namespace *identifier = qualified-namespace-specifier;*

qualified-namespace-specifier :
  ::$_{opt}$ *nested-name-specifier*opt *class-or-namespace-name*

using-declaration :
  using ::$_{opt}$ *nested-name-specifier unqualified-id*
  using :: *unqualified-id*

using-directive :
  using namespace ::$_{opt}$ *nested-name-specifier*$_{opt}$ *namespace-name*

Declarators

declarator-list:
  init-declarator
  declarator-list , init-declarator

init-declarator:
  ms-modifier-list$_{opt}$ *declarator initializer*$_{opt}$

declarator:
  dname
  ptr-operator declarator
  declarator (argument-declaration-list) cv-mod-list$_{opt}$
  declarator [constant-expression$_{opt}$ *]*
  (declarator)

cv-mod-list:
  cv-qualifier cv-mod-list$_{opt}$
  rmodel cv-mod-list$_{opt}$

ptr-operator:
  ms-modifier-list$_{opt}$ * *cv-qualifier-list*$_{opt}$
  ms-modifier-list$_{opt}$ **&** *cv-qualifier-list*$_{opt}$
  ms-modifier-list$_{opt}$ *complete-class-name* **::** * *cv-qualifier-list*$_{opt}$

cv-qualifier-list:
  cv-qualifier cv-qualifier-list$_{opt}$

cv-qualifier:
  const
  volatile

dname:
    name
    class-name
    ~ *class-name*
    typedef-name
    qualified-type-name

type-name:
    type-specifier-list ms-modifier-list$_{opt}$ *abstract-declarator*$_{opt}$

type-specifier-list:
    type-specifier type-specifier-list$_{opt}$

abstract-declarator:
    ptr-operator ms-modifier-list$_{opt}$ *abstract-declarator*$_{opt}$
    abstract-declarator$_{opt}$ (*argument-declaration-list*) *cv-qualifier-list*$_{opt}$
    abstract-declarator$_{opt}$ [*constant-expression*$_{opt}$]
        (*ms-modifier-list*$_{opt}$ *abstract-declarator*)

argument-declaration-list:
    arg-declaration-list$_{opt}$ ...$_{opt}$
    arg-declaration-list , ...

arg-declaration-list:
    argument-declaration
    arg-declaration-list , *argument-declaration*

argument-declaration:
    decl-specifiers ms-modifier-list$_{opt}$ *declarator*
    decl-specifiers ms-modifier-list$_{opt}$ *declarator* = *expression*
    decl-specifiers ms-modifier-list$_{opt}$ *abstract-declarator*$_{opt}$
    decl-specifiers ms-modifier-list$_{opt}$ *abstract-declarator*$_{opt}$ = *expression*

function-definition:
    decl-specifiers$_{opt}$ *ms-modifier-list*$_{opt}$ *declarator ctor-initializer*$_{opt}$ *fct-body*

fct-body:
    compound-statement

initializer:
    = *expression*
    = { *initializer-list* ,$_{opt}$ }
    (*expression-list*)

initializer-list:
    expression
    initializer-list , *expression*
    { *initializer-list* ,$_{opt}$ }

Classes

class-specifier:
>   *class-head* { *member-list*_{opt} }

class-head:
>   *class-key ambient-model*_{opt} *identifier*_{opt} *base-spec*_{opt}
>   *class-key ambient-model*_{opt} *class-name base-spec*_{opt}

member-list:
>   *member-declaration member-list*_{opt}
>   *access-specifier* : *member-list*_{opt}

member-declaration:
>   *decl-specifiers*_{opt} *member-declarator-list*_{opt} ;
>   *function-definition* ;_{opt}
>   *qualified-name* ;

member-declarator-list:
>   *member-declarator*
>   *member-declarator-list* , *member-declarator*

member-declarator:
>   *ms-modifier-list*_{opt} *declarator pure-specifier*_{opt}
>   *identifier*_{opt} : *constant-expression*

pure-specifier:
>   **= 0**

base-spec:
>   : *base-list*

base-list:
>   *base-specifier*
>   *base-list* , *base-specifier*

base-specifier:
>   *complete-class-name*
>   **virtual** *access-specifier*_{opt} *complete-class-name*
>   *access-specifier* **virtual**_{opt} *complete-class-name*

access-specifier:
>   **private**
>   **protected**
>   **public**

conversion-function-name:
>   **operator** *conversion-type-name*

C++ Language Reference

conversion-type-name:
 *type-specifier-list ptr-operator*_{opt}

ctor-initializer:
 : *mem-initializer-list*

mem-initializer-list:
 mem-initializer
 mem-initializer **,** *mem-initializer-list*

mem-initializer:
 complete-class-name **(** *expression-list*_{opt} **)**
 identifier **(** *expression-list*_{opt} **)**

operator-function-name:
 operator *operator*

operator: one of
 new **delete**
 + – * / % ^ & | ~
 ! = < > += –= *= /= %=
 ^= &= |= << >> >>= <<= == !=
 <= >= && || ++ — , –>* –>
 () []

Statements

statement:
 labeled-statement
 expression-statement
 compound-statement
 selection-statement
 iteration-statement
 jump-statement
 declaration-statement
 asm-statement
 try-except-statement
 try-finally-statement

labeled-statement:
 identifier **:** *statement*
 case *constant-expression* **:** *statement*
 default **:** *statement*

expression-statement:
 *expression*_{opt} **;**

362

compound-statement:
    { *statement-list*_{opt} }

statement-list:
    statement
    statement-list statement

selection-statement:
    if (*expression*) *statement*
    if (*expression*) *statement* **else** *statement*
    switch (*expression*) *statement*

iteration-statement:
    while (*expression*) *statement*
    do *statement* **while** (*expression*) ;
    for (*for-init-statement expression*_{opt} ; *expression*_{opt}) *statement*

for-init-statement:
    expression-statement
    declaration-statement

jump-statement:
    break ;
    continue ;
    return *expression*_{opt} ;
    goto *identifier* ;

declaration-statement:
    declaration

try-except-statement:
    __**try** *compound-statement*
    __**except** (*expression*) *compound-statement*

try-finally-statement:
    __**try** *compound-statement*
    __**finally** (*expression*) *compound-statement*

Microsoft Extensions

asm-statement:
    __**asm** *assembly-instruction* ;_{opt}
    __**asm** { *assembly-instruction-list* } ;_{opt}

assembly-instruction-list:
    assembly-instruction ;_{opt}
    assembly-instruction ; *assembly-instruction-list* ;_{opt}

nmodel:
    rmodel
    __**based** (*expression*)

ms-modifier-list:
    *ms-modifier ms-modifier-list*_{opt}

ms-modifier:
    __**cdecl**
    __**fastcall**
    __**stdcall**
    __**syscall** (reserved for future implementations)
    __**oldcall** (reserved for future implementations)
    __**unaligned** (reserved for future implementations)
    rmodel
    based-modifier

based-modifier:
    __**based** (*based-type*)

based-type:
    name

Microsoft-Specific Modifiers

Many of the Microsoft-specific keywords can be used to modify declarators to form derived types. (For more information about declarators, see Chapter 7, "Declarators").

Table B.1   Microsoft-Specific Keywords

Keyword	Meaning	Used to Form Derived Types?
__asm	Insert the following assembly-language code.	No
__based	The name that follows declares a 32-bit offset to the 32-bit base contained in the declaration.	Yes
__cdecl	The name that follows uses the C naming and calling conventions.	Yes
__declspec	The name that follows (**thread**, **naked**, **dllimport**, or **dllexport**) specifies a Microsoft-specific storage-class attribute.	No
__fastcall	The name that follows declares a function that uses registers, when available, instead of the stack for argument passing.	Yes
__stdcall	The name that follows specifies a function that observes the standard calling convention.	Yes

The following sections discuss the syntactic usage and semantic meaning of the Microsoft-specific modifiers.

Based Addressing

This section includes the following topics:

- __based
- Based pointers
- Pointers based on pointers

Using __based in 32-bit Compilations

Based addressing is useful when you need precise control over the segment in which objects are allocated (static and dynamic based data).

The only form of based addressing acceptable in 32-bit compilations is "based on a pointer" that defines a type that contains a 32-bit displacement to a 32-bit base or based on **void**.

Syntax

based-range-modifier:
      __**based** (*base-expression*)

base-expression:
      based-variable
      based-abstract-declarator
      segment-name
      segment-cast

based-variable:
      identifier

based-abstract-declarator:
      abstract-declarator

base-type:
      type-name

Based Pointers

Pointers based on pointer addresses are the only form of the __**based** keyword valid in 32-bit compilations. In such compilations, based pointers are 32-bit offsets from a 32-bit base.

When dereferencing a based pointer, the base must be either explicitly specified or implicitly known through the declaration.

Pointers Based on Pointers

The "based on pointer" variant of based addressing enables specification of a pointer as a *base-expression*. The based pointer, then, is an offset into the segment starting at the beginning of the pointer on which it is based.

One use for pointers based on pointers is for persistent objects that contain pointers. A linked list of pointers based on pointers can be saved to disk and reloaded to another place in memory, and the pointers will still be valid. The following example declares such a linked list:

```
void *vpBuffer;

struct llist_t
```

```
{
  void __based( vpBuffer ) *vpData;
  llist_t __based( vpBuffer ) *llNext;
};
```

The pointer, vpBuffer, is assigned the address of memory allocated at some later point in the program; the linked list is then relocated relative to the value of vpBuffer.

Pointers based on pointer addresses are the only forms of __based valid in 32-bit compilations. In such compilations, they are 32-bit displacements from a 32-bit base.

Calling and Naming Convention Modifiers

Calling conventions determine how functions are called; naming conventions determine how external names are treated. For more information, see "Calling Conventions Topics," in *Visual C++ Programmer's Guide* online.

Extended Storage-Class Attributes

This section describes extended attribute syntax, which simplifies and standardizes extensions to the Microsoft C and C++ languages. The storage-class attributes that use extended attribute syntax include **thread**, **naked**, **dllimport**, and **dllexport**. Use of these attributes is described later in this section.

Extended Attribute Syntax

The extended attribute syntax for specifying storage-class information uses the __declspec keyword, which specifies that an instance of a given type is to be stored with a Microsoft-specific storage-class attribute (**thread**, **naked**, **dllimport**, **dllexport, nothrow**, **property**, **selectany**, or **uuid**). Examples of other storage-class modifiers include the **static** and **extern** keywords. However, these keywords are part of the ANSI specification of the C and C++ languages, and as such are not covered by extended attribute syntax.

This is the extended attribute syntax for C++:

Syntax

decl-specifier :
        __**declspec** (*extended-decl-modifier-seq*)

extended-decl-modifier-seq :
        extended-decl-modifier$_{opt}$
        extended-decl-modifier extended-decl-modifier-seq

extended-decl-modifier :
        thread
        naked

dllimport
dllexport
nothrow
property
selectany
uuid(*"ComObjectGUID"*)

White space separates the declaration modifier sequence. Examples of the syntax appear in later sections.

The **thread**, **naked**, **dllimport**, **dllexport**, **nothrow**, **property**, **selectany**, and **uuid** storage-class attributes are properties only of the declaration of the object or function to which they are applied. Unlike the **__near** and **__far** keywords, which actually affect the type of object or function (in this case, 2- and 4-byte addresses), these storage-class attributes do not redefine the type attributes of the object itself. The **thread** attribute affects data and objects only. The **naked** attribute affects functions only. The **dllimport** and **dllexport** attributes affect functions, data, and objects. The **property**, **selectany**, and **uuid** attributes affect COM objects.

The thread Attribute

Thread Local Storage (TLS) is the mechanism by which each thread in a multithreaded process allocates storage for thread-specific data. In standard multithreaded programs, data is shared among all threads of a given process, whereas thread local storage is the mechanism for allocating per-thread data. For a complete discussion of threads, see "Multithreading Topics," in the *Visual C++ Programmer's Guide* online.

The C and C++ languages include the extended storage-class attribute, **thread**. The **thread** attribute must be used with the **__declspec** keyword to declare a thread variable. For example, the following code declares an integer thread local variable and initializes it with a value:

```
__declspec( thread ) int tls_i = 1;
```

You must observe these guidelines when declaring thread local objects and variables:

- You can apply the **thread** attribute only to data declarations and definitions, and classes that do not have member functions. It cannot be used on function declarations or definitions. For example, the following code generates a compiler error:

```
#define Thread __declspec( thread )
Thread void func();         // Error
```

- You can specify the **thread** attribute only on data items with static storage duration. This includes global data objects (both **static** and **extern**), local static objects, and static data members of classes. You cannot declare automatic data objects with the **thread** attribute. For example, the following code generates compiler errors:

```
#define Thread   __declspec( thread )
void func1()
{
    Thread int tls_i;              // Error
}

int func2( Thread int tls_i )      // Error
{
    return tls_i;
}
```

- You must use the **thread** attribute for the declaration and the definition of a thread local object, whether the declaration and definition occur in the same file or separate files. For example, the following code generates an error:

```
#define Thread   __declspec( thread )
extern int tls_i;    // This generates an error, because the
int Thread tls_i;    // declaration and the definition differ.
```

- You cannot use the **thread** attribute as a type modifier. For example, the following code generates a compiler error:

```
char __declspec( thread ) *ch;      // Error
```

- Classes can be instantiated using **thread** only if they contain no member functions. The **thread** attribute is ignored if no object is declared as part of the class declaration. For example:

```
__declspec(thread) class X {
public:
    int I; } x; // x is a thread object

X y;            // y is not a thread object
```

Because the declaration of objects that use the **thread** attribute is permitted, these two examples are semantically equivalent:

```
#define Thread   __declspec( thread )
Thread class B
{
    // Code
} BObject;         // Okay--BObject declared thread local.

class B
{
    // Code
}
Thread B BObject;  // Okay--BObject declared thread local.
```

- Standard C permits initialization of an object or variable with an expression involving a reference to itself, but only for objects of nonstatic extent. Although C++ normally permits such dynamic initialization of an object with an expression involving a reference to itself, this type of initialization is not permitted with thread local objects. For example:

```
#define Thread  __declspec( thread )
Thread int tls_i = tls_i;        // C and C++ error
int j = j;                       // Okay in C++; C error
Thread int tls_i = sizeof( tls_i )  // Okay in C and C++
```

Note that a **sizeof** expression that includes the object being initialized does not constitute a reference to itself and is allowed in C and C++.

The naked Attribute

For functions declared with the **naked** attribute, the compiler generates code without prolog and epilog code. You can use this feature to write your own prolog/epilog code sequences using inline assembler code. Naked functions are particularly useful in writing virtual device drivers.

Because the **naked** attribute is only relevant to the definition of a function and is not a type modifier, naked functions use the extended attribute syntax, described previously. For example, this code defines a function with the **naked** attribute:

```
__declspec( naked ) int func( formal_parameters )
{
    // Function body
}
```

Or, alternatively:

```
#define Naked  __declspec( naked )
Naked int func( formal_parameters )
{
    // Function body
}
```

The **naked** attribute affects only the nature of the compiler's code generation for the function's prolog and epilog sequences. It does not affect the code that is generated for calling such functions. Thus, the **naked** attribute is not considered part of the function's type, and function pointers cannot have the **naked** attribute. Furthermore, the **naked** attribute cannot be applied to a data definition. For example, this code sample generates an error:

```
__declspec( naked ) int i;      // Error--naked attribute not
                                // permitted on data declarations.
```

The **naked** attribute is relevant only to the definition of the function and cannot be specified in the function's prototype. For example, this declaration generates a compiler error:

```
__declspec( naked ) int func();  // Error--naked attribute not
                                 // permitted on function declarations
```

Rules and Limitations

- The **return** statement is not permitted in a naked function. However, you can return an **int** by moving the return value into the EAX register before the **RET** instruction.

- Structured exception handling constructs are not permitted in a naked function, because the constructs must unwind across the stack frame.

- The **setjmp** run-time function cannot be used in a naked function, because it too must unwind across the stack frame. However, use of the **longjmp** run-time function is permitted.

- Use of the **_alloca** function is not permitted in a naked function.

- To ensure that no initialization code for local variables appears before the prolog sequence, initialized local variables are not permitted at function scope. In particular, the declaration of C++ objects is not permitted at function scope. There can, however, be initialized data in a nested scope.

- Frame pointer optimization (the /Oy compiler option) is not recommended, but it is automatically suppressed for a naked function.

Considerations for Writing Prolog/Epilog Code

Before writing your own prolog and epilog code sequences, it is important to understand how the stack frame is laid out. It is also useful to know how to use the **__LOCAL_SIZE** symbol.

C++ Stack Frame Layout

This example shows the standard prolog code that might appear in a 32-bit function:

```
push      ebp                 ; Save ebp
mov       ebp, esp            ; Set stack frame pointer
sub       esp, localbytes     ; Allocate space for locals
push      <registers>         ; Save registers
```

The `localbytes` variable represents the number of bytes needed on the stack for local variables, and the `<registers>` variable is a placeholder that represents the list of registers to be saved on the stack. After pushing the registers, you can place any other appropriate data on the stack. The following is the corresponding epilog code:

```
pop       <registers>         ; Restore registers
mov       esp, ebp            ; Restore stack pointer
pop       ebp                 ; Restore ebp
ret                           ; Return from function
```

The stack always grows down (from high to low memory addresses). The base pointer (ebp) points to the pushed value of ebp. The locals area begins at ebp-2. To access local variables, calculate an offset from ebp by subtracting the appropriate value from ebp.

__LOCAL_SIZE

The compiler provides a symbol, **__LOCAL_SIZE**, for use in the inline assembler block of function prolog code. This symbol is used to allocate space for local variables on the stack frame in custom prolog code.

The compiler determines the value of **__LOCAL_SIZE**. Its value is the total number of bytes of all user-defined local variables and compiler-generated temporary variables. **__LOCAL_SIZE** can be used only as an immediate operand; it cannot be used in an expression. You must not change or redefine the value of this symbol. For example:

```
mov       eax, __LOCAL_SIZE            ;Immediate operand--Okay
mov       eax, [ebp - __LOCAL_SIZE]    ;Error
```

The following example of a naked function containing custom prolog and epilog sequences uses the **__LOCAL_SIZE** symbol in the prolog sequence:

```
__declspec ( naked ) func()
{
    int i;
    int j;

    __asm     /* prolog */
       {
       push  ebp
       mov   ebp, esp
       sub   esp, __LOCAL_SIZE
       }

    /* Function body */

    __asm     /* epilog */
       {
       mov   esp, ebp
       pop   ebp
       ret
       }
}
```

The dllexport and dllimport Attributes

The **dllexport** and **dllimport** storage-class modifiers export and import functions, data, and objects to and from a DLL. These modifiers, or attributes, explicitly define the DLL's interface to its client, which can be the executable file or another DLL. Declaring functions as **dllexport** eliminates the need for a module-definition (.DEF) file, at least with respect to the specification of exported functions. Note that **dllexport** replaces the **__export** keyword.

The declaration of **dllexport** and **dllimport** uses extended attribute syntax:

```
__declspec( dllexport ) void func();
```

Alternatively, to make your code more readable, you can use macro definitions:

```
#define DllImport __declspec( dllimport )
#define DllExport __declspec( dllexport )

DllExport void func();
DllExport int i = 10;
DllImport int j;
DllExport int n;
```

Definitions and Declarations

The DLL interface refers to all items (functions and data) that are known to be exported by some program in the system; that is, all items that are declared as **dllimport** or **dllexport**. All declarations included in the DLL interface must specify either the **dllimport** or **dllexport** attribute. However, the definition must specify only the **dllexport** attribute. For example, the following function definition generates a compiler error:

```
__declspec( dllimport ) int func()     // Error; dllimport
                                       // prohibited on definition.
{
    return 1;
}
```

This code also generates an error:

```
#define DllImport __declspec( dllimport )

__declspec( dllimport ) int i = 10;   // Error; this is a
                                      // definition.
```

However, this is correct syntax:

```
__declspec( dllexport ) int i = 10;   // Okay--export definition
```

The use of **dllexport** implies a definition, while **dllimport** implies a declaration. You must use the **extern** keyword with **dllexport** to force a declaration; otherwise, a definition is implied. Thus, the following examples are correct:

```
#define DllImport __declspec( dllimport )
#define DllExport __declspec( dllexport )

extern DllImport int k; // These are both correct and imply a
DllImport int j;        // declaration.
```

The following examples clarify the preceding:

```
static __declspec( dllimport ) int l; // Error; not declared extern.

void func()
{
    static __declspec( dllimport ) int s;    // Error; not declared
                                             // extern.
    __declspec( dllimport ) int m;           // Okay; this is a
                                             // declaration.
```

```
        __declspec( dllexport ) int n;          // Error; implies external
                                                 // definition in local scope.
        extern __declspec( dllimport ) int i;   // Okay; this is a
                                                 // declaration.
        extern __declspec( dllexport ) int k;   // Okay; extern implies
                                                 // declaration.
        __declspec( dllexport ) int x = 5; // Error; implies external
                                                 // definition in local scope.
}
```

Defining Inline C++ Functions with dllexport and dllimport

You can define as inline a function with the **dllexport** attribute. In this case, the function is always instantiated and exported, whether or not any module in the program references the function. The function is presumed to be imported by another program.

You can also define as inline a function declared with the **dllimport** attribute. In this case, the function can be expanded (subject to /Ob specifications), but never instantiated. In particular, if the address of an inline imported function is taken, the address of the function residing in the DLL is returned. This behavior is the same as taking the address of a non-inline imported function.

These rules apply to inline functions whose definitions appear within a class definition. In addition, static local data and strings in inline functions maintain the same identities between the DLL and client as they would in a single program (that is, an executable file without a DLL interface).

Exercise care when providing imported inline functions. For example, if you update the DLL, don't assume that the client will use the changed version of the DLL. To ensure that you are loading the proper version of the DLL, rebuild the DLL's client as well.

General Rules and Limitations

- If you declare a function or object without the **dllimport** or **dllexport** attribute, the function or object is not considered part of the DLL interface. Therefore, the definition of the function or object must be present in that module or in another module of the same program. To make the function or object part of the DLL interface, you must declare the definition of the function or object in the other module as **dllexport**. Otherwise, a linker error is generated.

  If you declare a function or object with the **dllexport** attribute, its definition must appear in some module of the same program. Otherwise, a linker error is generated.

- If a single module in your program contains both **dllimport** and **dllexport** declarations for the same function or object, the **dllexport** attribute takes precedence over the **dllimport** attribute. However, a compiler warning is generated. For example:

```
        __declspec( dllimport ) int i;
        __declspec( dllexport ) int i;          // Warning; inconsistent;
                                                 // dllexport takes precedence.
```

- In C, a compiler error is generated if you initialize a globally declared pointer with the address of a data object declared with the **dllimport** attribute. Similarly, you cannot initialize a static local function pointer with the address of a function declared with the **dllimport** attribute, or initialize a static local data pointer with the address of a data object declared with the **dllimport** attribute. The C++ compiler does not enforce this restriction, because C++ supports dynamic initialization of local and global static objects. For example, the following code generates errors when compiled with the C compiler, but not with the C++ compiler.

```
__declspec( dllimport ) void func1( void );
__declspec( dllimport ) int i;

int *pi = &i;                          // Error in C
static void ( *pf )( void ) = &func1;  // Error in C

void func2()
{
    static int *pi = &i;                   // Error in C
    static void ( *pf )( void ) = &func1;  // Error in C
}
```

However, because a program that includes the **dllexport** attribute in the declaration of an object must provide the definition for that object somewhere in the program, you can initialize a global or local static function pointer with the address of a **dllexport** function. Similarly, you can initialize a global or local static data pointer with the address of a **dllexport** data object. For example, the following code does not generate errors in C or C++:

```
__declspec( dllexport ) void func1( void );
__declspec( dllexport ) int i;

int *pi = &i;                          // Okay
static void ( *pf )( void ) = &func1;  // Okay

void func2()
{
    static int *pi = &i;                   // Okay
    static void ( *pf )( void ) = &func1;  // Okay
}
```

Using dllimport and dllexport in C++

You can declare C++ classes with the **dllimport** or **dllexport** attribute. These forms imply that the entire class is imported or exported. Classes exported this way are called exportable classes.

The following example defines an exportable class. All its member functions and static data are exported:

```
#define DllExport __declspec( dllexport )

class DllExport C
{
   int i;
   virtual int func( void )
   { return 1; }
};
```

Note that explicit use of the **dllimport** and **dllexport** attributes on members of an exportable class is prohibited.

dllexport Classes

When you declare a class **dllexport**, all its member functions and static data members are exported. You must provide the definitions of all such members in the same program. Otherwise, a linker error is generated. The one exception to this rule applies to pure virtual functions, for which you need not provide explicit definitions. However, because a destructor for an abstract class is always called by the destructor for the base class, pure virtual destructors must always provide a definition. Note that these rules are the same for nonexportable classes.

If you export data of class type or functions that return classes, be sure to export the class.

dllimport Classes

When you declare a class **dllimport**, all its member functions and static data members are imported. Unlike the behavior of **dllimport** and **dllexport** on nonclass types, static data members cannot specify a definition in the same program in which a **dllimport** class is defined.

Inheritance and Exportable Classes

All base classes of an exportable class must be exportable. If not, a compiler warning is generated. Moreover, all accessible members that are also classes must be exportable. This rule permits a **dllexport** class to inherit from a **dllimport** class, and a **dllimport** class to inherit from a **dllexport** class (though the latter is not recommended). As a rule, everything that is accessible to the DLL's client (according to C++ access rules) should be part of the exportable interface. This includes private data members referenced in inline functions.

Selective Member Import/Export

Because member functions and static data within a class implicitly have external linkage, you can declare them with the **dllimport** or **dllexport** attribute, unless the entire class is exported. If the entire class is imported or exported, the explicit declaration of member functions and data as **dllimport** or **dllexport** is prohibited. If you declare a static data member within a class definition as **dllexport**, a definition must occur somewhere within the same program (as with nonclass external linkage).

Similarly, you can declare member functions with the **dllimport** or **dllexport** attributes. In this case, you must provide a **dllexport** definition somewhere within the same program.

It is worthwhile to note several important points regarding selective member import and export:

- Selective member import/export is best used for providing a version of the exported class interface that is more restrictive; that is, one for which you can design a DLL that exposes fewer public and private features than the language would otherwise allow. It is also useful for fine-tuning the exportable interface: when you know that the client, by definition, is unable to access some private data, you need not export the entire class.

- If you export one virtual function in a class, you must export all of them, or at least provide versions that the client can use directly.

- If you have a class in which you are using selective member import/export with virtual functions, the functions must be in the exportable interface or defined inline (visible to the client).

- If you define a member as **dllexport** but do not include it in the class definition, a compiler error is generated. You must define the member in the class header.

- Although the definition of class members as **dllimport** or **dllexport** is permitted, you cannot override the interface specified in the class definition.

- If you define a member function in a place other than the body of the class definition in which you declared it, a warning is generated if the function is defined as **dllexport** or **dllimport** (if this definition differs from that specified in the class declaration).

C++ Inline Assembler

The inline assembler lets you embed assembly-language instructions in your C source programs without extra assembly and link steps. The inline assembler is built into the compiler—you don't need a separate assembler such as the Microsoft Macro Assembler (MASM).

Because the inline assembler doesn't require separate assembly and link steps, it is more convenient than a separate assembler. Inline assembly code can use any C variable or function name that is in scope, so it is easy to integrate it with your program's C code. And because the assembly code can be mixed with C statements, it can do tasks that are cumbersome or impossible in C alone.

The __asm keyword invokes the inline assembler and can appear wherever a C statement is legal. It cannot appear by itself. It must be followed by an assembly instruction, a group of instructions enclosed in braces, or, at the very least, an empty pair of braces. The term "__asm block" here refers to any instruction or group of instructions, whether or not in braces.

The following code is a simple **__asm** block enclosed in braces. (The code is a custom function prolog sequence.)

```
__asm
{
    push ebp
    mov  ebp, esp
    sub  esp, __LOCAL_SIZE
}
```

Alternatively, you can put **__asm** in front of each assembly instruction:

```
__asm push ebp
__asm mov  ebp, esp
__asm sub  esp, __LOCAL_SIZE
```

Since the **__asm** keyword is a statement separator, you can also put assembly instructions on the same line:

```
__asm push ebp    __asm mov  ebp, esp    __asm sub  esp, __LOCAL_SIZE
```

Microsoft-Specific Compiler COM Support Classes

Standard classes are used to support some of the COM types. There are four classes defined in COMDEF.H and the header files generated from the type library.

#include <comdef.h>

Class	Purpose
_com_error	Defines the error object thrown by **_com_raise_error** in most failures.
_com_ptr_t	Encapsulates COM interface pointers, and automates the required calls to **AddRef**, **Release**, and **QueryInterface**.
_bstr_t	Wraps the **BSTR** type to provide useful operators and methods.
_variant_t	Wraps the **VARIANT** type to provide useful operators and methods.

_com_error

A **_com_error** object represents an exception condition detected by the error-handling wrapper functions in the header files generated from the type library or by one of the COM support classes. The **_com_error** class encapsulates the **HRESULT** error code and any associated **IErrorInfo** object.

#include <comdef.h>

Construction	
_com_error	Constructs a **_com_error** object.

Operators	
operator =	Assigns an existing **_com_error** object to another.

Extractor Functions	
Error	Retrieves the **HRESULT** passed to the constructor.
ErrorInfo	Retrieves the **IErrorInfo** object passed to the constructor.
WCode	Retrieves the 16-bit error code mapped into the encapsulated **HRESULT**.

IErrorInfo functions

Description	Calls **IErrorInfo::GetDescription** function.
HelpContext	Calls **IErrorInfo::GetHelpContext** function.
HelpFile	Calls **IErrorInfo::GetHelpFile** function
Source	Calls **IErrorInfo::GetSource** function.
GUID	Calls **IErrorInfo::GetGUID** function.

Format Message Extractor

ErrorMessage	Retrieves the string message for HRESULT stored in the **_com_error** object.

ExepInfo.wCode to HRESULT Mappers

HRESULTToWCode	Maps 32-bit **HRESULT** to 16-bit **wCode**.
WCodeToHRESULT	Maps 16-bit **wCode** to 32-bit **HRESULT**.

Member Functions

_com_error::_com_error

_com_error(HRESULT *hr*, **IErrorInfo*** *perrinfo* **= NULL) throw( );**
_com_error(const _com_error& *that* **) throw( );**

Parameters

hr   **HRESULT** information

perrinfo   **IErrorInfo** object

that   An existing **_com_error** object

Remarks

Constructs a **_com_error** object. The first constructor creates a new object given an **HRESULT** and optional **IErrorInfo** object. The second creates a copy of an existing **_com_error** object.

_com_error::Description

_bstr_t Description( ) const throw ( );

Return Value

Returns the result of **IErrorInfo::GetDescription** for the **IErrorInfo** object recorded within the **_com_error** object. The resulting BSTR is encapsulated in a **_bstr_t** object. If no **IErrorInfo** is recorded, it returns an empty **_bstr_t**.

Remarks

Calls the **IErrorInfo::GetDescription** function and retrieves **IErrorInfo** recorded within the **_com_error** object. Any failure while calling the **IErrorInfo::GetDescription** method is ignored.

_com_error::Error

HRESULT Error( ) const throw( );

Return Value

Raw **HRESULT** item passed into the constructor.

Remarks

Retrieves the encapsulated **HRESULT** item in a **_com_error** object.

_com_error::ErrorInfo

IErrorInfo * ErrorInfo( ) const throw( );

Return Value

Raw **IErrorInfo** item passed into the constructor.

Remarks

Retrieves the encapsulated **IErrorInfo** item in a **_com_error** object, or **NULL** if no
IErrorInfo item is recorded. The caller must call **Release** on the returned object when
finished using it.

_com_error::ErrorMessage

const TCHAR * ErrorMessage( ) const throw( );

Return Value

Returns the string message for the **HRESULT** recorded within the **_com_error**
object. If the **HRESULT** is a mapped 16-bit **wCode**, then a generic message
"IDispatch error #<wCode>" is returned. If no message is found, then a generic
message "Unknown error #<hresult>" is returned. The returned string is either a
Unicode or multibyte string, depending on the state of the **_UNICODE** macro.

Remarks

Retrieves the appropriate system message text for **HRESULT** recorded within the
_com_error object. The system message text is obtained by calling the Win32
FormatMessage function. The string returned is allocated by the **FormatMessage**
API, and it is released when the **_com_error** object is destroyed.

_com_error::GUID

GUID GUID( ) const throw( );

Return Value

Returns the result of **IErrorInfo::GetGUID** for the **IErrorInfo** object recorded
within the **_com_error** object. If no **IErrorInfo** object is recorded, it returns
GUID_NULL.

Remarks

> Calls the **IErrorInfo::GetGUID** method. Any failure while calling the **IErrorInfo::GetGUID** method is ignored.

_com_error::HelpContext

> **DWORD HelpContext( ) const throw( );**

Return Value

> Returns the result of **IErrorInfo::GetHelpContext** for the **IErrorInfo** object recorded within the **_com_error** object. If no **IErrorInfo** object is recorded, it returns a zero.

Remarks

> Calls the **IErrorInfo::GetHelpContext** interface method. Any failure while calling the **IErrorInfo::GetHelpContext** method is ignored.

_com_error::HelpFile

> **_bstr_t HelpFile( ) const throw( );**

Return Value

> Returns the result of **IErrorInfo::GetHelpFile** for the **IErrorInfo** object recorded within the **_com_error** object. The resulting BSTR is encapsulated in a **_bstr_t** object. If no **IErrorInfo** is recorded, it returns an empty **_bstr_t**.

Remarks

> Calls the **IErrorInfo::GetHelpFile** interface method. Any failure while calling the **IErrorInfo::GetHelpFile** method is ignored.

_com_error::HRESULTToWCode

> **static WORD HRESULTToWCode(HRESULT *hr*) throw( );**

Return Value

> 16-bit **wCode** mapped from the 32-bit **HRESULT**

Parameters

> *hr*   The 32-bit **HRESULT** to be mapped to 16-bit **wCode**

Remarks

> Performs 32-bit **HRESULT** to 16-bit **wCode** mapping. See **_com_error::WCode** for more information.

> **See Also:**   _com_error::WCode, _com_error::WCodeToHRESULT

_com_error::Source

> **_bstr_t Source( ) const throw( );**

Return Value

Returns the result of **IErrorInfo::GetSource** for the **IErrorInfo** object recorded within the **_com_error** object. The resulting BSTR is encapsulated in a **_bstr_t** object. If no **IErrorInfo** is recorded, it returns an empty **_bstr_t**.

Remarks

Calls the **IErrorInfo::GetSource** interface method. Any failure while calling the **IErrorInfo::GetSource** method is ignored.

_com_error::WCode

WORD WCode ( ) const throw( );

Return Value

If the **HRESULT** is within the range 0x80040200 to 0x8004FFFF, the **WCode** method returns the **HRESULT** minus 0x80040200, else it returns zero.

Remarks

The **WCode** method retrieves a 16-bit error code which has been mapped into the encapsulated **HRESULT**.

The **WCode** method is used to undo a mapping which happens in the COM support code. The wrapper for a **dispinterface** property or method calls a support routine which packages the arguments and calls **IDispatch::Invoke**. Upon return, if a failure **HRESULT** of DISP_E_EXCEPTION is returned, the error information is retrieved from the **EXCEPINFO** structure passed to **IDispatch::Invoke**. The error code can either be a 16-bit value stored in the **wCode** member of the **EXCEPINFO** structure or a full 32-bit value in the **scode** member of the **EXCEPINFO** structure. If a 16-bit **wCode** is returned, it must first be mapped to a 32-bit failure **HRESULT**.

See Also: _com_error::HRESULTToWCode, _com_error::WCodeToHRESULT

_com_error::WCodeToHRESULT

static HRESULT WCodeToHRESULT(WORD *wCode*) throw( );

Return Value

32-bit HRESULT mapped from the 16-bit wCode.

Parameters

wCode   The 16-bit **wCode** to be mapped to 32-bit **HRESULT**

Remarks

Performs 16-bit **wCode** to 32-bit **HRESULT** mapping. See the **WCode** member function.

See Also: _com_error::WCode, _com_error::HRESULTToWCode

Operators

_com_error::operator =

_com_error& operator = (const _com_error& *that* **) throw ( );**

Parameters

    that   A **_com_error** object

Remarks

    Assigns an existing **_com_error** object to another.

_com_ptr_t

A **_com_ptr_t** object encapsulates a COM interface pointer and is called a "smart" pointer. This template class manages resource allocation and deallocation, via function calls to the **IUnknown** member functions: **QueryInterface**, **AddRef**, and **Release**.

A smart pointer is usually referenced by the typedef definition provided by the **_COM_SMARTPTR_TYPEDEF** macro. This macro takes an interface name and the IID, and declares a specialization of **_com_ptr_t** with the name of the interface plus a suffix of **Ptr**. For example,

```
_COM_SMARTPTR_TYPEDEF(IMyInterface, __uuidof(IMyInterface));
```

declares the **_com_ptr_t** specialization **IMyInterfacePtr**.

A set of function templates, not members of this template class, support comparisons with a smart pointer on the right-hand side of the comparison operator.

#include <comdef.h>

Construction

_com_ptr_t	Constructs a **_com_ptr_t** object.

Low-level Operations

AddRef	Calls the **AddRef** member function of **IUnknown** on the encapsulated interface pointer.
Attach	Encapsulates a raw interface pointer of this smart pointer's type.
CreateInstance	Creates a new instance of an object given a **CLSID** or **ProgID**.
Detach	Extracts and returns the encapsulated interface pointer.
GetInterfacePtr	Returns the encapsulated interface pointer.
QueryInterface	Calls the **QueryInterface** member function of **IUnknown** on the encapsulated interface pointer.
Release	Calls the **Release** member function of **IUnknown** on the encapsulated interface pointer.

Operators

operator =	Assigns a new value to an existing **_com_ptr_t** object.
operators ==, !=, <, >, <=, >=	Compare the smart pointer object to another smart pointer, raw interface pointer, or **NULL**.
Extractors	Extract the encapsulated COM interface pointer.

Member Functions

_com_ptr_t::_com_ptr_t

_com_ptr_t( ) throw( );
_com_ptr_t(Interface* *pInterface* **) throw( );**
_com_ptr_t(Interface* *pInterface***, bool** *fAddRef* **) throw( );**
_com_ptr_t(int NULL) throw(_com_error);
template< > _com_ptr_t(const _com_ptr_t& *cp* **) throw( );**
template<typename _InterfacePtr> _com_ptr_t(const _InterfacePtr& *p* **)**
  ↪ **throw(_com_error);**
template< > _com_ptr_t(const _variant_t& *varSrc* **) throw(_com_error);**
explicit _com_ptr_t(const CLSID& *clsid***, DWORD** *dwClsContext* **= CLSCTX_ALL)**
  ↪ **throw(_com_error);**
explicit _com_ptr_t(LPOLESTR *lpOleStr***, DWORD** *dwClsContext* **= CLSCTX_ALL)**
  ↪ **throw(_com_error);**
explicit _com_ptr_t(LPCSTR *lpcStr***, DWORD** *dwClsContext* **= CLSCTX_ALL)**
  ↪ **throw(_com_error);**

Parameters

pInterface   a raw interface pointer

fAddRef   if **true**, **AddRef** is called to increment the reference count of the encapsulated interface pointer

cp   a **_com_ptr_t** object

p   a raw interface pointer, its type being different from the smart pointer type of this **_com_ptr_t** object

varSrc   a **_variant_t** object

clsid   the **CLSID** of a coclass

dwClsContext   context for running executable code

lpOleStr   a Unicode string that holds either a **CLSID** (starting with "{") or a **ProgID**

lpcStr   a multibyte string that holds either a **CLSID** (starting with "{") or a **ProgID**.

Remarks

Constructs a **_com_ptr_t** object.

- **_com_ptr_t( )** Constructs a **NULL** smart pointer.

- **_com_ptr_t**(*pInterface*)   Constructs a smart pointer from a raw interface pointer of this smart pointer's type. **AddRef** is called to increment the reference count for the encapsulated interface pointer.

- **_com_ptr_t**(*pInterface*, *fAddRef*)   Constructs a smart pointer from a raw interface pointer of this smart pointer's type. If *fAddRef* is **true**, **AddRef** is called to increment the reference count for the encapsulated interface pointer. If *fAddRef* is **false**, this constructor takes ownership of the raw interface pointer without calling **AddRef**.

- **_com_ptr_t**(NULL)   Constructs a **NULL** smart pointer. The **NULL** argument must be a zero.

- **_com_ptr_t**(*cp*)   Constructs a smart pointer as a copy of another instance of the same smart pointer. **AddRef** is called to increment the reference count for the encapsulated interface pointer.

- **_com_ptr_t**(*p*)   Constructs a smart pointer from a different smart pointer type or from a different raw interface pointer. **QueryInterface** is called to find an interface pointer of this smart pointer's type. If **QueryInterface** fails with an **E_NOINTERFACE** error, a **NULL** smart pointer is constructed. Any other error causes a **_com_error** to be raised.

- **_com_ptr_t**(*varSrc*)   Constructs a smart pointer from a **_variant_t** object. The encapsulated **VARIANT** must be of type **VT_DISPATCH** or **VT_UNKNOWN**, or it can be converted into one of these two types. If **QueryInterface** fails with an **E_NOINTERFACE** error, a **NULL** smart pointer is constructed. Any other error causes a **_com_error** to be raised.

- **_com_ptr_t**(*clsid*, *dwClsContext*)   Constructs a smart pointer given the **CLSID** of a coclass. This function calls **CoCreateInstance**, by the member function **CreateInstance**, to create a new COM object and then queries for this smart pointer's interface type. If **QueryInterface** fails with an **E_NOINTERFACE** error, a **NULL** smart pointer is constructed. Any other error causes a **_com_error** to be raised.

- **_com_ptr_t**(*lpOleStr*, *dwClsContext*)   Constructs a smart pointer given a Unicode string which holds either a **CLSID** (starting with "{") or a **ProgID**. This function calls **CoCreateInstance**, by the member function **CreateInstance**, to create a new COM object and then queries for this smart pointer's interface type. If **QueryInterface** fails with an **E_NOINTERFACE** error, a **NULL** smart pointer is constructed. Any other error causes a **_com_error** to be raised.

- **_com_ptr_t**(*lpcStr*, *dwClsContext*)   Constructs a smart pointer given a multibyte character string which holds either a **CLSID** (starting with "{") or a **ProgID**. This function calls **CoCreateInstance**, by the member function **CreateInstance**, to create a new COM object and then queries for this smart pointer's interface type. If **QueryInterface** fails with an **E_NOINTERFACE** error, a **NULL** smart pointer is constructed. Any other error causes a **_com_error** to be raised.

_com_ptr_t::AddRef

void AddRef( ) throw(_com_error);

Remarks

Calls **IUnknown::AddRef** on the encapsulated interface pointer, raising an
E_POINTER error if the pointer is **NULL**.

_com_ptr_t::Attach

void Attach(Interface* *pInterface* **) throw( );**
void Attach(Interface* *pInterface*, **bool** *fAddRef* **) throw( );**

Parameters

pInterface   a raw interface pointer

fAddRef   If it is **true**, then **AddRef** is called. If it is **false**, the **_com_ptr_t** object
takes ownership of the raw interface pointer without calling **AddRef**.

Remarks

Encapsulates a raw interface pointer of this smart pointer's type.

- **Attach(** *pInterface* **)**   **AddRef** is not called. The ownership of the interface is
passed to this **_com_ptr_t** object. **Release** is called to decrement the reference
count for the previously encapsulated pointer.

- **Attach(** *pInterface*, *fAddRef* **)**   If *fAddRef* is **true**, **AddRef** is called to increment
the reference count for the encapsulated interface pointer. If *fAddRef* is **false**, this
_com_ptr_t object takes ownership of the raw interface pointer without calling
AddRef. **Release** is called to decrement the reference count for the previously
encapsulated pointer.

_com_ptr_t::CreateInstance

HRESULT CreateInstance(const CLSID& *rclsid*,
  ↪ **DWORD** *dwClsContext* = **CLSCTX_ALL**) throw( );**
HRESULT CreateInstance(LPOLESTR *clsidString*,
  ↪ **DWORD** *dwClsContext* = **CLSCTX_ALL**) throw( );**
HRESULT CreateInstance(LPCSTR *clsidStringA*,
  ↪ **DWORD** *dwClsContext* = **CLSCTX_ALL**) throw( );**

Parameters

rclsid   the **CLSID** of an object

clsidString   a Unicode string that holds either a **CLSID** (starting with "{") or a
ProgID

clsidStringA   a multibyte string that holds either a **CLSID** (starting with "{") or a
ProgID

dwClsContext   context for running executable code

Remarks

Creates a new running instance of an object given a **CLSID** or **ProgID**. This member functions calls **CoCreateInstance** to create a new COM object and then queries for this smart pointer's interface type. The resulting pointer is then encapsulated within this **_com_ptr_t** object. **Release** is called to decrement the reference count for the previously encapsulated pointer. This routine returns the **HRESULT** to indicate success or failure.

- **CreateInstance(** *rclsid*, *dwClsContext* **)**   Creates a new running instance of an object given a **CLSID**.

- **CreateInstance(** *clsidString*, *dwClsContext* **)**   Creates a new running instance of an object given a Unicode string which holds either a **CLSID** (starting with "{") or a **ProgID**.

- **CreateInstance(** *clsidStringA*, *dwClsContext* **)**   Creates a new running instance of an object given a multibyte character string which holds either a **CLSID** (starting with "{") or a **ProgID**.

_com_ptr_t::Detach

Interface* Detach( ) throw( );

Remarks

Extracts and returns the encapsulated interface pointer, then clears the encapsulated pointer storage to **NULL**. This removes the interface pointer from encapsulation. It is up to you to call **Release** on the returned interface pointer.

_com_ptr_t::GetInterfacePtr

Interface* GetInterfacePtr( ) const throw( );

Remarks

Returns the encapsulated interface pointer, which may be **NULL**.

_com_ptr_t::QueryInterface

template<typename _InterfaceType> HRESULT QueryInterface (const IID& *iid*, **↪ _InterfaceType*&** *p* **) throw ( );**
template<typename _InterfaceType> HRESULT QueryInterface (const IID& *iid*, **↪ _InterfaceType**** *p***) throw( );**

Parameters

iid   **IID** of an interface pointer

p   raw interface pointer

Remarks

Calls **IUnknown::QueryInterface** on the encapsulated interface pointer with the specified **IID**, and returns the resulting raw interface pointer in *p*. This routine returns the **HRESULT** to indicate success or failure.

_com_ptr_t::Release

void Release( ) throw(_com_error);

Remarks

Calls **IUnknown::Release** on the encapsulated interface pointer, raising an **E_POINTER** error if this interface pointer is **NULL**.

Operators

_com_ptr_t::operator =

_com_ptr_t& operator=(Interface* *pInterface* **) throw( );**
_com_ptr_t& operator=(int NULL) throw(_com_error);
template< > _com_ptr_t& operator=(const _com_ptr_t& *cp* **) throw( );**
template< > _com_ptr_t& operator=(const _variant_t& *varSrc* **)**
  ↪ **throw(_com_error);**
template<typename _InterfacePtr> _com_ptr_t& operator=
  ↪ **(const _InterfacePtr&** *p* **) throw(_com_error);**

Remarks

Assigns an interface pointer to this **_com_ptr_t** object:

- **operator=(** *pInterface* **)**   Encapsulates a raw interface pointer of this smart pointer's type. **AddRef** is called to increment the reference count for the encapsulated interface pointer, and **Release** is called to decrement the reference count for the previously encapsulated pointer.

- **operator=(NULL)**   Sets a smart pointer to **NULL**. The **NULL** argument must be a zero.

- **operator=(** *cp* **)**   Sets a smart pointer to be a copy of another instance of the same smart pointer of the same type. **AddRef** is called to increment the reference count for the encapsulated interface pointer, and **Release** is called to decrement the reference count for the previously encapsulated pointer.

- **operator=(** *varSrc* **)**   Sets a smart pointer to be a **_variant_t** object. The encapsulated **VARIANT** must be of type **VT_DISPATCH** or **VT_UNKNOWN**, or it can be converted to one of these two types. If **QueryInterface** fails with an **E_NOINTERFACE** error, a **NULL** smart pointer results. Any other error causes a **_com_error** to be raised.

- **operator=(** *p* **)** Sets a smart pointer to be a different smart pointer of a different type or a different raw interface pointer. **QueryInterface** is called to find an interface pointer of this smart pointer's type, and **Release** is called to decrement the reference count for the previously encapsulated pointer. If **QueryInterface** fails with an **E_NOINTERFACE**, a **NULL** smart pointer results. Any other error causes a **_com_error** to be raised.

_com_ptr_t Relational Operators

template<typename _InterfacePtr> bool operator==(_InterfacePtr *p*)
  ↳ throw(_com_error);
template<> bool operator==(Interface* *p*) throw(_com_error);
template<> bool operator==(_com_ptr_t& *p*) throw( );
template<> bool operator==(int NULL) throw(_com_error);
template<typename _InterfacePtr> bool operator!=(_InterfacePtr *p*)
  ↳ throw(_com_error);
template<> bool operator!=(Interface* *p*) throw(_com_error);
template<> bool operator!=(_com_ptr_t& *p*) throw(_com_error);
template<> bool operator!=(int NULL) throw(_com_error);
template<typename _InterfacePtr> bool operator<(_InterfacePtr *p*)
  ↳ throw(_com_error);
template<> bool operator<(Interface* *p*) throw(_com_error);
template<> bool operator<(_com_ptr_t& *p*) throw(_com_error);
template<> bool operator<(int NULL) throw(_com_error);
template<typename _InterfacePtr> bool operator>(_InterfacePtr *p*)
  ↳ throw(_com_error);
template<> bool operator>(Interface* *p*) throw( );
template<> bool operator>(_com_ptr_t& *p*) throw(_com_error);
template<> bool operator>(int NULL) throw(_com_error);
template<typename _InterfacePtr> bool operator<=(_InterfacePtr *p*)
  ↳ throw(_com_error);
template<> bool operator<=(Interface* *p*) throw( );
template<> bool operator<=(_com_ptr_t& *p*) throw(_com_error);
template<> bool operator<=(int NULL) throw(_com_error);
template<typename _InterfacePtr> bool operator>=(_InterfacePtr *p*)
  ↳ throw(_com_error);
template<> bool operator>=(Interface* *p*) throw(_com_error);
template<> bool operator>=(_com_ptr_t& *p*) throw(_com_error);
template<> bool operator>=(int NULL) throw(_com_error);

Remarks

Compares a smart pointer object to another smart pointer, raw interface pointer, or **NULL**. Except for the **NULL** pointer tests, these operators first query both pointers for **IUnknown**, and compare the results.

_com_ptr_t Extractors

operator Interface*( ) const throw( );
operator Interface&( ) const throw(_com_error);
Interface& operator*( ) const throw(_com_error);
Interface* operator->( ) const throw(_com_error);
Interface** operator&( ) throw( );
operator bool( ) const throw( );

Remarks

- **operator Interface***   Returns the encapsulated interface pointer, which may be **NULL**.

- **operator Interface&**   Returns a reference to the encapsulated interface pointer, and issues an error if the pointer is **NULL**.

- **operator***   Allows a smart pointer object to act as though it were the actual encapsulated interface when dereferenced.

- **operator->**   Allows a smart pointer object to act as though it were the actual encapsulated interface when dereferenced.

- **operator&**   Releases any encapsulated interface pointer, replacing it with **NULL**, and returns the address of the encapsulated pointer. This allows the smart pointer to be passed by address to a function which has an **out** parameter through which it returns an interface pointer.

- **operator bool**   Allows a smart pointer object to be used in a conditional expression. This operator returns **true** if the pointer is not **NULL**.

Relational Function Templates

template<typename _InterfaceType> bool operator==(int NULL,
↳ **_com_ptr_t<_InterfaceType>&** *p* **) throw(_com_error);**
template<typename _Interface, typename _InterfacePtr> bool operator==
↳ **(_Interface*** *i*, **_com_ptr_t<_InterfacePtr>&** *p* **) throw(_com_error);**
template<typename _Interface> bool operator!=(int NULL,
↳ **_com_ptr_t<_Interface>&** *p* **) throw(_com_error);**
template<typename _Interface, typename _InterfacePtr> bool operator!=
↳ **(_Interface*** *i*, **_com_ptr_t<_InterfacePtr>&** *p* **) throw(_com_error);**
template<typename _Interface> bool operator<(int NULL,
↳ **_com_ptr_t<_Interface>&** *p* **) throw(_com_error);**
template<typename _Interface, typename _InterfacePtr> bool operator<
↳ **(_Interface*** *i*, **_com_ptr_t<_InterfacePtr>&** *p* **) throw(_com_error);**
template<typename _Interface> bool operator>(int NULL,
↳ **_com_ptr_t<_Interface>&** *p* **) throw(_com_error);**
template<typename _Interface, typename _InterfacePtr> bool operator>
↳ **(_Interface*** *i*, **_com_ptr_t<_InterfacePtr>&** *p* **) throw(_com_error);**

```
template<typename _Interface> bool operator<=( int NULL,
    ↳ _com_ptr_t<_Interface>& p ) throw( _com_error );
template<typename _Interface, typename _InterfacePtr> bool operator<=
    ↳ ( _Interface* i, _com_ptr_t<_InterfacePtr>& p ) throw( _com_error );
template<typename _Interface> bool operator>=( int NULL,
    ↳ _com_ptr_t<_Interface>& p ) throw( _com_error );
template<typename _Interface, typename _InterfacePtr> bool operator>=
    ↳ ( _Interface* i, _com_ptr_t<_InterfacePtr>& p ) throw( _com_error );
```

Parameters

i   a raw interface pointer

p   a smart pointer

Remarks

They are function templates which allow comparison with a smart pointer on the right-hand side of the comparison operator. These are not member functions of **_com_ptr_t**.

_bstr_t

A **_bstr_t** object encapsulates the **BSTR** data type. The class manages resource allocation and deallocation, via function calls to **SysAllocString** and **SysFreeString**, and other **BSTR** APIs when appropriate. The **_bstr_t** class uses reference counting to avoid excessive overhead.

#include <comdef.h>

Construction

_bstr_t	Constructs a **_bstr_t** object.

Operations

copy	Construuts a copy of the encapsulated **BSTR**.
Length	Returns the length of the encapsulated **BSTR**.

Operators

operator =	Assigns a new value to an existing **_bstr_t** object.
Operator +=	Appends characters to the end of the **_bstr_t** object.
Operator +	Concatenates two strings.
Operator !	Checks if the encapsulated **BSTR** is a **NULL** string.
Operator ==, !=, <, >, <=, >=	Compares two **_bstr_t** objects.
Operator wchar_t*, char*	Extract the pointers to the encapsulated Unicode or multibyte **BSTR** object.

Member Functions
_bstr_t::_bstr_t

_bstr_t( ) throw( );
_bstr_t(const _bstr_t& *s1* **) throw( );**
_bstr_t(const char* *s2* **) throw(_com_error);**
_bstr_t(const wchar_t* *s3* **) throw(_com_error);**
_bstr_t(const _variant_t& *var* **) throw (_com_error);**
_bstr_t(BSTR *bstr***, bool** *fCopy* **) throw (_com_error);**

Parameters

s1   a **_bstr_t** object to be copied

s2   a multibyte string

s3   a Unicode string

var   a **_variant_t** object

bstr   an existing **BSTR** object

fCopy   if false, the *bstr* argument is attached to the new object without making a copy
by calling **SysAllocString**.

Remarks

Constructs a **_bstr_t** object.

- **_bstr_t( )**   Constructs a default **_bstr_t** object that encapsulates a **NULL BSTR**
  object.

- **_bstr_t(_bstr_t&** *s1* **)**   Constructs a **_bstr_t** object as a copy of another. This is a
  "shallow" copy, which increments the reference count of the encapsulated **BSTR**
  object instead of creating a new one.

- **_bstr_t(char*** *s2* **)**   Constructs a **_bstr_t** object by calling **SysAllocString** to
  create a new **BSTR** object and encapsulate it. This constructor first performs a
  multibyte to Unicode conversion.

- **_bstr_t(wchar_t*** *s3* **)**   Constructs a **_bstr_t** object by calling **SysAllocString** to
  create a new **BSTR** object and encapsulates it.

- **_bstr_t(_variant_t&** *var* **)**   Constructs a **_bstr_t** object from a **_variant_t** object
  by first retrieving a **BSTR** object from the encapsulated **VARIANT** object.

- **_bstr_t(BSTR** *bstr***, bool** *fCopy* **)**   Constructs a **_bstr_t** object from an existing
  BSTR (as opposed to a **wchar_t*** string). If *fCopy* is **false**, the supplied **BSTR** is
  attached to the new object without making a new copy via **SysAllocString**. This is
  the method used by the wrapper functions in the type library headers to encapsulate
  and take ownership of a **BSTR**, returned by an interface method, in a **_bstr_t**
  object.

_bstr_t::copy

BSTR copy( ) const throw(_com_error);

Remarks

Returns a newly allocated copy of the encapsulated **BSTR** object.

_bstr_t::length

unsigned int length ( ) const throw( );

Remarks

Returns the length of the encapsulated **BSTR** object.

Operators

_bstr_t::operator =

_bstr_t& operator=(const _bstr_t& *s1* **) throw ( );**
_bstr_t& operator=(const char* *s2* **) throw(_com_error);**
_bstr_t& operator=(const wchar_t* *s3* **) throw(_com_error);**
_bstr_t& operator=(const _variant_t& *var* **) throw(_com_error);**

Parameters

s1   a **_bstr_t** object to be assigned to an existing **_bstr_t** object

s2   a multibyte string to be assigned to an existing **_bstr_t** object

s3   a Unicode string to be assigned to an existing **_bstr_t** object

var   a **_variant_t** object to be assigned to an existing **_bstr_t** object

Remarks

Assigns a new value to an existing **_bstr_t** object.

_bstr_t::operator +=, +

_bstr_t& operator+=(const _bstr_t& *s1* **) throw(_com_error);**
_bstr_t operator+(const _bstr_t& *s1* **) const throw(_com_error);**
friend _bstr_t operator+(const char* *s2***, const _bstr_t&** *s1* **);**
friend _bstr_t operator+(const wchar_t* *s3***, const _bstr_t&** *s1* **);**

Parameters

s1   a **_bstr_t** object

s2   a multibyte string

s3   a Unicode string

Remarks

These operators perform string concatenation:

- **operator+=**(*s1*)   Appends the characters in the encapsulated **BSTR** of *s1* to the end of this object's encapsulated **BSTR**.

- **operator+**(*s1*)   Returns the new **_bstr_t** which is formed by concatenating this object's **BSTR** with that of *s1*.

- **operator+**(*s2*, *s1*)   Returns a new **_bstr_t** which is formed by concatenating a multibyte string *s2*, converted to Unicode, with the **BSTR** encapsulated in *s1*.

- **operator+**(*s3*, *s1*)   Returns a new **_bstr_t** which is formed by concatenating a Unicode string *s3* with the **BSTR** encapsulated in *s1*.

_bstr_t::operator !

bool operator!( ) const throw( );

Remarks

Checks if the encapsulated **BSTR** object is the **NULL** string. It returns **true** if yes, **false** if not.

_bstr_t Relational Operators

bool operator==(const _bstr_t& *str* **) const throw( );**
bool operator!=(const _bstr_t& *str* **) const throw( );**
bool operator<(const _bstr_t& *str* **) const throw( );**
bool operator>(const _bstr_t& *str* **) const throw( );**
bool operator<=(const _bstr_t& *str* **) const throw( );**
bool operator>=(const _bstr_t& *str* **) const throw( );**

Remarks

These operators compare two **_bstr_t** objects lexicographically. The operators return **true** if the comparisons hold, otherwise return **false**.

_bstr_t::wchar_t*, _bstr_t::char*

operator const wchar_t*( ) const throw( );
operator wchar_t*( ) const throw( );
operator const char*( ) const throw(_com_error);
operator char*( ) const throw(_com_error);

Remarks

These operators can be used to extract raw pointers to the encapsulated Unicode or multibyte **BSTR** object. The operators return the pointer to the actual internal buffer, so the resulting string cannot be modified.

_variant_t

A **_variant_t** object encapsulates the **VARIANT** data type. The class manages resource allocation and deallocation, and makes function calls to **VariantInit** and **VariantClear** as appropriate.

#include <comdef.h>

Construction

_variant_t	Constructs a **_variant_t** object.

Operations

Attach	Attaches a **VARIANT** object into the **_variant_t** object.
Clear	Clears the encapsulated **VARIANT** object.
ChangeType	Changes the type of the **_variant_t** object to the indicated **VARTYPE**.
Detach	Detaches the encapsulated **VARIANT** object from this **_variant_t** object.
SetString	Assigns a string to this **_variant_t** object.

Operators

operator =	Assigns a new value to an existing **_variant_t** object.
Operator ==, !=	Compare two **_variant_t** objects for equality or inequality.
Extractors	Extract data from the encapsulated **VARIANT** object.

Member Functions

_variant_t::_variant_t

_variant_t( ) throw( );
_variant_t(const VARIANT& *varSrc* **) throw(_com_error);**
_variant_t(const VARIANT* *pVarSrc* **) throw(_com_error);**
_variant_t(const _variant_t& *var_t_Src* **) throw(_com_error);**
_variant_t(VARIANT& *varSrc***, bool** *fCopy* **) throw(_com_error);**
_variant_t(short *sSrc***, VARTYPE** *vtSrc* **= VT_I2) throw(_com_error);**
_variant_t(long *lSrc***, VARTYPE** *vtSrc* **= VT_I4) throw(_com_error);**
_variant_t(float *fltSrc* **) throw( );**
_variant_t(double *dblSrc***, VARTYPE** *vtSrc* **= VT_R8) throw(_com_error);**
_variant_t(const CY& *cySrc* **) throw( );**
_variant_t(const _bstr_t& *bstrSrc* **) throw(_com_error);**
_variant_t(const wchar_t * *wstrSrc* **) throw(_com_error);**
_variant_t(const char* *strSrc* **) throw(_com_error);**

_variant_t(bool *bSrc* **) throw( );**
_variant_t(IUnknown* *pIUknownSrc***, bool** *fAddRef* **= true) throw( );**
_variant_t(IDispatch* *pDispSrc***, bool** *fAddRef* **= true) throw( );**
_variant_t(const DECIMAL& *decSrc* **) throw( );**
_variant_t(BYTE *bSrc* **) throw( );**

Parameters

varSrc   a **VARIANT** object to be copied into the new **_variant_t** object

pVarSrc   pointer to a **VARIANT** object to be copied into the new **_variant_t** object

var_t_Src   a **_variant_t** object to be copied into the new **_variant_t** object

fCopy   if false, the supplied **VARIANT** object is attached to the new **_variant_t** object without making a new copy by **VariantCopy**

lSrc, sSrc   an integer value to be copied into the new **_variant_t** object

vtSrc   the **VARTYPE** for the new **_variant_t** object

fltSrc, dblSrc   a numerical value to be copied into the new **_variant_t** object

cySrc   a **CY** object to be copied into the new **_variant_t** object

bstrSrc   a **_bstr_t** object to be copied into the new **_variant_t** object

strSrc, wstrSrc   a string to be copied into the new **_variant_t** object

bSrc   a **bool** value to be copied into the new **_variant_t** object

pIUknownSrc   COM interface pointer to a **VT_UNKNOWN** object to be encapsulated into the new **_variant_t** object

pDispSrc   COM interface pointer to a **VT_DISPATCH** object to be encapsulated into the new **_variant_t** object

decSrc   a **DECIMAL** value to be copied into the new **_variant_t** object

bSrc   a **BYTE** value to be copied into the new **_variant_t** object

Remarks

Constructs a **_variant_t** object.

- **_variant_t( )**   Constructs an empty **_variant_t** object, **VT_EMPTY**.

- **_variant_t(VARIANT&** *varSrc* **)**   Constructs a **_variant_t** object from a copy of the **VARIANT** object. The variant type is retained.

- **_variant_t(VARIANT*** *pVarSrc* **)**   Constructs a **_variant_t** object from a copy of the **VARIANT** object. The variant type is retained.

- **_variant_t(_variant_t&** *var_t_Src* **)**   Constructs a **_variant_t** object from another **_variant_t** object. The variant type is retained.

- **_variant_t(VARIANT&** *varSrc***, bool** *fCopy* **)**   Constructs a **_variant_t** object from an existing **VARIANT** object. If *fCopy* is **false**, the **VARIANT** object is attached to the new object without making a copy.

- **_variant_t(short** *sSrc***, VARTYPE** *vtSrc* **= VT_I2)** Constructs a **_variant_t** object of type **VT_I2** or **VT_BOOL** from a **short** integer value. Any other **VARTYPE** results in an **E_INVALIDARG** error.

- **_variant_t(long** *lSrc***, VARTYPE** *vtSrc* **= VT_I4)** Constructs a **_variant_t** object of type **VT_I4, VT_BOOL,** or **VT_ERROR** from a **long** integer value. Any other **VARTYPE** results in an **E_INVALIDARG** error.

- **_variant_t(float** *fltSrc* **)** Constructs a **_variant_t** object of type **VT_R4** from a **float** numerical value.

- **_variant_t(double** *dblSrc***, VARTYPE** *vtSrc* **= VT_R8)** Constructs a **_variant_t** object of type **VT_R8** or **VT_DATE** from a **double** numerical value. Any other **VARTYPE** results in an **E_INVALIDARG** error.

- **_variant_t(CY&** *cySrc* **)** Constructs a **_variant_t** object of type **VT_CY** from a **CY** object.

- **_variant_t(_bstr_t&** *bstrSrc* **)** Constructs a **_variant_t** object of type **VT_BSTR** from a **_bstr_t** object. A new **BSTR** is allocated.

- **_variant_t(wchar_t ****wstrSrc* **)** Constructs a **_variant_t** object of type **VT_BSTR** from a Unicode string. A new **BSTR** is allocated.

- **_variant_t(char*** *strSrc* **)** Constructs a **_variant_t** object of type **VT_BSTR** from a string. A new **BSTR** is allocated.

- **_variant_t(bool** *bSrc* **)** Constructs a **_variant_t** object of type **VT_BOOL** from a **bool** value.

- **_variant_t(IUnknown*** *pIUknownSrc***, bool** *fAddRef* **= true)** Constructs a **_variant_t** object of type **VT_UNKNOWN** from a COM interface pointer. If *fAddRef* is **true**, then **AddRef** is called on the supplied interface pointer to match the call to **Release** that will occur when the **_variant_t** object is destroyed. It is up to you to call **Release** on the supplied interface pointer. If *fAddRef* is **false**, this constructor takes ownership of the supplied interface pointer; do not call **Release** on the supplied interface pointer.

- **_variant_t(IDispatch*** *pDispSrc***, bool** *fAddRef* **= true)** Constructs a **_variant_t** object of type **VT_DISPATCH** from a COM interface pointer. If *fAddRef* is **true**, then **AddRef** is called on the supplied interface pointer to match the call to **Release** that will occur when the **_variant_t** object is destroyed. It is up to you to call **Release** on the supplied interface pointer. If **fAddRef** is false, this constructor takes ownership of the supplied interface pointer; do not call **Release** on the supplied interface pointer.

- **_variant_t(DECIMAL&** *decSrc* **)** Constructs a **_variant_t** object of type **VT_DECIMAL** from a **DECIMAL** value.

- **_variant_t(BYTE** *bSrc* **)** Constructs a **_variant_t** object of type **VT_UI1** from a **BYTE** value.

_variant_t::Attach

void Attach(VARIANT& *varSrc* **) throw(_com_error);**

Parameters

varSrc   a **VARIANT** object to be attached to this **_variant_t** object

Remarks

Takes ownership of the **VARIANT** by encapsulating it. This member function releases any existing encapsulated **VARIANT**, then copies the supplied **VARIANT**, and sets its **VARTYPE** to **VT_EMPTY** to make sure its resources can only be released by the **_variant_t** destructor.

_variant_t::Clear

void Clear( ) throw(_com_error);

Remarks

Calls **VariantClear** on the encapsulated **VARIANT** object.

_variant_t::ChangeType

void ChangeType(VARTYPE *vartype*, **const _variant_t*** *pSrc* = **NULL)**
↪ **throw(_com_error);**

Parameters

vartype   the **VARTYPE** for this **_variant_t** object

pSrc   a pointer to the **_variant_t** object to be converted. If this value is **NULL**, conversion is done in place.

Remarks

This member function converts a **_variant_t** object into the indicated **VARTYPE**. If *pSrc* is **NULL**, the conversion is done in place, otherwise this **_variant_t** object is copied from *pSrc* and then converted.

_variant_t::Detach

VARIANT Detach( ) throw(_com_error);

Return Value

The encapsulated **VARIANT**.

Remarks

Extracts and returns the encapsulated **VARIANT**, then clears this **_variant_t** object without destroying it. This member function removes the **VARIANT** from encapsulation and sets the **VARTYPE** of this **_variant_t** object to **VT_EMPTY**. It is up to you to release the returned **VARIANT** by calling the **VariantInit** function.

_variant_t::SetString

void SetString(const char* *pSrc* **) throw(_com_error);**

Parameter

pSrc   pointer to the multibyte character string

Remarks

Converts a multibyte character string to a Unicode **BSTR** object, and assigns it to this **_variant_t** object.

Operators

_variant_t::operator =

_variant_t& operator=(const VARIANT& *varSrc* **) throw(_com_error);**
_variant_t& operator=(const VARIANT* *pVarSrc* **) throw(_com_error);**
_variant_t& operator=(const _variant_t& *var_t_Src* **) throw(_com_error);**
_variant_t& operator=(short *sSrc* **) throw(_com_error);**
_variant_t& operator=(long *lSrc* **) throw(_com_error);**
_variant_t& operator=(float *fltSrc* **) throw(_com_error);**
_variant_t& operator=(double *dblSrc* **) throw(_com_error);**
_variant_t& operator=(const CY& *cySrc* **) throw(_com_error);**
_variant_t& operator=(const _bstr_t& *bstrSrc* **) throw(_com_error);**
_variant_t& operator=(const wchar_t* *wstrSrc* **) throw(_com_error);**
_variant_t& operator=(const char* *strSrc* **) throw(_com_error);**
_variant_t& operator=(IDispatch* *pDispSrc* **) throw(_com_error);**
_variant_t& operator=(bool *bSrc* **) throw(_com_error);**
_variant_t& operator=(IUnknown* *pSrc* **) throw(_com_error);**
_variant_t& operator=(const DECIMAL& *decSrc* **) throw(_com_error);**
_variant_t& operator=(BYTE *bSrc* **) throw(_com_error);**

Remarks

The operator assigns a new value to the **_variant_t** object:

- **operator=(** *varSrc* **)**   Assigns an existing **VARIANT** to a **_variant_t** object.
- **operator=(** *pVarSrc* **)**   Assigns an existing **VARIANT** to a **_variant_t** object.
- **operator=(** *var_t_Src* **)**   Assigns an existing **_variant_t** object to a **_variant_t** object.
- **operator=(** *sSrc* **)**   Assigns a **short** integer value to a **_variant_t** object.
- **operator=(** *lSrc* **)**   Assigns a **long** integer value to a **_variant_t** object.
- **operator=(** *fltSrc* **)**   Assigns a **float** numerical value to a **_variant_t** object.

- **operator=(** *dblSrc* **)**   Assigns a **double** numerical value to a **_variant_t** object.

- **operator=(** *cySrc* **)**   Assigns a **CY** object to a **_variant_t** object.

- **operator=(** *bstrSrc* **)**   Assigns a **BSTR** object to a **_variant_t** object.

- **operator=(** *wstrSrc* **)**   Assigns a Unicode string to a **_variant_t** object.

- **operator=(** *strSrc* **)**   Assigns a multibyte string to a **_variant_t** object.

- **operator=(** *bSrc* **)**   Assigns a **bool** value to a **_variant_t** object.

- **operator=(** *pDispSrc* **)**   Assigns a **VT_DISPATCH** object to a **_variant_t** object.

- **operator=(** *pIUnknownSrc* **)**   Assigns a **VT_UNKNOWN** object to a **_variant_t** object.

- **operator=(** *decSrc* **)**   Assigns a **DECIMAL** value to a **_variant_t** object.

- **operator=(** *bSrc* **)**   Assigns a **BYTE** value to a **_variant_t** object.

_variant_t Relational Operators

bool operator==(const VARIANT& *varSrc* **) const throw(_com_error);**
bool operator==(const VARIANT* *pSrc* **) const throw(_com_error);**
bool operator!=(const VARIANT& *varSrc* **) const throw(_com_error);**
bool operator!=(const VARIANT* *pSrc* **) const throw(_com_error);**

Parameter

varSrc   a **VARIANT** to be compared with the **_variant_t** object

pSrc   pointer to the **VARIANT** to be compared with the **_variant_t** object

Remarks

Compares a **_variant_t** object with a **VARIANT**, testing for equality or inequality.
Returns **true** if comparison holds, **false** if not.

_variant_t Extractors

operator short( ) const throw(_com_error);
operator long( ) const throw(_com_error);
operator float( ) const throw(_com_error);
operator double( ) const throw(_com_error);
operator CY( ) const throw(_com_error);
operator bool( ) const throw(_com_error);
operator DECIMAL( ) const throw(_com_error);
operator BYTE( ) const throw(_com_error);
operator _bstr_t( ) const throw(_com_error);
operator IDispatch*( ) const throw(_com_error);
operator IUnknown*( ) const throw(_com_error);

Remarks

Extracts raw data from an encapsulated **VARIANT**. If the **VARIANT** is not already the proper type, **VariantChangeType** is used to attempt a conversion, and an error is generated upon failure:

- **operator short( )** Extracts a **short** integer value.
- **operator long( )** Extracts a **long** integer value.
- **operator float( )** Extracts a **float** numerical value.
- **operator double( )** Extracts a **double** integer value.
- **operator CY( )** Extracts a **CY** object.
- **operator bool( )** Extracts a **bool** value.
- **operator DECIMAL( )** Extracts a **DECIMAL** value.
- **operator BYTE( )** Extracts a **BYTE** value.
- **operator _bstr_t( )** Extracts a string, which is encapsulated in a **_bstr_t** object.
- **operator IDispatch*( )** Extracts a dispinterface pointer from an encapsulated **VARIANT**. **AddRef** is called on the resulting pointer, so it is up to you to call **Release** to free it.
- **operator IUnknown*( )** Extracts a COM interface pointer from an encapsulated **VARIANT**. **AddRef** is called on the resulting pointer, so it is up to you to call **Release** to free it.

Charts

This appendix contains the following charts:

- ASCII Character Codes
- ASCII Multilingual Codes
- ANSI Character Codes
- Key Codes

ASCII Character Codes Chart

The ASCII character code tables contain the decimal and hexadecimal values of the extended ASCII (American Standards Committee for Information Interchange) character set. The extended character set includes the ASCII character set and 128 other characters for graphics and line drawing, often called the "IBM® character set."

ASCII Multilingual Codes Chart

There are a number of variants on the IBM character set, called "code pages." Systems sold in some European countries use the multilingual character set known as Code Page 850, which contains fewer graphics symbols and more accented letters and special characters.

ANSI Character Codes Chart

The ANSI character code chart lists the extended character set of most of the programs used by Windows. The codes of the ANSI (American National Standards Institute) character set from 32 through 126 are displayable characters from the ASCII character set. The ANSI characters displayed as solid blocks are undefined characters and may appear differently on output devices.

Key Codes Chart

Some keys, such as function keys, cursor keys, and ALT+KEY combinations, have no ASCII code. When a key is pressed, a microprocessor within the keyboard generates an "extended scan code" of two bytes. The first (low-order) byte contains the ASCII code, if any. The second (high-order) byte has the scan code—a unique code generated by the keyboard when a key is either pressed or released. Because the extended scan code is more extensive than the standard ASCII code, programs can use it to identify keys which do not have an ASCII code.

ASCII Character Codes Chart 1

Ctrl	Dec	Hex	Char	Code	Dec	Hex	Char	Dec	Hex	Char	Dec	Hex	Char
^@	0	00		NUL	32	20	SP	64	40	@	96	60	`
^A	1	01	☺	SOH	33	21	!	65	41	A	97	61	a
^B	2	02	☻	STX	34	22	"	66	42	B	98	62	b
^C	3	03	♥	ETX	35	23	#	67	43	C	99	63	c
^D	4	04	♦	EOT	36	24	$	68	44	D	100	64	d
^E	5	05	♣	ENQ	37	25	%	69	45	E	101	65	e
^F	6	06	♠	ACK	38	26	&	70	46	F	102	66	f
^G	7	07	•	BEL	39	27	'	71	47	G	103	67	g
^H	8	08	◘	BS	40	28	(	72	48	H	104	68	h
^I	9	09	○	HT	41	29	)	73	49	I	105	69	i
^J	10	0A	◙	LF	42	2A	*	74	4A	J	106	6A	j
^K	11	0B	♂	VT	43	2B	+	75	4B	K	107	6B	k
^L	12	0C	♀	FF	44	2C	,	76	4C	L	108	6C	l
^M	13	0D	♪	CR	45	2D	-	77	4D	M	109	6D	m
^N	14	0E	♫	SO	46	2E	.	78	4E	N	110	6E	n
^O	15	0F	☼	SI	47	2F	/	79	4F	O	111	6F	o
^P	16	10	►	SLE	48	30	0	80	50	P	112	70	p
^Q	17	11	◄	CS1	49	31	1	81	51	Q	113	71	q
^R	18	12	↕	DC2	50	32	2	82	52	R	114	72	r
^S	19	13	‼	DC3	51	33	3	83	53	S	115	73	s
^T	20	14	¶	DC4	52	34	4	84	54	T	116	74	t
^U	21	15	§	NAK	53	35	5	85	55	U	117	75	u
^V	22	16	▬	SYN	54	36	6	86	56	V	118	76	v
^W	23	17	↨	ETB	55	37	7	87	57	W	119	77	w
^X	24	18	↑	CAN	56	38	8	88	58	X	120	78	x
^Y	25	19	↓	EM	57	39	9	89	59	Y	121	79	y
^Z	26	1A	→	SIB	58	3A	:	90	5A	Z	122	7A	z
^[	27	1B	←	ESC	59	3B	;	91	5B	[	123	7B	{
^\	28	1C	∟	FS	60	3C	<	92	5C	\	124	7C	¦
^]	29	1D	↔	GS	61	3D	=	93	5D	]	125	7D	}
^^	30	1E	▲	RS	62	3E	>	94	5E	^	126	7E	~
^_	31	1F	▼	US	63	3F	?	95	5F	_	127	7F	⌂†

† ASCII code 127 has the code DEL. Under MS-DOS, this code has the same effect as ASCII 8 (BS). The DEL code can be generated by the CTRL+BKSP key.

ASCII Character Codes Chart 2

Dec	Hex	Char	Dec	Hex	Char	Dec	Hex	Char	Dec	Hex	Char
128	80	Ç	160	A0	á	192	C0	└	224	E0	α
129	81	ü	161	A1	í	193	C1	┴	225	E1	β
130	82	é	162	A2	ó	194	C2	┬	226	E2	Γ
131	83	â	163	A3	ú	195	C3	├	227	E3	π
132	84	ä	164	A4	ñ	196	C4	─	228	E4	Σ
133	85	à	165	A5	Ñ	197	C5	┼	229	E5	σ
134	86	å	166	A6	ª	198	C6	╞	230	E6	μ
135	87	ç	167	A7	º	199	C7	╟	231	E7	τ
136	88	ê	168	A8	¿	200	C8	╚	232	E8	Φ
137	89	ë	169	A9	⌐	201	C9	╔	233	E9	Θ
138	8A	è	170	AA	¬	202	CA	╩	234	EA	Ω
139	8B	ï	171	AB	½	203	CB	╦	235	EB	δ
140	8C	î	172	AC	¼	204	CC	╠	236	EC	∞
141	8D	ì	173	AD	¡	205	CD	═	237	ED	ø
142	8E	Ä	174	AE	«	206	CE	╬	238	EE	∈
143	8F	Å	175	AF	»	207	CF	╧	239	EF	∩
144	90	É	176	B0	░	208	D0	╨	240	F0	≡
145	91	æ	177	B1	▒	209	D1	╤	241	F1	±
146	92	Æ	178	B2	▓	210	D2	╥	242	F2	≥
147	93	ô	179	B3	│	211	D3	╙	243	F3	≤
148	94	ö	180	B4	┤	212	D4	╘	244	F4	⌠
149	95	ò	181	B5	╡	213	D5	╒	245	F5	⌡
150	96	û	182	B6	╢	214	D6	╓	246	F6	÷
151	97	ù	183	B7	╖	215	D7	╫	247	F7	≈
152	98	ÿ	184	B8	╕	216	D8	╪	248	F8	°
153	99	Ö	185	B9	╣	217	D9	┘	249	F9	∙
154	9A	Ü	186	BA	║	218	DA	┌	250	FA	·
155	9B	¢	187	BB	╗	219	DB	█	251	FB	√
156	9C	£	188	BC	╝	220	DC	▄	252	FC	ⁿ
157	9D	¥	189	BD	╜	221	DD	▌	253	FD	²
158	9E	₧	190	BE	╛	222	DE	▐	254	FE	■
159	9F	ƒ	191	BF	┐	223	DF	▀	255	FF	

ASCII Multilingual Codes Chart

0	32	64 @	96 `	128 Ç	160 á	192 └	224 ó
1 ☻	33 !	65 A	97 a	129 ü	161 í	193 ┴	225 ß
2 ☻	34 "	66 B	98 b	130 é	162 ó	194 ┬	226 ô
3 ♥	35 #	67 C	99 c	131 â	163 ú	195 ├	227 ò
4 ♦	36 $	68 D	100 d	132 ä	164 ñ	196 ─	228 õ
5 ♣	37 %	69 E	101 e	133 à	165 Ñ	197 ┼	229 Õ
6 ♠	38 &	70 F	102 f	134 å	166 ª	198 ã	230 µ
7 •	39 '	71 G	103 g	135 ç	167 º	199 Ã	231 Þ
8 ◘	40 (	72 H	104 h	136 ê	168 ¿	200 ╚	232 þ
9 ◊	41)	73 I	105 i	137 ë	169 ®	201 ╔	233 Ú
10 ◙	42 *	74 J	106 j	138 è	170 ¬	202 ╩	234 Û
11 ♂	43 +	75 K	107 k	139 ï	171 ½	203 ╦	235 Ù
12 ♀	44 ,	76 L	108 l	140 î	172 ¼	204 ╠	236 ý
13 ♪	45 -	77 M	109 m	141 ì	173 ¡	205 =	237 Ý
14 ♫	46 .	78 N	110 n	142 Ä	174 «	206 ╬	238 -
15 ☼	47 /	79 O	111 o	143 Å	175 »	207 ¤	239 ´
16 ►	48 0	80 P	112 p	144 É	176 ░	208 ð	240 -
17 ◄	49 1	81 Q	113 q	145 æ	177 ▒	209 Ð	241 ±
18 ↕	50 2	82 R	114 r	146 ff	178 ▓	210 Ê	242 =
19 ‼	51 3	83 S	115 s	147 ô	179 │	211 Ë	243 ¾
20 ¶	52 4	84 T	116 t	148 ö	180 ┤	212 È	244 ¶
21 §	53 5	85 U	117 u	149 ò	181 Á	213 ı	245 §
22 ▬	54 6	86 V	118 v	150 û	182 Â	214 Í	246 ÷
23 ↨	55 7	87 W	119 w	151 ù	183 À	215 Î	247 ¸
24 ↑	56 8	88 X	120 x	152 ÿ	184 ©	216 Ï	248 °
25 ↓	57 9	89 Y	121 y	153 Ö	185 ╣	217 ┘	249 ¨
26 →	58 :	90 Z	122 z	154 Ü	186 ║	218 ┌	250 ·
27 ←	59 ;	91 [	123 {	155 ø	187 ╗	219 █	251 ¹
28 ∟	60 <	92 \	124 ¦	156 £	188 ╝	220 ▄	252 ³
29 ↔	61 =	93]	125 }	157 Ø	189 ¢	221 ¦	253 ²
30 ▲	62 >	94 ^	126 ~	158 ×	190 ¥	222 Ì	254 ■
31 ▼	63 ?	95 _	127 ⌂	159 ƒ	191 ┐	223 ■	255

ANSI Character Codes Chart

0 ■	32	64 @	96 `	128 ■	160	192 À	224 à
1 ■	33 !	65 A	97 a	129 ■	161 ¡	193 Á	225 á
2 ■	34 "	66 B	98 b	ₜₜ130 ‚	162 ¢	194 Â	226 â
3 ■	35 #	67 C	99 c	ₜₜ131 ƒ	163 £	195 Ã	227 ã
4 ■	36 $	68 D	100 d	ₜₜ132 „	164 ¤	196 Ä	228 ä
5 ■	37 %	69 E	101 e	ₜₜ133 …	165 ¥	197 Å	229 å
6 ■	38 &	70 F	102 f	ₜₜ134 †	166 ¦	198 Æ	230 æ
7 ■	39 '	71 G	103 g	ₜₜ135 ‡	167 §	199 Ç	231 ç
8 ■	40 (	72 H	104 h	ₜₜ136 ˆ	168 ¨	200 È	232 è
9 ■	41)	73 I	105 i	ₜₜ137 ‰	169 ©	201 É	233 é
10 ■	42 *	74 J	106 j	ₜₜ138 Š	170 ª	202 Ê	234 ê
11 ■	43 +	75 K	107 k	ₜₜ139 ‹	171 «	203 Ë	235 ë
12 ■	44 ,	76 L	108 l	ₜₜ140 Œ	172 ¬	204 Ì	236 ì
13 ■	45 -	77 M	109 m	141 ■	173 -	205 Í	237 í
14 ■	46 .	78 N	110 n	142 ■	174 ®	206 Î	238 î
15 ■	47 /	79 O	111 o	143 ■	175 ¯	207 Ï	239 ï
16 ■	48 0	80 P	112 p	144 ■	176 °	208 Ð	240 ð
17 ■	49 1	81 Q	113 q	145 '	177 ±	209 Ñ	241 ñ
18 ■	50 2	82 R	114 r	146 '	178 ²	210 Ò	242 ò
19 ■	51 3	83 S	115 s	ₜₜ147 "	179 ³	211 Ó	243 ó
20 ■	52 4	84 T	116 t	ₜₜ148 "	180 ´	212 Ô	244 ô
21 ■	53 5	85 U	117 u	ₜₜ149 •	181 µ	213 Õ	245 õ
22 ■	54 6	86 V	118 v	ₜₜ150 –	182 ¶	214 Ö	246 ö
23 ■	55 7	87 W	119 w	ₜₜ151 —	183 ·	215 ×	247 ÷
24 ■	56 8	88 X	120 x	ₜₜ152 ˜	184 ¸	216 Ø	248 ø
25 ■	57 9	89 Y	121 y	ₜₜ153 ™	185 ¹	217 Ù	249 ù
26 ■	58 :	90 Z	122 z	ₜₜ154 š	186 º	218 Ú	250 ú
27 ■	59 ;	91 [	123 {	ₜₜ155 ›	187 »	219 Û	251 û
28 ■	60 <	92 \	124 |	ₜₜ156 œ	188 ¼	220 Ü	252 ü
29 ■	61 =	93]	125 }	157 ■	189 ½	221 Ý	253 ý
30 ■	62 >	94 ^	126 ~	158 ■	190 ¾	222 Þ	254 þ
31 ■	63 ?	95 _	127 ■	ₜₜ159 Ÿ	191 ¿	223 ß	255 ÿ

■   Indicates that this character is not supported by Windows.

ᵀₜ   Indicates that this character is available only in TrueType fonts.

Key Codes Chart 1

Key	Scan Code Dec	Scan Code Hex	ASCII or Extended† Dec	ASCII or Extended† Hex	ASCII or Extended† Char	ASCII or Extended† with SHIFT Dec	ASCII or Extended† with SHIFT Hex	ASCII or Extended† with SHIFT Char	ASCII or Extended† with CTRL Dec	ASCII or Extended† with CTRL Hex	ASCII or Extended† with CTRL Char	ASCII or Extended† with ALT Dec	ASCII or Extended† with ALT Hex	ASCII or Extended† with ALT Char
ESC	1	01	27	1B	ESC	27	1B	ESC	27	1B	ESC	1	01	NUL§
1!	2	02	49	31	1	33	21	!				120	78	NUL
2@	3	03	50	32	2	64	40	@	3	03	NUL	121	79	NUL
3#	4	04	51	33	3	35	23	#				122	7A	NUL
4$	5	05	52	34	4	36	24	$				123	7B	NUL
5%	6	06	53	35	5	37	25	%				124	7C	NUL
6^	7	07	54	36	6	94	5E	^	30	1E	RS	125	7D	NUL
7&	8	08	55	37	7	38	26	&				126	7E	NUL
8*	9	09	56	38	8	42	2A	*				127	7F	NUL
9(	10	0A	57	39	9	40	28	(				128	80	NUL
0)	11	0B	48	30	0	41	29	)				129	81	NUL
-_	12	0C	45	2D	-	95	5F	_	31	1F	US	130	82	NUL
=+	13	0D	61	3D	=	43	2B	+				131	83	NUL
BKSP	14	0E	8	08		8	08		127	7F		14	0E	NUL§
TAB	15	0F	9	09		15	0F	NUL	148	94	NUL§	15	A5	NUL§
Q	16	10	113	71	q	81	51	Q	17	11	DC1	16	10	NUL
W	17	11	119	77	w	87	57	W	23	17	ETB	17	11	NUL
E	18	12	101	65	e	69	45	E	5	05	ENQ	18	12	NUL
R	19	13	114	72	r	82	52	R	18	12	DC2	19	13	NUL
T	20	14	116	74	t	84	54	T	20	14	SO	20	14	NUL
Y	21	15	121	79	y	89	59	Y	25	19	EM	21	15	NUL
U	22	16	117	75	u	85	55	U	21	15	NAK	22	16	NUL
I	23	17	105	69	i	73	49	I	9	09	TAB	23	17	NUL
O	24	18	111	6F	o	79	4F	O	15	0F	SI	24	18	NUL
P	25	19	112	70	p	80	50	P	16	10	DLE	25	19	NUL
[{	26	1A	91	5B	[	123	7B	{	27	1B	ESC	26	1A	NUL§
]}	27	1B	93	5D	]	125	7D	}	29	1D	GS	27	1B	NUL§
ENTER	28	1C	13	0D	CR	13	0D	CR	10	0A	LF	28	1C	NUL§
ENTER£	28	1C	13	0D	CR	13	0D	CR	10	0A	LF	166	A6	NUL§
L CTRL	29	1D												
R CTRL£	29	1D												
A	30	1E	97	61	a	65	41	A	1	01	SOH	30	1E	NUL
S	31	1F	115	73	s	83	53	S	19	13	DC3	31	1F	NUL
D	32	20	100	64	d	68	44	D	4	04	EOT	32	20	NUL
F	33	21	102	66	f	70	46	F	6	06	ACK	33	21	NUL
G	34	22	103	67	g	71	47	G	7	07	BEL	34	22	NUL
H	35	23	104	68	h	72	48	H	8	08	BS	35	23	NUL
J	36	24	106	6A	j	74	4A	J	10	0A	LF	36	24	NUL
K	37	25	107	6B	k	75	4B	K	11	0B	VT	37	25	NUL
L	38	26	108	6C	l	76	4C	L	12	0C	FF	38	26	NUL
;:	39	27	59	3B	;	58	3A	:				39	27	NUL§
'"	40	28	39	27	'	34	22	"				40	28	NUL§
`~	41	29	96	60	`	126	7E	~				41	29	NUL§
L SHIFT	42	2A												
|	43	2B	92	5C	\	124	7C	|	28	1C	FS			
Z	44	2C	122	7A	z	90	5A	Z	26	1A	SUB	44	2C	NUL
X	45	2D	120	78	x	88	58	X	24	18	CAN	45	2D	NUL
C	46	2E	99	63	c	67	43	C	3	03	ETX	46	2E	NUL
V	47	2F	118	76	v	86	56	V	22	16	SYN	47	2F	NUL
B	48	30	98	62	b	66	42	B	2	02	STX	48	30	NUL
N	49	31	110	6E	n	78	4E	N	14	0E	SO	49	31	NUL
M	50	32	109	6D	m	77	4D	M	13	0D	CR	50	32	NUL
,<	51	33	44	2C	,	60	3C	<				51	33	NUL§
.>	52	34	46	2E	.	62	3E	>				52	34	NUL§

Key Codes Chart 2

Key	Scan Code Dec	Scan Code Hex	ASCII or Extended† Dec	ASCII or Extended† Hex	ASCII or Extended† Char	ASCII or Extended† with SHIFT Dec	ASCII or Extended† with SHIFT Hex	ASCII or Extended† with SHIFT Char	ASCII or Extended† with CTRL Dec	ASCII or Extended† with CTRL Hex	ASCII or Extended† with CTRL Char	ASCII or Extended† with ALT Dec	ASCII or Extended† with ALT Hex	ASCII or Extended† with ALT Char
/?	53	35	47	2F	/	63	3F	?				53	34	NUL§
GRAY /£	53	35	47	2F	/	63	3F	?	149	95	NUL	164	A5	NUL
R SHIFT	54	36												
*PRTSC	55	37	42	2A	*	PRTSC		††	16	10				
L ALT	56	38												
R ALT£	56	38												
SPACE	57	39	32	20	SPC	32	20	SPC	32	20	SPC	32	20	SPC
CAPS	58	3A												
F1	59	3B	59	3B	NUL	84	54	NUL	94	5E	NUL	104	68	NUL
F2	60	3C	60	3C	NUL	85	55	NUL	95	5F	NUL	105	69	NUL
F3	61	3D	61	3D	NUL	86	56	NUL	96	60	NUL	106	6A	NUL
F4	62	3E	62	3E	NUL	87	57	NUL	97	61	NUL	107	6B	NUL
F5	63	3F	63	3F	NUL	88	58	NUL	98	62	NUL	108	6C	NUL
F6	64	40	64	40	NUL	89	59	NUL	99	63	NUL	109	6D	NUL
F7	65	41	65	41	NUL	90	5A	NUL	100	64	NUL	110	6E	NUL
F8	66	42	66	42	NUL	91	5B	NUL	101	65	NUL	111	6F	NUL
F9	67	43	67	43	NUL	92	5C	NUL	102	66	NUL	112	70	NUL
F10	68	44	68	44	NUL	93	5D	NUL	103	67	NUL	113	71	NUL
F11£	87	57	133	85	E0	135	87	E0	137	89	E0	139	8B	E0
F12£	88	58	134	86	E0	136	88	E0	138	8A	E0	140	8C	E0
NUM	69	45												
SCROLL	70	46												
HOME	71	47	71	47	NUL	55	37	7	119	77	NUL			
HOME£	71	47	71	47	E0	71	47	E0	119	77	E0	151	97	NUL
UP	72	48	72	48	NUL	56	38	8	141	8D	NUL§			
UP£	72	48	72	48	E0	72	48	E0	141	8D	E0	152	98	NUL
PGUP	73	49	73	49	NUL	57	39	9	132	84	NUL			
PGUP£	73	49	73	49	E0	73	49	E0	132	84	E0	153	99	NUL
GRAY-	74	4A				45	2D	-						
LEFT	75	4B	75	4B	NUL	52	34	4	115	73	NUL			
LEFT£	75	4B	75	4B	E0	75	4B	E0	115	73	E0	155	9B	NUL
CENTER	76	4C				53	35	5						
RIGHT	77	4D	77	4D	NUL	54	36	6	116	74	NUL			
RIGHT£	77	4D	77	4D	E0	77	4D	E0	116	74	E0	157	9D	NUL
GRAY+	78	4E				43	2B	+						
END	79	4F	79	4F	NUL	49	31	1	117	75	NUL			
END£	79	4F	79	4F	E0	79	4F	E0	117	75	E0	159	9F	NUL
DOWN	80	50	80	50	NUL	50	32	2	145	91	NUL§			
DOWN£	80	50	80	50	E0	80	50	E0	145	91	E0	160	A0	NUL
PGDN	81	51	81	51	NUL	51	33	3	118	76	NUL			
PGDN£	81	51	81	51	E0	81	51	E0	118	76	E0	161	A1	NUL
INS	82	52	82	52	NUL	48	30	0	146	92	NUL§			
INS£	82	52	82	52	E0	82	52	E0	146	92	E0	162	A2	NUL
DEL	83	53	83	53	NUL	46	2E	.	147	93	NUL§			
DEL£	83	53	83	53	E0	83	53	E0	147	93	E0	163	A3	NUL

†   Extended codes return 0 (NUL) or E0 (decimal 224) as the initial character. This is a signal that a second (extended) code is available in the keystroke buffer.
§   These key combinations are only recognized on extended keyboards.
£   These keys are only available on extended keyboards. Most are in the Cursor/Control cluster. If the raw scan code is read from the keyboard port (60h), it appears as two bytes (E0h) followed by the normal scan code. However, when the keypad ENTER and / keys are read through the BIOS interrupt 16h, only E0h is seen since the interrupt only gives one-byte scan codes.
††   Under MS-DOS, SHIFT + PRTSC causes interrupt 5, which prints the screen unless an interrupt handler has been defined to replace the default interrupt 5 handler.

Index

Contributors to *C++ Language Reference*

Richard Carlson, Index Editor

David Adam Edelstein, Art Director

Roger Haight, Editor

Mark Hopkins, Editor

Marilyn Johnstone, Writer

Seth Manheim, Writer

Qian Wen, Writer

WASSER*Studios*, Production

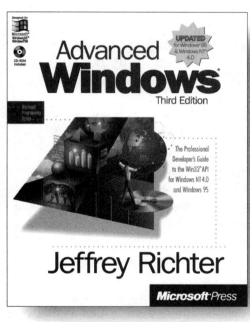

Preprocessor Reference

Microsoft®
Visual C++®
Language Reference

Microsoft Press

Contents

Tables

Introduction

This book explains the preprocessor as it is implemented in Microsoft® C/C++. The preprocessor is a tool you use to process C and C++ files before they are passed to the compiler. It allows you to:

- Define and undefine macros.

- Expand macros.

- Conditionally compile code.

- Insert specified files.

- Specify compile-time error messages.

- Apply machine-specific rules to specified sections of code.

Note For information on Microsoft product support, see the technical support help file, PSS.HLP.

Special Terminology

In this book, the term "argument" refers to the entity that is passed to a function. In some cases, it is modified by "actual" or "formal," which mean the argument expression specified in the function call and the argument declaration specified in the function definition, respectively.

The term "variable" refers to a simple C-type data object. The term "object" refers to both C++ objects and variables; it is an inclusive term.

CHAPTER 1

The Preprocessor

The preprocessor is a text processor that manipulates the text of a source file as part of the first phase of translation. The preprocessor does not parse the source text, but it does break it up into tokens for the purpose of locating macro calls. Although the compiler ordinarily invokes the preprocessor in its first pass, the preprocessor can also be invoked separately to process text without compiling.

Microsoft Specific →

You can obtain a listing of your source code after preprocessing by using the /E or /EP compiler option. Both options invoke the preprocessor and output the resulting text to the standard output device, which, in most cases, is the console. The difference between the two options is that /E includes **#line** directives and /EP strips these directives out.

END Microsoft Specific

Phases of Translation

C and C++ programs consist of one or more source files, each of which contains some of the text of the program. A source file, together with its include files (files that are included using the **#include** preprocessor directive) but not including sections of code removed by conditional-compilation directives such as **#if**, is called a "translation unit."

Source files can be translated at different times—in fact, it is common to translate only out-of-date files. The translated translation units can be kept either in separate object files or in object-code libraries. These separate translation units are then linked to form an executable program or a dynamic-link library (DLL).

Translation units can communicate using:

- Calls to functions that have external linkage.
- Calls to class member functions that have external linkage.
- Direct modification of objects that have external linkage.
- Direct modification of files.
- Interprocess communication (for Microsoft Windows®-based applications only).

The following list describes the phases in which the compiler translates files:

Character mapping   Characters in the source file are mapped to the internal source representation. Trigraph sequences are converted to single-character internal representation in this phase.

Line splicing   All lines ending in a backslash (\) and immediately followed by a newline character are joined with the next line in the source file, forming logical lines from the physical lines. Unless it is empty, a source file must end in a newline character that is not preceded by a backslash.

Tokenization   The source file is broken into preprocessing tokens and white-space characters. Comments in the source file are replaced with one space character each. Newline characters are retained.

Preprocessing   Preprocessing directives are executed and macros are expanded into the source file. The **#include** statement invokes translation starting with the preceding three translation steps on any included text.

Character-set mapping   All source-character-set members and escape sequences are converted to their equivalents in the execution-character set. For Microsoft C and C++, both the source and the execution character sets are ASCII.

String concatenation   All adjacent string and wide-string literals are concatenated. For example, `"String " "concatenation"` becomes `"String concatenation"`.

Translation   All tokens are analyzed syntactically and semantically; these tokens are converted into object code.

Linkage   All external references are resolved to create an executable program or a dynamic-link library.

The compiler issues warnings or errors during phases of translation in which it encounters syntax errors.

The linker resolves all external references and creates an executable program or DLL by combining one or more separately processed translation units along with standard libraries.

Preprocessor Directives

Preprocessor directives, such as **#define** and **#ifdef**, are typically used to make source programs easy to change and easy to compile in different execution environments. Directives in the source file tell the preprocessor to perform specific actions. For example, the preprocessor can replace tokens in the text, insert the contents of other files into the source file, or suppress compilation of part of the file by removing sections of text. Preprocessor lines are recognized and carried out before macro expansion. Therefore, if a macro expands into something that looks like a preprocessor command, that command is not recognized by the preprocessor.

Preprocessor statements use the same character set as source file statements, with the exception that escape sequences are not supported. The character set used in preprocessor statements is the same as the execution character set. The preprocessor also recognizes negative character values.

The preprocessor recognizes the following directives:

#define	**#error**	**#import**	**#undef**
#elif	**#if**	**#include**	
#else	**#ifdef**	**#line**	
#endif	**#ifndef**	**#pragma**	

The number sign (**#**) must be the first nonwhite-space character on the line containing the directive; white-space characters can appear between the number sign and the first letter of the directive. Some directives include arguments or values. Any text that follows a directive (except an argument or value that is part of the directive) must be preceded by the single-line comment delimiter (*//*) or enclosed in comment delimiters (*/* */*). Lines containing preprocessor directives can be continued by immediately preceding the end-of-line marker with a backslash (\).

Preprocessor directives can appear anywhere in a source file, but they apply only to the remainder of the source file.

The #define Directive

You can use the **#define** directive to give a meaningful name to a constant in your program. The two forms of the syntax are:

Syntax

#define *identifier token-string*$_{opt}$

#define *identifier*[(*identifier*$_{opt}$, ... , *identifier*$_{opt}$)] *token-string*$_{opt}$

The **#define** directive substitutes *token-string* for all subsequent occurrences of an *identifier* in the source file. The *identifier* is replaced only when it forms a token. (See "Tokens" in the *C++ Language Reference*.) For instance, *identifier* is not replaced if it appears in a comment, within a string, or as part of a longer identifier.

A **#define** without a *token-string* removes occurrences of *identifier* from the source file. The *identifier* remains defined and can be tested using the **#if defined** and **#ifdef** directives.

The *token-string* argument consists of a series of tokens, such as keywords, constants, or complete statements. One or more white-space characters must separate *token-string* from *identifier*. This white space is not considered part of the substituted text, nor is any white space following the last token of the text.

Formal parameter names appear in *token-string* to mark the places where actual values are substituted. Each parameter name can appear more than once in *token-string*, and the names can appear in any order. The number of arguments in the call must match the number of parameters in the macro definition. Liberal use of parentheses ensures that complicated actual arguments are interpreted correctly.

The second syntax form allows the creation of function-like macros. This form accepts an optional list of parameters that must appear in parentheses. References to the *identifier* after the original definition replace each occurrence of *identifier*(*identifier*$_{opt}$, ..., *identifier*$_{opt}$) with a version of the *token-string* argument that has actual arguments substituted for formal parameters.

The formal parameters in the list are separated by commas. Each name in the list must be unique, and the list must be enclosed in parentheses. No spaces can separate *identifier* and the opening parenthesis. Use line concatenation—place a backslash (\) before the newline character—for long directives on multiple source lines. The scope of a formal parameter name extends to the new line that ends *token-string*.

When a macro has been defined in the second syntax form, subsequent textual instances followed by an argument list constitute a macro call. The actual arguments following an instance of *identifier* in the source file are matched to the corresponding formal parameters in the macro definition. Each formal parameter in *token-string* that is not preceded by a stringizing (**#**), charizing (**#@**), or token-pasting (**##**) operator, or not followed by a **##** operator, is replaced by the corresponding actual argument. Any macros in the actual argument are expanded before the directive replaces the formal parameter. (The operators are described in "Preprocessor Operators" on page 23.)

The following examples of macros with arguments illustrate the second form of the **#define** syntax:

```
// Macro to define cursor lines
#define CURSOR(top, bottom) ((top) << 8) | bottom))

// Macro to get a random integer with a specified range
#define getrandom(min, max) \
    ((rand()%(int)(((max) + 1)-(min)))+ (min))
```

Arguments with side effects sometimes cause macros to produce unexpected results. A given formal parameter may appear more than once in *token-string*. If that formal parameter is replaced by an expression with side effects, the expression, with its side effects, may be evaluated more than once. (See the examples under "Token-Pasting Operator (##)" on page 25.)

The **#undef** directive causes an identifier's preprocessor definition to be forgotten. See "The **#undef** Directive" on page 22 for more information.

If the name of the macro being defined occurs in *token-string* (even as a result of another macro expansion), it is not expanded.

A second **#define** for a macro with the same name generates an error unless the second token sequence is identical to the first.

Microsoft Specific →

Microsoft C/C++ allows the redefinition of a macro, but generates a warning, provided the new definition is lexically identical to a previous definition. ANSI C considers macro redefinition an error. For example, these macros are equivalent for C/C++ but generate warnings:

```
#define test( f1, f2 ) ( f1 * f2 )
#define test( a1, a2 ) ( a1 * a2 )
```

END Microsoft Specific

This example illustrates the **#define** directive:

```
#define WIDTH       80
#define LENGTH      ( WIDTH + 10 )
```

The first statement defines the identifier WIDTH as the integer constant 80 and defines LENGTH in terms of WIDTH and the integer constant 10. Each occurrence of LENGTH is replaced by (WIDTH + 10). In turn, each occurrence of WIDTH + 10 is replaced by the expression (80 + 10). The parentheses around WIDTH + 10 are important because they control the interpretation in statements such as the following:

```
var = LENGTH * 20;
```

After the preprocessing stage the statement becomes:

```
var = ( 80 + 10 ) * 20;
```

which evaluates to 1800. Without parentheses, the result is:

```
var = 80 + 10 * 20;
```

which evaluates to 280.

Defining macros and constants with the /D compiler option has the same effect as using a **#define** preprocessing directive at the beginning of your file. Up to 30 macros can be defined with the /D option.

The #error Directive

Error directives produce compiler-time error messages.

Syntax

#error *token-string*

The error messages include the argument *token-string* and are subject to macro expansion. These directives are most useful for detecting programmer inconsistencies and violation of constraints during preprocessing. The following example demonstrates error processing during preprocessing:

```
#if !defined(__cplusplus)
#error C++ compiler required.
#endif
```

When **#error** directives are encountered, compilation terminates.

The #if, #elif, #else, and #endif Directives

The **#if** directive, with the **#elif**, **#else**, and **#endif** directives, controls compilation of portions of a source file. If the expression you write (after the **#if**) has a nonzero value, the line group immediately following the **#if** directive is retained in the translation unit.

Syntax

conditional:
> *if-part elif-parts*_{opt} *else-part*_{opt} *endif-line*

if-part:
> *if-line text*

if-line:
> **#if** *constant-expression*
> **#ifdef** *identifier*
> **#ifndef** *identifier*

elif-parts:
> *elif-line text*
> *elif-parts elif-line text*

elif-line:
> **#elif** *constant-expression*

else-part:
>   *else-line text*

else-line:
>   **#else**

endif-line:
>   **#endif**

Each **#if** directive in a source file must be matched by a closing **#endif** directive. Any number of **#elif** directives can appear between the **#if** and **#endif** directives, but at most one **#else** directive is allowed. The **#else** directive, if present, must be the last directive before **#endif**.

The **#if**, **#elif**, **#else**, and **#endif** directives can nest in the text portions of other **#if** directives. Each nested **#else**, **#elif**, or **#endif** directive belongs to the closest preceding **#if** directive.

All conditional-compilation directives, such as **#if** and **#ifdef**, must be matched with closing **#endif** directives prior to the end of file; otherwise, an error message is generated. When conditional-compilation directives are contained in include files, they must satisfy the same conditions: There must be no unmatched conditional-compilation directives at the end of the include file.

Macro replacement is performed within the part of the command line that follows an **#elif** command, so a macro call can be used in the *constant-expression*.

The preprocessor selects one of the given occurrences of *text* for further processing. A block specified in *text* can be any sequence of text. It can occupy more than one line. Usually *text* is program text that has meaning to the compiler or the preprocessor.

The preprocessor processes the selected *text* and passes it to the compiler. If *text* contains preprocessor directives, the preprocessor carries out those directives. Only text blocks selected by the preprocessor are compiled.

The preprocessor selects a single *text* item by evaluating the constant expression following each **#if** or **#elif** directive until it finds a true (nonzero) constant expression. It selects all text (including other preprocessor directives beginning with **#**) up to its associated **#elif**, **#else**, or **#endif**.

If all occurrences of *constant-expression* are false, or if no **#elif** directives appear, the preprocessor selects the text block after the **#else** clause. If the **#else** clause is omitted and all instances of *constant-expression* in the **#if** block are false, no text block is selected.

The *constant-expression* is an integer constant expression with these additional restrictions:

- Expressions must have integral type and can include only integer constants, character constants, and the **defined** operator.

- The expression cannot use **sizeof** or a type-cast operator.

- The target environment may not be able to represent all ranges of integers.

- The translation represents type **int** the same as type **long**, and **unsigned int** the same as **unsigned long**.

- The translator can translate character constants to a set of code values different from the set for the target environment. To determine the properties of the target environment, check values of macros from LIMITS.H in an application built for the target environment.

- The expression must not perform any environmental inquiries and must remain insulated from implementation details on the target computer.

The preprocessor operator **defined** can be used in special constant expressions, as shown by the following syntax:

Syntax

defined(*identifier*)

defined *identifier*

This constant expression is considered true (nonzero) if the *identifier* is currently defined; otherwise, the condition is false (0). An identifier defined as empty text is considered defined. The **defined** directive can be used in an **#if** and an **#elif** directive, but nowhere else.

In the following example, the **#if** and **#endif** directives control compilation of one of three function calls:

```
#if defined(CREDIT)
   credit();
#elif defined(DEBIT)
   debit();
#else
   printerror();
#endif
```

The function call to `credit` is compiled if the identifier `CREDIT` is defined. If the identifier `DEBIT` is defined, the function call to `debit` is compiled. If neither identifier is defined, the call to `printerror` is compiled. Note that `CREDIT` and `credit` are distinct identifiers in C and C++ because their cases are different.

The conditional compilation statements in the following example assume a previously defined symbolic constant named `DLEVEL`.

```
#if DLEVEL > 5
   #define SIGNAL  1
   #if STACKUSE == 1
      #define STACK   200
   #else
      #define STACK   100
   #endif
#else
```

```
    #define SIGNAL  0
    #if STACKUSE == 1
        #define STACK   100
    #else
        #define STACK   50
    #endif
#endif
#if DLEVEL == 0
    #define STACK 0
#elif DLEVEL == 1
    #define STACK 100
#elif DLEVEL > 5
    display( debugptr );
#else
    #define STACK 200
#endif
```

The first **#if** block shows two sets of nested **#if**, **#else**, and **#endif** directives. The first set of directives is processed only if DLEVEL > 5 is true. Otherwise, the statements after **#else** are processed.

The **#elif** and **#else** directives in the second example are used to make one of four choices, based on the value of DLEVEL. The constant STACK is set to 0, 100, or 200, depending on the definition of DLEVEL. If DLEVEL is greater than 5, then the statement

```
#elif DLEVEL > 5
display(debugptr);
```

is compiled and STACK is not defined.

A common use for conditional compilation is to prevent multiple inclusions of the same header file. In C++, where classes are often defined in header files, constructs like the following can be used to prevent multiple definitions:

```
// EXAMPLE.H - Example header file

#if !defined( EXAMPLE_H )
#define EXAMPLE_H

class Example
{
...
};

#endif // !defined( EXAMPLE_H )
```

The preceding code checks to see if the symbolic constant EXAMPLE_H is defined. If so, the file has already been included and need not be reprocessed. If not, the constant EXAMPLE_H is defined to mark EXAMPLE.H as already processed.

Microsoft Specific →

Conditional compilation expressions are treated as **signed long** values, and these expressions are evaluated using the same rules as expressions in C++. For example, this expression:

```
#if 0xFFFFFFFFL > 1UL
```

is true.

END Microsoft Specific

The #ifdef and #ifndef Directives

The **#ifdef** and **#ifndef** directives perform the same task as the **#if** directive when it is used with **defined(** *identifier* **)**.

Syntax

#ifdef *identifier*

#ifndef *identifier*

is equivalent to

#if defined *identifier*

#if !defined *identifier*

You can use the **#ifdef** and **#ifndef** directives anywhere **#if** can be used. The **#ifdef** *identifier* statement is equivalent to `#if 1` when *identifier* has been defined, and it is equivalent to `#if 0` when *identifier* has not been defined or has been undefined with the **#undef** directive. These directives check only for the presence or absence of identifiers defined with **#define**, not for identifiers declared in the C or C++ source code.

These directives are provided only for compatibility with previous versions of the language. The **defined(** *identifier* **)** constant expression used with the **#if** directive is preferred.

The **#ifndef** directive checks for the opposite of the condition checked by **#ifdef**. If the identifier has not been defined (or its definition has been removed with **#undef**), the condition is true (nonzero). Otherwise, the condition is false (0).

Microsoft Specific →

The *identifier* can be passed from the command line using the /D option. Up to 30 macros can be specified with /D.

This is useful for checking whether a definition exists, because a definition can be passed from the command line. For example:

```
// PROG.CPP
#ifndef test     // These three statements go in your source code.
#define final
#endif

CL /Dtest prog.cpp // This is the command for compilation.
```

END Microsoft Specific

The #import Directive

C++ Specific →

The **#import** directive is used to incorporate information from a type library. The content of the type library is converted into C++ classes, mostly describing the COM interfaces.

Syntax

#import *"filename"* [*attributes*]

#import *<filename>* [*attributes*]

attributes:

    attribute1, attribute2, ...

    attribute1 attribute2 ...

filename is the name of the file containing the type library information. A file can be one of the following types:

- a type library (.TLB or .ODL) file
- an executable (.EXE) file
- a library (.DLL) file containing a type library resource (such as .OCX)
- a compound document holding a type library
- any other file format that can be understood by the **LoadTypeLib** API

The *filename* is optionally preceded by a directory specification. The filename must name an existing file. The difference between the two forms is the order in which the preprocessor searches for the type library files when the path is incompletely specified.

Syntax Form	Action
Quoted form	This form instructs the preprocessor to first look for type library files in the same directory of the file that contains the **#import** statement, and then in the directories of whatever files that include (**#include**) that file. The preprocessor then searches along the paths shown below.
Angle-bracket form	This form instructs the preprocessor to search for type library files along the paths shown below.

The compiler will search in the following directories for the named file:

1. the **PATH** environment variable path list
2. the **LIB** environment variable path list
3. the path specified by the /I (additional include directories) compiler option

#import can optionally include one or more attributes. These attributes tell the compiler to modify the contents of the type-library headers. A backslash (\) symbol can be used to include additional lines in a single **#import** statement. For example:

```
#import "test.lib" no_namespace \
    rename("OldName", "NewName")
```

The **#import** attributes are listed below:

exclude	**high_method_prefix**
high_property_prefixes	**implementation_only**
inject_statement	**named_guids**
no_implementation	**no_namespace**
raw_dispinterfaces	**raw_interfaces_only**
raw_method_prefix	**raw_native_types**
raw_property_prefixes	**rename**
rename_namespace	

#import creates two header files that reconstruct the type library contents in C++ source code. The primary header file is similar to that produced by the Microsoft Interface Definition Language (MIDL) compiler, but with additional compiler-generated code and data. The primary header file has the same base name as the type library, plus a .TLH extension. The secondary header file has the same base name as the type library, with a .TLI extension. It contains the implementations for compiler-generated member functions, and is included (**#include**) in the primary header file.

Both header files are placed in the output directory specified by the /Fo (name object file) option. They are then read and compiled by the compiler as if the primary header file was named by a **#include** directive.

The following compiler optimizations come with the **#import** directive:

- The header file, when created, is given the same timestamp as the type library.

- When **#import** is processed, the compiler first checks if the header exists and is up to date. If yes, then it does not need to be recreated.

- The compiler delays initializing the OLE subsystem until the first **#import** command is encountered.

The **#import** directive also participates in minimal rebuild and can be placed in a precompiled header file. See "Creating Precompiled Header Files" in *Visual C++ Programmer's Guide* online for more information.

The Primary Type Library Header File

The primary type library header file consists of seven sections:

1. Heading boilerplate: Consists of comments, **#include** statement for COMDEF.H (which defines some standard macros used in the header), and other miscellaneous setup information.

2. Forward references and typedefs: Consists of structure declarations such as `struct IMyInterface`, and typedefs for any TKIND_ALIAS items.

3. Smart pointer declarations: The template class **_com_ptr_t** is a smart-pointer implementation that encapsulates interface pointers and eliminates the need to call **AddRef**, **Release**, **QueryInterface** functions. In addition, it hides the **CoCreateInstance** call in creating a new COM object. This section uses macro statement **_COM_SMARTPTR_TYPEDEF** to establish typedefs of COM interfaces to be template specializations of the **_com_ptr_t** template class. For example, for interface **IFoo**, the .TLH file will contain:

```
__COM_SMARTPTR_TYPEDEF(IFoo, __uuidof(IFoo));
```

which the compiler will expand to:

```
typedef _com_ptr_t<_com_IIID<IFoo, __uuidof(IFoo)> > IFooPtr;
```

Type `IFooPtr` can then be used in place of the raw interface pointer IFoo*. Consequently, there is no need to call the various **IUnknown** member functions.

4. Typeinfo declarations: Primarily consists of class definitions and other items exposing the individual typeinfo items returned by **ITypeLib:GetTypeInfo**. In this section, each typeinfo from the type library is reflected in the header in a form dependent on the TYPEKIND information.

5. Optional old-style GUID definition: Contains initializations of the named GUID constants. These are names of the form **CLSID_CoClass** and **IID_Interface**, similar to those generated by the MIDL compiler.

6. **#include** statement for the secondary type library header.

7. Footer boilerplate: Currently includes #pragma pack(pop).

All sections, except the heading boilerplate and footer boilerplate section, are enclosed in a namespace with its name specified by the **library** statement in the original IDL file. You can use the names from the type library header either by an explicit qualification with the namespace name or by including the following statement:

```
using namespace MyLib;
```

immediately after the **#import** statement in the source code.

The namespace can be suppressed by using the **no_namespace** attribute of the **#import** directive. However, suppressing the namespace may lead to name collisions. The namespace can also be renamed by the **rename_namespace** attribute.

The exclude attribute
exclude("*Name1***"[, "***Name2***",...])**

Name1   First item to be excluded

Name2   Second item to be excluded (if necessary)

Type libraries may include definitions of items defined in system headers or other type libraries. This attribute can be used to exclude these items from the type library header files being generated. This attribute can take any number of arguments, each being a top-level type library item to be excluded.

The high_method_prefix attribute
high_method_prefix("*Prefix***")**

Prefix   Prefix to be used

By default, high-level error-handling properties and methods are exposed by member functions named without a prefix. The names are from the type library. The **high_method_prefix** attribute is used to specify a prefix to be used in naming these high-level properties and methods.

The high_property_prefixes attribute

high_property_prefixes("*GetPrefix*"**,**"*PutPrefix*"**,**"*PutRefPrefix*"**)**

GetPrefix   Prefix to be used for the **propget** methods

PutPrefix   Prefix to be used for the **propput** methods

PutRefPrefix   Prefix to be used for the **propputref** methods

By default, high-level error-handling **propget**, **propput**, and **propputref** methods are exposed by member functions named with prefixes **Get**, **Put**, and **PutRef** respectively. The **high_property_prefixes** attribute is used to specify alternate prefixes for all three property methods.

The implementation_only attribute

The **implementation_only** attribute suppresses the generation of the .TLH header file (the primary header file). This file contains all the declarations used to expose the type-library contents. The .TLI header file, with the implementations of the wrapper member functions, will be generated and included in the compilation.

When this attribute is specified, the content of the .TLI header is in the same namespace as the one normally used in the .TLH header. In addition, the member functions are not declared as inline.

The **implementation_only** attribute is intended for use in conjunction with the **no_implementation** attribute as a way of keeping the implementations out of the precompiled header (PCH) file. An **#import** statement with the **no_implementation** attribute is placed in the source region used to create the PCH. The resulting PCH is used by a number of source files. An **#import** statement with the **implementation_only** attribute is then used outside the PCH region. You are required to use this statement only once in one of the source files. This will generate all the required wrapper member functions without additional recompilation for each source file.

Note   The **implementation_only** attribute in one **#import** statement must be use in conjunction with another **#import** statement, of the same type library, with the **no_implementation** attribute. Otherwise, compiler errors will be generated. This is because wrapper class definitions generated by the **#import** statement with the **no_implementation** attribute are required to compile the implementations generated by the **implementation_only** attribute.

The inject_statement attribute

inject_statement("*source_text*"**)**

source_text   Source text to be inserted into the type library header file

The **inject_statement** attribute inserts its argument as source text into the type-library header. The text is placed at the beginning of the namespace declaration that wraps the type-library contents in the header file.

The named_guids attribute

The **named_guids** attribute tells the compiler to define and initialize GUID variables in old style, of the form **LIBID_MyLib**, **CLSID_MyCoClass**, **IID_MyInterface**, and **DIID_MyDispInterface**.

The no_implementation attribute

The **no_implementation** attribute suppresses the generation of the .TLI header, which contains the implementations of the wrapper member functions. If this attribute is specified, the .TLH header, with the declarations to expose type-library items, will be generated without an **#include** statement to include the .TLI header file.

This attribute is used in conjunction with **implementation_only**.

The no_namespace attribute

The type-library contents in the **#import** header file are normally defined in a namespace. The namespace name is specified in the **library** statement of the original IDL file. If the **no_namespace** attribute is specified, this namespace is not generated by the compiler.

If you want to use a different namespace name, use the **rename_namespace** attribute instead.

The raw_dispinterfaces attribute

The **raw_dispinterfaces** attribute tells the compiler to generate low-level wrapper functions for dispinterface methods and properties that call **IDispatch::Invoke** and return the **HRESULT** error code.

If this attribute is not specified, only high-level wrappers are generated, which throw C++ exceptions in case of failure.

The raw_interfaces_only attribute

The **raw_interfaces_only** attribute suppresses the generation of error-handling wrapper functions and **__declspec(property)** declarations that use those wrapper functions.

The **raw_interfaces_only** attribute also causes the default prefix used in naming the non-property functions to be removed. Normally, the prefix is **raw_**. If this attribute is specified, the function names are directly from the type library.

This attribute allows you to expose only the low-level contents of the type library.

The raw_method_prefix attribute
raw_method_prefix(*"Prefix"*)

Prefix   The prefix to be used

Low-level properties and methods are exposed by member functions named with a default prefix of **raw_** to avoid name collisions with the high-level error-handling member functions. The **raw_method_prefix** attribute is used to specify a different prefix.

Note   The effects of the **raw_method_prefix** attribute will not be changed by the presence of the **raw_interfaces_only** attribute. The **raw_method_prefix** always takes precedence over **raw_interfaces_only** in specifying a prefix. If both attributes are used in the same **#import** statement, then the prefix specified by the **raw_method_prefix** attribute is used.

The raw_native_types attribute
By default, the high-level error-handling methods use the COM support classes **_bstr_t** and **_variant_t** in place of the **BSTR** and **VARIANT** data types and raw COM interface pointers. These classes encapsulate the details of allocating and deallocating memory storage for these data types, and greatly simplify type casting and conversion operations. The **raw_native_types** attribute is used to disable the use of these COM support classes in the high-level wrapper functions, and force the use of low-level data types instead.

The raw_property_prefixes attribute
raw_property_prefixes(*"GetPrefix"*,*"PutPrefix"*,*"PutRefPrefix"*)

GetPrefix   Prefix to be used for the **propget** methods

PutPrefix   Prefix to be used for the **propput** methods

PutRefPrefix   Prefix to be used for the **propputref** methods

By default, low-level **propget**, **propput**, and **propputref** methods are exposed by member functions named with prefixes of **get_**, **put_**, and **putref_** respectively. These prefixes are compatible with the names used in the header files generated by MIDL. The **raw_property_prefixes** attribute is used to specify alternate prefixes for all three property methods.

The rename attribute

rename("*OldName*"**,**"*NewName*"**)**

OldName   Old name in the type library

NewName   Name to be used instead of the old name

The **rename** attribute is used to work around name collision problems. If this attribute is specified, the compiler replaces all occurrences of *OldName* in a type library with the user-supplied *NewName* in the resulting header files.

This attribute can be used when a name in the type library coincides with a macro definition in the system header files. If this situation is not resolved, then various syntax errors will be generated, such as C2059 and C2061.

Note   The replacement is for a name used in the type library, not for a name used in the resulting header file.

Here is an example: Suppose a property named MyParent exists in a type library, and a macro GetMyParent is defined in a header file and used before **#import**. Since GetMyParent is the default name of a wrapper function for the error-handling **get** property, a name collision will occur. To work around the problem, use the following attribute in the **#import** statement:

```
rename("MyParent","MyParentX")
```

which renames the name MyParent in the type library. An attempt to rename the GetMyParent wrapper name will fail:

```
rename("GetMyParent","GetMyParentX")
```

This is because the name GetMyParent only occurs in the resulting type library header file.

The rename_namespace attribute

rename_namespace("*NewName*"**)**

NewName   The new name of the namespace

The **rename_namespace** attribute is used to rename the namespace that contains the contents of the type library. It takes a single argument, *NewName*, which specifies the new name for the namespace.

To remove the namespace, use the **no_namespace** attribute instead.

END C++ Specific

The #include Directive

The **#include** directive tells the preprocessor to treat the contents of a specified file as if those contents had appeared in the source program at the point where the directive appears. You can organize constant and macro definitions into include files and then use **#include** directives to add these definitions to any source file. Include files are also useful for incorporating declarations of external variables and complex data types. You only need to define and name the types once in an include file created for that purpose.

Syntax

#include *"path-spec"*
#include *<path-spec>*

The *path-spec* is a filename optionally preceded by a directory specification. The filename must name an existing file. The syntax of the *path-spec* depends on the operating system on which the program is compiled.

Both syntax forms cause replacement of that directive by the entire contents of the specified include file. The difference between the two forms is the order in which the preprocessor searches for header files when the path is incompletely specified.

Syntax Form	Action
Quoted form	This form instructs the preprocessor to look for include files in the same directory of the file that contains the **#include** statement, and then in the directories of whatever files that include (**#include**) that file. The preprocessor then searches along the path specified by the /I compiler option, then along paths specified by the INCLUDE environment variable.
Angle-bracket form	This form instructs the preprocessor to search for include files first along the path specified by the /I compiler option, then along the path specified by the INCLUDE environment variable.

The preprocessor stops searching as soon as it finds a file with the given name. If you specify a complete, unambiguous path specification for the include file between two sets of double quotation marks (" "), the preprocessor searches only that path specification and ignores the standard directories.

If the filename enclosed in double quotation marks is an incomplete path specification, the preprocessor first searches the "parent" file's directory. A parent file is the file containing the **#include** directive. For example, if you include a file named file2 within a file named file1, file1 is the parent file.

Include files can be "nested"; that is, an **#include** directive can appear in a file named by another **#include** directive. For example, file2, above, could include file3. In this case, file1 would still be the parent of file2 but would be the "grandparent" of file3.

When include files are nested, directory searching begins with the directories of the parent file and then proceeds through the directories of any grandparent files. Thus, searching begins relative to the directory containing the source currently being processed. If the file is not found, the search moves to directories specified by the /I compiler option. Finally, the directories specified by the INCLUDE environment variable are searched.

The following example shows file inclusion using angle brackets:

```
#include <stdio.h>
```

This example adds the contents of the file named STDIO.H to the source program. The angle brackets cause the preprocessor to search the directories specified by the INCLUDE environment variable for STDIO.H, after searching directories specified by the /I compiler option.

The following example shows file inclusion using the quoted form:

```
#include "defs.h"
```

This example adds the contents of the file specified by DEFS.H to the source program. The double quotation marks mean that the preprocessor searches the directory containing the parent source file first.

Nesting of include files can continue up to 10 levels. Once the nested **#include** is processed, the preprocessor continues to insert the enclosing include file into the original source file.

Microsoft Specific →

To locate includable source files, the preprocessor first searches the directories specified by the /I compiler option. If the /I option is not present or fails, the preprocessor uses the INCLUDE environment variable to find any include files within angle brackets. The INCLUDE environment variable and /I compiler option can contain multiple paths separated by semicolons (;). If more than one directory appears as part of the /I option or within the INCLUDE environment variable, the preprocessor searches them in the order in which they appear.

For example, the command

```
CL /ID:\MSVC\INCLUDE MYPROG.C
```

causes the preprocessor to search the directory D:\MSVC\INCLUDE for include files such as STDIO.H. The commands

```
SET INCLUDE=D:\MSVC\INCLUDE
CL MYPROG.C
```

have the same effect. If both sets of searches fail, a fatal compiler error is generated.

If the filename is fully specified for an include file with a path that includes a colon (for example, F:\MSVC\SPECIAL\INCL\TEST.H), the preprocessor follows the path.

For include files specified as **#include** "*path-spec*", directory searching begins with the directory of the parent file and then proceeds through the directories of any grandparent files. Thus, searching begins relative to the directory containing the source file containing the **#include** directive being processed. If there is no grandparent file and the file has not been found, the search continues as if the filename were enclosed in angle brackets.

END Microsoft Specific

The #line Directive

The **#line** directive tells the preprocessor to change the compiler's internally stored line number and filename to a given line number and filename. The compiler uses the line number and filename to refer to errors that it finds during compilation. The line number usually refers to the current input line, and the filename refers to the current input file. The line number is incremented after each line is processed.

Syntax

#line *digit-sequence* "*filename*"_{opt}

The *digit-sequence* value can be any integer constant. Macro replacement can be performed on the preprocessing tokens, but the result must evaluate to the correct syntax. The *filename* can be any combination of characters and must be enclosed in double quotation marks (" "). If *filename* is omitted, the previous filename remains unchanged.

You can alter the source line number and filename by writing a **#line** directive. The translator uses the line number and filename to determine the values of the predefined macros **__FILE__** and **__LINE__**. You can use these macros to insert self-descriptive error messages into the program text. For more information on these predefined macros, see "Predefined Macros."

The **__FILE__** macro expands to a string whose contents are the filename, surrounded by double quotation marks (" ").

If you change the line number and filename, the compiler ignores the previous values and continues processing with the new values. The **#line** directive is typically used by program generators to cause error messages to refer to the original source file instead of to the generated program.

The following examples illustrate **#line** and the **__LINE__** and **__FILE__** macros.

In this statement, the internally stored line number is set to 151 and the filename is changed to copy.c.

```
#line 151 "copy.c"
```

In this example, the macro ASSERT uses the predefined macros __**LINE**__ and __**FILE**__ to print an error message about the source file if a given "assertion" is not true.

```
#define ASSERT(cond)

if( !(cond) )\
{printf( "assertion error line %d, file(%s)\n", \
__LINE__, __FILE__);}
```

The Null Directive

The null preprocessor directive is a single number sign (**#**) alone on a line. It has no effect.

Syntax

```
#
```

The #undef Directive

As its name implies, the **#undef** directive removes (undefines) a name previously created with **#define**.

Syntax

#undef *identifier*

The **#undef** directive removes the current definition of *identifier*. Consequently, subsequent occurrences of *identifier* are ignored by the preprocessor. To remove a macro definition using **#undef**, give only the macro *identifier*; do not give a parameter list.

You can also apply the **#undef** directive to an identifier that has no previous definition. This ensures that the identifier is undefined. Macro replacement is not performed within **#undef** statements.

The **#undef** directive is typically paired with a **#define** directive to create a region in a source program in which an identifier has a special meaning. For example, a specific function of the source program can use manifest constants to define environment-specific values that do not affect the rest of the program. The **#undef** directive also works with the **#if** directive to control conditional compilation of the source program. See "The **#if**, **#elif**, **#else**, and **#endif** Directives" on page 6 for more information.

In the following example, the **#undef** directive removes definitions of a symbolic constant and a macro. Note that only the identifier of the macro is given.

```
#define WIDTH          80
#define ADD( X, Y )    (X) + (Y)
   .
   .

   .
#undef WIDTH
#undef ADD
```

Microsoft Specific →

Macros can be undefined from the command line using the /U option, followed by the macro names to be undefined. The effect of issuing this command is equivalent to a sequence of **#undef** *macro-name* statements at the beginning of the file.

END Microsoft Specific

Preprocessor Operators

Four preprocessor-specific operators are used in the context of the **#define** directive (see the following list for a summary of each). The stringizing, charizing, and token-pasting operators are discussed in the next three sections. For information on the **defined** operator, see "The **#if**, **#elif**, **#else**, and **#endif** Directives" on page 6.

Operator	Action
Stringizing operator (**#**)	Causes the corresponding actual argument to be enclosed in double quotation marks
Charizing operator (**#@**)	Causes the corresponding argument to be enclosed in single quotation marks and to be treated as a character (Microsoft Specific)
Token-pasting operator (**##**)	Allows tokens used as actual arguments to be concatenated to form other tokens
defined operator	Simplifies the writing of compound expressions in certain macro directives

Stringizing Operator (#)

The number-sign or "stringizing" operator (**#**) converts macro parameters (after expansion) to string constants. It is used only with macros that take arguments. If it precedes a formal parameter in the macro definition, the actual argument passed by the macro invocation is enclosed in quotation marks and treated as a string literal. The string literal then replaces each occurrence of a combination of the stringizing operator and formal parameter within the macro definition.

White space preceding the first token of the actual argument and following the last token of the actual argument is ignored. Any white space between the tokens in the actual argument is reduced to a single white space in the resulting string literal. Thus, if a comment occurs between two tokens in the actual argument, it is reduced to a single white space. The resulting string literal is automatically concatenated with any adjacent string literals from which it is separated only by white space.

Further, if a character contained in the argument usually requires an escape sequence when used in a string literal (for example, the quotation mark (") or backslash (\) character), the necessary escape backslash is automatically inserted before the character. The following example shows a macro definition that includes the stringizing operator and a main function that invokes the macro:

```
#define stringer( x ) printf( #x "\n" )

void main()
{
    stringer( In quotes in the printf function call\n );
    stringer( "In quotes when printed to the screen"\n );
    stringer( "This: \"  prints an escaped double quote" );
}
```

Such invocations would be expanded during preprocessing, producing the following code:

```
void main()
{
    printf( "In quotes in the printf function call\n" "\n" );
    printf( "\"In quotes when printed to the screen\"\n" "\n" );
    printf( "\"This: \\\" prints an escaped double quote\"" "\n" );
}
```

When the program is run, screen output for each line is as follows:

```
In quotes in the printf function call

"In quotes when printed to the screen"

"This: \" prints an escaped double quotation mark"
```

Microsoft Specific →

The Microsoft C (versions 6.0 and earlier) extension to the ANSI C standard that previously expanded macro formal arguments appearing inside string literals and character constants is no longer supported. Code that relied on this extension should be rewritten using the stringizing (#) operator.

END Microsoft Specific

Charizing Operator (#@)

The charizing operator can be used only with arguments of macros. If **#@** precedes a formal parameter in the definition of the macro, the actual argument is enclosed in single quotation marks and treated as a character when the macro is expanded. For example:

```
#define makechar(x)   #@x
```

causes the statement

```
a = makechar(b);
```

to be expanded to

```
a = 'b';
```

The single-quotation character cannot be used with the charizing operator.

Token-Pasting Operator (##)

The double-number-sign or "token-pasting" operator (**##**), which is sometimes called the "merging" operator, is used in both object-like and function-like macros. It permits separate tokens to be joined into a single token and therefore cannot be the first or last token in the macro definition.

If a formal parameter in a macro definition is preceded or followed by the token-pasting operator, the formal parameter is immediately replaced by the unexpanded actual argument. Macro expansion is not performed on the argument prior to replacement.

Then, each occurrence of the token-pasting operator in *token-string* is removed, and the tokens preceding and following it are concatenated. The resulting token must be a valid token. If it is, the token is scanned for possible replacement if it represents a macro name. The identifier represents the name by which the concatenated tokens will be known in the program before replacement. Each token represents a token defined elsewhere, either within the program or on the compiler command line. White space preceding or following the operator is optional.

This example illustrates use of both the stringizing and token-pasting operators in specifying program output:

```
#define paster( n ) printf( "token" #n " = %d", token##n )
int token9 = 9;
```

If a macro is called with a numeric argument like

```
paster( 9 );
```

the macro yields

```
printf( "token" "9" " = %d", token9 );
```

which becomes

```
printf( "token9 = %d", token9 );
```

Macros

Preprocessing expands macros in all lines that are not preprocessor directives (lines that do not have a **#** as the first non-white-space character) and in parts of some directives that are not skipped as part of a conditional compilation. "Conditional compilation" directives allow you to suppress compilation of parts of a source file by testing a constant expression or identifier to determine which text blocks are passed on to the compiler and which text blocks are removed from the source file during preprocessing.

The **#define** directive is typically used to associate meaningful identifiers with constants, keywords, and commonly used statements or expressions. Identifiers that represent constants are sometimes called "symbolic constants" or "manifest constants." Identifiers that represent statements or expressions are called "macros." In this preprocessor documentation, only the term "macro" is used.

When the name of the macro is recognized in the program source text or in the arguments of certain other preprocessor commands, it is treated as a call to that macro. The macro name is replaced by a copy of the macro body. If the macro accepts arguments, the actual arguments following the macro name are substituted for formal parameters in the macro body. The process of replacing a macro call with the processed copy of the body is called "expansion" of the macro call.

In practical terms, there are two types of macros. "Object-like" macros take no arguments, whereas "function-like" macros can be defined to accept arguments so that they look and act like function calls. Because macros do not generate actual function calls, you can sometimes make programs run faster by replacing function calls with macros. (In C++, inline functions are often a preferred method.) However, macros can create problems if you do not define and use them with care. You may have to use parentheses in macro definitions with arguments to preserve the proper precedence in an expression. Also, macros may not correctly handle expressions with side effects. See the `getrandom` example in "The **#define** Directive" on page 3 for more information.

Once you have defined a macro, you cannot redefine it to a different value without first removing the original definition. However, you can redefine the macro with exactly the same definition. Thus, the same definition can appear more than once in a program.

The **#undef** directive removes the definition of a macro. Once you have removed the definition, you can redefine the macro to a different value. "The **#define** Directive" on page 3 and "The **#undef** Directive" on page 22 discuss the **#define** and **#undef** directives, respectively.

Macros and C++

C++ offers new capabilities, some of which supplant those offered by the ANSI C preprocessor. These new capabilities enhance the type safety and predictability of the language:

- In C++, objects declared as **const** can be used in constant expressions. This allows programs to declare constants that have type and value information, and enumerations that can be viewed symbolically with the debugger. Using the preprocessor **#define** directive to define constants is not as precise. No storage is allocated for a **const** object unless an expression that takes its address is found in the program.

- The C++ inline function capability supplants function-type macros. The advantages of using inline functions over macros are:

  - Type safety. Inline functions are subject to the same type checking as normal functions. Macros are not type safe.

  - Correct handling of arguments that have side effects. Inline functions evaluate the expressions supplied as arguments prior to entering the function body. Therefore, there is no chance that an expression with side effects will be unsafe.

For more information on inline functions, see **inline, __inline**.

For backward compatibility, all preprocessor facilities that existed in ANSI C and in earlier C++ specifications are preserved for Microsoft C++.

Predefined Macros

The compiler recognizes six predefined ANSI C macros (see Table 1.1), and the Microsoft C++ implementation provides several more (see Table 1.2). These macros take no arguments and cannot be redefined. Their value (except for __LINE__ and __FILE__) must be constant throughout compilation. Some of the predefined macros listed below are defined with multiple values. Their values can be set by selecting the corresponding option in the development environment, or by using a command-line switch. See the tables below for more information.

Table 1.1 ANSI Predefined Macros

Macro	Description
__DATE__	The compilation date of the current source file. The date is a string literal of the form *Mmm dd yyyy*. The month name *Mmm* is the same as for dates generated by the library function **asctime** declared in TIME.H.
__FILE__	The name of the current source file. __FILE__ expands to a string surrounded by double quotation marks.
__LINE__	The line number in the current source file. The line number is a decimal integer constant. It can be altered with a **#line** directive.
__STDC__	Indicates full conformance with the ANSI C standard. Defined as the integer constant 1 only if the /Za compiler option is given and you are not compiling C++ code; otherwise is undefined.
__TIME__	The most recent compilation time of the current source file. The time is a string literal of the form *hh:mm:ss*.
__TIMESTAMP__	The date and time of the last modification of the current source file, expressed as a string literal in the form *Ddd Mmm Date hh:mm:ss yyyy*, where *Ddd* is the abbreviated day of the week and *Date* is an integer from 1 to 31.

Table 1.2 Microsoft-Specific Predefined Macros

Macro	Description
_CHAR_UNSIGNED	Default **char** type is unsigned. Defined when /J is specified.
__cplusplus	Defined for C++ programs only.
_CPPRTTI	Defined for code compiled with /GR (Enable Run-Time Type Information).
_CPPUNWIND	Defined for code compiled with /GX (Enable Exception Handling).
_DLL	Defined when /MD or /MDd (Multithread DLL) is specified.
_M_ALPHA	Defined for DEC ALPHA platforms. It is defined as 1 by the ALPHA compiler, and it is not defined if another compiler is used.
_M_IX86	Defined for x86 processors. See Table 1.3 for more details.
_M_MPPC	Defined for Power Macintosh platforms. Default is 601 (/QP601). See Table 1.4 for more details.

Table 1.2   Microsoft-Specific Predefined Macros *(continued)*

Macro	Description
_M_MRX000	Defined for MIPS platforms. Default is 4000 (/QMR4000). See Table 1.5 for more details.
_M_PPC	Defined for PowerPC platforms. Default is 604 (/QP604). See Table 1.6 for more details.
_MFC_VER	Defines the MFC version. Defined as 0x0421 for Microsoft Foundation Class Library 4.21. Always defined.
_MSC_VER	Defines the compiler version. Defined as 1100 for Microsoft Visual C++™ 5.0. Always defined.
_MT	Defined when /MD or /MDd (Multithreaded DLL) or /MT or /MTd (Multithreaded) is specified.
_WIN32	Defined for applications for Win32®. Always defined.

As shown in following tables, the compiler generates a value for the preprocessor identifiers that reflect the processor option specified.

Table 1.3   Values for _M_IX86

Option in Developer Studio	Command-Line Option	Resulting Value
Blend	/GB	**_M_IX86 = 500** (Default. Future compilers will emit a different value to reflect the dominant processor.)
Pentium	/G5	**_M_IX86 = 500**
Pentium Pro	/G6	**_M_IX86 = 600**
80386	/G3	**_M_IX86 = 300**
80486	/G4	**_M_IX86 = 400**

Table 1.4   Values for _M_MPPC

Option in development environment	Command-Line Option	Resulting Value
PowerPC 601	/QP601	**_M_MPPC = 601** (Default)
PowerPC 603	/QP603	**_M_MPPC = 603**
PowerPC 604	/QP604	**_M_MPPC = 604**
PowerPC 620	/QP620	**_M_MPPC = 620**

Table 1.5   Values for _M_MRX000

Option in Developer Studio	Command-Line Option	Resulting Value
R4000	/QMR4000	**_M_MRX000 = 4000** (Default)
R4100	/QMR4100	**_M_MRX000 = 4100**

(continued)

Table 1.5   Values for _M_MRX000 *(continued)*

Option in Developer Studio	Command-Line Option	Resulting Value
R4200	/QMR4200	**_M_MRX000 = 4200**
R4400	/QMR4400	**_M_MRX000 = 4400**
R4600	/QMR4600	**_M_MRX000 = 4600**
R10000	/QMR10000	**_M_MRX000 = 10000**

Table 1.6   Values for _M_PPC

Option in Developer Studio	Command-Line Option	Resulting Value
PowerPC 601	/QP601	**_M_PPC = 601**
PowerPC 603	/QP603	**_M_PPC = 603**
PowerPC 604	/QP604	**_M_PPC = 604** (Default)
PowerPC 620	/QP620	**_M_PPC = 620**

Pragma Directives

Each implementation of C and C++ supports some features unique to its host machine or operating system. Some programs, for instance, need to exercise precise control over the memory areas where data is placed or to control the way certain functions receive parameters. The **#pragma** directives offer a way for each compiler to offer machine- and operating-system–specific features while retaining overall compatibility with the C and C++ languages. Pragmas are machine- or operating-system–specific by definition, and are usually different for every compiler.

Syntax

#pragma *token-string*

The *token-string* is a series of characters that gives a specific compiler instruction and arguments, if any. The number sign (**#**) must be the first non-white-space character on the line containing the pragma; white-space characters can separate the number sign and the word **pragma**. Following **#pragma**, write any text that the translator can parse as preprocessing tokens. The argument to **#pragma** is subject to macro expansion.

If the compiler finds a pragma it does not recognize, it issues a warning, but compilation continues.

Pragmas can be used in conditional statements, to provide new preprocessor functionality, or to provide implementation-defined information to the compiler. The C and C++ compilers recognize the following pragmas:

alloc_text	**comment**	**init_seg**[1]	**optimize**
auto_inline	**component**	**inline_depth**	**pack**
bss_seg	**data_seg**	**inline_recursion**	**pointers_to_members**[1]
check_stack	**function**	**intrinsic**	**setlocale**
code_seg	**hdrstop**	**message**	**vtordisp**[1]
const_seg	**include_alias**	**once**	**warning**

[1] Supported only by the C++ compiler.

Pragmas Specific to the C++ Compiler

The following pragma directives are specific to the C++ compiler:

- **init_seg**
- **pointers_to_members**
- **vtordisp**

init_seg

C++ Specific →

#pragma init_seg({ **compiler** | **lib** | **user** | *"section-name"* [, *"func-name"*]} **)**

Specifies a keyword or code section that affects the order in which startup code is executed. Because initialization of global static objects can involve executing code, you must specify a keyword that defines when the objects are to be constructed. It is particularly important to use the **init_seg** pragma in dynamic-link libraries (DLLs) or libraries requiring initialization.

The options to the **init_seg** pragma are:

compiler   Reserved for Microsoft C run-time library initialization. Objects in this group are constructed first.

lib   Available for third-party class-library vendors' initializations. Objects in this group are constructed after those marked as **compiler** but before any others.

user   Available to any user. Objects in this group are constructed last.

section-name   Allows explicit specification of the initialization section. Objects in a user-specified *section-name* are not implicitly constructed; however, their addresses are placed in the section named by *section-name*.

func-name   Specifies a function to be called in place of exit() when the program exits. The function specified must have the same signature as the exit function:

```
int funcname(void (_ _cdecl *)(void));
```

If you need to defer initialization (for example, in a DLL), you may choose to specify the section name explicitly. You must then call the constructors for each static object.

END C++ Specific

pointers_to_members

C++ Specific →

#pragma pointers_to_members(*pointer-declaration*,
    [*most-general-representation*] **)**

Specifies whether a pointer to a class member can be declared before its associated class definition and is used to control the pointer size and the code required to interpret the pointer. You can place a **pointers_to_members** pragma in your source file as an alternative to using the /vmx compiler options.

The *pointer-declaration* argument specifies whether you have declared a pointer to a member before or after the associated function definition. The *pointer-declaration* argument is one of the following two symbols:

Argument	Comments
full_generality	Generates safe, sometimes nonoptimal code. You use **full_generality** if any pointer to a member is declared before the associated class definition. This argument always uses the pointer representation specified by the *most-general-representation* argument. Equivalent to /vmg.
Best_case	Generates safe, optimal code using best-case representation for all pointers to members. Requires defining the class before declaring a pointer to a member of the class. The default is **best_case**.

The *most-general-representation* argument specifies the smallest pointer representation that the compiler can safely use to reference any pointer to a member of a class in a translation unit. The argument can be one of the following:

Argument	Comments
single_inheritance	The most general representation is single-inheritance, pointer to a member function. Causes an error if the inheritance model of a class definition for which a pointer to a member is declared is ever either multiple or virtual.
Multiple_inheritance	The most general representation is multiple-inheritance, pointer to a member function. Causes an error if the inheritance model of a class definition for which a pointer to a member is declared is virtual.
Virtual_inheritance	The most general representation is virtual-inheritance, pointer to a member function. Never causes an error. This is the default argument when **#pragma pointers_to_members(full_generality)** is used.

END C++ Specific

vtordisp

C++ Specific →
#pragma vtordisp({on | off})

Enables the addition of the hidden vtordisp construction/destruction displacement member. The **vtordisp** pragma is applicable only to code that uses virtual bases. If a derived class overrides a virtual function that it inherits from a virtual base class, and if a constructor or destructor for the derived class calls that function using a pointer to the virtual base class, the compiler may introduce additional hidden "vtordisp" fields into classes with virtual bases.

The **vtordisp** pragma affects the layout of classes that follow it. The /vd0 and /vd1 options specify the same behavior for complete modules. Specifying **off** suppresses the hidden vtordisp members. Specifying **on**, the default, enables them where they are necessary. Turn off **vtordisp** only if there is no possibility that the class's constructors and destructors call virtual functions on the object pointed to by the **this** pointer.

```
#pragma vtordisp( off )
class GetReal : virtual public { ... };
#pragma vtordisp( on )
```

END C++ Specific

C and C++ Compiler Pragmas

The following pragmas are defined for both the C and C++ compilers:

alloc_text	**component**	**init_seg**[1]	**optimize**
auto_inline	**const_seg**	**inline_depth**	**pack**
bss_seg	**data_seg**	**inline_recursion**	**pointers_to_members**[1]
check_stack	**function**	**intrinsic**	**setlocale**
code_seg	**hdrstop**	**message**	**vtordisp**[1]
comment	**include_alias**	**once**	**warning**

[1] Supported only by the C++ compiler.

alloc_text

#pragma alloc_text(*"textsection"*, *function1*, ... **)**

Names the code section where the specified function definitions are to reside. The pragma must occur between a function declarator and the function definition for the named functions.

The **alloc_text** pragma does not handle C++ member functions or overloaded functions. It is applicable only to functions declared with C linkage—that is, functions declared with the **extern "C"** linkage specification. If you attempt to use this pragma on a function with C++ linkage, a compiler error is generated.

Since function addressing using __**based** is not supported, specifying section locations requires the use of the **alloc_text** pragma. The name specified by *textsection* should be enclosed in double quotation marks.

The **alloc_text** pragma must appear after the declarations of any of the specified functions and before the definitions of these functions.

Functions referenced in an **alloc_text** pragma should be defined in the same module as the pragma. If this is not done and an undefined function is later compiled into a different text section, the error may or may not be caught. Although the program will usually run correctly, the function will not be allocated in the intended sections.

Other limitations on **alloc_text** are as follows:

- It cannot be used inside a function.

- It must be used after the function has been declared, but before the function has been defined.

auto_inline

#pragma auto_inline([{on | off}])

Excludes any functions defined within the range where **off** is specified from being considered as candidates for automatic inline expansion. To use the **auto_inline** pragma, place it before and immediately after (not in) a function definition. The pragma takes effect at the first function definition after the pragma is seen. Pragma **auto_inline** does not apply to explicit inline functions.

bss_seg

#pragma data_seg(["*section-name*"[, "*section-class*"]])

Specifies the default section for unitialized data. The data_seg pragma has the same effect but works with initialized or unitialized data. In some cases, you can use **bss_seg** to speed up your load time by putting all unitialized data in one section.

```
#pragma bss_seg( "MY_DATA" )
```

causes uninitialized data allocated following the **#pragma** statement to be placed in a section called MY_DATA.

Data allocated using the **bss_seg** pragma does not retain any information about its location.

The second parameter, *section-class*, is included for compatibilty with versions of Visual C++ prior to version 2.0, and is now ignored.

check_stack

#pragma check_stack([{on | off}])

#pragma check_stack {+ | −}

Instructs the compiler to turn off stack probes if **off** (or −) is specified, or to turn on stack probes if **on** (or +) is specified. If no argument is given, stack probes are treated according to the default. This pragma takes effect at the first function defined after the pragma is seen. Stack probes are not a part of macros nor of functions that are generated inline.

If you don't give an argument for the **check_stack** pragma, stack checking reverts to the behavior specified on the command line. For more information, see "Compiler

Reference" in *Visual C++ Programmer's Guide* online. The interaction of the
#pragma check_stack and the /Gs option is summarized in Table 2.1.

Table 2.1   Using the check_stack Pragma

Syntax	Compiled with /Gs option?	Action
#pragma check_stack( ) or **#pragma check_stack**	Yes	Turns off stack checking for functions that follow
#pragma check_stack( ) or **#pragma check_stack**	No	Turns on stack checking for functions that follow
#pragma check_stack(on) or **#pragma check_stack +**	Yes or no	Turns on stack checking for functions that follow
#pragma check_stack(off) or **#pragma check_stack –**	Yes or no	Turns off stack checking for functions that follow

code_seg

#pragma code_seg(["*section-name*"[,"*section-class*"]] **)**

Specifies a code section where functions are to be allocated. The **code_seg** pragma
specifies the default section for functions. You can, optionally, specify the class as
well as the section name. Using **#pragma code_seg** without a *section-name* string
resets allocation to whatever it was when compilation began.

const_seg

#pragma const_seg(["*section-name*"[, "*section-class*"]] **)**

Specifies the default section for constant data. The data_seg pragma has the same
effect but works with all data. You can use this pragma to put all your constant data
in one read-only section.

```
#pragma const_seg( "MY_DATA" )
```

causes constant data allocated following the **#pragma** statement to be placed in a
section called MY_DATA.

Data allocated using the **const_seg** pragma does not retain any information about its
location.

The second parameter, *section-class*, is included for compatibilty with versions of
Visual C++ prior to version 2.0, and is now ignored.

comment

#pragma comment(*comment-type* [, *commentstring*] **)**

Places a comment record into an object file or executable file. The *comment-type* is
one of five predefined identifiers, described below, that specify the type of comment
record. The optional *commentstring* is a string literal that provides additional

information for some comment types. Because *commentstring* is a string literal, it obeys all the rules for string literals with respect to escape characters, embedded quotation marks ("), and concatenation.

compiler   Places the name and version number of the compiler in the object file. This comment record is ignored by the linker. If you supply a *commentstring* parameter for this record type, the compiler generates a warning.

exestr   Places *commentstring* in the object file. At link time, this string is placed in the executable file. The string is not loaded into memory when the executable file is loaded; however, it can be found with a program that finds printable strings in files. One use for this comment-record type is to embed a version number or similar information in an executable file.

lib   Places a library-search record in the object file. This comment type must be accompanied by a *commentstring* parameter containing the name (and possibly the path) of the library that you want the linker to search. Since the library name precedes the default library-search records in the object file, the linker searches for this library just as if you had named it on the command line. You can place multiple library-search records in the same source file; each record appears in the object file in the same order in which it is encountered in the source file.

linker   Places a linker option in the object file. You can use this comment-type to specify a linker option instead placing the option on the Link tab of the Project Settings dialog box. For example, you can specity the /include option to force the inclusion of a symbol:

```
#pragma comment(linker, "/include: _ _mySymbol")
```

user   Places a general comment in the object file. The *commentstring* parameter contains the text of the comment. This comment record is ignored by the linker.

The following pragma causes the linker to search for the EMAPI.LIB library while linking. The linker searches first in the current working directory and then in the path specified in the LIB environment variable.

```
#pragma comment( lib, "emapi" )
```

The following pragma causes the compiler to place the name and version number of the compiler in the object file:

```
#pragma comment( compiler )
```

Note   For comments that take a *commentstring* parameter, you can use a macro in any place where you would use a string literal, provided that the macro expands to a string literal. You can also concatenate any combination of string literals and macros that expand to string literals. For example, the following statement is acceptable:

```
#pragma comment( user, "Compiled on " _ _DATE_ _ " at " _ _TIME_ _ )
```

component

#pragma component(browser, { **on** | **off** }[, **references** [, *name*]])
#pragma component(minrebuild, on | **off**)

Controls the collecting of browse information or dependency information from within source files.

You can turn collecting on or off, and you can specify particular names to be ignored as information is collected.

Using **on** or **off** controls the collection of browse information from the pragma forward. For example:

```
#pragma component(browser, off)
```

stops the compiler from collecting browse information.

Note   To turn on the collecting of browse information with this pragma, browse information must first be enabled from the Project Settings dialog box or the command line.

The **references** option can be used with or without the *name* argument. Using **references** without *name* turns on or off the collecting of references (other browse information continues to be collected, however). For example:

```
#pragma component(browser, off, references)
```

stops the compiler from collecting reference information.

Using **references** with *name* and **off** prevents references to *name* from appearing in the browse information window. Use this syntax to ignore names and types you are not interested in and to reduce the size of browse information files. For example:

```
#pragma component(browser, off, references, DWORD)
```

ignores references to **DWORD** from that point forward. You can turn collecting of references to **DWORD** back on by using **on**:

```
#pragma component(browser, on, references, DWORD)
```

This is the only way to resume collecting references to *name*; you must explicitly turn on any *name* that you have turned off.

To prevent the preprocessor from expanding *name* (such as expanding **NULL** to 0), put quotes around it:

```
#pragma component(browser, off, references, "NULL")
```

The Visual C++ minimal rebuild feature requires that the compiler create and store C++ class dependency information, which takes disk space. To save disk space, you can use #pragma component(minrebuild, off) whenever you don't need to collect dependency information, for instance, in unchanging header files. Insert #pragma component(minrebuild, on) after unchanging classes to turn dependency collection back on.

data_seg

#pragma data_seg(["*section-name*"[, "*section-class*"]] **)**

Specifies the default section for data. For example:

```
#pragma data_seg( "MY_DATA" )
```

causes data allocated following the **#pragma** statement to be placed in a section called MY_DATA.

Data allocated using the **data_seg** pragma does not retain any information about its location.

The second parameter, *section-class*, is included for compatibilty with versions of Visual C++ prior to version 2.0, and is now ignored.

function

#pragma function(*function1* [, *function2*, ...] **)**

Specifies that calls to functions specified in the pragma's argument list be generated. If you use the **intrinsic** pragma (or /Oi) to tell the compiler to generate intrinsic functions (intrinsic functions are generated as inline code, not as function calls), you can use the **function** pragma to explicitly force a function call. Once a function pragma is seen, it takes effect at the first function definition containing a specified intrinsic function. The effect continues to the end of the source file or to the appearance of an **intrinsic** pragma specifying the same intrinsic function. The **function** pragma can be used only outside of a function—at the global level.

For lists of the functions that have intrinsic forms, see "intrinsic" on page 42.

hdrstop

#pragma hdrstop [("*filename*")]

Controls the way precompiled headers work. The *filename* is the name of the precompiled header file to use or create (depending on whether /Yu or /Yc is specified). If *filename* does not contain a path specification, the precompiled header file is assumed to be in the same directory as the source file. Any *filename* is ignored when /YX, the automatic precompiled header option, is specified.

If a C or C++ file contains a **hdrstop** pragma when compiled with either /YX or /Yc, the compiler saves the state of the compilation up to the location of the pragma. The compiled state of any code that follows the pragma is not saved.

The **hdrstop** pragma cannot occur inside a header file. It must occur in the source file at the file level; that is, it cannot occur within any data or function declaration or definition.

Note The **hdrstop** pragma is ignored unless either the /YX option is specified or the /Yu or /Yc option is specified without a filename.

Use *filename* to name the precompiled header file in which the compiled state is saved. A space between **hdrstop** and *filename* is optional. The filename specified in the **hdrstop** pragma is a string and is therefore subject to the constraints of any C or C++ string. In particular, you must enclose it in quotation marks as shown in the following example:

```
#pragma hdrstop( "c:\projects\include\myinc.pch" )
```

The name of the precompiled header file is determined according to the following rules, in order of precedence:

1. The argument to the /Fp compiler option

2. The *filename* argument to **#pragma hdrstop**

3. The base name of the source file with a .PCH extension

include_alias

#pragma include_alias("*long_filename*", "*short_filename*" **)**
#pragma include_alias(<*long_filename*>, <*short_filename*> **)**

Specifies that *short_filename* is to be used as an alias for *long_filename*. Some file systems allow longer header filenames than the 8.3 FAT file system limit. The compiler cannot simply truncate the longer names to 8.3, because the first eight characters of the longer header filenames may not be unique. Whenever the compiler encounters the *long_filename* string, it substitutes *short_filename*, and looks for the header file *short_filename* instead. This pragma must appear before the corresponding **#include** directives. For example:

```
// First eight characters of these two files not unique.
#pragma include_alias( "AppleSystemHeaderQuickdraw.h", "quickdra.h" )
#pragma include_alias( "AppleSystemHeaderFruit.h", "fruit.h" )

#pragma include_alias( "GraphicsMenu.h", "gramenu.h" )

#include "AppleSystemHeaderQuickdraw.h"
#include "AppleSystemHeaderFruit.h"
#include "GraphicsMenu.h"
```

The alias being searched for must match the specification exactly, in case as well as in spelling and in use of double quotation marks or angle brackets. The **include_alias** pragma performs simple string matching on the filenames; no other filename validation is performed. For example, given the following directives,

```
#pragma include_alias("mymath.h", "math.h")
#include "./mymath.h"
#include "sys/mymath.h"
```

no aliasing (substitution) is performed, since the header file strings do not match exactly. Also, header filenames used as arguments to the /Yu, /Yc, and /YX compiler options, or the **hdrstop** pragma, are not substituted. For example, if your source file contains the following directive,

```
#include <AppleSystemHeaderStop.h>
```

the corresponding compiler option should be

```
/YcAppleSystemHeaderStop.h
```

You can use the **include_alias** pragma to map any header filename to another. For example:

```
#pragma include_alias( "api.h", "c:\version1.0\api.h" )
#pragma include_alias( <stdio.h>, <newstdio.h> )
#include "api.h"
#include <stdio.h>
```

Do not mix filenames enclosed in double quotation marks with filenames enclosed in angle brackets. For example, given the above two **#pragma include_alias** directives, the compiler performs no substitution on the following **#include** directives:

```
#include <api.h>
#include "stdio.h"
```

Furthermore, the following directive generates an error:

```
#pragma include_alias(<header.h>, "header.h")  // Error
```

Note that the filename reported in error messages, or as the value of the predefined **__FILE__** macro, is the ame of the file after the substitution has been performed. For example, after the following directives,

```
#pragma include_alias( "VeryLongFileName.H", "myfile.h" )
#include "VeryLongFileName.H"
```

an error in VERYLONGFILENAME.H produces the following error message:

```
myfile.h(15) : error C2059 : syntax error
```

Also note that transitivity is not supported. Given the following directives,

```
#pragma include_alias( "one.h", "two.h" )
#pragma include_alias( "two.h", "three.h" )
#include "one.h"
```

the compiler searches for the file TWO.H rather than THREE.H.

inline_depth
#pragma inline_depth([0... 255])

Controls the number of times inline expansion can occur by controlling the number of times that a series of function calls can be expanded (from 0 to 255 times). This pragma controls the inlining of functions marked **inline** and **__inline** or inlined automatically under the /Ob2 option.

The **inline_depth** pragma controls the number of times a series of function calls can be expanded. For example, if the inline depth is four, and if A calls B and B then calls C, all three calls will be expanded inline. However, if the closest inline expansion is two, only A and B are expanded, and C remains as a function call.

To use this pragma, you must set the /Ob compiler option to 1 or 2. The depth set using this pragma takes effect at the first function call after the pragma. If you do not specify a value within the parentheses, **inline_depth** sets the inline depth back to its default value of 8.

The inline depth can be decreased during expansion but not increased. If the inline depth is six and during expansion the preprocessor encounters an **inline_depth** pragma with a value of eight, the depth remains six.

An inline depth of 0 inhibits inline expansion; an inline depth of 255 places no limit on inline expansion. If either pragma is used without specifying a value, the default value is used.

inline_recursion

#pragma inline_recursion([{on | off}])

Controls the inline expansion of direct or mutually recursive function calls. Use this pragma to control functions marked as **inline** and _ _**inline** or functions that the compiler automatically expands under the /Ob2 option. Use of this pragma requires an /Ob compiler option setting of either 1 or 2. The default state for **inline_recursion** is off. This pragma takes effect at the first function call after the pragma is seen and does not affect the definition of the function.

The **inline_recursion** pragma controls how recursive functions are expanded. If **inline_recursion** is off, and if an inline function calls itself (either directly or indirectly), the function is expanded only once. If **inline_recursion** is on, the function is expanded multiple times until the value of **inline_depth** is reached or capacity limits are reached.

intrinsic

#pragma intrinsic(function1 [, function2, ...])

Specifies that calls to functions specified in the pragma's argument list are intrinsic. The compiler generates intrinsic functions as inline code, not as function calls. The library functions with intrinsic forms are listed below. Once an **intrinsic** pragma is seen, it takes effect at the first function definition containing a specified intrinsic function. The effect continues to the end of the source file or to the appearance of a **function** pragma specifying the same intrinsic function. The **intrinsic** pragma can be used only outside of a function definition—at the global level.

The following functions have intrinsic forms:

_disable	**_outp**	**abs**	**strcat**
_enable	**_outpw**	**fabs**	**strcmp**
_inp	**_rotl**	**labs**	**strcpy**
_inpw	**_rotr**	**memcmp**	**strlen**
_lrotl	**_strset**	**memcpy**	
_lrotr		**memset**	

Programs that use intrinsic functions are faster because they do not have the overhead of function calls but may be larger due to the additional code generated.

Note   The **_alloca** and **setjmp** functions are always generated inline; this behavior is not affected by the **intrinsic** pragma.

The floating-point functions listed below do not have true intrinsic forms. Instead they have versions that pass arguments directly to the floating-point chip rather than pushing them onto the program stack:

acos	**cosh**	**pow**	**tanh**
asin	**fmod**	**sinh**	

The floating-point functions listed below have true intrinsic forms when you specify both the /Oi and /Og compiler options (or any option that includes /Og: /Ox, /O1, and /O2):

atan	**exp**	**log10**	**sqrt**
atan2	**log**	**sin**	**tan**
cos			

You can use the /Op or /Za compiler option to override generation of true intrinsic floating-point options. In this case, the functions are generated as library routines that pass arguments directly to the floating-point chip instead of pushing them onto the program stack.

message

#pragma message(*messagestring* **)**

Sends a string literal to the standard output without terminating the compilation. A typical use of the **message** pragma is to display informational messages at compile time.

The following code fragment uses the **message** pragma to display a message during compilation:

```
#if _M_IX86 == 500 #pragma message( "Pentium processor" ) #endif
```

The *messagestring* parameter can be a macro that expands to a string literal, and you can concatenate such macros with string literals in any combination. For example, the following statements display the name of the file being compiled and the date and time when the file was last modified:

```
#pragma message( "Compiling " __FILE__)
#pragma message( "Last modified on " __TIMESTAMP__)
```

once

#pragma once

Specifies that the file, in which the pragma resides, will be included (opened) only once by the compiler in a build. A common use for this pragma is the following:

```
//header.h
#pragma once
// Your C or C++ code would follow:
```

optimize

#pragma optimize("[*optimization-list*]", {on | off})

Feature Only in Professional and Enterprise Editions   Code optimization is supported only in Visual C++ Professional and Enterprise Editions. For more information, see "Visual C++ Editions" in the online documentation.

Specifies optimizations to be performed on a function-by-function basis. The **optimize** pragma must appear outside a function and takes effect at the first function defined after the pragma is seen. The **on** and **off** arguments turn options specified in the *optimization-list* on or off.

The *optimization-list* can be zero or more of the parameters shown in Table 2.2.

Table 2.2   Parameters of the optimize Pragma

Parameter(s)	Type of optimization
a	Assume no aliasing.
g	Enable global optimizations.
p	Improve floating-point consistency.
s or **t**	Specify short or fast sequences of machine code.
w	Assume no aliasing across function calls.
y	Generate frame pointers on the program stack.

These are the same letters used with the /O compiler options. For example,

```
#pragma optimize( "atp", on )
```

Using the **optimize** pragma with the empty string (" ") is a special form of the directive. It either turns off all optimizations or restores them to their original (or default) settings.

```
#pragma optimize( "", off )
 .
 .
 .
#pragma optimize( "", on )
```

pack

#pragma pack([*n*]**)**

Specifies packing alignment for structure and union members. Whereas the packing alignment of structures and unions is set for an entire translation unit by the /Zp option, the packing alignment is set at the data-declaration level by the **pack** pragma. The pragma takes effect at the first structure or union declaration after the pragma is seen; the pragma has no effect on definitions.

When you use **#pragma pack(***n***)**, where *n* is 1, 2, 4, 8, or 16, each structure member after the first is stored on the smaller member type or *n*-byte boundaries. If you use **#pragma pack** without an argument, structure members are packed to the value specified by /Zp. The default /Zp packing size is /Zp8.

The compiler also supports the following enhanced syntax:

#pragma pack([[**{push|pop}**,] [*identifier*,]] [*n*]**)**

This syntax allows you to combine program components into a single translation unit if the different components use **pack** pragmas to specify different packing alignments.

Each occurrence of a **pack** pragma with a **push** argument stores the current packing alignment on an internal compiler stack. The pragma's argument list is read from left to right. If you use **push**, the current packing value is stored. If you provide a value for *n*, that value becomes the new packing value. If you specify an *identifier*, a name of your choosing, the *identifier* is associated with the new packing value.

Each occurrence of a **pack** pragma with a **pop** argument retrieves the value at the top of an internal compiler stack and makes that value the new packing alignment. If you use **pop** and the internal compiler stack is empty, the alignment value is that set from the command-line and a warning is issued. If you use **pop** and specify a value for *n*, that value becomes the new packing value. If you use **pop** and specify an *identifier*, all values stored on the stack are removed from the stack until a matching *identifier* is found. The packing value associated with the *identifier* is also removed from the stack and the packing value that existed just before the *identifier* was pushed becomes the new packing value. If no matching *identifier* is found, the packing value set from the command line is used and a level-one warning is issued. The default packing alignment is 8.

The new, enhanced functionality of the **pack** pragma allows you to write header files that ensure that packing values are the same before and after the header file is encountered:

```
/* File name: include1.h
*/
#pragma pack( push, enter_include1 )
/* Your include-file code ... */
#pragma pack( pop, enter_include1 )
/* End of include1.h */
```

In the previous example, the current pack value is associated with the identifier enter_include1 and pushed, remembered, on entry to the header file. The **pack** pragma at the end of the header file removes all intervening pack values that may have occurred in the header file and removes the pack value associated with enter_include1. The header file thus ensures that the pack value is the same before and after the header file.

The new functionality also allows you to use code, such as header files, that uses **pack** pragmas to set packing alignments that differ from the packing value set in your code:

```
#pragma pack( push, before_include1 )
#include "include1.h"
#pragma pack( pop, before_include1 )
```

In the previous example, your code is protected from any changes to the packing value that might occur in include.h.

setlocale

#pragma setlocale("*locale-string***")**

Defines the locale (country and language) to be used when translating wide-character constants and string literals. Since the algorithm for converting multibyte characters to wide characters may vary by locale or the compilation may take place in a different locale from where an executable file will be run, this pragma provides a way to specify the target locale at compile time. This guarantees that the wide-character strings will be stored in the correct format. The default *locale-string* is "C". The "C" locale maps each character in the string to its value as a **wchar_t (unsigned short)**.

warning

#pragma warning(*warning-specifier* **:** *warning-number-list* [*,warning-specifier* **:** *warning-number-list*...]**)**

Allows selective modification of the behavior of compiler warning messages.

The *warning-specifier* can be one of the following:

Warning-specifier	Meaning
once	Display the specified message(s) only once.
Default	Apply the default compiler behavior to the specified message(s).
1, 2, 3, 4	Apply the given warning level to the specified warning message(s).
disable	Do not issue the specified warning message(s).
error	Report the specified warnings as errors.

The *warning-number-list* can contain any warning numbers. Multiple options can be specified in the same pragma directive as follows:

```
#pragma warning( disable : 4507 34; once : 4385; error : 164 )
```

This is functionally equivalent to:

```
#pragma warning( disable : 4507 34 )   // Disable warning messages
                                       //   4507 and 34.
#pragma warning( once : 4385 )         // Issue warning 4385
                                       //   only once.
#pragma warning( error : 164 )         // Report warning 164
                                       //   as an error.
```

For warning numbers greater than 4699, those associated with code generation, the **warning** pragma has effect only when placed outside function definitions. The pragma is ignored if it specifies a number greater than 4699 and is used inside a function. The following example illustrates the correct placement of **warning** pragmas to disable, and then restore, the generation of a code-generation warning message:

```
int a;
#pragma warning( disable : 4705 )
void func()
{
    a;
}
#pragma warning( default : 4705 )
```

Grammar Summary

This appendix describes the formal grammar of the preprocessor. It covers the syntax of preprocessing directives and operators discussed in Chapter 1, "The Preprocessor," and Chapter 2, "Pragma Directives."

The following topics are included:

- Definitions
- Conventions
- Preprocessor Grammar

Definitions for the Grammar Summary

Terminals are endpoints in a syntax definition. No other resolution is possible. Terminals include the set of reserved words and user-defined identifiers.

Nonterminals are placeholders in the syntax. Most are defined elsewhere in this syntax summary. Definitions can be recursive. The following nonterminals are defined in the "Grammar Summary" of the *C++ Language Reference*:

constant, constant-expression, identifier, keyword, operator, punctuator

An optional component is indicated by the subscripted $_{opt}$. For example, the following indicates an optional expression enclosed in curly braces:

{ *expression*$_{opt}$ }

Conventions

The conventions use different font attributes for different components of the syntax. The symbols and fonts are as follows:

Attribute	Description
nonterminal	Italic type indicates nonterminals.
#include	Terminals in bold type are literal reserved words and symbols that must be entered as shown. Characters in this context are always case sensitive.
opt	Nonterminals followed by $_{opt}$ are always optional.
default typeface	Characters in the set described or listed in this typeface can be used as terminals in statements.

A colon (:) following a nonterminal introduces its definition. Alternative definitions are listed on separate lines.

Preprocessor Grammar

#define *identifier token-string*$_{opt}$

#define *identifier*[(*identifier*$_{opt}$, ... , *identifier*$_{opt}$)] *token-string*$_{opt}$

defined(*identifier*)

defined *identifier*

#include "*path-spec*"

#include <*path-spec*>

#line *digit-sequence* "*filename*"$_{opt}$

#undef *identifier*

#error *token-string*

#pragma *token-string*

conditional:
> *if-part elif-parts*$_{opt}$ *else-part*$_{opt}$ *endif-line*

if-part:
> *if-line text*

if-line:
> **#if** *constant-expression*
> **#ifdef** *identifier*
> **#ifndef** *identifier*

elif-parts:
>*elif-line text*
>*elif-parts elif-line text*

elif-line:
>**#elif** *constant-expression*

else-part:
>*else-line text*

else-line:
>**#else**

endif-line:
>**#endif**

digit-sequence:
>*digit*
>*digit-sequence digit*

digit: one of
>**0 1 2 3 4 5 6 7 8 9**

token-string:
>String of tokens

token:
>*keyword*
>*identifier*
>*constant*
>*operator*
>*punctuator*

filename:
>Legal operating system filename

path-spec:
>Legal file path

text:
>Any sequence of text

Note The following nonterminals are expanded in Appendix A, "Grammar Summary," of the *C++ Language Reference*: *constant*, *constant-expression*, *identifier*, *keyword*, *operator*, and *punctuator*.

Index

Contributors to *Preprocessor Reference*

Chris Burt, Writer

Richard Carlson, Index Editor

David Adam Edelstein, Art Director

Roger Haight, Editor

Seth Manheim, Writer

Qian Wen, Writer

WASSER*Studios*, Production

Register Today!

Return this
Microsoft® Visual C++® Language Reference
registration card for
a Microsoft Press® catalog

U.S. and Canada addresses only. Fill in information below and mail postage-free. Please mail only the bottom half of this page.

1-57231-521-0A   *MICROSOFT® VISUAL C++®*   *Owner Registration Card*
                  LANGUAGE REFERENCE

_____
NAME

_____
INSTITUTION OR COMPANY NAME

_____
ADDRESS

_____

_____
CITY   STATE   ZIP

Microsoft ® *Press*
Quality Computer Books

For a free catalog of
Microsoft Press® products, call
1-800-MSPRESS